What Lutherans Are Thinking

A Symposium on Lutheran Faith and Life

Published under the auspices

of

THE CONFERENCE OF LUTHERAN
PROFESSORS OF THEOLOGY

Edited by

E. C. FENDT

Dean of the Theological Seminary and
Professor of Systematic Theology
Capital University, Columbus, Ohio

THE WARTBURG PRESS, COLUMBUS, OHIO

PRINTED IN U. S. A.

CONTENTS

(3)

PREFACE

In June, 1943, Augustana Theological Seminary, Rock Island, Illinois, was host to the first free conference of Lutheran Theological Professors in the United States and Canada. Seminary professors from every synod except one were present. One of the results of that conference was the resolution to project the publication of a volume on Lutheran faith and life which could serve as an introduction to the various fields of theological study.

The committee entrusted with this work solicited the cooperation of the authors brought together in this book. The authors were chosen irrespective of synodical affiliation, and each contributor was asked to write in the spirit of ecumenical Lutheranism. The aim of the committee was to publish a book which would give an accurate and informative presentation of the directions and the tendencies in contemporary American Lutheran thinking.

There has been no attempt to "harmonize" divergent opinions of various writers. That there are differing opinions within the Lutheran Church on many questions in theology is a fact not to be concealed, but that there is also an inner unity in the varied approaches used and in the conclusions reached by Lutheran scholars will also be evident to the reader of these chapters.

Lutheranism is not pledged to press all theological research into a rigid mold of expression but is fructified by the many streams of theological study as carried on in all the lands where the Lutheran Church is found. In past decades various European influences were transplanted within the groups in America which trace their ancestry to the Continental Lutheran Churches. In America there has come the opportunity to fuse this manifold religious heritage of European Lutheranism into the American branch of the Church of the Reformation. At present all Lutherans in America are interested not only in conserving and combining the treasured insights and doctrinal affirmations of their church in past centuries, but they are also eager to give testimony to their Lutheran faith in a world of chaos and unrest, which is seeking recovery from the effects of a destructive war and nationalistic hatreds.

The Lutheran Church looks to its theological seminaries for more than the training of its future clergy. It sees itself reflected in the theological seminaries through which it often gives expression to its innermost longings and convictions. A professor of theology, by virtue of the position accorded him, becomes a teacher and a leader of the entire church body which he serves, and his testimony can usually be taken as a reflection of the attitudes of the church in which he serves. If the professors who wrote the articles in this book have succeeded in giving expression to that which is fundamental and central in the theology and the life of the Lutheran Church, they will have made a notable contribution to Lutheran unity and ecumenical Christianity.

The purpose of this book was not to confine consideration to the problems of the church in the immediate present. Some questions in the forefront of contemporary religious discussion are not even mentioned. The aim of the book centers rather in this: to let the light of the past shed its rays upon the problems of the present and into the darkness of the future. And that light for Lutheranism is Jesus Christ, who speaks to His church through His Word and to the world through His church. To preach the gospel as God gave it, as God wants it proclaimed in every age, as God bears witness to its truth and its efficacy in the hearts and the lives of men and of nations, is still the mission of the church that puts the name evangelical before the name Lutheran given to it by its critics as people agreeing with Martin Luther in his understanding of the gospel.

The chapters in this book have a vital bearing on the crucial questions in every age of Christendom as to the origin, content, and application of the Christian gospel. Representative theologians within the Evangelical Lutheran Church of America have undertaken to indicate some of the theological data that must be evaluated by any and by all who are called upon to speak for Christ in His church and for Him to the world.

The members of the committee which planned the publication of this book are: E. C. Fendt, Theo. Graebner, C. G. Carlfelt, H. A. Preus, T. G. Tappert, and E. E. Flack. The undersigned was given the responsibility of preparing the manuscripts for the press.

EDWARD C. FENDT,
Chairman of the Committee.

Pentecost, 1946.

ABBREVIATIONS

W=Weimar Edition.

Wa=St. Louis Walch Edition of Luther's Works.

Tr.=*Concordia Triglotta*, St. Louis, 1921.

THE HERITAGE OF LUTHERANISM

W. H. T. DAU

A heritage implies a testator, a bequest, and an heir. Lutheranism denotes, in its proper meaning, "The principles of the Reformation as championed by Luther, or as embodied in the Lutheran churches; the doctrines peculiar to the Lutheran faith."[1] Thus understood, Luther, with his immediate co-workers and followers down to the year 1580, is the testator; the principles which he, together with them, adopted for reforming the church of his day, and the doctrines which he, together with them, professed and laid down in confessional writings collected in 1580 in the Book of Concord are the bequest or heritage; and all who accept those principles and doctrines unqualifiedly and enact them are the beneficiaries or heirs.

What are those principles?

The Formal Principle

By fairly universal consensus of the historians October 31, 1517, is designated as the beginning of Luther's reformatory activity. The very first of his ninety-five theses revealed the nature of his conscientious scruple, which he meant to remove by public discussion: he could not harmonize the sale of indulgences with the call to repentance with which Jesus began His public ministry, nor with the entire teaching of the Scriptures regarding forgiving men their sins.[2]

All his subsequent writings in explanation and defense of his theses, his lectures at the university, his sermons, his

---

[1] *Standard Dictionary.*
[2] W. 1, 229-238; Wa. 18, 70-81.

copious correspondence, are marked by his insistently en-
forcing the Scriptures. They are to him the Word of God,
the final and unalterable decision from heaven on all matters
pertaining to the true religion, by the only true God, Father,
Son, and Holy Spirit, and lastly proclaimed on earth with
finality by the incarnate Son of God, the God-man Jesus
Christ.[3]

On April 18, 1521, when he had his final hearing before
the Diet at Worms, Luther was thirty-seven years old. Up
to that time he had, according to Koestlin's computation,
published eighty-eight writings. He lived twenty-five years
longer and published three hundred and thirty-two more.[4]
But the solemn asseveration which he uttered in his final
address to the Diet expresses a deep-rooted conviction,
which he maintained to the end of his life:

"Unless I am overcome by testimonies of Scripture or by evident
reasons—for I believe neither the Pope nor the Councils alone, because
it is an established fact that they have erred a number of times, and
have contradicted one another—I am overcome by the Scriptures which
I have cited, and my conscience is caught in the words of God.
Recant I cannot and will not anything because it is uncertain and
insincere to act contrary to your conscience."[5]

For his Index to the St. Louis edition of Luther's writings
Editor Hoppe has recorded 1,221 references to the Scriptures.[6] These are not mere indications of places where the
terms "Scripture" and kindred terms occur in Luther's
writings, but they are condensed statements of judgments
and convictions which Luther expressed concerning the
Scriptures. In their entirety they form an exhaustive reader
on Luther's attitude toward the Bible. Every one of these

---

[3]Heb. 1:1.   [4]Koestlin-Kawerau, *Martin Luther*, 2, 718-723.
[5]W. 7, 816.
[6]Under "Heilige Schrift," 255; under "Bibel," 66; under "Altes
Testament," 41; under "Neues Testament," 51; not to mention allusions to particular books of the Bible. Nor does this include Luther's
quotations from Scripture.

references breathes profound reverence for the Scriptures as the Word of God; and they are uttered not only with reference to the Scriptures as a whole (Bibliology) but to every doctrine and even to minute details of Scriptural teaching.

A sampling of these utterances is found in Luther's last great effort of Scripture interpretation. Eight days after his last birthday Luther concluded his lectures on Genesis. In these lectures he remarks:

"Paul says I Cor. 2:15: 'He that is spiritual judgeth all things.' If I were the only one, then, in all the earth who was retaining the Word, I alone would be the Church, and would pass this judgment on all the world, that it was not the Church. For, although they have the official authority, yet they hold it without the Word, and, in truth, have nothing. On the other hand, we who have the Word, while authority we have nothing, still through the Word we have everything. Therefore, let the Pope, the cardinals, and the bishops either come over to us, or cease boasting that they are the Church, which cannot be without the Word, because it is begotten by the Word."[7]

Again: "We must come to a halt, where the Word stops. . . . The rest—whatever is not made plain by the Word—we must simply leave aside; such things cannot be ventured into without danger."[8]

Again: "Whoever takes away the Word, and does not accept it as spoken by God, takes away everything."[9]

Again: "Where the Word of God is, there is the true faith, and there are the true works; because there everything is being done in the Word, and under the direction of the Word."[10]

His last sermon, on Matt. 11:25-30, on February 15, 1546, at his birthplace Eisleben, Luther concluded with these words: "We must learn not to become wise in our own conceit, put all persons in high stations out of our sight, simply close our eyes, cling to the words of Christ, come to Him while He calls us in the friendliest manner, and say to Him: 'Thou alone art my dear Lord and Master, I am Thy pupil.' This, and much more could be said about this gospel. But I am too feeble. I will have to let this suffice."[11]

When Luther stresses the authority of the Word he means the Word in its plain, literal, grammatical sense. To

---

[7]W. 42, 334; Wa. 1, 555.   [9]W. 43, 70; Wa. 1, 1248.
[8]W. 42, 646; Wa. 1, 1084.   [10]W. 43, 431; Wa. 2, 124.
[11]W. 51, 194; Wa. 12, 1264.

the Romanist Emser, who contended for a "spiritual" meaning of the terms of Scripture, different from the literal one, Luther said: "The Holy Spirit is the simplest writer and speaker in heaven and on earth. Accordingly, His words too cannot have but one most simple meaning, which we call the written, or literal, meaning."[12] The literal meaning must be abandoned only when Scripture itself compels it. In 1520 the barefoot monk, Alveld of Leipzig, undertook to prove the papacy a divine institution. In his arguments he operated very much with allegories, types, and figures of speech. Replying to him, Luther wrote:

"Even if they had been so smart as to give the figure a spiritual complement [fulfilment], their argument could not stand, unless they had a plain passage of Scripture, which would bring the figure into harmony with its spiritual fulfilment. Otherwise everyone could interpret the figure as he pleased. That the serpent mounted by Moses signified Christ I am taught in the third chapter of the Gospel of John. If it were not for this, my reason might invent very strange, wild significations out of that figure. Again, that Adam was a figure of Christ, I have to learn, not from my own mind, but from Paul in Romans, ch. 5. Again, that the rock in the desert signified Christ, I am told, not by my reason, but by Paul in I Cor., ch. 10. Hence the figure may be interpreted by no one else than by the Holy Ghost, who has both set up the figure and brought about its fulfilment, so that the word and the effect, the figure and its fulfilment, may both be of God Himself, and not of men, and our faith may be well founded on divine, not on human, doings and sayings."[13]

Luther holds that Scripture must be self-interpretative. In his classic treatise of 1527 against the Sacramentarians Luther writes:

"In interpreting the Scriptures the pious teachers follow this method, that they take lucid, clear passages and with them make clear the dark, dubious passages. This is also the method of the Holy Spirit, to break up darkness by means of light. However, our fanatics act unreasonably: they wrench from a text a dark, dubious term which pleases their fancy, and at the same time skip what is written alongside of it, to make a lucid, clear text dark and dubious and wind up by

------

[12] W. 7, 650; Wa. 18, 1307.   [13] W. 6, 304; Wa. 18, 1027f.

saying that it is the pure truth. That is the method of the devil, who is a lover of darkness, and wants to obscure light."[14]

Luther, therefore, rejects rationalism: it does not comprehend, hence cannot interpret, Scripture. Substituting for Pastor Bugenhagen, who had gone to Luebeck to aid in the reformation of that city, Luther, on Saturday, January 27, 1531, preached a sermon on John 6:41, in which he said:

"John here records first this [murmuring of the Jews] to warn all of us, who hear this doctrine of the Christian creed concerning Christ, not to cast up many questions, and not to be inquisitive, as to how these things can be harmonized. For whoever wants to be a Christian and apprehend the articles of the Christian Creed, must not consult his reason or brain, as to whether it reads and sounds aright, but he must promptly declare: 'I do not ask how these things rhyme, but this one thing only I must know, viz., whether there is a word of God for it, or not. Next I ask, whether Jesus has said so. For you hear me often warning you, not to argue nor speculate with your reason in sublime matters which concern the Christian faith. For as soon as we want to make matters rhyme, harmonize, agree with, and fit into, our reason, we are undone."[15]

In his *Larger Commentary on Galatians* [1536] Luther remarks on chapter 3:6:

"When proposing articles of faith, God always proposes things which are impossibilities and absurdities, if you want to follow the judgment of reason. Thus, it certainly appears ridiculous and absurd to reason that in the Lord's Supper the body and blood of Christ should be presented to us; that baptism should be the washing of regeneration and renewing of the Holy Ghost; that the dead should rise on the last day; that Christ, the Son of God, should be conceived, carried in the womb of the virgin, be born, suffer the most ignominious death on the cross, be raised again, should now sit at the right hand of the Father, and have power in heaven and earth. (For Paul calls the gospel of Christ crucified the word of the cross and the foolishness of preaching, which the Jews consider scandalous, and the Greeks a foolish doctrine, etc.). Thus reason judges of articles of faith. For it does not understand that the highest worship is to listen to God speaking and to believe. But those things which reason itself chooses and does with a so-called good intention and proper devotion it considers God-pleasing."[16]

[14]W. 23, 225; Wa. 20, 856.   [15]W. 33, 118; Wa. 7, 2278.
[16]W. 40, I, 361f.; Wa. 9, 302.

Equally outspoken Luther is in rejecting new revelations which some claim to have received in ecstatic visions, dreams, or moments of deep emotion. During the Christmas season of 1543 Luther delivered a special course of lectures at the university on Isa. 9:2-7. During his remarks on v. 6 he said to the students:

"When you begin to love this little Child, then rest assured and assert as a certainty that you are of the number of the righteous, and one whom the 'Father has drawn,' not by some hyperphysical drawing, by revelations and visions. For you must not believe those peculiar illuminations, ecstasies, and visions such as the revelations which the monks have had at times. Of all such things the devil is often the author, and he is such a potent spirit that he can produce and inject into you the most delightful thoughts, making you think that you are among the angels, etc. But how delightful such thoughts may ever be, he pours them into the heart with a design and for an end far different from what men think. Such thoughts and illuminations are surely outside 'the Son that is given.' At this point many have broken their neck, and run into grave danger."[17]

Luther was convinced that aberrations of this kind were taking place in the perverted minds of the many religious fanatics with whom he had to deal. He called all who were handling religious matters without the Word of God "Schwaermer."[18] In his Table Talk he frequently refers to these people. He says that he has met more than thirty, at another time sixty of them, who all tried to remove him from his Scriptural position.[19] He charges them with having checked the victorious advance of the reformation against Romanism at many points. His judgment of them is summed up in these words:

"My Schwaermers prepare the way for completely denying Christ, God, and everything else, and some of them now begin to believe nothing. For they stride forth in the conceit of reason; that, forsooth,

---

[17]W. 40, III, 657; Wa. 6, 185.
[18]The English language has no exact equivalent for this term. "Mental ramblers" or "rovers" would express its meaning.
[19]Wa. 22, 1824, 1017.

is to be their trusted guide. Such mockery, however, serves but to rouse the mad rabble, who care nothing for Scripture."[20]

The Scripturalness of Luther's teaching is what won him his earliest co-workers and adherents. It gripped men's hearts in high and low estates and held them firm in convictions that were divinely wrought. *Nil nisi Scriptura!* (Nothing but Scripture!); *Nil ultra Scripturam!* (Nothing beyond Scripture!); *Quod non est biblicum, non est theologicum* (Whatever is not from the Bible is no part of theology)— these became slogans of Lutheran teachers. The Lutheran Confessions utter practically the same sentiment when the theologians assembled at Smalcald in 1537 adopted as their "rule" this: "The Word of God shall establish articles of faith, and no one else, not even an angel."[21] The Index of Scripture texts in the Triglot Concordia records 1,600 references.[22] This is, of course, a mere mechanical way of determining the use which the Lutheran confessors made of the Bible. The study of the Confessions themselves, however, evidences how completely the thought and diction of these men has become merged into that of the holy writers.[23]

The Scripturalness of its teaching is called the Formal Principle or Scripture Principle (*Formalprinzip* or *Schriftprinzip*) of Lutheranism. The meaning is, that anything which is presented as an article of faith, binding men's consciences, has the proper form, face, lineaments, shape, appearance, only when it is taken from the Scriptures; otherwise Lutherans regard it as a doctrinal abnormity, a phantasm, a monstrosity.[24] The old Norwegian Synod well

---

[20] W. 23, 127; Wa. 20, 800.   [21] Tr. p. 466.

[22] 382 to the Old Testament, 4 to the Apocrypha, 1,214 to the New Testament.

[23] They have, with Luther, made the world sing: "The Word they shall have let to stand."

[24] See Dau, "The Principium Cognoscendi in Theology"; "False Principia Cognoscendi in Theology"; "Luther's Theological Method," in *Concordia Theological Monthly*, August, September, and November, 1942.

expressed the mind and spirit of Lutheranism when it chose for its synodical seal the inscription: "It is Written."[25]

The Material Principle

The Scripture wrapping—metaphorically speaking—in which Lutheran teaching is presented certifies to its recipients its authenticity as God's message, a revelation from heaven to mankind. As such it is to secure for itself a reverent reception by all men. The wrapping may be counterfeited by a perverse use of Scripture. Truth may be made to serve as a specious cover for falsehood. The devil so employed it against the first Adam in Eden and against the second Adam in the wilderness. But the deception is discovered the moment the package is opened, and its contents are spread out for inspection. The container of God's truth is a priceless gift, but the contents are invaluable. Lutheran teaching presents "words fitly spoken, like apples of gold in baskets of silver."[26] When the teachings of Scripture are examined one by one, when their import, their harmony, their bearing on men's present and future life are fully apprehended, it is seen that they all rest on, spring from, a marvellously benign disposition toward renegade man on the part of his grossly insulted Creator. God's saving grace to fallen man streams out in all the wealth of knowledge, wisdom, and comfort which the Scriptures convey to despairing mankind. Luther felt that this wealth made all this world too narrow for gathering and storing all its treasure.[27]

---

[25]So did the Missouri Synod with its seal: *Verbum Dei Manet in Aeternum* (The Word of God Abideth Forever); Concordia Seminary of St. Louis with its seal: *Anothen to Phos* (The Light is from above); Valparaiso Lutheran University with its seal: *In Luce Tua Videmus Lucem* (In Thy Light Shall We See Light; Ps. 36:9). Other American Lutheran bodies very likely have adopted similar mottoes. I regret that I am not able to quote them.

[26]Prov. 25:11.   [27]W. 12, 235; Wa. 19, 1734.

It is impossible within the limits of this article to gather more than a few testimonies from Luther's and the confessional Lutheran writings to show how vigorously they have employed the material principle. To Luther the entire Scriptures, both of the Old and the New Testament, are one grand, harmonious testimony to Christ: to the mystery of His person, "without controversy great,"[28] and to the equally great mystery of the divine decree of redemption, which brought Christ into the world, to be the Savior of all mankind. "The entire Scriptures, through and through, tend to this, that Christ may be known."[29] "God is especially concerned about revealing and having men know His Son; for the Scriptures are given for the sake of the Messiah, the Woman's Seed, who is to restore everything that the serpent has corrupted, to take away sin, death, wrath, and to bring back innocence, life, the paradise, and kingdom of heaven."[30]

Accordingly, Luther holds: "Scripture must be understood, not against, but in favor of, Christ, and must either be related to Him or not be regarded as true Scripture."[31]

Luther studied Christ from every possible angle: the duality of His natures, the divine and the human, both unchanged by His incarnation; the unity of His person, one and the same individuality at all times and forever, not Christ the God alone, nor Christ the man alone, but the God-man. He studied the relation of Christ to the Holy Trinity, the operations of God within and without that sphere of unfathomable mystery. But Luther became com-

---

[28] I Tim. 3:16.
[29] W. 12, 438; Wa. 3, 18—from Luther's first sermon on Genesis, March 22, 1523.
[30] W. 54, 88; Wa. 3, 1958—from Luther's Exposition of the Last Words of David in 1543.
[31] W. 39, I, 47; Wa. 19, 1441. Thesis 41 of Luther's First Disputation on Rom. 3:28, at the promotion of Hieronymus Weller and Nicolous Medler, September 11, 1535. This, by the way, explains Luther's critical attitude toward some books of the Scriptures.

pletely absorbed in Christ's teaching. His messages regarding His mission from the Father for His work on earth, and the final application of that work to individual men through the operation of the Holy Spirit, in a word, the gospel.

This term "gospel" cost Luther many anxious hours of meditation until its meaning was flashed into his harassed mind. In his old age Luther remembered his agony as he had sat poring over the meaning of "the righteousness of God revealed in the gospel," Rom. 1:17. He had been taught to understand the righteousness of God as that attribute by which God is righteous in His essence, and by reason of which He abhors all unrighteousness and punishes sinners.

"At last," he relates, "after meditating day and night on this matter, I gave attention, by the mercy of God, to the connection, *viz.*, that the righteousness of God is revealed in this, that the just shall live by faith, as is written. Then and there I began to understand that the righteousness of God is this, by which the just lives by the gift of God, namely by faith, and that the meaning is this, that by the gospel is revealed the passive righteousness of God, namely that the merciful God makes men righteous by faith. . . . Then and there I perceived that I had been entirely reborn, and that I had entered the very paradise by open doors. Immediately the entire Scriptures appeared to me to have assumed an altogether different aspect."[32]

Paul's statement in Titus 3:4-7 now became the central thought in Luther's theology. Grace, grace alone, free grace, universal grace, is the mighty motive behind God's dealings with sinful man. "Grace," says Luther, "denotes the favor by which God accepts us when forgiving our sins and making us righteous gratis through Christ."[33] Grace requires no recompense, yea, it repudiates all efforts of men to merit it by their good works, good conduct, receptivity, etc. It cannot be purchased by bargaining for it; it is bestowed only on

---

[32]W. 54, 186; Wa. 14, 447. From the Preface of Vol. I of the first edition of Luther's Latin Writings, March 5, 1545.

[33]W. 40, II, 421; Wa. 5, 573. From lecture on Ps. 51:12, July 23, 1532.

the unworthy who have become convinced by the law of God and convicted by their own conscience of the utter worthlessness of their life from birth. Yea, in His unbelievable kindness God extends His grace only to His enemies. Human guilt and obstinacy are the Scriptural connotation of divine grace. Therefore grace is never comprehended nor apprehended except by persons who have all notions of their own worthiness crushed in them and are spiritually brought to the brink of despair.

Commenting on Romans, ch. 9, against Erasmus, Luther says:

"What else does this mean than that by the most evident example of both nations [the Jews and the Gentiles] and at the same time by the plainest testimony of Paul it is an established fact that grace is given for nothing to those who have not earned it and are most unworthy of it; and that it is obtained neither by tiny nor great studyings, strivings, achievements of the best and most upright men who seek and pursue righteousness with ardent zeal."[34]

What grace offers, faith must take. Believing means, not only to understand the promise of the gospel intellectually or know it, but also to yield a glad assent to it with the will and to rely on it with a firm trust under all conditions of life.

"Faith," says Luther, "is not the human notion and dream which some regard as faith; and when they see that no improvement of life nor good works come from it, while they hear the person still talk much about faith, they fall into this error that they declare: 'Faith is not sufficient; we must do works if we are to become godly and be saved.' The reason is: when people hear the gospel, they promptly manufacture for themselves by their own powers a notion in their hearts which asserts: 'I believe.' That they proceed to consider real faith. But since it is a human fiction and imagination, which never reaches the bottom of their hearts, it produces no effect on them, and no improvement of life follows from it.

"However, faith is a divine work in us, which divinely transforms and regenerates us, John 1:13. It mortifies the old Adam and makes us entirely new persons in our heart, will, understanding, and all our

[34] W. 18, 775f.; Wa. 18, 1948. From the treatise *On the Bondage of the Will*, 1525.

powers, and brings the Holy Spirit with it. Oh, there is something lively, busy, active, dynamic about it, which makes it impossible for faith not to work unceasingly what is good. Nor does faith inquire whether good works are to be done, but before that question is raised, it has already done them and is always at work. . . . Faith is a lively, bold trust in God's grace, so confident that it would die a thousand times for its own vindication. Such confidence and apprehension of divine grace make a person cheerful, defiant, buoyant in his dealings with God and all creatures. Such is the work of the Holy Spirit. Hence it is that a person is willing and alert, without constraint, to do good, to be of service to everyone, to suffer all manner of distress, from love of God and for His praise, who has manifested such grace to the believer."[35]

These factors, now, namely, the saving grace of God and man's faith in that grace, determine Luther's doctrine of justification, which he considers, not only "the loveliest of all doctrines," but also "the only doctrine that makes one a theologian."[36] "The article of justification," he says, "signifies that we are pronounced righteous by faith alone in Christ, without works."[37]

Justification, then, does not signify an inward change in man but a judgment on the part of God in His estimate of man. God really ought to pronounce on sinful man a verdict of condemnation; but for Jesus' sake, who has become the sinner's Proxy in His entire lifework and has atoned for the sinner's disobedience by His own obedience, God renders instead a verdict of exculpation: He declares the sinner "not guilty." This verdict the sinner accepts by taking God at His word although he is conscious that in himself he is still a sinner. Justification is not a medicinal act by which the sinner is supposed to be gradually purged from sin by making use of divine grace which is infused into him, but it is a forensic, judicial act like that of a judge who quashes an indictment against a criminal.

This faith, however, which accepts God's pardon in

---

[35]Wa. 14, 98f.
[36]W. 25, 375; Wa. 6, 802.
[37]W. 40, I, 355; Wa. 9, 296.

justification is the beginning of a new spiritual life in the sinner, who now starts, in cooperation with the Spirit of Christ that is in him, to sanctify his conduct in consecrated service to God and his fellow men. The commandments of God are no longer grievous to him because, following the leadership of Jesus, he loves God who has given them for his guidance in well-doing.

Every other doctrine of Scripture is in Lutheran theology correlated to the doctrine of justification, either as a cause or an effect. The Lutheran Confessions, echoing Luther's teaching, state:

> "This article concerning justification by faith (as the *Apology* says) is the chief article of the entire Christian doctrine, without which no poor conscience can have any firm consolation, or can truly know the riches of the grace of Christ, as Dr. Luther also has written: 'If this only article remains pure, the Christian Church also remains pure, and in goodly harmony and without any sects; but if it does not remain pure, it is not possible that any error or fanatical spirit can be resisted.' "[38]

The Material Principle of Lutheranism, then, is this, that no teaching can be essential to the life and well-being of the church, which does not present, clearly and unqualifiedly, Christ, the God-man, and His redemption by a vicarious atonement for men's sins; nor the saving grace of God as a free, unconditioned, and unlimited determination on the part of God to restore fallen man to his original destiny; nor human faith as a clear understanding, a welcome acceptance of, and a firm trust in the gospel of Christ as intended for, and applicable to, each believer individually.

The Apostolic Character of Lutheranism

If this is Lutheranism, what is there new about it? Answer: Nothing. Luther and his associates never intended anything new. They never proposed to form a new church

----

[38]Tr. 917, 6; 120, 2.

but only to reform the church of their day which had become deformed, corrupt, by remanding it back to the only
foundation that can be laid for it: the apostles and prophets,
with Jesus Christ Himself as the chief cornerstone. I Cor.
3:11; Eph. 2:20.

Luther challenged his adversaries: "I shall prove that we
have remained with the true, ancient church, yea, that we
are the true, ancient church. But you have fallen away from
us, that is, from the ancient church, and have set up a new
church in opposition to the old,"[39] and then proceeded to
submit the evidence in detail under twelve and more heads.
Lutherans have not in the past aimed, nor do they aim
today, at anything else than the pure teaching of the primitive church in apostolic times. They cannot admit any essential difference between Lutheranism and Christianity. Quite
properly Dr. F. Pieper, one of the leading theologians of the
past generation, issued his *magnum opus* under the title
Christliche Dogmatik, that is, Christian, not Lutheran,
Dogmatics, although the three volumes of his treatise are
filled with references to Luther, the orthodox Lutheran
theologians, and the Book of Concord.

But was not a grave impropriety committed when the
church which sprang from the Reformation adopted a name
that smacks of sectarianism? Answer: Lutherans never chose
the name "Lutheran." It never occurs as their designation in
their confessional writings. It was affixed to them in scorn
by their adversaries. Luther repudiated it indignantly. He
declared: "I beg not to have my name mentioned, and to
call people, not Lutheran, but Christian. What is Luther?
The doctrine is not mine, nor have I been crucified for
anyone."[40] Only when allegiance to the truth was involved,

---

[39] W. 51, 478ff.; Wa. 17, 1322ff. From Luther's invective against
Duke Henry of Brunswick "Wider Hans Worst." March, 1541.

[40] W. 8, 685; Wa. 10, 375. From Luther's *Faithful Warning to
Christians to Beware of Rioting and Rebellion*. 1522.

Luther, in accordance with II Tim. 1:8, warned people not to foreswear his name cowardly while in their hearts they were convinced of the truth of his teaching.[41] Lutherans today bear this name for this very reason. They do not believe in Luther but in his teaching and are convinced that because of their faith they are not a sect but are of "the one holy, catholic, and apostolic church" of the Nicene Creed.[42]

The Heirs of the Heritage

After the foregoing it seems almost supererogatory to discuss at length the beneficiaries of the work performed four centuries ago. Everyone who loves the truth as it is in Christ Jesus is welcome to claim his share in the Lutheran legacy and to operate with it to the glory of God for the upbuilding of His church and for a blessing to our beloved country which afforded an early haven of refuge and shelter to Lutherans.

It may not be out of place in this connection to recall Goethe's words:

> *Was du ererbt von deinen Vaetern hast,*
> *Erwirb es, um es zu besitzen.*
>
> [What from thy fathers thou hast inherited,
> Acquire it, that thou mayest possess it.]

The heritage is not a physical chattel that is handed over to a person in material bulk and entails no labor on the part of the recipient for getting hold of it. It is a spiritual bequest which only he can truly and fully possess who is filled with the spirit of the testator.

Lutheran teaching, because of its Scriptural and evan-

---

[41] W. 10, II, 40; Wa. 20, 91. From Luther's treatise *On Receiving the Sacrament in Both Kinds*, against Karlstadt. 1522.

[42] See Dau, "Lutheranism and Christianity," in *Four Hundred Years*, pp. 314-328.

gelical character, gripped the hearts of men when it began.
It was recognized as heaven's answer to the crying need of
the time. The late Dixie Professor of Ecclesiastical History
in the University of Cambridge has produced one of the
most recent and detailed portraitures of conditions in the
pre-Reformation church of Europe.[43] The distress there
pictured, even with professed restraint and *sotto voce,* aids
one in understanding the scope and the force of Lutheranism in its palmy days. It retains both in the present time.

> *Gottes Wort und Luthers Lehr'*
> *Vergehet nun und nimmermehr.*
> [The Word of God by Luther taught
> Shall nevermore be brought to naught.]

That is because Lutheranism is completely bound up in,
and definitely restricted to the Word of God. Let its present
heirs remember an axiom current among Lutherans in
Reformation times: *"Quo propior Luthero, eo melior theo-
logus"* (the more closely you approach Luther, the better
a theologian you are).

---

[43]See "Reformation" in *Encyclopedia of Religion and Ethics,* X,
609-622.

BIBLIOGRAPHY

Tschackert, Paul, *Die Entstehung der Lutherischen Kirchenlehre u. der Reformierten Samt Ihren Gegensaetzen.* (Gott., 1910).

Holl, Karl, *Gesammelte Aufsaetze zur Kirchengeschichte.* (Mohr, Tuebingen, 1932.)

Kahnis, K. F. A., *Die Deutsche Reformation.*

Wace and Buchheim, *Luther's Primary Works.*

Smith, Preserved, *Age of the Reformation.*

Koestlin, J., tr. by C. E. Hay, *The Theology of Luther.*

Dau, W. H. T., *Luther Examined and Reexamined,* a Review of Catholic Criticism and a Plea for Revaluation.

Pieper, Francis, *Luther's Doctrine of Inspiration,* in *Presbyterian and Reformed Review,* IV (1893), 249-66.

Elert, Werner, *Morphologie des Luthertums,* 1931.

Schmauk, Theodore, *The Confessional Principle,* Philadelphia: 1911.

Koberle, Adolf, *Rechtfertigung und Heiligung,* tr. by J. C. Mattes as *The Quest for Holiness.*

Sasse, H., *Was Heisst Lutherisch?* 1934, tr. by T. G. Tappert as *Here We Stand.*

Krauth, Charles Porterfield, *Conservative Reformation and Its Theology,* 1872.

THE WORD OF GOD

J. A. DELL

It has sometimes been said that the Reformation merely substituted an infallible book for an infallible church.[1] We should prefer to say that we have appealed from the decrees of fallible men to the Word of an infallible God.

The Augsburg Confession of the year 1530 has no separate article on the Word of God; not that the Word of God is ignored, however, or regarded as not binding upon Christians, but rather because the authority of God's Word is taken for granted as the frequent references to Scripture in the articles of the Confession show. But in the Formula of Concord, dated fifty years later, the very first words of the introduction are these: "We believe, teach, and confess that the prophetic and apostolic writings of the Old and New Testaments are the sole rule and norm according to which all teachings and teachers are to be estimated and judged."[2] And then, as each article is taken up, the affirmative statement of the doctrine will frequently have a subhead, "Pure doctrine, faith, and confession according to the above-mentioned norm," or "Pure doctrine of God's Word."

In the Lutheran Church in America the confessional article of the various synodical constitutions usually begins with a paragraph something like this: "We accept without

---

[1]"In the controversy against the Catholic principle of tradition on the one side, and on the other the principle of the Spirit of the individualistic enthusiast together with the newly arising rationalist principle, the temptation could not be withstood to create a system of assurances including the confessional dogma, the notion of verbal inspiration, and the Bible understood as a Book of revealed doctrine. The 'paper Pope' stands over against the Pope in Rome."—Emil Brunner, *The Divine-Human Encounter*, Westminster Press, 1943, p. 31. Translated by Amandus W. Loos.

[2]Mueller, *Die Symbolischen Bücher*, p. 517.

exception all the canonical books of the Old and New Testa·
ments as a whole, and in all their parts, as the divinely
inspired, revealed, and inerrant Word of God, and submit
to this as the only infallible authority in all matters of faith
and life."[3]

It is evident from the above that the position of the
Lutheran Church for four hundred years and down to the
present time has been that of Luther at Worms: "Show me
from the Word of God where I am wrong; otherwise I cannot and will not retract anything. Here I stand." It is also
evident how many and important points of doctrine are
involved in the simple statement, "For us the inspired Word
of God is the sole authority." Before one has sounded the
depth of that one brief sentence one must consider the
doctrine of revelation, the doctrine of inspiration, the problem of canonicity and the related problem of text criticism,
the question of the reliability and infallibility of the written
Word, and finally the group of doctrines of the Word as
means of grace, the efficacy of the Word, and the role of the
Holy Spirit. It is not the province of this chapter to cover
all these points. Subsequent chapters will deal with Text
Criticism, the Work of the Holy Spirit, and the Means of
Grace. What we are to consider now is the Word of God as
the source of authority in Lutheran theology. We begin
with a question:

WHAT DO WE MEAN BY THE WORD OF GOD?

1. A word is always traceable to a person. It is the
external symbol of a thought. Always the thought precedes
the word; the word is the externalized expression of the pre-
existent thought and is intended to convey that thought to
another person.

---

[3]From the Minneapolis Theses, basis of union of the five synods
comprising the American Lutheran Conference.

Applied to the Word of God, that means that the divine Word stems from a divine thought, a thought which God wishes to communicate to other persons. When the thought has been expressed in a form in which it may be apprehended by us it has become a Word.

Any word that is apprehended by us human beings is a revelation of and by another person. It is that for the simple reason that we cannot read other minds. We may form some general ideas of another person simply by observation, but we are unable to discern his thoughts. So by the observation of nature and by the exercise of natural reason we may form some conclusions in regard to God. But we are not able by natural powers to penetrate the mind of God and discern the thoughts of His heart. Even the natural knowledge that man has of God is not reliable, since, due to the fallibility of man's reason, he may arrive at wrong conclusions even when he starts with correct premises. Much less can we presume to say what are the specific details of God's thoughts toward us and His will for us. "No man hath seen God at any time."[4] "The natural man receiveth not the things of the Spirit of God."[5] "For who hath known the mind of the Lord?"[6] We can know only what God reveals to us of the counsels of His heart. Revelation is a voluntary act of God by which He, on His own initiative, removes the veil from that which we could not otherwise know.

2. This revelation has taken place in more than one way. There are recorded instances of God's speaking audibly to human beings. In Exodus we come upon the statement, "Moses spake, and God answered him by a voice."[7] Earlier in his experience with God, Moses had heard a voice that called to him from a burning bush.[8] Elijah also heard the

---

[4]John 1:18.   [5]I Cor. 2:14.
[6]Rom. 11:34.   [7]Exod. 19:19.
[8]Exod. 3:4.

voice of God.[9] In the Gospels several times the voice of God is heard from heaven as at the baptism and the transfiguration of Jesus.[10]

At other times God communicated with men through an angel as in the case of Mary and Joseph.[11] At times He revealed His mind through visions like that of Peter at Joppa or of Paul at Troas.[12] At times He made known future events by means of dreams as in the cases of Pharaoh and Nebuchadnezzar.[13]

3. So far we have been considering direct and immediate revelation, instances of God's speaking *to* men. But He also speaks *through* men, that is, mediately; and this constitutes the great bulk of revelation. We mean that the men to whom God communicated His thought were also agents through whom He conveyed that thought to others. "God . . . at sundry times and in divers manners spake in time past unto the fathers by the prophets."[14] "He spake by the mouth of His holy prophets which have been since the world began."[15] "God hath spoken by the mouth of all His holy prophets."[16]

The manner of God's making known to the prophets what they were to say is in most cases not revealed to us. Here and there we have the record of a vision or a voice, but for the most part the prophets simply say, "The Word of the Lord came unto me," without making clear how they knew it to be the Word of the Lord. But that they knew it to be a divine message entrusted to them is evident from their reluctance to accept the responsibility (Moses, Jonah); from their courage under persecution (Isaiah, Amos); and from their condemnation of false prophets (Jeremiah). Not being given the specific information, we do not pretend to be able

---

[9]I Kings 19:12ff.
[11]Luke 1:26; Matt. 1:20.
[13]Gen. 41; Dan. 4.
[15]Luke 1:70.

[10]Matt. 3:17; 17:5.
[12]Acts 10; Acts 16:9.
[14]Heb. 1:1.
[16]Acts 3:21.

to say in every instance how God gave the prophets their message; and if we speculate as to how it might have taken place—by direct inner illumination or otherwise—we realize that there is no authority in our speculations. In other words, we are here already making use of the Lutheran principle that the Word of God alone is the authoritative norm of faith, and where the Word is silent we do not presume to speak.

4. Both streams of revelation, God's speaking directly to men and God's speaking through men, blend into one in the person of our Lord Jesus Christ.[17] For on the one hand He is the Son of God in whom dwelleth all the fulness of the Godhead bodily,[18] and on the other hand He is our blood brother, the Word made flesh, who tabernacled among us and spoke with human lips to human ears. "God who at sundry times and in divers manners spake in time past unto the fathers by the prophets, hath in these last days spoken unto us by His Son."[19] "Have I been so long time with you and yet hast thou not known Me, Philip? He that hath seen Me hath seen the Father."[20] "No man hath seen God at any time; the only-begotten Son, which is in the bosom of the Father, He hath declared Him."[21] "This is My beloved Son . . . hear ye Him."[22] As in Christ the climactic act of what God *does* for us takes place, so in Him and around Him clusters the brightest, clearest revelation of what God *wills* for us. He is the living Word.

All of this is revelation. First there is a thought in God's mind which He wills to make known to us. When He does make it known, it is by an act of revelation on His part, not

---

[17]It is impossible here to avoid some anticipation of the doctrine of Christ, for theology is not a patchwork quilt but a seamless robe, "woven throughout from top to bottom."

[18]Col. 2:9.

[19]Heb. 1:1, 2.   [21]John 1:18.

[20]John 14:9.   [22]Matt. 17:5.

of discovery on our part. And when by an act of revelation,
which may take place in many ways, His inner thought is
communicated to us in language we can understand, it is a
Word of God. Sometimes that was a spoken Word. But
if it were no more than that it would probably be lost to us
today. We know what the audible voice from the burning
bush said to Moses because it is written down in Exodus.
We know what Jesus said because it is written down in the
Gospels. When we speak of the Word of God today we
mean the Bible.

The Written Word

How did the written Word come into being? Only of a
very small portion of it can we say that God wrote it. Of the
Ten Commandments Moses says, "The Lord delivered unto
me two tables of stone written with the finger of God."[23]
And when Belshazzar saw the handwriting on the wall,
Daniel interpreted it in this fashion: "The God in whose
hand thy breath is . . . hast thou not glorified. Then was
the part of the hand sent from Him, and this writing was
written."[24] But if these meager fragments were all the Word
of God we possessed, it would profit us little; for they are
only law and judgment.

Those who heard Jesus speak heard the Word of God
directly, for He said of His preaching: "He that is of God
heareth God's words. . . . I have given them Thy Word."[25]
But Jesus Himself wrote nothing.

The Word as we have it was written by men. Before it
was committed to writing it existed in the minds of the men
who wrote. Often the Word was current in an oral form
before it was written. The literary prophets probably proclaimed their messages from God orally before writing
them. After Pentecost the apostles and their followers

---

[23]Deut. 9:10.   [24]Dan. 5:23, 24.
[25]John 8:47; 17:14.

preached the Word far and wide for a while before any of the Gospels was written. When St. Paul wrote his epistles he wrote to confirm what he had previously preached and to correct any misapprehensions of the spoken Word.

Nor can we point to a direct command of the Lord to write the Word in more than a few instances. Moses is told, "Write thou these words."[26] Jeremiah records this command: "The Word that came to Jeremiah from the Lord, saying, Thus speaketh the Lord God of Israel, saying, Write thee all the words that I have spoken unto thee in a book."[27] Daniel receives the instruction, "But thou, O Daniel, shut up the words, and seal the book."[28] St. John, the Revelator, hears the Son of man say, "Write the things which thou hast seen."[29] But even so the portion of the written Word that is covered by these explicit commands is small. Those who do not hold the Lutheran position that the written Word is the sole norm of faith sometimes point out the absence of a command to write and use it as an argument for their view. These opponents are of two types: those who believe that the church is not only the custodian but also the judge of the Word, and that therefore the church can add to the Scriptures decrees, pronouncements, and interpretations whose authority is equal to or superior to that of the Bible; and those who believe that the Spirit of God speaks directly to and through "inspired" individuals today just as He in times past spoke to and through the prophets and the apostles.

With the fathers we say that such extra-Biblical pronouncements (whether of tradition or enthusiasm) either say the same thing as the Scriptures, in which case they are unnecessary; or they contradict the Scriptures, in which case they are untrue.

---

[26]Exod. 34:27.   [27]Jer. 30:1, 2.
[28]Dan. 12:4.   [29]Rev. 1:19.

How, then, do we know that these writings are sacred and divine and speak with the authority of God? We can easily perceive the motivation behind some of the writings. Sometimes the writers themselves tell us their reason for writing. Luke's introduction to the third Gospel says: "It seemed good to me . . . to write unto thee in order that thou mightest know the certainty of those things wherein thou hast been instructed."[30] And the fourth Gospel declares, "These are written that ye might believe that Jesus is the Christ, the Son of God; and that believing ye might have life through His name."[31] Many of the epistles are self-explanatory as to the cause of their being written.

But behind the various human motives for writing stands the Prime Mover, the eternal Spirit of God. Peter writes that "no prophecy of the Scripture is of any private interpretation. For the prophecy came not in old time by the will of man, but holy men of God spake as they were moved by the Holy Ghost."[32] Let us look a little closer at this important passage. It is not true that this refers to Old Testament prophecy only. The words translated "not in old time" are simply οὐ ποτέ, which means "not ever."[33] That the writer is referring to his own message and that of others associated with him is clear from the context. "We have a more sure word of prophecy, whereunto ye do well that ye take heed."[34] Nor does the apostle refer only to oral prophecy (men of God "spake," ἐλάλησαν); for he has just written, "Moreover I will endeavor that ye may be able after my decease to have these things always in remembrance."[35] His prophecy (proclamation of the will of God), which was oral, he is putting down in writing that they may still have it

---

[30]Luke 1:3, 4.   [31]John 20:31.
[32]II Pet. 1:21.
[33]Moffatt translates: "Prophecy never came by human impulse."
[34]II Pet. 1:19.   [35]II Pet. 1:12-15.

after he is dead; and of that prophecy, whether oral or written, he says that it comes by the moving of the Holy Spirit.

That the oral message of the prophets comes from the Spirit of God is a clear tenet of the Scriptures from Moses to Revelation. On one occasion, when certain men of Israel prophesied, Joshua said, "My lord Moses, forbid them." And Moses replied: "Enviest thou for my sake? Would God that all the Lord's people were prophets, and that the Lord would put His Spirit upon them."[36] Prophecy came by the moving of the Spirit. In the book of Nehemiah it is written: "Thou (God) gavest also Thy good Spirit to instruct them. . . . Thou didst testify against them by Thy Spirit in Thy prophets."[37] Ezekiel declares, "The Spirit entered into me when He spake unto me."[38] To His disciples Jesus said, "Ye shall receive power after that the Holy Ghost is come upon you, and ye shall be witnesses unto Me."[39] And introducing the last book of the Bible, John says, "I was in the Spirit on the Lord's day."[40]

But if the oral proclamation of the will of God came by the Spirit, then the written form of that prophecy must also be a gift of the Spirit. For on the one hand, the revelation of God's will that comes from the Spirit of truth is never given to deceive but to enlighten; therefore, it is not conceivable that the Spirit of truth would give them one message to proclaim orally and permit them to write another and different message. On the other hand, men who were moved by the Spirit were fully conscious of their responsibility to God; therefore, they would not have dared to write anything that varied from the message God gave them. The attitude of Balaam is the attitude of all the prophets: "If Balak would give me his house full of silver and gold, I can-

---

[36]Num. 11:28, 29.
[37]Neh. 9:20, 30.   [39]Acts 1:8.
[38]Ezek. 2:2.   [40]Rev. 1:10.

not go beyond the Word of the Lord my God. . . . Have I
now any power at all to say anything? The word that God
putteth in my mouth, that shall I speak. . . . Must I not take
heed to speak that which the Lord hath put in my mouth?"[41]

When, therefore, New Testament speakers or writers
refer to Old Testament Scriptures they speak of this *written*
Word of the prophets as the Word of the Spirit of God, a
Word which has authority and gives life. Jesus does so.
"How then doth David in Spirit call Him Lord?"[42] What
David wrote he wrote in the Spirit. "Ye do err, not knowing
the Scriptures."[43] A knowledge of the Scriptures keeps one
from error. "The Scriptures cannot be broken."[44] Their
authority cannot be questioned. "They have Moses and the
prophets; let them hear them."[45]This is the way to escape
condemnation. "There is one that accuseth you, even Moses
. . . if ye believe not his writings, how shall ye believe My
words?"[46] Moses' words and Jesus' teachings are placed on
the same level. Jesus is the last, perfect, and complete
revelation of God. If we do not accept His estimate of the
Scriptures, how can we accept anything else of the revelation God gives through Him?

The apostles speak of the Scriptures of the Old Testament in the same manner. Peter (and remember that he
himself is speaking in the Spirit) quotes Joel and David in
his Pentecost sermon.[47] He cites Psalm 16 and Joel 2 and
says that those writers foretold the resurrection of Christ
and the outpouring of the Spirit. Now God had said to
Moses, "When a prophet speaketh in the name of the Lord,
if the thing follow not, nor come to pass, that is the thing
which the Lord hath not spoken."[48] The fact that the written
prophecies of Joel and of David came true proves them to be

---

[41]Num. 22:18, 38; 23:12.
[42]Matt. 22:43.
[43]Matt. 22:29.
[44]John 10:35.

[45]Luke 16:29.
[46]John 5:45-47.
[47]Acts 2:16, 25.
[48]Deut. 18:22.

the Word of God. When Jesus says of a passage from the book of Isaiah, "This day is this Scripture fulfilled in your ears,"[49] He is confirming that what Isaiah wrote is of God. When thus Jesus and the apostles quote Moses, the Psalms, and the Prophets as inspired, we have all three sections of the Jewish Scriptures referred to as the Word of God: the Law, the Prophets, and the Writings.

From the New Testament we can adduce equal proof that the writings of the apostles and the evangelists are the Word of God. God says through Isaiah, "My Word shall not return unto Me void, but . . . it shall prosper in the thing whereto I sent it."[50] God's Word will be efficacious—to what end or in what way? For the saving of those who believe. For Jesus says, in the parable of the rich man and Lazarus, "They have Moses and the prophets; let them hear them" (if they will escape the place of torment). The same efficacy is ascribed to the *preaching* of the New Testament. "Go . . . preach the gospel to every creature. He that believeth and is baptized shall be saved."[51] "So then faith cometh by hearing, and hearing by the Word of God."[52] "When ye received the Word of God which ye heard of us, ye received it not as the word of men, but as it is in truth, the Word of God."[53] The preaching of the apostles was the Word of God.

Are their writings equally the Word of God? Paul writes to the Corinthians, "I delivered unto you that which I also received, how that Christ died for our sins according to the Scriptures," etc.[54] When he says, "I delivered," he is referring to his oral message; but then he immediately sets down what that oral message was. What he preached, that he also wrote. In another place he says, "If any man think himself to be a prophet, or spiritual, let him acknowledge that the

---

[49]Luke 4:21.
[50]Isa. 55:11.
[51]Mark 16:15, 16.

[52]Rom. 10:17.
[53]I Thess. 2:13.
[54]I Cor. 15:3ff.

things that I write unto you are the commandments of the Lord."[55] Again, "Seeing we have this ministry, as we have received mercy, we faint not; but have renounced the hidden things of dishonesty, not walking in craftiness, nor handling the Word of God deceitfully."[56] Could such a man write anything other than that he had preached? Or when he said, "Though we, or an angel from heaven, preach any other gospel unto you than that which we have preached unto you, let him be accursed"[57]—would he write a different gospel than he preached? Either he wrote the same gospel, or his writing falls under his own curse. We have seen that Peter also says, "I will endeavor that ye may be able after my decease to have these things always in remembrance."[58] And John writes: "Brethren, I write no new commandment unto you, but an old commandment which ye had from the beginning. The old commandment is the Word which ye have heard from the beginning."[59] What he writes is what he has preached. Or again: "These things write we unto you, that your joy may be full. This then is the message which we have heard of Him."[60] In the book of Revelation the message to each of the seven churches begins, "Unto the angel of the church in ———— write," and ends, "He that hath an ear, let him hear what the Spirit saith unto the churches."[61] What is *written* is spoken of as the message of the Spirit.

The Bible Is God's Word

Anyone who is a Christian will admit that what Jesus Himself says, or what God speaks directly through a prophet, or what is the immediate message of the Holy Spirit (as on Pentecost) is the Word of God. But some

---

[55]I Cor. 14:37.
[56]II Cor. 4:1, 2.
[57]Gal. 1:8.
[58]II Pet. 1:15.

[59]I John 2:7.
[60]I John 1:4, 5.
[61]Rev. 2 and 3.

Christians are of the opinion that, since the Word of God came through men who are fallible, something of the fallibility of men has been mingled with the infallibility of God. They would say that the Bible undoubtedly contains God's Word, but not that it is in all its parts the Word of God. It is the province of the critic to sift, to analyze, to weigh evidence pro and con, and to decide which portions of the Bible are reliable Word of God, and which are the additions of men.[62]

Lutherans prefer to say, "The Bible is God's Word," not, "The Bible contains God's Word." Of course, it is evident that other persons than God speak in the Bible. The wretched comforters of Job speak, Satan speaks in the temptation of Jesus, the rich man of Luke 12 speaks, the Pharisee in the parable of the Pharisee and the publican, Pilate in the trial of Jesus, and many others who are neither God nor the messengers of God. When we say that the Bible is God's Word we do not intend to say that the voice of Satan or of Pilate is the voice of God. But the inclusion of words that are not God's, for the sake of refuting or condemning them, does not make the whole any less the Word of God; just as the inclusion of the words of Dives in the parable of Lazarus and Dives does not make the whole parable any less the Word of the Lord.

It is true that the Scripture is not all of equal value to the believer. At the center of it is Christ, the Word made flesh, and at the center of the revelation of God's mind in Christ stands the cross. In concentric but ever-widening circles around that central fact of grace there are revelations of God of greater or less importance according to their nearness to the center. At the periphery there are some obscure passages that even scholars do not understand. It is not

---

[62]The subject of text criticism will be treated in Chapter III and is therefore only mentioned in passing here.

necessary for salvation that an individual know the entire
Bible. It is necessary only that through the Word he shall
have been brought face to face with the Son of God on the
cross and with the grace of God there manifested. In this
sense it is possible for Luthardt to say, "The Bible *is* the
normative Word of God, and it *contains* the saving Word
of God."[63]

The moment we yield to the theories of various schools
of criticism we have lost the authoritative ground of our
religion. There was, of course, an oral tradition before any
of the books of the New Testament was written. But to
suppose that the written New Testament varies from that
oral tradition is a tragic mistake. Then it becomes necessary
for the critics to winnow the material, to cast aside the chaff
and find the kernel of genuine original tradition. This they
do with great avidity, discarding this section as obviously
spurious and that verse as an editorial comment or "gloss,"
and another as an insertion at a later time, and another as
having been borrowed from a different document, and another as having been added in the interest of a theological
presupposition, and another as a myth lifted from some
heathen religion and added to the record for the purpose of
glorifying an important figure. What is left becomes increasingly meager as the years and the critics multiply. But that
is not the chief damage that is done. The great harm is in
the acceptance of the principle that men must decide on the
basis of human reasoning what is God's Word and what is
not. The final authority is the judgment of the critic, the
judgment of a man. We cannot accept the principle. The
Bible judges men; men do not judge the Bible. So Jesus also
declares to the Jews: "There is one that accuseth you, even
Moses, in whom ye trust."[64]

[63]See Meusel, *Handlexicon*, sub verbo *"Wort Gottes."*
[64]John 5:45.

The same holds true of any other human authority set up alongside of the authority of the Word of God. If the church, or any portion of the church, or any individual in the church can presume to speak with authority equal to that of the written Word, the objectivity of God's revelation has given place to the subjectivity of man's interpretation. The church speaks with authority only when it speaks out of God's Word and in full harmony with it. If that is not the case, then man's judgment of what is true has superseded God's. God is dethroned, and man is enthroned. Therefore Luther demanded that his opponents prove his errors, if any, from the Word of God. Therefore St. Paul exhorts Timothy to "hold fast the form of sound words."[65] And therefore the Formula of Concord says that we hold the Scriptures to be the sole norm according to which all teachings and teachers are to be judged.

Inspiration

The foregoing thoughts lead directly to the subject of inspiration. Why is the written Word of God the sole norm of faith and life so that no critic or pope or enthusiast can add to it or subtract from it? Because it is inspired.

We have seen that in the Bible both the oral messages of the prophets and their written form are ascribed to the working of the Spirit of God. Accordingly we say that the Spirit's moving of the men of God pertains both to the content and the form of their message. This is the doctrine of inspiration.

Over against those who hold that only the content of the prophetic message is inspired and not the form Lutherans sometimes add another word and speak of the doctrine of *verbal* inspiration. More of that presently; but first let us

---

[65]II Tim. 1:13.

inquire why some theologians are reluctant to speak of anything more than an inspiration of content. Because, they
say, the form varies so widely. Paul writes with Paul's
vocabulary, and Mark writes with Mark's. Whether the
vocabulary of any given author be rich or poor, he uses only
that vocabulary which is his. That is true; but it is no argument against the Spirit's having used all vocabularies to
accomplish His purpose. The argument for an inspiration of
content only is based upon a misapprehension, namely, that
if the Spirit controlled also the form, the whole Bible would
be written in the same style, the Holy Spirit's style. That
does not follow. A musician can express himself on a violin
with four strings or on a piano with eighty-eight; but in
either case it is the musician who controls the sounds that
are made and produces the effect that he desires. By verbal
inspiration we mean only that when the Spirit of God used
any man as His instrument, He took what that man had
and, allowing the man to use his own vocabulary, the Spirit
so controlled the use of that vocabulary that what the man
wrote actually conveyed the sense that the Spirit wanted
conveyed.

There has even been some quibbling about the term
"verbal inspiration" on the ground that such a term pre-
scribes a method to the Spirit. It does not have anything to
do with method. No one knows anything about the method
of inspiration. That is something for the Holy Spirit to
know, who searches all things, yea, the deep things of God.
He has not seen fit to reveal to us anything about the method
He uses, and therefore every mouth is stopped on that point.
The use of the term "verbal inspiration" does not refer to the
dictation theory or any other theory as to method. It refers
only to the *fact* of inspiration, a fact clearly revealed in
Scripture, and says that the act of inspiring controlled both
content and form. The Holy Spirit conveyed to His chosen

instrument the thought that God wanted expressed (content) and so controlled the human instrument's use of his own vocabulary that what was written down actually did express and does express God's thought (form).

Why do we believe in inspiration in this sense?

1. Because if the Spirit does not control the form in which His thought is expressed He does not control the thought. However the Spirit imparts the thought to the prophet, the prophet cannot accurately convey it to other men except in words. In fact, the prophet cannot even conceive the thought of the Spirit clearly in his own mind without words. One may have a vague impression, a dim presentiment of a truth, but it is not possible to pass on to other men vague impressions and feelings. Before the prophet can be certain himself what God wants him to say, the message must be clearly apprehended by his mind, and a clear apprehension is not possible in a human mind without a formulation of some kind.[66] Further, if what the Spirit imparted to the prophet were only a vague and an unformulated idea, leaving it to the prophet to translate the general urge into specific language, then we could never be sure that the prophet had hit upon the exact words to convey the Spirit's meaning. But since the whole tenor of Scripture demands of the reader and the hearer that it be accepted as accurate truth, it implies that it has been accurately conveyed and transmitted. Since the whole Bible is composed of words, we cannot speak of an inspired Bible without speaking of inspired words.

2. Because of the way in which Scripture is used in the Scriptures. For example, an argument will be used in the New Testament which hinges upon an exact wording in the

---

[66]"What he cannot express he cannot conceive." (From a description of the human mind by Susanne K. Langer, *Fortune* magazine, January, 1944, p. 142.)

Old. Thus Jesus proves to the Sadducees that there is a life after death by quoting God's words to Moses from the burning bush, "I am the God of Abraham and the God of Isaac and the God of Jacob," and adding, "He is not the God of the dead, but of the living."[67] St. Paul, in like manner, bases an argument on the number of a noun. "He saith not, And to seeds, as of many; but as of one, And to thy seed, which is Christ."[68] Since the Word of God was going to include important arguments based on the form of words, the form of words could not have been a matter of indifference to the Holy Spirit.

3. Because of direct statements of the Scriptures.

a. Consider the passage, "All Scripture is given by inspiration of God," etc.[69] Various exegeses of these words have been offered, but for our present purpose the exegesis is not important. Just take the words πᾶσα γραφὴ θεόπνευστος. Any student, no matter what his interpretation of the passage, will agree that γραφή (writing) and θεόπνευστος (God-breathed) belong together. The point is that it is *writing* (not thinking or speaking) of which inspiration is here predicated. And writing is the form; writing is words.

b. The classic statement of the Apostle Paul which includes the words as well as the thoughts in the gift of the Holy Spirit. "Now we have received, not the spirit of the world, but the Spirit which is of God; that we might know the things that are freely given to us of God. Which things also we speak, not *in the words* which man's wisdom teacheth, but *which the Holy Ghost teacheth;* combining spiritual things with spiritual (words)."[70]

c. The Word of the Lord to Jeremiah, a phrase that is often repeated elsewhere also: "Behold, I have put My

---

[67]Matt. 22:31, 32.   [69]II Tim. 3:16.
[68]Gal. 3:16.   [70]I Cor. 2:12, 13.

words in thy mouth."[71] In the mouth they are words, not mere impressions or impulses.

d. The promise of the Lord to His disciples: "But when they deliver you up, take no thought how or what ye shall speak; for it shall be given you in that same hour what ye shall speak."[72] This does not refer to the Scriptures but to the oral statements of disciples before human courts. The Lord tells His followers that the very words shall be given them. The argument here is *a minori ad majus:* if, in defending themselves, the very words would be given them when only their earthly life was at stake, how much more in writing the testimony of the Lord, upon which the eternal life of future generations would depend!

The Preached Word

We have spoken of the original revelation and of the written form of that revelation. Both are the Word of God. There is still a third sense in which we can speak of the Word of God, namely, the preached Word.

There is a difference here between the preaching that precedes the written Word and that which follows it. Before the letter to the Romans was written, for example, St. Paul preached the doctrine of justification by grace for Christ's sake which is therein contained. And after the letter to the Romans was written, nineteen centuries of preachers have proclaimed justification by faith on the basis of that letter. We do not place the two types of preached Word on the same level. In the one case we have to do with directly inspired persons and special gifts of the Spirit; not so in the other.

The apostles had the advantage of personal contact with the Lord,[73] they were promised special enlightenment by

[71]Jer. 1:9.
[72]Luke 21:15.
[73]I John 1:1-3.

the Lord,[74] and at Pentecost and after they were given special gifts of the Spirit.[75] They were also conscious of the Spirit's nearness and guidance.[76] Those charisms were necessary because that generation was to formulate the revelation of God in Christ in the New Testament for all time. That formulation having been completed, the special gifts of the Spirit are no longer necessary in the same degree. That they are not present now as they were in the first generation of the Christian Church is clear to any observer.

How then, and in what degree, is the preaching of the church of today the preaching of the Word of God? It is the proclamation of God's Word in so far as it conveys to the modern hearer the original meaning of God revealed through Christ or His Spirit. Here again we are driven back to the doctrine of an authoritative and reliable written Word. Everyone knows that in the name of the Christian religion all kinds of statements are made from pulpits. Some of them are directly contradictory to other statements similarly made so that both cannot be true. How can we know the true from the false? Here is the ultimate and unfailing criterion: it is true if it agrees with the original revelation made in the written Word under the guidance of the Spirit of God, and it is untrue if it does not.

The apostles, that is to say, the Holy Spirit, wrote that criterion into the record. Paul writes to the Galatians, "Though we, or an angel from heaven, preach any other gospel unto you than that which we have preached unto you, let him be accursed."[77] And then he proceeds to set that gospel down very clearly in writing. Peter does the same thing. He warns his readers, "There shall be false teachers among you, who privily shall bring in damnable heresies,

---

[74]John 14:26; 15:26, 27; 16:13; Acts 1:8.
[75]I Cor. 12:8-11; 14:18.   [77]Gal. 1:8.
[76]Acts 13:2; 15:28.

even denying the Lord that bought them."[78] How does he aim to safeguard them against such false teachers? He has just told them: "I will endeavor that ye may be able after my decease to have these things always in remembrance. . . . We have a more sure word of prophecy."[79] John also insures his readers against being led astray: "Beloved, believe not every spirit, but try the spirits whether they are of God; because many false prophets are gone out into the world. Hereby know ye the Spirit of God: every spirit that confesseth that Jesus Christ is come in the flesh is of God. . . . This is the record, that God hath given to us eternal life, and this life is in His Son. . . . These things have I written unto you . . . that ye may know."[80]

One thing needs to be said yet. Every argument here set forth for an inspired, authoritative, and reliable Word of God is an argument that presupposes faith. For every appeal is to the written Word, the very Word that is under examination. Far from being ashamed of such reasoning, we are ready to assert that it must be so. Every appeal in law is from a lower court to a higher; but when the highest tribunal has been reached, there is nothing to which we may compare its statements but its own statements. When men swear to the truth they swear by a higher being; but when God would affirm His promises He swears by Himself,[81] because there is no higher being. The Scriptures must be proved true by the Scriptures. They cannot be proved true by reason to reason. They are proved true by faith to faith. As the Son of God said, "If any man will do His will, he shall know of the doctrine, whether it be of God."[82]

---

[78]II Pet. 2:1.   [81]Heb. 6:13.
[79]II Pet. 1:15, 19.   [82]John 7:17.
[80]I John 4:1, 2; 5:11, 13.

BIBLIOGRAPHY

Boettner, Loraine, *The Inspiration of the Scriptures*, Wm. B. Eerdmans Co., 1940.

Brunner, Heinrich Emil, *The Divine-Human Encounter*, Westminster Press, 1943.

Dallmann, William, *Why Do I Believe the Bible Is God's Word?* Concordia Publishing House (reprint), 1937.

Engelder, Theodore, *Scripture Cannot Be Broken*, Concordia Publishing House, 1944.

Ihmels, Ludwig, *Centralfragen der Dogmatik*, 1912.

Meusel, *Handlexicon*, sub verbo *"Wort Gottes."*

Patton, Francis L., *Fundamental Christianity*, Macmillan Co., 1928.

Pieper, F., *Christliche Dogmatik*, Concordia Publishing House, (edited by J. T. Mueller), 1934.

Rohnert, W., *Inspiration der Heiligen Schrift*, 1889. *Die Dogmatik der Evangelisch-Lutherischen Kirche*, H. Wollerman, Leipzig, 1902.

Walther, W., *Das Erbe der Reformation*, Vol. I, *"Der Glaube an das Wort Gottes,"* 1903.

THE SACRED TEXT

The Lutheran Evaluation of Biblical Criticism

E. E. FLACK

As divine revelation the Bible has one Author, the Holy Spirit; as the most human of books it is the product of many inspired men who wrote under varying conditions and circumstances and exhibited in their writings their own peculiarities of language, style, and modes of thought.[1]

Biblical Criticism is the examination of the human and historical aspects of the Scriptures, which, like all other literary remains, lend themselves to scientific analysis. It deals only indirectly with matters of faith. Such investigation, if honestly and reverently pursued, is not only legitimate and desirable; it is even indispensable in theological knowledge.

Literary Criticism is generally classified under two heads: 1) Textual Criticism or Lower Criticism, which seeks to ascertain as nearly as possible the exact words of the original writers; and 2) Higher or Historico-Literary Criticism, which goes beyond the text of a writing in the effort to solve such questions as its authorship, sources, structure, chronology, and circumstances of origin. Of the two types of investigation, the former is more precise, being limited to definite principles of literary procedure; the latter, more subjective and indefinite. Both approaches are helpful to a clear understanding of the text and historical setting of Scripture.

A. The Textual Criticism of the Scriptures

The original manuscripts of the books of the Bible have all become lost; in fact, not a single passage has been preserved to us in the handwriting of the author. If the church

---

[1] Cf., Heb. 1:1; II Tim. 3:16; II Pet. 1:21.

were in possession of the autographs in their entirety, it would be practically unnecessary to resort to the science of Textual Criticism, which seeks primarily to recover the words of the author. But since no original autograph of any portion of Scripture has survived, it is desirable to employ this science in the effort to reconstruct the basic text by the aid of the numerous extant copies, all of which are far removed from the time of writing and are encumbered by many obvious variations from the original.[2] The task is quite complicated, requiring the cumulative contributions of painstaking scholars.

I. *The Textual Criticism of the Old Testament*

1. Comparatively few ancient Hebrew manuscripts of the Old Testament have been preserved. The so-called *Papyrus Nash* (c. 150 A.D.) embraces only the Decalog[3] and the Shema.[4] A larger manuscript, a codex of the Prophets, is dated at 916 A.D. The oldest complete manuscript of the Old Testament extant[5] is generally assigned to the year 1010 A.D. The practice of the Jews in burying or otherwise concealing manuscripts which were damaged or worn or which contained errors accounts in large measure for the paucity of early copies of the Hebrew Scriptures surviving to our day. It was the rule that any manuscript of the Torah which contained more than three errors had to be concealed.

In their labors on the text early Jewish scholars sought to perfect a standard type. Soon after the public recognition of the Canon of the Old Testament in the second century A.D.,[6] a text known as the text of the Sopherim became fixed as

---

[2] It is estimated that the extant manuscripts of Scripture embrace as many as 200,000 variations. The majority of these, however, are insignificant.

[3] Deut. 5:6ff.

[4] Deut. 6:4.

[5] A manuscript belonging to the Firkowitzsch collection.

[6] The Councils of Jamnia, 90 and 118 A.D.

the official pattern.[7] This text was consonantal: it did not
originally embrace the Hebrew vowel marks. Gradually it
came to be regarded as the sacred text,[8] the type to which
all others were made to conform. Manuscripts containing
even the slightest deviation from this standard were for the
most part destroyed.

In the next several centuries the Jewish scribes studied
the text laboriously, copying on the margins of their codices
notes dealing with such matters as alternate readings, spell-
ing, pronunciation, and the number of words and even
letters in the documents. In the Masorah or tradition they
handed down cumulative evidences in support of the sacred
text. They employed the aid of the Targums, Aramaic para-
phrases of the Hebrew, and the Talmud, or commentaries on
the text. Eventually, about the seventh century A.D., they
introduced the Hebrew vowel marks into the consonantal
text in order the more accurately to transmit their sacred
Scriptures. However, by the tenth century the number of
alterations in the text had become so great that a new
standard codex was called forth. This revision, prepared by
Ben Asher, is the parent Palestinian recension. The parent
Babylonian recension, prepared by Ben Naphtali, appeared
about the same time. In spite of their legalistic and mechanical approach, the Masoretic scribes rendered an inestimable
service to the science of textual criticism.

Since the transmitted text thereafter carried the vowel
marks, it was commonly held at the time of the Reformation
that they were a part of the original. A Jewish scholar, Elias
Levita (1468-1549), first in Reformation times advanced the
theory that the vowel points were a late addition.[9] Luther
readily accepted this conclusion. But in spite of cumulative

---

[7]The scribes were called Sopherim (Heb. *saphar,* meaning to
count), because they counted the letters and words in their Scriptures.
[8]Cf. Josephus: *Contra Apionem,* 1:8.
[9]Levita's book was entitled *A Masorah of the Masorah.*

evidence, this view did not gain general acceptance for centuries.

2. The transmission of the related texts and versions has been of great aid in the reconstruction of the basic text. The Samaritan Pentateuch is an independent Hebrew text which owes its origin to the separation of the Samaritans from the Jews (c. 400 B.C.). The oldest extant manuscript of this text dates from the tenth century A.D. It differs from the standard text in about 6,000 readings, comparatively few of which, however, are of any particular significance.

The Greek versions of the Old Testament are very important. Foremost among them is the Septuagint (LXX), which is older than the text of the Sopherim, having been undertaken in Alexandria in the time of Ptolemy Philadelphus (285-247 B.C.), though not completed for almost two centuries. The translators took considerable liberty with the text, particularly in the latter sections of the Old Testament. They even added a number of books, the so-called Apocrypha. But in spite of its variations and additions, LXX is a very important guide toward the determination of the original. Many manuscripts of LXX antedate by several centuries the earliest extant Hebrew texts.[10]

Besides LXX, which the early Christians on Gentile soil adopted as their Bible, certain other Greek versions of the Old Testament, namely, those of Aquila, Theodotion, and Symmachus, are noteworthy. They appeared about the second century A.D. A monumental undertaking was the Hexapla of Origen, embracing six texts in parallel columns.[11]

---

[10] Among these are *Codex Sinaiticus* (Aleph) and *Codex Vaticanus* (B) of the fourth century, and *Codex Alexandrinus* (A) of the fifth. The first printed text of the LXX appears in the Complutensian Polyglot (1514-17). Modern critical editions include those of Swete (3 vols. 1887-94), Brooke and McLean (Cambridge, 1906 . . .), and Rahlfs (1935).

[11] The Hebrew, Greek-lettered Hebrew, Aquila, Symmachus, LXX in revised form, and Theodotion.

Chief among the Latin versions was Jerome's Vulgate (390-404 A.D.), which became the standard. Other versions included the Syriac, Egyptian, Gothic, Arabic, and Slavonic, all of which have served to throw further light upon the original.

3. The invention of printing contributed greatly to the preservation of the sacred text of Scripture. The first complete Hebrew Bible containing the Tiberian vowel pointing came from the press at Soncino in 1488. A second edition appeared at Naples in 1491-1493. In 1494 the third edition, the *Brescia Bible*, which Luther later employed in preparing his German translation, appeared. The first printed rabbinic Bible, containing vowel marks and accents, the Masorah and comments, was issued at Venice by Daniel Bomberg in 1516-1517. The second edition of this work, published in 1524-1525, is known as the *editio princeps*, the standard text for later times. The first text of the Hebrew Bible appearing under Christian influences is that issued in the Complutensian Polyglot in 1514-1517.

Since Reformation times many critical editions of the Hebrew Bible have appeared under both Jewish and Christian influences. This process, which has involved the employment of such aids as chapter divisions, numbering, paragraphing, and versification, has resulted in the multiplication of variations from the *editio princeps*. However, by careful comparison of the variants and the elimination of readings obviously inferior, scholars have approximated the original text. The work of textual critics in assembling the variant readings[12] has served to indicate more clearly the remarkable accuracy of the fixed text of the Sopherim of the second century A.D., with which the reconstructed text is for the

---

[12]Kenicott, *e.g.*, in 1776-80 assembled the variant readings of 694 manuscripts, and De Rossi in 1784-98 issued in several volumes the variant readings of 732 manuscripts and 310 printed editions.

most part identical. The best modern edition with critical apparatus is Kittel's *Biblia Hebraica.*[13]

Since the standard text of the Sopherim was itself a reconstructed text, which, though remarkably pure, obviously embraced many variations from the original, the task of the textual critic has been not merely to present a text in conformity with this imperfect pattern, but to endeavor to recover as nearly as possible the text of the autographs. To this end he is under obligation to make use of all available resources. This painstaking, yet rewarding, work will never cease so long as linguistic pursuits, historical investigation, and archæological discovery keep bringing to light fresh truths bearing upon the Scriptures.

II. *The Textual Criticism of the New Testament*

1. The *materials* available for the critical study of the text of the New Testament are older and far more extensive than those relating to any other ancient book. More than 4,000 Greek manuscripts of the New Testament in whole or in part have been brought to light. Added to these are twice as many Latin manuscripts. The list of materials includes: a) papyri or early paper documents;[14] b) uncials or majuscles, manuscripts of large-letter script dating down to the ninth century;[15] c) cursives or minuscles, small-script manuscripts dating largely from the ninth century on;[16] d) lectionaries or service books carrying pericopes; e) patristic quotations; f) versions such as the Syriac, Latin, Egyptian, Armenian, Ethiopic, Gothic, Arabic, and Slavonic; g) ostraka or fragments of pottery or limestone bearing

[13]Third edition, Stuttgart, 1929-1937.
[14]*E.g.,* the important Chester Beatty Papyri, brought to light in 1930.
[15]Chief among them are Aleph, B, A, D, C, and W.
[16]Cursives number about 3,000. Among the more important are Nos. 1, 13, 69, 124, and 346.

Scriptural passages;[17] and g) similar talismans or charms. Each of these materials contributes something to our knowledge of the text of the New Testament.

2. The *mechanical arrangement* of the text is also an aid in the effort to date documents, determine their relationships, and decide upon the best readings. Among the devices handed down in New Testament materials are: a) *kephalaia majora* or *titloi*, titles or headings widely represented in manuscripts from the fifth century on; b) Ammonian Sections, introduced by Ammonius of Alexandria to indicate parallel passages; c) Eusebian Canons, a revision of Ammonius' work made by Eusebius (d. 340 A.D.);[18] d) Euthalian Sections, divisions of Acts and Epistles of Paul made by Euthalius near the end of the fourth century A.D.; e) *stichoi* or lines devised to guide the reader as well as copyists; f) punctuation; and g) versification.

The modern chapter division of the New Testament was arranged about 1205 A.D. by Stephen Langdon, Archbishop of Canterbury (d. 1228). Robert Stephanus (Fr. Estienne), a Paris printer, first introduced the modern verse division in a Greek New Testament published in Geneva in 1551.

3. *Printed texts* of the Greek New Testament are very numerous. Cardinal Ximenes prepared the first edition for the Complutensian Polyglot, completed January 10, 1514. However, Pope Leo X withheld his authorization for its publication for several years. Meanwhile Erasmus issued his Greek New Testament early in 1516. Though inferior to the work of Ximenes, this edition was cheaper and more popular as a single volume. By 1522 it had reached its third edition; by 1535, its fifth. Robert Stephanus issued several

---

[17]These were in use between the sixth century B.C. and the fourth century A.D. Cf. II Cor. 4:7, "We have this treasure in earthen (*ostrakinois*) vessels."

[18]Eusebius divided the Gospels into 1,165 sections, which he arranged into ten canons or tables.

editions between 1546 and 1555. The third edition of 1550 marked an advance in textual criticism by reason of his use of readings of several manuscripts, including Codex Bezæ (D). Between 1565 and 1604 Theodore de Beza produced as many as nine editions, no one of which, however, marked any appreciable advance over the text of Erasmus.

From 1624 to 1678 the Elzivir brothers, printers at Leyden and Amsterdam, brought out seven editions, which were also largely reproductions without significant improvements. Their second edition, issued in 1633, carried in its preface this advertisement: *"Textum ergo habes nunc ab omnibus receptum."*[19] This statement, though supported by no ecclesiastical authority, marked this edition as the *Textus Receptus*, the standard on the continent for two centuries. In England Stephanus' edition of 1550 was regarded as the received text. As in the case of the Hebrew text of the Sopherim, the *Textus Receptus* became so fixed that any suggested alterations met with vigorous opposition. The only significant advance in the textual criticism of the New Testament made in the seventeenth century appeared in the London Polyglot, issued by Bishop Walton in 1657. For this edition Archbishop Ussher made collations of several newly discovered manuscripts, among them Codex Alexandrinus (A).

In the eighteenth century many new manuscripts were brought to light and numerous collations were made with the received text. In 1707 John Mill issued at Oxford an edition with as many as seventy-eight fresh collations. In his Prolegomena he published a critical apparatus which paved the way for later advances. Richard Bentley of Cambridge, convinced that the received text should be abandoned in favor of a better critical text, issued in 1720 his *Proposals for Printing a Critical Edition of the New Testament.*

---

[19] "You now have therefore the text received by all."

On the continent advances were made by John A. Bengel (1687-1752), who in 1734 published at Tuebingen a Greek New Testament in which he not only made use of new variants but also included a critical apparatus giving the first suggestions relative to the classification of manuscripts. His contemporary, J. J. Wettstein (1693-1754), who collated many manuscripts and developed an ingenious system of manuscript notation, issued a critical text in 1751-1752. Griesbach (1745-1812), who carried forward historical research, particularly on the recensions, patristic quotations, and ancient versions, published in all three editions of the Greek New Testament.[20]

But in spite of the progress made in the eighteenth century in the collecting and collating of manuscripts, very little advance was made in the editing of the text, so deeply rooted in public opinion was the tradition of the perfection of *Textus Receptus*. It remained for scholars in the nineteenth century to point out the superiority of the text of the early uncials.

In 1831, two centuries after the publication of TR (1633), Karl Lachmann (1793-1851), a classical philologist of Berlin, issued the first critical text marking a definite break with the received text. In his second edition with a Prolegomena (1842-1850) he set forth what was regarded as the fourth-century readings on the basis of the earliest extant uncial codices, Alexandrinus (A), Vaticanus (B), and Ephraem (C), and relegated the variant readings of TR to a secondary position at the end. This meant in substance the downfall of TR.

Constantin Tischendorf (1815-1874), the foremost collector and editor of manuscripts in the century, followed with eight critical editions of the Greek New Testament,

---

[20] One at Halle, 1774-7; 2nd rev. ed., Jena, 1796-1806; 3rd ed., 1805.

issued between 1841 and 1872. The discoverer of Codex Sinaiticus (Aleph),[21] Tischendorf made extensive use of this important uncial in his eighth edition (1869-1872), which is still recognized as indispensable to students of the critical text. His pupil, Caspar Rene Gregory (1846-1917), completed and published in 1884-1894 his masterly Prolegomena, which set new standards in textual criticism.[22]

S. P. Tregelles (1813-1875), an English contemporary of Tischendorf, published in 1857-1872 an edition of the Greek New Testament, which, though inferior to the eighth edition of the German scholar, nevertheless rendered a distinct service in diverting the attention of English scholars from their received text. The way was now open for the two great Cambridge scholars, B. F. Westcott (1825-1901) and F. J. A. Hort (1828-1892), to win lasting recognition through their work, *The New Testament in the Original Greek*, published in 1881 after twenty-eight years of critical study and research.

This text superseded the *Textus Receptus* as the standard, though not without opposition from many quarters. Employing the results of critical studies made up to their time, Westcott and Hort distinguished in their critical apparatus four types or families of texts: Neutral, Alexandrian, Western, and Syrian.

In 1898 Eberhard Nestle (1851-1913) issued a Greek New Testament based on the texts of Tischendorf, Westcott and Hort, and Weymouth.[23] Through fortunate publishing arrangements this text with critical apparatus has become very popular.[24]

---

[21]Discovered in 1859, though some leaves were found in 1844.
[22]Revised and enlarged edition in German appeared in 1900-09 under the title, *Textkritik des Neuen Testaments*.
[23]*The Resultant Greek Testament,* 1886, though after 1901 the third text was replaced by that of Bernhard Weiss, 1894-1900.
[24]Sixteen editions appeared between 1898 and 1936.

The work of textual criticism continues. The discovery of many new manuscripts and particularly papyri, fresh research on the text, the appreciation of the *Koine,* the Greek of the New Testament, and the results achieved in criticism of the text called forth in the early decades of this twentieth century numerous revisions of the New Testament in English.[25]

4. The *methods* employed by textual critics in their endeavor to recover the original wording of Scripture involve four distinct processes: 1) An examination is made of each manuscript by itself with the intent of removing all obvious errors, unintentional and intentional. Among the unintentional errors are those of the ear, eye, pen, memory, and judgment. The intentional errors include deliberate linguistic or rhetorical changes, historical corrections, harmonistic alterations, particularly in the Synoptic Gospels, doctrinal and liturgical corrections.

2) The second step involves the comparison of manuscripts to which the first process has been applied and the arrangement of them in various groupings according to resemblances in errors, with the aim of determining the ancestors or archetypes. 3) The next step deals with the comparison of archetypes and the construction of a provisional text. 4) The final process is the conjectural emendation of the reconstructed text. This step is properly employed only in the case of those rare readings which cannot otherwise be resolved.

5. The *principles* governing the determination of the critical text are very complex. In general, those readings are to be preferred which are: a) the older, *i.e.,* nearer in point of time to the original; b) shorter, since it is the tendency

---

[25]Among these are: *The American Standard Version* (1901), now revised; *The New Testament in Modern Speech* by Weymouth (1902); *A New Translation* by James Moffatt (1913); and *The American Translation* by E. J. Goodspeed (1923).

of copyists to enlarge upon the text; c) more difficult, free from explanatory additions; d) more free from doctrinal bias; e) more widely supported; and f) more in harmony with the original writer's style and habits of thought.

In the final analysis, what the scholar is seeking in textual criticism is not necessarily the text of the oldest manuscripts, for a fourth-century manuscript, for example, may be a copy of a very corrupt text of the same period while a sixth-century manuscript, in comparison, may be a direct copy of a third-century ancestor; nor the text of the greatest number of manuscripts since the multiplication of copies tends to increase the probability of error; nor even the oldest text since the oldest recensions which are known are centuries removed from the original autographs; but rather, the purest text possible, the text which according to all the tested canons of criticism reproduces the *ipsissima verba* of the original writers.

B. The Higher Criticism of the Scriptures

Behind the text of Scripture lie, humanly speaking, areas of investigation inviting to inquiring minds. Who was the author of this or that book of the Bible? When and under what circumstances did he write? What sources did he employ in the composition of his work? What were his aims and motives? To whom did he address his thought? Such inquiries into the Holy Scriptures, when carefully and prayerfully made, are quite proper and are conducive to a better understanding and appreciation of the Word of God.

This type of investigation is known as Documentary or Historico-Literary Criticism, Source Criticism, or Higher Criticism—a term which is widely held in disrepute. The expression arises from the fact that the investigations are made higher up the stream, that is, back of the text. It is a type of criticism which readily lends itself, particularly in the hands of unscrupulous and unbelieving men, to intricate analysis, subjective hypotheses, and wide speculation. Under such circumstances it has often been negative and subversive of faith. When properly employed in subordination to the religious use of Scripture, it is a real asset in Biblical study.

At no time in its history has the Bible been free from criticism. Students of Scripture in every age have sought to solve such problems as the authorship, date, sources, and literary structure of Biblical books. The early Jews examined their literature meticulously to ascertain its human origin. The early Christians did likewise. Certain traditions, not always in accordance with the facts, were handed down from early times. Martin Luther examined the traditions current in his day very critically and expressed courageously his honest convictions regarding Biblical questions, though always in relation to Christ as the center and living substance of Scripture. Concerning the Book of Esther he writes: "I am so hostile to the book and to Esther that I wish they did not exist at all; for they Judaize too much and have much heathen perverseness."[26] In his German Bible of 1534 he relegated the Apocrypha to a secondary position in relation to the Canonical Scriptures though he regarded them as "useful for reading." In his prefaces to the several books of the Bible he often spoke critically.[27]

Yet in all his critical study of Scripture Luther had an approach which preserved him from both liberalism and legalism: the principle of justification by faith. As he declared, "All the genuine sacred books agree in this, that all of them preach Christ and deal with Him."[28] Furthermore, in one of his sermons he says: "He who would read the

[26]*Tischreden*, Weimar Edition, Vol. I, No. 475, p. 208.
[27]Cf., Preface to James, *Works of Martin Luther*, Holman Ed., Vol. VI, pp. 444 and 477.
[28]*Works of Martin Luther*, Holman Edition, Vol. VI, p. 478.

Bible must simply take heed that he does not err, for the Scripture may permit itself to be stretched and led, but let no one lead it according to his affects, but let him lead it to the source, *i.e.*, the cross of Christ, then he will surely strike the center."[29]

Anyone holding firmly to this Lutheran principle of justification by faith in Christ may examine the hypotheses of Higher Criticism without fear of losing the Word of God.

I. *The Higher Criticism of the Old Testament*

The modern Higher Criticism of the Bible, much of which has been speculative and negative, began with the investigation of Old Testament problems, particularly questions relating to the authorship and the structure of the Pentateuch. In 1670 Benedict Spinoza, a liberal Jewish philosopher, issued his *Tractatus,* which was the first extensive analytical criticism of the Old Testament. He advanced numerous arguments to disprove the rabbinical tradition that Moses wrote the Pentateuch. In the century following Spinoza criticism was for the most part rationalistic and destructive. In 1753 Jean Astruc, a French physician, published his notable *Conjectures,* in which he called attention to the appearance of different divine names, *Elohim* and Jehovah (or *Yahwe*), in particular sections of Genesis, concluding that back of the present text lie distinct documents. Johann Gottfried Eichhorn (1752-1827), who has been called "the founder of modern Biblical Criticism," in his three-volume work, *Introduction to the Old Testament* (1770-1773), noted that in addition to the distinction in the use of names for God other related literary peculiarities appear in the Pentateuch. The way was now open for wide speculative inquiry. To this interest philosophy, philology, and historical research made large contributions.

---

[29]Weimar Edition, Vol. I, p. 52.

The nineteenth century marked the greatest progress thus far reached in Old Testament criticism. Contributing to this development were many factors such as archæological discovery, which for the first time made possible a firsthand knowledge of the vast Egyptian and Babylonian civilizations and literary remains antecedent to and contemporary with the Hebrews;[30] the organization of Bible societies, which disseminated and popularized the Scriptures;[31] the development of the Sunday school movement, which called forth commentaries, lesson helps, maps, and outlines for Bible study; progress in philosophical thought, which promoted scientific criticism; advances in lexicography and comparative philology;[32] the application of the theory of evolution to history and literature;[33] and numerous other developments taking place in an expanding scientific age.

Employing the new materials and methods, Old Testament critics pressed the investigations initiated in the seventeenth and the eighteenth centuries to the point of crystallizing the theory of the presence of four main documents, J, E, D, and P, in the Pentateuch or rather Hexateuch since Joshua, as was later observed, presents the same literary phenomena. A number of noted critics contributed to the characterization of these supposed documents. Among them were: Wilhelm de Wette (1780-1849), who posited a late and independent dating (c. 621 B.C.) for Deuteronomy; Johann Vatke (1806-1882), a late origin of the Levitical laws; Abraham Kuenen (1828-1891), further distinctions in the documents; and Julius Wellhausen (1844-1918), who in his *Prolegomena zur Geschichte Israels* applied the evolu-

---

[30]The Rosetta Stone, discovered in 1799, afforded insight into Egyptian hieroglyphics; and the Behistun Inscription, 1835, into Babylonian cuneiform writing.

[31]The British and Foreign Bible Society was organized in 1804.

[32]William Gesenius (1786-1842) was the great pioneer in Hebrew lexicography; Ewald (1803-1875), in comparative philology.

[33]Darwin published his *Origin of Species* in 1859.

tionary theory to the whole of Old Testament literature, history, and religion. In Wellhausen the more radical criticism reached its zenith.

In opposition to this development stood such conservative scholars as Ernest Wilhelm Hengstenberg (1802-1869), who set forth his *Christologie des Alten Testaments;* Heinrich A. C. Hævernick (1811-1845), who stood for the doctrinal interpretation; Johann Heinrich Kurtz (1809-1890), a sane historical method; Franz Delitzsch (1813-1890), a sound exegesis on philological and historical bases; and Gustav Friedrich von Oehler (1812-1872), a conservative yet progressive Old Testament theology.

The close of the nineteenth century witnessed three schools of critics: the advanced, the mediating, and the conservative, all contending for the recognition of their complex theories of the dates and the relations of the documents J, E, D, and P, which they continued to investigate and elucidate.

Developments in the twentieth century thus far have included both the popularization and the modification of higher critical views. At first there was wide dissemination of these views through critical commentaries,[34] general works on Old Testament Introduction,[35] and ardent advocates. This led to a conservative reaction observable in America in the conflict between Modernism and Fundamentalism. Though seriously affecting Reformed churches, this failed in general to disturb Lutherans, primarily by reason of their balancing principle of justification by faith in Christ, the center of Scripture.

More recent advances in archæological discovery and

---

[34]Cf., the International Critical Commentary series.
[35]Cf., works on Old Testament Introduction by Bewer, Briggs, Cornill, Creelman, Driver, Gray, McFadyen, Oesterley and Robinson, and Pfeiffer.

excavation in Palestine and the ancient East[36] have brought
forth evidences of a larger amount of earlier materials in the
Pentateuch than critics had hitherto been wont to recognize.
A further modification of the critical hypothesis has become
manifest in a clearer understanding, arising from a study of
the sources, of the early religious and cultural development
in Israel. The increasing appreciation of early in comparison
with supposedly very late origins continues to modify critical hypotheses.

Briefly, what is true in Pentateuchal criticism applies in
general to other parts of the Old Testament. Criticism
today has better apparatus than formerly and proceeds more
cautiously, having found many of its "assured results" to be
only vanishing hypotheses. While it has constructively
pointed out the progressive character of Old Testament history, literature, and thought it has left many problems still
unsolved. The way is still open for further research.

II. *The Higher Criticism of the New Testament*

The modern Higher Criticism of the New Testament
arose in the latter part of the eighteenth century in the
publication by Lessing (1729-1781) of Reimarus' *Fragmente*
(1778). The nineteenth century saw the whole of early
Christian literature and history subjected to critical study
and investigation. As in the case of the Old Testament, the
early criticism of the New Testament was to a large extent
negative. Later, however, it found expression in saner views.
Ferdinand Christian Bauer (1792-1860), founder of the
famous Tuebingen School of criticism, proposed the ingenious hypothesis that the New Testament owes its origin
to an unresolved conflict between Peter and Paul, reflected
in a few genuine epistles, Galatians, Corinthians, and Romans, the remaining books appearing very late as efforts

---

[36]Cf., *e.g.*, Barton, Archaeology and the Bible.

toward conciliation. Although this theory was not without its influence for a time it has since been fully discredited. Thorough investigation of the evidence, both internal and external, has resulted in the restoration to Paul of the majority, if not all, of the epistles which bear his name.

Modern criticism of the Gospels has dealt minutely with the Synoptic Problem. Through the maze of conflicting hypotheses there has emerged the two-source theory, Mark and Q (*Quelle,* source), which, with varying interpretations, has been the most widely accepted conclusion in modern times. Papias, a church historian (c. 120 A.D.), bears testimony to Mark as Peter's interpreter and writer of his memoirs, and to Matthew as the author of the *Logia,* Sayings of our Lord, written in Aramaic.

Among the many recent approaches to the interpretation of the Gospels is the so-called Form Criticism (*die formgeschichtliche Methode*),[37] which seeks to analyze the motives for the crystallization of the materials in the Gospels in the life of the early church, in preaching, evangelism, religious instruction, missionary service, controversies with the Jews, and worship. The method throws some light upon the Gospels, yet, like many other hypotheses, it is too naturalistic and speculative to gain general approval.

Constructively, New Testament criticism has established irrefutably the genuineness of many New Testament writings, the historicity of New Testament characters, and the reality of the experiences of the early church; it has thrown light upon the social, historical, and literary background of the New Testament; and it has opened up innumerable new avenues of thought and investigation. But it has also left many problems still unsolved.

In recent decades theological study, and particularly the new Luther research, has clearly shown the inadequacy of

---

[37]Advocated by Dibelius, Bultmann, Kundsin, Grant, *et al.*

historical and literary criticism fully to solve the problems of Scripture and Christian experience. The approaches of the history, philosophy, and psychology of religion have all but yielded the field to the theological approach with its emphasis upon the unity and the dynamic character of Scripture.[38] The radical view of the recognition of "strata of reliability" in the Gospels in the "doubly attested sayings" and other critical categories, *e.g.*, has given place to the certitude of the Savior in every section of the Synoptics. There is no longer a bold contrast between "the Jesus of history" and "the Christ of faith" such as engaged the thinking of critics a generation ago.[39] Furthermore, Paul's theology is not the evolutionary reproduction of the tenets of the mystery cults abounding in his environment but the revelation of the Incarnate One, whose presence and power he, and others in the primitive church, had personally experienced, and to whom with one mind and one spirit they bore a unified and incontrovertible testimony in the thought patterns of the period. At the center of their *kerygma,* apostolic preaching, stood the cross.

In so far as Biblical Criticism contributes to a clearer understanding and appreciation of this unity, continuity, and living character of revelation in the Scriptures, it is constructive. A purely human approach, it naturally has limitations which must always be recognized.

C. CONCLUSION

This survey of Biblical Criticism from the point of view of Lutheran faith and confession may be summarized as follows:

1. *The Holy Scriptures are complete and final.* As stated by the *Formula of Concord:* "We believe, teach, and confess

---

[38]Cf., *Religion in Geschichte und Gegenwart,* 2nd ed., also Kittel's *Theologisches Woerterbuch zum Neuen Testament.*

[39]Cf., Schmidt *et al: Jesus Christus im Zeugnis der Heiligen Schrift,* 1936.

that the only rule and standard according to which at once all dogmas and teachers should be esteemed and judged are nothing else than the prophetic and apostolic Scriptures of the Old and of the New Testament. . . . "[40]

Although the formation of the Canon was a historical process involving centuries, that process under Providence has yielded the ultimate revelation for all the ages to come. The church confidently points to a Canon of Scripture which is universally acknowledged, and which will never be altered. The Apocrypha and other writings received temporarily in certain quarters are "useful for reading," as Luther suggested, but they must always be regarded as secondary and subordinate to the canonical Scriptures, which alone are authoritative.

2. *The text of Scripture is essentially trustworthy.* Transmitted to us in an accumulation of varying manuscripts, versions, quotations, and printed editions, and reconstructed in accordance with tested canons of criticism, the text of both the Old Testament and the New Testament represents for all intents and purposes the *ipsissima verba* of the original. So accurately has the text of the Scripture been transmitted and preserved in history under the guidance of the Holy Spirit, its divine Author, that the remaining unresolved variations, however extensive, fade into insignificance in the light of the authoritative truths conveyed. No doctrine of the Christian faith, no important teaching, no moral precept hinge upon any disputed passage of the Bible. The living Word of God has come down to us in history through all the mazes of human transcription in a record which is eternally true. The Scriptures, which we possess today in more than a thousand tongues, and not merely the original autographs, which have long since become irretrievably lost, constitute the veritable Word of God. Men in all lands have definitely

---

[40] *The Book of Concord,* edited by Jacobs, p. 491.

experienced the dynamic truth of the Word written in their own tongues.

3. *The Scriptures cannot be destroyed.*[41] An impregnable Rock, the Bible will always stand the test of rigid scientific analysis. It requires no human defense, for it carries its own apologetic. The presence of the Holy Spirit in the Word makes it self-evidencing. Critics may come and go, their hypotheses endure for a time and then give place to more plausible theories, but all the while the Bible stands securely, the never-failing source and guide for faith and life. No matter how viciously diabolical or unbelieving minds may attack the Scriptures, "the Word they still must let remain. . . ." *"Gottes Wort bleibt ewig!"*

4. *Biblical Criticism, properly employed, serves useful purposes.* It throws light upon the historical, social, and literary sources of Biblical materials. It points out the progressive character of revelation in history from early times as delineated in the Old Testament to its culmination in Christ and the New Testament record. It explodes numerous erroneous traditions transmitted from earlier times. It serves also as a corrective of many false inferences of credulous interpreters. In brief, it provides a very useful approach to the documentation of divine truth. Though at times it has been destructive and subversive of faith, criticism has undoubtedly yielded positive results in contributing to a better understanding and appreciation of the Bible. It will never resolve all the difficulties of Biblical interpretation, but it will throw increasing light upon obscure parts and passages. The revision of erroneous traditions and tenets and the verifying of sound judgments are wholesome processes. The positive values of the critical achievements represented in such a work as Nestle's sixteenth critical edition of

---

[41] Cf., John 10:35.

the Greek New Testament cannot be estimated. The church welcomes thorough, discriminating study of the Bible.

5. *The test of Scriptures lies, not in criticism, but in its office and function as the Means of Grace.* Criticism, however scholarly, can never generate grace and faith nor provide spiritual insight. Erudition has never had the key to revelation.[42] It is the Holy Spirit who imparts to believing hearts the truths of grace. "He has a peculiar congregation in the world, which is the mother that bears every Christian through the Word of God, which He reveals and preaches, and through which He illumines and enkindles hearts. . . . "[43] In the Scriptures we hear *Deus loquens.* God has spoken, is speaking, and will continue to speak. "Scripture was divinely inspired not only while it was being written, God breathing through the writers, but also while it is being read, God breathing through the Scriptures, and the Scriptures breathing Him."[44] Criticism is a human approach and must therefore always be kept subordinate to the religious use of Scripture. Biblical scholarship is a real blessing only when pervaded by the illuminating influences of the Holy Spirit.

6. *The discrimination between law and gospel is of greater significance than documentary analysis.* Criticism may point to the diversities in the literary structure and strata of Scripture, but it is unable adequately to differentiate between the legal and evangelical elements. For this spiritual discernment faith is essential. As Luther frequently maintained, the ability to distinguish between law and gospel is the highest art in Christianity.[45] Every Christian should know and exercise this art, which is learned in the school of the Holy Spirit.

---

[42]Cf., I Cor. 1:18ff.
[43]Martin Luther, *The Large Catechism, Book of Concord,* Jacobs, p. 444.   [44]Bengel, *Gnomon of the New Testament,* Vol. II, p. 553.
[45]See Walther, *The Proper Distinction Between Law and Gospel,* p. 46ff.

7. *Jesus Christ, the Incarnate Word, is the living center of all Scripture.* In Him lie its unity, analogy, and energy.[46] Books of the Bible have their relative place as they are occupied with Christ. The Old Testament is less central than the New Testament; Judges, than John; Chronicles, than Corinthians. The proper approach to Scripture, therefore, is through justification by faith in Christ, the material principle of the Reformation, which alone leads to the formal acceptance of the Bible as the Word of God. "The Christian does not have faith in Christ because he believes that Scripture is divinely inspired, but he believes that Scripture is divinely inspired because through the truth revealed in it he has attained to faith in Christ."[47] This is the approach of a standing or falling church.

BIBLIOGRAPHY

I. GENERAL WORKS

Kenyon, F. G., *Our Bible and the Ancient Manuscripts,* 4th ed., 1938.

Norlie, O. M., *The Translated Bible,* 1934.

Reu, M., *Luther and the Scriptures,* 1944.

Robinson, H. Wheeler, *et al, Record and Revelation,* 1938.

Robinson, H. Wheeler, *The Bible and Its Ancient and English Versions,* 1941.

II. WORKS ON OLD TESTAMENT INTRODUCTION AND CRITICISM

Albright, F. W., *Archaeology and the Religion of Israel,* 1942.

Cartledge, S. A., *A Conservative Introduction to the Old Testament,* 2nd ed., 1944.

Eissfeldt, Otto, *Einleitung in das Alte Testament,* 1934.

Hempel, Johannes, *et al, Werden und Wesen des Alten Testaments,* 1936.

Kennedy, James, *An Aid to the Textual Amendment of the Old Testament,* 1928.

---

[46]Cf., John 1:1; Heb. 4:12.

[47]Th. Harnack, *Canon and Inspiration,* p. 351.

Meinhold, Johannes, *Einfuehrung in das Alte Testament*, 2nd ed., 1926.

Oesterley, W. O. E. and Robinson, T. H., *An Introduction to the Books of the Old Testament*, 1934.

Pfeiffer, Robert H., *Introduction to the Old Testament*, 1941.

Sellin, E., *Introduction to the Old Testament*, tr. by Montgomery, 1923.

Weiser, A., *Einleitung in das Alte Testament*, 1939.

III. WORKS ON NEW TESTAMENT INTRODUCTION AND CRITICISM

Behm, Johannes, *Feine's Einleitung in das Neue Testament*, 1936.

Buechsel, Friederich, *Die Hauptfragen der Synoptikerkritik*, 1941.

Cartledge, S. A., *A Conservative Introduction to the New Testament*, 1938.

Clogg, F. B., *An Introduction to the New Testament*, 1937.

Dodd, C. H., *History and the Gospel*, 1938.

Filson, Floyd, *The Origins of the Gospels*, 1938.

Goodspeed, E. J., *Introduction to the New Testament*, 1937.

Goodspeed, E. J., *Problems of New Testament Translations*, 1945.

Grobel, K., *Formgeschichte und Synoptische Quellenanalyse*, 1937.

Hatch, R., *The Principal Uncial Manuscripts of the New Testament*, 1939.

Kenyon, F. C., *Handbook to the Textual Criticism of the New Testament*, 1938.

Kittel, Gerhard, *et al*, *Theologisches Woerterbuch zum Neuen Testament*, 1933.

Milligan, George, *The New Testament and Its Transmission*, 1932.

Robertson, A. T., *An Introduction to the Textual Criticism of the New Testament*, 1925.

Scott, E. F., *The Literature of the New Testament*, 1932.

Thiessen, H. C., *Introduction to the New Testament*, 1943.

Vaganay, Leon, *An Introduction to the Textual Criticism of the New Testament*, 1937.

REVELATION TODAY

ALBERT A. JAGNOW

"Jesus Christ, the same yesterday, and today, and forever," Hebrews 13:8.

In his little pamphlet directed against natural theology Karl Barth suggests that the theological task of this generation is to understand revelation as grace and grace as revelation. This appears to be a timely reminder. When one seeks to define revelation in nontechnical terms and to show its contemporary, dynamic function one becomes aware of its close relationship to the means of grace, especially to the Word.

At the very outset it may be well to state one's point of view and approach. The Christian speaks as one who stands under the effect of revelation, within the Christian Church. His is the point of view of faith—faith in the living God who has revealed Himself to him in the fellowship of His church as Ruler, Redeemer, and Sanctifier. His is a confessional and Biblical point of view therefore. As a Christian he speaks to Christians. And this is all the more necessary because, as will appear later, revelation cannot be understood from without by a mere scientific observer. It must be experienced from within, through the personal commitment of faith.

Such an approach frankly admits the relativity of all human knowledge. Even theology is fragmentary and piecemeal work! This admission does not, however, militate against faith in the absoluteness of the personal God who reveals Himself to man. He is in heaven; man on earth. Man cannot climb to Him by means of his religious genius; but He stoops to man in love and mercy. The relationship between such a God and sinful man is the theme of all theology based on revelation. And here, surely, it is necessary to speak reverently and with deep humility as becomes the greatness of this subject and the fragmentariness of personal experience. Yet this is not merely personal experience, but experience backed up by Scripture and by the history of the Christian Church.

What, then, do Christians know concerning that revelation which has asserted itself over them? How shall they define revelation? If the answer seem brusque and dogmatic at times, ascribe such seeming dogmatism to the necessity for brevity and not to any presumption of omniscience on their part. All theology is fallible, human work. But God's revelation is absolute. As Augustine said, "God is more truly thought than He is uttered, and exists more truly than He is thought."

Revelation

Revelation is the self-disclosure of God to man. In the event of revelation God, the absolute Person, graciously stoops to man, judging him, and challenging him to a new life in Himself. Not cosmic force but personal challenge is involved here. God, the transcendent One, whose existence cannot really be proven by philosophy and whose nature cannot be rationally fathomed, here comes to man to make him His. He Himself bridges the gap which man cannot bridge because of sin and finitude. And as He challenges each one individually and personally He graciously offers to free man from the slavery of sin and to bestow upon him the perfect freedom and peace of those who serve Him alone. Revelation in its true sense, then, really is the "unveiling" of that God who cannot by His very nature ever be fully "revealed"; but who, even in His revelation, must be apprehended by faith.

The Threefold Form of the Word of God

God reveals Himself to man through His Word. One needs to examine the threefold form of the Word of God in order to understand more clearly what this means. On the lowest level—if one may speak of levels here—stands the proclamation of the church or *the preached Word of God*. Preaching, if it is to be real proclamation of the Word, must be based on Scripture and will be judged by Scripture. It is the task of the church to examine her message ever anew in the light of Scripture and to make whatever corrections are needed by further study of the written Word. Here theology finds her task. Theology is a normative science, which seeks to make the proclamation of the church correspond to the teaching of Scripture. If the saving message of Scripture is called "dogma," and human words about this message are called "dogmas," then the function of "Dogmatics" is to conform dogmas to Dogma.

The church and the pastor are servants of the Word of God. Where this is not understood, preaching becomes ineffectual, for it does not speak of God and for God. Sermons on political, social, and purely moral themes are, therefore, not likely to interest the man in the pew; for the great expectation of the churchgoer is that he may hear God speak to him, even now, in and through and behind the words of the preacher and of the Scripture. And where the voice of God has really been heard in the sermon, there the Holy Spirit has made the proclamation of the church effective to the believing heart; past revelation has become a present event; and the preached Word has really become a means of grace.

Scripture or *the written Word* is the second form of the Word of God. If preaching is mediate (or secondhand) witness to the Word, Scripture must be called immediate (or firsthand) witness to the Word of God. In Scripture the witness of those who had direct contact with God's revelation is found recorded. These prophets and apostles wrote their experiences for the sake of the church which should come after them. In other words, Scripture may be regarded as the history of revelation. But, humanly speaking, it is more than this, for it also shows history interpreted according to revelation. In the light of revelation the prophets of old saw the history of their people transformed, and every contemporary event spoke to them of the rule and the will of God.

Although revelation clearly occurs in history and is conditioned by its own times, it is just as clearly not of history. If the prophets, for example, were the products of their own times (as is sometimes assumed on the basis of evolutionary principles), one should expect them to represent the upthrust of the dominant social consciousness of their own age. But this is true only of the false prophets. True prophets most often swim against the stream of their times and are willing to say, "Thus saith the Lord" even though their penalty be exile or death. Surely, this is no evolutionary phenomenon and cannot be explained save on the basis of objective revelation.

All the books of Scripture do not seem to have equal value. On the whole, the Old Testament is a history of God's dealing with the Chosen People and shows the divine preparation for the coming of Jesus Christ. In some of the Old Testament books (as in the prophets) this preparatory function stands clearly in the foreground while other books are mere historical footnotes, as it were, showing certain attitudes, problems, and customs of the Chosen People. The New Testament, on the other hand, bears witness to the Christ who has come and who will come again in glory to judge both the quick and the dead. In the New Testament this witness to Him sounds forth more clearly than any-

where else. For this reason the New Testament especially
has been *the* book of the Christian Church, her inspiration
and constant source of witness, light, and strength. Still it is
hard to imagine doing without the Old Testament, for
without it we should not know the early history of revelation, nor could we understand how the law and the prophets
were fulfilled in Christ.

It is necessary to remember, however, that the unity of
the Bible is not a mechanical one. Luther said, "The Bible
is the cradle in which Christ is laid." Here lies the unity of
Scripture: it is a history of revelation, preparation for Christ,
witness to Christ. In short, Jesus Christ is He who unifies
Scripture. Therefore Scripture must be the constant and
only source of Christian preaching and the only true norm of
Christian faith and life. In order to value the Bible aright
one need only reflect that there would be no knowledge of
revelation without Scripture.

The third form of the Word of God is the living, *transcendent Word, Jesus Christ.* He is the One who was to
come: the Word witnessed to in Scripture and proclaimed
by the church. He is the culmination of revelation, God's
last word to man as the writer to the Hebrews suggests.
Without Him the Old Testament would be pointless and
fruitless, and the New Testament would never have come
into being. He is the final revelation of God's will and
heart, showing the believer the face of the Father and
calling him back to the Father's home. Yet even in Christ
God's self-disclosure is veiled. He, the Son, became man in
unbelievable humility. Nay more, He, the Son, became
"flesh," which suggests that He had a human body with all
the weaknesses which are characteristic of man under sin.
Yet He had no sin, and through His humanity shone the
glory of God.

But God's glory here was veiled in "flesh." It is interest-

ing to note that Christ never compelled faith in Himself
though He showed many tokens of revelation. Through His
wondrous words and His deeds of kindness and love the
character of the Father was revealed. Through His miracles
the power of God was seen. At the beginning and the end
of His life stood the great tokens of the virgin birth and the
empty tomb, so deeply appreciated by the church. But
during His earthly career it was always possible to close
one's heart and mind. Many believed in Him; but many
heard and saw Him and believed not. The leap of faith was
necessary even then; and unbelief condemned, then as now.
Apparently, God was not interested in forcing anyone into
His kingdom by compelling proof such as is offered in physical science or in mathematics. From our Lord's day to our
own God still remains hidden, even in His revelation.
Through Christ, witnessed to in Scripture and proclaimed
by the church, God still comes to man to call man to Himself. But this is a personal matter. Every man must make
the personal commitment of faith if he would pierce the
veil and see behind the tokens of revelation the living
Word, Jesus Christ.

This suggests why no scientific proof of revelation is
possible. Revelation occurs in the realm of personal life,
where personal experience brings assurance, but where
scientific proof to a mere observer is out of the question.
One cannot measure faith and hope and love. As Ritschlians
like to remind us, man seeks to explain nature; but he
must appreciate and value the life of the soul without
being able to explain it.

In closing this section on the threefold form of the Word
of God *the unity of the Word* must be emphasized. These
three forms go together. But they are three forms of the
Word, not three words. It appears that neither form could
be known without the others. And because of their necessary

interrelation Karl Barth suggests that this is the only real analogy to the Trinity in the whole field of theology.

The diagrams on this page are an effort to make clear in visual form what has just been presented. Figure "A" shows the three forms of the Word without reference to time. At the top stands revelation as a transcendent event, culminating in the living Word, Jesus Christ. Below it appears Scripture as firsthand witness to this revelation. Then comes the preaching of the church, which is based on Scripture. Preaching is a reminder of past revelation and a promise that this revelation can become effective even here and now through faith. Scripture and preaching may be called phenomenal forms of the Word since they are open to inspection and observation. The event of revelation, which is God's gift to faith, is transcendent and not open to scientific observation as such.

Figure "B" is an effort to show these same three forms of the Word of God arranged over a time line. Here it is more clearly seen how preaching points back to Scripture and forward with the promise held out to faith that revelation can become a reality here and now to the believing soul.

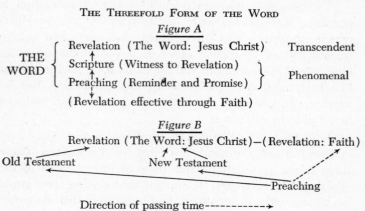

THE THREEFOLD FORM OF THE WORD

Figure A

THE WORD { Revelation (The Word: Jesus Christ)   Transcendent
Scripture (Witness to Revelation) }
Preaching (Reminder and Promise) } Phenomenal
(Revelation effective through Faith)

Figure B

Revelation (The Word: Jesus Christ)—(Revelation: Faith)

Old Testament   New Testament

Preaching

Direction of passing time----------→

The Content and Scope of Revelation

Revelation means God speaks, God acts. The content of revelation is the Triune God Himself. By the power of the Holy Spirit the words of apostles and prophets and the person of Jesus Christ become revelation for the Christian today. In the event of revelation the Christian learns to know God as Creator, Preserver, Redeemer, Sanctifier. He accepts His grace and yields himself to His saving will shown in Christ. God's principles of action begin to bear fruit in the lives which are transformed according to His will. More and more one learns to be pleasing unto God, obedient unto His will, and helpful to one's fellow man.

All of this is, of course, not as simple as it sounds, for revelation does not furnish man with a complete set of Pharisaic laws. It is a misconception to speak of "the new law of love" as though it were similar to an Old Testament code. Rather, revelation through Jesus Christ gives man a new set of attitudes ("a new heart") and new principles of action, which must be applied by every Christian in every contemporary situation. Instead of giving a series of commands, Jesus Christ shows His children the life of love and obedience. This certainly does not make religion any easier. But it does make it forever contemporaneous in its application. The challenge now is, "Be ye perfect, as your Father in heaven is perfect"; and each one must see for himself, in the light of revelation, what this means here and now. One might say revelation shows a man the image of Jesus Christ and asks him by the grace and power of God to conform his life and his world to that image from moment to moment. In this sense revelation is never complete but always contemporaneous and progressive. Therefore the Christian, like Saint Paul, always remains one who has not yet attained, but who follows after.

Concerning the scope of God's self-disclosure little can be said here. It would not be difficult to show that revelation is an absolutely unique category, that it is the key to God, man, the world, and history. It is the living relationship to God that gives meaning and purpose to life, that answers man's last questions about himself and his world, that sets up aims and ideals, and transforms all values, so that man may live in the light of eternity. There is no real solution to the problems of life without revelation. And revelation makes all the difference between triumphant hope and black, unreasoning despair.

This difference appears not only in ethics but in history and its interpretation. Compare, for instance, Wellhausen's *Prolegomenon to the History of Israel* with the history of the Chosen People as told by itself under the impact of revelation in the Old Testament. Or compare Professor Case's book, *Jesus,* with the story of the Lord as told in the Gospels. What accounts for the difference in the same story when told in two ways? Revelation. The Old Testament and the Gospels look at history from the point of view of revelation.

The Autonomy of the Word of God

But if revelation, the Word of God, is such a purely personal event which cannot be measured scientifically from without, how can anyone be certain that he really knows the living God? The answer is found in the autonomy of God's Word. Faith is the God-given key to revelation. It has been described as a mortal leap in the dark. Faith is absolute despair of one's self, coupled with absolute trust in God. It is always a serious question whether one actually stands in the faith. But when the decision for God has been made, when one has entered the fellowship of the body of Christ which is the church, then the heart knows with the trembling but absolute assurance of faith that God is gracious unto *me*. Then no philosophical or pseudo-scientific argument can shake the conviction that God Himself has stooped to me, personally, and made me His child.

In other words, the Word of God, the event of revelation, proves itself to the Christian in faith. And this is the only possible proof that can be demanded, for revelation takes place in the secret meeting of the soul with God, as the Holy Spirit works through the means of grace. And only the soul and God know what has taken place. A scientific observer would be totally at loss. This is not illogical. For, surely, any god which science or philosophy could demonstrate objectively would be a part of the world, an idol, and not the living, transcendent God. One cannot, therefore, demand unreasonable proof in this area just as one cannot demand objectively valid proof of love or friendship or beauty. In the intimately personal event of revelation one knows God through faith. But only after the event of revelation does one really know Him.

This is not as solipsistic as it appears to be. Contemporary Christians are not the only ones who have stood under revelation. The Old Testament is the history of many individuals and of a nation conditioned by revelation. The New Testament enshrines similar experiences. And the whole history of the Christian Church displays a countless fellowship of those who have had essentially the same experience of revelation which Christians today cherish. The believer is not alone therefore. He has the history of revelation and the saints of all the ages on his side. And "we know and are sure that Thou art the Christ, the Son of the living God." Just as the unbelief of a Caiaphas or a Pilate did not shake the faith of the disciples who had seen the risen Lord, so the unbelief of the world need not shake the Christian's faith. He knows Him because he has stood before Him in the event of revelation; others do not know Him because they do not care to see Him. And God forces no one into His kingdom. Yet, "he that doeth the will shall know of the doctrine."

At this point a footnote ought perhaps to be added concerning the uniqueness and the absoluteness of God's revelation culminating in Jesus Christ. In the incarnation the living God stooped to become man in order to reveal Himself to men. More than this cannot possibly be hoped for. The New Testament and the church have always insisted that no new or higher revelation is to be expected until Christ returns in glory. Anything which might be said concerning the progressiveness of revelation in the present situation must, therefore, be construed as referring to man's increasing understanding of the content of revelation. "We know in part." The church still waits for the Spirit to lead her into clearer knowledge. This is the reason for continued theological study. And from this human, relative point of view revelation may be looked upon as progressive.

Revelation Today

When the preached Word or the Scripture brings a man face to face with the living Christ, revelation takes place for him. God speaks. He hears. And when he yields himself to God through Christ, by the power of the Holy Spirit, the mortal leap of faith is made, time falls away, and Christ becomes his eternal contemporary. Henceforth He is "my Lord, who has redeemed me, purchased and won me from all sins, from death and from the power of the devil, that I might be His own, and live under Him in His kingdom, and serve Him in everlasting righteousness." Here, then, the means of grace have been used by the Spirit to mediate revelation to the believer and to place him under God's present will. And through this ever-recurring process God speaks to him from day to day, showing him new duties in new situations, as he seeks to obey God's will for him. So revelation is seen to be dynamic, life-giving, forever contemporaneous. No longer can one worship the dead letter or cling to ancient shibboleths. To be sure, history and revelation go together. Many things have been learned by the church which cannot be despised by the individual Christian. He will cherish Scripture and the history of the church, for they show him how others have lived under revelation. But he cannot rest in a mere repetition of the history or in routine observance of ancient custom. He must press on to seek the vital experience of living faith, which hears God speaking to him here and now. Such an experience of faith may not always come in the same way, and one can make no rules about it. One cannot say that it must contain a certain emotional tinge or bring conscious conversion. God still works in secret, and His ways are past finding out. But, "he that doeth the will shall know of the doctrine."

What of the church? Surely, there are special tasks which God would lay upon His church in this hour of distress. If the church often seems at a loss in our day, if she speaks with hesitancy, if she does not enjoy the full confidence and rapt attention of those to whom she is speaking, may it not be that she herself has too often forgotten her real function as minister of the Word? May it not be that the members and the leaders of the church need more consecration to Jesus Christ; that they need to study the Scripture much more intently; that they need to look much more carefully at God's deed in their own history? The church needs to recover the feeling of the prophets for the contemporaneity of revelation and to speak boldly as they did, judging each present problem in the light of the Word. If the church is unable to utter a relevant word for Him in this moment, the fault lies not in Him but in the church. She needs to place herself more fully under revelation and to serve the Word more fully: "Jesus Christ, the same yesterday, and today, and forever."

BIBLIOGRAPHY

Karl Barth, *Kirchliche Dogmatik: Prolegomena: Die Lehre vom Wort Gottes:* I, 1. München: Kaiser, 1932. 514 s. (English: *The Doctrine of the Word of God.*)

H. Richard Niebuhr, *The Meaning of Revelation.* Macmillan, 1941. 191 pp.

F. W. Camfield, *Revelation and the Holy Spirit:* An essay in Barthian theology. London: Elliot Stock, 1933. 298 pp.

Revelation, A Symposium, edited by Baillie and Martin. London: Faber and Faber, 1937. 310 pp.

E. F. Scott, *The New Testament Idea of Revelation.* Scribners, 1935. 250 pp.

R. Bultmann, *Der Begriff der Offenbarung im Neuen Testament.* (Sammlung gemeinverständlicher Vorträge, 135) Tübingen: J. C. B. Mohr, 1929. 48 s.

OLD TESTAMENT THEOLOGY

C. UMHAU WOLF

I. The Trend of Old Testament Theology[1]

A. *Theological Writings*

For some twenty years in Germany, and for two score years in England and America, the study of Old Testament theology was replaced by the study of the history of the religion of Israel. The very terms were and are significant of trends of thinking. In the 1890's there were completed the last works which freely use the title, "Theology of the Old Testament."[2] The difficulty of combining the "assured results of criticism" with a unified theology was recognized.

"An idea that is found now only in a late writing might really belong to an earlier time, if we only had a more extensive literature covering that time. But the effect of the criticism referred to is to cut up the writings, particularly the prophecies, with a multitude of fragments and to introduce the greatest uncertainty into exegesis."[3] Surely, here the feeling of the futility of maintaining a theology in the face of the development hypothesis of criticism is strongly in evidence.

During the period of eclipse the new titles which appear utilize the word "religion" or the phrase "religious history"

---

[1]James Smart, "Death and Rebirth of Old Testament Theology," *Journal of Religion*, 1943, Vol. 23, Nos. 1 and 2. Emil Brunner, "Die Bedeutung des Alten Testaments für unsern Glauben," *Zwischen den Zeiten*, 1930, Vol. 8, p. 30ff. (Both of these articles contain a more detailed historical development of the trend in Old Testament Theology.)

[2]G. F. Oehler, *Theology of the Old Testament*, 1884. Herman Schultz, *Old Testament Theology*, 1892, 2 vols. A. B. Davidson, *Old Testament Theology*, published posthumously 1904, ed. Salmond.

[3]A. B. Davidson, *op. cit.*, p. 30.

and capitalize on comparative studies. The Schleiermacher interpretation of the worth of the Old Testament for Christianity prevails.[4] There is no place for any revelation in discussions of the religion of Israel. All the facts and the beliefs are traced to an origin in other peoples, with only the occasional admission that Israel's version may have reached higher levels or even partakes of any greater significance for the rise of Christianity than that of many other religions of paganism and their sundry literatures.

In the 1920's the beginnings of a healthy reaction were noted in Germany, reaching its climax in the period 1930-1939. Here again the titles are indicative of a change in emphasis.[5] As usual, the shift has been slower in England, Scandinavia, and America.[6] It must be noted that some of these reactions are to be found in the writings of men who are not primarily Old Testament scholars but Christian theologians. The rise of dialectical theology and the popular response given "crisis" theology have a direct part to play in the present trend of Old Testament study. The Old Testament concept of history under God lends itself readily to an interpretation of crises.

"Throughout the Bible we have the story of God's action

---

[4]Examples of this type are many. A few are here noted. Robertson Smith, *Lectures on the Religion of the Semites*, 1889. Karl Budde, *Religion of Israel to the Exile*, 1899. Karl Marti, *Religion of the Old Testament*, 1910. J. R. Frazer, *Folklore of the Old Testament*, 1918. H. T. Fowler, *Origin and Growth of the Hebrew Religion*, 1917. W. E. Oesterley and T. H. Robinson, *Hebrew Religion*, 1930.

[5]E. König. *Theologie des Alten Testaments*, 1923. E. Kautzsch, *Die Bleibende Bedeutung des Alten Testaments*, 1922. Otto Eissfeldt, "Israelitisch—jüdische Religionsgeschichte und alttestamentliche Theologie," ZAW, 1926, No. 44, p. 1. Walter Eichrodt, "Hat die alttestamentliche Theologie noch selbständige Bedeutung innerhalb der alttestamentlichen Wissenschaft?" ZAW, 1929, No. 47, p. 83ff. Emil Brunner, "Die Bedeutung des Alten Testaments für unsern Glauben," *Zwischen den Zeiten*, 1930, Vol. 8, p. 30ff. Walter Eichrodt, *Theologie des Alten Testaments*, Vol. I, 1933; Vol. II, 1935; Vol. III, 1939. Ludwig Köhler, *Theologie des Alten Testaments*, 1936. Ernst Sellin, *Theologie des Alten Testaments*, 1936. Wilhelm Vischer, "Die Bedeu-

in history, of his struggle with the recalcitrant will of man to bring order into the latter's chaotic soul and society. Little wonder, then, that the Old Testament presents us with a continuous series of crises!"[7]

B. *Critical Trends*

Criticism with its literary and historical analysis, its documents, fragments, and supplements could hardly be expected to contribute to the interpretation of a unified theology of the Old Testament. It is to be regretted that, while gaining in the secondary skills of research and criticism, some Christian scholars have lost sight of the primary purpose (and only excuse for their effort)—the faith.[8] The reaction in the field of criticism has been neither as rapid nor as complete as in the field of dialectical theology. In 1926 Otto Eissfeldt noted the fallacy of trying to use the historical method on revelation. Historical method can handle facts, he suggests, but theology handles revelation.[9] Perhaps recognition of the barren and sterile result, as far as the faith was concerned, brought about this trend.[10]

tung des Alten Testaments für das christliche Leben," *Theologische Studien*, 1938, No. 3.

[9]J. Phythian-Adams, *The Call of Israel*, 1934. G. S. Hendry, *God the Creator*, 1935, Hastie Lectures. C. H. Dodd, *History and the Gospel*, 1938. Anders Nygren, *Agape and Eros*, I, 1932; II, 1938. A. H. Herbert, *The Throne of David*. Wheeler Robinson, ed. *Record and Revelation*, 1938. Joh. Lindblom, "The Old Testament in the Christian Church," *Expository Times*, May, 1940, Vol. 51, No. 8, p. 374ff. Cp. Beiheft No. 66, ZAW, 1936. W. F. Albright, *From the Stone Age to Christianity*, 1942. G. E. Wright, *The Challenge of Israel's Faith*, 1944. Paul Minear, "Wanted a Biblical Theology," *Theology Today*, April, 1944. H. H. Rowley, *The Relevance of the Bible*, 1944. R. B. Scott, *The Relevance of the Prophets*, 1944.

[7]G. E. Wright, *Challenge*, p. 21, cf. Scott, RB, *op. cit.*, p. 14.

[8]Cf. Paul Minear, *op. cit. passim.* and Jacob Myers, "The Old Testament Today," *Lutheran Church Quarterly*, October, 1943.

[9]Otto Eissfeldt, *op. cit.*, p. 10.

[10]C. H. Dodd, *Op. cit. passim.* and C. H. Dodd, "The Gospels as History," *Bulletin of John Rylands Library*, April, 1938, Vol. 22, No. 1, p. 3, and G. S. Hendry, *op. cit.*, p. 40.

The task is thus not finished when we have labelled a passage, "late," "spurious," or otherwise. Whether the *shema'* in Deuteronomy, for example, is from the time of Moses, David, Josiah, Ezra, or Simon Maccabee, little affects its theological significance for us. Criticism does not destroy the didactic values of the Old Testament.[11] There may be disagreements on the date of a text in the Old Testament, but there is only slight disagreement as to that body of beliefs by the grace of God now presented to us as basic to the Apostolic Church and to our church. Even those thinkers from the liberal wing of Christianity, who have themselves departed from these beliefs, acknowledge their uncompromising presence in the Old Testament. The text, document, or doctrine are still in our canon and must be interpreted.[12] The Old Testament is still our Bible, not having been deposed by nor having absconded before Marcion, Schleiermacher, Harnack, Delitzsch, or Hirsch.

For the Christian, for the theologian, to whom the linguist and the historian must needs be assistants, the question remains to be faced.

"Thus, while entering upon an important and yet never-ending search into antiquity for the correct rendering, we actually may evade the central issue: Is this really God's Word, and does it speak to us? . . . Regardless of who wrote it or when, we still must face the issue. Some prophet wrote it. Is he correct; and if so, what have his words to do with us?"[13]

The newer criticism, the fuller appreciation of oral tradition, archæology, and a less dogmatic evolutionary

---

[11]S. L. Brown, "The Study of the Old Testament" in *The Priest as Student*, H. Box ed. 1939, p. 47. Cf. Wheeler Robinson, *Religious Ideas of the Old Testament*, 1913.

[12]Ernest Colwell, *The Study of the Bible*, 1937, p. 163. Cf. Joh. Hempel, "Content of Literature" in *Record and Revelation*.

[13]G. E. Wright, *Challenge*, p. 3.

concept of history and religion today point to an essential unity of the Old Testament despite literary analysis.[14] The bulk of the Old Testament offers a striking uniformity no matter how it is divided.[15] Even if, as suggested by many, the Old Testament books have undergone many redactions and editings, it would be expected that these editors would do a relatively complete job, and so gradually even these texts would become harmonized. Such unity is found although the answer cannot be said to lie only in literary editing or in men, but its unity is God.

The Old Testament is not the theology or religion of the average Israelite of any particular period. It speaks of itself as normative, but the people for the most part departed from the norm. The Old Testament could be called the "theology of the remnant." Therefore "the total impression of the combined work is dominantly that of the higher stage" of the spirit of prophecy, inspired, pointing to a noble meaning.[16] This from the hand of one who continues to speak in terms of religion and religious development. Until the incarnation of Christ the Old Testament remained the fullest revelation of God.

C. *Anti-Semitism*

In addition to all this there is a newer, dramatic comprehension of the source and origin of many of the more diabolic attacks. Anti-Semitism is directly responsible for much of the abuse of the Old Testament. But Anti-Semitism does not stop with the Old Testament.[17] It must of necessity go on to show that the writers of the New Testament were also

---

[14]W. R. Taylor, in *Journal of Religion*, Vol. 23, No. 4, p. 236.

[15]G. E. Wright, *op. cit.* Forward, p. vi.

[16]H. B. Streeter, *The God Who Speaks*, 1937, pp. 99-100.

[17]Joh. Lindblom, *op. cit.*, p. 374. Cf. the strenuous efforts of German Christians to eliminate the Semitic, *e.g.*, George Wehrung, "Christentum und Deutschtum," 1937, *Tübinger Studien zur systematischen Theologie*, No. 6.

Jews[18] as was Jesus Christ Himself. The German National Church, under Rosenberg's decrees, attempted to purge Christianity of the Semitic strands. To eliminate the Old Testament we open the door for others to eliminate the New. Almost every argument used against the Old, whether literary, historical, or philosophical, can be directed with equal cogency against the New Testament.[19]

II. PRIMARY THEOLOGICAL ELEMENTS IN THE OLD TESTAMENT

A. *Introduction*

In the Old Testament we have a religion which is primarily theological. It is not philosophic or speculative. It derives its meaning entirely from its belief in God. All the other divisions of dogmatics such as anthropology and soteriology are properly only subdivisions of theology and can be rightly understood only by a proper comprehension of the doctrine of God in the Old Testament.[20] The Old Testament may be called theonomous; it is surely not heteronomous. Variation and diversity are seldom, if ever, contradictory but a matter of completeness or emphasis. The religion of the Old Testament may seem heterogeneous to some, but the essential elements of its theology are homogeneous.

B. *God*

The Hebrew Bible nowhere speculates on the origin or existence of God. God is.[21] Whoever doubts this basic fact of Old Testament theology is considered a fool by the psalm-

---

[18]Jacob Myers, *op. cit.*, p. 368.

[19]G. S. Hendry, *op. cit.*, p. 40. Cf. a recent example of such criticism in the New Testament field, R. Hawkins, *The Recovery of the Historical Paul*, 1943.

[20]A. B. Davidson, *op. cit.*, p. 13.; Ernst Sellin, *op. cit.*, p. 9; G. E. Wright, *op. cit.*, p. 55.

[21]G. E. Wright, *op. cit.*, p. 55.

ist. Even the fool quoted may not be expressing doubt of God's existence but of His immanence. That God is and lives becomes the center of the unity of the theology of the Old Testament. In the midst of a world which knew many gods and every day created further gods this is a remarkable belief that cannot have come purely from human experience but by God's own teaching. The theology of the Old Testament presupposes the belief in the existence of God, but no attempt is made to prove it.[22] Köhler makes this the key to his treatment of Old Testament theology.[23] This statement is not elaborated in the New Testament, for the same God is and lives for all time.

In the Hebrew Bible God is Creator, King, and Lord.[24] No philosophy is used to demonstrate this principle. It is suggested that the covenant name Yahweh expresses this belief, i.e., "He causes what comes into existence."[25] The account of creation in Genesis I is not first in position as only the beginning, initium, but as the principle, principium, for the theological understanding of and ground for the faith of all that follows.[26]

C. God's Self-Revelation

If a creator is taken for granted by the writers of the Old Testament, it follows that His ability to reveal Himself is also taken for granted.[27] The Lord speaks the word: "Thus saith the Lord."[28] This is the primary difficulty in the purely

---

[22]A. B. Davidson, op. cit., p. 31; Ernst Sellin, op. cit., p. 12.
[23]Ludwig Köhler, op. cit., p. 1ff.; cf. p. 39.
[24]Otto Eissfeldt, op. cit., passim.; Joh. Lindblom, op. cit., p. 375. Cf. Count Baudissin, Kyrios, Vol. I.
[25]W. F. Albright, Op. cit., p. 198.
[26]Ludwig Köhler, op. cit., p. 71.; G. S. Hendry, op. cit., p. 131; Emil Brunner, op. cit., p. 37.
[27]Emil Brunner, op. cit., p. 37.
[28]H. H. Rowley, op. cit., p. 137; Ernst Sellin, op. cit., p. 46, L. Köhler, op. cit., pp. 83-89. Cf. Chapter, "Thus Saith the Lord," in G. E. Wright, Challenge.

historical method of Old Testament study. "Historical criticism cannot reach the depths of the Old Testament revelation."[29] The unique life, history, and faith of Israel (or the remnant of Israel as above) cannot be explained solely by evolutionary, developmental hypotheses. The unity of the Old Testament likewise depends on the source of its theology. "It can only be explained as the result of a self-disclosure of the deity to the receptive leaders of the chosen people."[30] In fact, even the historical approach would grant to certain men late in the series special endowments as innovators and seers, such as Amos and Second Isaiah, thus being inconsistent with their clear-cut development theories. The New Testament reaffirms this fact of self-revelation.

The culmination of this revelation of God is to be found in the expressions of monotheism in Genesis, Deuteronomy, Amos, Isaiah, and elsewhere. It matters only slightly from the theological point of view whether this clear teaching was first told forth by Moses, the eighth-century prophets, or unknown prophets of the Exile. However, each passage of the Old Testament declares that such knowledge and belief are the product of revelation, not of philosophy, of religious contemplation, or human experience. The fact of monotheism as the religion of the remnant in Israel and as the theological background for Christianity cannot be gainsaid.

Monotheism was not the result of philosophical speculation on the part of Hebrews in any age. It was the revealed impact of the living God in the experiences of national and individual life. For the Israelite the co-existence of other deities was irrelevant in theology and in life.[31] Although it was once thought that such an idea as monotheism had to be the late evolutionary capstone of Hebrew religion,[32] it is

[29]Walter Eichrodt, ZAW, p. 83.
[30]S. L. Brown, op. cit., p. 60.
[31]R. H. Kennett in Peake, ed. The People and the Book, p. 390.
[32]W. E. Oesterley and T. H. Robinson, op. cit., Vol. II, p. 272.

more and more being suggested that such practical monotheism may yet be Mosaic in origin.[33] Thus men may see
development yet recognize that the Old Testament in its
revelation testifies clearly that there is a unity of which
analytic criticism and historical theories were in danger of
losing sight.[34] The unity is maintained in the New Testament
so that we have not two books speaking about God but one
complete revelation. The Old Testament rightly keeps Christianity from degenerating into pantheism or tritheism.

D. God's Grace

The revelation of the one Creator God to man in the
Old Testament and in Israel's history is not a matter of law
but of grace. The Old Testament has suffered long and is
suffering today under the stigma of "legalism." It truly had
been made into a legalistic system and handbook of laws
by pre-Christian Jews just as it is sometimes used today
by Adventists and Fundamentalist sects. But Judaism in
Christ's time or our own time is not the true representative
or interpreter of Old Testament theology.

The writers of the Hebrew Bible teach clearly that all is
a matter of grace.[35] Self-revelation on the part of the Creator
God is the beginning of such grace. The covenant itself, far
from being merely a legal code, is originally the gracious
offering of the great God to a people who deigned to know
no worthiness in themselves.[36] The children of Abraham did
not deserve the covenant. They immediately broke it at

---

[33]Ernst Sellin, op. cit., p. 12. Cf. subtitle to W. F. Albright, op. cit.
"Monotheism and the Historical Process."

[34]James Smart, op. cit., pp. 135-136.

[35]G. F. Oehler, op. cit., p. 175f; Ernst Sellin, op. cit., p. 30.

[36]Ludwig Köhler, op. cit., p. 43; Anders Nygren, op. cit., I, pp. 48-
51; Joh. Lindblom, op. cit., p. 375f.   Joh. Pedersen, Israel Its Life
and Culture, Vol. I., p. 264. Joh. Hempel, Gott und Mensch, 1926, p.
126f.

Sinai and thereby released God from the covenant, but out of His grace He continued to pursue them in love.[37]

"The Old Testament is pervaded and indeed dominated, by the thought of the transcendent God on whom man utterly depends and who is ever seeking to reveal Himself to man. Hen and Hesed show the essential teaching of God. The word now used in English translations should be grace."[38] Man's Hesed is the behavior obligated by his acceptance of the covenant responsibilities. God's Hesed is His redemption, His faithfulness, and His mercy in the covenant.[39] The *leitmotif* of Eichrodt's *Theologie des Alten Testaments* is based on this covenant theme.[40]

The law for the covenant people is not only judgment but also a means of salvation.[41] The sending of the prophets to recall the people is out of God's grace. The promise of a victory to a despised and exiled people is from grace. The change from death to life in the Old Testament comes by the grace of God. Grace cannot be eliminated from the theology of the Old Testament.[42] Neither can law and the wrath of God be eliminated from Christianity. The gospel is the fulness of grace from the same Lord of love and mercy and righteousness and judgment.

III. THE RELATION OF THE OLD TO THE NEW TESTAMENT

A. *Common Ground in Both Testaments*

It has already been noted that the Old Testament teaches quite clearly the self-disclosure of the Creator. The New Testament is usually accepted in the Christian Church

[37]G. E. Wright, *op. cit.*, p. 75. Emil Brunner, *op. cit.*, p. 41.

[38]C. J. Wright, "Grace, Constructive Theology III," in *Expository Times*, December, 1939, p. 129.

[39]G. E. Wright, *op. cit.*, p. 74. Nelson Glueck, "Das Wort Hesed im Alten Testament," Beitrag ZAW, 1927, No. 47.

[40]Walter Eichrodt, *Theologie*, Vol. I, "Gott und Volk."

[41]G. F. Oehler, *op. cit.*, p. 184; Ludwig Köhler, *op. cit.*, p. 198.

[42]Wilhelm Vischer, *op. cit.*, pp. 8-14.

as the final revelation of God in Jesus Christ. Thus it has been said that the Old Testament "is not preparation for, but part of, the communication of God to man which is the eternal gospel."[43] There is an over-all unity of the Bible which is not divided between Malachi and Matthew. The beginning of Genesis demands the end of Revelation. The same God is acting in love and justice according to His living being in all history.

The revelation of God is the same in both Testaments. Even those who speak from a historical standpoint see the "same degree of revelation" in both Testaments.[44] The revelation of the Old Testament commended itself to the early church and the Evangelists. The same revelation is still transmitted through it to us. "Because it is part of the record of the divine revelation, the Old Testament is to be regarded as Christian Scriptures."[45] As Christians we dare not interpret the Old Testament neutrally.

In the Bible God is personal. God is not a platonic idea or a vague force in either Testament. Here is a living God in living contact and vital relationship with His people.[46] This is in evidence throughout the whole of sacred history.

"The common factor is: God is the God of history, working freely in history as a personal will to realize a certain goal of ethical nature, imparting the salvation of mankind. The relation of God to man is of a free and personal nature."[47]

---

[43]Godfrey Phillips, *Old Testament in the World Church*, 1942, p. 85.

[44]Wheeler Robinson, *Ideas*, p. 225. Note that the New Testament, as above, is subject to these same attacks.

[45]James Wood, "Is the Old Testament Christian Scripture?" *Expository Times*, April, 1942, Vol. 53, No. 7, p. 239. Cf. H. C. Alleman, "The Bible as the Word of God," *Lutheran Church Quarterly*, July, 1944, p. 216ff.

[46]D. B. Macdonald, *Hebrew Philosophical Genius*, 1936, p. 3.

[47]Joh. Lindblom, *op. cit.*, p. 376, cf. R. B. Scott, *op. cit.*, Chap. X.

The primary message of the Bible is the gospel of salvation. This doctrine of the initiative of grace and of the divine redemption in love is born in the Old Testament.[48]

"The unity of the Old Testament is to be found in the proclamation of the saving acts of God by those who have been delivered out of the hands of the enemy. . . . It is surely the gospel of the saving acts of God which forms the center of the unity in the Old Testament, and there are signs that a recognition of this fact may well lead to a rediscovery of the vital place of the Old Testament in the whole sweep of God's revelation to mankind."[49]

Although the Old Testament has often been condemned as legalistic and as teaching exclusively a God of wrath, from what has been stated previously it should be evident that these are utterly false accusations. In the Hebrew Bible the mutual relationship of love and wrath is clearly shown. The fundamental paradox of Christianity—a God of tender mercy and awful majesty—is found already in the Old Testament.[50] Hosea 11 may be paralleled with Romans 11. Even God's wrath emerges from His character encompassing holiness and love.[51]

Sin is personal or national disobedience to the will of God. It separates from the Holy One. This is clearly expressed in both Testaments.[52] The idea of sin determines much of the idea of judgment and of the eschaton.[53] The

---

[48]H. H. Rowley, *op. cit.*, p. 88. Cf. Translator's Preface in Anders Nygren, Vol. I, p. xii, and the author himself in Vol. II, p. 39f.

[49]F. W. Dillistone, "The Rediscovery of the Gospel," *Theology Today*, April, 1944, p. 71.

[50]S. L. Brown, *op. cit.*, p. 49. Note: Christianity must retain the proper balance between these two.

[51]Joh. Lindblom, *op. cit.*, p. 376.

[52]*Ibid.*

[53]H. Cunliffe-Jones, "Constructive Theology V-Eschatology," in *Expository Times*, February, 1940, p. 241. Cf. F. W. Dillistone, *op. cit.*, p. 73, and R. B. Scott, *op. cit.*, p. 216.

Bible reveals the world to be what it ought not to be because of sin. Life is opposed to God. Such an interpretation of life is perhaps nearer our present war-born philosophies than the former optimism of the champions of the social gospel, the gospel of education, and so forth.[54] The whole promise of the Old and the message of the New Testament is God's gracious victory over sin.

Once again the unity of the Testaments is being brought to the fore. Together the Old and New Testaments make a self-contained whole. They are united by God's unique, real revelation to mankind during a particular historical period and almost exclusively through a special cultural unit. In fact, there is danger that the dialectical theology may over-emphasize this unity.[55]

"What characterizes the attitude of the dialectical theology to the Bible is the idea that the Old and New Testaments contain quite the same revelation. There is no difference between them. . . . Emphasis on the unity of the Old and New Testaments must lead consequently to emphasis on the identity of the concept of God in the Old and New Testaments. The God concept of Paul, Jesus, and the Old Testament was the same."[56] We must always hold to the unity of the Testaments through the oneness of revelation but avoid identity.

B. *The Essential Difference between the New and Old*

The old Augustinian expression of the relationship of the covenants is being revived. The New Testament is *latent* in the Old, and the Old Testament is *patent* in the New. In the Old we find the germ of the gospel of grace. But the

---

[54]G. E. Wright, *op. cit.*, pp. 18-19; D. B. Macdonald, *op. cit.*, p. 9; J. E. McFayden, *Message of Israel*, 1931, p. 23.

[55]Cf. Karl Barth and followers.

[56]Joh. Lindblom, *op. cit.*, pp. 375-375. For a sane interpretation cf. A. H. Herbert, *op. cit.*

Old Testament does not fulfill itself. In the Old we have a real hope but in the New a hopeful realization. Thus the fundamental difference between the two Testaments is one of clarity of vision, fullness of expression, and completeness of realization. The Messianic hope is fulfilled in Jesus Christ, the Lord and Savior.[57]

In the Old Testament the grace of God appears primarily in the covenant with Israel. To be sure, that covenant was intended to show others this grace and to attract them to God. But in the New Testament the grace of God is shown toward all sinners. In the Old, God's love is especially experienced by the children of the covenant, but in the New, God's love may be experienced by all sinners.

In the gracious covenant of the Old Testament man is never completely certain whether he has lived up to the obligations of the covenant or has broken it. This means there is uncertainty.[58] Of course, by the time of Christ there were those self-satisfied legalists who felt a mistaken certainty, but generally before His age even the called prophets had to be anxious about their departure from the covenant lest God withdraw also from His freely accepted and promised obligations. In the New Testament certainty is not based on keeping the obligations of the New Covenant but on the certain hope in the victory of Christ. In the Old Covenant man was to live faithfully according to the laws given him out of God's grace. In the New man was to have faith in the crucified and risen Christ.

The blessings of the Old Covenant are generally understood in material ways. The true Israelite knew that back of the material benefits of *shalom* stood the inner blessing of God. But in the New Testament there is no mistaking it,

---

[57]Joh. Lindblom, *op. cit.*, p. 377; Emil Brunner, *op. cit.*, p. 33.
[58]Joh. Lindblom, *op. cit.*, p. 377.

material blessings are entirely secondary. The "peace of God" in the New Covenant is spiritual and inward.

C. *The Need for the Old in the New Testament Church*

The knowledge of the Hebrew Bible is essential to a proper understanding of the Greek Testament. Many of our New Testament Greek Lexicons have made the error of deriving meanings from classical Greek alone. Much of the Hellenizing of the church is traceable to faulty lexicography and exegesis. The writers of the New Testament were primarily Semitic. They were steeped in the Old Testament.[59] Even if the Aramaic origin of the Gospels is not completely proved, the Greek is primarily the translation of Semitic words and ideas. This is especially true of Jesus' own words.[60] The New Testament is almost a Semitic literature written in Greek. The newer dictionaries are recognizing this fact.[61]

Certain phrases used in the New Testament cannot be understood except as they are translated from the Hebrew. Thus we find that "Messiah," "Son of God," "Shepherd" are understandable only in the light of the Old Testament. How can one understand the phrases and the analogies of the Book of Hebrews without a knowledge of the Old Testament? Or who can appreciate the Book of Revelation and other apocalyptic passages of the New Testament without a knowledge of Semitic apocalyptic?[62] The Lord's Supper,[63] the sacrifice of the Pascal Lamb,[64] the gift of tongues,[65] the

[59]S. L. Brown, *op. cit.*, p. 40.
[60]W. F. Lofthouse, "Old Testament and Christianity," in *Record and Revelation*, p. 461.
[61]Cf. Kittel's *Wörterbuch zum NT.*
[62]C. H. Dodd, *History and the Gospel*, p. 60.
[63]H. H. Rowley, *op. cit.*, p. 94; W. Vischer, *op. cit.*, p. 21.
[64]H. H. Rowley, *op. cit.*, p. 90.
[65]H. B. Streeter, *op. cit.*, p. 159.

spiritual Israel,[66] etc., cannot be interpreted or discussed on the basis of New Testament Greek alone. Before one can understand the New Testament he must know the Hebrew Bible.

Many ideas in the New Testament are derived from the Law, the Prophets, and the Writings. An Anglican, perhaps overemphasizing, notes the following:

"From the Old Testament are derived: Fatherhood of God, worth of the individual, Servant of the Lord, Messiah, Kingdom of God, Covenant, mystical union, High Priest, efficacy of atoning blood, apocalyptic imagery."[67]

The foundations of the gospel are found in the Old Testament teachings of redemption, forgiveness, peace, and the kingdom of God.[68] The first Christian theology in the Gospels and the Church Fathers was based on the interpretation of Christ as the Messiah of Israel.[69] The Old Testament, therefore, provides the key for understanding the Christ and the idea of the agape of the cross, to the Greek foolishness and to the Jew a stumbling block.[70] To understand the fulness of New Testament grace we must have the background of the Old Testament doctrines of God, man, and sin.

"No Christian who understands his faith will make light of this legacy. He will not indulge in unimaginative statements to the effect that a doctrine of Divine Grace is only found in the Christian religion. On the contrary, he will gladly acknowledge that the historical foundation for Christian teaching is in the Old Testament. Without the doctrine of God and man found in those Scriptures, the Christian doctrine of grace has no secure standing ground."[71]

[66]G. E. Wright, op. cit., p. 98.
[67]S. L. Brown, op. cit., p. 39.
[68]F. W. Dillistone, op. cit., p. 63.
[69]E. Kautzsch, op. cit., pp. 32-33; W. Vischer, op. cit., p. 4.
[70]Anders Nygren, op. cit., II, pp. 38-40.
[71]C. J. Wright, op. cit., p. 130.

The idea of the covenant and the "people of God" is essential to an understanding of the New Testament teach-ings concerning the kingdom of God, ecclesia, and the new covenant.[72] "Ecclesia in the New Testament is only a trans-lation of the Old Testament 'people of God.' The same will of God is to direct the community."[73]

Jesus and the Evangelists add little to our idea of God already derived from the Old Testament.[74] The same God is witnessed by the Prophets, Evangelists, and Christ. The same God reveals Himself in both Old and New Testaments. This revelation has a beginning and an end. The New Testament presupposes the knowledge of God as creator and the creator-relationship to the world clearly expressed in the Old Testament.[75] The New Testament emphasizes the fatherhood of God, which had only occasional utterance in the Old Testament revelation.[76] The doctrine of God in the Old Testament assumed in the New keeps the latter from becoming pure sentimental universalism.

Thus we are already anticipating the final necessity for reaffirming the place of the Old Testament in the New Testament church. The Old is an antidote to many errors which inhere in a teaching based solely on the New Testa-ment. The early church more fully realized this fact than do many today. For this reason it did not accept Marcion's suggestion to abandon the Old Testament.[77] To have done so would have given ready entrance to many errors concern-ing God and salvation. To abandon the Old means of neces-sity the abandonment of much of the New.[78]

---

[72]G. E. Wright, op. cit., p. 98.
[73]E. Brunner, op. cit., p. 46. Cf. Newton Flew, Jesus and His Church, 1938, discussing the basis of ecclesia in the covenant.
[74]Wheeler Robinson, Ideas, p. 224.
[75]G. S. Hendry, op. cit., pp. 41-42.
[76]Joh. Lindblom, op. cit., p. 377. Cf. G. E. Wright, "The Termi-nology of the Old Testament Religion and Its Significance," Journal of Near Eastern Studies, 1942, Vol. I, p. 404ff.
[77]Anders Nygren, op. cit., II, p. 41. [78]H. H. Rowley, op. cit., p. 95.

The belief in external revelation from God protects the Christian Church from subjectivism. Too often Christians have depended on introspection and speculation in their strivings for a clearer insight of God, man, and the destiny of the world.[79] The Old Testament speaks forth against the possibility of such human endeavors' ever succeeding. Historic Christianity is not a sentimental humanism regarding the noble aspirations and worthy efforts of man. The New Testament emphasis on the love and fatherhood of God must be counterbalanced by the synthesis found in the God of the Old Testament. God is both holiness and love. There is no universalism but a doctrine of the Remnant.[80] Such modern sentimentalism is guarded against by the Old Testament.[81]

"We must remember that the father-son conception is in doctrinal danger of degenerating into sentimentality, as has so often happened in modern times. It needs to be united with the master-servant picture to give it backbone and support."[82]

In line with the Old Testament correctives to the modern tendencies concerning the doctrine of God the Old Testament is a sure defense against pantheism.[83] God is not nature or any natural force. He is creator and controller of nature. God is not one with life. He is not solely immanent in life. In the Old Testament the balance between transcendence and immanence is maintained. Here is a personal God, a

---

[79]Joh. Lindblom, *op. cit.*, pp. 377-378; E. Kautzsch, *op. cit.*, p. 24.

[80]G. E. Wright, *Challenge*, p. 90. Note: There has been little danger of this in some Fundamentalist sects and certain portions of Lutheranism, but the modern Protestant spirit has often lost sight of the wrath of God.

[81]E. Brunner, *op. cit.*, p. 43.

[82]G. E. Wright, "Terminology," *JNES*, p. 414. Cf. Christian Science and Universalism.

[83]Joh. Lindblom, *op. cit.*, p. 378.

God who creates and controls the world, and who will also judge the world.[84]

The world created by God is the world of man. The Hellenistic dualism which some would read into Paul is counterbalanced by the Old Testament. There are not two eternal forces, good and evil, nor two opposing powers, flesh and spirit. The world is the world of God even if it is ruled presently by sin. The Old Testament never speculates on the ultimate origin of evil or sin but preaches the ever-present reality of sin. God created both the material and the spiritual. He continues to control both. He will judge both. In the Old Testament one can find no philosophic basis for withdrawal or asceticism such as many read into the New Testament conflict. "There is a defense against such false dualism in the Old Testament belief in God as Creator."[85]

Likewise a dichotomy of body and soul is often emphasized in the teachings of the church. The Old Testament knows man only as one being. He is the whole self. The Hebrew Bible knows no immortality of the one part over against the other or the whole. This treatment of life, *in toto,* a whole individual personality, is perhaps the reason that the Old Testament has no clear expression of the resurrection of the body, for there was no possibility for the Hebrew to conceive of the continuance of "half-of-life" but only of the whole. God is the creator of the whole man, so likewise He is the judge and savior of the whole.

The Old Testament has often been maligned for its so-called nationalism. But the covenant was to be an example to other nations. Ruth, Jonah, and passages in other books preach against those narrow interpretations which were common then as now. The Old Testament clearly teaches that God created all peoples, that He is the God of

---

[84]E. Kautzsch, *op. cit.,* p. 25; E. Brunner, *op. cit.,* p. 37.
[85]Joh. Lindblom, *op. cit.,* p. 377.

all history, and that He judges all men. "This is a guard against false individualism, and against the temptations of making God into a God for just small private interests."[86]

The Old Testament is needed in the New Testament church because it still points to Christ when many are ignorant of promise and fulfillment. It still shows men their complete disobedience to God's law. It convicts of sin. It is still through the law a pedagogue to bring men to Christ. The Old Testament shows men the need for grace, not justice. It continues to offer hope in the midst of a despairing life situation. Together with the New Testament it gives men a hope certainly realized. For those who have heard the call and have been converted the Old Testament contains teaching and devotion for all occasions. Without the Old we should lose much of the dynamic of Christianity, and without the New there could be only expectant hope.

Perhaps it is not too much to say with the editor of the *Expository Times*, "The Bible will play a greater part in the future; not only of our religion, but of our culture."[87] We pray that this may be so. The grace of God, the Lord and Father of us all, will assuredly bring us through hope and faith into life. *Soli Deo Gloria!*

---

[86]*Ibid*, p. 378. F. W. Dillistone, *op. cit.*, p. 77.
[87]*Expository Times*, December, 1941, p. 99.

BIBLIOGRAPHY

BOOKS

Oehler, G. F., *Theology of the Old Testament*, 1884.

Schultz, Herman, *Old Testament Theology*, 1892, 2 vols.

Davidson, A. B., *Old Testament Theology*, 1904, ed. Salmond.

Fowler, H. T., *Origin and Growth of the Hebrew Religion*, 1917.

Oesterley, W. E. and Robinson, T. H., *Hebrew Religion*, 1930.

Eichrodt, Walter, *Theologie des Alten Testaments*, 1933-1939, 3 vols.

Phythian-Adams, J., *The Call of Israel*, 1934.

Köhler, Ludwig, *Theologie des Alten Testaments*, 1936.

Sellin, Ernst, *Theologie des Alten Testaments*, 1936.

Robinson, Wheeler, ed. *Record and Revelation*, 1938.

Albright, W. F., *From the Stone Age to Christianity*, 1942.

Wright, George, *The Challenge of Israel's Faith*, 1944.

Rowley, H. H., *The Relevance of the Bible*, 1944.

Scott, R. B., *The Relevance of the Prophets*, 1944.

ARTICLES

Emil Brunner, "Die Bedeutung des Alten Testaments für unsern Glauben," *Zwischen den Zeiten*, 1930, Vol. 8, p. 30ff.

Otto Eissfeldt, "Israelitisch-jüdische Religionsgeschichte und alttestamentliche Theologie," *ZAW*, 1926, No. 44, p. 1ff.

Walter Eichrodt, "Hat die alttestamentliche Theologie noch selbständige Bedeutung innerhalb der alttestamentlichen Wissenschaft?" *ZAW* 1929, No. 47, p. 83ff.

Wilhelm Vischer, "Die Bedeutung des Alten Testaments für das christliche Leben," *Theologische Studien*, 1938, No. 3.

Johannes Lindblom, "The Old Testament in the Christian Church," *Expository Times*, May, 1940, Vol. 51, No. 8, p. 374ff.

James Smart, "Death and Rebirth of Old Testament Theology," *Journal of Religion*, 1943, Vol. 23, Nos. 1 and 2.

William Irwin, "The Reviving Theology of the Old Testament," *Journal of Religion*, 1945, Vol. 25, October.

NEW TESTAMENT THEOLOGY

THEODORE S. LIEFELD

The science of Biblical Theology is a product of the Protestant Reformation. As distinguished historically from the medieval conception of authoritative, tradition-based dogma, it proceeds on the premise that a uniquely and absolutely authoritative Bible warrants and demands an exclusively Scripture-based theology. That means more than a dogmatic with complete Scriptural substantiation. The distinction is rather one of approach and method than of degree of Biblical proof. Biblical Theology is exegetical; its "given" is not the preconceived formulæ of rationalistic dogmatism but the revealed Word itself. Its sole concern is discovering and objectively presenting the truths revealed in the Scriptures.

By self-evident deduction, then, New Testament Theology is "the scientific representation of the religious ideas and doctrines which are contained in the New Testament."[1] That would seem to offer plain directive for procedure and guarantee at least a measure of uniformity in results. But the development of this Protestant science has followed many devious paths.

In the period of Protestant orthodoxy felt need for systematic apologetic led to the theological textbook with proof passages. Such remains in common use in Lutheran circles today. As a teaching and confessional medium it is desirable; and as representative of a distinct, dogmatic discipline it is justified. But it is increasingly recognized today that a doctrine-initiated study is not a substitute for the analysis of

---

[1] Bernhard Weiss, *Biblical Theology of the New Testament,* vol. 1, Intro., p. 1.

the historical documents of the New Testament. The exegetical method, heritage of the Reformation, is indispensable to the life and the work of a Scripture-centered church.

On the other hand, the development of a theological method that unqualifiedly relies on a historical-critical interpretation of the New Testament books has brought results equally inimical to the nature and the purpose of Biblical revelation. Beginning with F. C. von Baur and the Tuebingen School in the middle of the nineteenth century, the increasing tendency has been to study the New Testament from the preconceived viewpoint of documentary diversity. In the case of Baur application of the Hegelian philosophy of history led to the postulating of conflict between the writers of the New Testament. The premise of opposing Petrine and Pauline parties in the early history of the church supposedly revealed Judaistic, universalistic, and irenic (as found in John) tendencies, conforming to the thesis, antithesis, and synthesis pattern.

As a basis for dating the writings of the New Testament the Tuebingen method has fallen into disrepute. But other elements in its viewpoint have continued to influence New Testament scholarship.[2] One is the Baur contention that a diversity of doctrinal systems in the New Testament inevitably means antitheses and contradictions, which destroy any unity in the whole. Types of patterns other than the historical have been superimposed on the New Testament with further disuniting result. So men, like De Wette and Holtzmann, distinguishing a variety of New Testament religions, endeavor to explain their differences by means of contemporary religious influences coming from outside the Christian tradition. Others have stressed social, cultural,

---

[2]For a historical survey of nineteenth-century works reflecting this tradition, see B. Weiss, *Biblical Theology of the New Testament*, Intro., p. 26ff.

psychological, and literary factors as determinative of the disparity among the New Testament writings.

As a consequence of this popular tendency it has become common practice to speak of types of theology within the New Testament frame, the number characterized depending only on the fineness of microscopic analysis. Contemporary New Testament scholars speak of Petrine, Pauline, Johannine, Apocalyptic, Synoptic, and Jacobean theology, to mention only the commoner classifications. Other specialists seem to see a distinguishable theological entity in each of the twenty-seven documents comprising the New Testament canon. The implications of such compartmentalizing are evident. One is expressed in a recent publication by E. F. Scott:

"No book, indeed, could be less fitted to serve as a touchstone for orthodox belief (than the New Testament). . . . The New Testament is not a single book but a miscellany. It is made up of a number of writings which, for the most part, have nothing to do with each other. The writers were men of different minds and interests; they were scattered over a period of about a century, during which all conditions were changing; they wrote for various circles of readers and adapted their teaching to the special needs and problems which happened at the time to be most urgent. In a work of this kind it is vain to look for any uniformity: The New Testament doctrines have become blended in our minds, so that they all seem to hang together; but the unity we find in them is that of a composite photograph, which does not correspond, when taken as a whole, with any definite object. Our religion is derived from the New Testament, but the elements of it have been combined by an artificial process. No New Testament writer thought of Christianity in just the way that we do now."[3]

The popular, current approach reflected in the foregoing raises serious questions for the New Testament scholar, to say nothing of perplexity for the layman. Is there any justification for even speaking of a "theology of the New Testament," or have we only a heterogeneous collection of theologies? If the latter, which particular type has the best

---

[3]*The Varieties of New Testament Religion*, p. 2.

claim to be accounted truly Christian? Furthermore, what
ground is there then for the fundamental principle of Reformation exegesis—*"Scriptura ex Scriptura explicanda est"*
(the self-interpreting character of the Scriptures)—or for its
dogmatic counterpart— the *"analogia fidei"*? The postulate
of many New Testament theologies effectively removes any
single interpretative standard, leaving only the context of
the individual document as point of reference.

That the New Testament writings show considerable
diversity is, of course, indisputable. When one considers the
fact of their composition over a period of at least two generations, by ten or more writers, it would be strange if it
were otherwise. Additional factors of personality, cultural
variation, deliberate and distinctive emphasis, and the fact
that various stages of a growing church are being reflected,
particularly in the epistles, contribute further to what B.
Weiss calls an "individually and historically conditioned
manifoldness."[4]

Hence justice to both the distinctive character of each
document as well as to its origin in a historical context
requires that the method of Biblical study be primarily
analytical. Any approach which sets aside individual analysis of the books in favor of mere harmonization of the whole
does violence to the historical character of the testimony
presented in the New Testament. In the effort to affirm
unity it creates the illusion of singularity.

On the other hand, a similar distinction must be maintained between legitimate analyzing and that sort of frag-
mentizing which sees only individual, humanly conceived
documents, each with little or no relationship to the rest.
The analytical expert who zealously focuses his microscope
on a documentary segment without seeing or revealing the
connections of his particular study with the rest of the New

---

[4] *Ibid*, vol. 1, p. 1.

Testament fosters an isolationism which conceals the very essence of Spirit-given revelation. As A. M. Hunter points out: "It leads to a piecemeal treatment of early Christian thought; it makes men propound unreal dilemmas, like 'Jesus or Paul'?; it produces 'Gospel scholars,' 'Paulinists,' 'Johannine authorities,' excellent men all, but men ever in danger of not seeing the wood for the particular trees on which their gaze is focused."[5]

Perhaps four scalings or variations of scholarly approach to the New Testament have been suggested as reflected in the extensive literature of this century as well as of the previous one. At one extreme lies the view which sees only diversity in unrelated, mutually independent historical documents; at the other extreme there is perception only of dogmatically formulated oneness of ideas and principles, lifted out of a static, canonical record. Intermediate are two bifocal emphases, differing only slightly in weighting and approach. The one stresses diversity, yet is conscious of some unifying factor in the New Testament such as the concept of revelation, or the common devotion and religious experience of the early church, or the person of Christ. Lutheranism takes yet a fourth, the other intermediate position. It recognizes with the great Reformer the historical life-situation character of the documents comprising the New Testament canon and therefore the need for historico-grammatical study of each as a distinct record. But it sees as even more significant that perceived by the early church—that each document is an integral part of a greater sum-total, and that total as not only a historical record of man's religious experience but a divinely appointed means to a greater end.

There is only one divine purpose throughout human history: that is the saving will of God. Hence God's revela-

---

[5] A. M. Hunter, *The Message of the New Testament,* p. 16.

tion of Himself must be an organic whole. The Scriptures
are that revelation and so constitute a unity. All of the
New Testament canon, as the medium of His direct speaking then and now, is not many words but one Word, the
voice of God Himself. Its component parts—the individual
documents—cannot be fully understood or rightly interpreted save in the light of the whole message. The emphasis
therefore belongs on the organic unity of the New Testament in the midst of its diversity. And that can be discovered and adequately delineated only by a method which
combines both analysis and synthesis.

One further consideration must precede a direct approach to the theology of the New Testament itself. It has
already been suggested in speaking of one sacred Scripture,
comprising both Old and New Testaments. Evidently some
close connection must exist between the two canons. What
is the nature of that relation, and what significance does it
hold for the interpretation of the New Testament message?

Probably no more succinct, yet comprehensive, answer
can be given than the now-famous formula of St. Augustine:
"*Novum Testamentum in Vetere latet: Vetus Testamentum
in Novo patet.*" That statement says more than that a number of Old Testament prophecies, Messianic in character,
find their fulfillment in the person, experience, and work of
Jesus Christ. It testifies rather to the fact that the whole of
the Old Testament forms the basis and the rootage of the
New Testament. Without an understanding of that background it is impossible to attain a proper perspective on the
meaning of the New Testament, and it further follows that
"a church which thinks that it can dispense with the Old
Testament cuts away its own roots."[6]

The heritage is many-sided; it includes religious concepts, institutions, and language itself. When Jesus, accord-

---

[6]Otto Piper, *God in History*, p. 23.

ing to the Gospel of Mark (1:14, 15), began His Galilean ministry, preaching the gospel of God and saying, "The time is fulfilled, and the kingdom of God is at hand," He was not introducing new ideas to His Jewish listeners. Rather, He was taking hold of concepts long established in their minds and central to both their expectations and aspirations. The whole history of God's dealing with Israel had been a progressive unfolding of the divine purpose to establish His dominion over man. Each prophet in turn had directed Israel's eyes to that future day when the kingdom, long promised and covenanted, would be theirs. And central to the realization of that hope was the coming of a person, the Messiah. So Jesus not only speaks of the kingdom as something already quite familiar to His audience; but by act and verbal claim He identified Himself as the expected Messiah, thereby qualifying as the proclaimer of the advent of the kingdom of God. Not only did Jesus find His own destiny portrayed in the Old Testament Scriptures, but they always constituted for Him the authority for His message and mission and the recommended touchstone for the judgment of others. "Ye search the Scriptures, for in them ye think ye have eternal life; and they are they which testify of Me," John 5:39.

Christianity, then, was not a radically new revelation thrust into a spiritual vacuum but was the climax of a history of redemption, moving through centuries of cumulative revelation and religious preparation, recorded in the Old Testament.

"The lofty Jewish Monotheism, the incorporeal spirituality and the kingly supremacy of God, and the corresponding horror of Nature worship—above all, the holiness of God, *i.e.*, His separation from impurity—are all ideas carried over from Judaism to Christianity. The blending of morality with religion, which distinguishes Christianity from most pagan cults, is also a distinctive mark of Judaism. The mercy of God to sinners, His compassion, longsuffering, and redeeming love, forgiving the penitent and rescuing the lost, are seen in the Old

Testament. Lastly, the essentially Christian thought of a King and Savior, sent by God to establish the kingdom of heaven on earth, deliver the needy, and finally judge the nations, comes down from Old Testament prophecy and is accepted by our Lord who claims to be this Savior and King, the long-looked-for Messiah. In regard to all these ideas the New Testament absorbs and confirms the highest thought of the Old Testament while it also goes further, correcting what is narrow and materialistic in Judaism and showing its own richer truth against the background of the earlier religion."[7]

It is sometimes argued that the Judaism which provides background for Jesus' teaching was not so much the Old Testament Scriptures as such but rather that revelation as reflected and modified by the religious developments of the Inter-Testament period. It is evident enough that such post-exilic institutions as the synagogue, the teacher, and the distinctive sects of Judaism are significant factors in the New Testament scene. But rather than providing Jesus with His message, as some contend, these Inter-Testament developments appear most prominently in connection with Jesus' criticism of the religious life of His day. His standard was not current thought and practice but the authoritative Old Testament itself, from which message contemporary Judaism was guilty of many departures.

So then, there is not only a similarity between the Old and the New Testament, but there is a reciprocal relation between the two, establishing them as an organic whole— one Book, composed of two parts. And the degree of dependence of the New on the Old necessitates interpretation of the later through the medium of the earlier. It is increasingly evident that much of the terminology used by Jesus and His disciples—expressive of such central concepts as truth, righteousness, Lord, church, etc.—can be properly understood only in terms of its Old Testament usage. And, conversely, the Old Testament finds its fulfillment, com-

[7]W. F. Adeney, *The Theology of the New Testament*, pp. 3, 4.

pletion, and therefore its meaning in the New. The latter brings Judaism to its highest, fullest development.

Yet alongside the continuity of the twofold revelation there is seen also a uniqueness in the New Testament itself. It is epitomized in the trenchant observation of John's Gospel: "No man hath seen God at any time; the only-begotten Son, who is in the bosom of the Father, He hath declared Him," John 1:18. The presence of God in Jesus Christ is a unique event which has type and symbol but no analogy in the Old Testament. In the words of a contemporary: "The new point of view in the New Testament in contrast to the Old is that God proffers us His Word no longer only in the words of the prophets but in the Word become flesh."[8]

What has just been stated leads into the very heart of the New Testament message. It is that Jesus Christ is the Revealer of God to men. While God in various and partial ways revealed His nature in previous generations, the very secret and mystery of His purpose were not spoken to mankind until Jesus Christ spoke them. "Jesus came preaching." What was the nature of the message which He declared publicly and imparted to His disciples, and which was in turn transmitted to the teachers and the prophets of the early church?

The commonest New Testament designation is the term *kerygma*. The verb from which it derives, *keryssein*, occurs over sixty times in the New Testament books. While it is found most prominently in the Synoptic Gospels and in Paul it appears also in the Acts, I Peter, and the Apocalypse. Most translations of the New Testament render the word "to preach," which has today taken on a rather humanistic and anemic tone; its more exact meaning is to perform the function of a herald, to proclaim with authority and fidelity a message with which one has been entrusted. The noun

---

[8]E. Brunner, *The Divine-Human Encounter*, p. 109.

kerygma, then, signifies both the act of proclamation and the message proclaimed, and in the New Testament stress is more commonly on the latter. Terms which are used as synonyms by the New Testament writers are "gospel," "good tidings," the "word." So the *kerygma* is the word that God speaks to mankind, proclaimed by Christ. It is the message of salvation. It is a proclamation containing "good news," the news of an event, which is the saving act of God in and through Jesus Christ.

A historical study of the New Testament documents makes it evident that a considerable time before any of our written gospels, or even the epistles of Paul were produced, the apostles were proclaiming this *kerygma* or message of salvation. Reconstructors of the Gospels in our own generation have claimed to "recover" this early Christian tradition from the early Petrine speeches of Acts and from fragmentary portions of the Pauline letters (chiefly Romans 1:2-5; 4:24, 25; 10:8, 9; I Cor. 15:3ff.). That the message of the early church is reflected in these passages is evident enough. But what is equally observable, though often missed, is that this *kerygma* is not a fragmentary element in a few records but runs through and dominates the whole New Testament. For the gospel is not just a message brought *by* Christ and passed on by Him as a body of doctrine or ethic to the evangelists of the New Testament. Nor is it a narrative *about* Him. Rather, that *kerygma is* Jesus; He is the gospel, the good tidings that God proclaims to mankind. Hence, while this message embraces the historical record of the earthly life and teaching of Jesus it is more than either biography or pedagogy—it is rather Christology.

It is true that in the matter of approach, emphasis, and language the New Testament writers seem to offer different characterizations of the Christ. According to Mark He is the Son of man, for Matthew, the Messiah of Israel; in Luke and

Paul He is revealed as the second Adam who restores man. John sees Him as the incarnate Logos, and the writer to the Hebrews, as the great High Priest. And yet, in this many-sided way they all tell the Christ-centered story of salvation under the guidance of one divine Spirit. "We preach Christ," says Paul. "Jesus is the Christ, the Messiah," say the evangelists.

"It must be understood that all the apostles present one and the same doctrine; and it is not correct to speak of four evangelists and four Gospels, for all which the apostles wrote is one gospel. But gospel means nothing but a proclamation and heralding of the grace and mercy of God through Jesus Christ, merited, and procured through His death. And it is not properly that which is contained in books, and is comprehended in the letter, but rather an oral proclamation and living word, and a voice which echoes through the whole world, and is publicly uttered that it may universally be heard. Neither is it a book of laws, containing in itself many excellent doctrines, as has hitherto been held. For it does not bid us do works whereby we may become righteous, but proclaims to us the grace of God, bestowed freely, and apart from any merit of our own; and it tells how Christ has taken our place, and rendered satisfaction for our sins, and cancelled them, and by His own works justifies and saves us.

"Whoever sets forth this, by preaching or writing, he teaches the true gospel, as all the apostles did, especially St. Paul and St. Peter, in their Epistles. So that all, whatever it be, that sets forth Christ, is one and the same gospel. . . ."[9]

There are several aspects of the gospel in Christ that are so dominant in the New Testament revelation that, though already implied, they require more detailed consideration. One is expressed in what was perhaps the earliest confessional formula of the church: "Jesus is Lord." "God hath made that same Jesus, whom ye have crucified, Lord as well as Christ," says Peter in his Pentecostal sermon (Acts 2:36), and Paul already in his earliest extant letter, I Thessalonians, applies this title, *kyrios*, to Jesus at least twenty times.

It should be observed that the assigning of this title to

---

[9]Martin Luther, *Commentary on Peter and Jude,* in the Lenker edition of 1904, p. 9ff.

Jesus by His early followers was in large measure a consequence of the resurrection. The fact of His return from and victory over death and the personal experience of the working of the risen Christ convincingly proved to them His unique divine Sonship and compelled acknowledgment of His Lordship over their lives. Yet it did not mean to them a Sonship attained but a Sonship manifested—an identity anterior to His human history. He did not come out of humanity but into it, the eternal Word; that is the meaning of the incarnation. And as the meaning of that Lordship was unfolded by the Spirit, especially to Paul, it assumed far greater proportions. It was a Lordship not only over the individual but over the church and beyond that over all things.

The attainment of such an all-embracing sovereignty is represented by Paul as the ultimate purpose of God in history and the main end of Jesus' life and death. "To this end Christ died and rose again, that He might be Lord of both the dead and living," Rom. 14:9. Contemplation of the cosmic significance of that Lordship moves him to write to the Philippians (2:9-11): "God hath highly exalted Him, and given Him a name which is above every name; that at the name of Jesus every knee should bow, of things in heaven, and things on earth, and things under the earth, and that every tongue should confess that Jesus Christ is Lord, to the glory of God the Father."

But the mere fact of Christ's return from death does not adequately account for the evangelists' estimate of their Lord. The son of the Nain widow and Jairus' daughter and Lazarus had also been restored to life under the witnessing of the disciples, without consequent deification or phenomenal prestige. We must look farther for the key to the matter.

That key falls under our eyes on almost every page of the New Testament. "The Son of man came not to be ministered unto, but to minister and to give His life a ransom for

many," Mark 10:45. "Our Savior Jesus Christ, who gave
Himself for us, that He might redeem us from all iniquity,
and purify unto Himself a peculiar people," Titus 2:13, 14.
"Who was delivered for our offences, and was raised again
for our justification," Rom. 4:25. "And having made peace
through the blood of His cross, by Him to reconcile all
things unto Himself," Col. 1:20. "Neither is there salvation in
any other, for there is none other name under heaven given
among men, whereby we must be saved," Acts 4:12. "Whom
God hath set forth to be a propitiation through faith in His
blood, to declare His righteousness for the remission of sins
that are past," Rom. 3:25.

The heart of the gospel lies in the meaning of Christ's
death. It is a gospel because it is a gospel of salvation. That
kerygma centers not only in Jesus but in "Him crucified";
He is Lord but also Savior. The early church has and
preaches a "Word of the cross." And it may fairly be said
that the central message of the New Testament is redemption or atonement.

But notice, the New Testament approach to this issue is
not so much conceptual and theological as it is personal and
active. Attention centers, not primarily in the fact that Jesus
preached a doctrine of the atonement, but on what He did
so that there might be an atonement to preach. And that
voluntary "doing" is cast always in the framework of the
eternal will of God—His will for restored fellowship with man.

The passages quoted three paragraphs earlier are not just
illustrative of New Testament emphasis on the atonement
idea. They are also representative of the variety of terminology through which the writers of the New Testament gave
expression to the meaning of the cross. Five terms predomi-
nate in their language; as commonly translated they are
"ransom," "redemption," "justification," "propitiation," and
"reconciliation." A sixth, expressive of end result, is "salva-

tion." These words, expressive of image and metaphor, are probably used by the writers more for descriptive than definitive purpose; but they have been treated as abstract terms in the history of the church's thinking, and highly elaborated theories of the atonement have been fabricated out of them. The doctrinal result has had two unfortunate effects; by emphasis on one aspect to the minimizing or excluding of others the composite view, which taken together they furnish, has been violated. And attention has been directed away from the effect of Christ's work for and on men and focused in non-Biblical fashion on the method of that work itself.

Strictly speaking, there are no theories of soteriology in the New Testament. There is rather an account of how and why Jesus died for man, and what that means for us. The simple fact, basic to every Biblical elaboration, is that Christ died for us, that is, instead of as well as in behalf of us. The further New Testament portrayal is that the cross, the consequence of the sins of men, has the power to redeem those who see in it both the love of God and His condemnation of sin.

The message of the cross, then, is a message of judgment, the holy God's judgment on sin. That judgment Jesus took upon Himself, the innocent suffering for the guilty, the just for the unjust. But the counterbalancing message is that of divine love—*agape*. The God of love who takes upon Himself sin's judgment in man's behalf thereby becomes the universal sufferer. In consequence of Christ's vicarious self-sacrifice God's final word to mankind is His offer of forgiveness rather than His judgment. And since God takes the initiative and goes the whole way to restore helpless man to life and righteousness and to Himself, the New Testament speaks of salvation as by grace alone. As E. H. Wahlstrom suggests, we find in the New Testament revelation the most radical doctrines of both God and man ever proclaimed.[10]

And finally, the cross is characterized in the New Testament as an expression and agency of power. It represents Christ's own victory over Satan, sin, and death. God's enemies are put to flight. The Lord who suffers is not a helpless, human victim but Christus Victor. But again, the emphasis is placed in the New Testament on the fact that this was for man; it is our victory. "He was raised for our justification." Through Christ's triumph there is victory for all who by God's grace accept Him in faith and unite their lives with His. He is the founder of a new humanity, redeemed from evil and raised into newness of life.

So again, the object of God's atoning work in Christ comes into focus. Whereas it has originated in the gracious will of God and has been necessitated by man's sin, its purpose is restoration of the living and loving fellowship between God and man. When Jesus, as well as His ambassadors in Acts, promised the forgiveness of sins in His name to those who responded with repentance and faith, they offered a renewed fellowship with God. The great Johannine concept of "eternal life" as the fruit of Christ's death is in its essence fellowship with God in Christ. Though Paul uses many words to describe the spiritual end effected by the Lord such as justification, peace with God, joy, and access to Him, certainly two of his favorite terms are reconciliation and life. Taken together, they express both the immediate and the ultimate effect of the gospel, received and appropriated by the individual. By His own creative act God produces a new life in the believer. "If any man is in Christ, he is a new creature." That life is in the Spirit, which means that all the powers of the Spirit are available to the Chris-

---

[10]E. H. Wahlstrom, *The Message of the New Testament, The Augustana Quarterly,* vol. 15, April, 1936, No. 2, p. 167.

tian. The new man is given capacity for obedience to the divine will. As the Spirit is dynamically operative, the Christian life is also dynamic. Not only does the child of God know forgiveness of sin; he learns freedom from sinning, which is growth in holiness. Already fellowshipping with God in Christ, he "presses on" in his God-given grace and power toward the goal of that perfection in oneness and communion which shall mark the consummation of God's purpose in eternity.

But while God deals savingly with the individual, it is yet true that His purposes are carried out by the Spirit in a social situation. "The New Testament knows nothing of unattached Christians,"[11] nor of isolated, solitary believers. So we find the earthly program of Jesus, which centered in the establishment of the kingdom, providing for the instrumentality of the church.

. Even the casual reader is impressed with the prominence given the concept of the kingdom of God (kingdom of heaven is the equivalent expression in Matthew) in the Synoptic record of Jesus' ministry. Excluding parallel versions, there are still about sixty sayings and parables in which Jesus speaks of the *basileia*. This is a fruitful field for Gospel study in contrast to that of the church (*ecclesia*), which appears in only two Gospel passages (Matt. 16:18; 18:17)—and some present-day critics of the Gospels even question their reliability.

The tendency of recent Protestant Biblical research in this area has been to reject the traditional identifying of the kingdom and the church.[12] It is pointed out that the word used by Jesus and translated *basileia* ("kingdom") was in the Aramaic *malku*, in the Hebrew *malkuth*, and that it

---

[11]A. M. Hunter, *The Message of the New Testament*, p. 81.
[12]For a representative modern treatment see *Jesus and His Church*, by R. N. Flew, 1938.

means primarily "kingly rule" or "kingship" or "sovereignty."
It therefore denotes the authority that God as ruler possesses
along with the actual exercise of that authority and only by
way of secondary and derived meanings suggests the territory or domain governed by Him or an organization of men.
In contrast to the traditional identifying of the two some
scholars arrive at so social and external a reading of the
epistolary ecclesia concept—in terms of human institution,
fellowship, brotherhood—as to make kingdom and church
almost mutually exclusive ideas.

Exegesis that recognizes and follows the analogy of
Scripture arrives at a conclusion intermediate between these
extremes. Linguistically the New Testament terms "kingdom" and "church" are not synonymous. But they cannot be
so simply distinguished as representing the divine as against
the human, the individual as against the collective, or the
invisible in contrast to the visible. They are rather closely
interrelated aspects of the same fulfillment of the divine
purpose in human history.

Jesus, in His incarnate person, in His preaching and
teaching, and above all in His redemptive activity revealed
and established the power and the authority of God on
earth. In Him the kingdom had come, both as a fact and as
a dynamic process to be consummated and completely realized only with the triumphant return of the King in glory.
Those who responded to that revelation and power experienced the redemptive sovereignty of God; they acknowledged the King. But that meant subjects governed by God;
historically it meant disciples, followers of the Master, the
Twelve; it meant a corporate group which under His sovereignty would function as instrument of God's saving purpose for mankind. In a word, it meant the church, the body
of Christ, the continuing sphere of His presence and activity,
and the dwelling of the Spirit.

The church, no less than the kingdom, is the work of Christ through the Spirit in the ongoing history of Christendom. Those to whom the kingdom has come, acknowledging God's rule, are members of the church; that is, they belong to Christ. A comparison of New Testament emphases reveals that being "in the kingdom" (Synoptic Gospels), or "in Christ" (Paul), or having "eternal life" (John), or being members "of the church" (cf. I Cor. 1:2) all have the same essential mark in common: that is, faith in Christ, the revelation of God's redemptive love.

Whatever is productive of such faith is constitutive of the church, that is, the chief distinguishing mark of the church is not the nature of its organization, or its common devotion, or its sense of continuity, or its conception of world brotherhood; it is its Christ-given function. It has been established by Jesus for the purpose of proclaiming the gospel, God's good tidings, to the world. That means bringing others into the fold of the Good Shepherd and sustaining those who are already His sheep.

And in terms of the means which Christ provided His first disciples to such an end it means preaching the Word of God and administering the sacraments of baptism and the Lord's Supper. These are the living media through which the exalted Christ, working through the Spirit, comes to man, engendering, sustaining, perfecting faith; their vital use distinguishes the church from every other society and agency.

A few representative passages will serve to establish both the mission entrusted to the church and the means it is to use. "God was in Christ, reconciling the world unto Himself . . . and hath committed unto us the word of reconciliation," II Cor. 5:19. "Being born again . . . by the word of God," I Peter 1:23. "For I am not ashamed of the gospel of Christ; for it is the power of God unto salvation to every one that believeth," Rom. 1:16. "Sanctify them through Thy truth.

Thy word is truth," John 17:17. "Receive with meekness the engrafted word, which is able to save your souls," James 1:21. "Go ye into all the world, and preach the gospel to every creature. He that believeth and is baptized shall be saved," Mark 16:15, 16. "For as many of you as have been baptized into Christ have put on Christ," Gal. 3:27. The meaning of the Lord's Supper, in relation to the foregoing, can be seen not only in the Synoptic words of Jesus' institution (Matt. 26:26-28; Mark 14:22-24; Luke 22:19, 20) but in the question which Paul addresses to the church regarding the Sacrament: "The cup of blessing which we bless, is it not the communion (*koinonia*) of the blood of Christ? The bread which we break, is it not the communion of the body of Christ?" I Cor. 10:16.

God effects His saving purpose through the Word, the incarnate Christ. But that Word is present in and operative through the entire gospel message, the Scriptures. And He is also present in and operative through the sacraments which Augustine called "the visible Word." Through these "means" God offers, bestows, covenants His grace to mankind. Through them as forms of communication the Spirit convinces of sin and releases from its bondage, regenerating and sanctifying man. Through them Christ comes to the believer and takes possession of his personality that he may henceforth live in Christ, as Christ in him. So man through faith is saved, and God is glorified.

The church, then, in the light of the early Christian community portrayed in the Acts, is both the depository of the gospel message and in a sense the fulfillment of it. And since there is but one gospel and one faith as one Lord, there can be but one church, the single community of God's people everywhere, knowing a common fellowship with one another. That fellowship is not man-made but divinely established and maintained. It experiences in common the grace and the love of God in Christ and the empowerment of the Spirit. It reflects the light and the love of Christ as an ethic and a leaven in every human enterprise and relationship. It shares the sufferings of its Lord at the hands of an ungodly world. But though it has no continuing city here it looks toward the fulfillment of Christ's promises and the consummation eschatologically of God's purpose, when He shall return to judge the world and subdue all enemies and "make all things new," including the resurrected child of God. Then that fellowship of saints shall enter into full and permanent possession of its destiny, which is the perfect, unmitigated joy of oneness with God.

That is the message of the New Testament. It is neither a philosophy nor a theological system but a *Heilsgeschichte*— a story of salvation with two historical foci. It begins with the incarnation, the miracle of the eternal God coming in His Son Jesus Christ into human life and history that He might share our sorrows and sufferings and take upon Himself the burden of our sins so that through the triumph of His death and resurrection we might be delivered and brought into saving fellowship with God. And it ends with the Parousia, when the fellowship of the faithful with God shall be perfected, and He shall be "all in all."

BIBLIOGRAPHY

Adeney, W. F., *The Theology of the New Testament*, London: Hodder and Stoughton.

Beyschlag, W., *New Testament Theology*, 2 vols., Edinburgh: Clark, 1895.

Bowman, J. W., *The Intention of Jesus*, Philadelphia: Westminster, 1943.

Branscomb, H., *The Teachings of Jesus*, Nashville: Cokesbury Press, 1931.

Brunner, E., *The Divine-Human Encounter*, Philadelphia: Westminster, 1943.

Deissmann, G. A., *The Religion of Jesus and the Faith of Paul*, London: Hodder and Stoughton, 1923.

Enslin, M. S., *Christian Beginnings*, New York: Harper, 1938.

Feine, Paul, *Theologie des Neuen Testaments*, Leipzig: Hinrichssche Buchhandlung, 1922.

Filson, F. V., *One Lord—One Faith*, Philadelphia: Westminster, 1943.

Flew, R. N., *Jesus and His Church*, London: Epworth, 1938.

Gould, E. P., *The Biblical Theology of the New Testament*, New York: Macmillan, 1900.

Hoskyns, E. C., and Davey, N., *The Riddle of the New Testament*, London: Faber, 1936.

Hunter, A. M., *The Message of the New Testament*, Philadelphia: Westminster, 1944.

Kepler, T. A., *Contemporary Thinking About Jesus*, New York: Abingdon-Cokesbury, 1944.

Major, H. D. A., Manson, T. W., and Wright, C. J., *The Mission and Message of Jesus*, London: Nicholson and Watson, 1937.

Nygren, A., *Agape and Eros*, translated by A. G. Hebert, London: Society for Promoting Christian Knowledge, 1932.

Parsons, E. W., *The Religion of the New Testament*, New York: Harper, 1939.

Piper, O., *God in History*, New York: Macmillan, 1939.

Porter, F. C., *The Mind of Christ in Paul*, New York: Scribner, 1930.

Rawlinson, A. E. J., *The New Testament Doctrine of the Christ*, New York: Longman's Green and Co., 1926.

Reu, M., *Luther and the Scriptures*, Columbus, O.: Wartburg Press, 1944.

Schlatter, A., *Die Theologie der Apostel*, 1922.

Schmid, C. F., *Biblical Theology of the New Testament*, Edinburgh: Clark, 1882.

Schodde, G. H., *Biblical Hermeneutics*, Columbus, O.: Lutheran Book Concern, 1917.

Scott, E. F., *The Kingdom of God in the New Testament*, New York: Macmillan, 1931.

Scott, E. F., *The Varieties of New Testament Religion*, New York: Scribner, 1943.

Stevens, G. B., *The Theology of the New Testament*, New York: Scribner, 1899.

Stevens, G. B., *The Pauline Theology*, New York: Scribner, 1892.

Taylor, Vincent, *Forgiveness and Reconciliation*, London: Macmillan and Co., Ltd., 1941.

Weidner, R. F., *Biblical Theology of the New Testament*, 2 vols., Chicago: Revell, 1891.

Weiss, Bernhard, *Biblical Theology of the New Testament*, 2 vols., Edinburgh: Clark, 1882-1883.

Weiss, B., *The Religion of the New Testament*, New York: Funk and Wagnalls, 1905.

Zahn, Theodor, *Introduction to the New Testament*, 3 vols., New York: Scribner, 1917.

PERIODICALS

Carlson, E. M., "The Interpretation of Luther in Modern Swedish Theology," *Augustana Quarterly*, vol. 23, no. 3, July, 1944.

Heick, O. W., "The New Testament in the Light of Recent German Scholarship," *Lutheran Church Quarterly*, vol. 6, no. 4, October, 1933.

Heick, O. W., "The Gospel According to Paul," *Lutheran Church Quarterly*, vol. 13, no. 3, July, 1940.

Wahlstrom, E. H., "The Message of the New Testament," *Augustana Quarterly*, vol. 15, no. 2, April, 1936.

GOD

T. A. KANTONEN

"To have a God means to have something in which the heart puts all its trust."[1] "God has no divinity where there is not faith."[2] "Faith is darkness which sees nothing, and yet in that darkness sits Christ."[3] "I should not, and I will not know of any other God except Him who is in my Lord Christ."[4]

These statements, selected from various writings of Martin Luther, are typical of the way in which the modern rediscoverer of the gospel approached the fundamental doctrine of all religion, the doctrine of God. There are, of course, many other approaches such as the metaphysical, the ethical, and the social. All the avenues, in fact, by which man thinks his way to an organizing principle of existence or of value, if pursued far enough, eventuate in some kind of idea of God. Christians have no monopoly on the word "God." Melanesian savages may use it as a synonym for "mana," the wonder-working energy which makes certain objects "tabu." And naturalistic philosophers in America may speak of a "cosmic drift toward integration" as God. Christ introduced no new word to describe or to define God. What God meant to Him was presented within the existing conceptual framework just as He brought the kingdom into the existing social framework. Scientific and philosophical analyses of the sources and the meaning of the general concept of God are therefore quite beside the point in Christian

---

[1] *Large Catechism*, comment on First Commandment, paragraph 4.
[2] *Weimar Ausgabe* of Luther's complete works (hereafter designated WA), XL, 1, 360.
[3] WA, XL, 1, 229.
[4] WA, XXVIII, 100.

(128)

theology. A theology based upon the gospel, as Luther saw, has a method of its own. It is the method of faith in Christ. If we must have a technical name for it we may call it "Christocentric existentialism." Let us first examine this method, then observe the main features of the portrait of God which it presents, and finally study the unique concept which it yields when logically developed.

I.   THE METHOD: CHRISTOCENTRIC EXISTENTIALISM

The method of Christian theology is, first of all, *existential.* This means that we have no significant knowledge *about* God unless we have first responded *to* God. He is not the end-result of a logical or moral process. He is the primary reality from which everything else is derived. "In the beginning God." It would be foolish presumption to speak about such a reality, especially in personal terms, had He not first made Himself known to us, and had we not actually stood in His presence. As Luther insists, unless God Himself precedes men's idea of God, "instead of the true and natural God, they worship the dreams and imaginations of their own heart."[5] As distinguished from speculation and wishful thinking, *faith* is this concrete, existential relation in which man as man stands before God and responds to Him as person to person. Where it does not exist, God indeed has no divinity. Four centuries before William James distinguished between knowledge by description and knowledge by acquaintance Luther clearly applied this distinction to bring out the existential meaning of faith: "We should note that there are two ways of believing. One way is to believe about God as I do when I believe what is said of God is true. . . . The other way is to believe in God as I do when I not only believe that what is said about Him is true but

---

[5]*Commentary on Galatians*, Middleton translation, London: 1839, p. 319.

put my trust in Him, surrender myself to Him, and make
bold to deal with Him."[6]

The existential starting point was not invented but only
rediscovered by Luther. It is the clear and consistent teaching of the Bible. The Scriptural writers nowhere undertake
to demonstrate the existence of God by means of intellectual
arguments. To belabor such an obvious point as whether
there is a God is no concern for serious-minded men. It is
left to fools (Ps. 53:1) and devils (James 2:19). One who
has faced life on a level worthy of human personality does
not ask whether God is but how he can square himself with
God, discover His will and do it. No matter whither he
turns, be it nature or history or his own inner life, he is so
unmistakably confronted by God that he knows no place to
flee from the divine presence. The pertinent question is how
to obtain the cleanness of hands and heart that will enable
a man to stand in God's presence. For existential knowledge
of God is morally conditioned. You know what you know
about God because you are what you are. "Blessed are the
pure in heart, for they shall see God," Matt. 5:8. "If any man
willeth to do His will, he shall know of the teaching, whether
it is of God," John 7:17. Faith, the living contact between
man and God, thus takes place in conscience (II Cor. 4:2;
I Tim. 3:9). It is there that man enters into a person-to-
person relation to God, for conscience means essentially that
God addresses each man as an individual "thou" and calls
him to give an account of himself.

When a man honestly faces God with his whole being
and in terms of personal responsibility he is bound to discover that there is something radically wrong with his relation to God. Man is a sinner, and as such he is cut off from
God. God remains veiled because man lacks the purity of
heart with which to pierce the veil. Instead of serving as a

---

[6]*Works* of Martin Luther, Holman ed., II, p. 368.

bridge to God conscience reveals tension, distress, and maladjustment, thus only showing that the bridge has been destroyed. If, therefore, our theology is to be something more than an expression of our needs and aspirations, God Himself must pierce the veil, overcome our sin, and bring about a new positive orientation of man to Himself. We not only need God but we need an incarnate and reconciling God. The heart of the gospel is that this need has been met. "God was in Christ reconciling. . . . " Hence Christian knowledge of God is not only existential but also Christocentric. Christianity proclaims in earnest what no philosophy would dare to say for fear of being ridiculed as a superstitious and irrational fable, namely, that God has taken on flesh, entered history in a definite place and time, walked as a man among men, and even died a criminal's death. The living gospel, which alone gives Christian theology its *raison d'etre*, throbs in such statements as: "He that hath seen Me hath seen the Father," John 14:9. "No one cometh unto the Father but by Me," John 14:6. "In Him dwelleth all the fullness of the godhead bodily," Col. 2:9. True theology does not begrudge the heathen whatever awareness of God they may sense from nature or human nature, nor deny that God spoke to Israel through the law and the prophets, but it walks with Paul and Luther in the "light of the knowledge of the glory of God in the face of Jesus Christ," II Cor. 4:6.

A modern non-Lutheran theologian has pleaded earnestly for "the all-decisive insight—stressed with such power by Luther—that God must be conceived wholly according to Christ."[7] Since Paul, no one has indeed grasped the Christocentric existentialism of the gospel as clearly and as firmly as the great Reformer. The powerful Luther research of our century, based upon the discovery of rich prereformatory

[7]H. R. Mackintosh, *The Christian Apprehension of God,* New York: Harpers, 1929, p. 87.

writings such as the *Lectures on the Epistle to the Romans,*
has shed new light upon Luther's own religious crisis and
the basic method growing out of it. We can now appreciate
afresh the vitality and the depth of the new approach which
makes Luther such a pivotal figure in the history of Christian thinking. Seeberg calls it "realism of conscience." I have
preferred to use the Kierkegaardian term "existentialism."
But to Luther, still more than to Kierkegaard, are applicable
the words with which Professor Swenson has characterized
the latter thinker: "He has . . . effected for theological
thinking a veritable Copernican revolution, one . . . infinite-
ly more significant than the much heralded astronomical
one, the same Copernican revolution which is effected in the
soul of every man, when he becomes mature in the consciousness that it is not so much he that cross-examines
existence, as existence that cross-examines him."[8] Luther's
recurrent phrase for the divine cross-examination is to stand
coram Deo, in the presence of God. This outlook, maintained with costly but penetrating honesty, enabled the
Reformer to see through the religious as well as intellectual
and moral pretensions behind which men hide from the true
God. Whether he professes belief in God or not, before
God's Word arrests him man is a practical atheist. Either
he is self-satisfied in his detachment from God and looks
upon Him only in a cool, academic way, or else he seeks his
own good even in God, thus using God as a means to his
own end.[9] Such self-centered atheism Luther calls "godlessness to the right." But there is also a "godlessness to the
left," making for despair. When a genuine contact with God
has taken place in a man's conscience, and he has to stand

---

[8]D. F. Swenson, *Something about Kierkegaard,* Minneapolis: Augsburg, 1941, p. 86.
[9]Current religious thinkers have learned to speak in the same vein.
To many men, according to Halford Luccock, God is a "glorified
aspirin tablet," while Harry E. Fosdick deprecates the use of God as
a "cosmic electric fan" turned on when life becomes too hot.

coram Deo, he sees himself as a sinner who has incurred the wrath of God. He would like to believe in a fatherly God, but what he actually encounters is an offended Majesty. He tries now to flee from God's presence, to forget the whole encounter, but finds that he cannot. Not even by dying can he escape God, for death only opens the door into the divine judgment hall. In this crisis man can take either the false road of self-sanctification, trying to build his own ladder to heaven, or the true road of pure grace. The latter is the way of the gospel which offers Christ for sinners only. Man is and remains a sinner, but paradoxically enough, such is the God whom we see in Christ that He loves sinners and bestows His favor upon the godless. In Christ the hidden, terrifying majesty of God, *Deus absconditus,* becomes *Deus revelatus,* God revealed as unconditioned forgiving love.

The Protestant scholasticism, which fell heir to the legacy of Luther, was unable to rise above the static intellectualism and legalism of prevailing thought forms and do justice to Luther's basic insight. It was almost lost in the rationalism of the eighteenth century, nor was it recovered in the thought systems popular in the nineteenth: the romanticism of Schleiermacher, the speculative idealism of Hegel, the moralism of Kant and Ritschl, to say nothing of the various currents generated by scientific evolutionism. The credit for its recovery must be given to Kierkegaard, the greatest Christian thinker since Luther, who postulates God as a personal necessity, demands that man face God with wholehearted sincerity, recognizes the humanly unbridgeable gulf which separates the sinner from God, and finds faith to be "existential communication" on the basis of the divine gift of grace. The conception of God based on the Christian gospel has come to its own in our day in a vital and ecumenical theology flourishing where the insights of Luther and of Kierkegaard have been understood and followed.

II. THE RESULT: THE GOD PORTRAIT OF CHRISTIAN THEOLOGY

"There is one divine essence which is called and is God, eternal, without body, indivisible, of infinite power, wisdom, and goodness, the Maker and Preserver of all things." Such is the definition of God given in the First Article of the Augsburg Confession. If God can be encompassed within a definition, this one will probably serve the purpose as well as any. If God is God, however, and man is man, then by the very nature of the case any attempt on the part of man to define God must end in failure, a fact generally admitted even by the staunch seventeenth-century adherents of the Confession. Moreover, the use of the Eleatic-Platonic term "essence" or such variants as "being" or "substance" to describe God introduces a point of view foreign both to Scripture and to faith. The essence-attribute ideology is a survival from a form of thinking which reasoned in terms of space-filling objects and their properties instead of the volitional activity of persons. The dynamic God of the gospel is better expressed by verbs than by nouns, and poorest of all by abstract nouns. He is more easily dramatized than conceptualized. "The Highest cannot be spoken," said Goethe, to which a theologian has added, "Nonetheless it may be lived out in act, in personal being."[10] Just as William James could not define spirituality except by pointing to Phillips Brooks, so existential Christianity, confronted with the question, "What is God like?" can only point to Christ. "The content of faith," says Aulen, "must reflect uninterruptedly the picture of God which is given through the Christ-deed."[11] Farther than that we cannot go. Christianity rests upon the axiom that once man, in Luther's words, "has looked Christ

---

[10]Mackintosh, op. cit., p. 108.

[11]Quoted in N. Ferre, Swedish Contributions to Modern Theology, New York: Harper, 1939, p. 104.

in the heart," faith is *given* to him, *i.e.*, God discloses Himself as an incontrovertible fact. "To ask for proof that what shines to us through Christ is God, is like asking for proof that luminous objects are visible."[12]

Abandoning, then, the whole essence-attribute point of view and seeking simply to trace the features of the Christ-revealed God as they are reflected in faith, let us examine first the form and then the content of the picture thus given to us.

What God is in Himself, apart from His self-disclosure in Christ, faith does not presume to say. As in Luther's concept of *Deus absconditus*, it allows God to be God instead of robbing Him of His divinity by transposing Him into some rational or moral category of our own. On the other hand, as Ritschl correctly saw, "personality is the form in which the idea of God is given through revelation."[13] In the language of Scripture, "God is Spirit," John 4:24. Were it not for the necessity of repelling foreign influences, Christian theology would find it as unnecessary to demonstrate the personality of God as to argue for His existence. To stand in the presence of a person and to respond when he has spoken calls for a higher form of recognition than a rational demonstration of his existence as a person. The only relevant response to God is worship. But the attitude of reverence, the motive power for worship, cannot long be maintained before an impersonal object. In the words of Kant, "reverence refers always to persons only as its object, never to things."[14] Without a personal God there can be no true life of faith, expressing itself in heartfelt commitment, trust, prayer, and loyalty. Thus the Bible speaks constantly about a "living God" as the objective correlate of living

---

[12]Mackintosh, *op. cit.*, p. 198.
[13]*Justification and Reconciliation*, p. 237.
[14]*Kritik der Praktischen Vernunft*, I, IB, 111.

religion. Religion as a rite, or a code, or a surmise, may be possible without that kind of God, but not religion in the Christian sense of "fellowship." To be capable of fellowship is to be personal. The revelatory communication upon which this fellowship is based has the same presupposition. Finally, the God revealed by a person, Jesus Christ, can Himself be nothing less than a person.

To conceive of God under the form of personality is to give Him the highest form of expression of which we are humanly capable. But faith never forgets the divine warning: "To whom will ye liken God?" Isa. 40:18, and, "My thoughts are not your thoughts," Isa. 55:8. Man has been created in the image of God and thus has in the structure of his own being his best clue to God. But, by simple logic, this does not mean that the converse is also true, i.e., that God is to be created in the image of man. To Strauss and Biedermann, who claimed that personality itself is an expression of finitude and therefore inapplicable to God, Lotze demonstrated incontrovertibly that complete personality is possible only to God while we are at best only fragmentary personalities. Analogies drawn from *human* personality will carry just so far, and it is fallacious to draw further inferences where these analogies no longer hold. Thus to conceive God as finite in the sense of being limited by a "given" element in His own nature, as Professor Brightman does, is to stop short of a true God, for it is to read a human limitation into God. We start with a *given* nature, but God is the ground of His own being. The old orthodoxy guarded against undue anthropomorphism with its doctrine of divine "aseity," while modern theologians express the same thought by the terms "absoluteness" and "sovereignty."

No one has stressed more uncompromisingly the absolute sovereignty of God than Luther in *The Bondage of the Will*. The "inscrutable will" of the divine majesty can never be

subject to cross-examination by man; it is "only to be feared
and adored." But the central insight in Luther's doctrine of
God, and the central theme of the gospel, is this: God's
sovereignty is the sovereignty of love. Apart from Christ
God is pure sovereignty, a terrifying, concealed majesty before whom we can only tremble. As revealed in Christ, God
is pure love, unconditioned and inexhaustible, whose royal
gifts we can in no way deserve but only accept with amazed
gratitude. Just as "God is Spirit" expresses the form in
which the gospel presents God, so "God is love," I John 4:8,
is the essential content of the divine nature, or, to be more
accurate, the fundamental activity of the divine will. The
New Testament word for love, *agape*, has a meaning all its
own, sharply different from any natural emotion or spiritual
aspiration of man. It has no cause except the richness and
the fullness of its own being, and its movement is a spontaneous outreach, independent of the worth or worthlessness
of its object. It is a flowing down, not a struggling up. It
leads to the incarnation of God, not to an apotheosis of man.
As taught by Jesus in the Sermon on the Mount, it is poured
upon the evil and good alike and has the same disregard for
merit as rain and sunshine have for fences. It is concretely
manifested in Jesus' love of sinners.

The difference between the portrait of God thus given
and the opposite one derived from considerations of reason
and value may be illustrated by a comparison of Aristotle's
God and the "father" in Jesus' story of the prodigal son.
Aristotle's God, abiding by rational and moral proprieties,
cannot contaminate himself with the imperfections of the
world; and, since he is himself the only worthy object for
his thinking, he is engaged in a solitary contemplation of his
own perfection. The God of Thomas Aquinas is cast in the
same mold, a fitting expression of the Roman Catholic emphasis on merit. But the father of the prodigal not only

receives a sinner who has forfeited every right to fellowship but actually runs down the road to embrace one whose associations have been with harlots and swine. A God as undignified as that is quite inconceivable apart from revelation. But He alone can do more than offer a reward for those who have achieved. He can bring hope to those who have failed. The father love of God is revealed, above all, in the death of Christ for sinners. "God commendeth His own love toward us," declares Paul, "in that, while we were yet sinners, Christ died for us," Romans 5:8. This "agape of the cross," viewed specifically in the light of the worthlessness and the godlessness of man as undeserved love, is *grace*. This word portrays God in the full sovereignty of His love. "It is love to the indifferent and disloyal, whose one claim is their need."[15] It is a love which finds sin and creates worth. Here is the living center of the entire gospel: man is delivered from his sinful preoccupation with himself by a love which seeks him while he is still careless or hostile, encompasses him in the midst of his sin, and lifts him into fellowship with God. Here lies also the solution of the intellectual problem of divine transcendence and divine immanence. It is the nature of agape to be sovereign and exalted, beyond the reach of any natural limitation, and yet to give itself freely and recklessly, to communicate, to share, to be accessible, to create fellowship.

In Luther's rediscovery of the gospel the centrality of agape was given full and rich expression. Luther's God was "nothing but an abyss of love." Why He loved sinners had no other explanation than this: it is God's nature to do so, for love is *opus Dei proprium*, God acting as God. Every element of constraint was removed from God just as every element of merit was removed from man. Hence Luther did not hesitate to proclaim the sovereignty of love *contra legem*

---

[15]Mackintosh, *op. cit.*, p. 198.

et contra rationem, against every legalistic and rationalistic limitation. But both law and reason came back with the Lutheran orthodoxy, which proceeded to reduce his dynamic insights into conceptual form. The resulting alterations in the God portrait are especially evident in the doctrines of election and the atonement. To Luther election or predestination stood simply for God's sovereign purpose to save, an elaboration of the text, "Ye have not chosen Me, but I have chosen you," John 15:16, a safeguard of *sola gratia,* redemption by grace alone. God's love may be a *verlorene Liebe,* a love wasted upon people who despise and reject it, but it continues to be poured upon the unworthy. Intellectualistic orthodoxy, while resenting the arbitrary sovereignty of Calvin's God, could not comprehend a God who chooses to love the godless. Hence it removed the paradox in favor of a bit of clever reasoning: God chooses only those whose faith He foresees. In the atonement Luther's emphasis was upon the God who "gave His only-begotten Son," who puts forth every resource of His love to conquer the powers of destruction and to redeem man. Orthodoxy, on the other hand, fell back upon the legalism of St. Anselm: punishment had to be borne before God's mercy was free to act. Such considerations as these are the result of conceiving love and justice as separate, even antithetical, elements within God, needing to become reconciled. It was under a similar misconception that Luther struggled in bitter anguish of soul, and it was by removing it that he restored the true gospel portrait of God. To this critical question of the relation of God's love and God's holiness or justice we must now turn.

That God is not only a loving God but also a holy and righteous God is clearly an integral part of the Christian revelation. Thus our Lord does not speak of God only as Father but as "holy Father" and "righteous Father." In the Old Testament holiness is indeed the dominant trait of God.

Again and again we find there the conception of holiness as an incomprehensible, wonderful, awe-inspiring power, a view common to all religion as masterfully shown in R. Otto's *Das Heilige*. It was the contribution of the Hebrew prophets to portray the transcendent power and majesty of the Holy One in terms of ethical perfection and righteousness which made Him the supreme good, "the moral law alive." In the New Testament "holy" is used consistently in the prophetic sense. Thus it is a personal characteristic both of Jesus and of the sanctifying Spirit. When holiness is conceived under the form of personality instead of impersonal law, the idea of divine "wrath" is inescapable. If God is a holy person He must actively oppose evil. Outside of revelation this wrath is totally arbitrary and mysterious. In the "law and the prophets" the norms according to which it operates are revealed. But if man's actual contact with God takes place in conscience, as the existential approach postulates, then man's first impression of God must be that of a righteous Judge whose will he has violated and whose wrath he has therefore justly deserved. Facing God while standing amid the wreckage of His broken laws and listening to His voice through the accusations of an outraged conscience, it is not obvious to man that God is love. To living religion the question of the relation of God's holiness and God's love becomes the acute personal one: how can I, a sinner, find a God of grace?

This question marked the long, hard trail so thoroughly explored by Luther, at the end of which he came upon that insight into the heart of God by which evangelical theology lives but which it must rediscover again and again. The insight came, as the new Luther research has shown, while the future Reformer was preparing his lectures on the Psalms in 1513 or 1514.[16] In Psalm 31:1 the scholarly young

---

[16]See Luther's own account of this experience in WA, LIV, pp. 179-187.

seeker after grace encountered the prayer: "Deliver me in Thy righteousness." But on what ground, pondered he, can a *sinner* ask a *righteous* God for *deliverance?* Does not divine righteousness demand rather the *punishment* of the sinner? The answer came from Romans 1:17: "For therein is revealed a righteousness of God from faith unto faith: as it is written, But the righteous shall live by faith." God's righteousness is of a higher order than ours. It is a *redeeming righteousness,* which freely gives us Christ in all His saving power. God does all the giving, we only receive. God saves sinners, not in spite of His holiness, but because of His holiness. God's justice is a paradoxical justice which justifies the unjust and which must therefore be identified with His love. "Note this fact carefully," insists Luther, "that when you find in the Scriptures the word God's justice . . . it means the revealed grace and mercy of God through Jesus Christ."[17]

Once this discovery of a completely Christlike God is made, a master key for unlocking the entire Scriptural revelation is placed in our hands. We learn to appreciate the truth that began to dawn upon Israel after the sufferings of the Exile, that God's holiness is consummated in forgiveness: "Thou art holy . . . our fathers trusted in Thee . . . and Thou didst deliver them," Ps. 22:3-40; "Our Redeemer . . . the Holy One of Israel," Isa. 47:4. "There is no God beside Me, a just God and a Savior; look unto Me, and be ye saved," Isa. 40:21, 22. We can see why Jesus should call the Father "righteous" in sending a Savior to make known the divine agape (John 17:25, 26). And a new radiance shines from such a passage as "If we confess our sins, He is faithful and righteous to forgive us our sins and to cleanse us from

---

[17]"Sermon on the Gospel, First Sunday in Advent," Lenker ed., X, section 37.

all unrighteousness," I John 1:9. Inconsistencies and tensions which we have read into God disappear when all other aspects of God are seen in the light of His sovereign, redeeming purpose in Jesus Christ. God is still holy, but we now see Him as Holy Love bent upon seeking and saving that which is lost.

God, then, as the living Thou of faith, is the absolutely sovereign and holy will revealed in Christ to be redeeming love. The "attributes" not already included in this portrait are simply ways in which faith has sought to sharpen these basic features. Thus mercy, patience, and faithfulness are other words for describing the love of God. The holiness of His love is described, not only as righteousness and justice, but also as goodness or ethical perfection. As absolute personality, transcending temporal, spatial, and human limitations, He is immutable, eternal, omnipresent, and omniscient. To faith, however, these are never formal or static concepts; they stand for complete dependability, which invites complete trust. Detached from their living interrelatedness as activities of the one Christlike God, the various "attributes" become meaningless abstractions, often inconsistent with one another. An important case in point is "omnipotence." It is an expression of sovereignty, the indispensable form for conceiving God. But taken by itself as omnipotence instead of omnipotent love, it becomes involved in intellectual absurdities as well as in a conflict with love itself. As theology has acknowledged ever since St. Augustine, if God is God, there are many things which He cannot do, e.g., He cannot act in contradiction of Himself or of the nature of the things He has made. A God capable of being evil is not God. What God is determines what is possible, not vice versa. Faith, therefore, is not interested in random speculation about the possible and the impossible but only in the omnipotence of holy love. The philosophers who first separate omnipotence and love and then find it necessary to limit omnipotence in order to preserve love are guilty, as Berkeley would say, of first stirring up the dust and then complaining that they cannot see. It was in answer to "Who can be saved?" that Christ said, "All things are possible with God," Mark 10:26, 27. The God of Christian faith is almighty to save. No other God can give this assurance.

III. THE INTERPRETATION: THE TRINITY

We have studied the method of Christocentric existentialism and the God portrait which it presents. When man faces this God with his whole being, standing, as Kierkegaard said, "in an absolute relation to the Absolute," then the only adequate acknowledgment of His presence is the unconditioned commitment of faith. "Love so amazing, so divine, demands my soul, my life, my all." But when he is asked to conceptualize the meaning of this revelation of God, to engage in intellectual interpretation instead of worship and service, then he is on the road which leads inevitably to the doctrine of the Trinity.

The first Christians confessed, "Jesus is Lord," and they lived by the gifts of His Spirit. They constituted a fellowship of the Spirit, which their Lord Jesus Christ had given them after returning to the Father who had sent Him. Their faith was thus clearly Trinitarian although no necessity as yet existed for thinking it through and coining a word for the conclusion. In this faith they would encourage one another, for example, to "be filled with the Spirit, giving thanks for all things in the name of our Lord Jesus Christ to God, even the Father," Eph. 5:18-20.[18] The clearest expressions of the

---

[18]See also: Eph. 1:17; Rom. 8:11; Heb. 10:29; I Cor. 12:3-6; I Pet. 1:1, 2; John 14:16.

Trinitarian faith are found in the baptismal formula (Matt. 28:19) and the apostolic benediction (II Cor. 13:14).

The doctrine of the Trinity, however, does not rest on any specific, isolated passages of Scripture but on the content of the Christian revelation as a whole. It is the entire gospel in an intellectual nutshell. As such it has been recognized to be the specifically Christian conception of God by the church universal from Athanasius to Barth. Although the apostles did not raise the intellectual question of divine unity and triplicity, once the question was raised, the church could be true to itself only by replying in terms of the Trinity. It is the only answer which does justice both to the Christocentrism and to the existentialism of the church's faith.

The Trinity is, first of all, the church's affirmation of the reality of its Christ-centered revelation of God. Worship of the one God whom Jesus worshipped and whom He revealed as "Father" is, of course, self-evident and uncontested. But historically and empirically the key member of the Trinity is the Second Person. The Father is the "Father of our Lord Jesus Christ," and the Spirit does not speak of Himself but of Christ. The first Christians, like Luther, thus had no existential knowledge of God apart from Christ. Had the church not felt constrained to assert emphatically that Christ is nothing less than "very God of very God," there would have been no need for the doctrine of the Trinity. Greek antiquity was familiar with various "sons of God," from Aesculapius to Apollonius of Tyana, a contemporary of Jesus, men who had achieved the rank of deity or at least of demigod. But when such thinking was applied to Him whom the church worshipped as her Lord, "in whom dwelt all the fullness of the godhead bodily," it was so infuriatingly inadequate that the 318 Fathers assembled at Nicea could not help literally tearing to pieces an Arian confession written in such vein. To the church Christ was no demigod, nor even a full deification of man, but the very incarnation of God, the Word become flesh. But the moment the philosophical term "Logos" had been applied to Jesus, to interpret the meaning of the incarnation, it became necessary to go still farther and to seek to define the relation between the divine Speaker and His incarnate Word, and the doctrine of the Trinity was in the making. Against its own will, perhaps even against its better judgment, the church was thus forced into the realm of metaphysics, but only because the center of its faith, "God in Christ," was challenged. So it has been through the centuries, and so it is today: only to a thoroughly Christ-centered theology is the concept of the Trinity a fundamental necessity.

Without the *existential* approach to Christ, however, the church's faith could have assumed a binitarian instead of a trinitarian form. Had the manifestation of God in Christ been only a historical reality, apprehended directly only by the few who were privileged to know Jesus "after the flesh," there would have been no need for a third person of the Trinity. The doctrine of the true divinity of the Holy Spirit is the church's witness to the living and abiding reality of the Christ-revealed God. Through the Spirit Christ continues to be present in the communion of believers and to afford them person-to-person experience of God and not mere knowledge about God. Giver of life and power, the Spirit reveals "God in Christ" to be Redeemer in fact as well as in name. Thus He makes possible a genuine and a vital *witnessing* on the part of the church. In His creative fullness the Spirit stands for the personal inwardness and subjectivity of the Christian experience of God and at the same time constitutes the bond which binds together into a fellowship those who have this experience.

The Trinity, then, is the church's interpretation, in the philosophical language of an ancient day, of the existential contact with God which her Lord continues to give. The language has changed; the word "person," for example, has today quite another connotation than it has in the Athanasian Creed. Today the unchanging content of the Trinity may perhaps be expressed in such words as those of Troeltsch: "the revelation of God, given in Christ, and operative in the Spirit."[19] Viewed in the existential perspective, it reflects the dynamic and the transforming richness of the Christian revelation. Before we can speak of God as being one we must revise our ordinary concepts of unity. God is one, not in any barren sense of singularity, but one in a higher, threefold sense in which God remains God although He has revealed and continually communicates Himself to us. The unity of God is not the unity of a static category but the unity of an energizing and redeeming purpose having its own dialectic: The Father gives the Son, the Son redeems, the Spirit makes redemption real in experience. It is the kind of logic that can be grasped only from the center of the gospel: God is love. "You have an insight into Trinity," said Augustine, "if you have an insight into love." Just as agape is revelation's last word about God, so Trinity, its conceptual counterpart, is fittingly theology's last word in the doctrine of God. The greatest thinkers of the church such as Augustine and Luther are reluctant to go farther than that, showing a chaste reticence in dealing with the unfathomable relations within the Godhead. A more rash intellectualism emboldened the Protestant orthodoxists to speak of the *ad intra* and *ad extra* operations of the three persons and to assign them personal characteristics and definite spheres of activity. The tendency, for instance, to restrict the Father to creation and providence overlooks, on the one hand, that Christ is the revelation of the creative as well as of the redemptive principle (John 1:3) and, on the

---

[19]*Glaubenslehre*, 1925, p. 124.

other hand, that the Father can be known only through the Son. Apart from Christ both nature and history remain enigmas. Seen through His eyes, both reveal the fatherly heart of God.

The doctrine of the Trinity, as the Athanasian Creed holds, shows a Christian how he is to *think about God*. The church clings to this concept because no acceptable substitute has been offered. But any concept of God is a poor substitute for God Himself. The Trinity means little or nothing to a man until the Spirit, operating in the Christian fellowship, has led him to acknowledge in living personal faith: "Jesus is Lord."

BIBLIOGRAPHY

G. Aulen, *Den kristna gudsbilden genom seklerna och i nutiden*, 1927.

J. Baillie, *Knowledge of God*, 1939.

Karl Barth, *The Doctrine of the Word of God*, tr., 1936.

T. Bohlin, *Gudstro och Kristustro hos Luther*, 1927.

T. Bohlin, *Kierkegaards dogmatiska åskådning*, 1925.

E. S. Brightman, *The Problem of God*, 1930.

E. Brunner, *Gott und Mensch*, 1930.

H. H. Farmer, *Towards Belief in God*, 1943.

A. E. Garvie, *The Christian Doctrine of the Godhead*, 1925.

Charles Gore, *Belief in God*, 1922.

E. Hirsch, *Luthers Gottesanschauung*, 1918.

Leonard Hodgson, *The Doctrine of the Trinity*, 1943.

F. Kattenbusch, *Deus absconditus bei Luther*, 1920.

A. C. Knudson, *Doctrine of God*, 1930.

Martin Luther, *The Bondage of the Will*, tr., 1931.

H. R. Mackintosh, *The Christian Apprehension of God*, 1929.

A. Nygren, *Agape and Eros*, tr., 3 vols., 1932, 1938, 1939.

R. Otto, *The Idea of the Holy*, tr., 1926.

A. S. Pringle-Pattison, *The Idea of God in the Light of Recent Philosophy*, 1917.

E. Seeberg, *Luthers Theologie, Motive, und Ideen. I Gottesanschauung*, 1918.

N. Söderblom, *Das Werden des Gottesglaubens*, 1916.

N. Söderblom, *The Living God*, 1930.

W. R. Sorley, *Moral Values and the Idea of God*, 1918.

W. Temple, *Nature, Man, and God*, 1934.

C. C. J. Webb, *God and Personality*, 1919.

MAN

E. THEODORE BACHMANN

This brief study of man centers on the perennial question: "What is man?" Every man thinks he knows the answer, for none would deny his own humanity. But what man is, is really the question of the centuries. Forcefully, among the modern theologians, Emil Brunner has said: "The most powerful of all spiritual forces is man's view of himself, the way in which he understands his nature and his destiny; indeed it is the one force which determines all the others which influence human life. For in the last resort all that man thinks and wills springs out of what he thinks and wills about himself, about human life and its meaning and its purpose."[1]

Those who have sought to answer the riddle of man's existence have approached the subject from various directions. The most modern approach, stemming from an earlier naturalism, is the way of *science*. "No former age," says Ernst Cassirer in his provocative *Essay on Man*, "was ever in such a favorable position with regard to the sources of our knowledge of human nature. Psychology, ethnology, anthropology, and history have amassed an astoundingly rich and constantly increasing body of facts." This scientific endeavor, however, has not only failed to find a method for the mastery of such vast material, but it is also discovering that a "wealth of facts is not necessarily a wealth of thoughts."[2]

---

[1]The Oxford Conference Report, *The Christian Understanding of Man*, Chicago: Willet Clark, 1938, p. 146.

[2]Ernst Cassirer, *An Essay on Man, An Introduction to a Philosophy of Human Culture*, New Haven: Yale University Press, 1944, p. 22. The provocative thinking of the author commends this book for general reading.

These mountainous scientific data radiate influences
which outstrip the bounds of modern man's thought and
invade every area of his being. A well-known British hu-
manist has termed this the "implacable offensive of science"
which present-day moralists either dodge or underestimate.[3]
Yet the danger lies, not in science as such, but in the use to
which it may be applied by men who are possessed, not by
a passion for morality, but for power. As such, the gospel of
harnessing the powers of nature is perverted into a legalism
which is devastating to man and associates him no longer
with his Creator but with the dust of the earth.[4]

Perversity of this sort points to a phenomenon which
pervades all human history. It is man's ambivalence. It
finds expression in his ability to create and to destroy. It
involves him in fundamental contradictions whose disso-
nance shakes the core of his being. This self-transcendence
through creativity and self-abasement through destructive-
ness can be studied scientifically as "the problem of evil."
But this problem can never be solved scientifically so long

---

[3] E. M. Forster, quoted by Leslie Paul, *The Annihilation of Man,
A Study of the Crisis in the West*, New York: Harcourt, Brace, 1945,
p. 160. The author is favorable to Christianity, but his critique of
modern civilization, including the church, is unsparing.

[4] Among the many books dealing with this general theme are Harry
Elmer Barnes, *Society in Transition*, New York: Prentice-Hall, 1941.
Pitrim A. Sorokin, *Man and Society in Calamity*, New York: Dutton,
1943. For the practical application of power in modern times the
writings of Marx, Lenin, Hitler are revealing. From the standpoint of
psychology the works of Carl G. Jung, *e.g.*, *Modern Man in Search of
a Soul*, New York: Harcourt, Brace, 1933, interpret the dynamic in
man's life as a "will to power." With prophetic vision Rudolph Sohm,
the Lutheran historian of church law, declared in 1887: "To what shall
I compare the society in our day? It is like the earth on which we
live. A thin crust around a great volcanic, seething, revolutionary heart
of liquid fire. Outwardly all is flourishing and thriving in peace and
order; but another moment, and the titanic elementary forces of the
underworld have changed all this splendor into dust and ashes." *Outlines of Church History*, London: Macmillan, 1913, pp. 243-244; 244-
254 contain a vivid summary of the modern situation in the making.

as man is the measure and his spiritual life, if acknowledged at all, is regarded as autonomous.[5]

A much older approach to the study of man, which is often congenial to mysticism, is the way of *philosophy*. Here the wealth of human thought becomes evident, not simply as relating man to himself, but as projecting his conscious thinking to personal and universal ultimates. As human wisdom made articulate, philosophy throws much significant light on the study of man. The ordinary person like the intellectual contrives his philosophy of life. According to it he governs much of this thought and action. This is true even of such widely imitated philosophers as Aristotle, Marx, or John Dewey. Herein the limitations of the philosophical approach to man's life become clear. Every philosopher believes he has found the basic truth about human nature. Yet each gives his own picture of his discovery. Systems of philosophy reveal not only subjective preferences but also basic contradictions. Each philosophy, moreover, as it seeks to fathom the depths of human life, founders on the treacherous rock of man's evil. It cannot solve the problem of man's sin.[6]

----

[5]Paul, *op. cit.*, pp. 162-175, on the limitations of the scientific attitude. For a study of man from the biological standpoint and not antagonistic to religion, see John M. Dorsey, *The Foundations of Human Nature*, New York: Longmans Green, 1935. A basic work from the side of psychology is William Healy and Augusta F. Bronner, *The Structure and Meaning of Psychoanalysis: As Related to Personality and Behavior*, New York: Knopf, 1938. Cf. the profitable study toward a Christian understanding of psychology by Fritz Kunkel, *In Search of Maturity, An Inquiry into Psychology, Religion, and Self-Education*, New York: Scribner's, 1943. Also the four essays on the nature of personality by Emil Brunner, *God and Man*, London: Student Christian Movement Press, 1936.

[6]Cassirer, *op. cit.*, pp. 20-21. Among the many philosophical concepts of human life two may be singled out: Aristotle, *The Nichomachean Ethics* (several editions) especially Book III; and John Dewey, *Human Nature and Conduct*, New York: 1923. See also Paul Arthur Schilpp, *The Philosophy of John Dewey*, Chicago: Northwestern University Press, 1939, in "The Library of Living Philosophers,"

An equally venerable approach to the study of man, frequently permeated with philosophy, is the way of *theology*. Its basic concern has been with the conquest of evil and the triumph of good. Behind it lies the panorama of man's diverse religions which eloquently attests to the seriousness of his desire to hurdle the problematic evil standing between him and the better life. Within this theological approach lies the testimony of conscience, that persistent reminder that man is not alone.[7] No discerning missionary or student of the history of religions can doubt the sincerity of man's quest for supernatural assistance in overcoming evil and in satisfying life's deepest longing. But the spiritual wealth represented by the religions of mankind is cancelled by their theological relativism. Left to himself, man cannot—even by theologizing—form a living relation between himself and the divine. Even Christianity, in mortal hands and conditioned by human thought, often gives the appearance of sharing in this general failure.[8]

With science, philosophy, and theology all displaying their weaknesses, might not these approaches—if taken col-

which includes others as George Santayana, Bertrand Russell, and Alfred North Whitehead. For a global outlook on the philosophical scene, also with reference to the "problem of evil," p. 6, see Charles E. Moore, ed., *Philosophy—East and West*, Princeton: Princeton University Press, 1944.

[7]James H. Breasted, *The Dawn of Conscience*, New York: Scribner's, 1939, p. 123. As the title indicates, the author regards conscience as a social product. See also the sharp appraisal of modern man's attitude toward conscience in Reinhold Niebuhr, *The Nature and Destiny of Man, A Christian Interpretation*, Volume I, *Human Nature*, New York: Scribner's, 1941, pp. 93-122.

[8]Hendrik Kraemer, *The Christian Message in a Non-Christian World*, New York and London: Harper, 1938, pp. 101-228, where the author deals with the non-Christian religions. Cf. the contrary emphasis in William E. Hocking, *Living Religions and a World Faith*, New York: Macmillan, 1940. A balanced presentation is that of Edmund D. Soper, *The Philosophy of the Christian World Mission*, New York and Nashville: Abingdon-Cokesbury, 1943, pp. 129-231. See also, Gordon H. Smith, *The Missionary and Anthropology*, Chicago: Moody, 1945.

lectively—lead to a definitive appraisal of modern man and to a possible prescription for his permanent well-being? This would be an attractive hypothesis were it not that our age, in thinking about man, lacks an intellectual center. Lacking such a center, there can be little effective communication across lines of specialization. One of the first to describe this contemporary dilemma was the thoughtful Roman Catholic philosopher, Max Scheler, who in 1928 declared: "In no other period of human knowledge has man ever become more problematic to himself than in our own days. We have a scientific, a philosophical, and a theological anthropology that know nothing of each other. Therefore we no longer possess a clear and consistent idea of man."[9]

The historic occasion of this modern unclarity and inconsistency lies in the seventeenth century. It was there that the revival of classical paganism in the Renaissance manifested its ultimate divisiveness. There science, philosophy, and theology parted company while each thereafter strove for autonomy.[10] The present anthropological confusion is therefore part of our intellectual inheritance. But coupled with it is a new and somewhat shattering self-consciousness which has become widespread in our time. Man impatiently wants to know more about himself; his age-old thirst for salvation by knowledge propels him on his quest.

---

[9]*Die Stellung des Menschen im Kosmos,* Darmstadt: Reichl, 1928, p. 13. Quoted by Cassirer, *op. cit.,* p. 22.

[10]Jacob Burckhardt, *The Civilization of the Renaissance,* Vienna: The Phaidon Press, n.d., especially the fourth part, "The Discovery of the World and of Man," pp. 146-185. More generally significant is his compelling work, *Force and Freedom, Reflections of History,* edited by James Hastings Nichols, New York: Pantheon, 1943, especially pp. 100-101, 165-254, 311ff. "Since the sixteenth century . . . science has been one of the paramount criteria of the genius of an age," p. 101. Cf. the illuminating presentation of subsequently decisive developments by George Norman Clark, *The Seventeenth Century,* Oxford: The Clarendon Press, 1929. See also James H. Randall, *The Making of the Modern Mind,* Boston: Houghton Mifflin, 1926, Books II and III.

At this point Christianity enters. It challenges both man's motivation, which is egocentric, and his means, which are finite. In their place Christianity proposes the ultimate approach to an understanding of man. Its source is God, and its goal is God. Its dynamic is the gospel, which is "God's saving power for everyone who has faith."[11] Out of this Christocentric faith there emerges a unique understanding of man. It is communicated fundamentally not from man to man, nor from man to deity, but from the living God to mortal man. Speaking out of the catastrophic experiences of two global wars within one generation, a group of courageous Christians in Germany has declared: "Man in our time has abandoned belief in his divine origin and in his divine destiny, and just for that reason his self-consciousness has increased extravagantly. Now that man realizes that this [abandonment] has all been a satanic deception, despair has followed. No biological, historical, or moral valuation of man can provide a basis for the reassurance of his humanity. Only Jesus Christ can do that."[12] Those who can make such an affirmation stand once more in the heritage of the Reformation. Their words are prophetic, suggesting the Biblical understanding of man as recovered by Martin Luther.

The motivation for this understanding, as Luther persistently affirmed, lies not in the human desire to know something about God, but in God's intention to know something about each individual man. From his Creator, not from himself, man derives his self-knowledge. In making this assertion Luther was restoring the Biblical understanding of man. He was laying the matter of man's relation to

[11]Romans 1:16 (Moffatt tr.). For an intensive study see Gerhard Kittel, *Theologisches Wörterbuch zum Neuen Testament*, Stuttgart: Kohlhammer, 1933ff, vol. I, "akouo," pp. 216-225; vol. II, "dunamis," pp. 286-318; "euaggelion," pp. 705-735; Vol. III "kerugma," pp. 682-717.

[12]*International Christian Press and Information Service*, Geneva: Twelfth Year, No. 35, September, 1945, p. 6.

God upon the conscience of each individual. He insisted that man cannot make his religion merely a constituent element in his culture; when he does, it is no longer religion that he is cultivating but self-gratification.[13]

In the sixteenth century, therefore, while philosophy, theology, and science were still superficially agreed about man, Luther became the great protagonist of the awakened religious conscience. In fulfilling this role he rendered timely service not only to his contemporaries but also to men of our day.[14] In view of his enduring significance in the field of theological anthropology, and because the twentieth-century phase of the "Luther renaissance" in Europe has reproduced his thinking on man in the manner of a timely critique, I shall follow two major considerations: Luther's understanding of man, and the need of a more dynamic understanding of man for our time.

I. LUTHER'S UNDERSTANDING OF MAN

Much of the distinctiveness of Lutheran anthropology, as one might expect, is derived from Luther himself. One will misunderstand or miss altogether the evangelical emphases of Lutheran theology as a whole if one does not grasp the fundamentals of Luther's understanding of man. In order to do that, one must know 1) where Luther begins his theology, 2) how he persists in pointing out man's human limitations, 3) how he discerns man's basic limitation in the unfree will, 4) how he recovers the sinner in man, and 5) what role he assigns to conscience in man's relation to God.

---

[13]Karl Holl, *Gesammelte Aufsätze zur Kirchengeschichte, I. Luther,* Tübingen: Mohr, 1923, p. 109.

[14]Below, Part II, (Ms. p. 20ff). Holl, *op. cit.,* p. 35f. Also Emil Brunner, *Man in Revolt, A Christian Anthropology,* New York: Scribner's, 1939, pp. 93-96, 525-526, together with other references wherein he shows his indebtedness to Luther. Cf. Niebuhr, *op. cit.,* i, pp. 17, 265ff, 160-162, almost succeeds in covering up his indebtedness to Luther for many of his own anthropological insights.

1

Luther begins his theology not above, in an absolute concept of God, as does Thomas Aquinas or John Calvin; but his starting point is below, in the humanity of Christ. "I have often told you," he preached to the students at Wittenberg, "and I tell you again, and when I am dead, remember it, that all the doctors whom the devil rides and guides, begin at the top and preach a God apart from Christ (as we ourselves did once in the schools). . . . Begin your wisdom and your knowledge with Christ, and say: 'I know no other God than Him who is in that man.' "[15] Again he declared: "God cannot be apprehended save only in the flesh of Christ. . . . He who has Christ stamped upon his heart can assuredly thereafter mount up to the Father."[16]

Conversely, what is Luther's primary concern with the God who "has created me and all that exists"? It is a functional concern whose attention focuses on the relation of God to the sinner. His theology "is concerned always and exclusively with God in His relation to the sinful world." Therefore his starting point is not God in His general relation to the world as its Creator and Sustainer but God, the Redeemer, in His specific relation to man.[17]

---

[15]Luther, Sermon on John 17 (1530), *Werke*, Weimar Ausgabe (WA), 28:101. Quoted by George S. Hendry, *God the Creator*, Nashville: Cokesbury, 1938, p. 87. Also Theodosius Harnack, *Luthers Theologie*, Erlangen: Blaesing, 1862, pp. 91-110. He is one of the first to set forth this functional approach of Luther to the study of theology.

[16]Hendry, *op. cit.*, p. 101, quoting Luther from WA 25; 107. This little book, by a Scottish scholar who confesses an affinity to Continental theology, is unusually rich and stimulating.

[17]*Ibid.*, 83-84. Harnack, *op. cit.*, pp. 89, 90, 92. An appreciation of this book by the father of the famous Adolf Harnack reappeared with the renewed study of Luther after 1918. It was published in a new two-volume edition in 1927, but all references here are to that of 1862.

2

Having located him in this divine-human relationship, how does Luther keep man in his place? Man is never, according to Luther, unrelated to God. He is always a creature, and he can never escape his Creator.[18] All men, moreover, have been endowed with an intellect which distinguishes them from animals. This "natural light" sustains man's striving after the good. Its brightest manifestation is human reason, which is "among all other things of this life the very best and something divine. It is the discoverer and ruler of all the arts. . . . " Even after Adam's fall "God has not deprived reason of this majesty."[19] In secular affairs, in matters of law and order, reason enables man to make intelligent use of his freedom of action and to govern himself without falling into anarchy.[20] On the basis, therefore, of what he has and is, man is a responsible creature.

Philosophy, likewise, has its rightful place in man's thought processes. But Luther relentlessly opposes any noticeable intrusion of philosophy into the realm of theology. He anathematizes the philosophical theology of scholasticism. When human speculation offers substitutes for the theology based upon God's self-disclosure in Christ, then philosophy is guilty of usurping the place and short-circuiting the power of the revealed Word. Aristotle, that pagan philosopher who was "baptized" by Aquinas, has been the

---

[18] Holl, op. cit., 75, 76.

[19] Luther, "Theses de homine" (1536), WA, 39(1): 175f. Quoted by Emanuel Hirsch, *Hilfsbuch zum Studium der Dogmatik*, Berlin und Leipzig: Gruyter, 1937, pp. 150-151. This book is an invaluable and convenient collection of source material on the Protestant Reformation in regard to both the Lutheran and the Calvinistic movements.

[20] Luther, "Secular Authority, To What Extent It should be Obeyed" (1523), *Works of Martin Luther* (Philadelphia Edition), vol. III, pp. 223-274; "A Sermon on Keeping Children in School" (1530), vol. IV, pp. 133-180. See also Carl Stange, *Studien zur Theologie Luthers*, vol. I, Gütersloh: Bertelsmann, 1928, pp. 20-33, "Die reformatorische Lehre von der Freiheit des Handelns."

most guilty. For, by employing his metaphysical principles, the scholastic theologians have perverted Christian theology. Therefore Luther reverses the Roman Catholic dictum and asserts: "No one can become a theologian unless he dispenses with Aristotle."[21]

In the philosophical perversion of theology Luther detected the most subtle and vicious attack upon the uniqueness of Christ—who came also to save the theologians from their sin. He regarded this intellectual aberration as symptomatic of man's actual condition. Reason has made man proud; by philosophizing he has projected himself to the heights of deity. From that illusory vantage point he has interpreted his own relation to God. With imagined competence he has deemed himself capable of achieving a right relationship with God. Consequently Luther seeks to unmask man's presumptuousness and to indicate the limits within which man is competent to handle his own affairs. On this point Theodosius Harnack, a pioneer among modern authorities on the Reformation, has summed up Luther like this: "The natural knowledge of God, derived from reason, conscience, and the law, may in itself be objectively warranted, nevertheless it is not the right knowledge of God because it does not avail the sinner for salvation; instead, as misused by him, it makes him secure in his sins, easy-minded and self-righteous."[22]

According to Luther man's knowledge of God apart from Christ is and remains a purely "legal cognition." Neither the law of Moses nor the testimony of the conscience can do anything but accuse man of failure. Inasmuch as the moral law can indict but not save, so likewise reason's ultimate contribution to man's condition is not enlightenment but deception. For the fact is that "all men are oppressed under

---

²¹Hendry, *op. cit.*, 85. ²²Harnack, *op. cit.*, 94, 96.

the sovereignty of the devil." Even the common man who hardly ventures into the realm of abstract thought falls under the same indictment. He may wish to possess God, but his desires are preoccupied with material goods and human approval. He indeed has a god, but his name is Mammon.[23]

3

While man has "freedom of action in externals" and can of his own volition behave himself acceptably in company with his fellow men he does not have such freedom in determining his relation to God. Man's basic limitation lies in his unfree will, or—to give the Latin term *arbitrium* a more precise connotation—in his incompetence.[24] Here Luther and the Reformers broke with the medieval interpretation of freedom which had grown out of the semi-pelagianism of the Roman Church and which had atomized man's behavior into individual acts. Such acts might in themselves appear praiseworthy and thus give rise to an undue optimism in appraising human nature. But for Luther such mosaic interpretation of behavior seemed as the very thing which prevented man from seeing his life as a whole; that is, as a person in relation to God.[25]

In his polemic, *De servo arbitrio*, Luther attacks not only Erasmus but all others who presume that man is competent to determine his own destiny. What folly it is for man, with the help of "Mistress Reason," to think

[23]See Luther's explanation to the First Commandment, Large Catechism. *Triglot Concordia*, St. Louis: Concordia, 1921, pp. 581ff. WA, 39(1): 175f. Hirsch, *op. cit.*, p. 150. Harnack, *op. cit.*, pp. 91ff.

[24]Hendry, *op. cit.*, p. 123. See also Stange, *op. cit.*, pp. 20ff, who supplies the often overlooked emphasis of the Reformers on the corollary of the doctrine of the unfree will, *i.e.*, man's freedom of action and his duty among his fellow men.

[25]Stange, *op. cit.*, p. 28. Brunner, *God and Man*, p. 164, "God the creator calls man into being through His creative Word. . . ." Cf. Hendry, *op. cit.*, 150.

nothing but human thoughts about God, and then to equate these with God's self-disclosure in Christ. Luther, on the contrary, means to magnify Christ in order to keep man in his proper relation to God. Free will, so far as it concerns man, can never be anything more than a concept, a relativism upon which he may wish to set his wishful thinking but which is powerless in the face of God's omnipotence. God alone can have free will or complete competence to deal with man's nature and destiny. Hence, freedom of the will "is exclusively a divine attribute."[26]

Luther deliberately goes to an extreme in order to demonstrate that God's grace is the sole agency of man's conversion. One must understand this emphasis as set over against the desire of natural man to participate in his own salvation and thus to save his face (his ego) with a show of merit. Conformity, insists Luther, with the divine will brings the "liberty wherewith Christ hath set us free." The inner peace that follows submission then becomes the true strength of man's life. In commenting on the word of Christ, "Without Me ye can do nothing," John 15:5, Luther says: "Since God has taken my salvation out of my own will and received it into His, and has consented to save me—not by my own doings or chasing about but rather through grace and mercy—I am certain and rest secure that He is truthful and will not lie to me. For in this He is mighty and great, so that neither devils nor adversaries can break Him or tear Him from me."[27]

From this serene center amid the turbulence of life Luther draws a final conclusion. God's will is at work, not

---

[26]WA, 1:359, 365f. Found also in Hirsch, *op. cit.*, p. 147. This is Thesis 13 in Luther's Heidelberg Theses of 1518.

[27]Harnack, *op. cit.*, pp. 174-198, an excellent discussion of *De servo arbitrio*. For a thorough study of the background of this treatise see WA, 18:551-596. Henry Cole's English translation of this work (1823), partly corrected and reprinted, appeared as, Martin Luther, *The Bondage of the Will*, Grand Rapids: Eerdmans, 1931. Also Hirsch, *op. cit.*, p. 150.

only in the incompetence of evil men, but also in that
demonic power which competes with God for the possession
of man's will. Figuratively, Luther sees the human will as
a horse which both God and Satan are trying to ride.
Elsewhere he says: "The devil is the lord of the world,
and I myself have never been able to believe it, that the
devil should be the lord and god of the world, until I
have now experienced it as an article of faith: *Princeps
mundi, deus huius saeculi. . . .*" Luther even dares to speak
of "God's devil" who is permitted to ply his nefarious craft
among men, but always within limits set by God.[28]

By this realistic inclusion of the demonic within the prerogative of the divine Luther extends the boundary of faith.
He knows that Christian faith, in order to be effective in a
sinful world, dare not be limited to a half-god who is only
sweetness and light. It must rather be attached without
reservation to "the Father of our Lord Jesus Christ," who is
the God of righteous wrath over man's sin as well as the just
and merciful One. If, as Luther maintains, the believer
cannot praise God for everything—even as Job exclaimed in
the depths of bereavement (1:20-22)—then his trust is
shaken to its foundations, and his faith is an illusion.[29]

Faith, as Luther observes in connection with man's
will, is the radical remedy which alone can save. Faith
is the possession in advance of the things we hope for.[30]

---

[28]*Ibid.*, p. 148. See also WA, 50:473. Cf. *The Bondage of the
Will*, p. 390, sec. 167. In regard to the devil there is a worth-while
study by Hermann Obendiek, *Der Teufel bei Martin Luther*, Berlin:
1931; quoted by Karl Heim, *Jesus der Herr, Die Führervollmacht Jesu
und die Gottesoffenbahrung in Christus*, Berlin: Furche, 1935, p. 114.

[29]Heim, *op. cit.*, p. 116. Heim has reaffirmed the need for a more
realistic satanology, like that of Luther, if man is to understand both
himself and the God who rescues him from sin. To the tender-minded
such an affirmation may be a shock.

[30]Georg Helbig, tr., *Martin Luther, Vorlesung über den Hebräer-
brief, 1517/1518*, Leipzig: Dietrich, 1930, pp. 134-136, on Hebrews
11:1.

It is "of things which do not appear. Therefore, that there be room for faith, it is necessary that all things which are believed should be hidden. They cannot, however, be hidden more remotely than under their contrary object, sense, and experience. Thus when God makes us alive He does it by killing us; when He justifies us He does it by making us guilty; when He carries us up to heaven He does it by leading us down to hell."[31]

4

With the humanity of Christ as his starting point, and with the determination to impress upon man the reality of his human limitations, Luther did what man only at his best can ever do—he recovered man, the sinner.

In his lectures on Romans, Luther unfolds the anthropology of St. Paul and with profound insight interprets the meaning of sin. What the scholastic teachers had glossed with superficial comments Luther replaced with the penetrating indictment that all men are under sin (Rom. 3:9). This charge is leveled not simply at the behaviorism of good deeds but at its motivation. "The outward man," said Luther, "is constantly practicing good works, but the inner man fairly bubbles over with sinful desires and lusts, which tend to the contrary. For if he could do it with impunity, or if he knew that no laurels or peace would reward him, he would rather omit the good and do the evil. What difference then is there before God between him who does evil and him who wants to do evil . . . ?"[32] His sharp analysis then leads to an appraisal

---

[31]WA, 18:633. Quoted by Hendry, *op. cit.*, pp. 110-111. For a helpful recovery of the New Testament understanding of the demonic, see Kittel, *Theologisches Wörterbuch*, vol. II, pp. 1-21, "daimon."

[32]Michael Reu, *Luther's German Bible, An Historical Presentation together with a Collection of Sources*, Columbus: Lutheran Book Concern, 1934, p. 122.

of the plight in which the man finds himself who wants
to appear outwardly good but is perversely motivated.
Such a man's "works are doubly evil, first because they
are not done out of good will and therefore are evil, and
second, because in a new pride they are held to be good
and are defended."[33] This leads to Luther's ultimate definition of sin: "Man can seek only that which he is; he
can love only himself above all things. Therein lies the
root and essence of all sinfulness." Men without Christ
"seek, even in their good and virtuous acts, only to please
and applaud themselves."[34]

The will in man, whereby he challenges the omnipotent
will of God, is for Luther synonymous with the human ego.
He speaks of it as *der Ichwille* or ego-will and recognizes
it as being always first on the scene when any decision is to
be made. It lobbies for action favorable to its own interests.
It is both persistent and powerful because it is lodged in
man's elemental nature and can therefore subvert the good
intention of nobler resolves. It is subtle because, for the
most part, it does not express itself openly or consciously but
is at home in the realm of the unconscious. Yet it is none
the less genuine will. It strives to subject the entire personality to its crafty ends. This ego-will, mostly submerged
like an iceberg, is the seat of man's self-assertion against
God and is the basis of his life and behavior as a sinner.[35]

Luther's concept of the ego-will gave new depth to the
meaning of concupiscence. Contrary to the teaching of the
Roman Church but in agreement with St. Paul and the
Fathers, Luther contended that the propensity to sin, which

---

[33]*Ibid.*, p. 123.
[34]*Ibid.*, p. 125.
[35]Holl, *op. cit.*, pp. 60-62. See also Charles L. Hill, *The Loci
Communes of Philip Melanchthon*, Boston: Meador, 1944, pp. 69-110,
"On the powers of man, especially free will."

remains even after baptism, is truly sin.[36] No mere summoning of the higher virtues nor adherence to the moral law can liberate man from this fundamental perversity. Such confidence in human virtue and law only makes men hypocrites.[37] The cause of this perversity lies in each individual's origin.

Original sin, as Luther understands it, is not simply the lack of the original righteousness in which man was created and which is beyond man's comprehension. But, in relation to God, it is "the total loss of the whole rectitude and the capability of all the powers of the body as well as the soul and the whole inner and outward man." God not only hates the self-inflicted loss of uprightness but also "this whole concupiscence by which we disobey the command: Thou shalt not covet (Exod. 20:17). . . . For this commandment shows us sin, as the Apostle says: I would not have known that concupiscence is sin, if the law did not say: Thou shalt not covet (Rom. 7:7)."[38]

If concupiscence or the ego-will is innate, can man be charged with guilt? Luther says: yes. For he sees Adam's sin not simply as a determining event in the history of the human race but as a fact in the origin of each individual's personal history. Original sin, which Luther sometimes calls

---

[36]The King James version translates concupiscence as "lust." Moffatt, Goodspeed, Weymouth translate it as "covet," which in our day sounds innocuous. For the official Roman Catholic interpretation of concupiscence see Philip Schaff, *The Creeds of Christendom*, New York: Harper, 1877, 1919, vol. II, p. 88, "This concupiscence, which the apostle sometimes calls sin (Rom. 7:7), the Holy Synod declares that the Catholic Church has never understood it to be called sin . . . in those *born again*." From *The Canons and Decrees of the Council of Trent*, Fifth Session (1546). For Luther's interpretation, see Reu, *op. cit.*, pp. 126, 128. Luther clinched his understanding of the abiding contradiction even in the life of the sinner in the statement: *"Ideo simul sum peccator et justus, quia facio malum et odio malum."* Johannes Ficker, ed., *Luthers Vorlesung über den Römerbrief, 1515/1516*, Leipzig: Dieterich, 1925, Teil I., p. 65, comment on Rom. 7:16.

[37]Holl, *op. cit.*, p. 63.

[38]Reu, *op. cit.*, pp. 131-132.

Personensünde, originates in the will and therefore makes every man personally responsible and guilty before God.[39]

This profound grasp of the meaning of sin grew out of Luther's personal experience and an unsparing analysis of his spiritual torture. The recurring temptation (*tentatio*) which assailed him vivified original sin into a fundamental anthropological premise. As a result Luther went beyond the teachings of St. Paul as commonly interpreted.[40] Driven to despair by the question: "How can I get me a gracious God?" he experienced the meaning of sin as separation from God. In "the God-forsaken winter of his soul" he realized how man's separation from God threatens him with destruction. Amid such trials Luther found his chief adversary not the devil but God, who must always be the self-assertive sinner's ultimate opponent.[41] "In such moments the soul is utterly unable to believe that it can be saved; it only thinks that the pains of hell are not yet complete.[42]

For a time the young Luther misunderstood the meaning of "the righteousness of God." He resented the apparently impossible demands God made on the sinner. Therefore, "as I could not depend on my satisfactions for my own reconcil-

---

[39]WA, 10(1): 508-509. In a sermon on the Gospel for New Year's, 1522, (Luke 2:21), Luther says: "Original sin or natural sin (*personensund*) [is] the chief sin; were it not for this, then there would be no actual sin either." Quoted by Holl, *op. cit.,* p. 66.

[40]Paul Althaus, *Paulus und Luther über den Menschen,* Gütersloh: Bertelsmann, 1938, shows how Luther differed from Paul in emphasizing that even the believer "sins daily," (see Luther's explanation on baptism in the Small Catechism). Moreover, Luther interprets the "I" in Rom. 7 as pertaining not simply to the man without Christ but also to the Christian—which most exegetes do not admit, pp. 68-69, 86-87. A valuable study is that of James Stewart, *A Man in Christ, The Vital Elements of St. Paul's Religion,* New York: Harper, n.d., pp. 99-103.

[41]Holl, *op. cit.,* pp. 66-69. See also Walther von Loewenich, *Luthers Theologia crucis,* München: Kaiser, 1933, pp. 21-53. This is a fruitful and suggestive study of Luther's concept of the *Deus absconditus,* whose wrath is revealed against the sinner.

[42]Reu, *op. cit.,* p. 104; n. 62, p. 334.

iation I did not love Him but actually hated that righteous and sin-avenging God, if not with silent blasphemy, then with great murmuring."[43]

Having experienced divine wrath, Luther discerned afresh the meaning of Christ, who endured this wrath in man's behalf. The glad news of the gospel is that, because of Christ, God bestows righteousness upon man. By faith in Christ, who took man's punishment upon himself and was "made sin for us" (II Cor. 5:21), God reconciles the world to Himself (v. 19). Though humanly he remains a sinner and is daily in need of repentance and forgiveness, the penitent believer is justified—declared by God to be in a right relationship with Him. Indeed, as Luther exults, "the just shall live by faith!"[44]

5

Luther's recovery of the sinner was not simply a personal experience but a matter which was to be laid upon the conscience of every man. Conscience, if obeyed, is the lever which pries man out of his state of complacency. Conscience accuses man; it gives him no rest because its testimony shows that he has not lived up to his best. Its character has the force of law. Its function, like that of the Decalogue or of moral law in general, is to convict man of sin.[45] Every man, when he takes his conscience seriously, must feel himself personally responsible to God. Luther himself was deeply moved by a sense of personal responsibility, as though the impending Last Judgment was a present and daily reality.[46]

[43]*Ibid.*, p. 107; n. 71, p. 336.

[44]Gustaf Aulen, *Christus Victor*, London: S.P.C.K., 1931, pp. 77-96, 117-138, is a careful discussion of Luther and what the author calls the "classic" doctrine of the atonement. What has happened to this doctrine in Lutheran teaching since Luther (the Osiandrian controversy) follows, pp. 139ff.

[45]*Triglot Concordia*, pp. 121, 479.   [46]Holl, *op. cit.*, pp. 18, 35.

In the writings of Luther and in the Confessions conscience—good, bad, or terrified—recurs so frequently that this interpretation of Christianity has been called the "religion of conscience."[47] One of its chief demands is that man accept the full claim of the law and the gospel.

Like conscience, but to a far higher degree, the divine law is intended to "reveal original sin with all its fruits." It must "tell man that he has no God nor cares for God, and [that he] worships other gods, a matter which before and without the law he would not have believed. In this way he becomes terrified, is humbled, desponds, despairs, and anxiously desires aid, but sees no escape; [then] he begins to be an enemy of God. . . . That is what Paul says, Rom. 4:15: The law worketh wrath. And Rom. 5:20: Sin is increased by the law."[48]

Luther understands that the law magnifies sin in order that the work of Christ may appear in its true glory. He opens his lectures on Romans, asserting: "The sum total of this letter is: to destroy, to ferret out, and to obliterate all wisdom and righteousness of the flesh . . . and in its place to implant, to engraft, and to magnify sin, whether it does not exist at all, or whether one only thinks that it exists."[49] Through the law God is actually challenging man to be what his ego-will makes him, namely, a rival to his Creator. But man cannot step out of character. The law, as it were, calls his bluff. But he must be able to stand in the face of his own condemnation long enough to recognize the righteousness and justice of God's position. Then, and only then, will

---

[47]*Ibid.*, 35.

[48]*Triglot Concordia*, p. 479.

[49]Ficker, *op. cit.*, Teil II, p. 1, on Rom 1:1. Also in Reu, *op. cit.*, p. 111. There is a German translation of Luther's lectures on Romans, but none in English—except the few portions published by Reu. See Eduard Ellwein, *Martin Luther, Vorlesung über den Römerbrief, 1515 /1516*, (based on the Ficker Latin edition, above), München: Kaiser, 1937.

he be able to understand the meaning of "nevertheless," whereby God, in His infinite mercy and for Christ's sake, promises to save him.[50] The law from without and conscience from within bring man to this decisive moment.

God's promise to save His enemy, man (Rom. 5:10), and to forgive his sin is indeed "glad news." Such mercy and forgiveness, says Luther, is contrary to reason; it is too good to be true, except that God Himself does it. Therein lies the miracle of forgiveness. This is the gospel. This is *Christus pro nobis.* Only by faith can man accept this priceless gift while to the sophisticated world, which turns a deaf ear to its own conscience (Rom. 1:18-32), it will always remain foolishness (I Cor. 1:18ff).[51]

To believe that God can and does forgive sin for Christ's sake is a challenge to faith proclaimed by the gospel and opposite to that given by the law.[52] Is it really true that the God of righteous wrath, from whom the sinner cannot escape even in hell, is also the God of forgiving love? And that in Christ He does this "in order that I might be His own, live under Him in His kingdom, and serve Him in everlasting innocence, righteousness, and blessedness"? Yet "this is most certainly true."

The faith by which I now accept this new life of *Christus in nobis* demands the response of my whole being. A total claim rests upon me.[53] It is no longer that of sin which enslaves but of grace which adopts (Rom. 8:15). My conscience, moreover, is not terrified but at peace. It becomes

---

[50]Holl, *op. cit.*, p. 74.
[51]*Ibid*, pp. 75-78.
[52]Above (Ms. p. 18).
[53]Luther, Small Catechism, explanation to the Second Article of the Creed. See also Kittel, *op. cit.*, vol. I, "agapao," pp. 20-55; cf. "hamartano/hamartia," pp. 267-320, both of which are basic studies. In stimulating theological form the concept of divine love has been set forth by Anders Nygren, *Eros and Agape*, 2 vols., London: S.P.C.K., 1938-1939.

the constant and controlling factor in the life which has learned to say YES to God. Its testimony affirms my abiding obligation to God and declares that in doing His will I have found perfect freedom.[54] This is the climax of Luther's anthropology. The recovery of the sinner has no purpose unless it points to something greater, the restoration of divine sonship. The image of God which the first Adam lost is now restored by Christ, the "Second Adam," while "we all, with open face beholding as in a glass the glory of the Lord, are changed into the same image from glory to glory, even as by the Spirit of the Lord."[55]

II. THE NEED OF A MORE DYNAMIC UNDERSTANDING OF MAN FOR OUR TIME

Luther's anthropology, it seems, made its tremendous impression for two major reasons. One was that he sought to understand the Bible as few men ever have. The late Michael Reu has shown how profoundly Luther's intensive preoccupation with the Scriptures determined his whole theological outlook.[56] Others have indicated how Luther absorbed the Biblical anthropology into his very being, and how inevitably he interpreted it with certain variations caused by his own experience.[57] But at all times Luther strove to maintain a double emphasis: correct exegesis of a

[54]*Triglot Concordia*, pp. 193, 339-341, 551, 723. Holl, *op. cit.*, pp. 35-37.
[55]Romans 5, II Cor. 3:18. See the discussion in Brunner, *Man in Revolt*, pp. 96f, 501ff. Also above, Note 14, on Niebuhr. For the manner in which Lutheran dogmaticians have been tempted to elaborate on man's state of original righteousness see Heinrich Schmid, *Doctrinal Theology of the Evangelical Lutheran Church*, Philadelphia: Lutheran Publication Society, 1889, pp. 225-238. Also, Henry E. Jacobs, *A Summary of the Christian Faith*, Philadelphia: General Council Publication House, 1905, pp. 95-96.
[56]Reu, *op. cit.*, pp. 75-145, "Luther and the Bible." See also his last work, *Luther and the Scriptures*, Columbus: Wartburg Press, 1943, especially pp. 13-37.
[57]Althaus, *Paulus und Luther*, pp. 9, 86.

given passage and a personal re-experiencing of its content.[58] His analysis of man was always Biblical in that he could never conceive of a basic understanding of man apart from God.

The other reason for the effectiveness of Luther's anthropology was that he always related it to life. What God was saying to Luther through His Word was meant for all men. And if this is true, then men must hear about it. Perhaps his greatest significance "lies in the fact that he made it plain once and for all that when Christian faith is brought in harmony with human thought, no matter of what age that thought may be, it is deprived of its essential character; for the faith is basically contrary to human thought and cannot be accommodated with it." This is so because Christian faith is based on revelation. Revelation is not a category of thought or an extension of it but moves in a direction contrary to that thought.[59] Indeed, "My thoughts are not your thoughts," Isa. 55:8.

A man's friends sometimes do him more harm than good, and the Lutheran dogmaticians, unwittingly and with best intentions, modified the dynamic character of Luther's anthropology as well as of his theology in general. As everyone knows, Luther was no systemizer. Consequently, when his understanding of man became systematized and placed in increasingly elaborate theological structures (reared on the principles of Aristotelian logic!), something vital was lost. The standardized sinner of Lutheran scholasticism bears little resemblance to the individual whom the living God addresses with the inescapable Word: "Thou art the man!" For erudition in the Scriptures, as well as supplying many minor deficiencies, the dogmaticians hold us in their debt. Indeed, from Melanchthon on down Lutheranism has grown more out of interpretations than out of the writings of

---

[58]Holl, *op. cit.*, p. 578f.
[59]Hendry, *op. cit.*, pp. 132-133.

Luther himself. But for a vital grasp of man, the sinner, the standard works with which Lutherans in America are familiar leave something to be desired.[60]

How can we recover a more dynamic understanding of man for our time? The need of the hour is for theologians in the best sense of the term. In Luther's own words: "Prayer, meditation, and struggle make a theologian." Moreover, just as Luther attacked the misconceptions about man in his day at their source, so the Christian today, who is a spiritual descendant of the Reformation, will fail to do his duty if he thinks that the Reformation is finished also in respect to its anthropology. The Biblical principles of this anthropology remain valid; but these, to be effective, must be addressed to popular misconceptions about man in our day. The pontificating theology and the complacent psychology of the sixteenth-century schoolmen have given way to the confused theology and autonomous psychology of the modern schools. Today the results of the intellectual revolution of the seventeenth century are all too apparent. Theology, challenged by philosophy and science, has been powerless to prevent the progressive dismemberment of man by dissociated and often mutually antagonistic investigators. The attacks upon the anthropology of Christianity in the nineteenth century, from which it but partly recovered, have been increased in the twentieth.[61]

More than we may as yet know, anthropology is the decisive question of the age. Around it centers a struggle

---

[60] Along with such standard works as Jacobs, *op. cit.*, and the English translation of Schmid, *op. cit.*, there is the most ambitious of all dogmatical books produced in America, Franz Pieper, *Christliche Dogmatik*, 3 vols. and Index, St. Louis: Concordia, 1924-1928.

[61] Werner Elert, *Der Kampf um das Christentum, seit Schleiermacher und Hegel*, München: Beck, 1921, is both penetrating and pessimistic, particularly in respect to the situation in Germany and the Lutheran Church. Also, Randall, *op. cit.*, Book IV; and Merle Curti, *The Growth of American Thought*, New York: Harper, 1943, Parts VI and VII.

of superhuman proportions and of demonic fury, for the destiny of man's soul is at stake. The Christian today, like the prophet of old, must know his generation, speak the language of his contemporaries, and proclaim among them the divine law and gospel. The man-made challenges of materialistic science and of humanistic philosophy, so popular and widespread among all peoples, must be studied and grasped in their full significance and then answered out of a clear understanding of the Word of God and an unconquerable faith in His gospel.

A renewed and much more vigorous study of man, from this Christian perspective, is urgent. As possessors of the Lutheran heritage our responsibility for such a study is twofold. On the one hand, Lutheranism at large has been embarrassed by the rise of a vicious totalitarianism among a people more than half of whom were baptized members of the Lutheran Church.[62] On the other, Lutheranism has produced leaders who have recognized the terrible contradiction between haughty paganism and Christian faith, and who have fearlessly fought the pagan terror with the sword of the Spirit. The Lutheran Church, as in the age of the Reformation, has opportunely been placed at the very center of the epoch-making struggles of our time, where it has produced modern martyrs who, together with fellow Christians, have bravely fought against "the dethronement of God and the enthronement of man."[63]

[62]Paul B. Means, *Things that are Caesar's, The Genesis of the German Church Conflict*, New York: Round Table, 1935. Wilhelm Hauer, Karl Heim, Karl Adam, (in Eng. tr.) *Germany's New Religion, The German Faith Movement*, New York: Abingdon, 1937. Kressmann Taylor, *Until that Day*, New York: Duell, Sloan and Pearce, 1942. Stewart W. Herman, *It's Your Souls We Want*, New York: Harper, 1943. To these four illuminating books should be added the theological comparison by Walter Marshall Horton, *Contemporary Continental Theology*, New York: Harper, 1938.

[63]Theophilus Wurm, Lutheran Bishop of Württemberg, in *International Christian Press and Information Service* (ICPIS), Twelfth Year, No. 19, 20, May, 1945, p. 2. Also No. 25, July, 1945, pp. 2-3.

Our danger, as Christians in America, may not be so
much that of succumbing in some titanic conflict as that
of failing to realize the nature of the spiritual testing to
which we shall be increasingly subjected. Can we thoroughly repent of our own failings? Can we gain such an
understanding of our human situation that we shall be able
to speak to our people in the churches and to our contemporaries aloof from the church those words of prophetic
judgment, as Luther proclaimed them in his day, that will
call men to their senses and bring them to true repentance
and faith in Christ before this time of grace is ended?[64]

[64]"A Letter to the German Churches," circulated and read in most
of the Protestant churches in August, 1945: "God's wrath has broken
upon us. . . . Today we admit: Long before God spoke in wrath, He
sought us with the word of His love, and we did not listen. Long
before our churches became piles of rubble, our pulpits were restricted
and our prayers silenced. . . . Long before men were murdered, men
had become mere cyphers. . . . When a man's life becomes worthless,
he thinks nothing of taking human life. . . . Cowardice in the face of
men's suffering has brought upon us this measureless grief." This is but
one indication among many how courageously thoughtful Lutherans
in Germany are appealing for a new and powerfully Christian understanding of man.

BIBLIOGRAPHY

Althaus, Paul, *Paulus und Luther über den Menschen*, Gütersloh: 1938.

Brunner, Emil, *Man in Revolt, A Christian Anthropology*, New York: 1939.

Buber, Martin, *I and Thou*, New York: 1937.

Calhoun, Robert Lowry, *God and the Common Life*, New York: 1935.

Elwein, Eduard, *Martin Luther, Vorlesung über den Römerbrief, 1515/1516*, Munich: 1937.

Harnack, Theodosius, *Luthers Theologie*, Erlangen: 1862; reprint, 1927.

Heim, Karl, *Jesus der Herr*, Berlin: 1935.

Hill, Charles L., *The Loci Communes of Philip Melanchthon*, Boston: 1944.

Holl, Karl, *Gesammelte Aufsätze zur Kirchengeschichte*, i, *Luther*, Tübingen: 1923.

Jacobs, Henry Eyster, *A Summary of the Christian Faith*, Philadelphia: 1905.

Kierkegaard, Soren, *The Concept of Dread*, Princeton: 1944.

————, *Fear and Trembling*, Oxford: 1939.

————, *The Sickness unto Death*, Princeton: 1941.

Kittel, Gerhard, *Theologisches Wörterbuch zum Neuen Testament*, Stuttgart: 1933ff.

Köstlin, Julius, *The Theology of Luther in Its Historical Development and Inner Harmony*, tr. C. E. Hay, 2 vols. Philadelphia: 1897.

Luther, Martin, *The Bondage of the Will*, Grand Rapids: 1931.

Neve, J. L., and Heick, O. W., *A History of Christian Thought*, 2 vols., Philadelphia: 1943ff.

Niebuhr, Reinhold, *The Nature and Destiny of Man*, i, *Human Nature*, New York: 1941.

Oxford Conference Report, *The Christian Understanding of Man*, Chicago: 1938.

Reu, J. Michael, *Luther's German Bible*, Columbus: 1934.

Schmid, Heinrich, *Doctrinal Theology of the Lutheran Church*, tr. H. E. Jacobs and C. E. Hay, Philadelphia: 1889.

Seeberg, Reinhold, *Textbook of the History of Christian Doctrines*, tr. C. E. Hay, 2 vols., Philadelphia: 1905.

Stewart, James, *A Man in Christ, The Vital Elements of St. Paul*, New York: n. d.

Stange, Carl, *Studien zur Theologie Luthers*, Gütersloh: 1928.

Triglot Concordia, St. Louis: 1921.

SALVATION

W. ARNDT

(REDEMPTION, JUSTIFICATION, ELECTION)

Whoever wishes to evaluate correctly the Lutheran teaching on salvation should bear in mind that Luther, whom the church bearing his name follows in this teaching, did not arrive at his convictions on this subject through any speculative process but through his eager searching in the Scriptures for light and help when his sins had prostrated him.

Everybody acknowledges that in dealing with this matter we are considering the very heart of Luther's message. It is not so generally known that what Luther set forth on this point were not truths that he "discovered" *after* eyes had come to be fixed on him and the question was asked whether he was possibly the long-awaited reformer of the church. If anybody should think that Luther had somehow arrived at the conviction that God wanted him to be the needed reformer and that, in examining the church's teachings, he found that what it taught on salvation was altogether wrong and unscriptural and would have to be changed, and that hence he demolished the church's teaching in this sphere and substituted for it the old Pauline gospel, he would totally misjudge what occurred.

Luther did not approach the Scriptures as a reformer at this stage but as a poor sinner who was not at all thinking of carrying on a dashing crusade against the church and the hierarchy, steeped in error, but who felt deeply his own unworthiness and was anxiously inquiring whether there was any help for him. This happened, it should be said, years before the celebrated 95 Theses were posted on the door of the Castle Church in Wittenberg and the world was told by an unusual and bold arraignment of abuses connected with the indulgence traffic. Not a scholarly urge, not the zeal of the reformer, but practical religious necessity drove Luther to investigate what the Scriptures teach on salvation. Accordingly, it cannot be stated too strongly that the Lutheran doctrine on this all-important subject is not intended to satisfy the philosopher or the scholar, that it is not speculative teaching, but is intended to be regarded as a message of good cheer for the weary and the heavy-laden, pointing them to the rest their hearts crave.[1]

I

Salvation, as the word is used in the Scriptures, means to rescue (*sooteeria*)—to rescue from sin and its consequences, from the wrath of God, and from eternal death. One of the important emphases in the Lutheran doctrine of salvation is the truth that this salvation had to be and was accomplished by God Himself. Man had plunged himself into a mælstrom of spiritual destruction; of his own free will he had sinned and alienated himself from God. He had no strength, not even the desire to emerge from the waters of death and to return to the shore of safety at the side of God. One mightier than man had to achieve the rescue if it was to become a reality. In words of triumph the Lutheran teaching proclaims that God Himself became the Rescuer, that He, the very Sovereign who had been disobeyed, provided the means by which His subjects might be freed from the consequences of their disobedience.

Soli Deo gloria! To God alone be glory! is a well-known slogan of Christians, one which the Lutheran Church is happy to use in speaking of man's salvation. "By grace are ye saved through faith, and that not of yourselves; it is the

---

[1]See the interesting and helpful remarks of H. Sasse, *Here We Stand*, pp. 61ff., where the passages from Luther's writings that bear on this point are quoted.

gift of God, not of works, lest any man should boast,"[2] it exclaims with the Apostle Paul. Precisely as the work of creation was performed independently of any human help, so the work of salvation is from beginning to end God's own achievement.[3]

The question naturally arises, "What induced God to provide a rescue for His guilty subjects from the misery into which they had cast themselves?" When we help a person who is in distress we may do it because the person whom we aid has at some time come to our own assistance, or because we know him to be particularly worthy of receiving support. That no such considerations operated in the case of God is the definite assertion of Lutheran teaching. The expression that occurs most frequently, when the motive actuating the Creater in His course is considered, is *the grace of God.* "All have sinned and are justified without merit *by His grace,*" says Luther in the Smalcald Articles.[4]

In one of his early hymns the Reformer gives this thought forceful poetic form:

> Then God beheld my wretched state
> With deep commiseration;
> He thought upon His mercy great
> And willed my soul's salvation;
> He turned to me a Father's heart—
> Not small the cost!—to heal my smart,
> He gave His best and dearest.

---

[2] Eph. 2:8f.

[3] The Formula of Concord, Epitome, Art. IV par. 5, *Trigl.*, p. 799, says emphatically: "We believe, teach, and confess also that good works should be entirely excluded, just as well in the question concerning salvation as in the article of justification before God, as the apostle teaches with clear words when he writes as follows: 'Even as David also describeth the blessedness of the man unto whom God imputeth righteousness without works, saying, Blessed is the man to whom the Lord will not impute sin,' Rom. 4:6ff. And again: 'By grace are ye saved through faith; and that not of yourselves, it is the gift of God; not of works, lest any man should boast,' Eph. 2:8, 9."

[4] *Trigl.*, p. 461.

The grace of God, that is, His favor and kindness, altogether unmerited by those to whom it was exhibited, the love of God for the poor, lost world—that is the basis of the divine work of salvation.

II

When we let the Lutheran teachers analyze what had to be done if man was to be rescued we find that everything they point to can be listed under two heads: something had to be done *for* man, and something had to be done *in* man. The former is completed; the latter is going on and will go on until Judgment Day. In this chapter we are chiefly interested in what God did *for* us.

The comprehensive statement of the Fourth Article of the Augsburg Confession must be noted here: "Also they [that is, our churches] teach that men cannot be justified before God by their own strength, merits, or works, but are freely justified for Christ's sake through faith, when they believe that they are received into favor and that their sins are forgiven for Christ's sake, who by His death has made satisfaction for our sins. This faith God imputes for righteousness in His sight, Rom. 3 and 4." Christ and faith are the pivotal points of that statement—Christ representing what was done for us, faith appropriating what God has provided and offers.

The doctrine of salvation takes us to the cross of Christ; in fact, the New Testament makes that cross central, all-important. "We preach Christ crucified," Paul stated in characterizing his message; and the Lutheran Church, following him, has made the cross of Jesus its chief theme. In speaking of it we are taken to what Paul calls the blessed mystery which "eye hath not seen, ear hath not heard, and which hath not entered the heart of man,"[5] but which God

---

[5] I Cor. 2.

has revealed through His Spirit. The plan of salvation is unfolded in that grand revelation. God's justice had condemned the sinner; that justice could not be disregarded; it had to be satisfied; punishment had to be meted out. From the point of view of justice there seemed to be no help for man.

But divine love solved the difficulty. What man could not do, the Son of God, Jesus Christ, did for him. He took man's sin upon Himself and paid the penalty which this sin entails. In the suffering which He bore, especially during the dread hours on the cross, He made amends for man's wrongdoing and expiated his disobedience toward, and defiance of, the divine majesty.[6]

A term was coined which tersely designates what Christ accomplished through His suffering and death—the vicarious atonement. It explains that an atonement, a reconciliation, was brought about between God and man, and that this work of indescribable significance was accomplished through a substitute, one who shouldered man's burdens and fulfilled his obligations. Another term was used to designate the same thing, the passive obedience of Christ. Christ submits obediently, willingly to the suffering which man has brought upon himself; He travels the road which divine love has mapped out for the salvation of sinners. "He became obedient unto death, even the death of the cross."[7] These words are spoken lightly by us. But what a world of meaning they contain, what an ocean of divine love they lead us to see! No wonder that Paul speaks of these divine matters in terms of holy ecstasy as in Romans 5.

---

[6]The beautiful words of the Formula of Concord, Thorough Declaration, Art. V, Par. 20, *Trigl.*, p. 959, should be compared. "The Son of God, our Lord Christ, has taken upon Himself and borne the curse of the Law, has expiated and paid for all our sins, through whom alone we again enter into favor with God, obtain forgiveness of sins by faith, are delivered from death and all the punishments of sins, and eternally saved."   [7]Phil. 2:8.

In addition, Jesus fulfilled the law for us, again acting as our substitute, and for this part of His work the Lutheran teachers have used the term "active obedience."[8]

One of the chief terms to designate the atonement of Christ is the word *redemption*. Because of their sins men were in a condition of slavery or imprisonment, a condition constituting the antechamber of eternal death. If they were to be freed, a price had to be paid, a price sufficient to satisfy divine justice. Christ came and paid the price, by this act purchasing or redeeming men from the sad state into which their natural sinfulness and their many evil deeds had placed them. Probably the term redemption is used most frequently in the Lutheran Church in reference to Christ's divine work in our behalf. It draws attention beautifully to the ransom that was paid, Christ's suffering and dying, or more simply, the blood of Christ, and to the result that was accomplished, our freedom from the sentence of condemnation, from the prison cell in which our wrongdoing had placed us.

Again, the Scriptures speak of Christ's death as a sacrifice. In the Old Testament the Israelites offered animals to God to make satisfaction for their sins. These sacrifices were but types that pointed forward to the great work of Christ in which He offered the all-sufficient sacrifice for the sins of the world.[9]

What Christ has earned for all of us through His work in our behalf is called forgiveness of sins. We may picture the divine tribunal. Before the awful throne of God stands the sinner, arraigned because of what he is and what he did.

---

[8]See Formula of Concord, Thorough Declaration, Article III, *Trigl.*, p. 919.

[9]In the Apology, III, 58, *Trigl.*, p. 171, Christ is directly called a "Victim," the offering of the sacrifice. "The Law condemns all men, but Christ, because without sin He has borne the punishment of sin and been made a Victim for us, has removed the right of the Law to accuse and condemn those who believe in Him."

The sentence of "guilty" is being spoken. But now comes the substitute who takes man's place, and divine justice says to man, "You are freed; your sins are forgiven." The announcement resounds through the hall of justice; the guilty is pardoned.[10]

There is another name given to this forgiveness of sins; it is *righteousness*. Paul frequently speaks of the righteousness that God provides for the sinner. The offender is clothed with righteousness; God regards him as possessing the righteousness which is demanded by the law. Hence the charges against him are dropped. Of this act on the part of God, Paul says, "God hath made Him to be sin for us, who knew no sin, that we might be made the righteousness of God in Him."[11]

The Scriptures, especially in the writings of Paul, employ a special term to designate this bestowal of forgiveness of sins, of righteousness, on the sinner—*justification*. When God accepts Jesus as the substitute for man and declares that the sinner now, through the work of Christ, is free from the consequences of his wrongdoing, from the guilt and the penalty of sin, He justifies the sinner, that is, He declares the sinner just and righteous. When the penalty for the offences of mankind had been paid on Good Friday, there rang through the universe the divine sentence of justification for the whole world (universal or objective justification). "It is finished," the Savior said on the cross. "Yes, it is finished," the divine majesty said in heaven, "and now I bestow forgiveness and righteousness on the whole world." And that the work of obtaining forgiveness of sins for men was indeed finished God declared most gloriously and convincingly on Easter morning when He raised the substitute for mankind from the dead.[12]

---

[10]Cf. Rom. 3:21-28.   [11]II Cor. 5:21.

[12]The Scriptures declare likewise that Christ has freed us from the power of sin, breaking the dominion of the tyrant. Cf. I Pet. 1:18f.

In this way the gulf that had been created between God
and mankind through the sin of Adam and all the evil
deeds that followed was closed; God and the sinners were
reconciled. The work that had to be done for man outside
of himself was accomplished. Although the men that lived
at the time were unaware of it, although we had not yet
been born, the work of redemption, of atonement, of reconciliation, was performed. The people who saw Christ dying
on the cross had no conception of the vast significance of
that terrible scene. Many realized that a sad miscarriage of
justice had occurred; and that is where their understanding
of the cross of Jesus stopped. But divine revelation teaches
us the true meaning of the event on Golgotha, saying,
"Christ redeemed us from the curse of the law, being made
a curse for us."[13]

III

It is true that this teaching, which brings us the assurance of the existence of help in our misery, is much attacked.
Many people call it crude, medieval, outworn, hopelessly
out of date. This criticism does not disturb us. The question
is not whether this teaching is in keeping with modern ideas

We cannot do better than quote Luther on this point. In words
vibrant with deep emotion he says in the Large Catechism, explaining
the Second Article of the Creed (*Trigl.*, p. 685): "When we had been
created by God the Father and had received from Him all manner of
good, the devil came and led us into disobedience, sin, death, and all
evil, so that we fell under His wrath and displeasure and were doomed
to eternal damnation, as we had merited and deserved. There was no
counsel, help, or comfort until this only and eternal Son of God in His
unfathomable goodness had compassion upon our misery and wretch-
edness and came from heaven to help us. Those tyrants and jailers,
then, are all expelled now, and in their place has come Jesus Christ,
Lord of life, righteousness, every blessing, and salvation, and has
delivered us poor lost men from the jaws of hell, has won us, made us
free, and brought us again into the favor and grace of the Father, and
has taken us as His own property under His shelter and protection,
that He may govern us by His righteousness, wisdom, power, life, and
blessedness."
[13]Gal. 3:13.

and satisfactory to our age, but whether it is Scriptural. Let the Bible be searched without prejudice, and it will be found that this doctrine is presented in its sacred pages.

More serious, perhaps, some will find the criticism that this teaching makes God grossly unjust because the sins of the world were expiated by an innocent person. This objection would be valid if Christ had been forced into suffering and death against His will. But the whole New Testament testifies that the Son of God most willingly entered upon the career of suffering, eager to do the will of the heavenly Father. We may think of His going up to Jerusalem in spite of His knowledge about the dreadful events that were before Him.[14] It may be said, then, that this objection, too, is not valid.

Other critics state that it is impossible for one person to become a substitute for another in moral matters. If a person has sinned he is guilty. How can anybody become guilty in his stead? Can one man become corrupt in the place of another? But this objection, too, does not bear close scrutiny. Jesus did not become corrupt, but the sins of the world were laid upon Him; they were imputed to Him as if He had committed them, and the guilt they entailed was made to rest on Him. Jesus was made sin for us, the Scriptures state definitely, and He is at the same time called the Holy One of God.

It will, of course, always remain a great mystery how He, who committed not a single sin, could nevertheless be treated as if He had committed all the sins of the world. Special attacks are leveled against the words of the Augsburg Confession,[15] where Lutheran churches declare: "Our works cannot reconcile God or merit forgiveness of sins, grace, and justification, but we obtain these only by faith when we believe that we are received into favor for Christ's

---

[14]Mark 10:32.   [15]Article XX.

sake, who alone has been set forth the Mediator and Propitiation, I Tim. 2:5, in order that the Father *may be reconciled through Him.*"

It is wrong to say, so we are told, that God was reconciled through Christ. How can anyone say that God was the object of the work of reconciliation? In reply we admit that the world was reconciled to God.[16] But what does it mean that the world was reconciled to God? Does that mean that all men drop their enmity and become friends of God? Not at all. It means that God, through Christ, did something for the world so that He could look upon it with favor and grant it forgiveness of sins. Divine justice then viewed the world with wrath as the facts required. Now, on the basis of the work of Christ, God views the world with satisfaction because the right relation has been restored. It was God Himself who restored the right relation when His Son paid the penalties that were due; hence, the divine revelation says, "God reconciled the world to Himself." The terminology of the Lutheran Confessions is not wrong; it expresses the truth of St. Paul's teaching in II Cor. 5.

But, it may be said, God must not be represented as a Being who is angry with the world; He is love, and the Lutheran teaching is wrong because it speaks of the wrath of God which had to be appeased. We gladly subscribe to the statement that God is love. What more comforting truth can be found in the Scriptures! But let no one forget that this is a moral universe, that wrongdoing must be punished, that God is not a weak, indulgent father, condoning whatever wrong deeds are committed by His children. The teaching of the substitutionary atonement takes sin seriously; it gives full due to the justice of God; but it at the same time does not disregard His love and mercy.

---

[16]II Cor. 5:19.

Many opponents of this teaching have dwelt on what they call the impossibility of removing all the sins of the world through one person's suffering which lasted merely a few hours. The objection, though it at first appears impressive, loses its validity when we consider that Jesus is the Son of God, true God Himself. His sacrifice was of infinite value because of who He was. "The blood of Jesus Christ, His Son, cleanseth us from all sin."[17] Jesus, the Savior, was not only human but was likewise divine. Therefore His sacrifice had this tremendous power. Compare the eloquent passage Heb. 7:26, 27, in which the divine nature of Jesus is emphasized.[18]

IV

Now the question arises: "If Jesus earned righteousness and life for all, and if the whole world has been justified, must it not follow that everybody will be saved?" When this question is asked, definite Scripture passages at once come to mind which state with utmost clearness the stern and sad truth that not all people will enter into everlasting bliss. Our Lord's account of the final judgment shows that, whereas some are saved, others are not.[19]

This consideration leads to another important doctrine, that of the justification of the individual sinner through

---

[17] I John 1:7.
[18] The Formula of Concord in the Thorough Declaration, Art. 8, 44, *Trigl.*, pp. 1029f., quotes important words of Dr. Luther bearing on this point: "We Christians must know that if God is not also in the balance and gives the weight, we sink to the bottom of our scale. By this I mean: If it were not to be said, 'God has died for us, but only a man,' we should be lost. But if 'God's death' and 'God died' lie in the scale of the balance, then He sinks down, and we rise up as a light, empty scale. But indeed, He can also rise again or leap out of the scale; yet He could not sit in the scale unless He became a man like us, so that it could be said: 'God died,' and again, 'God's passion,' 'God's blood,' 'God's death.' For in His nature God cannot die; but now that God and man are united in one person, it is correctly called God's death, when the man dies who is one thing or one person with God."   [19] Matt. 25:31-46.

faith. The Scripture declares with one voice that, although forgiveness of sins has been earned for all, and in the gospel is offered freely to all men, those only will become its beneficiaries who accept what God offers. God is gracious, but He deals with men as with moral beings; hence He does not force them into life or bliss against their will. Heaven is open, but man is not driven through its gates. It is necessary for man to accept the gracious gift of god. This acceptance is the only thing necessary, but it is indeed necessary. The acceptance of the gift of God is of the very essence of what Scripture calls faith. We are not speaking of the origin and the nature of saving faith. What must be emphasized in this chapter is that God offers the righteousness earned by Christ to every sinner; and when the sinner by faith accepts the gift of God, then the Lord pronounces him righteous.

The technical term which the Bible uses for this act of God's is called justification. It may well be borne in mind that this word, which has played a tremendous role in the teachings of the church, is not an ecclesiastical term like "trinity" but is taken directly from the Bible itself.[20]

In so using the term justification the Lutheran Church has always held that the Bible employs a term that has a forensic or judicial connotation. Justification literally signifies the act of making just or righteous. Taken by itself, the word is ambiguous. It may mean to make somebody personally, in his own essence and being, a righteous and good person. It may, however, likewise mean to declare somebody righteous, pronounce him innocent of a charge. If the term is used in the latter sense, it has a significance that is taken from court procedure, and the Lutheran Confessions assert that such is the view which we must take of justification. The sinner is declared righteous by God. Personally he is an altogether unworthy being, but he grasps the forgive-

---

[20]Cf. especially Rom. 3:21-28 and Gal. 2:16-21.

ness which God offers him, and in the same moment that the sentence is pronounced by the divine Majesty, the guilty is acquitted. When justification is viewed in this fashion, we call it subjective justification. It will be noted that objective or universal justification takes place antecedent to faith on the part of man. It occurred when the work of Jesus was completed. It was declared a great fact through the resurrection of Christ. The faith of man had nothing to do with it. But when the personal appropriation of this free gift of God, or righteousness of Christ, or the forgiveness of sins, is considered, faith does, indeed, enter into the discussion.

Faith does not come before us as a moral act. Its only role is that of a hand which takes what God offers. No merit whatever attaches to it. The honor and the glory belong entirely to God. This, of course, becomes all the more clear when we contemplate the truth that this faith is itself a gift of God, bestowed in love. But that truth is not now before us. What we are concerned with is the very definite teaching of the Scriptures that works do not justify. Hence faith cannot enter into the justification process as a good work. Let the reader ponder the strong antithesis between faith and works in Romans 3:28.

The doctrine of justification has always been called the chief article of Lutheran doctrine. Works of reference point out that the Lutheran Church is known for this teaching as its most characteristic feature. Every Lutheran will be glad to have the teaching of his church described in this fashion even though the description expresses a criticism. Lutherans themselves call this teaching the article of faith with which the church stands or falls. If this teaching is kept pure, so Luther declared, all articles will be kept intact or can be restored to their pristine purity. But if this article is vitiated, the whole Christian doctrine will collapse. There is the most intimate relation between this article and all the other doctrines that are taught in the Scriptures. Here is the center from which all radiate.

V

Both the redemption of Christ and the justifying verdict of the divine majesty are acts of God which take place outside of us. They have occurred in time, that is, since the creation of the world. When we reflect on the greatness of God's mercy which manifests itself in what He has done for us, the question arises whether it was only since the world was called into being or only at the time when the sentence of acquittal was spoken in our behalf that God thought of or does think of us. When He makes us believers in Jesus Christ, is that due to a loving decision with respect to us which He has made only then and there? The reply is obvious. He, the great God, who is from everlasting to everlasting, before whom the past, the present, and the future are an open book, thought of us before there was a universe and resolved to make us His own. Before the foundations of the earth were laid He decided not only that we, like our fellow men, should be redeemed, but that we should be regenerated by the Spirit and brought into the kingdom of God. In other words, He chose us to be His children and to inherit everlasting life.

In teaching this doctrine the Lutheran Church relies entirely on divine revelation. It quotes God's Word to show that there has been such an election or predestination. It points to passages[21] where the Apostle Paul speaks of God as having chosen us in Christ before the foundation of the world and as having predestinated us unto the adoption of children; and to passages[22] where there is a golden chain of divine acts with respect to us Christians: God's foreknowing

---

[21] Eph. 1:4-6.
[22] Rom. 8:28-30. Other passages quoted by Lutheran theologians are Matt. 22:14; II Thess. 2:13, and I Pet. 1:2.

(that is, His electing us as His own), His predestinating, His calling, His justifying, His glorifying.[23]

On the basis of these Scripture texts the Christian can say that God thought of him from eternity and resolved to make him a believer and to lead him to glory. This teaching is submitted in the Scriptures, not as a matter of religious speculation, or to round out some system of doctrine, but to comfort our hearts and to give us the assurance that God will not forsake us.

In thinking of this act of God's the Christian cannot but marvel at God's grace and goodness. He acknowledges that he is not one whit better than any of his fellow men, that in the sight of God he is as guilty of transgressions of the law as all other human beings are, and that God has still chosen him to be His own, has converted him and kept him in the faith. The thought humbles him and leads him to magnify divine mercy.

In this brief chapter it is obviously impossible to dwell on the numerous questions which have been raised and debated in discussions of the subject of predestination. A few remarks will have to suffice.

It should be noted that the Lutheran teaching of predestination is by no means identical with that of Calvin. Whereas Calvin taught an absolute election, the Lutheran doctrine holds that God elected us in Christ, in view of the merits of Christ. Whereas Calvin taught that God elected some people to life and others to death, the Lutheran doctrine says that election pertains only to the children of God and consists solely in an election to salvation.[24] The Re-

---

[23]The term "God's foreknowing," which occurs in this passage signifies, as is now quite universally admitted by scholars, not merely an act of cognition, a knowing beforehand, but a knowing that involves an act of the will, an acknowledging and accepting as one's own.

[24]Formula of Concord, Art. I (Thorough Declaration), Par. 5, *Trigl.*, p. 1065, says: "The eternal election of God or predestination, that is, God's ordination to salvation, does not extend at once over the

formed theology has a twofold predestination: Election and Reprobation. In Lutheran theology the terms predestination and election are identical in meaning, and reprobation is not a divine decree at all but God's dealing with the self-hardened sinner.

It must furthermore be emphasized that according to Lutheran teaching the divine election or predestination embraces, or pertains to, the whole way of salvation, from the creation of faith to the entrance into heaven, and not merely the final glorification of the believer. The Formula of Concord is explicit on this point.[25]

The Lutheran teaching has often been criticized because, pertaining only to the believers, it apparently lacks the consistency and the comprehensiveness of the view of those who teach a double election, holding that some have been elected to life and others to damnation. The Lutheran reply is that when the Bible speaks of election it speaks of an election to life and nowhere says that God has predestinated one part of mankind to salvation and the other part to perdition. The Lutheran teaching stops where the Scriptures stop. That may not be satisfactory to speculative human

---

godly and the wicked, but only over the children of God, who were elected and ordained to eternal life before the foundation of the world was laid, as Paul says, Eph. 1:4, 5: 'He hath chosen us in Him, having predestinated us into the adoption of children by Jesus Christ.' " Hence there were two considerations that moved God to elect us, 1) His love, 2) the work of Christ.

[25]*ibid.* Pars. 13-23, *Trigl.,* p. 1069. Note in particular: "Therefore if we wish to think or speak correctly and profitably concerning the eternal election or the predestination and ordination of the children of God to eternal life, we should accustom ourselves not to speculate concerning the bare, secret, concealed, inscrutable foreknowledge of God, but how the counsel, purpose, and ordination of God in Christ Jesus, who is the true Book of Life, is revealed to us through the Word, namely, that the entire doctrine concerning the purpose, counsel, will, and ordination of God pertaining to our redemption, call, justification, and salvation should be taken together; as Paul treats and has explained this article, Rom. 8:29f.; Eph. 1:4f., as also Christ in the parable Matt. 22:1ff."

reason but it should satisfy all who are willing in humility to take the Scriptures as their guide.

As we in retrospect view the teachings we have considered we see in the Scriptures a magnificent structure that has been erected for our salvation. Every stone of this building has been obtained in a divine quarry which we call the love of God. All of them bear a crimson mark made by the blood of Christ. Not man but God has been the Builder. And the humble Christian in grateful rapture exclaims with the Apostle Paul: "I am persuaded, that neither death, nor life, nor angels, nor principalities, nor powers, nor things present, nor things to come, nor height, nor depth, nor any other creature, shall be able to separate us from the love of God, which is in Christ Jesus, our Lord."[26]

---

[26]Rom. 8:38f.

BIBLIOGRAPHY

Althaus, Paul, *Mysterium Christi.*

Aulen, G., *Christus Victor.*

Berkhoff, L., *The Atonement.*

Boettner, L., *The Atonement.*

Brunner, A., *The Mediator.*

Bushnell, H., *The Vicarious Sacrifice.*

Campbell, McLeod, *The Nature of the Atonement.*

Franks, R., *History of the Doctrine of the Work of Christ in Its Ecclesiastical Development.*

Harnack, Theodosius, *Luthers Theologie mit besonderer Beziehung auf seine Versoehnungs und Erloesungslehre.*

Holl, Karl, *Gesammelte Aufsaetze zur Kirchengeschichte.*

Koeberle, Adolf, *The Quest for Holiness.*

Luther, M., *Brief an die Roemer* (C. G. Eberle).

Luther, M., *Commentary on Galatians.*

Neve, J. L., *A History of Christian Thought.*

Pieper, F., *Christi Person und Werk.*

Preuss, Ed., *Justification of the Sinner before God.*

Ritschl, A., *Justification and Reconciliation.*

Sasse, Hermann, *Here We Stand.*

Stewart, James S., *A Man in Christ.*

Soederblom, N., *The Mystery of the Cross.*

Symposium, A Theological, *The Atonement in Modern Religious Thought,* London: James Clarke & Co., 1902.

Taylor, Vincent, *Forgiveness and Reconciliation.*

Warfield, B., "Christ Our Sacrifice," *Princeton Theological Review,* Vol. 15.

THE PERSON AND THE WORK OF CHRIST

J. BODENSIECK

Jesus Christ is the center of Christianity. He is our only Savior, our all-sufficient Redeemer, our Glory and our sure Defense, our Shepherd and Friend, our Master and Teacher, our High Priest and Prophet and King, our gracious, omnipotent Lord.

Christ's Coming Planned in Eternity

From eternity God had foreseen that mankind would fall from fellowship with Him. Moved by unspeakable love and unfathomed grace, He decided, from eternity, to restore mankind to His fellowship. He planned the method whereby fallen mankind might be restored and then chose and foreordained the Son to become the Redeemer of the world. Christ's coming into the world, His life, His sufferings and death, His resurrection, in short, every phase of His redemptive work, are the result of the divine decree of salvation. There was nothing accidental in Christ's coming, suffering, and dying; these were an integral part of the divine plan that reaches back into eternity.

Preparation

God is a God of history; His very name, *Yahweh*, implies that He intervenes in human affairs and events. He is also a God of order and pedagogy. He did not send the Redeemer without definitely preparing the world for His coming. In fact, the entire history of mankind, beginning with the expulsion from Paradise, was a preparation for the coming of the Redeemer. This preparation, so far as the heathen world is concerned, was chiefly negative: the course of heathendom issued in moral and intellectual bankruptcy and a longing for help, often suppressed and often concealed but also often expressed in pathetic words.[1] Israel's preparation was much more positive; its entire history was a preparation: the choice of Abraham, the deliverance from bondage in Egypt, the giving of the law, the return from the Babylonian Captivity, all these events are elements of the preparation for the Redeemer's coming. Along with this preparation went the preparation of the people of Israel for the arrival of the Savior, particularly in the following three factors:

1) The law separated Israel from all other nations and "kept it in custody" until faith should come and impart inward holiness; it served as the "boy-ward,"[2] keeping Israel in the right direction toward Christ; it showed men their sin and by means of the commandments tended to arouse the corruption slumbering in men's hearts, revealing to them what a sorry secret they really carried in their bosoms; and it demonstrated to men that they were utterly unable to keep the law and to come to communion with God by the way of legal righteousness. The numerous sin and guilt offerings also kept alive the sense of a need for reconciliation and roused a longing for deliverance.

2) The second factor was prophecy. The prophets' function was twofold: they viewed the events of their times in the light of God's expressed will, exposed Israel's shortcomings, and thus became the preachers of repentance;[3] but they also directed Israel's eyes to the future, showing by specific predictions that salvation was to be brought and by this message kindling faith in the hearts of the people.[4] There are two lines of prophecy in particular which must be noted in this connection: the one which predicts that

---

[1]Isa. 2:3; 42:4—the waiting of the isles; Acts 16:9. Compare the Babylonian penitential psalms, e.g., the prayer to the goddess Ishtar given in Barton, Archaeology and the Bible, pp. 458f.

[2]Gal. 3:24.

[3]II Sam. 12:7; Amos 2:4ff.; Isa. 1:2-17, etc.

[4]Isa. 40:31; 49:23; 25:9.

Yahweh will come in person to visit His people, the other which promises the coming of a true son of David who is to bring salvation and blessedness. The meeting place of these two lines of prophecy was Bethlehem.

3) The third factor was the collection of writings known as the Old Testament. The purpose of these writings was to preserve the knowledge of God's deeds and words both for the people of Israel and for all believers in subsequent generations and to lead all believers to a proper understanding of Christ and His mission. The Spirit of God moved men in proclaiming and writing their messages so that believers possess in the Old Testament a trustworthy, coherent, and sufficient record, which is approved by Christ and the apostles.

Miracle

Since Christ's coming into the world is the highest point of divine revelation, and since revelation is always new and foreign as compared with the natural order of things, it is to be expected that we here meet with the element of the miraculous more frequently than at any other stage of the history of salvation. By a miracle we understand an event which resulted from the entrance of higher forces into the course of history; an event which can therefore never be explained on the basis of natural laws, and which is invariably connected in some way with God's saving will. To the natural man this whole realm is unknown; further, to him it is offensive, not only in its totality but also in every phase. To the Christian, however, who has experienced in his own heart the miracle of regeneration, this world of miracle is blessed reality and assured certainty.

Jesus Christ, True God

Jesus Christ is God manifested in the flesh. The Gospels, as well as the other New Testament writings, leave no room for uncertainty on this fundamental fact of our faith. Christ's own words reveal 1) that His consciousness is God-consciousness. He assumes titles and functions which in the Old Testament were ascribed exclusively to *Yahweh, e.g., the* physician,[5] *the* shepherd,[6] *the* bridegroom,[7] *the* judge,[8] the forgiver of sins,[9] the source of rest.[10] 2) He knew Himself to be "the Son of God," not merely in the sense of Messianic fellowship with God,[11] but in the sense of a unique personal relationship to God which has its origin in an essential unity with the Father. Whereas most of Jesus' assertions of this nature are recorded by John,[12] who alone has recorded the all-inclusive claim, "He who hath seen Me hath seen the Father,"[13] this line of testimony is not unknown to the Synoptists.[14] As a result, Christ never collectively spoke of the heavenly Father as "our" Father but always distinguished His relation to God from that of others to God.[15] 3) He had been in existence prior to His coming into the flesh. This is clearly set forth in a number of Johannine passages,[16] especially 3:16, where we should empty the statement of its meaning if we were to interpret that Christ became the Son of God by virtue of His being sent. 4) He ascribed to Himself strictly divine functions when He claimed that He would be eternally present with

[5]Mark 2:17 and parallels; cf. Exod. 15:26.
[6]Mark 14:27; John 10:12, 14; cf. Ps. 23:1.
[7]Mark 2:19f.; cf. Isa. 54:4f.; Ezek. 16:8-14; Hosea 2:21.
[8]Matt. 25:31; cf. Ps. 75:7; Gen. 18:25.
[9]Matt. 26:28; cf. Exod. 34:7; Ps. 130:4.
[10]Matt. 11:28; cf. Hosea 13:9.
[11]As, *e.g.*, John 1:49; 6:69; cf. Exod. 4:22; Hosea 11:1; Jer. 31:20, and Ps. 2:7; II Sam. 7:14.
[12]Concerning His life Christ claims an immediate relation to the Father in 5:26; His work in 5:17ff.; His power, 10:37; His existence in 10:30; 14:10.
[13]John 14:9.
[14]Matt. 26:63; Luke 22:66-70; and especially the significant text Matt. 11:27.
[15]John 20:17; Matt. 5:48; 6:4, 8, 32.
[16]John 8:58; 17:5, 24.

His disciples, that He will answer the prayers of His followers, and that the Holy Spirit, whom He and the Father will
send, shall be in His, Christ's, service.

The apostles' testimony agrees with Christ's own statements. The fact that they worshipped Him, that the early
Christians were known as "those who call on the name of
Jesus Christ," that they asked Jesus Christ to supply those
very gifts which were formerly asked only of God, show
definitely that they regarded Him as divine, more specifically as divinely pre-existent because the idea of an apotheosis of man was an abomination to Jews. The apostles speak
of Jesus Christ as "the Son of God," not merely in the historical sense, according to which Psalm 2:7 had been fulfilled
in His resurrection,[17] but also in the metaphysical, eternal
sense.[18] They actually call Christ "God." Thomas uses this
address without being rebuked by Him for exaggeration.
Paul so speaks of Christ a number of times[19] and declares
that the fulness of the Godhead dwells in Him bodily[20] and
that He is the image of God, the image by which the invisible God made Himself visible.[21] In declaring that the creation of the world is mediated through Christ the apostles
attest His pre-existence.[22] It is not impossible that Hebrews
1:3 is an assertion concerning the pre-existent One. Christ
represents the effulgence of the divine Being, all its rays are
gathered in Him, and thus the divine Being becomes com-
prehensible in Christ as its expression. The most complete
apostolic testimony is found in the prologue of John's Gospel,[23] where Christ is called "Logos," or "Word," because

---

[17]Heb. 5:5; Acts 13:33.
[18]Gal. 4:4; Heb. 1:2.
[19]Tit. 2:13; quite likely also in Rom. 9:5, and, if the critical text is
correct, in Acts 20:28.
[20]Col. 2:9.
[21]Col. 1:15.
[22]John 1:3; I Cor. 8:6; Col. 1:16; Heb. 1:2, 10.
[23]John 1:1-8.

God has spoken in Him and revealed Himself in a personal manner, and where it is said concerning this Logos: a) that He existed already at the beginning, before creation, in all eternity, b) that He was at that time in living relationship with God, c) that He was God at that time, d) that after "tenting" among men for a while He is again with God, e) that He is the inexhaustible fountain of grace for all believers, and finally, f) that He is the "only-begotten God."[24]

Jesus Christ, True Man

The Scriptures, however, represent Jesus Christ, not merely as true God, born of the Father from eternity, but also as a true, genuine man. They tell of His lowly birth in the stable in Bethlehem,[25] of the development of His physical and His mental powers, of His exercise of the human faculties of perception and volition, of His being subject to emotion, to hunger, thirst, fatigue, pain, compassion, anger, agony, and fright at the sight of death. They tell of His submission to the various forms of divinely established authority: His parents, the law of Judaism, and the heathen rulers, and of His relations to His brothers and His countrymen. He is exposed to all the ills and the difficulties which have their origin in human sin such as the hatred of men, the ingratitude of His fellow men, and the stupidity of His disciples. He was tempted to sin, like all men,[26] and, like all mortals, He passed through death. His attitude toward God was that of a man serving Him in a life of holy obedience and prayer. It never occurred to His contemporaries to doubt His humanity or to deny it.

Christ did not cease being a true and genuine man when He died; this appears from the various accounts of His

---

[24] 1:18, critical text.
[25] Luke 2:1; Luke 2:40, 52.
[26] Matt. 4:1-11; Luke 4:1-13; and note the expression, "for a season," in Luke 4:13.

resurrection and His appearances;[27] and also from the statements concerning His function as Priest and as Intercessor, seated at the right hand of God.

Jesus Christ, One Person

Just as clearly as the Bible sets forth Christ's divinity and His true and full humanity, so clearly it describes Jesus Christ as one person. Whether Jesus is speaking of Himself, or whether others speak about Him, at no time is there a distinction made between a divine personality and a human personality, a divine will and a human will, a divine ego and a human ego. His ego is one, His personality is one. Christ was not even aware of an interruption of His self-consciousness when He became man, for He declares, "Before Abraham was, I am,"[28] although He certainly did not exist before Abraham so far as His human nature is concerned but only as God. Yet He did not say, "Before Abraham was, my deity existed," or, "Before Abraham was, I existed as the second person in the Trinity," but, "I am," I, the person whom you see before you at this moment here in the Temple, the same person who had declared earlier in the same discussion, "I proceeded forth and came from God; neither came I of Myself, but He sent Me."[29] The same view is expressed by Christ in His great sermon on the Bread of Life[30] and in His parting discourses,[31] especially in the high-priestly prayer.[32] The prologue of John's Gospel is instructive in this respect: the subject throughout is "the Word"; there is no change of subject whether statements are made concerning the pre-existent, the incarnate, or the exalted One.

The use of these expressions shows conclusively that

---

[27]Note particularly Luke 24:39, according to which text He, the Risen One, had "flesh and bones."
[28]John 8:58.
[29]John 8:42.
[30]John 6:38, 46.
[31]John 16:28.
[32]John 17:5, 24.

there existed in Christ, not two consciousnesses, one divine and one human, but only one consciousness. He was conscious of being one person. This consciousness reached back into His pre-existent state and covered both phases of His being, the divine and the human, and included all the realities of His experiences in both phases. He recognized both of these phases as His own, and He predicated of His own person all the properties and the experiences which may be said originally to pertain only to His divinity or to His humanity. These two phases—the dogmatical term is "natures"—have been so intimately and inseparably united in Christ in a vital union that they completely permeate one another, without, however, losing their own peculiar identity. As a piece of iron in the furnace is pervaded and permeated by the fire and is all aglow with heat and yet remains iron, so the human nature is pervaded and permeated by the divine nature, yet each remains itself. As the human soul dwells in a human body, directs it and shapes it, penetrates it and gives it life, yet does not fuse with it so as to create a third something which is neither soul nor body, so also the divine nature in Christ permeates the human nature so that we may say, "Neither the divine is outside the human nor the human outside the divine," yet neither surrenders its identity. This perfect union is called, in dogmatical language, the "communion of natures."

If the two natures of Jesus Christ are really united, and if they truly permeate one another, that is to say, if the total complex of divine properties, functions, abilities, and states is united with the total complex of human properties, functions, abilities, and states, then there must of necessity have occurred what amounts to an impartation or "communication" of these properties. The dogmaticians of the Lutheran Church have developed this phase of Christian doctrine with admirable thoroughness and painstaking precision under the head of *communicatio idiomatum, i.e.,* communion of properties.[33] Three kinds or aspects of communication are distinguished: 1) the idiomatic aspect, when properties of the one or the other of the two natures are ascribed to the person, *e.g.,* "they crucified the Lord of glory."[34] Being crucified is a peculiarity of the human nature; yet it is here predicated of the entire person which, in this case, is named according to its divine nature. Or, "Jesus Christ, the same yesterday, today, and forever,"[35] where to the person of Jesus Christ eternity is ascribed which is really a property only of the divine nature. 2) The majestic aspect, when properties of the divine nature are communicated to the human nature so that the human nature shares in the majestic properties of Christ's divine nature, *e.g.,* the statement, "All power is given to Me,"[36] means that omnipotence has been given to Christ according to His human nature since it did not need to be given to Him in His divine nature. Or the statement, "Where two or three are gathered together in My name there am I in the midst of them,"[37] means that the human nature shares in the majestic property of omnipresence. This is one reason why in the Holy Communion the body and the blood of Christ may be really present everywhere. 3) The third aspect, called apotelesmatic, is in reality merely the application of the other two kinds of communication to the work of redemption. The name is derived from the Greek word for "official act." It refers to all those functions which Christ performed as the Savior of mankind, *e.g.,* dying for the sins of the world,[38] destroying the works of the devil,[39] laying down His life.[40]

---

[33]For summaries of this part of Christology see Schmid, *Doctrinal Theology of the Evangelical Lutheran Church,* 4th ed., pp. 309-337, or Mueller, *Christian Dogmatics,* pp. 272-286.

[34]Acts 3:15.
[35]Heb. 13:8.
[36]Matt. 28:18.
[37]Matt. 18:20.
[38]I Cor. 15:3.
[39]I John 3:8.
[40]John 10:17.

The importance of this aspect becomes clear when we consider that Christ could accomplish the work of redemption only if at every stage it was the result of the perfect cooperation of His two natures, if both factors, the human and the divine, constantly worked together, if the two natures were perfectly united. There is at stake here nothing less than the sweetest comfort of the gospel: "The blood of Jesus Christ, His Son, cleanseth us from all sin."[41]

The Incarnation

The only explanation of the unique person of Jesus Christ which the Bible presents is the Biblical doctrine of the incarnation: God became man—the miracle of all miracles. In what did the incarnation consist? The answer most often given by the Scriptures is this: "Jesus Christ came into the world because the Father sent Him, His pre-existent Son."[42] Paul's classic text in Philippians 2:7 ("being made in the likeness of man") shows that "taking the form of a servant" was by no means a mere assumption of human form but the entrance of the Pre-existent One into a real, actual, human existence. Hebrews 2:14 offers another element of explanation when it declares that the Incarnate One is a partaker of flesh and blood in the same manner in which children are partakers of flesh and blood, viz., their parents' flesh and blood. In other words, we may infer that by means of His birth Christ became a sharer of human flesh and blood. No such inference from the state of incarnation to the act of incarnation is needed when we read in John 1:14: "The Word became flesh." The Word—the Eternal, the Mediator of creation, the Light of the world, the Life of the universe, the Second Person in the Trinity—became flesh; He became something in addition to what He had been before; He became man so that His spiritual, uncorporeal

---

[41] I John 1:7. [42] John 8:42; Rom. 8:3; Gal. 4:4.

form of existence henceforth is found only in the physical existence of a living man; He became flesh, not merely resembling it, but taking upon Himself humanity and all that it implies; He became a true man.

The Sinless One

In one significant respect, however, the humanity that Christ took upon Himself in the act of incarnation differs from that of the rest of mankind: Christ remained free from sin. There is not only no record of any transgression on the part of Jesus, but, on the contrary, unanimous testimony concerning His sinlessness. Pilate found no guilt in Him.[43] Christ Himself challenged His enemies to convict Him of a single misdeed,[44] a challenge that remained unanswered because His conduct and His words were holy and pure and undefiled and above any possible reproach. He was not free from temptation[45] but did not succumb to any sinful stimulus. There was no inner discord in Him. He had no illicit desires, hence St. Paul can declare that "He knew no sin,"[46] i.e., sin was no part of His consciousness as it unfortunately is in the case of all men. He had no "evil conscience" at any time, which is the reason no prayer for pardon was ever uttered by Him[47] and why He can assert that "the prince of this world will find no point of contact" in Him.[48] St. Paul succinctly and completely expresses this fact when he writes that God "sent His Son in the likeness of the flesh of sin,"[49] which means that Christ has taken upon Himself the nature

---

[43]Matt. 27:24; Luke 23:4; John 18:38.
[44]John 8:46.
[45]Heb. 4:15.
[46]II Cor. 5:21.
[47]This is all the more remarkable because the "best" and "noblest" men have been those with the most tender conscience, e.g., Paul and Luther.
[48]John 14:30.
[49]Rom. 8:3. Paul does not say, "in the flesh of sin," nor, "in the likeness of flesh."

of man in its completeness, together with all the limitations and weaknesses to which man is subject since the fall, and that there is one point of distinction between Him and all men, namely, His sinlessness, because it was precisely this fact that He was a true and genuine but sinless man that demonstrates St. Paul's argument that flesh and sin are by no means inseparable, and that sin has no right to rule over the flesh. But this very text refers to Christ's coming into the world, His birth; it reads like a theological formulation of the angelic message to Mary, "The holy thing that shall be born of thee shall be called the Son of God."[50] If the reading of the "Western Text" in John 1:13 is correct,[51] we should have there the clear statement that Christ "became flesh" by birth indeed but not according to ordinary physiological or biological processes, i.e., through the mixture of the blood of two persons, nor through the decision of man's will, nor through the action of human impulses, but was begotten and born "out of God."

Born of the Virgin Mary

It is in perfect harmony with the consciousness of Christ and the testimony of the disciples when the Scriptures declare that He was born in a miraculous manner of the Virgin Mary.[52] It is likewise in harmony with the Old Testament predictions according to which the Savior was to belong to the house of David.[53] Mary was, at least by the law of inheritance, a member of the house of David.[54] And He was to come forth from the congregation of those who sincerely longed for the coming of the Lord,[55] and Mary

---

[50]Luke 1:35.

[51]It reads, "He was born" instead of "who were born." The problem is fully discussed in Zahn's *Kommentar zum Neuen Testament*, Excursus I, pp. 700ff.; see also Lenski, *The Interpretation of St. John's Gospel, ad loc.*

[52]Luke 1:35; Matt. 1:20.   [54]Matt. 1:24; Luke 2:5f.

[53]Ps. 110:1; Isa. 11:1.   [55]Isa. 25:9; Ps. 25:5.

certainly belonged to this pious group.[56] While it is conceivable that a child born in wedlock could, by special divine intervention, have been spared the taint of sin which now affects all children of men,[57] and while it must be admitted that the mere absence of a human father did not necessarily assure the sinlessness of the child, yet it is easy to see that in this virgin birth, effected by the power of the most high God, the element of human sin was completely removed from the process of conception and birth, and that a perfectly holy, sinless child was born at Bethlehem, God's "unspeakable gift" to mankind.[58] Christ was sinless from the earliest dawn of consciousness, nay, He was holy and sinless from birth; He did not become sinless at some point during His life but was perfectly free from every suggestion of sin all the time.

This incarnation of the Godhead was necessary if the divine plan of salvation was to be accomplished. If mankind, lost in sin and excluded from fellowship with the holy and righteous God, is to be restored, a way must be found whereby God's holiness is satisfied, and human sin is punished; someone who is Himself without sin and yet represents the entire human race, like another Adam,[59] must suffer the penalty of sin and at the same time freely and voluntarily and perfectly fulfill the will of God. No man could possibly bear the full weight of mankind's sin and yet offer his life in constant obedience to God. Only God could do this. The sin-bearer must, therefore, be both God and man. In this sense the incarnation of God was necessary.[60]

---

[56]Luke 1:28ff., 47-55.

[57]John 3:6.

[58]II Cor. 9:15.

[59]Christ is presented as the Second Adam in Rom. 5:14ff. and I Cor. 15:22, 45ff.

[60]In substance Anselm's theory concerning the necessity of Christ's incarnation, proposed in *Cur Deus Homo*, c. 1098, is correct; it, however, needs to be purged of certain incorrect and fanciful elements.

It should be noted that the term "incarnation" denotes both an act and a state. The act of Christ's incarnation took place when He was conceived by the Holy Ghost, when He became man. The state of His incarnation did not end at His death, or His burial, or His resurrection, or His ascension. Christ has assumed human nature and possesses it even now and will keep it in all eternity. He is the glorified, exalted God-man, seated at the right hand of God, ruling all things and returning at the end of time to judge the quick and the dead as the God-man Jesus Christ.

The State of Humiliation

If Christ assumed human nature with all its limitations and weaknesses (though without the blemish of sin), it is clear that we are face to face with a most gracious act of condescension. It is conceivable that the second person of the Godhead could have become incarnate and yet have appeared with great power and glory even as He will appear at the end of time with great might.[61] But at His first coming He combined with His incarnation an exinanition, a renunciation of the exercise of certain divine powers, a *"kenosis,"* so that He lived His life on earth in a state of humiliation, a state of constant dependence upon the Father in heaven.[62] The words of Jesus in the high-priestly prayer, "And now, O Father, glorify Thou Me with Thine own self with the glory which I had with Thee before the world was,"[63] presuppose that Christ had possessed the glory, *i.e.*, the manifestation of the divine essence, until a certain point in time and at that point in time had surrendered it. The two texts, Philippians 2:6, 7 and II Corinthians 8:9, likewise presuppose such a point in time when an act of exinanition occurred.

---

[61] Mark 13:26.
[62] John 5:19, 36; 7:16; 8:28; 11:41; 12:49; 14:28; Luke 2:40, 52; Matt. 8:10; Heb. 4:15; Gal. 4:4; Rom. 5:6-10, etc.
[63] John 17:5.

Had there been no such exinanition, Christ could, indeed, have been incarnate, but He could not have lived a genuinely human life, nor could He have borne the sin of the world and the hatred of men and the curse of God, nor could He have suffered and died for us. This act of humiliation is, therefore, an essential presupposition of our salvation.

There has been much discussion on the problem of in what Christ's *kenosis* consisted. According to some writers it was the pre-existent Son of God who at the time of the incarnation surrendered the possession of His divine powers; according to others, He merely gave up the use of these powers; according to still others, it was not the Pre-existent One at all that performed the act of exinanition but rather the human nature of Christ by surrendering either the possession or the use of the prerogatives and the powers of the divine nature. Whereas it may be difficult to give a precise definition of the exinanition, this much should be clear: any explanation which infringes upon the true divinity of Christ, or involves any moral defect, or lowers His authority as the Revealer of God, or lessens the meaning of His voluntary, self-sacrificing grace and love, or reduces His sufferings to a sham performance or a sort of tragic stage act, any such explanation must be rejected. Our comfort is that, while our mind can never reach the miracle of Christ's incarnation, we know by faith that Christ, our one and only Savior, has come into the flesh to save us from our sins.[64]

Christ's Perfect Obedience

When Christ combined the exinanition with His incarnation He entered into a state of total dependence upon the Father. This state is described by Paul as "obedience,"[65]

---

[64]For a fuller discussion of the *kenosis* see Mueller, *op. cit.*, pp. 287-295, or Mackintosh, *The Doctrine of the Person of Jesus Christ*, pp. 230-246 and 463-486.

[65]Rom. 5:18f., the grand antithesis between the first Adam's disobedience and Christ's perfect obedience; also Phil. 2:8.

and this fully agrees with Jesus' own statements.[66] At every stage, in every moment, Christ's life was perfect obedience. His circumcision, the discipline in the parental home, His baptism by John, His victory over the tempter, His revelation of the Father's will in the prophetic ministry, His submission to the hostility and the hatred of the leaders of the people, and especially His suffering and death—every one of these acts was done in obedience to the Father and because He recognized that such obedience was indispensable if the salvation of mankind was to be effected.

This obedience is described in the Scriptures, on the one hand, as passive submission, not only to unfavorable circumstances and the misunderstanding and hatred of the people, nor only to the pains and the anguish of suffering and death, but especially to the divine judgment[67] in all its severity, including expulsion from His communion, death, and damnation; and, on the other hand, as Christ's own voluntary act. The divine judgment did not overtake Him, did not come upon Him as an unavoidable necessity; He rather Himself fully resolved to take upon Himself our sins and to bear our punishment; and so, in perfect freedom, He fulfilled the Father's saving will and voluntarily went into death.[68] It is because these aspects—passive submission and free choice—are characteristic of Christ's life that the Scriptures designate Christ's lifework as "sacrifice";[69] for sacrifice involves that the penalty for sin is suffered (the sacrificial animal must be killed) and that a voluntary offering is brought (the sacrificial blood is brought before God).

---

[66]John 4:34 and especially Matt. 20:28, where Christ declares Himself to be the fulfillment of the Old Testament prophecies concerning the Servant of *Yahweh,* Isa. 42, 49, 53, 61.

[67]Gal. 3:13; II Cor. 5:21.

[68]John 10:18; 19:30; Heb. 2:14; 9:14; 10:7; I Pet. 2:24.

[69]John 1:29; Eph. 5:2; Heb. 9:14; I Pet. 1:19.

Christ's Obedience Vicarious

That Christ offered His perfect obedience to the Father for the benefit of mankind is asserted in numerous Bible texts, not only apostolic declarations,[70] but also words of Jesus Himself, especially His statements that He has come to give His life as a ransom for many,[71] that His blood is shed for many,[72] and that the good Shepherd lays down His life for the sheep.[73] It is in agreement with John the Baptist's statement that Jesus is "the lamb that bears the sin of the world"[74] and with Isaiah's words, "Surely He hath borne our griefs and carried our sorrows. . . . He was wounded for our transgressions, He was bruised for our iniquities; the chastisement of our peace was upon Him, and with His stripes we are healed."[75]

The words of Isaiah just quoted and particularly those which follow immediately, ". . . the Lord hath laid on Him the iniquity of us all . . . it pleased the Lord to bruise Him, He hath put Him to grief,"[76] advance beyond the idea that Christ suffered for our benefit; they indicate that His suffering was substitutionary, that Christ suffered not only in our behalf but in our stead.[77] In the last analysis, this is also the rationale of sacrifice.[78] A careful exegesis of Paul's statement, "Christ ransomed us from the curse of the law becoming

---

[70] Rom. 3:25; 4:25; Gal. 3:13; II Cor. 5:15, 21; I Pet. 1:19; 2:24; 3:18; I John 2:2; Heb. 2:14; 9:14, and many others.
[71] Matt. 20:28.
[72] Matt. 26:28; Mark 14:24.
[73] John 10:11, 15.
[74] John 1:29.
[75] Isa. 53:4, 5.
[76] Isa. 53:6, 10.
[77] It should be noted that the Greek preposition *hyper*, found in John 10:11; I Tim. 2:6; Gal. 3:13, and II Cor. 5:15, 21, has been shown to occur in the sense of substitution, cf. Deissmann, *Licht vom Osten*, 4 Aufl., p. 285, where a letter is reproduced which was written for someone else, *i.e.*, in his stead, and where Deissmann adds that this substitutionary *hyper* occurs in numerous similar texts.
[78] Lev. 16:21.

accursed for us,"[79] will ultimately arrive at the conclusion
that Christ has taken the place of those who lay under the
curse of the law, and that is what is called substitution. The
designation of Christ as the "second Adam"[80] points in the
same direction, for if He is the second Adam, then He is
mankind's all-embracing representative, and then His actions are those of all mankind, and if He subjects Himself
to the curse He acts as mankind's substitute. That is the
reason Paul is justified in saying, "If one died for all, therefore all died,"[81] and later in the same chapter he can say,
"Christ was made sin for us." If Christ has taken our place
just as the sacrificial lamb takes the sinner's place, then our
sin is laid upon Him just as the sinner's guilt is placed upon
the lamb. He was "made sin," *i.e.*, our sins were imputed to
Him, and He, though personally sinless and guiltless and
holy, willingly acquiesced in being treated as the sinner, He
took our sins upon Himself, carried them in His body to the
tree in order to remove them from us,[82] and nailed the
"bond" (the certificate of guilt, as it were) to the tree as
proof that it has been paid in full.[83]

Christ's vicarious obedience is the sublimest demonstration of divine love, the love of the Father who sent His Son
into the world[84] as well as the love of the Son who laid down
His life for the sins of mankind,[85] and its final act of voluntary death on the cross marks the accomplishment of the
eternal saving decree of God. Precisely because Christ, out
of love, willed to take mankind's sins upon Himself and
acquiesced voluntarily in the imputation of our sins to Him,
there is no "crying injustice" involved in this transaction as

[79]Gal. 3:13.
[80]Rom. 5:12ff.; I Cor. 15:21ff.
[81]II Cor. 5:14.
[82]I Pet. 2:24.
[83]Col. 2:14.
[84]John 3:16; I John 4:9f.; Rom. 5:8; 8:32.
[85]John 10:15; 15:13; 13:1; Gal. 2:20.

Ritschl and other rationalists said; moreover, we must remember that Christ is no mere person among many, no "foreigner" or "third person," but the second Adam, the personal and all-embracing representative of the human race, and as such His acts are representative of all mankind.[86] If we should surrender the conception of Christ's vicarious obedience, then His suffering and His death become dark and unsolved problems, and we have lost the ground for our assurance of salvation.

Satisfying Propitiation

The effect of Christ's vicarious obedience is satisfying propitiation, satisfaction of the demands of God's punitive righteousness and propitiation or covering up of our sins, satisfaction and propitiation in one. These two phases can be separated only in the abstract; they are in reality inseparably connected just as Christ's active obedience and His passive obedience must not be conceived as two different modes of action but as being constantly joined together.

As the Absolute One, God must insist that His will be acknowledged. When He declares, "Ye shall be holy," He means it, and He insists that men admit the justice of this demand. But mankind sinned, ignored His demand of holiness, and exalted its own will at the expense of God's will. Therefore, God must punish mankind. He excluded men from His presence, for a demand, especially a divine demand, must be acknowledged and satisfied; but a demand may be satisfied by execution or, if it is not heeded, by punishment. In the latter event the demand receives its due, for the punishment meted out to the disobedient shows

---

[86] It is quite likely that Jesus designated Himself as "the Son of man" on the basis of His conviction that His mission had significance for the totality of mankind. For a brief but comprehensive statement on the meaning of this term see Zahn, *Grundrisz der neutestamentlichen Theologie*, pp. 19ff.

that the demand may not be ignored with impunity. In other words, the absoluteness and the holiness of God, *i.e.*, His punitive righteousness, would have been satisfied if all men had been compelled to suffer the penalty of everlasting damnation for their sin.[87] But God did not choose to satisfy His righteousness in this manner but sent His Son into the world that He might be man's substitute, bear the full weight of the penalty of sin, and take upon Himself the divine judgment including the banishment from God's presence. Christ thus actually bore, by His passive obedience unto death, the full measure of the divine wrath. Thereby He completely satisfied the demand of the absolute and holy God. Christ's suffering is a most unambiguous demonstration of the divine reaction against sin, but it at the same time fully satisfied the punitive righteousness of God. This satisfaction was indispensable not only for the sake of God but also for the sake of men. Nothing is so likely to arouse in men's hearts a burning sense of the awfulness of sin, so likely to impress upon their consciences the fact of God's extreme hatred of sin as the sight of their Substitute, who submits to their penalty and in their place is forsaken of God.

Satisfaction alone would, however, not have been sufficient to cancel our sin and our guilt and to restore us to fellowship with God. Satisfaction alone would not have carried out completely the decree of salvation. For punishment merely satisfies retributive justice; it cannot cancel or destroy sin. In most cases punishment merely makes the punished individual still more violent in his opposition to justice. Christ's obedience, however, was more than passive submission to the penalty. Voluntarily He took the penalty upon Himself. Without the slightest trace of resistance He acknowledged the justice of God's wrath and curse. He was excluded from communion with God and yet is for God

---

[87] Rom. 3:25.

every moment. Thus Christ satisfied not merely God's punitive righteousness but also His saving righteousness[88] and
thus actually achieved the propitiation[89] for our sin. Our sin
is now "covered over" in the sight of God and cancelled. By
constantly clinging to God our Substitute, Christ, retracted,
as it were, our rebellion against Him; His obedience covered
our disobedience, removed it from His sight, and neutralized
its effect upon God's holiness. This covering over of our sin
through Christ's active obedience is the essence of propitiation.

Reconciliation

Christ's work of satisfying propitiation had two results:
with reference to God it resulted in reconciliation or atonement; with reference to the powers to whose dominion we
were subjected on account of our sin it resulted in redemption.[90]

"Reconciliation," when it is used in ordinary English
today, denotes the termination of hostilities between two
parties and the establishment or re-establishment of friend-

---

[88]Rom. 3:25.

[89]The term *hilasterion* used in Rom. 3:25 signifies "means of
propitiation," and *hilasmos* in I John 2:2 is "propitiation." In non-
biblical Greek the verb *hilaskesthai* always means "to render someone
propitious, to appease someone," but in Biblical language it is never
used in the sense of appeasing God but in the very opposite sense; for
it is God who, in spite of His hatred of sin, still fervently loves the
sinner and seeks to save him, and it is as unnecessary as it is impossible for man to transform God's disposition toward him. Although
God is gracious and loves man, nevertheless communion between Him
and man cannot be established until man's sin is "covered over"
(compare Hebrew *kipper*; the sacrifices prescribed in Lev. 16 and 17,
and the *yom kippur*, the day of atonement, literally, the day of covering over). It is on the basis of these ideas that Paul declares in Romans
3 that God Himself set forth His Son, who shed His blood on the
cross, as *hilasterion, i.e.,* God has applied Him as a means of covering
over our sins in His own sight to the end that His saving righteousness
might be revealed, and that He might justify him that has faith in
Jesus; and that John declares in I John 2:2 that Christ's blood covers
over all the sins of the world.

[90]All these terms, it should be noted, are at times used in the
Scriptures in a wider sense to denote the entire saving work of Christ.

ship and harmony between them. The word is not used in this sense in the Bible. A change of this nature need not take place in the heart of God, for—in spite of His wrath against sin—He was never hostile toward man, and He longed continually for communion with him; and such a change could not take place in the heart of man because he is unable by his own strength to terminate that enmity against God which dwells in him.[91] In the Bible "reconciliation" does not refer to a change of attitude, either that of God toward man or that of man toward God,[92] but refers to a change in the relationship between God and man. The relation of wrath, which despite God's unintermittent love existed because of man's sin, was ended by God's own intervention when He gave His Son into death and has been changed into a relationship of peace and good pleasure. That this is the meaning of reconciliation becomes clear when we observe that the Scriptures establish an inseparable connection between the reconciliation and the work and death of Christ;[93] for it certainly cannot be maintained that a change of heart occurred in men or even in the whole universe the moment Christ died on the cross. The Biblical concept of reconciliation is therefore this: God is the acting subject; it occurred at the time of Christ's death; it took place by means of Christ's death; the world is its object; it consists in a new relationship between God and man, the relation of peace.[94]

---

[91]Rom. 5:15ff.; 7:17-24; 8:6-8; Eph. 2:1ff.; Col. 2:13, etc.

[92]It is, of course, true that God acts upon the heart of man in order to bring about a change of attitude, but this change of mind is never called "reconciliation" but "repentance" (metanoia). Even in the text where Paul declares that the Christian preacher pleads with men, "Be ye reconciled with God" (II Cor. 5:20), i.e., "Enter by repentance and faith into the new relationship with God!" he presupposes that the reconciliation has already been completely accomplished by the Father.

[93]II Cor. 5:19-21 and especially Rom. 5:10, "reconciled by the death of His Son," and Col. 1:20, "to reconcile all things unto Himself, having made peace through the blood of His cross."

[94]Note that Paul interprets the reconciliation in Col. 1:20 by the word "making peace." Cf. Eph. 2:13-18.

Because Christ has accomplished this reconciliation He is actually called "our peace."[95] The new relationship is just as real and actual as was the previous wrath-relation; it is by no means an imaginary concept or the result of wishful thinking. It is rather a necessary consequence of the work of propitiation, for if our sins have been covered over by Christ's blood, then the cause of God's wrath has been covered over, and He no longer beholds that which made us His enemies, and the wrath-relation has been superseded by a new and blessed peace-relation. It is not improper to designate the reconciliation as "the justification of the world." And the expression "all things" or "the universe" used by Paul in at least one pertinent text may well indicate that by virtue of Christ's obedience even those consequences of sin have been removed to which the irrational creation, by reason of man's sin, had been subjected. This was done at least in principle at the time of Christ's death even though their actual, tangible removal will not occur before the end of time.

Redemption

The second result of Christ's work of propitiation is our "redemption" (using the term in its narrower, Biblical sense)[96] from those powers to which men were subjected on account of their sin. Imprisonment and bondage have given way to freedom. There are four such powers from which we have been delivered. We have been freed from the guilt of

---

[95] Eph. 2:14; cf. Micah 5:4.

[96] "Redemption" is the equivalent of the Greek word for "ransom" and means "deliverance on the basis of the payment of a ransom price." The context usually indicates whether the deliverance is an act of releasing someone upon receipt of the ransom price or an act of redeeming someone by paying the ransom money. The idea of a ransom paid to secure our deliverance is frequently applied to Christ's work and its results. Christ's blood or His life is called ransom or price in Matt. 20:28; Mark 10:45; I Tim. 2:6; I Cor. 6:20; 7:23. The corresponding verbs are found in I Pet. 1:19f.; I Cor. 6:20; 7:23; Gal. 3:13; 4:5; Tit. 2:14 to show what Christ did for the benefit of mankind by

sin. Many Bible passages[97] express this thought; it follows also from those texts which declare that the blood of Christ cleanses us from sin, and that His blood has sprinkled our hearts and our consciences; and also from those texts where "forgiveness of sins" and "redemption" are used interchangeably, and where it is asserted that our sins are forgiven or blotted out through Christ.

We have also been redeemed from the dominion of sin. Paul declares that "Christ gave Himself for us with the purpose of redeeming us from all lawlessness and purifying for Himself a people of His own possession, zealous unto good works,"[98] and leaves no doubt as to whether or not Christ actually carried out this intended act of redemption. Peter states the same truth as an incontestable fact and bases his admonition on this act of redemption from the dominion of sin. The writer of Hebrews combines both when he declares that the blood of Christ cleanses us from sin and gives us the strength to serve the living God.[99]

Christ has also redeemed us from death, the penalty of sin; He has abolished death, *i.e.*, made it ineffectual, and has brought life and immortality to light. The Christian must, indeed, pass through the experience of death. Physical death has not been removed, but it has "lost its sting"[100] and frightens us no longer; in fact, it is only "the form of death" that is left.

Finally, Christ has redeemed us from the dominion of Satan. Christ has overcome the enemy and taken away

means of His blood. The nouns indicate what Christ has done for us or what we possess in Him: Heb. 9:12-15; I Cor. 1:30; Rom. 3:24; Eph. 1:7; Col. 1:14. If the question is raised, "Who received the ransom price?" the only possible answer is—God; for it was He who for the sake of our sins gave us over into the power of sin, death, and Satan. God was entitled to the ransom, and He alone could release the prisoners.

[97]*E.g.* Matt. 20:28; Col. 1:14; Rom. 3:24; Heb. 9:12, 15.
[98]Tit. 2:14. [100]I Cor. 15:55, 56.
[99]Heb. 9:14.

his armor.[101] He has delivered us from the powers of darkness, utterly defeated them and triumphed over them.[102]

This complete redemption is a necessary consequence of propitiation. If sin is covered over in God's sight, He could not possibly leave us under the cruel dominion of those powers to whom He had subjected us on account of our sin. Christ completed His task of saving mankind; He did not stop at any halfway mark. Triumphantly Christ emerged from the grave as the eternal, living proof that satisfying propitiation, reconciliation, redemption have been achieved in every respect. His grand work of salvation was finished.

Now any sinner who hears the message of propitiation may subjectively enter into the new relationship of peace with God on the sole condition that the message kindles faith in his heart. In the same moment he will receive that Christ in whom there are propitiation, reconciliation, and redemption forever and for every child of man.

The Exaltation

His work completed, the God-man laid aside the infirmities of the flesh and assumed the full exercise of His divine majesty. This exaltation is the logical consequence of His work of redemption; it is the most cogent proof of His divinity. It is also a reward for His obedience, the divine seal attesting His work of redemption as actually completed.

The exaltation occurred gradually, by a series of steps, *viz.*, the descent into Hades, the resurrection, the ascension, and the session at the right hand of God, and was so revealed to men. It is also the condition for the introduction of mankind into the communion with God which Christ had made possible by His work. As King He will now gather citizens into His kingdom and as High Priest represent them before His Father. At present He is chiefly engaged in expanding

---

[101]Luke 11:21; I John 3:8.   [102]Col. 1:13; 2:15.

His kingdom of grace on earth. He sends His Spirit into the world for that purpose and is efficacious in the Word and the Sacraments. He created the New Testament. He guides His followers and employs the service of the entire church for the accomplishment of His purposes. And He will eventually usher in the kingdom of glory, the final consummation of all things.

No wonder each of us confesses eagerly, gratefully, joyfully: "I believe that Jesus Christ, true God, begotten of the Father from eternity, and also true man, born of the Virgin Mary, is my Lord; who has redeemed me, a lost and condemned creature, bought me and freed me from all sins, from death, and from the power of the devil; not with silver and gold, but with His holy and precious blood, and with His innocent sufferings and death; in order that I might be His own, live under Him in His kingdom, and serve Him in everlasting righteousness, innocence, and blessedness; even as He is risen from the dead, and lives and reigns to all eternity. This is most certainly true."

[NOTE: In the preparation of this chapter the author wishes to acknowledge his indebtedness to the fourth part of the unpublished Dogmatics of the late Dr. Michael Reu.]

BIBLIOGRAPHY

Otto Borchert, *The Original Jesus,* New York: 1933.

Alexander Bruce, *The Humiliation of Christ,* New York: n.d.

A. T. Cadoux, *The Theology of Jesus,* London: 1940.

Charles Gore, *The Incarnation of the Son of God,* London: 1903.

A. A. Hodge, *The Atonement,* Philadelphia.

E. E. Hoskyns and F. N. Davey, *The Riddle of the New Testament,* London: 1931.

Thomas S. Kepler, *Contemporary Thinking about Jesus,* Nashville: 1944.

J. Gresham Machen, *The Virgin Birth of Christ,* New York: 1930.

James Moffatt, *Jesus Christ the Same,* Nashville: 1940.

Herbert M. Relton, *A Study in Christology,* London: 1922.

Richard Roberts, *The Contemporary Christ,* New York: 1938.

Wm. Childs Robinson, *Our Lord,* Grand Rapids: 1937.

John Schaller, *Biblical Christology,* Milwaukee: 1919.

Geerhardus Vos, *The Self-disclosure of Christ,* New York: 1926.

THE WORK OF THE HOLY SPIRIT

(Conversion, Regeneration, Sanctification)

C. G. CARLFELT

In His discussion with Nicodemus, Jesus indicates that the workings of the Holy Spirit are of such a nature that they cannot be completely comprehended by men. It is evident, on the one hand, that we cannot prescribe the order according to which the Holy Spirit must work in connection with the application of redemption in each individual case; but, on the other hand, certain acts or steps in the process of salvation are also discernible, and this makes it possible for us to speak of an *ordo salutis,* an order of salvation, indicating the separate elements that are involved in the process of salvation. For the sake of clarity and as an aid toward an understanding of what takes place when a sinner is saved we are accustomed to present the various steps herein involved in a logical sequence, and, superficially viewed, it would seem as if each such step would be distinctly separated in time from that which follows. This need not, however, be the case in all instances because individual experiences may and do differ also with respect to salvation, and the various acts or steps involved in this experience may overlap in time.

Concerning the proper order of these acts of salvation there is some disagreement among various Lutheran theologians, depending mainly on their understanding of what is involved in the concept of regeneration. Some define regeneration in a broader sense so as to include the awakening of faith. Others view it in a stricter sense so as to mean the beginning of the new spiritual life and the adoption of man as a child of God. It would seem more logical to place justification before regeneration inasmuch as justification takes place in the mind of God and is therefore causative, and regeneration is experienced in the heart of man and is then the effect of the foregoing justification. It is emphasized, however, that some of these phenomena may, indeed, occur simultaneously. Although each one of these acts cannot always be definitely fixed as to time they yet occur, and the principle features of each are experienced in some way. It should also be remembered that no act of grace is ever fully completed in this life. Man, even though he is justified in the sight of God, is yet also a sinner who needs a constant application of all the acts of grace. To use a phrase of Luther, man is *simul justus et peccator*—he is justified and yet a sinner.

The various acts involved in the work of the Holy Spirit in connection with man's salvation are the following: vocation, illumination, conversion, justification, regeneration, mystical union, sanctification, and conservation. This chapter will deal with the three main concepts of conversion, regeneration, and sanctification; but these, by their very nature, also include a number of other principles that are connected with what has been termed "the order of salvation."

CONVERSION

A.   Preliminary Considerations

1. *The Need of Conversion.*

In Luther's explanation of the Third Article of the Apostles' Creed we read that we cannot by our own strength believe in Jesus Christ or come to Him. In other words, man does not and can not effect his own salvation. This we hold to be a true presentation of the condition of man as he is in his natural state. This is amply born out by the testimony of Scripture as can be seen from the following quotations: "The

natural man receiveth not the things of the Spirit of God";[1]
"Ye were dead in trespasses and sins";[2] "The carnal mind
is enmity against God";[3] "No man can say that Jesus is
Lord but in the Holy Spirit."[4]

This has its explanation in the fact that the will of man,
because of the existence and the power of original sin, is not
inclined toward God, not in harmony with His will, but
rather, as in a state of rebellion, turned away from God.
From this state, which is the very opposite of that for which
he was created, man cannot liberate himself even though he
may at times recognize that he is going in the wrong direction, and that his life is not what it ought to be. In temporal
matters man possesses a certain degree of freedom of will
though even in this sphere there are many forces and circumstances that influence the choices and the decisions that
are made. In spiritual matters, however, the will of man is
so enslaved by sin, so centered upon self, that man cannot
by his own determination or on his own initiative seek God
or begin the process that ultimately leads to salvation. If
man is, therefore, to be saved, that is, to possess and to enjoy
the fruits of the redemption accomplished in Jesus Christ,
the initiative must come from God; and it is in this connection that we discern the work of the Holy Spirit in
and through the various acts that we have already mentioned in the introductory paragraphs.

In addition to the proponents of a false optimism who,
basing their opinion on the principles of a moral and a
cultural evolution, would maintain that through a constant
process of self-development man is able to arrive at his
ultimate destination both here and now and in the world to
come, there are also others who claim that the roads that
lead to Christ and to salvation are both many and various.

---

[1] I Cor. 2:14.   [3] Rom. 8:7.
[2] Eph. 2:1.   [4] I Cor. 12:3.

While it is true that the preparatory steps may differ, and that rather widely, in the case of different individuals, it is also true that in the last analysis there is but one road that leads to Christ, and that is the road whereby one comes to a knowledge of sin, to a longing for better things, and to the assurance that salvation is obtainable in and through Christ.

Now this knowledge of sin and of salvation in Christ is not a part of the endowment of natural man but is wrought by the Holy Spirit, especially through those activities which we term Vocation and Illumination. Through the former the Spirit makes known the will of God concerning salvation, sets forth the promise of forgiveness, and invites men to accept these gifts of grace. This invitation or call is primarily extended through the Word, but other helpful means may also be used. Christians often perform a valuable service in this connection, both directly, by speaking to others about Christ, and indirectly, by the very tenor and quality of their lives. Special events in life, both good and evil, may also be used by the Spirit to cause the sinner to become aware of his own needs and of the fact that the grace of God is available also for him personally.

We believe that this call of God is both universal and earnest, for God "would have all men to be saved, and come to the knowledge of the truth."[5] Jesus invited ALL who labored and were heavy laden,[6] and He directed His immediate followers to go and make disciples of all nations.[7]

Through the act of illumination, in which both the law and the gospel are used, the Holy Spirit seeks to influence the intellectual, the volitional, and the emotional life of man so as to prepare him actually to receive the salvation that is offered. To this end the natural disinclination of man toward the things of God must be removed together with existing

---

[5]I Tim. 2:4.   [7]Matt. 28:18.
[6]Matt. 11:28.

prejudices. The knowledge of sin is deepened to the extent that the individual concerned sees *himself* as a sinner and thus guilty before God and worthy of His condemnation. It is evident that this would result in despair were it not for the fact that the illumination by the gospel also makes known the saving grace of God in Christ.

2. *Contrition.*

When man recognizes the failure of his life and realizes that in his selfishness he has sinned against God, the normal result is that he comes into the state of contrition. He now senses even more clearly than he did before that as a sinner he is not deserving of grace but of condemnation. Man now experiences anguish and fear in his conscience; his pride subsides, and its place is taken by a true humility, and he is willing to acknowledge that God is "in the right," that He is the sovereign Lord of life and death to whom he can offer nothing by way of self-commendation. The words now become true that "nothing in my hand I bring," and that there is no other recourse left but a confession of sin and a reliance on the grace of God—"simply to Thy cross I cling."

This is a very critical period in the life of a person who is undergoing the experience of a spiritual awakening. It is not true that this experience will in every instance lead to a true confession of sin before God. Through the confluence of a number of circumstances and principles, psychological and otherwise, a person who has up to this point been under the influence of the Holy Spirit may simply revert to his former natural state. It is also possible that the recognition of the fact that one's life is not what it ought to be may lead to a bondage under the law, and in this case there will be a constant, and possibly also very earnest, attempt to correct existing flaws of life so as to achieve some degree of perfection and thus to arrive at a greater harmony between the external details of one's life and the will of God and on the basis of these achievements to establish a communion with God and be recognized as His good and acceptable child. While these possibilities are present, the normal effect of the experience hitherto described should lead the person who is in the state of contrition to that poverty of spirit which marks the beginning of faith and thus results in conversion.

3. *Faith in Relation to Conversion.*

Without faith it is impossible to please God or to have fellowship with Him, but not all that we may at times designate as faith can be pleasing to God. Our notion as to the meaning of faith is frequently quite erroneous or mistaken. In general we often look on faith as being a rather strong opinion but lacking in absolute certainty. Again it may be viewed as a firm conviction that is based on some accepted testimony or experience whereby we might, for instance, place our trust and confidence in some person whose trustworthiness or ability we have learned to know. Moreover, faith is often conceived as being very much akin to hope, and Hebrews 11:1 is then referred to as a proof text. Faith, to some, may consist merely in the intellectual apprehension of some truth but be entirely lacking in moral and spiritual implications. The teachings of Scripture, traditional formulations of Christian doctrine, or the opinion of this or that school of religious thought become the object of faith, and the whole process of faith becomes intellectually qualified. By still others faith is apprehended as being a power, usually one to be employed in the working of some miracle, especially in connection with physical healing.

It is evident that considerations such as we have mentioned thus far do not adequately describe or characterize Christian faith. They contain some elements of truth and might therefore be acceptable to some persons even though they do not contain or state the whole truth. Our intellect certainly has a part to play in connection with Christian faith. In a certain sense faith and hope may be very closely akin, and we do believe that the prayer of faith is not without avail. All of this is, however, but a part of the picture, and in its essence Christian faith is greater and more profound than any one of these elements.

We are accustomed to list knowledge, assent, and trust as the component elements of Christian faith. The first two might be viewed as the primary requisites without which it is not possible to have a real faith. We must know that God is, and we must give our intellectual assent to this truth before we can arrive at that which is the real essence and function of faith, namely, a genuine *trust* in God. When this state obtains, man will recognize God as his sovereign Lord and himself as nothing before Him. In other words, there will be a true experience of the Creator-creature relationship. Instead of making himself the center of his life man will now look away from himself and to someone else, in this case to God to whom he desires to commit his life. This also involves that man cease to offer anything to God as if to appease Him, and that he be willing and ready to accept the grace of God as His free gift.

"Faith," says Luther, "is a listening to the Word telling us what God is. It is a going to and a reliance on the love of God." It is this truth that our Lutheran Church emphasizes with her statement of *sola fide*—by faith alone—which constitutes the so-called material principle of the Reformation. This guards against the idea that man should be able to accomplish his own salvation. It precludes the idea that, by ascending from the natural state in which he finds himself, man is enabled to establish a communion with God, to convert himself, and thus to merit salvation. The intrinsic nature and quality of faith is therefore trust, a confident trust in the mercy of God as revealed in Christ Jesus, and not a deed among other deeds. It consists of that self-surrender and that acceptance of Christ through which all our thoughts, our words, and our deeds receive a new aim and direction. It is our trustful "yes" to and our humble affirmation of the will of God as this has been revealed in our Lord. It is the revelation of God that both calls faith into being and bestows upon it its own particular content. It can, therefore, not be isolated so that it could exist as a separate entity apart from God's disclosure of Himself.

By stating that faith is our affirmation to the will of God it may seem as if faith constitutes an activity entirely on the part of man, but it does not necessarily follow that this is the case. The beginning of faith takes place when God touches inner and hidden strings in the life of man with the result that man sees God in a new and a different light. The awakening of faith is thus an *opus externum*, an external work, a victory over man by the Spirit; but at some moment in this process, at the time when man's opposition to the work of the Spirit ceases, this external work, wrought by the Spirit on the human personality, becomes the bold "yes" of man's affirmation to the will of God. This in no way means that we subscribe to the idea of synergism, that God and man cooperate in the matter of salvation. The redemptive activity of God alone is that which makes salvation possible. The decisive element in faith is that man is overcome by God. He is moved out of the circle where he himself has been the center and the object of his thought and consideration. To speak with Luther, man is no longer *incurvatus in se*, no longer turned in toward himself in self-seeking but turned toward God and ready to accept the gifts that He so willingly bestows.

B. CONVERSION

Conversion always denotes a change or an exchange as when a sum of money is, for instance, converted into the corresponding currency of some other country. In the religious sense a change in the state of mind takes place in and through conversion.

It has been pointed out that the Greek word μετάνοια, *metanoia*, which is most commonly used as a designation for conversion in the New Testament, carried a fourfold connotation in classical usage. It implied that a person reviewed his former course of life, and that, on the basis of the "after-knowledge" thus arrived at, his mind was changed. This included also a regret of the former course pursued together with a change of conduct as a result of the change of mind that had taken place. It is evident that this process touches the entire life of man so as to affect not only his intellect but also his emotions and his will.

Defining conversion in its religious sense, we might say that it means a change of mind on the part of man so that he, who thus far by reason of sin has been turned away from God, is by the grace of God turned again toward God, and by the love and the grace of God now permits himself to be brought into a closer fellowship with God. It has also been described as that act of the Holy Spirit through which the sinner meets God and experiences the religious reality in such a way that he is overcome by God with the result that, turning from the former aims of his own selfish will, he now subjects himself to the will of God.

When we say that in the experience of conversion man is overcome by God we do not intend to indicate that the grace of God is irresistible, or that by the use of His omnipotence God forces anyone to be converted. We must distinguish between the omnipotence of God as this may be seen in the realm of nature and His loving will as this is active in the realm of the personal life and in connection with man's conversion. The depravity of man consists ultimately in this—that his will is in bondage under the power of evil. Evil does not exist apart from a will that is in opposition to God and to good. If man is to be liberated from his bondage, this must be done by a will that is not only in opposition to evil but is also able to draw the will of man unto itself. This is done by the loving will of God which is revealed in our world by our Savior Jesus Christ.

All of this, however, takes place within the sphere of personality, and because man is a person, he does have the power to withstand the grace of God. Since the whole matter of salvation depends on a personal relationship between God and the sinner, it follows also that grace cannot be viewed as sort of an impersonal substance or power, a *gratia infusa* that is simply poured into the life of man. Grace is a function of the will of God, and its effects are therefore to be found within the realm of man's personal life.

It is indeed God who is the *auctor principalis* in the process of conversion, but He does not thrust His grace on those who are not willing to receive it. Luther expresses the matter both tersely and truly when he states that in conversion God does not draw man as the hangman draws a criminal to the gallows but by softening and changing his heart through the means of grace. For this reason the responsibility rests with man as to the outcome of this gracious activity on the part of the Spirit. The possibility of turning from sin and to God is given by the Spirit, but this possibility must be realized by man if a conversion is to take place. In other words, man must permit the power of the Spirit to become operative in his life if he is to be converted.

With respect to the element of time there is no set pattern that conversion must follow. It might be either instantaneous or gradual. Paul and Augustine may be referred to as examples of persons who experienced an instantaneous conversion, though also in these instances preparatory elements were not entirely lacking. In the lives of the disciples of Jesus, on the other hand, we do not find such violent or instantaneous experiences of conversion. In the case of these men it was rather a slow development. And how slow they were to grasp the full significance of the meaning of Jesus for their lives!

Those who remain in the grace of baptism need not be alarmed if they have not experienced the violent emotional upheaval that is so often associated with an abrupt conversion. If we believe in the efficacy of the means of grace we must hold also that it is possible for a person to remain in the state of baptismal grace; in fact, this should constitute the normal experience of a Christian who was received into communion with God by baptism and has been constantly fostered and nurtured in the church.

In the case of those who have broken this original fellowship with God, who have left the Father's house and wandered out into the world, a conversion is necessary if that communion with God is to be re-established. This, as we have said above, may take place either by a gradual process or more abruptly. With respect to this much depends on the point of view taken. There must be some certain moment when, through the activity of the Holy Spirit, faith comes into being in the human heart. If, on the other hand, all the steps leading to conversion are taken into account, conversion may be looked on as a process that extends over a period of time. There are doubtless many Christians who cannot point to any one specific time when their conversion occurred, that is, they cannot designate the day or the hour when they became converted by means of some extraordinary experience. This has, indeed, been made the criterion in certain quarters as to whether a person is really converted or not, but the important matter in this connection is not that a man is able to name the hour of his conversion, but that he is able to know with assurance that he has turned from darkness to the light, from a life of sin and selfishness to God.

REGENERATION

In defining the meaning of the Sacrament of the Altar, Luther states that "where there is remission of sin, there is also life and salvation." When a sinner has experienced a genuine conversion he is also aware of the fact that a change has taken place in his life. Not only has the direction of his life been altered so that instead of being self-centered— *incurvatus in se*—he is now turned toward God, but his entire being has been so changed that this experience can best be described as a change from death to life. The state of spiritual death, in which man finds himself aside from and prior to a communion with God, now no longer obtains. In connection with the acts of justification and reconciliation the person who has undergone this experience has received a new life; he has been regenerated. It now remains for us to indicate what is meant by regeneration. But before doing that it may be necessary to designate what regeneration does *not* mean.

1. *Some Misconceptions Regarding Regeneration.*

Throughout the history of the Christian Church there seems to have been some confusion concerning the real meaning of the term under consideration, and as a result various explanations have been given. In some instances the very inception of faith in a human heart has been looked on as being synonymous with regeneration, and this has been termed a regeneration in the wider sense. In other instances regeneration has been described in terms that would define it as an illumination of the mind and an excitation of the will with the result that man, more or less by his own efforts, embarks on a new way of life.

Existing confusions in this connection may, in the main, be attributed to a rather common failure to distinguish properly between conversion and regeneration. This seems to be the case especially with regard to scholars in the field of psychology of religion. William James, for instance, speaks of regeneration in the following manner: "To be converted, to be regenerated, to receive grace, to experience religion, to gain assurance, are so many phrases which denote the process, gradual or sudden, by which a self hitherto divided, and consciously wrong, inferior and unhappy, becomes unified and consciously right, superior and happy, in consequence of its firmer hold upon religious realities."[8] It may be possible that James describes only the subjective experience of regeneration, but the conclusion is nevertheless valid that for him the characteristic element in regeneration is that a divided personality becomes integrated; instead of discord there will be harmony, and instead of having an inferiority complex man will now be "superior and happy." This, it seems, is too narrow as a description of regeneration since the main emphasis is placed on the effects which this experience will have on man's emotional life. These effects cannot, however, be confined to any one area of life since by the act of regeneration man's whole personality is changed.

It is also quite possible to go too far in another direction. This is done if we hold that in the act of regeneration some new substance is infused into man as if some new physical property were added to his life, or if we claim that the nature of man is so completely changed that he is no longer capable of sin. This was taught by the fanatics in the days of Luther and is still held by sects that might be described as

---

[8] James, William, *Varieties of Religious Experience*, p. 189.

being more or less fanatical in their zeal for complete holiness in this life. Even the regenerated individual, if he is sincere, must acknowledge that neither the substance nor the nature of his life has undergone such a radical change that there is nothing left of his old self. The Bible also testifies against such ideas of "perfectionism," for we read that "if we say that we have no sin, we deceive ourselves, and the truth is not in us."[9] This has also been verified by Christian experience, and the most saintly among men have always been deeply conscious of their failure to reach the goal of perfection. To illustrate this point Luther states that a Christian is *justus,* justified, and yet also *peccator,* a sinner.

2. *The Meaning of Regeneration.*

As Luther pointed out, the forgiveness of sin is closely connected with life and salvation. The possession of life and salvation rests on forgiveness or posits that forgiveness and reconciliation have taken place. When a sinner is justified by the grace of God, a new life principle is implanted in that individual by God. A brief and simple definition of regeneration would be that it is that act of grace through which the converted sinner in and through justification receives a new spiritual life. This means that the person undergoing this experience becomes a child of God, and that a new life is quickened within him. He is not a new ego but a new kind of man. His whole life has been affected so that his attitude, direction, love, hope, and aspiration have been changed from what they were previously to something new and different. A number of New Testament references, notably in Paul, describe or characterize the change that takes place in regeneration. Faith in Christ Jesus results in sonship with God.[10] The Father has given us an inheritance with the saints in light, removed us from the power of

---

[9] I John 1:8.   [10] Gal. 3:26.

darkness, and transplanted us into the kingdom of the Son of His love.[11] Anyone who is in Christ is a new creature.[12] Those who have been baptized into Christ Jesus have been buried with Him in order that they, like Him, might also rise and walk in newness of life.[13] Dying to the old and arising to a new life mean also that the powers of that life should be expressed in a new kind of service, a service in the Spirit.[14]

From all of this it is evident that salvation means *life,* a life that now is and not only one to be revealed and bestowed at the end of time. As sin and death have always been inseparably connected in our thinking, so we can also connect salvation and life. Salvation ultimately leads to a still greater life, but it is also a life in the present. Jesus had much to say regarding salvation as life and regarding Himself as mediating this life. He is the "bread of life," "the resurrection and the life." He that hears Him has passed out of death into life and *has* eternal life.[15]

This life is not something that is inherent in man, or that he himself has called into being; it is a gift from God that is bestowed through the Holy Spirit. We say, therefore, that the Holy Spirit is the efficient cause of regeneration, and that it is He who works this miracle in the heart of the individual concerned. This act of the Spirit is instantaneous in character and is not, like sanctification, an extended process that is to cover the entire period of life. There can be no intermediate state between death and life. When a person is removed from the realm of death he is thereby also translated into the kingdom of life. All life is and remains a mystery, and the spiritual life engendered in regeneration is no exception to this rule. We cannot tell, therefore, by what process this im-

[11]Col. 1:13.   [14]Rom. 7:6.
[12]II Cor. 5:17.   [15]John 5:24.
[13]Rom. 6:1-11.

planting of the new life occurs, *i.e.*, the *modus operandi* of the act of regeneration is God's own secret, which He has not revealed to us.

Beneath all definitions and descriptions we meet the mystery of life itself and the mystery of the action of the Spirit of God upon the spirit of man. The act of regeneration itself possibly takes place in such a way that man is not conscious of the moment when it occurs. What man knows is the consequence of regeneration. Jesus likens this activity of the Spirit to the wind that blows where it will.[16] We discern the results of the wind, but we know not whence it comes or whither it goes. It is with this as it is with many of our deepest religious experiences. The region where they transpire lies so deep in our personality that by reason of this very fact they defy our attempts at an actual definition. This seeming obscurity does not, however, need to trouble or confuse us, for, even if the act itself cannot be adequately described, we know by its attendant consequences if and when it has taken place.

We have stated that regeneration is the work of the Holy Spirit in the heart of man, but we have not thereby denied that certain means are at the disposal of the Spirit or are used by Him in accomplishing this work. On the contrary, both baptism and the Word are the means whereby this new life of the spirit is engendered. We believe that baptism is a sacrament in the real sense of that word. It is an act through which God does something in and for the person who is baptized. A child who is baptized is, therefore, by that very act taken into a fellowship with God, and the new life is implanted into its heart. We should designate this as the normal way of regeneration within the Christian community of the church, and we know that it is possible for a person to remain in baptismal grace. In that case the life received in

---

[16]John 3:8.

baptism is nurtured and fostered, especially through the Word and the Sacrament of the Altar, but a prayer fellowship with God is also of great importance in this connection.

In a case where the baptismal covenant has been broken, resulting in separation from God and consequent spiritual death, the Word becomes the means employed by the Spirit in the kindling of the new spiritual life. The covenant of baptism is not abrogated on God's side, and it is therefore not necessary for a person who has been baptized but has fallen from the grace of baptism to be re-baptized at the time of his conversion in order that he might become regenerated. In that sense baptism is a pledge of the willingness and readiness of God again to receive the contrite sinner and to re-instate him in that covenant relationship which also entails the bestowing of a new life.

In either of these instances, whether regeneration comes about through the sacrament of baptism or through the Word, the very act itself cannot be further described. In speaking of the *means* employed in this connection care must be taken lest this activity of the Holy Spirit become mechanized to such an extent that the spontaneity of the Spirit be denied. To guard against this it might better be said that we here deal with a work that is dependent on a *mediated immediacy* of the Holy Spirit.

3. *The Effects of Regeneration.*

Life normally expresses itself in power and in activity, and the life of a regenerated Christian also follows this pattern. He will be conscious of the love and the grace of God as a power in his life, and this again expresses itself in a twofold way: negatively in the overcoming of sin and positively in enabling man to show forth some fruits of the Christian life in loving service to God and to fellow men. Inasmuch as God is in constant and most radical opposition to all evil, the presence of His Spirit and His love in a human life also results in a struggle against sin and evil. No one can, however, become completely victorious in this struggle, and from this point of view it is true that here on earth the Christian life is in a constant process of being. It is never a fully finished product.

The new life is thus also one of hope. The Christian both hopes and strives in his effort to become more and more like his Master in the purity of life, and he has not only the hope but also the firm assurance that as Christ became victorious over even the power of death, so he also shall at last gain the final victory. This is a hope, however, that is mingled with fear, for it is possible for a Christian to lose the life bestowed on him in baptism or through regeneration if by neglect or willful disobedience he nullifies the covenant relationship that was once established.

On the positive side the life implanted through regeneration expresses itself in loving service. Man becomes an instrument whereby the love of God can express itself in the world. The constraining power of that love becomes the motive force for any good work that a regenerated man may perform. The power of Christ is made perfect in man's weakness.[17] Paul knew the constraining power of the love of Christ,[18] and that love still seeks its way into humanity at large through those who have become new men by the act of regeneration.

The person who has been led unto life and salvation by the love of God and has tasted of the fulness of that divine love will, as a result, earnestly endeavor to realize God's loving purpose and will in and through his own life and will also be constrained to become a witness for God and His love. Luther felt deeply and spoke clearly on this subject and uses rather strong language in setting forth this part of

---

[17]II Cor. 12:9.   [18]I Cor. 5:14.

a Christian's calling in the world. A Christian is to be "a
Christ for his neighbor." As the nature of God is nothing
else than love, so through love and beneficence the Christian
reveals God to his fellow men.[19]

It should be underscored, however, that the power
through which a Christian can in some measure discharge
the obligation to live a Christlike life in love and good works
does not come from himself. It is all the fruit of that new
life which is the gift of God through the act of regeneration,
and this precludes any thought of merits in connection with
the good works that a Christian may perform, or that he has
been able to perform these in his own power and wisdom.
A man is regenerated through the love and the power of
God, and in the last analysis it is also through these that he
is enabled to remain a Christian and bring forth some fruits
of the Christian life, and it is not without significance that
these have been called the "fruits of the Spirit."[20]

Apart from fellowship with God man lives in a state of
disharmony. Charlotte Elliot describes this aptly in the
following lines from a well-known hymn:

> "Just as I am, though tossed about
> With many a conflict, many a doubt,
> Fightings and fears within, without."

As long as man is in bondage under the tyranny of his own
egocentricity, there can be neither peace nor an inner
harmony in his life. When he is released from that tyranny
in and through the bestowal of the new life in Christ he will
also experience the peace that passeth understanding.[21]
Jesus promised His followers that He would give them a
peace that would differ from anything that the world
could give.[22] Peace and blessing, or blessedness, are then
among the effects of the regenerated life.

---

[19]W.A. 10, I, 1, p. 100.   [21]Phil. 4:7.
[20]Gal. 5:22.   [22]John 14:27.

In our activistic mode of life we are in no small danger
of losing sight of this important aspect of the Christian life.
In our constant doing, even in connection with the work of
the church, we might become so preoccupied that we have
no time to let Christ do for us what He has promised. The
Christian life should touch all the faculties of our personality, including also the emotional side of our nature. Not
that we can live constantly in a state of spiritual ecstasy or
daily enjoy what has been termed "a mountaintop experience," nor yet measure the validity of our Christian life in
accordance with the intensity of our feelings.

The Christian will also be conscious of the fact that life
is a struggle. He, too, will have moments of uncertainty and
sorrow, but underneath all of this there is, nevertheless, a
peace that rests on a firmer foundation than that of mere
feelings, namely, on Him who is our Peace and on His
promises. It is rather a peace in the midst of strife, and this
underlying peace and harmony of life is in itself a factor in
the maintaining of the spiritual life. Concerning this the late
Einar Billing of Sweden speaks in the following manner:
"Our peace is not a frail treasure that we must anxiously
guard in order to protect it from the world. It is rather the
strong power that guards us, and in whose company we can
securely walk through the world. It is not a weak and
delicate mood that comes and goes, but a secure and objective
reality that surrounds us wherever we go. It is not the last,
concluding, and highest element in the Christian life, but the
first, the foundation—and yet also the highest experience."[23]

Only he who lives in fellowship with God can know the
meaning of this peace. Possessing it, he will also be aware
that it is a source of power, power to do and to suffer for the
sake of Christ. "Only when we are conscious of an inner
possession, surpassing all else, and which nothing, not even

---

[23]*Herdabrev,* p. 17.

death, can take away from us, and concerning which we do not have to fight with others, because it is given us by grace, and for this reason it also increases as we share it with others; only when we realize this will our heart be able to lay hold on something that liberates it from its frantic grasp on itself. When peace and blessedness are rooted in a human heart, then that heart will have a power not only to guard itself against the powers that would defile it, but also to share its life with others."[24]

SANCTIFICATION

Every human heart harbors some kind of aspiration for a better life, but there is by no means unanimity among men as to how that better life is to be attained. There are those who hold to the idea of human progress, believing that man possesses some inherent qualities which, by the process of evolution, will finally lead to the perfection of life. That there is progress in life certainly cannot be denied, but it does not follow that the direction of this progress will always be toward the good. Experiences of life testify to the fact that also evil can increase and be developed to a new and even terrifying degree.

Christianity, too, believes in and preaches the principle of the betterment of life, both individual and communal, but it knows that this cannot come about by any mere human developments, and that it must rest on a more secure foundation than the inherent perfect ability of man. The Bible is explicit in its demand that the life of a Christian increase and develop in goodness, and the ultimate goal of this progress is nothing less than perfection and holiness as expressed in the words of Jesus: "Ye therefore shall be perfect, as your heavenly Father is perfect."[25] The Bible also draws a clear distinction between the Christian life and that

---

[24]Billing, Einar, *op. cit.,* p. 22.   [25]Matt. 5:48.

of the "world." Paul admonishes his readers that they should
not be fashioned according to this world but be transformed
by the renewing of their mind so as to be able to prove what
is the good, acceptable, and perfect will of God.[26] "This is
the will of God, even your sanctification."[27] In both of these
instances Paul speaks to *Christians, i.e.,* to persons who had
accepted Christ as their Savior and on whom, therefore, the
new life of the Spirit had been bestowed. Consequently, it
is evident that sanctification presupposes conversion and regeneration, and these again have as their foundation the
redemptive activity of God through Christ Jesus. Through
the new birth there has been a transforming of the whole
personality of the person concerned; a new content and a
new direction have been given to his intellectual, emotional,
and volitional life. It is on the basis of this experience that
there can and must be a betterment of life along ethical and
spiritual lines. Only in this connection will man's search for
the good life finds its ultimate answer, for that answer does
not depend on any intrinsic and natural goodness of man
himself but on the grace of God, revealed in Christ and
mediated through the Holy Spirit.

By sanctification we mean that activity of the Holy Spirit
in the life of a believer whereby the power and the influence
of sin are diminished, with the result that he is enabled to
live in closer harmony with the will of God. This is effected
through the means of grace and with the cooperation of the
regenerated person.

Sanctification thus involves the following aspects:

1) Negatively, it consists in subduing and overcoming
the power of sin together with all evil inclinations and habits.

2) Positively, it refers to the growth and the development of the Christian life in conformity with the will of God

---

[26]Rom. 12:2.   [27]I Thess. 4:3.

so that the believer acquires a more Christlike way in all
his relationships, in thought, word, and deed.

3) Sanctification differs from other elements in connection with man's salvation in that it to a certain extent involves
a cooperation between the believer and the grace of God.

We have stated that in the new birth there is a transformation of the personality of man, but we have not thereby affirmed that man's nature has been entirely changed. A
change has taken place in the very center of his being, but
the old life of man with its predilections has not been fully
uprooted or put to death. It still lives on alongside the new
man even though it is no longer in full control, and there is
constant struggle between these two as to which shall be
predominant. Through regeneration the power of sin has
been broken, but sin itself has not been completely eradicated
from the heart. In the sight of God the converted sinner is
justified, but he nevertheless finds that in his own life there
is a residue of sin that must constantly be overcome, restricted, as it were, to an ever-widening periphery of life.

If we ask how long this struggle shall continue we in
reality propound the same question that Paul raised: "Who
shall deliver me out of the body of this death?"[28] The
answer to this inquiry is twofold. With Paul also the believer
can say: "I thank God through Jesus Christ, our Lord."[29]
He knows that the assurance of his salvation rests on the
grace of God in Christ, but he also knows that the warfare
between the old and the new life will not terminate this side
of death. Sanctification in the sense of overcoming the power
of sin is therefore a *process* and not an act that takes place
once and for all. The believer, too, each day faces some
"existential moment" when he must make a choice between
right and wrong, between the desires of the old man and the
will of God. There are temptations from within and without

---

[28] Rom. 7:24.   [29] Rom. 7:25.

that must be conquered. Natural inclinations and temptations presented by our environment are ever ready to make their assaults upon the citadel of the inner life whence they have been dethroned but whither they constantly seek to return as the masters of life. The struggle between these two forces in the Christian life may become so severe that it may be characterized as a "struggle unto death," but it is not a warfare that ends in defeat, providing the person involved does not willfully sever himself from the grace of God.

In this connection we meet one of the paradoxes of the Christian life, namely, that our sense of sin may increase as we make progress on the road of sanctification. This will cause anxiety to those who are deeply concerned about the status of their spiritual lives, but under normal circumstances it should not lead to despair if we realize that the more we learn to know of Christ, the more we shall become conscious also of the differences between His life and ours. As the light of His grace falls more and more upon our hearts, we shall become aware of new areas where sin still lurks, and where its power has not become entirely broken. Even then we need not doubt the ultimate outcome, "because if our heart condemn us, God is greater than our heart, and knoweth all things."[30]

On the positive side sanctification means a closer approximation of the life of the believer to the will of God so that he will in all his relationships more closely emulate the example set by the Lord. There is thus not only the forsaking of the evil but also the actual doing of the good. To this belong the training of one's thought and will and the direction of the affections toward a more Christlike way of living. Externally this issues forth in good works, which may be called the fruits of sanctification, or, to use Pauline phraseology, the "fruits of the Spirit."[31]

---

[30]I John 3:20.   [31]Gal. 5:22.

There has at times been an undue reluctance among Lutherans to emphasize the idea of good works, fearing, no doubt, that they might be led into the fallacy of work-righteousness. We need not, however, be dissuaded by any such inhibitions if we bear in mind the oft-quoted statement of Luther that "good works do not make a man good, but a good man does good works." We do not depend on our good works for our salvation, but if good works do not follow as a result of our faith, it is evident that our faith is not what it ought to be.

Good works have been defined as the free acts of justified persons,[32] and they should be as free and as natural to the Christian as is, for instance, the act of breathing. They are done, not under the compulsion of external constraints, but are the natural results and consequences of a regenerated and sanctified life. The power to perform good deeds is indeed from God; it is the love (*agape*) and the grace of God that are energizing the Christian, but he must be willing to use that power if it is to result in deeds of love.

Man is not an irresponsible automaton but a responsible personal being who is accountable for his life in all its details. This responsibility extends also into the realm of the Christian life. It is true that man is saved by grace, and that whatever progress he may make in Christian living is also dependent on an inflow of this same grace, but this does not nullify man's responsibility in the matter of sanctification. The new life implanted in regeneration needs attention and nurture, and there are some things that man can and must do to further this process. It is paramount for the Christian to live a normal and natural physical life so that his powers of body and of mind are at their best, for it is a recognized fact that temptations may have greater influence over us when these powers are weakened. Furthermore, he must

---

[32]Hollazius.

avoid associations and places where he might be subjected
to the temptations of evil, for "he who throws himself into
danger will often perish thereby."

But the Christian must also be aware of the more positive
aspects of his life and should therefore endeavor, as Paul
states,[33] "to put on a heart of compassion, kindness, lowli-
ness, meekness, longsuffering; forbearing one another, and
forgiving each other." To do this he must needs make a
faithful use of the means of grace, and all of this belongs to
the cooperation that a regenerated person is called on to
render in connection with his sanctification. This is certainly
not a cooperation between two equal forces or persons. The
believer needs a power greater than his own in order to fight
the good fight and to become victorious, but he can never
forget that he, too, has a part to play, and that responsibility
for his own life has by no means ceased by reason of the
fact that he has experienced a regeneration, that he now
lives his life "in the Lord."

The ancients used to say that *extra ecclesiam nulla salus*
(outside the church there is no salvation), and, rightly understood, this is a truth that cannot be denied. We could
also add that aside from the church and the means of grace
there can be no sanctification. Christian life, as all other life,
is corporate in its nature in so far as the Christians are
members of the body of Christ, for which He gave Himself
that He might sanctify it and present to Himself a glorious
church, holy and without blemish.[34] The purely personal
element of the Christian life is not submerged in but enriched by this corporate fellowship. Through it the believer
shares in the tradition of the church and in the fellowship
of the saints, past and present; he is instructed and edified
as he takes part in the common worship; and at the Table
of the Lord he receives not only assurance but also that

[33]Col. 3:12, 13.   [34]Eph. 5:25-27.

renewal of spiritual energy which he needs for his daily walk and living as a Christian.

The importance of the church as an aid toward sanctification is seen most clearly in connection with its administration of the means of grace. The Word and the sacraments are the channels through which the illuminating and vitalizing grace of God is made available to men, and all endeavors to develop and improve life apart from these means are not only utterly futile in themselves but the expressions of a spirit that is in sharp contrast to that which is at home within Christianity. For the Christian the question is not that of self-expression but of an expression of the grace and the love of God, active in and through his life. Where there are growth and development, there must also be the corresponding replenishing of the powers and the potentialities that make growth possible. Anyone, therefore, who desires to grow in the grace and the knowledge of the Lord Jesus Christ toward his own sanctification will seek that grace where it is to be found, namely, in and through the means of grace as administered by the church. It is thus that God strengthens us and keeps us steadfast in our faith even unto the end.

BIBLIOGRAPHY

These subjects are generally treated in works on Systematic Theology such as Jacobs, *A Summary of the Christian Faith* and Stump, J., *The Christian Faith.*

The following books deal with these subjects either wholly or in part:

Baltzly, Oliver, D., *Catechetical Evangelization*, Burlington: 1928, p. 249.

Bergendoff, Conrad, *The Secular Idea of Progress and the Christian Doctrine of Sanctification*, Rock Island: 1933, p. 16.

Engstrom, L. M., *Christ Our Sanctification*, Rock Island: 1928, p. 31.

Eyster, Wm. T., *The Doctrine of Sanctification as Taught by the Sacred Scriptures and Lutheran Theology*—a reprint from *Lutheran Quarterly*, July, 1919, p. 15.

Golladay, Robert E., *Sermons on the Catechism*, Columbus: 1917, p. 461.

Gerberding, G. H., *New Testament Conversions:* A Series of Sermons, Philadelphia: 1889, p. 283. *Lutheran Fundamentals*, Rock Island: 1925, p. 321. *The Way of Salvation in the Lutheran Church*, Philadelphia: 1887, p. 276

Keyser, L. S., *Election and Conversion*, Burlington: 1914, p. 184.

Koeberle, Adolf, *The Quest for Holiness*, New York: Harper, 1936, p. 268.

Hallesby, O., *Infant Baptism and Adult Conversion*, Minneapolis: Lutheran Free Church Publishing Co., 1924, p. 94.

Flew, Newton, *The Idea of Perfection in Christian Theology*, London: 1934, p. 422.

Kuyper, Abraham, *The Work of the Holy Spirit*, New York: Funk, 1900, p. 664.

Warfield, B. B., *Perfectionism*, New York: 1931, 2 volumes.

Whitley, W. T. (Editor), *The Doctrine of Grace*, Macmillan, 1931, p. 396.

THE CHURCH

ERIC H. WAHLSTROM

The Lutheran doctrine of the church must be understood as an integral part of the total conception of the gospel. Our conception of the nature of grace determines our conception of the church. Any attempt, therefore, to approach the subject from the point of view of the church as an institution, or an assembly, or from the religious and moral character of the members must inevitably fail. Only when the intimate connection between the gospel and the church is clearly grasped can the Lutheran doctrine of the church be rightly understood and appreciated.

The gospel is the message of God's redemptive love. It declares that God is active in history to redeem man and to create for Himself a people for His own possession. God reveals Himself in this creative activity. The Bible is *Heilsgeschichte,* and the *Heil* is God's activity in the world. God always has been, is now, and ever will be a God who redeems and creates new life. Wherever God is active to seek and to save the lost, there the church comes into being. When we see the church clearly as the result of God's redemptive activity we are able to develop a conception of the church which is true to its nature and its function. We shall then not be in danger of underestimating the church, for it is God's church; He creates, maintains, and sustains it. And we shall likewise be prevented from saying too much, for the church can never be anything in its own right; it can never be separated from or independent of the redemptive activity of God.

THE NATURE OF THE CHURCH AS SEEN IN ITS ORIGIN

The church is described in the Augsburg Confession, Article VII, as "the communion of saints, in which the gospel is rightly preached, and the sacraments rightly administered." We may perhaps take as a commentary on this article what. Luther has to say relative to the clause, "I believe in the holy Christian Church," in his explanation of the Third Article of the Creed: "The Holy Spirit has called me through the gospel, enlightened me with His gifts, and sanctified and preserved me in the true faith; *in like manner* as He calls, gathers, enlightens, and sanctifies the whole Christian Church on earth, and preserves it in union with Jesus Christ in the one true faith." The church comes into being *in like manner* as an individual becomes a believer, through the activity of the Spirit who "calls, enlightens, and sanctifies" him. As Luther ascribes the redemption of the individual to the gracious activity of the Spirit, so he likewise ascribes the creation of the church to the activity of the same Spirit. The expression "in like manner" does not imply that we are dealing with two different kinds of action. The activity of the Spirit in calling the individual is at the same time the activity which creates the church. The work of the Spirit is to create a redeemed community, and whoever is redeemed is by that act also made a member of the church.

When the Augsburg Confession speaks of the gospel being preached and the sacraments administered it refers to this activity of the Spirit, or the redemptive activity of God. That the gospel is preached and the sacraments are administered means that God is present in and through these means to seek and to save the lost. God comes to man in mercy and grace to set him free from sin, destroy death, and create new life. The gospel is "the power of God unto salvation" exactly because in it God comes to save man and to create for Himself a redeemed humanity, a people for His own possession. The Word of God is God Himself active in the world for the redemption of man.

The church is, therefore, not a human construction. Its origin cannot be found in some supposed, innate, religious tendency in man. It does not arise out of the actions of men banding themselves together in a search for God or for the meaning of life. It is perhaps significant that the idea of the church is confined to the Biblical tradition. Other religions have temples, priests, sacraments, liturgies, moral teachings, etc., but the idea of the church as the redeemed people of God is limited to the Jewish-Christian tradition. Here God has revealed himself as the One who creates and maintains the church.

Nor is the church a human construction in the sense that the true believers, "the new men," join themselves together to start the church. Such a view would separate redemption from the doctrine of the church. God would then presumably save man by His grace, but this "saved man," since he feels the need of communion, would then seek out others who have had a similar experience and together with them organize a church. The founding of the church would then go back ultimately to a decision of the immediate disciples of Jesus to organize the church, and each believer would decide for himself whether he wanted to join the church or not. The church on earth would then become merely a human institution, and its true nature as "a people for God's own possession" would be obscured. The Lutheran doctrine of the church implies that to be redeemed is to become incorporated into the people of God and thus to be made a member of the church.

The origin and the reality of the church rest upon the gospel of the grace of God. It is the nature of the gospel, or, which is the same thing, it is the purpose of God, to create a redeemed people who are to live in communion

with Him. God has always been engaged in this creative
and redemptive activity. The God who redeemed Israel out
of Egypt and constituted it by this act His people is the
same God who "was in Christ reconciling the world unto
Himself," and the same God who today "calls, gathers,
enlightens, and sanctifies the whole Christian Church on
earth." The church is thus a fellowship of the redeemed, a
"communion of saints," created by God through the gospel.

The constitutive elements of the church are therefore the
Word and the sacraments through which the gospel is proclaimed. Since the gospel is "God's power unto salvation,"
and God through it redeems men, the church is where the
gospel is proclaimed and the sacraments are administered.
"Where baptism and the gospel are, no one may doubt that
there are saints, even if it were only the babes in their
cradles." "Wherever, therefore, you hear or see this Word
preached, believed, confessed, and acted on, there is no
doubt that there must be a true *ecclesia sancta catholica.*"[1]
Wherever God is at work in grace and mercy to forgive sins
and create new life, the church comes into being. No matter
how far into the future we go, the foundation of the church
will always remain that same grace of God. Even "the new
song" which the redeemed in heaven sing has for its theme
the redemption secured by "the Lamb that was slain." The
church has no other origin in time or in eternity than the
grace of God.

If we ask specifically when the church began we cannot
answer by declaring that Pentecost was its birthday, or that
Jesus founded it during His lifetime. It began in and with
God's redemptive activity in the world. Jesus could not
possibly have "founded" what was already in existence.
Only from the religious-theological point of view, when
Jesus is confessed as the living Lord, the Logos, the Redeem-

---

[1] Luther.

or, Atoner, and Reconciler, can we speak of Him as founding
the church. In Him the redemptive activity of God reached
its climax and culmination. The foundation of the church
was laid once for all in His life and in His vicarious suffering
for our sins. But His atoning death was not simply an event
in history; nor can it be separated from the continuing,
redemptive activity of God. The cross is the central manifestation in time and in history of God's redemptive activity
and the victory of life over death. "God was in Christ reconciling the world unto Himself." He is "the chief cornerstone"
on whom patriarchs and prophets, evangelists and apostles,
and all the saints of God in all ages have built.

The fact that in Him the redemptive process reaches its
climax gives to His life a supreme and decisive importance.
What had been a promise now became fulfilment; what had
been occasionally and darkly seen was now manifested in
the light; what had been a hope now became a realization.
God had been conceived as the Redeemer of a chosen
people; He is now revealed as the universal Redeemer of all
nations and all tongues. When we say that the church is
created by the gospel we mean the gospel of the vicarious
suffering and death and the victorious resurrection and life
of the Lord Jesus Christ. It is this gospel which is the power
of God unto salvation and through which God creates and
maintains His church in all ages and to all eternity.

We may regard the fellowship which Jesus gathered
around Himself as the nucleus of the new Israel, the faithful
remnant, who were to become the bearers of God's revelation to men. How much of group consciousness and actual
organization there was among them, and how much instruction, if any, Jesus gave to them about the future organization
and program of the church, are questions which the Gospels
fail to answer clearly. The fellowship was informal. They
were held together by loyalty to the Master; and, although

there may have been recognized leaders among them, there were no officers in the strict sense of the word. But we cannot be far wrong if we assume that those who "had been with Jesus" continued to develop the movement in the spirit and along the lines which they had learned from Him. What Jesus created was a new life, a new sense of communion, and a new conception of fellowship; but He left the organization to be developed later as the occasion and the circumstances might demand.

II

THE NATURE OF THE CHURCH AS SEEN IN ITS FELLOWSHIP

A. *The Boundaries of the Church.*

If the origin of the church rests on the activity of God in prevenient grace, then the boundaries of the church cannot be drawn by anything else than by this same grace of God. Wherever God comes in Word and sacrament to "call, gather, enlighten, and sanctify," there He establishes and maintains the church. This is what the Augsburg Confession declares in saying that "the church is the communion of saints in which the gospel is rightly preached and the sacraments are rightly administered." It is obviously impossible for anyone to say at what point a person to whom this word of grace comes ceases to be the "old man" and becomes one of the people of God. Even the individual is usually unable to point to any definite time. Since God is continually active both to call and to sanctify, the church is in a constant state of becoming.

Our conception of the church must, therefore, find room within its fellowship for those who are—both literally and figuratively—children; for those who are only vaguely conscious of their lack of a solid foundation giving peace and security to life, as well as for the aged saint who can say,

"I have finished the course, I have kept the faith." Yes, we may even have to include those to whom God comes in prevenient grace, who are as yet only vaguely conscious of Him who stands without knocking at the fast-closed door of the heart. The boundaries of the church extend as far as the redemptive activity of God.

The church in its proclamation of the gospel is the agency of the prevenient grace of God, and this must be made evident in its attitude to those whom it seeks to invite into its fellowship. The church must not lay down rules of admission into its fellowship which deny its character as a creation of grace. It must not, for instance, in admitting adults demand as a condition of membership that the applicant shall have arrived at a certain stage of maturity either in regard to confession, knowledge, religious experience, or moral life. The most that can possibly be demanded is simply that the applicant shall be serious in his desire to become the object of the ministration of the church in its proclamation of grace.[2] The church cannot compel anyone to belong, nor does it refuse anyone; but it gladly invites all without distinction or examination to come and to partake freely of the riches of grace which God offers through His church. The very fact that he comes indicates that God has reached and called him. If certain requirements should be demanded, what should they be? How much of knowledge, experience, and moral improvement is sufficient? To ask these questions indicates at once the arbitrariness of all other boundaries except those set by the prevenient grace of God.

If we take the idea of grace seriously we see the church as an institution into which God continually calls and gathers new members, and in which He continually enlightens and sanctifies those who are members. The church is both evangelistic and educational; both an agency of

---

[2]Billing, *Folkkyrkan*, p. 136.

grace and a communion of saints. As God's redemptive activity continues, the possibilities of external expansion and inner growth remain unlimited.

If this conception be held as the ideal and real, it is possible to grant that in actual practice some external criteria may be required. The church may perhaps demand that he who says, "I need the grace of God," shall give some tangible evidence of this conviction. It is simply good and proper order that the applicant shall be given time to acquire a rudimentary understanding of the nature of the church and its teaching, and that he give his consent to its doctrine and practice. But the impression must not be given that this knowledge and confession *entitle* a person to membership in the church. The right to belong to the church never rests on confession, obedience, contributions, attendance at worship and Communion, or on any subjective attitude or achievement, but solely on the grace of God.

B. *The Church as the Communion of Saints.*

In the Lutheran Church the word "saint" does not refer to the holiness of the person but to his status as a forgiven sinner. The conception underlying sainthood in Catholicism and in Pietism is that the "new man" uses the endowment of grace to produce fruits of righteousness which he can present before God. He who is able to do this to a remarkable degree earns for himself the title "saint."

When grace is understood as being the foundation of the whole of life, the possibility of sainthood in this sense is denied. Luther's *sola fide* stands guard against all Pelagian attempts to interpret salvation as man's work; and his formula, *simul iustus et peccator,* shuts out the possibility of the new man taking pride in its own achievements. The Christian never gets beyond forgiveness of sin; he lives continually under a pardon, and his relation to God is predicated, not on his holiness, but on grace alone. The word "saint," therefore, in the Lutheran sense means a forgiven sinner, one who lives by daily forgiveness, and who is at the same time *totaliter iustus* and *totaliter peccator*.[3]

The church as the communion of saints is the fellowship of forgiven sinners, who live continually by grace alone. It is from this point of view immaterial whether we understand *communio sanctorum* as participation in holy things or as congregation of saints. What they participate in is the means of grace or grace itself; and by this participation they are saints, *e.g.*, forgiven sinners. Wherever the gospel of forgiveness is proclaimed, there are the saints, and there is the church.

C. *The Church as an Object of Faith.*

The existence and the reality of the church are known to faith only. Since the church is where God is active through Word and sacrament, no other element, be it apostolic succession, the excellent character of the members, the common confession, or the New Testament pattern of organization, etc., can be either substituted for this or admitted as valid. But this means that only he who has experienced the work of God, *i.e.*, he who has faith, is able to perceive the reality of the church. The believer has himself experienced the reality of God's redemptive work through the gospel and therefore knows that the church in which this gospel is proclaimed is the true church of Jesus Christ because and in so far as it is a creation of the gospel. Faith knows that this is the church because here God is active in Word and sacrament to seek and to save the lost.

When the church is seen from this point of view, the troublesome problem of "the visible and the invisible church" can be solved. In what persons and to what extent God's call is really effective only God Himself knows. No man is

---

[3]Nygren, A., *Till Gustav Aulen*, p. 117.

competent to separate the wheat from the tares and in that way establish the boundaries of the church. God knows those who are His. Since God, however, makes use of visible means of grace to create His church in the world, the church becomes visible to that extent. The preaching of the Word, the administration of the sacraments, and the members' fellowship with one another in the Word are visible and tangible activities. But faith alone perceives in these the presence and the reality of the church. The outsider sees a group of people with similar interests, but he notes also the presence of hypocrites and the sins of those who profess to be true believers. Faith knows this also, but it perceives, what no one else can see, the redemptive activity of God which creates the church.

There is only one church, the creation of the gospel, where God is at work to forgive sins and to create new life. Since God's work in the soul is hidden, but since He, nevertheless, makes use of visible means of grace, the church must remain in this world both visible and invisible. Only in the final state, as the church triumphant, can it become wholly visible as the finished creation of God.

D. *The Church Is One, Holy, Catholic.*

Since the church is created through the redemptive activity of God, it is one in all ages and in all times. It is that body of believers, the redeemed people of God, who have become the object of God's redemptive activity through Word and sacrament. The unity of the church exists already, for it centers in Him who is its Creator and Head. In so far as the church acknowledges and realizes its true nature as a creation of grace, the divisive elements will be eliminated, and a visible unity achieved.

The church is "holy" because the holy God is present in it to sanctify His people. This holiness is not inherent in the church as an institution, nor is it meant to call attention to the "holy" character of its members. The reason the church can be called "holy" lies entirely in the fact that the Holy Spirit is present to sanctify it.

That the church is "catholic" (universal) is strongly set forth in the Lutheran conception of it as the sphere of the prevenient grace of God. When the church is conceived as including all to whom God comes in grace and mercy, then it becomes a free gift offered to all men. God's purpose and His activity include all men, "there is neither Jew nor Greek, neither bond nor free, neither male nor female, for all are one in Christ Jesus."

III

THE NATURE OF THE CHURCH AS SEEN IN ITS FUNCTIONS

A. *The Organization of the Church.*

Since it is the nature of the gospel to create a communion, the church cannot remain simply a spiritual entity. God creates the new life, but this life expresses itself in the world in tangible and visible forms. This new life creates for itself such forms as are congenial and suitable to its own nature. Consequently no forms can be prescribed for this life, nor can these forms be judged except in reference to the nature of the new life in grace. The organization must be judged true or false, good or bad, simply on the basis of whether it helps or hinders the new life in its effort to articulate itself in the world. That form of organization is good and true in any age and in any place which, in accordance with time and the circumstances, brings out the nature of the church as a creation and an agency of the grace of God.

It is quite evident, therefore, that even Jesus Himself could not give to the church a complete form of organization, and also that we cannot make the New Testament forms binding on the church today. The primitive church developed a flexible organization which differed according to locality and circumstances. It found help and guidance in the patterns of contemporary society although the decisive element was its own spiritual life and the presence of the Spirit. The organization was designed to facilitate the preaching of the gospel and to express the consciousness of unity and fellowship within the church. While the historic forms are of great value and should not be lightly set aside, there is no reason the church should maintain a form of organization because it is old, or because it is mentioned in the New Testament.

The office of the ministry, too, rests on the nature of the gospel. Although Jesus in a sense instituted the ministry by calling and training those whom He sent forth to preach, the office has its ground in the redeeming activity of God through Word and sacrament. God who "was in Christ reconciling the world unto Himself" has also given to us "the ministry of reconciliation." This office rests on the nature of the gospel as a proclamation of grace as is indicated in Paul's words: "How shall they believe in Him whom they have not heard? and how shall they hear without a preacher? and how shall they preach, except they be sent?"[4] The Spirit who "calls, gathers, enlightens, and sanctifies the whole church" also on the one hand calls men into the ministry and on the other guides the church in the selection and the preparation of those who are to be ordained as ministers of the Word. The church and the ministry belong together; the one is not primary or secondary to the other. The gospel creates the office of the ministry even as it creates the church. The ministry is not a self-perpetuating order but a divinely appointed office within the church.

---

[4]Rom. 10:14, 15.

B. *The Function of the Church in Regard to Its Members.*

The function of the church is to lead its members into a fuller and deeper realization of their Christian life. We may say that the church is concerned that the members understand the true nature of the Christian life, and that they live this new life. The means which the church uses for this purpose are the means of grace, and all its manifold activity in preaching, teaching, worship, service, etc., has this goal in view.

The function is twofold. On the one hand, the church must never let anyone forget that he owes his right to a place in the church solely to God's gracious forgiveness. The member is called into the church through the grace of God, and he remains in the church also by grace. He never comes to a place where he has grace and forgiveness behind him. No matter how long he lives and how much of Christian experience he may acquire, his relation to God remains predicated on forgiveness. The message of the church is *Sola Fide* both for the beginner and for the aged saint.

On the other hand, the grace of God is for the whole of life. The church always insists that, if the members *are* Christian, they must *live* as Christians. It welcomes all without distinction or examination, but it also declares to all, "Let everyone that nameth the name of the Lord depart from iniquity."[5] Paul was serious in his demand that "the works of the flesh" must be "put off," and that the new life should manifest itself in the exercise of the Christian virtues which are the fruit of the Spirit.[6] The new life is God's creation, and if it is true to its nature it must be a life in truth and holiness. "A good tree bears good fruit." This moral character is not a demand imposed from without by law; it rests on the very nature of the new life. It is simply unthinkable to Paul that those who "have died to sin should

---

[5]Billing, *Svenska Folkkyrkan,* p. 43.
[6]Col. 3:5-17.

any longer live in it." The church's moral teaching must not be presented as "a new law" but be a development from and an amplification of the spiritual transformation worked by the grace of God. The new life creates its own forms of expression, for "it is God that worketh in you both to will and to do." The church insists that the new man should live in accordance with the nature of the new life, and for this reason it has to make clear what that nature is, but it cannot lay down rules and regulations for this life. Each Christian has his own "calling" given him by God, and he must himself find and determine what the will of God is for his life.

The church also provides a sphere in which the members live in fellowship, sharing the riches of God's grace and mutually serving one another. Luther made a great deal of this; he even spoke of the members' conversation and intercourse as a means of grace. In this fellowship the Christian lives and practices the Christian life created in him by grace.

C. *The Function of the Church in Regard to the World.*

a. Mission.

The church is both a creation of God's grace and an agency for the proclamation of this grace in the world. From the point of view of its nature as the redeemed people of God the church is identical with God's kingdom of grace where His will to save is being carried out. But from the point of view of function the church is the agency for the establishment of the kingdom. God has given to the church the Word and the sacraments for the extension of His kingdom into all the world.

The message of the church is the good news that "God was in Christ reconciling the world unto Himself." This message includes both judgment and grace, both law and gospel. In the proclamation of law the church declares that God is the Creator and Ruler of all the universe, and that His will is supreme. Man's great sin is that he fails to recognize God as God and give thanks to Him. He imagines that he can stand alone as the captain of his own fate. In thus severing himself from the ultimate ground of his being man has brought upon himself all the evils that are comprehended in Paul's phrase, "dead in trespasses and sins." The church declares that man in this state lives under the wrath of God and is subject to eternal condemnation. It proclaims the judgment of God on all sin, individual and social, without respect of person.

On the other hand, in the proclamation of the gospel the church bears witness by word and deed to the reality of God's saving grace in the creation of new life. It declares that God alone saves from sin, and that He is present in the Word to "call, gather, enlighten, and sanctify" His people. Through this proclamation of "the whole counsel of God" the church becomes, as Luther says, "the mother who bears every Christian through the Word of God which He (the Holy Spirit) reveals and preaches, and through which He illumines and enkindles hearts, that they understand and accept it, cling to it, and persevere in it."

b. The relation of the church to the state and society.

Since the relation of the church to state and society is discussed in two separate chapters in this book, it is not necessary to deal with these problems here. It is clear, however, that this relation, too, must be determined on the basis of the nature of the church as a creation of grace. The state is neither the servant nor the lord of the church; it is a servant to God to whom it is ultimately responsible. The church does not presume to legislate for the state, but it does insist on its freedom to proclaim both law and gospel, to proclaim the judgment of God upon all sin, individual and social, and to call upon all to recognize their dependence upon God. The church must maintain this witness even when the state adopts harsh and repressive measures against it.

c. The church and the churches.

Since the Lutheran doctrine declares that the church is found wherever God is active through Word and sacrament to seek and to save the lost, the church must be recognized wherever the gospel is preached even though this may not be done "in truth and purity." Differences in organization, polity, and rites do not form an impassible barrier to unity. It would seem to be natural and inevitable that historical, social, and geographical factors should create different forms of organization and life. The new life created by grace expresses itself in different ways as times and circumstances determine. These differences can become an obstacle to unity only by insisting that they belong to the essence of the church.

The deeper we can penetrate to the center of the gospel message of grace, the clearer we can apprehend the nature of the church. "For the true unity of the church it is enough to agree concerning the doctrine of the gospel and the administration of the sacraments. Nor is it necessary that human traditions, rites, and ceremonies, instituted by men, should everywhere be alike."[7] The sense in which the authors of the Augsburg Confession understood "the doctrine of the gospel" may be illustrated by a quotation from the Edinburgh Conference report: "Man's salvation and welfare have their source in God alone, who is moved to His gracious activity towards man not by any merit on man's part, but solely by His free, out-going love."[8] When the nature of the church as a creation of grace is clearly seen, and this is applied seriously and humbly to the whole life of the church, the elements which now divide the churches will lose their significance, and the true unity of the Body of Christ will be realized.

[7] Augsburg Confession, Article VII.   [8] E. R., Ch. II, par. 1.

Conclusion

An effort has been made in this paper to present the Lutheran doctrine of the church from the point of view of the New Testament message of grace and in accordance with the Lutheran emphasis on *Sola Gratia* and *Sola Fide*. The author may not have succeeded in these brief paragraphs in making this viewpoint clear and consistent. But he hopes that his intention is clear. If the grace of God is central, it means that the doctrine of the church and the church itself are to reflect clearly and unmistakably this grace of God. Everything in the church—its message, program, organization, government, and actions—must be judged in reference to this vital center. Anything in the church which limits and obscures the grace of God must be declared false and detrimental.

This conception is admittedly an ideal toward which we may strive but never hope fully to realize. In actual practice the ideal must be held in a tension with forces which tend to draw the church away from this vital center. The advocates of a "pure" church will stress the experience and the conduct of the members; those who think in terms of "orthodoxy" will emphasize pure doctrine; and those who want the church to be an aggressive agency for social reform in the world will place the emphasis on social programs and activities. These emphases are legitimate and necessary, but they are not the church's main concern. As long as the church maintains its hold on the vital center of grace, there is room within it for many different emphases and interests. The church is much more broad, liberal, inclusive, and tolerant than some of its most devoted members realize. It is as broad and inclusive as the redemptive activity of God and as tolerant as He who said: "He that is not against us is for us."

BIBLIOGRAPHY

Althaus, Paul, *Communio Sanctorum*, München: 1929.

Aulén, Gustaf, *Till belysning af den lutherska kyrkoiden*, Uppsala: 1912.

Billing, Einar, *Den svenska folkkyrkan*, Stockholm: 1930.

Brilioth, Yngve, *Svensk kyrkokunskap*, Stockholm: 1933.

Holl, Karl, *Gesammelte Aufsätze zur Kirchengeschichte*, I. Luther, Tübingen: 1932. *Die Entstehung von Luthers Kirchenbegriff. Luther und das landesherrliche Kirchenregiment.*

Kattenbusch, F., *Die Doppelschichtigkeit in Luthers Kirchenbegriff*, Gotha: 1928.

Köstlin, Julius, *The Theology of Luther*, Philadelphia: 1897., tr. by C. E. Hay.

Luther, Martin, Holman Edition, Philadelphia: 1915. "The Papacy at Rome," vol. I; "On the Councils and the Churches," vol. V.

Wahlstrom, Eric, "The New Testament Teaching on the Church," *Minutes of the Continuation Committee of Faith and Order*, 1939, pp. 55ff.; "The Kingdom of God and the Church," *Christendom*, vol. V., 1940, pp. 54ff.; "Conceptions of the Church," *J. of Theol. of the Am. Luth. Conference*, April, 1942, pp. 263ff.

THE MEANS OF GRACE

J. T. MUELLER

In Lutheran theology the doctrine of the means of grace occupies an important place, and rightly so, for without these means the redeeming grace of God through the substitutionary atonement made by Christ Jesus would be entirely unknown and therefore of no avail to sinful man.

Lutheranism acknowledges, above all, two fundamental acts of divine love performed in the interest of fallen man, helpless in the guilt and the condemnation of his sin: first, the merciful God has procured a full and free salvation for all men; and second, He bestows this salvation upon men freely, without cost or effort on their part. The latter He does through the means of grace, and this fact establishes the importance of these means in the *ordo salutis*.

Lutheranism neither overemphasizes nor underestimates the value and the function of the means of grace but accords to them the position which is rightfully theirs according to the clear revelation of Scripture. The purpose of this essay is to show what importance Scripture attaches to the doctrine that God works through means to convey His saving grace to men.

I. EVALUATION OF THE DOCTRINE

To many students of the history of doctrine the Lutheran teaching concerning the means of grace seems hopelessly complex; in reality, however, it is clear and simple. It rests upon the twofold Scriptural basis of God's objective justification and of His institution of the means of grace as vehicles of His forgiveness.

Clear understanding and unqualified acceptance of the *objective justification* are fundamental. Scripture reveals that God's grace is universal, that He has obtained perfect reconciliation for all men through Christ's vicarious atonement. St. Paul writes, "God was in Christ, reconciling the world unto Himself, not imputing their trespasses unto them,"[1] and again, "As by the offence of one, judgment came upon all men to condemnation, even so by the righteousness of one, the free gift came upon all men unto justification of life."[2] There is then, according to Scripture, a universal reconciliation. As Luther says, there is "in the heart of God" full and free forgiveness for all mankind.[3] His wedding feast of salvation is spread out and ready for all to take so that not a single sinner in this world need go hungry. There is pardon for all, grace for all, heaven for all. This is the gospel of universal grace.

The second basis on which the doctrine of the means of grace rests is Christ's expressed *institution* of the means of grace. According to Scripture, God has ordained that the forgiveness procured for all men should be offered and imparted to them through the gospel. Of the gospel as the divinely ordained means of grace St. Paul speaks immediately after he has described the glorious truth of God's objective justification as follows: "And hath committed unto us the Word of reconciliation [that is, the Word by which the reconciliation of Christ is presented and imparted to men]. Now then we are ambassadors for Christ, as though God did beseech you by us; we pray you in Christ's stead, be ye reconciled to God."[4] In accordance with this doctrine St. Paul calls the gospel "a power of God unto salvation."[5] God thus offers and imparts reconciliation to men through the gospel as His appointed means of grace. Since baptism is comprehended in God's command and connected with God's

---

[1] II Cor. 5:19.
[2] Rom. 5:18.
[3] Rom. 4:25.

[4] II Cor. 5:19, 20.
[5] Rom. 1:16.

Word, that is, His precious gospel promise of forgiveness,[6] it, too, is a means of grace as will be shown later. The same is true of the Holy Supper.[7] When our church teachers say that the means of grace are the Word and the sacraments, they (properly speaking) mean by the term "Word" the gospel or the "Word of reconciliation." The law, though it is also God's Word, is not properly a means of grace since it does not offer forgiveness of sins but only demands and condemns. St. Paul calls the law "the letter that killeth," "the ministration of death," "the ministration of condemnation."[8] The law is then the very opposite of a means of grace; it offers for sin, not forgiveness, but damnation.

The means of grace accordingly derive their essence and their efficacy from Christ's vicarious atonement and from His divine institution. The Augsburg Confession recognizes this when it declares: "The Sacraments and the Word are effectual by reason of the institution and commandment of Christ."[9] Prof. E. W. A. Koehler says well: "The means of grace presuppose that God is gracious and reconciled to all men for Christ's sake. A denial of universal justification is necessarily reflected in the doctrine of the means of grace. If God is not reconciled and has not forgiven all sins, there can be no means by which grace and forgiveness are offered."[10]

The means of grace as the divinely appointed vehicles of pardon possess a twofold power: an *offering* and an *operative* power. On the one hand they exhibit and offer the forgiveness of sins which Christ has earned for perishing mankind by His substitutionary suffering and death. This important fact is taught in Luke 24:37, where Christ declares that repentance and remission of sins should be

---

[6] Matt. 28:19f.; John 3:5; Tit. 3:5.
[7] Matt. 26:28.
[8] II Cor. 3:6-9.
[9] Augsburg Confession, Art. VIII; Concordia *Triglotta*, p. 47.
[10] E. W. A. Koehler, A *Summary of Christian Doctrine*, p. 172.

preached in His name among all nations. The Word of God should thus be preached for the salvation of men; the law for repentance,[11] the gospel for the remission of sins.[12] John the Baptist was "to give knowledge of salvation unto His people by the remission of their sins."[13] The apostles were to preach the gospel to every creature[14] that men might be saved. St. Paul makes the claim that through the gospel he begat the believing Corinthians.[15] The gospel, being the joyous message of God's free and plenary pardon in Christ Jesus, thus has a collative or offering power. It is not a dead but a living Word by which the Holy Spirit of His good pleasure offers the blessings of regeneration and sanctification to men.[16]

But the gospel has also an *operative* power. This effective power is nothing else than God's own power connected with and exerted through the gospel and the sacraments, by which these means of grace produce and sustain faith in men and thus actually bring about their regeneration and sanctification. In view of its effective power St. Paul declares that the Word of God "effectually worketh in you that believe."[17] So also, by virtue of its operative power, baptism is "for the remission of sins"[18] and "washes away sins,"[19] and the Lord's Supper conveys and seals to the communicant "remission of sins."[20] Prof. Joseph Stump says well: "The Word of God is not simply informing and directive, but it is a power. . . . It is God speaking to men, and therefore it possesses a supernatural power not possessed by any merely human word, however eloquent. It is 'quick and powerful,' searching out the innermost recesses of the soul.[21] It has a

---

[11]Rom. 3:20, "knowledge of sin."
[12]Acts 20:24, "gospel of the grace of God."
[13]Luke 1:77.
[14]Mark 16:15, 16.
[15]I Cor. 4:15.
[16]John 6:63.
[17]I Thess. 2:13.
[18]Acts 2:38.
[19]Acts 22:16.
[20]Matt. 16:18.
[21]Heb. 4:12.

power to convert, regenerate, and sanctify, which is utterly foreign to the mere words of men. . . . And because of this inseparable connection of the Holy Spirit with the Word, it is always efficacious; that is, it always possesses the power to accomplish the result at which the Holy Spirit aims."[22] In this connection Prof. A. G. Voigt calls attention to a very important fact. He says: "This truth that the Spirit speaks to man through the Word is distinctive of Lutheran doctrine; for outside of the Lutheran Church the action of the Spirit is conceived as only concurrent with the use of the Word, and sometimes not concurrent."[23]

The operative power of the means of grace, just as their offering power, however, must not be conceived as a sort of magical force; the means of grace are effective only because it has pleased God indissolubly to connect with them His own omnipotent power. In the spiritual realm the means of grace are means for restoring, nurturing, and sustaining the soul just as in the realm of nature secondary causes are used by God for restoring, nurturing, and sustaining the body. While the illustration is, perhaps, not altogether fitting since the realm of the earthly is not in every way identical with that of the heavenly, the governing principle in both is essentially the same. The gospel and the sacraments engender, strengthen, and preserve in us faith and spiritual life because the Holy Spirit graciously works effectually through these means of grace. But in no case is the effectiveness of the means of grace dependent on man's effort or worthiness. To regard the efficacy of the means of grace as dependent on the recipient's attitude or feeling means, as Luther says, to teach pagan and antichristian doctrine."[24] The righteousness by which we are saved is always "outside of us" and never "in

---

[22]Joseph Stump, *The Christian Faith*, p. 301.
[23]A. G. Voigt, *Biblical Dogmatics*, p. 202.
[24]Luther, St. Louis Edition, XIX, 943.

us" since it consists in Christ's perfect righteousness offered and imparted to us by God through the means of grace.

On the other hand, man's unbelief never renders the divine offer of forgiveness, exhibited in the means of grace, invalid. Man may reject God's pardon, but in Christ Jesus His gracious offer of forgiveness to every sinner stands forever. Salvation is thus always by grace, and man's damnation always through his own fault; for God's call to repentance is always serious, always meant to save sinners and always meant for all sinners.

The means of grace are the source and fountainhead of all spiritual blessings which the believer enjoys since they engender faith and through faith work regeneration, conversion, and sanctification.[25] The Christian thus owes to the means of grace his entire sanctification, or good works, his love toward God and the neighbor, membership in the Christian Church, the mystical union, preservation in faith, victory over the devil, the world, and the flesh.[26] In short, the Christian owes his entire state of grace and salvation to the power of the gospel, whether this be heard or read or applied by absolution, whether it be administered in baptism or the Lord's Supper, whether it be presented to him in the form of a symbol or in some other way. It is always the gospel, and only the gospel, that is God's power to salvation.[27]

To demonstrate this truth and make it a living, vital principle was, on its formal side, the outstanding accomplishment of the Lutheran Reformation. The Augsburg Confession condemns all "who think that the Holy Ghost comes to them without the external Word, through their own preparations and works."[28] In the Smalcald Articles Luther writes: "We must firmly hold that God grants His Spirit or grace to

---

[25] Rom. 10:17; Acts 16:14ff.
[26] John 17:17; 14:23; Heb. 4:12; Jas. 1:21; Luke 11:28.
[27] Rom. 1:16.
[28] A. C., Art. V; *Trigl.*, p. 45.

no one except through or with the preceding outward Word."[29] So also the Formula of Concord declares: "The Father will not do this [draw anyone to Himself] without means, but has ordained for this purpose His Word and Sacrament as ordinary means and instruments."[30] This Biblical thought, so deeply rooted in the Lutheran mind, explains why in their practice Lutheran pastors place so much stress upon Christian indoctrination. The Christian lives in and by the Word, and from it he draws all his spiritual nurture and strength.

In this connection the question has been asked in what manner the means of grace justify and save. Advocates of work-righteousness contend that the means of grace justify by the sanctification which they produce. But Lutheran theology, maintaining the *sola gratia*, teaches that the means of grace do not save by the renewal which they work but by working regeneration or conversion. The teaching of justification by way of sanctification is a pernicious error which Christians must avoid at all costs.[31] According to Scripture justification does not follow sanctification, but sanctification follows justification. In other words, by the faith which the Holy Ghost creates through the means of grace the sinner is regenerated, converted, justified.[32] So also the believing child of God is sanctified by the faith engendered and preserved by the Holy Ghost in his heart through the means of grace. It was by faith that the jailor at Philippi was justified and saved; but as a converted child of God he at once manifested true fruits of faith in his new, sanctified life.[33]

The sacraments have the same effect as the spoken or written Word because they are nothing else than the visible

---

[29]Smalcald Articles, Part III, Art. VIII, 3, *Trigl.*, p. 495.
[30]Formula of Concord, Art. XI, 76, *Trigl.*, p. 1087.
[31]Gal. 5:4.
[32]These terms denote the same act of removal from spiritual death to spiritual life.   [33]Acts 16:30ff.

Word or the gospel, proclaimed in sacred action in connection with visible signs. For this reason the sacraments offer, convey, and seal to the recipients forgiveness of sins, life, and salvation just as the gospel does when it is spoken or read.[34] It is not in agreement with Scripture to ascribe to baptism regeneration exclusively and to the Lord's Supper, as a special function, the implanting of the germ of the resurrection body. The gospel regenerates also when it is read or preached to men.[35] In short, the sacraments possess efficacy only because, by virtue of Christ's institution, the gospel is active in them through their external signs; and it is always the gospel that does the "great things."

Luther is fully in accord with Scripture when regarding baptism he says, "It is not the water indeed that does them, but the Word of God which is in and with the water"; and regarding the Lord's Supper, "In the Sacrament forgiveness of sins, life, and salvation are given us through these words." In the Smalcald Articles Luther explains more fully why "the gospel not merely in one way gives us counsel and aid against sin; for God," he says, "is superabundantly rich in His grace," so that He aids us first "through the spoken Word, by which the forgiveness of sins is preached in the whole world, which is the peculiar office of the gospel; secondly, through baptism; thirdly, through the holy Sacrament of the Altar; fourthly, through the power of the keys (absolution), and also through the mutual conversation and consolation of the brethren."[36] According to Luther the gospel, preached or read or applied in baptism, in the Lord's Supper, in absolution, and in special forms by Christian laymen, is always the saving agency so that in every case there is the same effect, so far as God is concerned, namely, the gracious offering and imparting of forgiveness of sins.

---

[34]Acts 2:38; Tit. 3:5; Matt. 26:28.   [35]I Pet. 1:23.
[36]S.A., Part III, Art. IV, *Trigl.*, p. 491.

There are only two sacraments since there are but two divinely ordained sacred actions in which God has attached to visible elements His gospel promise of forgiveness, life, and salvation. These are baptism and the Lord's Supper. The term "sacrament" is, of course, ecclesiastical and not Biblical so that from his point of view it was not unscriptural for Melanchthon to enumerate among the sacraments also absolution as the sacrament of repentance. Of the three sacraments he says: "These rites have God's command and the promise of grace, which is peculiar to the New Testament."[37] But Melanchthon's definition was confusing, and so neither Luther nor the Lutheran dogmaticians, nor even Melanchthon himself, held to the definition given in the Apology. Lutheranism has always taught that there are only two sacraments given to the church by the divine Master.

Against the Roman view of the *opus operatum* Lutheranism maintains that the sacraments do not profit without faith since the gospel promises of forgiveness are received only by faith, considered as personal trust in God's promises. "On the part of the receiving Christian the sacraments demand faith or trust in the saving promises, just as the gospel in general demands faith."[38] Prof. J. A. Singmaster writes: "The Lutheran professes to rest his faith on the divine promises, regardless of physical and philosophical objection. Perhaps those who have disputed his belief have betrayed him at times into an attempted explanation of what he holds to be inexplicable. Luther himself was immovable in his faith though he realized the price it cost him. He might have purchased union among Protestants by accepting a lower view, but he was bound by conscience to maintain his conviction."[39]

While, however, the sacraments do not profit without

---

[37] Apology to the Augsburg Confession, XIII (VII), *Trigl.*, p. 309.
[38] J. T. Mueller, *Faith of Our Fathers*, p. 98.
[39] J. A. Singmaster, *A Handbook of Christian Theology*, p. 282.

faith, faith must not be regarded as belonging to the essence of the sacraments. By this we mean that it is not our faith or anybody else's faith that makes baptism or Holy Communion a sacrament. The means of grace are grounded on Christ's free and universal atonement, the objective atonement, and they have their being in their divine institution. Baptism and the Lord's Supper are sacraments simply because Christ has instituted them as such. In connection with the institution of the sacraments Stump says, "It is a special mercy of God out of consideration for our human weakness, that He has instituted the sacraments in addition to His Word."[40] Since, then, the sacraments are entirely objective, that is, efficacious in themselves inasmuch as God ordained them to be effective means of grace by His divine institution, man cannot unmake a sacrament by his unbelief. The sacraments, as God's own signs and bearers of His gracious forgiveness, always stand even though man repudiates them by unbelief.

II.   HOLY BAPTISM AS A MEANS OF GRACE

Baptism is a true means of grace. This statement does not contradict the truth that in a strict sense the gospel is the only means of grace. Baptism is no more and no less than gospel preaching in a special form. Luther says that baptism is water comprehended in God's command and connected with God's Word. That is to say, on the one hand, that God has instituted or commanded baptism. In this sense baptism is a part of the divine law or of God's will telling us what we are to do. But baptism does not save as law; that is, it does not save by our act of obedience to the divine baptismal command. Baptism saves only because it is connected with God's Word, that is, with His gospel promise.[41] Baptism saves us as a "vehicle of grace."[42] This is the basic Lutheran

---

[40]Stump, *op. cit.*, p. 323.   [42]Singmaster, *op. cit.*, p. 268.
[41]Mark 16:16.

principle regarding baptism (as, of course, also regarding the Lord's Supper). Baptism is pure gospel just as is Holy Communion. That explains both its efficacy and its necessity. The necessity is, of course, not absolute but only relative; it is a necessity from the viewpoint of God's command and the sinner's need of forgiveness.

The Lutheran Church rejects the doctrine that baptism is a "mere Jewish ceremony" or a "mere church institution" since its divine institution is so clearly attested in Scripture.[43] In agreement with its divine institution the apostles constantly enjoined it for diligent, holy use.[44] The Christian Church has always accepted baptism as a divinely instituted sacrament and has confessed it as such in its creeds. The Nicene Creed, for example, voices the doctrine of the church when it says: "I acknowledge one baptism for the remission of sins." Dr. W. E. Schramm is right when he writes: "It is in obedience to this plain command that the Christian Church administers baptism."[45]

It is immaterial how the water is applied in baptism since the Greek word *baptizein* signifies not merely immersing but also washing, sprinkling, pouring, in fact, any application of water, and that not merely in Biblical but also in secular Greek.[46] The words of the *Didache:* "Pour water three times on the head," furnish sufficient testimony that the church even in ancient times administered baptism also by pouring water upon the head of the person baptized. If it is said in objection to this mode of applying the water that baptism has the significance or the symbolical meaning of drowning the Old Man, for which reason immersion should be used, Lutheranism readily admits this meaning. Luther says of

[43]Matt. 28:19, 20.
[44]Acts 2:38; 10:48; 8:38; Rom. 6:3ff.; Gal. 3:27.
[45]W. E. Schramm, *What Lutherans Believe*, p. 135.
[46]Mark 7:3f.; Eph. 5:26; Matt. 3:11; Acts 2:17; Heb. 9:10 compared with Num. 19:13, 19.

baptism: "It signifies that the Old Adam in us should, by daily contrition and repentance, be drowned and die with all sins and evil lusts and, again, a new man daily come forth and arise, who shall live before God in righteousness and purity forever."[47] This significance is, indeed, of the greatest importance, and the Christian believer should heed and live his baptism every day of his life. But baptism symbolizes not only immersion but also the washing away of sins and the outpouring of the Holy Ghost. For this reason it is going beyond Scripture to insist upon one mode of applying the water as the only valid one.

The phrase "to baptize into the name of Christ"[48] means the same as "to baptize into the name of the triune God."[49] Scripture passages that speak of baptizing in the name of Christ do not contradict the Trinitarian formula. Prof. H. E. Jacobs correctly interprets the phrase "in the name" thus: "It is baptism into the One Name, which all three share," and he rightly explains the phrase "into the name of Christ" or "into Christ" as: "This means, through baptism to enter into life-communion with all that Jesus is and has done and to surrender oneself, with implicit faith and obedience, to the revelation of God that has been made in and through Jesus Christ, as the Israelites were 'baptized into Moses.' "[50, 51]

Of paramount importance is the question as to the benefit of baptism. Some claim that Luther goes too far when in his Small Catechism he writes of this sacrament: "It works forgiveness of sins, delivers from death and the devil, and gives eternal salvation to all who believe this, as the words and promises of God declare." But this doctrine rests upon clear and sure Scripture proof. If, for example, Scripture tells us that persons are baptized "for the remission of sins," or that "baptism washes away sins," or that a man is "born of water

---

[47]Cf., Rom. 6:3, 4.   [48]Acts 10:48.
[49]Matt. 28:19.   [50]I Cor. 10:2.
[51]H. E. Jacobs, A *Summary of the Christian Faith*, p. 327.

and of the Spirit," or that in baptism "we put on Christ," or
that we are "baptized into one body," or that we are "buried
with Him by baptism into death," or that "baptism saves us,"
and the like,[52] it is obvious that the Bible itself teaches that
baptism works the great blessings which Luther ascribes to
it. Again, when Scripture says that baptism is "the washing
of regeneration and renewing of the Holy Ghost,"[53] or that
Christ "sanctifies and cleanses His church with the washing
of water by the Word,"[54] it is clear that the Christian believer owes his entire state of grace and salvation to holy
baptism. Through baptism a person is regenerated, sanctified, implanted into the body of Christ, preserved in faith,
and finally saved. Stump puts it thus: "The purpose of
baptism, as of the Word, is to offer to men and to bestow
upon the believer the benefits of Christ's redemption. It is a
baptism into Christ's death[55] and thus into a participation in
all benefits acquired by that death. It is a covenant relation
into which God enters with the baptized person, and in
which God assures the baptized person that all the blessings
of redemption have been acquired for him and actually
belong to him if he accepts them by faith."[56] This is, of
course, not said exclusively of the gospel but inclusively, for
a person is regenerated and sanctified in baptism through
the gospel, the living Word of God, connected with this
sacred act. The efficacy of baptism, therefore, does not lie in
any physical potency or quality of the water but in its gospel
promise of grace and pardon. Luther writes: "Baptism is
efficacious for the forgiveness of sins and for regeneration
because it has pleased God to convey His forgiveness to us
not only in the audible but also in the visible Word."[57]

---

[52]Acts 2:38; 22:16; John 3:5; Gal. 3:27; I Cor. 12:13; Rom. 6:3,
4; I Pet. 3:21.
[53]Tit. 3:5.
[54]Eph. 5:26.
[55]Rom. 6:3.
[56]Stump, *op. cit.*, p. 336f.
[57]Luther, St. L., XVI, 2292f.

Whatever benefits baptism offers and conveys it offers and conveys through the gospel of which it is only a visible form.

In baptism God establishes a covenant of grace with the baptized person, which endures forever.[58] Luther emphasizes this truth in his simple but striking way when he writes, "Though we are baptized but once, nevertheless, baptism endures forever."[59] But while baptism is to be administered no more than once it should be used by the Christian throughout his life for daily repentance, the assurance of God's grace, and sanctification.[60] In his daily life the believer constantly appropriates the forgiveness of sins and the power to lead a holy life granted to him in baptism. When he falls into sin he penitently returns to baptism, laying hold of the forgiveness that is sealed to him in the baptismal covenant. Confirmation is not a supplement to baptism, but its purpose is to instruct the catechumen concerning the meaning of baptism and to impress upon him its full glory.

Infant baptism is fully in accord with Holy Scripture. In the first place, children are included in Christ's command to baptize all nations.[61] Again, since baptism has taken the place of circumcision,[62] it is wrong to exclude children from this divine ordinance of grace. Then, too, children are in need of baptism because they are flesh born of flesh.[63] Moreover, Scripture tells us of entire families that were baptized, and these certainly included children.[64] All these and other arguments have been used by Lutheran theologians in defense of infant baptism. Schramm writes: "In

---

[58] I Pet. 3:21; Isa. 54:10.
[59] Luther, *op. cit.,* IX, 1508.
[60] I Cor. 6:11; 12:13; Gal. 3:26, 27; Rom. 6:3, 4; Eph. 4:5; Col. 2:11, 12; Tit. 3:5, 6.
[61] Matt. 28:19.
[62] Col. 2:11, 12.
[63] John 3:6, and baptism is the divinely prescribed means of regeneration. Tit. 1:3-5.
[64] I Cor. 1:17; Acts 16:15, 33.

holy baptism we may bring our children to Jesus. We lay them in His arms, and they receive His blessing. We know of no way, other than baptism, by which infants may be brought to Jesus and laid in the arms of His grace."[65] Dr. Mellenbruch sums up the whole argument when he says, "The plan of salvation includes them."[66]

III. THE LORD'S SUPPER AS A MEANS OF GRACE

The doctrine of the Lord's Supper has been much in controversy, yet the dogma, as it is presented by the Lutheran Church, is not at all complex. The Formula of Concord summarizes the doctrine in the following words: "We maintain and believe, according to the simple words of the testament of Christ, the true, yet supernatural eating of the body of Christ, as also the drinking of His blood, which human senses and reason do not comprehend, but as in all other articles of faith our reason is brought into captivity to the obedience of Christ, and this mystery is not apprehended otherwise than by faith alone, and revealed in the Word alone."[67] Ultimately that is all that can be said of the essence of this mysterious, yet comforting, sacrament. In his Small Catechism Luther positively sets forth all that is necessary for Christians to know about this sacrament for its salutary use.

The names of the sacrament are taken partly from Scripture, from which have been derived such expressions as "The Lord's Supper,"[68] "The Lord's Table,"[69] "The Breaking of Bread,"[70] and others, and partly from church usage as, for example, "The Sacrament of the Altar." The name Mass is not widely used in the Lutheran Church today since the term now designates the Roman Catholic interpretation

---

[65]Schramm, *op. cit.*, p. 141.
[66]Mellenbruch, *The Doctrines of Christianity*, p. 157.
[67]F.C., VII, 42, *Trigl.*, p. 817.   [69]I Cor. 10:21.
[68]I Cor. 11:20.   [70]Acts 2:42.

of the Lord's Supper, and Christians therefore might be confused by this term.

As holy baptism, so also Holy Communion is divinely instituted as a sacrament to be in force throughout the New Testament.[71] The divine institution of the sacrament has been denied on various grounds, but it is fully attested by the historical Christian Church ever since the days of the apostles.[72] *The New Schaff-Herzog Encyclopedia of Religious Knowledge* states that "the real ground for the denial of the institution as an ordinance for the church lies elsewhere than in the discrepancy of the accounts," and then proceeds to show that after all none is valid since all are based on extrascriptural considerations.[73] Stump is right when he says, "The Lord's Supper was instituted by Christ on the night in which He was betrayed, while He sat with His disciples in the upper room after eating the Passover with them."[74] That is the claim of Scripture and the belief of the Christian Church.

For all practical purposes the simple definition of the Holy Supper, given by Luther in his Small Catechism, suffices since it answers every question regarding the essence of this sacrament. More complete and satisfactory from a scientific point of view is Leonhard Hutter's definition: "The Lord's Supper is a sacrament of the New Testament, instituted by Christ, in which the true body and blood of our Lord Jesus Christ, in and under the bread and wine, are truly distributed to all who eat and drink, and the promise of grace (forgiveness) is applied and sealed to every believer."[75]

---

[71]Matt. 26:26ff.; Luke 20:19; Acts 2:42; I Cor. 11:25ff.
[72]I Cor. 10:16; 11:20ff.
[73]Vol. VII, 2, p. 25.
[74]Stump, *op. cit.*, p. 347.
[75]Leonhard Hutter, *Loci Theologici*, 230; tr. by Drs. Hay and Jacobs, *Doctrinal Theology of the Ev. Luth. Church*, p. 560.

The Lord's Supper has been called the "sacrament of confirmation" in contradistinction to baptism, which has been called the "sacrament of initiation." Rightly understood, this distinction is permissible, for through baptism infants are received into the covenant of God whereas through the Lord's Supper Christian adults are confirmed in it. But the same gospel which renders baptism efficacious renders also the Holy Supper efficacious, and the same forgiveness which is offered in baptism is offered also in Holy Communion. The distinction is made from the viewpoint of the recipient and not from that of the efficacy or the purpose of the two sacraments. Neither baptism nor the Holy Supper should be regarded as unnecessary in the case of the adult believer, but both should be used according to Christ's institution because through both these means of grace the Holy Spirit engenders or strengthens faith and sanctifies the believer.[76]

Lutheranism teaches the real presence of Christ's true body and blood in the Lord's Supper, and does this in opposition to both Roman Catholic transubstantiation and Reformed symbolism. Its polemics against Romanism may be summed up as follows: In the Holy Supper the bread remains bread and the wine, wine,[77] but with the consecrated bread and wine the communicant receives Christ's body and blood; the consecrated bread is to be eaten and not adored;[78] the sacrament is to be administered *sub utraque specie*, all communicants receiving both the bread and the wine;[79] the sacrament does not work *ex opere operato*, but its blessings are received by faith. Lutheranism very emphatically rejects the charge of consubstantiation or the commixture of the substances, for although there is a sacra-

---

[76]Rom. 10:17; I Pet. 1:23; Acts 2:38; Matt. 26:28.
[77]I Cor. 10:16.
[78]Matt. 26:26.   [79]Matt. 26:27; I Cor. 11:28.

mental union between the bread and the body and between the wine and the blood, the substance of Christ's body and blood remains unmixed.[80]

Most of the Reformed churches see in the Holy Supper only a memorial meal in which the believer establishes contact with the absent body of Christ, enthroned in heaven at the right hand of God the Father, merely by faith or spiritual eating. No matter where in the words of institution they find the figure of speech, their interpretation always amounts to this, that in the Holy Supper the earthly elements represent the body and blood of Christ, who is to be received spiritually or by faith. In his masterly treatment of the doctrine in the *Conservative Reformation and its Theology*, Dr. C. P. Krauth has once for all demonstrated that such symbolism does not do justice to the words of institution, and that the Lutheran doctrine has the clear and explicit Scripture proof on its side.[81] The teaching of Paul in I Cor. 10 and 11 cannot be understood as symbolical representation. Unmistakably these passages teach the sacramental union between the bread and the body and the wine and the blood and so confirm the simple meaning of the words of institution: "Take, eat; this is My body. Drink ye all of it; for this is My blood of the new testament, which is shed for many for the remission of sins."[82] Lutheranism certainly does not try to render intelligible to reason the mystery of the real presence, but it does desire to do justice to Christ's words. Even the phrase "in, with, and under" is not used to explain the mode of Christ's presence in the sacrament, but its purpose is to reject transubstantiation and to assert the real presence, which rests upon Christ's absolute promise. If the objection is raised that by His ascension Christ has removed

[80]H. Schmid, *Doctrinal Theology*, p. 571.
[81]C. P. Krauth, *The Conservative Reformation and Its Theology*, p. 585ff.   [82]Matt. 26:26-28.

the presence of His body from this earth, He Himself assures us definitely of His continued gracious presence as the God-man.[83] In addition, Scripture declares that after His session Christ fills all things according to His human nature.[84] This is, of course, to be understood, not after the manner of a "local ubiquity" or a physical, local presence, but after that of a "supernatural ubiquity" or Christ's divine, incomprehensible omnipresence.

The heavenly elements in Holy Communion consist in the body and blood of Christ as the words of institution declare. These must not be replaced by substitutes such as "the whole Christ" or "the person of Christ" or "the merits of Christ," and the like. The whole Christ with all His merits is indeed present in the sacrament and is received by faith or the spiritual eating. But what, according to the clear words of Scripture, the communicant receives by the sacramental eating is Christ's body and blood.

The earthly elements in the Lord's Supper are, of course, bread and wine, for which, too, no substitutes should be used. The earthly elements should be consecrated,[85] distributed, and received by the communicants in order that there may be a true communion. Consecration merely for adoration is unscriptural since "nothing has the nature of a sacrament outside the use instituted by Christ."

The purpose of the Lord's Supper is the same as is the application of the gospel in every other form as, for example, in public preaching, absolution, and baptism. Accordingly our church teachers have called Holy Communion a means of justification or remission of sins. The proof for this purpose they find in the words of Christ: "Shed for you, for the remission of sins," which are an actual offer and seal of God's gracious pardon. Stump says rightly: "As each com-

---

[83]Matt. 19:20.   [85]I Cor. 10:16.
[84]Eph. 1:22; 4:10.

municant individually receives the bread and along with it the body of Christ, and as each communicant individually receives the wine and along with it the blood of Christ, so to each communicant individually is spoken the comforting assurance that the body of Christ was given for him and the blood was shed for him for the remission of sins."[86]

The words, "This do in remembrance of Me," do not mean merely that the communicant is to remember the absent Christ who atoned for his sins, but they invite the communicant to accept the gracious forgiveness offered in the Holy Supper. So the Apology explains the words when it says, " 'In remembrance of Christ' means to 'remember Christ and receive Him by faith.' "[87]

The precious gospel promise in the Holy Supper, moreover, strengthens the faith of the communicant, promotes his sanctification, increases his love toward God and the neighbor, gives him patience in tribulation, confirms his hope of eternal life, and deepens his union with Christ and His mystical body, the church.[88] Lastly, the Holy Supper serves also a confessional purpose.[89]

All these blessings are received by the communicant through faith in the gospel promise of forgiveness sealed to him in the sacrament so that faith in the promise of Christ or the spiritual eating is indeed required of the communicant to obtain the benedictions of the sacrament. Luther says: "He is truly worthy and well prepared who has faith in these words: 'Given and shed for you, for the remission of sins.' " In view of its lofty purpose everyone who neglects the Holy Supper trifles with God's grace and puts himself in danger of ultimately losing his faith and his salvation.

---

[86]Stump, *op. cit.*, p. 358.
[87]Apology, Art. XXIV, 72, *Trigl.*, p. 409.
[88]I Cor. 10:17; Eph. 3:16; I Cor. 11:28.
[89]I Cor. 10:20, 21; 10:17; 11:26; Acts 2:42.

The salutary purpose of the Holy Supper urges and encourages Christians to administer Holy Communion only to penitent believers who are able to examine themselves.[90] Worthy reception of Holy Communion requires both adequate knowledge of the sacrament and sincere faith in its promises. Let it be remembered also that sacramental worthiness demands not only faith in Christ in general but above all faith in the gospel promise of the sacrament, faith in the words, "Given and shed for you." Hence the qualification of the Augsburg Confession: "None are admitted, except they first be examined."[91] There is a reason for this; for in the Lord's Supper the promise of forgiveness is not only individualized, but it is sealed by the special pledge of Christ's body and blood, and this the communicant must know and believe.

In spite of its high purpose the Lord's Supper should not be overemphasized in a Romanizing manner as if divine grace were offered us merely or chiefly through the sacraments. The Apology is indeed Scriptural when it writes, "Of all acts of worship that is the greatest, most holy, most necessary, and highest, to preach the Word."[92] Dr. C. F. W. Walther stresses this thought when he says, "Preaching is the most important function assigned to the minister."[93]

But neither should the sacrament be neglected; and not only the pastor but also the congregation is responsible that the Lord's Supper is held in that high honor which it deserves as Christ's last testament to His church. Communion attendance is the thermometer showing a church's spiritual ardency or indifference, its consecration to or repudiation of Christ's saving gospel.

---

[90] I Cor. 10:17; 11:28f.
[91] A.C., Art. XXIV, 6, *Trigl.*, p. 65.
[92] Apology, Art. XV, 42, *Trigl.*, p. 327.
[93] C. F. W. Walther, *The Proper Distinction between Law and Gospel*, p. 247.

It goes without saying that Christians who are weak in faith should be encouraged to receive the Holy Supper frequently since it is the very means by which their faith is strengthened. Just at this point the proper distinction and application of the law and the gospel on the part of the pastor is most vital. To the weak Christian Luther says: "Do not flee from the sacrament, but seek help in it that your faith may be confirmed and strengthened. Your desire for the sacrament will be the stronger, the more frequently you use it."[94] Of special importance in this connection is also the confessional element involved in attending Holy Communion,[95] and Dr. Schramm's words deserve careful consideration: "Because partaking of the Lord's Supper affords us an opportunity to witness for Him, this is an additional reason for communing regularly and frequently."[96]

It is well for all Lutherans to heed Dr. Stump's closing words in his presentation of the doctrine of Holy Communion in *The Christian Faith*. He writes: "The early church administered the Communion on every Lord's Day. . . . Where the spiritual state is what it ought to be, the Christian will be glad to come to the Lord's Supper whenever it is administered, in order that he may have the comfort which it brings with its individual promise of grace and forgiveness to him."[97]

---

[94] Luther, St. L., XI, 654.
[95] I Cor. 11:26.
[96] Schramm, *op. cit.*, p. 152.
[97] Stump, *op. cit.*, p. 358.

BIBLIOGRAPHY

Althaus, P., *Die Heilsbedeutung der Taufe im Neuen Testament*. Guetersloh: 1897.

Engelder, Theo., *Popular Symbolics*. Concordia Publishing House, St. Louis, Mo.: 1934. Cf. articles on "Means of Grace," "Baptism," and "Lord's Supper," in the various sections of the book.

Fritz, J. H. C., *Pastoral Theology*. 1st ed. Concordia Publishing House, St. Louis, Mo.: 1932. "The Sacrament of Baptism," pp. 113ff.; "The Sacrament of the Altar," pp. 129-154.

Elert, W., *Morphologie des Luthertums*, I. Muenchen: C. H. Beckssche Verlag, 1931, pp. 255ff.

Gerhard, J., *Loci Theologici*. Gustav Schlawitz: Berlin, 1866. Vols. IV-VI, "De Sacramentis," pp. 137ff.

Harless und Harnack, *Die Kirchlich-religioese Bedeutung der reinen Lehre von den Gnadenmitteln*. Erlangen: 1869.

Herzog-Hauck, Jackson, S. M., editor. *The New Schaff-Herzog Encyclopedia of Religious Knowledge.* Funk and Wagnalls Co., I, pp. 435ff.; "Lord's Supper," Vol. VII, pp. 24ff.

Hoenecke, A., *Ev.-Luth. Dogmatik*. Northwestern Publishing House, Milwaukee, Wis.: 1909. Vol. IV. "Die Mittel zur Aneignung des Heils," pp. 1-146.

Jacobs, H. E., *A Summary of the Christian Faith*. General Council Publication House, Philadelphia, Pa.: 1919. "The Word as the Means of Grace." pp. 265ff. (Including the sacraments.)

Koehler, E. W. A., *A Summary of Christian Doctrine*. Koehler Publishing Co., River Forest, Ill.: 1939. Part VIII. "Salvation through the Means of Grace." pp. 172ff.

Krauth, C. P., *The Conservative Reformation and Its Theology*. General Council Publication Board, Philadelphia, Pa.: 1871. "Baptism, Lord's Supper." pp. 518ff.

Luther, M., "Wider die himmlischen Propheten von den Bildern und Sacrament." (St. L. Ed.), Concordia Publishing House, St. Louis, Mo.: 1890. XX, pp. 133ff. "Dass diese Worte Christi: 'Das ist mein Leib' usw. noch fest stehen wider die Schwaermgeister." XX, pp. 762ff.

Luther, M., "D. Martin Luthers Bekenntnis vom Abendmahl Christi." St. L. Ed. XX, 894ff.

Luther, M., "D. Martin Luthers kurzes Bekenntnis vom heiligen Sacrament wider die Schwaermer." St. L. Ed. XX, 1765ff.

Mellenbruch, P. L., *The Doctrines of Christianity*. Fleming H. Revell Co., New York, N. Y.: 1931. pp. 150ff.

Mueller, J. T., *Christian Dogmatics*. Concordia Publishing House, St. Louis, Mo.: 1934. "The Doctrine of the Means of Grace." pp. 441ff.

Mueller, J. T., *Faith of Our Fathers*. Wm. B. Eerdmans Publishing Co., Grand Rapids, Mich.: 1939. pp. 89ff.

Pieper, F., *Christliche Dogmatik*. Concordia Publishing House, St. Louis, Mo.: 1920. Vol. II. "Die Gnadenmittel," pp. 121-458.

Schmid, H., *The Doctrinal Theology of the Ev. Luth. Church*. Tr. by C. A. Hay and H. E. Jacobs. Northern Publication Society, Philadelphia, Pa.: 1875 (1889-1899), pp. 500ff.

Schramm, W. E., *What Lutherans Believe*. Lutheran Book Concern, Columbus, Ohio: pp. 134ff.

Seeberg, R., *Lehrbuch der Dogmengeschichte*. A Deichertsche Verlagsbuchhandlung, Leipzig: 1933. Vol. IV, 1, "Die Lehre Luthers." pp. 377ff.

Singmaster, J. A., *A Handbook of Christian Theology*. The United Lutheran Publication House, Philadelphia, Pa.: 1927. pp. 262ff.

Sommerlath, E., *Der Sinn des Abendmahls*. Doerffling & Francke Verlag, Leipzig: 1930. "Nach Luthers Gedanken ueber das Abendmahl," 1527-1529.

Stange, C., *Studien zur Theologie Luthers*. I, 1928. pp. 345ff.

Stump, Jos., *The Christian Faith*. The Macmillan Co., New York, N.Y.: 1920. "The Means of Grace," pp. 289ff.

Voigt, A. G., *Biblical Dogmatics*. Lutheran Board of Publication, Columbia, S. C.: 1917, pp. 199ff.

Walther, C. F. W., *The Proper Distinction between Law and Gospel*. Tr. by W. H. T. Dau. Concordia Publishing House, St. Louis, Mo.: 1929.

Walther, W., *Lehrbuch der Symbolik*. A. Deichertsche Verlagsbuchhandlung, Erlangen: 1924. Articles on "Gnadenmittel" in the sections on the four representative churches.

PERIODICALS

Creager, Harold L., "The Lord's Supper, Then and Now," *The Lutheran Church Quarterly*, Vol. XVIII, No. 2, April, 1945, pp. 196ff.

Rasmussen, Carl C., "The Lutheran Doctrine of Baptism," *The Lutheran Church Quarterly*, Vol. XVIII, No. 2, April, 1945, pp. 131-150.

Religion in Geschichte und Gegenwart. Cf. Articles on "Means of Grace," "Baptism," "Lord's Supper."

THE MINISTRY

T. F. GULLIXSON

I. GENERAL CONSIDERATIONS

Concerning the holy ministry a body of doctrine is taught with remarkable unanimity by the Lutheran churches of the world whether they are national churches under partial control of the state or free churches unfolding their polity in liberty quite on their own initiative. That body of doctrine was reborn in the storm of stress arising when the ecclesiastical despotisms engendered through the centuries in a wrong overemphasis were confronted by the evangelist with his finger on the open Bible saying, "It is written." "Thus saith the Lord."

The great errors in Christian teaching are usually one side of given truths overstressed, overemphasized until they have been pushed across the line from truth.

The ministry is of God.

The ministry of the Word is the Lord's gift to the church.

Those who are called of the churches to preach the Word and administer the sacraments are to be heard and heeded inasmuch as they are truly heralds of the Lord.

This is truth. What one side of this truth has become after centuries of human emphasis in mixture of noble purpose and ambition for power is set out in the canons of the Council of Trent thus:

"If anyone saith that in the Catholic Church there is not a hierarchy by divine ordination instituted, consisting of bishops, priests, and ministers: let him be anathema.

"If anyone saith, that by sacred ordination . . . a character is not imprinted by that ordination; or, that he who

(289)

has once been a priest can again become a layman: let him
be anathema."[1]

Pushed on to farther extremes you have the canons on
Apostolic Succession and the Papal Decree of Infallibility.

The consequences of this overemphasis are revealed in
many ways, in church architecture, church polity, in history.

So far-reaching are the consequences of right and wrong
attitude here that it has been well said: "The various
theories of the Christian ministry are the key to the entire
history of Christendom."[2]

Freedom of speech for the Word of God brought rebirth
for the Biblical doctrine of the ministry. Its truth, speaking
from the open pages written by Evangelists and Apostles
without benefit of tradition or of priest, will keep such concept of ministry in spiritual things alive and healthy.

A. *The Ministry Is of Our Lord Jesus Christ.*

He it was who said to His first ministers, "I will make you
fishers of men," and kept His word. He sent His twelve disciples. He appointed other seventy also and sent them two
by two. He trained His loyal band and promised them the
Comforter, "He shall teach you all things, and bring all things
to your remembrance, whatsoever I have said unto you."[3]

He came, though doors were locked, to them on Easter
Eve, "to the eleven gathered together and them that were
with them."[4] "Then were the disciples glad when they saw
the Lord. Then said Jesus unto them again, Peace be unto
you: as My Father hath sent Me, even so send I you."[5]

To the Eleven as they sat at meat, to the Eleven on the
hilltop, came the command, "Go ye into all the world and
preach."[6] "Go ye and make disciples of all the nations, bap-

---

[1]Creeds of Christendom, Vol. II, pp. 191-192.
[2]W. B. Pope, quoted by Kern.
[3]John 14:26.   [5]John 20:21, 22.
[4]Luke 24:33.   [6]Mark 16:15.

tizing them in the name of the Father and of the Son and of the Holy Ghost; teaching them to observe all things whatsoever I have commanded you, and lo I am with you alway, even unto the end of the world."[7]

He acknowledged their ministries: "They went forth and preached everywhere, the Lord working with them, and confirming the word with signs following."[8]

Though ascended and glorified, He was still the giver of ministries and of ministers. Let Paul tell it: "And I said, Who art Thou, Lord? And He said, I am Jesus whom thou persecutest. But rise, and stand upon thy feet: for I have appeared unto thee for this purpose, to make thee a minister and a witness both of these things which thou hast seen, and of those things in the which I will appear unto thee."[9]

Our Lord, whose own prophetic ministry is carried on by His servants, does not overlook the congregation as a mediating agency in the furtherance of His purpose: "Now there were in the church that was at Antioch, certain prophets and teachers; as Barnabas, and Simeon that was called Niger, and Lucius of Cyrene and Manæn, which had been brought up with Herod the tetrarch, and Saul. As they ministered to the Lord, and fasted, the Holy Ghost said, Separate me Barnabas and Saul for the work whereunto I have called them."[10]

At the conclusion of this first missionary journey we read: "And thence sailed to Antioch, from whence they had been recommended to the grace of God for the work which they fulfilled. And when they were come, and had gathered the church together, they rehearsed all that God had done with them, and how He had opened the door of faith unto the Gentiles. And there they abode long time with the disciples."[11]

[7]Matt. 28:19, 20.
[8]Mark 16:20.
[9]Acts 26:15, 16.
[10]Acts 13:1, 2.
[11]Acts 14:26-28.

The needs of the churches beyond the apostolic generation were met, are still being met. "And He gave some, apostles; and some prophets; and some evangelists; and some pastors and teachers; for the perfecting of the saints, for the work of the ministry, for the edifying of the body of Christ."[12]

"And all things are of God, who hath reconciled us to Himself by Jesus Christ, and hath given to us the ministry of reconciliation; to wit, that God was in Christ, reconciling the world unto Himself, not imputing their trespasses unto them; and hath committed unto us the ministry of reconciliation."[13]

B. *This Heaven-given Ministry, God's Gift to the Churches, Is in Each Congregation a Double Gift.*

Drawn together in faith and in a purpose to further hear and proclaim God's truth, there is established in the midst of this fellowship of believers the throne of grace, the mercy seat, which is there through the proper use of Word and sacrament. This prerogative, the "ministry of reconciliation," is a privilege which rests upon such an assembly so long as it is a real fellowship of believers and merits the name Christian congregation. It is a solemnly earnest matter to call into being a Christian congregation. It is a still more serious business to let a congregation die.

That churches may be called into being and may live the Spirit with the grace of God has gone on before to touch with the finger of divine purpose some Christian brother to "speak to him with a mighty hand" that he may turn and say, "Here am I, send me." Such a one, nurtured, trained, tested, and found to be suited to the exacting assignments of the ministry, is given to the congregation in response to its call.

The minister, as he faces his holy dispensation task, can

---

[12]Eph. 4:11, 12.　　　　　　　　[13]II Cor. 5:18, 19.

truly say, "To me is this grace given to preach here." The congregation can say, "The Lord has sent us a servant to serve Him here."

C. *This Ministry Has Continuity.*

The living succession within the Apostolic Church runs on through succeeding generations of spiritual priests and priestesses in the fellowship of believers founded on the apostolic Word.

Nor is that fellowship chopped up into isolated segments called local congregations. Each properly constituted church is a complete unit of a complete whole after the similitude of the complete presence of Christ at the right hand of glory and His complete presence in my Communion service and in ten thousand other Communion services of the same day and hour and moment.

The ministry roots in the living stream of apostolic faith taught, believed, lived. The responsibility for maintaining this gift, the ministry of Word and sacrament, ends only if the local community of spiritual life has ended.

The ministry has continuity for the man of God to whom it is given.

There is, indeed, no statement of Scripture to support the "character indelible" alleged to be conferred by ordination as little as there is aught in Scripture or in life's experience to support a similar claim for the rite of confirmation.

While it is, indeed, the call of a congregation which establishes the ministry of a man of God, it does not necessarily follow that he ceases to be a minister if for some right reason an interval of time elapses between that ministry in one congregation and the ministry in another. Nor does it follow, when ripeness of years has brought resignation, that his status or his responsibilities as a clergyman are gone from him.

Truly, his ministry properly relates to a single local parish.

It also relates, by virtue of the hidden unity indicated above, to the whole fellowship of believers, particularly to that co-operative union of congregations called a synod through which matters pertaining to the training, the testing, the calling and ordination of pastors are normally implemented.

What may one say of his ordination who is years away from active parish ministry?

"God gave me this grace to be called into the ministry."

"I am held to the end of life by my ordination promises."

"Though others have entered into the labors of the parish which called me, I will hold myself, and be held of others, to be a man of God and keeper of the continuity of my life's witness 'till life's last breath."

D. *The Ministry of Word and Sacrament Has Unity and Equality.*

Tradition and ecclesiastical canons have much to say about gradations in spiritual authority; but the lips of Jesus spoke thus: "But be not ye called Rabbi: for one is your Master, even Christ, and all ye are brethren. . . . Neither be ye called masters; for one is your master even Christ."[14]

In exalting certain types of church polity endeavors are put forth to fix special meanings for the words *episkopos, presbyteros, diakonos;* but the Spirit in the Word moves freely, still unbound by concepts of polity makers.[15]

---

[14]Matt. 23:8, 10.

[15]We are indebted here to Vinet's *Pastoral Theology* where in the introduction appears a brief study of the New Testament names for the ministry: pp. 29-30: "*Bishop* appears to be the synonym of *Elder* in Titus 1:5 and 7: 'That thou shouldest ordain *Elders* . . . now a *Bishop* must be without blame'; and in Acts 20:17 and 28: Paul calls the *Elders* of Ephesus and commends to them the flock over which the Holy Ghost has made them *Bishops*. See also Phil. 1:1; I Tim. 3:2. This does not forbid that there should be bishops over other bishops, inspectors of inspectors. . . . But this does not suppose an institution, it was only an expedient."

E. *The Christian Ministry Is an*
   Office of Service not of Lordship.

This is at the outset indicated by the word *diakonos*
which predominates among New Testament words for the
office. The Master's declaration, "He that heareth you heareth Me"[16] is still in effect, and our confession, too, has its
article on Ecclesiastical Power as has our Catechism its part
on the Office of the Keys.

Great is the minister's share of the duty "to try the spirits
whether they are of God,"[17] but the task is not his alone.

"According to divine right the function of passing judgment on doctrine belongs indeed to the ministry of preaching. However, also the laymen have this right, and for this
reason they also have a seat and vote with the preachers
in church courts and counsels."[18]

The pastor is at the very forefront, facing responsibility
in guarding the sanctity of the altar; but it is not an exclusive
responsibility, nor does the required authority finally apper-
tain to him.[19]

Bishop Skagestad speaks for the Church of Norway thus:
"The power of the keys therefore, as concerns forgiveness
and retention of sins, is exclusively a function of the primary
assignment of the office: the proclamation of the gospel, and
not a formal authority granted in a statutory manner to the
minister to loose and bind sins. And this power, moreover, *is*
not with the minister alone, but it is after all an effect of
the gospel, whosoever may proclaim it just so that its
proclamation is pure and right."[20]

"When the congregation has committed the administration of the office to one or more men, then no one except

[16]Luke 10:16.   [19]Matt. 18:17, 18.
[17]I John 4:1.   [20]*Pastorallaere,* p. 111.
[18]*Walther and the Church,* p. 185.

in an emergency shall publicly teach or administer the sacrament without the call of the congregation."[21]

"There is no doubt but that the Lutheran reformation sustains the church's or rather the believing congregation's primacy as a principle in relation to the office. The principle is the decisive thing, and the principle is this that it is not the office which is primary and the church, the congregation, secondary, but the reverse; that accordingly the office devolves from the congregation; that it possesses and administers nothing which the church, the congregation, did not originally possess through the gift of God by virtue of the priesthood of believers.' "[22]

II.   IN THE SANCTUARY

"Now then we are ambassadors for Christ as though God did beseech you by us; we pray you in Christ's stead, be ye reconciled to God."[23]

The ministry which we cherish is a ministry of reconciliation. We come as beseeching ambassadors. We come pleading in Christ's stead.

Every function of the Christian ministry relates itself to this central purpose, and real achievement in any pastoral field is determined by it.

A. *Preaching.*

"They went forth and preached everywhere." Thus did the first ambassadors; and so will the latest generation of faithful preachers go. Preach in His name repentance and forgiveness of sin! The assembled apostles and disciples on Easter evening could never forget that program. When the later church has forgotten, or remembering has ignored, the Lord has not been able to work with forgetful or with wilfully disobedient preachers. The church in large part has been sick, deathly sick with such ministries.

---

[21]Articles of Union, Norwegian Lutheran Church of America.
[22]Skagestad, *Pastorallaere*, p. 97, quoting Achelis.   [23]II Cor. 5:20.

This program does not sentence the preacher to wearisome repetition of phrases unrelated to life. "Sin, righteousness, judgment to come": here are the materials of the Greek tragedies, of Shakespeare, of Gœthe, of Ibsen, the materials of human living, its fears and hopes, its calamities and triumphs.

Here are themes more up to date than tomorrow's headlines. Their implications reach beyond tomorrow. God as He is. Man as he really is. God's solution through a method which even the angels never dreamed of. God's Son living for the world, dying for the world, reigning now, and coming again to judge.

The faithful preacher will not tell dreams and fancies, appending the name of God to them, but will declare His word in truth. He will not jumble together civil, ceremonial, and moral law. He will not hamper the edge of the sword of the law by wrapping it in advance with evangelical promises; nor will he rob the gospel of its consolations by making it something else than gospel.

His teaching ministry in and out of the pulpit will seek its authority and its basic materials in the Bible. He will not merely repeat the sayings of Jesus, blessed though they be; nor just retell the sayings about Jesus, precious as they are; nor will his sermons be mere restatements of conclusions and findings concerning Jesus; but he will relentlessly be seeking to lose himself more and more in knowledge, love, and trust in Jesus Christ that his preaching, like St. Paul's, shall evidently set Him forth as though the very cross stood beside his pulpit for all God's children to see.

B. *At the Baptismal Font.*

Too well and too long satisfied with intruding rationalisms, our fellow Protestants have looked away from the grace of God in the sacraments.

The Lutheran ministry still stands at the baptismal font, ministering not the shadows of a symbol but the realities of sacramental grace. We stand so, not because the vast majority of Christian churches stand with us at this point, but because the Lord, our Savior, has chosen to use means for His spiritual miracles of grace.

Such a concept of the sacrament will lay heavy obligation on him who ministers.

It behooves us to remember that the authority and the command to baptize, whether infant or adult, have inseparably joined instruction with baptism, and what God has joined together must not be put asunder, that we are stewards of a mystery which is a living reality and does relate itself to continuity and manifest growth in spiritual life.

The reading of the service and all details in connection with baptism, from acceptance of sponsors to the recording of baptismal data, will be done with such earnestness and care as befits an agency of grace established by the Lord now at the right hand of God.

C. *At the Communion Table.*

In our churches are found a wide variety of altars, some elaborate, some severe in their simplicity. It should be remembered in the service of Communion that our altar is essentially a table where the Christ, who offered Himself once for all, is Host, and we His guests at table, and not, despite the name, an altar where repeated sacrifice is either a fact or a necessity.

Here, too, our ministry stands in a place between. On the one hand there is the constantly increasing shadow of the priestly office of the Mass, the alleged bloodless re-sacrifice of our Savior, which is the heart of all Roman Catholic worship; on the other hand there is the effect again of minor rationalisms intruding their many interpretations upon the words and the promises of Christ until the only invisible grace attaching to the Eucharist in so many Protestant churches is that subjective contribution which the worshipper himself makes in his spiritual communion.

That influences from either side are diffusing themselves over our place between and upon our ministries at the altar of Communion is apparent.

It is evident that not all of the ceremonial procedures of the Mass are properly adaptable to the Evangelical Lutheran Communion service.

It is just as evident that many of the phrases, sentiments, hymns current in the Communion practices of our fellow Protestants do not fit the concepts which we confess and declare in our Communion. He who today ministers the Eucharist will need first of all to be a minister of the Word and a devotee of the things plainly written there concerning the Lord's Supper.

Obviously his ministry and his stewardship of this mystery of God extend beyond the prescribed rubrics to encompass the preparatory service, the absolution private or general, the Communion records, and such indoctrination as shall continually raise up a fellowship of believers, a congregation which is a worthy honor guard for this high and holy privilege, the true body and blood of our Lord Christ.

D. *The Ministry of Intercession.*

While the Word of God itself is living and powerful and the sacraments in their very nature efficacious, the ministry is properly related to the priesthood of believers and does not function effectively out of relation with that true spiritual fellowship.

As himself a personal member of that priesthood of believers, the minister will crave for himself a personal share in that ministry of intercession which our great High Priest is ever fulfilling. This spirit of intercession will breathe through every rubric in his leadership of worship. It is a constant recourse as he moves among the pastoral responsibilities of his parish. There is everywhere for him an inner room, a secret place, where all the burdens of his people may be brought and shared in sympathy and laid before the mercy seat.

This holy habit, the ministry of intercession, will make his face shine in the eyes of people as did the countenance of Moses just down from the mountain of the presence of God.

E. *The Ministry of Teaching.*

The pulpit work in the normal parish represents a major segment of the teaching ministry. However, indoctrination is so vital and so constant a part of the true pastor's work that special emphasis is in order.

Our Lord joined, in His command to "make disciples," baptism and teaching. The two must never be put asunder. A parish may be ever so large and have diverse gifts and forces available, but still the ordained ministry must be at heart a teaching ministry. There are the little children to be made wise unto salvation through faith in Jesus Christ. There are the catechumens to be kept growing in grace and in the knowledge of our Lord. There are the adult enquirers ever needing to be taught the way more fully. There are the tottering steps and the feeble doctrinal knees made so from walking where the world is so much with us as it is in church life now.

The true man of God will be ever learning, ever teaching.

III. PASTORAL MINISTRY

The evangelical preacher, priest, pastor, are one and the same man of God whether in or outside the sanctuary. Numerals and chapter divisions do not divide them.

The sacristy is a mighty stronghold of pastoral ministry if this is the place for conference with those approaching Communion, with those making appointments for the marriage service, with catechumens, with the anxious, with all the many on the errands of joy or sorrow which mark the days of the church's contact with mortals on life's swiftly changing pathways.

A. *Confession and Absolution.*

Our Heavenly Father has been kind, indeed, in ordaining as a valid help for His troubled children confession and absolution. A privilege it is. Not a compulsion. The burdened Christian who carries, by the normal ministries of Word and sacrament, his load straight to the mercy seat there to hear the Savior say, "Son, be of good cheer, thy sins are forgiven thee," should certainly not be restrained by mediating human ordinances and rerouted by way of a compulsory confessional.

But not all saints are strong saints, and many struggling sinners dare not call themselves saints at all. These should not be left without those human helpers which a Father, knowing the frailty of us all, wishes them to have.

We should be reminded, by the virtues still residing in the Catholic confessional in spite of the adhering abuses, by the gushing tides of the late Oxford Movement with its emphasis on the blessing of "sharing," by the principles and the practices of psychiatry, to know our own Lutheran heritage and to use it. Each generation in turn should fully know that help for health of soul which lies in the act of personal confession of sin and in that individual application of the gospel to the penitent, which is absolution.

No place where two may talk together in deep confidence is unsuited to that help which the man of God can give to burdened souls in the ministry of listening, the ministry of understanding sympathy, the ministry of forgiveness spoken in the Redeemer's name, the ministry of counsel.

Personal work is a new name for an old, old reality in the Church of Jesus Christ, and woe be it if the clergyman engenders about him an odor of worldliness to walk therein, if he wraps himself in an aura of fussy professionalism, if he wears as an unseen coat the reputation of a pastoral humorist, or so girds himself with puritanic sanctimoniousness that the lowly around him will not or cannot break through to the hidden shepherd to get help for loads that are too heavy.

The Word is not obsolete when it says: "Brethren, if a man be overtaken in a fault, ye which are spiritual restore such an one in a spirit of meekness."[24] "Confess your faults one to another, and pray one for another."[25] "If he shall hear thee, thou hast gained thy brother."[26]

B. *The Ministry of Consolation.*

"Preach to broken hearts" said one of America's pulpit princes. If these be in the pews every Sunday, the shepherd on his parish rounds will be finding them on Monday. Going in His name who said, "The Spirit of the Lord is upon Me; because the Lord hath anointed Me to preach the gospel to the poor; He hath sent Me to heal the brokenhearted, to preach deliverance to the captives, and recovering of sight to the blind, to set at liberty them that are bruised," the pastor will be very busy in the world of today and tomorrow.

The world is so full of bruised and battered, hampered and hamstrung pilgrims. Disappointment and frustration will be found on any city street, and the view from the garden gate on many a country road is the same. The pastor on his round should be quick to discern and to bring the

---

[24]Gal. 6:1. [26]Matt. 18:15.
[25]James 5:16.

healing word from Christ, who has rest for all the weary and heavy-laden who will hear Him. Between and beyond two world wars are so many wounded men and loyal women for whom the rest of life is a long, long pull against the tide. They need God and strengthening in their faith. Those who go down into the valley of the shadow of death need to hear again and again the voice of the Good Shepherd.

Normal death rates plus all the gold stars will fill our land, too, with mourners. To cause them to hear the Shepherd's comforting voice is to bring blessing indeed.

Along the road of his going down the years the pastor will hear the clamor of such as are envious, of such as nurse suspicion and jealousies, the words of them that are bitter, and the noises of them that quarrel. "Blessed are the peacemakers," and blest is the peace that is made in Jesus' name.

C. *Ministry to Troubled Minds.*

"He has given me my reason and all my senses and still preserves them." Wondrous Providence, patient loving-kindness, how worthy of praise and thanksgiving!

How delicate the balance between normal and abnormal! What awesome difference the pressure of a hidden tumor can make, the hardening of an artery, a blow upon the head, hidden abscesses, malnutrition, consequences from yesterday coming alongside today, "quick coming fancies that rob of sleep and balance," phobias and delusions, exaltedness and depression.

Should the pastor know about these things, and should he come by the homes where such deep troubles live? Exacting, indeed, are the demands for fine discernment, for balanced ministries; but no one ought to be more willing to help, and in some cases none more able to help, than a pastor who comes speaking words of hope and assurance in a world going black.

D. *The Ministry of Holy Living.*

"But be thou an example of the believers in word, in conversation, in charity, in spirit, in faith, in purity."[27]

"Adorn the doctrine of God our Savior in all things."[28] Indeed, we do not believe in dividing all things into "sacred" and "secular," or dividing between the "religious" and the "common" man. Slaves were being exhorted to "adorn the doctrine" in the words just above.

But there is a ministry of holy living, and the pastor is to exemplify it and encourage to multiplication of it in life.

The works of the flesh were very manifest in that vast environment of hard paganism when little groups of the lowly in Galatia began to walk like Christian soldiers with the cross of Jesus going on before. The works of the flesh are manifest now with the growing encroachments of neopaganism, with its banner "man is an animal" going on before. The effective, collective answer of the churches that are in God is now as it was in Galatia: "They that are Christ's have crucified the flesh with the affections and the lusts."

"The fruit of the Spirit is love, joy, peace, longsuffering, gentleness, goodness, faith, meekness, temperance."

The modern world poses many new problems in Christian life and witness. Formerly there were Christian neighborhoods and Christian settlements in fairly complete fellowship of ideals and purpose; now the world has its radio facilities for contact with every home; Hollywood fashions in dress, in morals, in matrimony, have their advocates nearly everywhere; a dollar's worth of gas will carry almost any family in America into crassest contacts with sinful living.

Ministry of holy living is not attained by causing a minister to live in a puritanical strait jacket of others' devising, but it will require that the man of God does gird

---

[27] I Tim. 4:12.   [28] Titus 2:10.

himself with sanctified earnestness to go before his flock in truly Christian living.

E. *Ministry to the Congregation as a Whole.*

"Take heed therefore unto yourselves, and to all the flock."[29]

The call to a parish ministry sets up responsibility toward a group, the whole and all its parts. Public ministry of Word and sacrament meets a major requirement, but the very name pastor suggests watchful care over the fringes of the flock. The strays are the constant anxiety of the sheepherder. Too tempting is the way where one walks intimately with a few members who fit one's own spiritual pattern while others are neglected; too easy it is to forget those who come not regularly to the still waters and the green pastures of worship services.

Young catechumens and new members need watchful encouragement. The tempted, and they are many, need earnest reminders. Voices of those who have departed from the truth are crying and calling away from the old fellowship and must be countered by the faithful pastor's words. The agents of the evil one lurk like wolves in the sagebrush to snatch away the unwary.

F. *Ministry to Environment.*

"Walk in wisdom toward them that are without."[30]

"Give none offense, neither to the Jews, nor to the Gentiles, nor to the church of God."[31] These words were directed to churches but bear most weightily on him who is pastor of the congregation and usually is to the fore in public contacts and relationships.

It is no light task so to direct the collective impact of a

---

[29]Acts 20:28.
[30]Col. 4:5.

[31]I Cor. 10:32.

congregation upon its environment that it shall be a constant witness for God and His Christ, that fellow men shall see goodness and glorify the Father which is in heaven. To have no salty savor for life, to send no gleaming lights as from a city set on a hill, to send forth no leavening influence for good, to exert no compulsion in the highways and the hedges that strangers may come in is to be awaiting judgment from Him who still watches over the churches and over the angels of the churches, their pastors.

BIBLIOGRAPHY

Loehe, William, *Three Books Concerning the Church.*

Lenski, R. C. H., *Kings and Priests.*

Walther, C. F. W., *Kirche und Amt.*

Vinet, A. R., *Pastoral Theology.*

Schaff, Philip, *The Creeds of Christendom.*

Skagestad, G., *Pastorallaere.*

Walther, C. F. W., *Pastorale.*

Jefferson, Chas. E., *The Minister as Shepherd.*

Faunce, William H. P., *The Educational Ideal in the Ministry.*

Gerberding, G. H., *The Lutheran Pastor.*

Jensen, Gustav, *The Ministry.*

Gotzsche, Johannes, *Prestens Sondags Gudstjeneste.*

THE LIFE EVERLASTING

E. C. FENDT

The Christian life is both a present gift and a future possession. The gospel of Christ is not only soteriological but also eschatological in content and in application. The Christian in this world is already a child of God, but it is not yet manifest what he shall be.[1] His life on earth is lived between the two advents of the Savior.

Since the close of the apostolic era theology has had difficulties in developing the necessary perspective and proper balance in grounding the incentive to sanctification in the *two* advents of Christ. Theologians usually stressed the one advent to the neglect of the other in developing the spiritual motivation of the Christian life. Some found the sole reason for the Christian's cooperation with the Spirit of God in the purpose and the effect of Christ's first advent, centering in His incarnation, atonement, and resurrection. They were inclined to relegate eschatology to a position of secondary importance, making it an appendix or an addendum to the body of Christian doctrine.

Other theologians stressed the importance of Christ's second advent to the point where Christians were led to believe that their salvation still lay in the future, that Christ in His first advent only made possible what He in His second advent will first make real. These men were inclined to minimize the purpose and the effect of Christ's first advent and centered their faith in Him whose second coming would bring realization to all their hopes (or fears).

The New Testament is not one-sided in its presentation

---

[1] I John 3:2.

of the Christian life. As a good example, the Epistle for Christmas Day may be cited:

"For the grace of God that bringeth salvation hath appeared to all men, teaching us that, denying ungodliness and worldly lusts, we should live soberly, righteously, and godly in this present world; looking for that blessed hope, and the glorious appearing of the great God and our Savior Jesus Christ; who gave Himself for us, that He might redeem us from all iniquity, and purify unto Himself a peculiar people, zealous of good works."[2]

The admonition and the incentive to holy living are here centered in both advents.

Another observation can be made. By stressing the all-inclusiveness of Christ's atonement some men never felt the compelling necessity of abstaining from sin. They reasoned (without Scriptural warrant) that God expected them to keep on sinning since they could not attain perfection in holiness in this life, and that God had forgiven all their sins when Christ died, long before they had been committed. Their dogmatics usually contain a short section on, or a very superficial treatment of, the Christian doctrine of sanctification. In their presentation of the atonement the element of propitiation looms much larger than the element of reconciliation. At times there is even a striking insistence that God became differently minded toward mankind as a result of Christ's atonement without emphasizing that "God was in Christ reconciling the world unto Himself."[3] It is certainly not without foundation to observe that the practical effect of many theories of the atonement was to conclude that the world was in Christ reconciling God to itself. The Spirit indeed kept the church from formulating its dogma on the atonement thus and always kept alive in the church regard for the divine reason and result of the Mediator's function.

---

[2] Titus 2:11-14.   [3] II Cor. 5:19.

But all too often the doctrine of justification by grace was misread to mean only payment for sin and not redemption from sin.

During the last two centuries evangelical theology has undergone developments that have brought eschatology into a position of commanding importance again. Lutheran theology has not been unaffected. In Europe, Lutheran theologians were often found in the vanguard of movements centering attention on certain phases of Christian truth and building systems of theology with these phases in central position. The effect of Kant, Schleiermacher, and Ritschl in theology was to emphasize the ethical to the exclusion of the eschatological. The history of Christendom is replete with evidences of reaction. When an important part of the body of Christian truth is omitted, there is always a reaction. That reaction came first in Schweitzer,[4] later in Barth.[5] They insist that the gospel cannot be divested of its eschatological content and still be known as the gospel of Christ. If the New Testament, as we have it, is used as a judge between these contending theological *Richtungen*, the latter must be awarded the verdict of understanding the message of the New Testament better than the former.

Because the promises of God relating to the last things were despised by philosophizing theologians, Bible-reading Christians felt the lack of them. Many unqualified interpreters, lacking in understanding of the church's dogma and its history, deficient in knowledge regarding canonics and Biblical criticism, arose to meet the need. The last century has witnessed more variations of millennialism than any preceding century in the history of Christendom. One of the reasons, and by no means the least, for the rise of the many sects advocating distinctive forms of millennialism was the

---

[4]*The Quest for the Historical Jesus.*
[5]*Roemerbrief,* p. 298.

neglect of eschatology by the great bulk of the church's teachers and leaders. In particular, it was because of over-looking the great importance of Christ's second advent in God's plan of salvation as revealed in the New Testament.

Lutheran theology, in common with all Christian theology, is today confronted with problems in eschatology because of millennial influences that are not readily solved without invoking the differentiation between protocanonical and deuterocanonical books in the New Testament canon, so well known to theologians of decades ago but at present lost in the statements regarding the inspiration of the Scriptures. Such a directive for Biblical interpretation as the one stating that no doctrine in the analogy of faith is to be derived from a book that is deuterocanonical, which is not clearly revealed in a book that is protocanonical, is no longer universally applied in Lutheranism. Martin Luther would have thought he was being deprived of one of his most prized rules of exegesis if he had been asked to forget this. And the fathers insisted that unclear passages of the Bible must be interpreted in the light of clear passages. In much of the literature on eschatology there is evidence that this rule is applied in reverse. Individualistic interpretations on unclear prophetic sections of the Scripture, often negating plainly revealed truth, are applied to historical sections of Scripture, with the result that there is confusion in the church about that which the Spirit is saying to the church.

A further defect in Biblical interpretation appears when statements are taken out of their context and made to say what their writer never intended them to say. When, for example, the statement, "The dead in Christ shall rise first,"[6] is used to teach a resurrection of Christians prior to the general resurrection of all the dead, the violence done to

---

[6] I Thess. 4:16.

the context is apparent to anyone reading on in Paul's letters. It is in relation to those living on the earth that Paul speaks of the "dead in Christ rising first," not in relation to other departed spirits.

It remains a serious problem for the Lutheran theologian correctly to evaluate and to utilize the many sections of Holy Scripture depicting the future. He cannot pass them by because he is pledged to teach the whole counsel of God. He notices the variety of interpretations already offered and is loath to follow just any beckoning guide. His Lutheran Confessions are silent on many of the doctrines of eschatology. They were not in controversy in the day when the Confessions were written. Without some help in correlating and summarizing the many Scriptural allusions he is tempted to steer his course away from the disputed areas of eschatology. But he cannot teach or preach the New Testament (or live with it) very long until eschatology again claims his attention. "If in this life only we have hope in Christ, we are of all men most miserable."[7] The gospel of Christ is more than an ethic for this life only. It is more than an invitation to a future life. It embraces and conveys the Life Everlasting.

There are three successive stages in that life everlasting, which are essential parts of the gospel, with the same emphasis throughout on God's accomplishing His eternal purposes with respect to mankind redeemed by Christ. From the viewpoint of the Christian these can be designated very simply as follows:

I. *To be in Christ while yet in a world of sin and death.*

II. *To be with Christ away from the world of sin and death.*

III. *To be under Christ in a world without sin and death.*

---

[7] I Cor. 15:19.

I

To be in Christ while yet in a world of sin and death. To be "in Christ" means to share in the life of Christ. It means more than reaping benefits from the earthly life and death of Jesus. "In Him was life,"[8] and, "Because I live, ye shall live also,"[9] are Scriptural statements pregnant with meaning and are reassuring in the faith of Christians. "I lay down My life that I may take it up again. No man taketh it from Me, but I lay it down Myself. I have power to lay it down, and I have power to take it up again."[10] These words of Jesus before His death have always been remembered in the church as the prelude to the central event in the mediatorial work of the Savior, His resurrection from the dead.

Anders Nygren of Lund makes this comment:

"The decisive moment in the history of man lies, as far as Paul is concerned, in the resurrection of Christ. Here God revealed the exceeding greatness of His power. While the life of humanity had previously stood under the sovereign power of death, life has emerged triumphant through the resurrection of Christ. It is this tremendous contrast to which Paul wants to give expression when in Romans 5:12 he places Adam and Christ in opposition to each other. . . . As through one man, Adam, death has come to all men, so God gives life to us through one man, the man Jesus Christ."[11]

With the resurrection of Christ a new age began for mankind. Life conquered death. Death no longer held sway over the descendants of Adam. The power of sin and death had been broken. Paul summarizes it thus: "If Christ hath not been raised, your faith is vain; ye are yet in your sins."[12] If Christ had not been raised, mankind would have contin-

---

[8]John 1:3.   [10]John 10:17, 18.
[9]John 14:19.
[11]Nygren, "This Age and the Age to Come," *Augustana Quarterly*, Vol. XXI, p. 105.   [12]I Cor. 15:17.

ued in sin and death. "But now hath Christ been raised from the dead, the first fruits of them that slept."[13] And as a result of His resurrection Paul could write, "If any man is in Christ, he is a new creature: the old things are passed away; behold they are become new."[14] For himself Paul expressed the hope "to be found in Him, not having mine own righteousness, which is of the law, but that which is of God by faith: that I may know Him, and the power of His resurrection, and the fellowship of His sufferings, being made conformable unto His death; if by any means I might attain unto the resurrection of the dead."[15]

In Paul's theology there is a close connection between Christ's resurrection, the believer's "walk in newness of life,"[16] and the believer's bodily resurrection at Christ's second coming. With the resurrection of Christ the life everlasting has been firmly established. "The powers of the resurrection-life are already at work in the world through our union with the risen Christ. The resurrection of the dead is already in progress, but only, to be sure, in its mere beginning, in respect to the 'first fruits of them that slept.' "[17]

It was at this point that the theologians of "the ethical kingdom idea" failed to see the nature of the kingdom of God, which Jesus proclaimed "at hand." They thought the kingdom would be built by men conforming more and more to the ethical standards of Jesus, both individually and collectively. Many of them attached no importance to the bodily resurrection of Christ other than to deny it. Their interest lay in men's remembering the ethical teaching of Jesus, and some even identified His resurrection with this act of recollection. They failed to see that God's kingdom is not an immanent reign of God in the world but rather an escha-

---

[13] I Cor. 15:20.
[14] II Cor. 5:17.
[15] Phil. 3:9-11.

[16] Rom. 6:4.
[17] Nygren, *op. cit.*, p. 106.

tological event, introduced into the world by God in the person and the work of Jesus Christ. Their gospel centered in man's reaction to Jesus' ethics rather than in God's intervention in man's world of sin and death by sending Jesus Christ into that world. Jesus said: "I am come that they might have life, and that they might have it more abundantly."[18] And in the same conversation He proceeds to show how He gives His life for the sheep, laying it down that He might take it up again. This commandment He received of the Father.[19]

While the rest of the world is still under the power of sin and death, those who are "in Christ" are no longer in that condition. Christ shares His life with them. He called them into fellowship with Himself and keeps them in that fellowship. He gives unto them that which He alone can give, life everlasting. They have it already in this life, never to lose it except through their own rejection of it. "They shall not perish, neither shall any man pluck them out of My hand."[20] To all believers in Christ, whether still on earth or away from the earth, Jesus promises: "I am the resurrection and the life, he that believeth in Me, though he were dead, yet shall he live. And whosoever liveth and believeth in Me shall never die."[21]

II

To be with Christ away from the world of sin and death. This is the second stage of the Christian's life everlasting. As long as he remains on the earth he is surrounded by sin and death. In his body he experiences mortality and corruptibility. His body, which is the temple of the Holy Ghost, wears out, ceases to function as the organ of expression of his personality. He finally experiences the separation of his soul and his body, removal from the earth, for which he was created by God.

---

[18]John 10:10.
[19]Cf. John 10:18.
[20]John 10:28.
[21]John 11:25, 26.

The world refers to this experience as death, but for the believer in Christ it has always held an attraction as a transition from this world of sin and sorrow to an unencumbered sinlessness with Christ. "To die is gain,"[22] and to have "desire to depart and to be with Christ"[23] are two expressions we immediately associate with Paul, but they cannot be limited to Paul. They have been the conviction of many Christians who were no more at home in a world of sin and weary in their service to God on the earth.

While scientists study the natural causes of death, finding such causes in the physical nature of man, and busy themselves with attempts to postpone (or perhaps circumvent) death, human sorrow over the passing of a loved one has often been postponed by medical skill. But there is no desire to avert death completely as long as sin continues in men. Should men continue to live too long on the earth in its present sinfulness, this might conceivably become an unbearable state. Philosophers have sought to beautify death as a passing of the soul from the limitations and the corruptibility of the body. They think of death as bringing rest to a tired soul, freeing that soul from the ills and the woes of a suffering mankind. They have assumed an immortality of the soul as being an essential characteristic of man. But the hope that every man will come to a better state of existence after he leaves this earth cannot be proved by them. It remains an unfounded hope.

Lutheran theology has always scanned the Scriptures to find the answers to the questions about the existence and the activity of the disembodied soul. It has sought to remain within the limitations of the divine revelation. The first question relative to the status of the believer's disembodied soul has been answered in the Scriptural assurances as exemplified in Paul's conviction:

---

[22] Phil. 1:21.   [23] Phil. 1:23.

"I am persuaded, that neither death, nor life, nor angels, nor principalities, nor powers, nor things present, nor things to come, nor height, nor depth, nor any other creature, shall be able to separate us from the love of God, which is in Christ Jesus our Lord."[24]

Death does not separate from the love of God in Christ. A gracious God does not omit removal from the earth for His saints but promises to retain the saints in fellowship with Himself away from the earth. Christians have always known this haven of continued fellowship with God as heaven.

Paul Althaus of Erlangen has emphasized the important differences between a pagan hope for the immortality of the soul and the Christian's faith in the resurrection of the body, going so far as to say: "The Christian faith knows nothing of an immortality of the person—that would mean a denial of death, not recognizing it as a judgment of God—but only of an awakening from a real death through the power of God: there is existence after death only by way of awakening, resurrection."[25]

Another quotation from the same theologian:

"In no event can the question regarding the dead be answered differently than by pointing to death and the day of resurrection. No word more than that. . . . And whoever desires a further answer, giving more information than this, he can be directed only to death. We know of nothing before the resurrection other than death, and that the dead are in God's hand. That is enough."[26]

The great majority of Lutheran theologians would question Althaus' implication that the disembodied soul does not enjoy existence (or self-expression) in God's presence. They are not certain that Althaus' observation is entirely correct regarding views of death entertained by Luther and Ger-

---

[24]Rom. 8:38, 39.
[25]Translated from Althaus, *Die Letzten Dinge*, p. 126.
[26]Althaus, *op. cit.*, p. 152.

hard. "The difference is noteworthy. In Luther man sleeps (death means that). In Gerhard only the body sleeps."[27]

The outstanding truth in the Biblical portrait of the disembodied soul of the believer in Christ is its waiting for the resurrection of its body. This fact has often been overshadowed by the contemplation of being taken away from the sin and sorrow of this world to a life of sinlessness in heaven. But the entrance of the disembodied soul into heaven is not the end of God's work of redeeming mankind from sin and death. It constitutes but a stage of experiencing the life everlasting. It is not the permanent state of the redeemed and sanctified believer in Christ. God's work is not completed until He has reunited the disembodied soul with its resurrected body, incorruptible and immortal. The disembodied souls of the believers in Christ are safe in God's presence from the day of departure from the earth until God brings them with Him on the day of resurrection. Althaus will find general agreement among Lutheran theologians when he observes, "We do not know an immortality of the (disembodied) soul, but an immortality of our relationship with God."[28]

In Lutheran theology the state of the souls of unbelievers is likewise clear. God has revealed no plan of bringing the disembodied souls of those who have rejected fellowship with Him during their earthly sojourn to fellowship with Himself later. Theology cannot supply a plan of salvation for such where God is silent in His Word. The Scriptures necessitate the conclusions that their sins remain in them. They remain estranged from God. They are in hell. They continue to exist separated from God because of their persevering preference to remain thus in spite of God's earnest and repeated invitations to be reconciled to Him while on earth. And a theology that purports to be faithful to Holy

[27]*Op. cit.*, p. 144.   [28]Althaus, *op. cit.*, p. 105.

Scripture cannot shirk from announcing God's judgments there recorded.

III

To be under Christ in a world without sin and death. Christian theology has designated the inauguration of this stage of the life everlasting variously. It is most frequently known as the Second Advent of Christ. Connected with this coming are the resurrection of the dead and the judgment of the nations.[29] This Second Advent is also portrayed as ushering in the new heaven and the new earth, wherein dwelleth righteousness.

Christ's return to the earth in a manner visible to all men will thus mark the termination of this world's history, the eradication of sin and death from the renovated and recreated world of God and His redeemed mankind.

It is difficult to describe in detail what shall then transpire. We possess all our information in Biblical prophecy, in which chronological sequence is lacking. There are many "signs" given in Scripture preceding the coming again of the Savior. The universal proclamation of the gospel, the continued growth and sudden decline of the church in membership, the final Antichrist, the tribulation of the nations at war, and frightening manifestations in the heavens are portrayed as ushering in the time when the Son of man, coming in the clouds of heaven with power and glory,[30] will appear.

Some commentators have included among these signs a national or mass conversion of the Jews, but a careful study of Romans 11 in the Greek text warrants the conclusion that the continued unbelief on the part of most Jews is there put down as a condition still obtaining when Christ returns.[31] Paul's emphasis is not on a final mass conversion of the Jews but on the sole way of salvation, *viz.*, through faith in Christ,

---

[29]Cf. I Thess. 4:16; Matt. 25:31, 32; John 5:27-29; Acts 17:31.
[30]Matt. 24:30.   [31]Cf. Matt. 24:34.

both for Jew and Gentile, in the time of the Gentiles including the end of that age when the last human soul shall have been won for God's kingdom.[32]

The majority of Lutheran theologians has identified Christ's Second Advent with the resurrection of all the dead and their final judgment. Some have entertained ideas of a millennium preceding the final judgment. They distinguish between His appearing to gather together His saints and to rule with them on earth and His final coming to judge the world. There have been a few Lutherans who embraced premillennialism because they were convinced that it was revealed in the Scriptures. Some few have also taught post-millennialism, in which they held the hope of the church's growth in members and in influence to become so strong as to rule the world for Christ and with Christ. But the great bulk of Lutherans still accepts the verdict of the Augsburg Confession:

"They condemn also others, who are now spreading certain Jewish opinions that, before the resurrection of the dead, the godly shall take possession of the kingdom of the world, the ungodly being everywhere suppressed"[33] as being in harmony with the doctrine of Scripture. Both forms of millennialism tend to accentuate peripheral items. The premillennialist's interest in "signs" preceding Christ's appearing usually leads him to expect the Lord momentarily, and he is inclined to think all his contemporaries not so aroused as indifferent to the purposes of Christ's Coming Again. The postmillennialist, finding little to corroborate his dream of a Christian world at present, necessarily thinks of Christ's return as in the far-distant future and busies himself with building this new world order, omitting all references

---

[32]For a further treatment see Hove, *Christian Dogmatics*, Augsburg Publishing House, 1930, pp. 423-440.

[33]Augsburg Confession, Article XVII.

to an immanent return of Christ in his preaching and his
activity. That there is a middle road, which is characterized
by expectancy as well as patience, awareness of the Lord's
promise to return as well as fulfilling present obligations, is
hard for the extremist to understand. Yet that is precisely
where the Biblical message of the end of the age and the
world to come centers. The extremist is always in danger
of putting more faith in his own interpretation or hope
than in the Lord, whose Word abides forever.

Lutheran theology sees in Christ's Second Advent the
consummation of His kingdom on earth. All believers in
Christ shall be raised from the dead and restored to the
earth to remain on earth forever. In this act God will
achieve His will regarding a mankind on which He can
bestow His love and will have a mankind living in perfect
fellowship with Himself on earth. God's original will for
mankind as expressed in His creation of man, which mankind in sin sought to set aside and vitiate, will be realized. It
will be God's earth again, with all traces of sin and death
removed, God dwelling with men on earth, and men, raised
from the dead or changed in the twinkling of an eye from
mortal to immortal dwellers on the earth, will behold
Him as He is.

It would be idling away precious hours dedicated to
work to ask, "How can these things be?" It would be
presumptuous to describe the body of the resurrection
further than to predict characteristics of incorruption and
immortality promised by God. Whatever is asserted must
remain in the confines of the revelation of God given
through Paul:

"The first man is of the earth, earthy: the second man is
from heaven. As is the earthy, such are they also that are
earthy: and as is the heavenly, such are they also that are
heavenly. As we have borne the image of the earthy, we

shall also bear the image of the heavenly. Now this I say, brethren, that flesh and blood cannot inherit the kingdom of God; neither doth corruption inherit incorruption. . . . For this corruptible must put on incorruption, and this mortal must put on immortality. So when this corruptible shall have put on incorruption, and this mortal shall have put on immortality, then shall be brought to pass the saying that is written, Death is swallowed up in victory."[34]

There is one further item to be mentioned. No theologian in any age has been able to explain it or elaborate on it. It does not merely belong to the *opera ad extra* of the Trinity; it is a future act within the Trinity. There is only one reference to it in the entire Scripture, but it is enough to assure us of the final outcome of all things in God's providence and way of salvation. It follows the promise of Christ's reign as being planned and ordained to conquer the last enemy, death. We remember Christ's resurrection and believe also our resurrection; up to this point our minds can follow. But then follows the statement which is to eschatology what John 3:16 is to the entire Christian faith. It is God's last word and summary to us on the life everlasting, which is in Him, and which He shares with us through Jesus Christ:

"And when all things shall be subdued unto Him, then shall the Son also Himself be subject unto Him that put all things under Him, that God may be all in all."[35]

---

[34] I Cor. 15:47-55.
[35] I Cor. 15:28.

BIBLIOGRAPHY

Althaus, Paul, *Die Letzten Dinge*, 4th ed., 1933, C. Bertelsmann, Gütersloh.

Barth, K., *Roemerbrief*, 4th ed., 1924.

Elert, W., *Morphologie des Luthertums*, Vol. I, 1931.

Hall, George F., "Luther's Eschatology," *Augustana Theological Quarterly*, Vol. XXIII, No. 1, 1944.

Heim, K., *Zeit und Ewigkeit*, 1928.

Hove, E., *Christian Doctrine*, Augsburg Publishing House, 1930.

Kliefoth, Th., *Christliche Eschatologie*, Leipzig: 1885.

Nelson, Clifford Ansgar, "The Eschatological Element in Contemporary Preaching," *Augustana Theological Quarterly*, Vol. XXII, No. 2, 1943.

Nygren, Anders, "This Age and the Age to Come," *Augustana Theological Quarterly*, Vol. XXI, No. 2, 1942.

Reu, M., *Die Vollendung der Gottesgemeinschaft*, 1926.

Salmond, S. D. F., *The Christian Doctrine of Immortality*, Edinburgh: 1901.

Schweitzer, Albert, *The Quest of the Historical Jesus*, 1906.

Scott, E. F., *The Book of Revelation*, 1939.

Seiss, J. A., *Last Times*, Philadelphia: 1878.

Sommerlath, E., "Unsre Zukunftshoffnung," in *Allgemeine Evangelische Lutherische Kirchenzeitung*, Leipzig: Vol. 60, No. 50.

Stange, K., *Das Ende aller Dinge*, 1930.

Troeltsch, Ernst., "Eschatologie IV" in *Die Religion in Geschichte und Gegenwart* and "Ewiges Leben" in Vol. II.

Wendland, D. H., "The Kingdom of God and History," VI in *Oxford Conference Series*.

The *Dogmatics* of Luthardt, Vilmar, Rohnert, Philippi, and Pieper.

FAITH AND REASON

THEODORE GRAEBNER

There is scarcely a subject in the range of religious discussion which is more completely encrusted with clichés than the subject announced at the head of this chapter. From Tertullian's *Credo quia absurdum* to the behaviorist conception of thought as verbalized muscle and gland action, every interpretation of the epistemological principle bears some relation to the problem of Reason and Faith. Even stating the subject thus seems to imply some kind of preconceived solution. There is a large school which would prefer the heading: *Reason—or Faith?* indicating that the two are simply mutually exclusive, irreconcilable opposites. The attempt will be made in this chapter to give a brief survey of the various interpretations which have been placed upon the relationship of faith and reason. The rationalistic and the skeptical interpretations will first engage our attention, and a brief statement of the Scriptural view as set forth in Lutheran theology will conclude the chapter.

I

Rationalism as a historic phenomenon is the attempt to secure for natural man a position of authority in the field of Christian doctrine and ethics. In his *Religion Within the Limits of Pure Reason* Kant described a rationalist as "one who regards only natural religion as morally necessary and a principle of ethics." K. G. Bretschneider, voluminous author in the field of systematic theology (died 1848), defined rationalism as "the mode of thought which accepts no supernatural revelation but subscribes only to the philosophical dogmas of religion." Very properly Carl Meusel in his

(323)

Kirchliches Handlexicon (s.v. "Rationalismus") finds the historical explanation of rationalism in the departure of theology from the two pivots in the faith of Augustine and Luther, the contrast between sin and grace. Ignore or deny this contrast, and the world had to relapse into the Pelagian position of the fifth century, had to postulate an inborn perfectibility of man, an ability to discover religious truth by his own effort and become his own savior through his acknowledgment of duty, required, simply, an intellect elevated through rational training.

It is impossible to ignore the influence of the Kantian critical philosophy on religious belief. Kant gave a most significant role to the concept of reason (*Vernunft*). On the one hand his philosophy distinguishes between pure reason and empirical reason and in the *Critique of Pure Reason* passes destructive sentence on the powers of reason in the field of speculation, metaphysics, religion. Yet he gave reason an autonomy, a sufficiency, which cancels the need of revelation; and although he never went the length of denying the historic existence of revelation he recognized as truly divine only those elements which it contained that are demonstrable by reason. Morality, too, has its true, absolute standards in human reason, and conscience is not governed by an awareness of divine law but has its high principle in the categorical imperative of duty. At that, the rationalism of the Kantian epoch ranks high above the so-called enlightenment and its "natural theology" which at best discoursed philosophically on truth and morality.

On the other hand, the period which followed the acceptance of Kantian criticism by the philosophers was marked by a relapse of rationalistic thought to the level of the British Deism of the early eighteenth century. By an easy generalization revealed religion, particularly the theology of western Europe, was given the blame for the fanatical

quarrels, the persecutions, the religious burnings and mas-
sacres reported during the Middle Ages and even during the
first centuries of the modern era whereas the study of religion "in the works of the Creation produces a direct contrary
effect. The mind becomes at once enlightened and serene, a
copy of the scene it beholds: information and adoration go
hand in hand; and all the social faculties become enlarged."

The words are those of Thomas Paine (1737-1809).
Again we note the optimism of the enlightenment when
Paine looks forward to the day "when God and men may
join forces to make a better world, in which God and men
may live more happily together."[1] Set forth with constant
references to the new discoveries of the immensity of the
siderial universe, which had just captured the imaginations,
Paine's *Age of Reason* was read by the masses and made
Paine the recognized leader of the deistic movement that
swept the country.[2] But like the earlier Deism of the disciples of John Locke, the philosophical constructs of naturalism supplied no God with whom the soul could have
communed. It could sustain the universe by motion but
supplied no fulcrum on which the human heart could
sustain the weight of its troubles. The deistic movement
waned and finally disappeared. An important outgrowth was
the New England transcendentalism. It denied the need of
miracle, revelation, dependence on an outward standard of
faith; it affirmed the need of intuition, mystic ecstacy, inward dependence upon an immanent life. As the philosopher
of Concord exclaimed: "Here is now a perfect religion,
which can be set in an intelligible and convincing manner
before all men by their reason."

The discoveries of the last century in the field of physics

---

[1] Quoted in the *Scientific Monthly*, February, 1944, p. 104.
[2] Its most prolific and distinguished opponent in the United States
was President Timothy Dwight of Yale University.

and chemistry brought the interest of the scholar back to earth, and transcendentalism long before the end of the century passed away like a mist.

II

The enthronement of reason as supreme arbiter in the field of religious truth has remained the major premise of all naturalistic thinking on this subject. The claim that reason shall decide what is to be believed and what is to be rejected is the basis of such discussions as Arthur E. Murphy's book on *The Uses of Reason,* published in 1943. Prof. Murphy is head of the Department of Philosophy at the University of Illinois, and his book is a scholarly and well-written treatise on the ability of reason to undertake the guidance of men in their efforts to understand the world and to live a worth-while life in it. The concluding part of the book urges the claims of philosophic reason. Here Prof. Murphy contends that "religion, like any other human activity, is subject to the principles of philosophic reason and rightly judged by the standards they provide." In other words, he undertakes to make reason the court of final appeal in every province of human life. He had, indeed, stated, "We have . . . no standard of antecedent rationality which would justify us in rejecting the supernatural as incredible," but then, by applying "a standard of comprehensive reasonableness," he came to the conclusion that any religion, to qualify for good standing, must admit "the secular autonomy of both factual inquiry and responsible moral judgment." We understand this to mean that religion has no authority in its own field whatsoever.

Really, the position here taken that religion should be "reasonable" enough to submit to this demand of "comprehensive reasonableness" voids any claim of religion to command the respect of thinking people. There is a loophole in the statement of the author that he has sought to interpret the claims of reason "in such fashion as to render them compatible with relevant experience elsewhere." The Christian will demand a hearing under this clause since he has indeed experiences in the spiritual field which will move him to judge the claims of reason so as to make them compatible with those experiences. In other words, on the basis of his experiences under the Holy Spirit's influence he demands the right to judge to what extent reason may operate in the field of Christian teaching.

We shall next proceed to review briefly the attempts of that school of thought which has solved the Faith-Reason problem by dissolving it—agnosticism.

III

The most elaborate argument for agnosticism is that submitted by Herbert Spencer in the first volume of his *Synthetic Philosophy*. In Part I of *First Principles* he discusses The Unknowable under four heads: 1. Ultimate Religious Ideas; 2. Ultimate Scientific Ideas; 3. The Relativity of all Knowledge; 4. The Reconciliation. The ultimate religious ideas are sifted by the criterion or test of all knowledge or "Universal Postulate," to wit, "the inconceivableness of its negation." Now, what did Spencer mean by "inconceivability"? An inconceivable proposition to him is "one, of which the terms cannot, by any effort, be brought before consciousness in that relation which the proposition asserts between them." An example of it would be that one side of a triangle is equal to the sum of the other two sides.

But the fundamental error of Spencer's agnosticism is revealed in this definition of the inconceivable. With him all knowledge is conveyed through the senses alone, is imaged; all knowledge can therefore be re-presented or re-imaged or called up by the imagination. Now, there are certainly ideas that can be "framed in thought" or "represented in imagination"; but there are vastly more important ideas that cannot be so framed and re-presented such as the notions causation, time, goodness, moral obligation—to mention but a few. But only a sensationalist can reason on the assumption that what cannot be pictured in the imagination cannot be thought or understood. Innumerable instances prove the contrary. The mind clearly conceives of the force of gravity, varying inversely as the square of the distance between two attracting bodies, but this thought cannot be imaged. On the other hand, there are, indeed, inconceivables of which, however, the mind is conscious, and in whose universal and necessary conclusions its faith can never be shaken. No sane man can escape the conclusion that "a thing cannot both be and not be at the same time and in the same sense"; that "two straight lines can never enclose a space"; that twice five cannot make any other number than ten; that ingratitude can in no circumstances be a virtue. "Unimaginable" though they are, that is, although no mental picture can be formed of them, yet they come home to every sane mind with a positive and direct force as universal and necessary truths, the most certain of all our knowledges. It is clear, then, that the agnosticism of Spencer is based on a begging of the question. The major premise of all his reasoning is that there is no knowledge except that received by the avenue of our sense organs. Naturally, God must be to him an Unknowable.

The illogical nature of this reasoning is evident from the application which Spencer makes of his "Universal Postulate" to the problem of Creation. He argues that the commonly received, theistic belief that the world was created by external agency is based on unthinkable premises. It assumes, he says, the existence of the original material, and the creation of space whose nonexistence is unthinkable.

Not only that, he says, but the entire religious view of the nature of the world suffers from the same malady. To quote Spencer's own words: "If from the origin of the universe we turn to its nature, the like insurmountable difficulties rise up before us on all sides—or rather, the same difficulties under new aspects. We find ourselves on the one hand obliged to make certain assumptions; and yet on the other hand we find these assumptions cannot be represented in thought."[3]

Operating with the argumentation of Dean Mansell's lectures on *The Limits of Religious Thought,* Spencer points out that the Absolute or First Cause is unthinkable, hence cannot be the object of knowledge as little as the idea of the Infinite can pass the test of analysis. Both Spencer and Mansell commit the error of assuming that the Infinite is something quantitative—a pure fiction—which they substitute for the qualitative Infinite, a genuine reality. It is no limitation of infinite love and truth that they are not to be measured by a yardstick or a comet's orbit. One infinite attribute does not necessarily interfere with another infinite attribute. Infinite knowledge does not exclude infinite power; infinite justice does not clash with infinite love. In this whole argumentation the capital words are used in a twofold sense—of God, the one Absolute Being; and of the all-inclusive Whole, including God, man, everything.

In the following sections Spencer deals with the ultimate ideas of science, discovers also here inscrutable mysteries, but offers a reconciliation of religion and science on "this deepest, widest, and most certain of all facts: that the Power which the Universe manifests to us is utterly inscrutable"—!

Hence, the only sensible attitude for both philosopher and religionist is agnosticism. We had imagined that our divine religion, Christianity, had stood the test of nineteen

---

[3]*First Principles,* I., p. 36.

centuries. But synthetic philosophy puffed out the light with a few metaphysical breaths and consigned the world to total darkness. All that was left of religion was reverence for the "fundamental verity," the Inscrutable Power, the impersonal philosophic mist of the universe. Everything beyond this is delusion and superstition. To think of God as the Christian habitually thinks of Him, attributing to Him such attributes as intelligence or will, justice or benevolence, is not only highly unphilosophical but extremely impious and blasphemous as well.

In looking over the results we are inclined to agree with one of the keenest critics of Spencer's agnosticism when he says: "We do not ourselves see the practical value of such a 'reconciliation.' What is the value of a mystery, of a problem to be solved, of an inscrutable power that only manifests itself to us in the formula of evolution as applied to the homogenous? It is of no scientific value. We ask, 'Has it a religious value?' Since in Mr. Spencer's view, this question would mean, 'Has it any value in explaining the origin of things?' we would reply, 'It has no value. It is no item in our emotional nature; it is no item in our environment to which it is necessary to adapt ourselves. Its interest to us is nil.'"[4]

Spencer's "far more transcendent mystery," "Inscrutable Power," furnishes us very little aid in the problem of faith and reason. All the God he or any other agnostic would leave us is a power or force, concerning which (not *whom*) we can know absolutely nothing, which has neither intelligence nor will, which, in fact, cannot be regarded even as a force since matter and force "are mere symbols," generalized modes of the manifestation of an inscrutable something, "no more real existences than the x and y of the algebraist are real existences."

---

[4] Guthrie, *On Mr. Spencer's Formula of Evolution.*

IV

From 1850 to 1900 the physical universe, and this includes the world of man, was viewed under the aspect of mechanism. The past forty years have witnessed the gradual disappearance of the materialistic view from physical science and with it a rebound from the agnosticism of the nineteenth century. By the discovery of the electronic structure of the atom, matter became far more fine-structured, elusive, one might perhaps say spiritual, than we once thought. And so the tight mechanism of nineteenth-century theory has been given up. More and more the very concept of matter disappears, and the most up-to-date scientific speculation is proceeding along lines of idealism, the recognition of the supernatural if not of the divine. The world is not only the product of intelligence but is receiving its inexhaustible flow of energy from a divine source. Behind all waves of cosmic energy is God.

J. Winternitz, author of *Relativitætstheorie und Erkenntnislehre,*[5] has this notable expression signalizing the end of the skeptical attitude:

"Light may perhaps be thrown upon this darkness (the problem of knowledge) when we consider that not only is our reason a part of nature, but that nature must also in some way be concerned in reason. If we no longer see in nature and reason two realms, worlds apart, which have nothing in common, we are not therefore obliged to put reason on a level with a mindless nature, and so reduce it to a mere biological tool, to the 'lantern of the will'; we have equally good grounds for believing to be effective in the world external to us that power for which, and through which alone, there is a world, namely reason."[6]

---

[5] Leipzig, 1923.
[6] Quoted in *The Natural Sciences* by Bernard Bavink, tr. by H. S. Hatfield, 1932, p. 245.

Edgar Sheffield Brightman has more recently (1930) said in his thought-provoking volume *The Problem of God:*

"Whatever shows the universe to be rational shows it to be what one would expect from the handiwork of a Supreme Mind. It is true that rationality is a very general term, and it does not necessarily follow that a rational order in the universe implies such a God as religion worships; but an irrational universe would exclude the possibility of a God, and we must show the universe to be rational if there is to be a God. Is the universe rational? Does it embody laws and meanings which mind can discover? It seems like a vast and proud assumption of human reason to assert that the entire universe, past, present, and future, conforms to a reason in some way akin to the human. Yet human reason is a real part of the universe and must partake of the nature of the whole in some measure. When we object to thinking of the universe as in any man anthropomorphic, we forget that man is to some extent cosmomorphic; the same laws are everywhere. Yet can we be sure that the same laws are everywhere? Do we know with absolute certainty that the universe is not a lawless chaos? We know in part. All knowledge of what extends beyond the present moment of experience rests on faith in reason. By distrusting reason, we can undermine science or morality or religion. But if we distrust reason, we have taken away the basis from skepticism itself; for doubt which rests on no reason is meaningless. It is both logically and practically necessary for us to trust reason and to assume the rationality of the universe. It is only on the basis of this assumption that science can lay claim to having found any laws which extend at all beyond the data that have actually been examined."

If the universe were rational, and we were not, of course we could not understand the universe. Therefore, there must be one rational order in the universe and in us. But this is only another way of saying that the universe is ordered by a rational Mind to which our minds are similar.

"The laws of geometry are laws normal to the human mind; how significant then the fact that these laws have been followed in the construction of the universe; so that if we give to the constructive Mind the name God, we shall say with Aristotle that 'God geometrizes.' Every step in the progress of physical science is taken in pursuance of this kinship between our minds and the rational Mind that framed the universal order, and every conclusion that is reached in science confirms this kinship. Without such kinship science would be impossible; and the vaster and richer our knowledge of the universe, the more solid is the certainty that we and the universe are alike, the universe bearing the impress of a Mind like ours. Eternal Being is intelligent. The intelligibleness of the universe to us is strong and ever-present evidence that there is an all-pervading rational Mind, from whence the universe received its character. Beside the famous argument, 'Cogito, ergo sum,' may be placed this other, 'Intelligo, ergo Deus est.' "[7]

A remarkable address was given at Columbia University in 1943 by Dr. Willard H. Dow of the Dow Chemical Company when he received the Chandler Medal for distinguished service in the field of science. He said: "Is there a scientist who does not appreciate the concept of an omnipotent plan? . . . It is not without significance that the capable scientists of today tend to be devoutly religious; whereas many of those who claimed to be scientists only a generation or two ago took pride in proclaiming themselves as agnostics or atheists, for they could not correlate religion and science."

"Sixty or seventy years ago the majority of scientists believed—and the belief often caused them considerable distress—that the product of their special incompetence was identical with reality as a whole. Today this belief has begun to give way, in scientific circles, to a different and obviously truer conception of the relation between science and total experience."

The last quotation is from Aldous Huxley's *Ends and Means*.[8] The book is worthy of attention for our present study. Mr. Huxley records a radical change which has in recent years taken place in his thinking. He says that a few years ago he had taken for granted that the world has no meaning. This, he says, was partly due to the fact that he had shared the common materialistic belief of the scientists. But he acknowledges other reasons, nonintellectual ones. "I had motives for not wanting the world to have a meaning; consequently assumed that it had none, and was able without difficulty to find satisfying reasons for this assumption."

[7]A. H. Clark, *Outline of Christian Theology.*   [8]1937.

And he says that he was not alone in that respect. "Those who detect no meaning in the world generally do so because, for one reason or another, it suits their books that the world should be meaningless." He cites, as an instance, the "pornographic day dreams" of certain writers, the theoretical justification of abnormal, erotic practices. "The philosopher who finds no meaning in the world is not concerned exclusively with a problem in pure metaphysics. He is also concerned to prove that there is no valid reason why he personally should not do as he wants to do, or why his friends should not seize political power and govern in the way that they find most advantageous to themselves. The voluntary, as opposed to the intellectual, reasons for holding the doctrines of materialism, for example, may be predominantly erotic, as they were in the case of Lamettrie (see his lyrical account of the pleasures of the bed in *Le Volupté* and at the end of *L'Homme Machine*), or predominantly political, as they were in the case of Karl Marx." To justify the selfish life, to set themselves free from a system of morality, to "justify ourselves in our political and erotic revolt," men denied that the world had any meaning whatsoever.

We are not interested so much here in Aldous Huxley's conversion from these views. ("It was the manifestly poisonous nature of the fruits that forced me to reconsider the philosophical tree on which they had grown.") But we are interested in his testimony that "the mind is so constituted that a philosophy of meaninglessness is accepted only at the suggestion of the passions." In other words, it is the depraved nature of man which prevents his reason from acknowledging the existence of the spiritual, of the supernatural, of God. This comes close to the reasoning of Paul in the letter to the Romans:

"The wrath of God is revealed from heaven against all ungodliness and unrighteousness of men, who hold the truth in unrighteousness!"

[Suppress the truth by an unrighteous life.] "Because that which may be known of God is manifest in them; for God hath showed it unto them. For the invisible things of Him from the creation of the world are clearly seen, being understood by the things that are made, even His eternal power and Godhead; so that they are without excuse: Because that, when they knew God, they glorified Him not as God, neither were thankful; but became vain in their imaginations, and their foolish heart was darkened. Professing themselves to be wise, they became fools."[9]

Read also the following verses in which the idolatry, agnosticism, and pantheistic speculations of current Greek and Roman philosophy are placed by Paul in a direct line of effect with the sexual perversions practiced by the heathen.

Behind the agnosticism of the schools there is only one cause: a mind alienated from God.

And the philosopher professes himself an agnostic primarily for the same reason as any unbelieving barber. They both love darkness more than the light.

V

The return of liberal theology from the agnosticism of Mansell to the acknowledgment of a supernatural revelation could be illustrated from the expressions of many contemporary writers. The Archbishop of Canterbury, early in 1944, contributed to Dr. Oldham's *London Christian News-Letter* an article entitled "Christians in the Secular World." The archbishop startled the representatives of the liberal theology by making basic a return to the conception of the world as alienated from God. Liberalism had taken over from the physics of the nineteenth century the contrasting view of the world as moving steadily "upward and onward forever," under a supposed Law of Progress. The archbishop, while making no profession of the evangelical doctrine of the Fall, makes the idea of an alienated world a prime consideration in settling the Christian's attitude to the world. He denies

[9]Rom. 1:18-22.

that the world of man, as it presents itself to human reason, "makes sense." Apart from the Christian revelation the world is "largely nonsense," he says. It is a "disordered chaos waiting to be reduced to order as the Spirit of God gives it shape." That is to say, any attempt to find the meaning of the world of man which proceeds on any level of inquiry below that of the Christian revelation of ultimate reality is doomed to futility. Unless and until the meaning of the world and of life is thrust upon human attention by God's own action in history and apprehended as divine revelation by man's response, no searching into the secrets of nature and of history by man's cognitive intelligence can ever discover it.

This is still quite a remove from the orthodox evangelical conception of revelation but is significant in two respects. It rejects the notion of man's ability to attain to valid judgments even in the natural sphere and, secondly, in sharp contrast with the liberal theology, reinstates the authority of revelation. Moreover, the archbishop finds in revelation the true nature of the realities within which the moral ideal must operate, which limit the full expression of the moral ideal, and which bring all human action, including all Christian action, under the judgment of God. The significance of this retreat from the evolutionistic position was set forth by Dr. C. C. Morrison[10] when he summarized the archbishop's conclusions thus:

"God's revelation is progressive, said liberal theology. Science is the divine instrument by which human intelligence discovers reality. Jesus was not a scientist. There was no scientist among his fishermen disciples. Why should we who stand at the peak of centuries of scientific development with a knowledge far exceeding that of any who went before us—why should we retrace the path of the centuries in a childish quest for the meaning of our lives and of our world?

"To which Christian orthodoxy answers that those events of nineteen hundred years ago do as a matter of fact tell us something that

[10]*Christian Century*, March 1, 1944.

science has not told us and can never tell us. Our cognitive intelligence, which is the instrument of science, cannot tell us the meaning of history or the meaning of our world or the meaning of our lives, for meaning comes not by cognition but by faith, and human faith is the organ of the divine creativity in history. It was through the faith of the initial Christian community, a faith evoked by their companionship with Jesus, that the creative God who is ever at work in history thrust into the full stream of history a revelation of himself whose vitality and finality constitute the point at which it emerged as the very center of history."

In the opinion of Dr. Morrison, this is "Christian orthodoxy." He calls it "a new orthodoxy that is now in the making." But he comes nearer the truth when he takes the archbishop's position as an indication that "the transition from liberal theology to orthodox Christianity is farther advanced than has been generally supposed."

VI

The universe is rational.

And the Holy Scriptures are rational.

The Bible is to be read like any other book.

Archbishop Trench says in his *Notes on the Parables*:[11] "In the interpretation of Scripture, grammar and the laws of human speech should first be respected, and the doctrine can and will take care of itself."

We have a branch in our theological curriculum which we call hermeneutics. It teaches the rules of interpretation to be followed in Scriptural exegesis. Essentially it directs us to the laws of thought, of language, of common sense. From this standpoint the Bible must be read like any other book. The first principle of language is that words are intended to be understood. And the Bible is written with this purpose in the mind of its divine author. Philip, the evangelist, asks the eunuch, "Understandest thou what thou

---

[11]p. 248.

readest?" The man had difficulty in understanding Isaiah 53.
But in order to help him out of his predicament Philip did
not direct him to a mystical, allegorical key or offer some
esoteric interpretation of the passage. The process of indoctrination which followed is described in Acts 8:34, 35.
It is the same process which Paul used on his journeys when
he preached the New Testament message in the synagogues.
The best illustration is the address made at Antioch as recorded in Acts 13. It is throughout based on Old Testament
history and prophecy. When people believed Paul and Barnabas, it was because they understood the message. They
were held to be without excuse when they rejected Jesus as
the Messiah because the Word of God had been spoken to
them. There is no excuse for failing to comprehend the
doctrine of the gospel messengers.

"Whoso readeth, let him understand."[12]

"Consider what I say; and the Lord give thee understanding in all things."[13]

"Whatsoever was written aforetime was written for our
learning."[14]

Throughout the sayings of Jesus the assumption is that
His Word and the words of His apostles require simply a
knowledge of human language to be understood in their
intended sense. Unbelief and perversity may cause men to
miss the saving message. The word is dark to those who do
not want to see.[15] "Through faith we understand," says the
author of Hebrews.[16] It is when we have "cast down imaginations, and every high thing that exalteth itself against the
knowledge of God, and bring into captivity every thought
to the obedience of Christ,"[17] that we can find Christ and
His salvation in the Word. That word itself requires no key

---

[12]Matt. 24:15.   [14]Rom. 15:4.
[13]II Tim. 2:7.
[15]II Cor. 4:3f.; John 8:43-47; Matt. 13:11; 6:22f.; I Tim. 1:7.
[16]Heb. 11:3.   [17]II Cor. 10:5.

like that of Mrs. Mary Baker Eddy nor a Science of Correspondence as offered by Swedenborg.

The Bible is to be read like any other book. The Holy Scriptures are rational.

The Bible does not require any interpretation by the church in order that its meaning, whether of historical, ethical, or doctrinal matters contained in it, be understood. This was the point on which Luther had his clash with Rome when faced with the demand for recanting certain doctrines he had professed. The second article of the Creed of Pius IV reads:

"I do admit the Holy Scriptures in the same sense that Holy Mother Church hath held and doth hold, whose business it is to judge the true sense and interpretation of them. Nor will I ever receive or interpret them except according to the unanimous consent of the Fathers." As the Holy Mother Church publishes no commentaries on the Holy Scriptures nor any "authorized interpretation," and as "the unanimous consent of the Fathers" is impossible (they have commented freely, each according to his ability), the layman might as well despair of ever understanding the Scriptures even if he had permission to read them.

Cardinal Gibbons in *The Faith of Our Fathers*,[18] says that the Scriptures are "not of themselves clear and intelligible, even in matters of highest importance." When the Roman Church presents its interpretation of Scripture it sometimes goes as far afield from reasonable exegesis as the key of Mrs. Eddy and the *Arcana Cœlestia* of Swedenborg. It is arbitrary, consistently ignores context, and never shrinks from mistranslation. The argument against celibacy derived from Paul's, "A bishop . . . the husband of one wife," is met thus: "St. Paul means that a man who has been married twice should not be raised to the dignity of bishop. In those

[18]92nd ed., p. 89.

days they had to choose some married men to the priesthood because they could not find enough single men to administer to the increasing number of the faithful."[19] Luke 15:10 is consistently translated "doing penance" instead of "that repents." The tremendous cult of Mary is based upon the angel's address, "Hail, Mary!" the angel's blessing being made to furnish proof that we should pray to the Virgin, and that she will help those who petition her. Gregory VII based his exercise of spiritual and civil power on Gen. 1:16. In all Catholic handbooks it is asserted that John 21:15, 16, "Feed My sheep," gives the pope power over the priests; "Feed My lambs," power over laymen. Chemnitz's *Examen* is a brilliant refutation of the use of Scripture made by the Council of Trent.

VII

When we refer to the authority of Scripture as the formal principle of the Reformation (*unicum principium cognoscendi* in theology) we merely restate the law that the truth of revelation is available to human apperception. This, too, is the meaning of the dogma regarding the clarity of Scripture. The Augsburg Confession itself is regarded only as a symbol to which adherence is required "not because it was composed by our theologians, but because it has been taken from God's Word and is founded firmly therein."[20] Any attempt, therefore, to make the tradition of the church, be it Catholic or Protestant, or the resolutions of councils, or the definitions of the dogmaticians, or the dogmas and definitions of the confessional writings themselves a standard by which the Scriptures are to be read and their true sense to be obtained would be a denial of the first principle of Protestant theology—that the Scriptures are rational, that they are given us to be understood.

---

[19]*Questions Asked by Protestants*, p. 42.
[20]*Formula of Concord, Triglotta*, p. 850, 5.

As a corollary to this position we must quote the Lutheran definition of faith which finds in that concept three marks—knowledge, acceptance, and trust. The wide gap which separates the theology of the Reformation from that of Rome is again evident. In Catholic teaching faith is a purely intellectual acknowledgment of the doctrine of the church. It may even exist when a person has become worthy of damnation through unrepented mortal sin.[21] Faith is in its very nature certainty, assurance, the opposite of doubt.[22] The New Testament defines faith as the knowledge of Christ, the Savior.[23] ("This is life eternal, that they might know Thee, the only true God, and Jesus Christ, whom Thou hast sent.")

Because of this attitude toward the Scriptures as given for our understanding and toward faith as in one respect an act of the understanding, we have in Lutheranism the tremendous emphasis on indoctrination. Our entire work of gaining members for the local congregation is based upon an appeal to the understanding. This gives the Lutheran Church an ecumenicity transcending all differences of race, nationality, and even culture. It asks as a condition for its appeal only normal, human reasoning faculties. Hence its aversion to methods which make their appeal to the emotions. Hence the church membership class and not the revival. Hence confirmation and not "decision day."

In other chapters of this volume the limitation of the understanding as a factor in our relation to the truth is adequately dealt with. Reason as a means of receiving what God offers, Yes; reason as a seat of authority, No. Reason unregenerated, reason without the illuminating power of the Holy Spirit receives nothing of the wisdom of God, and all the clearness of the teachings of Scripture is lost upon him

---

[21]*Trid.*, Sess. VI, chap. XV.   [22]Heb. 11:1; Rom. 4:20; Jas. 1:6.
[23]John 17:3; Luke 1:77; Gal. 4:9; Phil. 3:8; I Tim. 2:4.

who does not read it as he reads no other book, as the inerrant Word of God.

BIBLIOGRAPHY

Sheldon, Henry C., *Unbelief in the Nineteenth Century*, A Critical History. Eaton & Mains, 1907.

Bridges, H. J., *Taking the Name of Science in Vain*, Macmillan, 1928.

Jacks, L. P., *Revolt Against Mechanism*, Macmillan, 1934.

Kohler, W., *Gestalt Psychology*, Liveright, 1929.

Wickham, H., *The Misbehavorists*, Dial Press, 1928.

Ellis, W. D., *Gestalt Psychology and Its Meaning*, Sathergate Bookshop, 1930.

Bavink, B., *The Natural Sciences*, The Century Co., 1932.

Keyser, C. J., *Science and Religion*, Yale Univ. Press, 1914.

Topinard, P., *Science and Faith*, The Open Court Pub. Co., Chicago: 1899.

Brown, W. Adams, *Pathways to Certainty*, S. C. M. Press, London.

Cairns, D. S., *The Reasonableness of the Christian Faith;* also, *The Faith that Rebels*, S. C. M. Torch Library, London.

Grattan, C. H. and others, *The Critique of Humanism*, Brewer and Warren, New York.

Johnson, W. H., *Humanism and Christian Theism*, Fleming H. Revell, New York.

King, W. P., and others, *Humanism Another Battle Line*, Cokesbury Press, Nashville, Tenn.

Royce, J., *The Religious Aspect of Philosophy*, Boston and New York: Houghton, Mifflin and Company, 1913.

Wright, W. K., *A Student's Philosophy of Religion*, New York: The Macmillan Co., 1922.

Has Science Discovered God? A Symposium of Modern Scientific Opinion. Thomas Y. Crowell Company, Edward H. Cotton, Editor.

Fries and Schneider, *Religion in Various Cultures*, Henry Holt and Company.

Briault, Rev. M., *Polytheism and Fetishism*, London and St. Louis, Mo.: 1931.

LeRoy, Alexander, *Religion of the Primitives*, trans. by Newton Thompson, New York: 1922.

Sayce, A. H., *The Religions of Ancient Egypt and Babylonia*, Edinburgh: 1902.

Schmidt, W., *The Origin and Growth of Religion*, New York: 1931.

THE SYMBOLS OF THE CHURCH

THEODORE G. TAPPERT

There are signs today that the historic creeds and confessions of Christendom are once again coming back into currency. A generation ago these documents were quite generally brushed aside with gestures of scorn or impatience. Today they seem to be regarded with respectful consideration even if they are not always embraced with conviction.

Lutherans in America have not remained unaffected by the shifting attitudes toward creeds and confessions which have marked Christendom as a whole. In the middle of the last century Lutherans were involved in tremendous doctrinal controversies. For the most part these were exaggerated extensions of similar struggles which had unsettled the churches in Europe. In America, even more than in Europe, they revolved around the confessions of the sixteenth century. Epithets like "symbolist," "antisymbolist," "hypersymbolist," "open counterfeiters," "theological proletarians," "croaking Old Lutherans," "reckless innovators," "enthusiasts," "moth-eaten symbolists," "wolves in sheep's clothing," and "dead formalists" reflect how zealously, and also how bitterly, the Lutherans contended for one or another kind of confessional platform. After decades of such strife, which left permanent wounds and divisions, lines of separation became fairly fixed. Within these lines, and even between them, controversies over the confessions gradually subsided when other issues and activities supplanted them.

Since about the turn of the century there has been a noticeable decline in the use of and enthusiasm for the confessions. It is true that every Lutheran body in America had by this time officially declared its adherence to the

Augsburg Confession, but resolutions which are in conflict
with it and which are sometimes innocently adopted by
synods would suggest that it is often forgotten that this
confession is supposed to be a statement of guiding principles. It is also true that several substantial books on the
history and the interpretation of the confessions were published, but some of these were dying echoes of past controversies, others were purely historical, and there is little evidence that any of them has had any profound effect on the
life of the church. It is true, too, that candidates for the ministry continued to read and to subscribe to the confessions,
but some did this mechanically and simply as a matter of
course; others, with but dim appreciation of their real
significance; and still others, with serious scruples of conscience and mental reservations.

I believe that this is a fair description of conditions as
they have existed throughout the Lutheran Church in America during the last few decades. To a very large extent—
gratifying to some and alarming to others—the confessions
have lost their vitality even in those synods in which ecclesiastical authorities have been most vigilant and strict. The
Book of Concord has been read without enthusiasm, if not
with great reluctance, by students of theology, and it has been
allowed to gather dust on the shelves of pastors' libraries.

It is possible, if not probable, that Lutherans in America
will once again turn with new interest to their confessions.
Currents in the life and the thought of Christendom have a
way of penetrating eventually to even the most isolated and
self-sufficient circles. It is especially unlikely that Lutherans
in America can long remain untouched and unmoved by the
experiences of their fellow Lutherans in Europe. It would
be a pity, however, if a return to the confessions would
embroil the American church in contentions similar to those
which disturbed its peace a century ago. It would be a

tragedy if a return to the confessions plunged the church into a new era of repristination punctuated by orgies of mutual recrimination and excommunication. Or, to put it in different terms, it would be unfortunate, indeed, if the church had learned nothing from its earlier painful struggles in this sphere.

* * * *

One can distinguish among the Lutherans in America during the nineteenth century four sharply divergent attitudes toward the confessions. For the sake of concreteness these can be attached to the names of four men. And in order to focus attention on the contrasts particular stages in the careers of these men will serve to illustrate the divergence. It should be remembered, however, that these four men were in varying degrees representative of larger schools of thought.

One of these, John August Probst, a pastor near Easton, Pennsylvania, was a typical advocate in his day of the abandonment of all creeds and confessions. "To Christian people in general," he wrote,[1] "dogmas about which the preachers of former days quarreled in their publications no longer matter. Such writings are now of interest only to scholars. All the old confessional writings, too . . . are with time become obsolete and have only historical value. Those times and circumstances are past. . . . Consequently we are not bound to them, but to the Bible. . . . All enlightened and informed preachers are mutually agreed in this, that much in the hitherto existing confessional writings must be stricken as obsolete and absurd."

A second position with regard to the confessions grew, in part, out of opposition to such men as Probst and, in part,

---

[1] J. A. Probst, *Die Wiedervereinigung der Lutheraner und Reformirten*. Allentown: 1826, pp. 76-77, 80.

out of a partially successful effort to stem the tide of rationalism. Samuel Simon Schmucker, professor of theology in Gettysburg, proposed, not abandonment, but revision of the confessions. Early in his career he came to the conviction that "the Augsburg Confession should again be brought up out of the dust, and everyone must subscribe to the twenty-one articles and declare before God, by his subscription, that it corresponds with the Bible."[2] Yet he, too, was concerned "to throw off the shackles of traditionary, patristic, and symbolic servitude," and accordingly he rejected the "obsolete authority" of all the church's "enormous symbols" except the ecumenical creeds and the Augsburg Confession.[3] He advocated and defended the adoption of "only the twenty-one doctrinal articles [of the Augsburg Confession], omitting even the condemnatory clauses of these, and also the entire catalogue of Abuses corrected." To this statement these words were added: "No minister, however, considers himself bound to believe every sentiment contained in these twenty-one articles; but only the foundamental doctrines."[4] By "fundamental doctrines" Schmucker evidently meant those which were common to all Christendom, not the "peculiar doctrines of his [own] sect."[5] He assumed the right, therefore, to alter the historic confessions.[6] The principle on which he based his famous "American Recension of the Augsburg Confession" was this: "To omit the several portions which are rejected by the great mass of our churches in this country, and to add nothing in their stead."[7]

[2]P. Anstadt, *Life and Times of S. S. Schmucker*. York: 1896, p. 63.
[3]S. S. Schmucker, *The American Lutheran Church . . . Delineated in Several Occasional Addresses*, Fourth Edition. Springfield: 1852, pp. 247, 204, 168-69, 67.
[4]S. S. Schmucker, *Elements of Popular Theology*. Baltimore: 1842, p. 33.
[5]*American Lutheran Church*, p. 229.
[6]*Ibid.*, pp. 189-204.
[7]S. S. Schmucker, *Definite Platform . . . for Evangelical Lutheran District Synods*. Philadelphia: 1855. The text is reprinted in M. Reu,

A third attitude toward the confessions, developed independently of the two already mentioned but afterward consciously set over against these, was expressed by C. F. W. Walther, the mentor of the Missouri Synod. A revision was as unacceptable to Walther as an abandonment of the Augsburg Confession. The whole Augsburg Confession, and with it all the other confessions in the Book of Concord, were embraced. Moreover, these documents were received as literally binding. The suggestion that fundamental articles could be distinguished from nonfundamental was met with the assertion that "if in the Lutheran Church we permit departure from any one point of the confessions, we tear down the Lutheran Church itself. We betray ourselves as traitors who have taken a position within its walls, under pretense of repairing them, in order to raze its fortifications, and open the gate for the enemy to enter over the ruins."[8] Walther required "unconditional subscription" to the confessions, and this was defined as a solemn declaration by a candidate that "he acknowledges the doctrinal contents of the symbolical books of our church, and these without any exception, as in full agreement with the Scriptures, and in conflict with them at no point (whether a primary or a secondary point). . . . Accordingly, no matter what the location of a teaching may be in the doctrinal system of the symbols, and no matter in what form it may appear—whether it be treated as an *ex professo* topic or as an incidental remark—the unconditional subscription applies to every one of them; none of them is accepted with reservations by the subscriber. . . . All the elaborations of doctrine included in

The Augsburg Confession: a Collection of Sources with an Historical Introduction. Chicago: 1930, pp. 479-86. Schmucker rejected all or parts of Articles II, IX, X, XI, XXV, and XXVIII. Cf. *The Lutheran Observer,* October 16 and November 19, 1849.

[8] *Der Lutheraner,* XI. St. Louis: 1854, p. 203.

the symbols become, by virtue of the reception of these [symbols] by the church, parts of its confession."[9]

A fourth attitude toward the confessions was developed in protest against what was deemed the extravagant dogmatism of Walther. George M. Grossmann, one of the founders and the first president of the former Iowa Synod, was the man who gave this fourth position its earliest expression. He, too, stressed the authority of all the confessions, but he insisted upon interpreting them "historically" and "practically" rather than "dogmatically." "The church," he wrote,[10] should embrace the confessions "because it acknowledges all the symbolical decisions, in matters which were in dispute before and during the age of the Reformation, as being in accord with the Word of God." This was a clear assertion of the historical character of the confessions and at the same time an acceptance of the historical decisions as correct. Grossmann then threw further light on his position when he added: "Inasmuch as there are several tendencies [*Richtungen*] within the Lutheran Church in America, it [the Iowa Synod] professes its adherence to the one which, on the basis of the Scriptures and guided by the Confessions, strives toward the development and perfection of the Lutheran Church." The "tendencies" against which this statement is directed are those represented by Schmucker and Walther.[11] The former, it seemed to him, rejected light from the past while the latter denied that there could be "new light in later times." As for himself, Grossmann "could not but declare that it is contrary to the whole history of the church to say that

---

[9]Reported in *Synodalbericht der deutschen ev.-luth. Synode von Iowa*, 1858, pp. 8, 16.

[10]Georg J. Fritschel, ed., *Quellen und Dokumente zur Geschichte und Lehrstellung der ev.-luth. Synode von Iowa u. a. Staaten*. Chicago: n.d., 223-28. Cf. Georg J. Fritschel, *Aus den Tagen der Väter*. Chicago: 1930, pp. 134-42.

[11]*Quellen und Dokumente*, pp. 204ff. *Aus den Tagen der Väter*, pp. 138-42.

the time of symbolical formulation has terminated in the year 1580," that is, with the publication of the Book of Concord.[12]

❈ ❈ ❈ ❈

These four attitudes toward the confessions, it deserves to be reiterated, were taken by the afore-mentioned men at specific stages in their careers and in the context of certain historical situations. I am not here concerned with an analysis or evaluation of the motives of these men. Nor do I propose to inquire whether or in what measure any or all of these positions were defensible or justified in the given situations. I have intentionally selected concrete conceptions which were held in the church during a past century in the hope that they might be discussed with the greatest possible impartiality and perspective and in the expectation that something might be learned from such a discussion for our own day. This purpose requires an initial readiness to subject each of the four positions to candid criticism. I propose to do no more here than suggest the lines which such criticism might take.[13]

John A. Probst took up the cry for a creedless church which was common in the early nineteenth century and which was usually associated with a plea for church union. In his desire to be rid of the confessions Probst urged the sufficiency of the Scriptures. The slogan, "Back to the Bible," exercised a strong appeal and still does so for all those who acknowledge the authority of the Scriptures. But it rests on a theory of the contemporaneity of the apostolic church and of the New Testament which overlooks the chasm of the

---

[12]*Quellen und Dokumente,* p. 225.

[13]By limiting myself to criticism of these four divergent positions I do not mean to imply that other contemporaneous interpretations were invulnerable. Compare, for example, Charles Porterfield Krauth's favorite expression that we must receive the confessions "in their own, true, native, original, and only sense."

centuries which separates them from us. Completely forgotten, too, is the church, for we know God in Jesus Christ, not from the bare Scriptures, but from the Scriptures as they are mediated to us by and in the Christian community. This slogan is at the same time a virtual denial of the continued activity and guidance of the divine Spirit in the unfolding apprehension, in history, of the revelation recorded in the Scriptures.

More than that, Probst betrayed a misapprehension of the character and the function of a confession of faith. When Bishop Johannes Dræseke attempted, in 1836, to make the Prussian Union palatable to J. A. A. Grabau, the latter declared that he could not feel at home in a church which possessed no commonly received symbol. Bishop Dræseke replied, much in the manner of Probst, that the Holy Scriptures were the Prussian Union's confession. Grabau's response to this was pointed and significant: "The Holy Scriptures are God's confession to us, not our confession to God. The church needs a confession in which it professes its own faith before God."[14] The assumption that at least the primitive church had managed to get along without a confession of some kind is untenable; the New Testament documents themselves record the preaching of the gospel and its confession in contrast with contemporaneous religions and philosophies. Nor is it valid to insist on Biblical language; St. Paul used Judaistic notions to interpret the Christian faith to the Jews even as the Nicene church later employed the terminology of Hellenistic philosophy and the Reformation church used the categories of scholastic theology to make their faith intelligible to their times. Just as the individual cannot exist without expressing self-consciousness, so the church cannot exist without expressing its Christian

---

[14] J. A. Grabau, *Lebenslauf des Ehrwürdigen J. An. A. Grabau.* Buffalo: 1879, p. 19.

consciousness, and it has always done this in some form of confession.

S. S. Schmucker sensed at least something of this. In his earlier years he defended the Augsburg Confession against and among its detractors. Later, among men who went beyond him in their adherence to the whole Augsburg Confession, Schmucker clarified his position by distinguishing between fundamentals and nonfundamentals and then by revising the Augsburg Confession so that his recension included only what he deemed the fundamental articles. Schmucker was not an innovator when he espoused a distinction between fundamentals and nonfundamentals.[15] But he succumbed to the same dangers and difficulties which his predecessors confronted (but did not always succumb to) when they thought in such terms. It may, indeed, be said that there is only one absolute fundamental: the grace of God in Jesus Christ. This is the heart and center. As soon as one moves outward from this center, relativity begins. But the relation between the center and that which lies beyond it is an organic one. An evangelical confession of faith is not simply a catalogue of separate and unrelated statements, some of which are important, and others are not. It is a living organism in each of whose members pulsates the heart-blood of the whole. Accordingly one cannot amputate one's good pleasure without hacking the whole organism to pieces and inflicting mortal wounds upon it.[16] But Schmucker exposed himself to further criticism when, in his recension, he tampered with an historical document. It is true that this had been done before in the case of the Augsburg Confession, notably by Philip Melanchthon him-

---

[15]See the illuminating booklet by Theodore Graebner, *The Historic Lutheran Position in Non-Fundamentals*. St. Louis: 1939.

[16]Cf. Werner Elert, "Zur Frage eines neuen Bekentnisses," in *Luthertum*, Vol. XLV. Leipzig: 1934, p. 36. Also F. H. R. Frank, *Die Theologie der Concordienformel*. Erlangen: 1858, Vol. I, pp. 1-49.

self.[17] But when Schmucker did this he lost sight of the official and historical character of the confession. He put his own private confession in place of the public confession of the church, and in so doing he silenced the testimony of the church of the sixteenth century. For the Augsburg Confession is "a witness and declaration of the faith" which sets forth "how the Holy Scriptures have been understood and explained in the articles in controversy in the church of God by those who then lived."[18] If need be, the church can compose a new confession. But there must be no Marcionitic meddling with the texts of the historic confessions, and any new confession must inevitably stand on the ground of those which preceded if the continuity of the church is to be preserved.

C. F. W. Walther developed his attitude toward the confessions in an atmosphere of severe struggles and controversies both in Europe and America. He had a profound sense that it was his mission "to make the teaching, treasures, and history of the Lutheran Church known" in America.[19] And he certainly knew the teaching and the treasures of his church, particularly in their sixteenth- and seventeenth-century forms, better than either Probst or Schmucker. However, he had a rather extravagant opinion of the finality of the doctrinal formulations which those ages had produced. In this he could appeal to the preface to the Book of Concord, which expressed scruples about departing "even a finger's breadth, either from the subjects themselves [in the confessions], or from the phrases which are found in them."[20] However much such a stand may be justified in

---

[17] I refer to the Variata of 1540. C. J. Nitzsch made a proposal similar to Schmucker's at the First General Synod of Prussia in 1846, but it was not adopted.

[18] *Concordia Triglotta: the Symbolical Books of the Evangelical Lutheran Church*, ed. by F. Bente. St. Louis: 1921, p. 779. *The Book of Concord*, ed. by H. E. Jacobs. Philadelphia: 1882, I, p. 492.

[19] *Der Lutheraner*, I. St. Louis: 1844, p. 1.

[20] *Concordia Triglotta*, p. 23; ed. Jacobs, p. 19.

times of controversy it is untenable in times of calmer reflection and becomes increasingly assailable with the passing of centuries. It fails to do justice to the fact that a historical situation is unrepeatable, that it occurs only once. Each of the confessions comes out of a particular, unrepeatable historical situation in which concrete answers were given to concrete questions. To turn these concrete testimonies into dogmatic abstractions is to transform the confessions into laws. The Formula of Concord expressly states that the Augsburg Confession is a "symbol of our time."[21] To ignore this is to close one's eyes to the temporary and accidental character of the terminology, and also of the framework into which this whole confession (and the others too) was cast. To overlook this must inevitably lead, if consistently pursued, to a sterility which reduces theology to an exegesis of the confessions.

George M. Grossmann recognized the danger which lay in this path. He charged that Walther had "a mechanical, legal conception" of the confessions. Over against this he and his synod later maintained that "the church did not set up, in the Book of Concord, a kind of symbolical dogmatics in which every sentence has the weight of an article of faith. . . . Our synod acknowledges the articles of faith witnessed in the symbols as the church's confession, and accepts these as the norm of the teaching and faith of its members. It uses the argumentation and elaboration [in the symbols] to ascertain the right sense of the articles of faith established therein; it also esteems these and will not allow them to be treated with contempt; yet it does not consider them essential parts of our confession."[22] Apart from the

---

[21]*Concordia Triglotta*, p. 777; ed. Jacobs, p. 492.
[22]*Denkschrift verfasst zur Gedächtnisfeier der vor zehn Jahren geschehenen Gründung der deutschen ev. luth. Synode von Iowa.* Ansbach: 1864, p. 28. It is a pity that this important document is not better known.

reintroduction here of a milder form of the distinction between fundamentals and nonfundamentals, the difficulties in
which have already been suggested in connection with
Schmucker's views, there are two weaknesses in Grossmann's original statement. The first is that it is not enough
to subscribe the "symbolical decisions in matters which were
in dispute" in the sixteenth century, for the confessions also
contain articles of faith concerning which "there is no contention or dispute, since we on both sides confess them."[23]
To forget the latter is to lose sight of the ecumenical character of Lutheranism. The second weakness is connected
with the identification of a church with one of several "tendencies" or schools of thought when Grossmann was ready to
recognize other tendencies than his own as truly Christian
and Lutheran. The church must have room in it for a variety
of *Richtungen*, provided these tendencies are not in conflict
with the basic confession. To deny this measure of theological freedom within the church would transform the church
into a sect.

* * * *

None of these four positions has, to my knowledge, official standing in any Lutheran body in America today. This
is in itself an evidence that some good came out of the bitter
wrangling of the last century. It must also be said that the
four men mentioned had the grace to contribute, although
in different ways, to the modification of their own views during their lifetime. Unfortunately this did not always result
in the exercise of larger charity and patience toward those
who differed from them. Yet each of the four men emphasized elements which have a permanent place in the attitude
toward the confessions which may be said to have been
emerging, since their time, out of the older differences.
Probst centered attention on the primacy of the Scriptures,

---

[23]*Concordia Triglotta*, p. 461; ed. Jacobs, p. 311.

Schmucker on the relation between the confessions and later theological apprehension, Walther on the confessions as official expositions of the Scriptures, and Grossmann on the historical and secondary character of the confessions.

The large measure of agreement which exists in the Lutheran Church in America today has been achieved by the converging of approaches from two directions. On the one hand there was steady progress throughout the nineteenth century toward an appreciation of the historical creeds and confessions of the church as correct exhibitions of the Christian faith. The views of Probst, Schmucker, and Walther reflect some of the steps taken in this direction. On the other hand there has been a growing awareness of the human and historical limitations of these documents without thereby robbing them of their meaning for our day. Grossmann gave a great impetus in this direction, and many others have followed in his train. The significance of this second direction requires some further attention.

It is fortunate that the Book of Concord, which assembled the various documents which comprise the confessional standards of the Lutheran Church, included a preface, and that the prefaces of the Augsburg Confession (1530), the Apology of the Augsburg Confession (1531), and the Smalcald Articles (1537,) the Small and Large Catechisms of Luther (1529), and the Formula of Concord (1577) were retained in the official collection. These have served to remind the church of the historical character and the settings of the various symbols. Beyond the inclusion of the prefaces, however, there are many specific things in the Book of Concord which any careful reader must recognize as historically conditioned.

First of all, there are unlovely and abusive references to contemporary opponents. In the Apology the Roman confutators of the Augsburg Confession are called "rude asses,"

"godless sycophants," "windbags," and "worthless sycophants."[24] Certain noblemen are elsewhere berated as "louts
and scrimps."[25] Some of the evangelical clergymen are characterized as "shameful gluttons and servants of their own
bellies who ought more properly to be swineherds and dog-
tenders than curates of souls and pastors." As such they
deserve to be "driven out, being baited with dogs and pelted
with dung."[26] The pope is described as "a miserable Judas,"
"the very anti-Christ," a "false, mischievous, blasphemous,
and arrogant" man who had been "raised up by the devil."[27]

In the second place, in addition to such language which
has all the flavor of the robust sixteenth century, there are
patent errors of fact. A reference to Revelation 12 in the
Smalcald Articles should read Revelation 10, and in the
same document Jerome is misquoted, probably from memory.[28] The title of the so-called "appendix" to the Smalcald
Articles ascribes this treatise to "the theologians assembled
at Smalcald" when in reality it was written by Philip Melanchthon.[29] A "ridiculous" etymology of the word "Mass" is
rejected on the ground that the opponents are "asses"—"nor
do the asses know any grammar." Then an equally ridiculous
etymology is offered when the word "Mass" is traced to a
Hebrew origin.[30] Somewhat similar is the apparent accept-

---

[24]Cf. F. Bente's "Historical Introductions" in *Concordia Triglotta*,
p. 45.
    [25]*Concordia Triglotta*, p. 567; ed. Jacobs, p. 381.
    [26]*Concordia Triglotta*, p. 571; ed. Jacobs, p. 385.
    [27]*Concordia Triglotta*, pp. 469, 471, 473, 475; ed. Jacobs, pp. 316,
318, 319, 320. The original draft of the Smalcald Articles had included
the phrase *"Pfui dein mal an!"* (equivalent to *Pfui über dich!*), but
Luther deleted this phrase and contented himself with the expression,
"The Lord rebuke thee, O Satan!" See the only good critical edition
of the Book of Concord in Latin and German: *Die Bekenntnisschriften
der evangelisch-lutherischen Kirche*, herausgegeben vom Deutschen
Evangelischen Kirchenausschuss. Göttingen: 1930, Vol. I, p. 433.
    [28]*Concordia Triglotta*, pp. 473f.; ed. Jacobs, pp. 318, 319f.
    [29]*Concordia Triglotta*, p. 503; ed. Jacobs, p. 338.
    [30]*Concordia Triglotta*, p. 413; ed. Jacobs, p. 276.

ance, by the authors of the Formula of Concord, of the hoary "scientific" notion that "when a magnet is smeared with garlic-juice, its natural power is not thereby removed, but only impeded."[31]

More serious than such lapses of seemliness or memory and such shortcomings in historical, philological, and scientific knowledge, are dubious statements of a third kind. These are directly or indirectly doctrinal in their implications. The Augsburg Confession, in its tendentious opposition to the Anabaptists, declares flatly, without any qualifying "ordinarily," that baptism is "necessary to salvation."[32] With an apparently unconditional endorsement of Aristotle's *Ethics*, the Apology affirms that "Aristotle wrote concerning civil morals so learnedly that nothing further concerning this need be demanded."[33] The Latin text of the Smalcald Articles alludes to the mother of Jesus as the "pure, holy, and ever virgin Mary,"[34] perhaps because the customary mediæval ascription was inserted from force of habit. The Apology contains a statement which reads that "Baptism, the Lord's Supper, and Absolution, which is the sacrament of Repentance, are truly sacraments,"[35] although the nature of confession and absolution receives different treatment elsewhere. The Apology also asserts that "if ordination be understood as applying to the ministry of the Word, we are not unwilling to declare ordination a sacrament."[36] Melanchthon's treatise, "Of the Power and Primacy of the Pope" (the so-called appendix to the Smalcald Articles), teaches a conception of the relation between church and state which has no adherents among Lutherans in America. This treatise calls

---

[31]*Concordia Triglotta*, pp. 783, 865; ed. Jacobs, pp. 495, 543.
[32]*Concordia Triglotta*, p. 47; ed. Jacobs, p. 39.
[33]*Concordia Triglotta*, p. 123; ed. Jacobs, p. 86.
[34]*Concordia Triglotta*, p. 461; ed. Jacobs, p. 311.
[35]*Concordia Triglotta*, p. 309; ed. Jacobs, p. 214.
[36]*Concordia Triglotta*, p. 311; ed. Jacobs, p. 215.

upon kings and princes, "as the chief members of the
church," to "guard the interests of the church and to see to
it that errors [heresies] be removed and consciences be
healed."[37] That this is not simply Melanchthonian is apparent from Luther's preface to the Small Catechism, which
suggests that, in the case of "those who are unwilling to
learn" the Catechism, "their parents and employers should
refuse them food and drink, and . . . notify them that the
prince will harry such rude people out of the land."[38]

These examples should suffice to illustrate to what an
extent the Lutheran symbols are historically conditioned.
Each of the confessions is occasional in character. All of
them contain words, phrases, and sentences which, if we
were writing such documents today, we would use more
guardedly. All of them make some historical allusions or
employ incidental Scriptural exegesis or apply occasional
arguments of logic which strike us today as unfortunate,
mistaken, or vulnerable. But to conclude from such evidence
that these symbols have nothing to say to us today, or that
we cannot heartily embrace them as our confession, would
be a very grave mistake. Martin Luther called the Augsburg
Confession a *Leisetreterin* which passed too lightly over the
papacy and the doctrine of purgatory; yet he could endorse
it *ex animo* as "our confession."[39] The fact of the matter is
that the confessions do not claim to be logically infallible,
exegetically perfect, and historically final systems of doctrine. Indeed, they do not presume to be *systems* of doctrine
at all. They are nothing more and nothing less than "testimonies," "declarations," and "statements" which record a
subjective apprehension of the objective revelation of God in
Jesus Christ. The Augsburg Confession takes the subjective,

---

[37]*Concordia Triglotta,* p. 519; ed. Jacobs, p. 347.
[38]*Concordia Triglotta,* p. 535; ed. Jacobs, p. 360.
[39]W. A., *Briefwechsel,* Vol. V, pp. 435f., 440, etc.

experiential element for granted when, for example, it explains that "the term 'faith' does not signify merely the knowl- of the history . . . but signifies a faith which believes; not merely the history, but also the effect of the history."[40]

*   *   *   *

The Lutheran Church in America must insist upon an adherence to the confessions which is cordial and vital because it is informed and intellectually honest. The confessions have become dead letters in the church whenever they have been neglected or celebrated simply as museum pieces. They have also become dead letters whenever they have been interpreted with such rigid literalism that the consciences of men have been burdened with intolerable doubts and scruples. The symbols of the Lutheran Church deserve to live and to speak to us across the centuries about the abiding truths of our faith. They can do this if we read them in the light of three major points of reference.

The first of these is Martin Luther. Three of the six Reformation symbols in the Book of Concord were written by him. The others rest squarely and unmistakably upon him. The Formula of Concord calls Luther "the most distinguished teacher of the churches which confess the Augsburg Confession" and claims that his "entire doctrine, as to sum and substance, is comprised in the articles of the frequently mentioned Augsburg Confession." It goes even farther to suggest that, in the case of real or alleged obscurities and difficulties, "the proper meaning and sense of the oft-mentioned Augsburg Confession can and should be derived from no other source more properly and correctly than from the doctrinal and polemical writings of Dr. Luther."[41] The Apology refers to a treatise of Luther in order "to consider that book as reiterated" in connection with the discussion of

---

[40]*Concordia Triglotta*, p. 55; ed. Jacobs, p. 45.
[41]*Concordia Triglotta*, p. 985; ed. Jacobs, p. 608.

monastic vows.[42] Except in the Formula of Concord, which cites Luther forty-nine times, there are no other express appeals to Luther's writings, but the unexpressed dependence is manifest throughout.

This does not mean that Luther is an authority above the confessions, but that the confessions are a historical expression of the Reformation of which he was the guiding spirit. And in so far as this is so, it is impossible to adhere to the confessions and not affirm the Reformation; it is impossible to subscribe the confessions and repudiate the "sum and substance" of Luther's theology. To be sure, there is a distinction to be observed between Luther's teaching and the teaching of the confessions. Luther's teaching is the theology of an individual, and as such his opinions are not binding upon the church. The confessions, on the other hand, define the teaching of the church, and Luther, like every other teacher of the church, is subject to the confessions. This distinction is not only important but also very illuminating, for although the confessions modify Luther's teachings at some points and are prudently silent at others, Luther is by no means read out of the church as a heretic. And this is so because the church agrees with Luther in the "sum and substance" of his theology. This is so because the church believes that "in these last times God, out of especial grace, has brought the truth of His Word to light again from the darkness of the Papacy through the faithful service of the precious man of God, Dr. Luther."[43] To understand the "truth of His Word," therefore, as this is confessed in the Lutheran symbols, inevitably requires an understanding of Martin Luther.

The second point of reference in the light of which we must read the confessions is the pre-Reformation church.

---

[42]*Concordia Triglotta*, p. 423; ed. Jacobs, p. 283.
[43]*Concordia Triglotta*, p. 851; ed. Jacobs, pp. 535-36.

The Augsburg Confession professed to set forth "the sum of our doctrine" in which "there is nothing that departs from the Scriptures, or from the Church Catholic, or from the Church of Rome as known from its writers."[44] The writers here referred to were the Fathers of the ancient church. The three so-called ecumenical creeds were expressly cited in the Augsburg Confession, the Apology, the Smalcald Articles, and the Formula of Concord, and the full texts were incorporated at the very beginning of the Book of Concord. The Formula of Concord speaks of these creeds as "glorious confessions of the faith, brief, devout, and founded upon God's Word, in which all the heresies which at that time had arisen in the Christian Church are clearly and unanswerably refuted."[45] The Apostles' Creed was afforded additional attention in the Small and Large Catechisms. In fact, the three traditional parts of the catechism—Ten Commandments, Creed, and Lord's Prayer—were consciously preserved because they "have remained in Christendom from of old."[46] In the same unity of the one church, the confessions, without express explanation, retained the traditional canon of "the prophetic and apostolic Scriptures."[47] In all of these ways the confessions identified themselves with the church in the past, and here, too, they followed closely in the footsteps of Luther. In 1538 he "decided, as a matter of supererogation, to issue conjointly . . . the three symbols, or creeds, which have been received, read, and chanted throughout the church." Luther did this, as he put it, "for the purpose of affirming once more that I am at one with the true Christian Church which has maintained these symbols, or confessions, to this day."[48] In 1532 he defended his interpretation of the

---

[44]*Concordia Triglotta*, p. 59; ed. Jacobs, p. 46.
[45]*Concordia Triglotta*, p. 851; ed. Jacobs, p. 535.
[46]*Concordia Triglotta*, p. 575; ed. Jacobs, p. 387.
[47]*Concordia Triglotta*, p. 777; ed. Jacobs, p. 491.
[48]W. A., Vol. L, p. 262.

Eucharist on this ground, among others, that it "has been
unanimously believed and held by the Christian Church in
all the world from the very beginning even unto this hour.
. . . It is dangerous and terrible to hear or believe something
contrary to the unanimous witness, faith, and teaching of
the one holy Christian Church—something that has been
received unanimously in all the world ever since the beginning, now more than 1500 years."[49]

The assertion that the ecumenical creeds were acknowledged in the Book of Concord "primarily for apologetic
reasons"[50] receives support from the belief, in the sixteenth
century, that an acceptance of the Nicene Creed would
assure legal status in the empire.[51] But this is not the whole
truth. The entire history of the Lutheran Reformation testifies to a profound and very genuine concern for the continuity of the church. The confessions accordingly assumed a
positive rather than a negative position with respect to the
development of Christian thought and life, rejecting only
what had "been erroneously accepted by the corruption of
the times."[52] In like manner Luther maintained that the true
church continued to exist even under the papacy.[53] This conviction has a bearing on the status which Lutherans accord
to tradition, for the confessions reject both the extravagant
overemphasis on tradition by Rome and the extreme depre-
ciation of tradition by radicals. At the same time this conviction has given the Lutheran Church an ecumenical outlook
and responsibility which have not always been appreciated
by those within it. In the sixteenth century the Lutherans

---

[49]*W. A.*, Vol. XXX, 3, p. 552.
[50]F. Bente, in *Concordia Triglotta*, pp. 9f.
[51]Ferdinand Kattenbusch, *Luthers Stellung zu den oecumenischen
Symbolen*. Giessen: 1883; Werner Elert, *Morphologie des Luthertums*.
München: 1931, I, pp. 240-55.
[52]*Concordia Triglotta*, p. 59; ed. Jacobs, p. 47.
[53]*W. A.*, Vol. L, p. 563; Vol. XXVIII, p. 221.

confessed their faith "in the sight of God and of all Christendom."[54] Lutherans dare not do less than this today.

The third point of reference in the light of which we must read the confessions is the Bible. The authority of the Scriptures is taken for granted in all the symbols. The preface to the Augsburg Confession states that this document attempts to show "what manner of doctrine" was "taught in our churches" on the basis of "the Holy Scriptures and the pure Word of God."[55] A formal statement on this subject was not offered until 1577 when the Formula of Concord included this statement: "We believe, teach, and confess that the sole rule and standard according to which all dogmas, together with all teachers, should be esteemed and judged are the prophetic and apostolic Scriptures of the Old and of the New Testament alone."[56] The Scriptures are also called "the pure, clear fountain of Israel, which is the only true standard by which all teachers and doctrines are to be judged."[57] Incidental allusions in other confessions ascribe the origin of the Scriptures to the Holy Ghost, but, unlike the Calvinistic confessions, the Lutheran symbols contain no dogmatic theory of inspiration, nor do they contain a list of the books which are received as canonical. The remarkable casualness of the references concerning the Scriptures in the earlier confessions may be accounted for only by the fact that the authority of the Bible was, in itself, not a matter in dispute.

What was in dispute was the *interpretation* of the Scriptures. And ultimately the whole significance of the Lutheran confessions lies right here. They stand or fall according to the correctness of their interpretation of the Scriptures. The starting point of this interpretation, for Luther as for the confessions, was Jesus Christ. For Luther it was "beyond

---

[54]*Concordia Triglotta*, p. 1103; ed. Jacobs, p. 670.
[55]*Concordia Triglotta*, p. 39; ed. Jacobs, p. 34.
[56]*Concordia Triglotta*, p. 777; ed. Jacobs, p. 491.
[57]*Concordia Triglotta*, p. 851; ed. Jacobs, p. 535.

question that all the Scriptures point to Christ alone."[58] This was the central value which he found in the ecumenical creeds, for in his treatise on these creeds Luther wrote in 1538: "He who does not find God in Christ will never find Him. He will not find God outside of Christ, even if he mounts up above the heavens, or descends below hell itself, or goes beyond the limits of the world."[59] "But what is the knowledge of Christ," the Apology asks, "unless to know the benefits of Christ, the promises which by the gospel He has scattered abroad in the world?"[60] Thus Jesus Christ is intimately identified with the gospel, and the gospel with justification by faith. "That we are justified freely by faith" is, according to the Apology, "the principal matter of all Epistles, yea, of the entire Scriptures."[61] The doctrine of justification "alone shows the way to the unspeakable treasure and right knowledge of Christ, and alone opens the door to the entire Bible."[62] This, then, is the heart and center of the Scriptures: Jesus Christ, the gospel, reconciliation with God in Christ, justification by faith.

This and all the teachings which, as expanding concentric circles, revolve around this center must be judged by "the sole rule and standard," the Scriptures. "Other writings, however, of ancient or modern teachers, whatever name they bear, must not be regarded as equal to the Holy Scriptures, but all of them together be subjected to them, and should not be received otherwise or further than as witnesses, which are to show in what manner after the time of the apostles, and at what places, this pure doctrine of the prophets and apostles was preserved."[63] Thus Luther and

---

[58]*Works of Martin Luther.* Philadelphia: 1915, Vol. II, p. 432.
[59]*W. A.*, Vol. L, p. 267.
[60]*Concordia Triglotta*, p. 151; ed. Jacobs, p. 100.
[61]*Concordia Triglotta*, p. 147; the edition of the Book of Concord by Jacobs omits this reading from the German text on p. 99.
[62]*Concordia Triglotta*, p. 121; ed. Jacobs, p. 84.
[63]*Concordia Triglotta*, p. 777; ed. Jacobs, p. 491.

the tradition of the pre-Reformation church were reduced to a secondary status, subject to the Scriptures—and with them the confessions themselves. All these symbols and writings and teachers are "not judges, as are the Scriptures, but only a testimony and declaration of the faith."[64] In other words, the Scriptures are the primary point of reference in the light of which the confessions must be read.

In so far as the science of theology remains vital, the three points of reference to which the confessions direct us must be subjected to unrelenting study and scrutiny. The Church of the Augsburg Confession, which repudiates moral perfectionism, cannot claim intellectual or theological perfectionism. If this means anything at all, it means that we have not yet achieved a perfect understanding of the ancient church, or of Luther, or of the Scriptures. Yet, although imperfectly, we do understand. And according to the measure of our understanding we can embrace the confessions and pray in the words of the Formula of Concord: "May Almighty God, Father of our Lord Jesus, grant the grace of His Holy Ghost that we all may be one in Him, and constantly abide in this Christian unity, which is well pleasing to Him. Amen."[65]

---

[64] *Concordia Triglotta,* p. 779; ed. Jacobs, p. 492.
[65] *Concordia Triglotta,* p. 837; ed. Jacobs, p. 528.

BIBLIOGRAPHICAL NOTES

1. TEXTS OF THE SYMBOLS

There is only one critical edition of the Book of Concord, and this is basic for any study of the Latin and the German texts today: *Die Bekenntnisschriften der evangelisch-lutherischen Kirche,* herausgegeben vom Deutschen Evangelischen Kirchenausschuss, 2 vols., Göttingen: 1930. An English translation, accompanied by Latin and German texts in parallel columns, is conveniently presented in the *Concordia Triglotta: the Symbolical Books of the Evangelical Lutheran Church,* edited by F. Bente, St. Louis: 1921. The translation in this volume is based, with revisions which have greatly improved it, on the older work, *The Book of Concord; or, The Symbolical Books of the Evangelical Lutheran Church,* edited by Henry E. Jacobs in two volumes, Philadelphia: 1883. The second volume of Jacobs' work is devoted largely to documents pertaining to the symbols and to extensive indexes. Bente's edition also appears in English alone, and there is a one-volume "People's Edition" of Jacobs' text of the confessions, somewhat revised.

2. GENERAL HISTORIES AND EXPOSITIONS

Each of the above works contains historical introductions. The more significant additional historical and expository treatments in English are the following: Charles Porterfield Krauth, *The Conservative Reformation and its Theology,* Philadelphia: 1871, is a rather rhetorical and, in some areas, antiquated volume which has served a good purpose in its time and is still useful today. James W. Richard, *The Confessional History of the Lutheran Church,* Philadelphia: 1909, is based on more careful and independent research and represents a decidedly more sympathetic interpretation of Melanchthonianism. This is again counteracted sharply in Theodore E. Schmauk, *The Confessional Principle and the Confessions of the Lutheran Church,* Philadelphia: 1911, a large and very diffuse volume which has the special value of making the investigations of Theodor Kolde accessible to English readers. Much more modest in its purpose is J. L. Neve, *Introduction to the Symbolical Books of the Lutheran Church,* Columbus: 1926, which is intended as a guide for students of theology. The great work of Philip Schaff, *The Creeds of Christendom with a History and Critical Notes,* 3 vols., sixth edition reworked by David S. Schaff, New York: 1931, discusses the Lutheran symbols in relation to those of other communions. A fresher treatment from this angle is available in William A. Curtis, *A History of Creeds and Confessions of Faith in Christendom and Beyond,* Edinburg: 1911. For comparative studies of various denominations and their statements of faith see E. H. Klotsche, *Christian Symbolics*, Burlington, Iowa: 1929, and J. L. Neve, *Churches and Sects of Christendom*, second edition, Burlington, Iowa: 1944.

3. PARTICULAR SYMBOLS

There are several recent studies in English which deal with individual symbols. M. Loy, *The Augsburg Confession: an Introduction to its Study and an Exposition of its Contents*, Columbus: 1908, is a rambling and an excursive treatment. Compact and popular is J. L. Neve, *The Augsburg Confession: a Brief Review of its History and an Interpretation of its Doctrinal Articles*, Philadelphia: 1914. M. Reu, *The Augsburg Confession: a Collection of Sources with an Historical Introduction*, Chicago: 1930, is an exceedingly valuable aid for an appreciation of the setting of this symbol. More readable is the brief sketch by Conrad Bergendoff, *Making and Meaning of the Augsburg Confession*, Rock Island: 1930.

An excellent work, by a specialist in the field, is M. Reu, *Dr. Martin Luther's Small Catechism: a History of its Origin, its Distribution, and its Use*, Chicago: 1929. The same may be said of George J. Fritschel, *The Formula of Concord: its Origin and Contents*, Philadelphia: 1916. Attention should also be called, because of their bearing on the symbols, to M. Reu, *Luther's German Bible*, Columbus: 1934, and *Luther and the Scriptures*, Columbus: 1944, and to P. E. Kretzmann, *The Story of the German Bible*, St. Louis: 1934.

LUTHERAN UNITY

CONRAD BERGENDOFF

It was a brusque reply which the president of the Augustana Synod sent in April, 1911 to Robert H. Gardiner of the Episcopal Church concerning the proposed World Conference on Faith and Order.[1] Since, in a sense, the modern ecumenical movement may be dated from the action of the General Convention of the Protestant Episcopal Church at Cincinnati in October, 1910, stimulated by the great World Missionary Convention at Edinburgh earlier in the same year, it may be of value to investigate the reaction of the Lutheran Church to this initial proposal, and from that point to trace the development of Lutheran participation in ecumenical endeavors. At the Cincinnati Convention a commission had been "appointed to bring about, if possible, a conference for the consideration of questions touching Faith and Order, and to ask all Christian Communions throughout the world which confess our Lord Jesus Christ as God and Savior to unite with us in arranging for and conducting such a Conference."[2] The Augustana Synod received, accordingly, an invitation to take part, and the Episcopal Church Commission expressed the hope that a commission might be set up in the Augustana Synod to act for the synod in this matter.

To this request Eric Norelius, just then retiring from the presidency of the synod after a lifelong period of service in the synod, stretching back to the pioneer days, replied that the synod "has no Committee authorized to deal with any question in regard to the unity of different churches, and I am sure that the Synod will not appoint any such Commit-

---

[1] *Minutes* of Augustana Synod, 1911, p. 37.
[2] *Ibid.* p. 38.

tee. We certainly believe in Christian unity, and there has always been such a unity among true Christians, and there will always continue to be such a union; but an outward union of different churches on a platform such as is proposed by the Episcopal Commission we consider to be futile and no union at all."

Probably Norelius could not treat the Episcopal Commission's proposal entirely in an impartial mood. For he remembered that as long ago as 1867[3] a bishop of the Episcopal Church had visited Sweden and had sought to have the Church of Sweden direct its emigrant sons and daughters to the Episcopal Church in America, despite the presence there of the Augustana Synod. And the index of the synodical minutes bears references in 1901 and 1907 to the Episcopal Church coupled with the ugly word, "proselyting." So the patriarch of the synod in his declining days may be pardoned for not sensing in the proposals of the Episcopal Church something other than a scheme to ensnare American Lutherans of Scandinavian background who might be misled by liturgy and Prayer Book to believe that the proper home for Swedish Lutherans in America was a church with bishops.

But it is quite likely that the answer would have been much the same even if the invitation had come from a different quarter. For the reply of the Augustana Synod was remarkably similar to that of the General Council of the Evangelical Lutheran Church in North America. The Augustana Synod was a member of the Council, then headed by Theodore Schmauk, and had for forty years felt at home in the doctrinal atmosphere of the Council. We may believe that President Norelius would second the words of President Schmauk as we find these in a series of reports to the biennial meetings of the Council during the last decade of its history.

In 1909 President Schmauk reported the arrangements

[3]*Minutes,* 1910, p. 36.

being made for the World's Missionary Conference. "With
its wide and earnest outlook, and with its appeal to the
power of prayer for the Foreign Field, the General Council
is in unison, and we regret our inability on account of our
sound fundamental principle, of unity as a pre-requisite to
cooperation, to enter in as one of the active elements in such
a meeting."[4] Two years later the president described his
reaction to the invitation of the Episcopal Commission.

"In the correspondence which I have had with the Secretary of
the Commission, I said, on behalf of the General Council, that we fully
agree with the view of the Commission, 'that the beginnings of unity
are to be found in the clear statement of those things in which we
differ, as well as of those things in which we are at one'; and that we
are in accord with the Commission in the desire 'to lay aside self-will,
and to put on the mind which is in Christ Jesus'; that, however, we do
not regard 'Faith' and 'Order' as being on the same essential plane;
that we do not believe that a Unity of 'Order,' or the union of the
Church Visible, i.e., of ecclesiastical denominations, is the unity to
which our Saviour referred in His prayer to the Father; that we do not
believe that there is any unity in the Church which is not a unity of
principle; that we do not believe that unity in Faith can be reached by
any agreement to agree; that we do not regard a unity of government
or of order, or that 'outward and visible reunion' of Christendom which
is the ultimate object of this Conference, as important, or as desirable,
in advance of a unity of principle; that we do not look on other Protestants as rivals, from whose ranks we should make proselytes; that we
believe in acting on our faith as a matter of conscience, until such a
time, if the Lord brings it about, as the consciences of Christians be
cleared to hold the same faith; and that, meantime, we do not regard
an externally divided Protestantism as a disgrace to Christendom, in
so far as differences are a matter of faith and conscience; and that an
official invitation to cooperate in this movement would probably be
referred to a committee of our body to be considered fundamentally
and report at a later stage."[5]

That the president spoke for the Council as a whole may
be gathered from the action of the Council in approving his

[4]*Minutes of General Council*, Thirty-second Convention, Minneapolis, 1909, p. 10.
[5]*Minutes of General Council*, Thirty-third Convention, Lancaster,
1911, p. 13.

statements and appointing a committee which reported in 1913. The report of this committee, furthermore, is entirely in accord with President Schmauk's words both in 1911 and 1913.[6] It stated that "the General Council heartily welcomes discussions on the subject of Christian unity," claims, "that there has been, is, and will be abiding through all time, one holy Christian Church" and that "to the true unity of the Church it is sufficient that there be agreement touching the doctrine of the Gospel—and the Sacraments. The General Council, therefore, believes that questions touching Faith or Doctrine are on a higher plane and should have a prior consideration to questions touching Order, which are secondary." Though "unable to unite—in arranging for and conducting a Conference on Faith and Order," it advocated a "Committee on the Unity of Faith which shall be authorized, without participating in the organization or arrangement of any conference, to present and set forth the Lutheran Faith."[7]

Beyond this point the General Council never advanced. It did appoint a standing committee, but the committee had no authority to participate in any conference. Nor was any conference held before the war put a temporary end to international gatherings. Meanwhile the Council itself ceased to be while the United Lutheran Church inherited the stand of the Council on the matter of ecumenical relations.

The discussion had the advantage, however, of clarifying the position of most of the Lutheran Churches in America. Between the stand of the Episcopal Church and the Lutheran a wide difference had become apparent. The Lutheran Church questioned the concept of unity as defined by the Episcopal Commission, doubting that visible union was essential or even contemplated by Christ, and strongly dissenting from the Episcopal claim that "Faith" and "Order"

---

[6]*Minutes of General Council,* Thirty-fourth Convention, Toledo, 1913, pp. 10 and 11.

[7]*Ibid.,* 227-228.

were on the same plane. There were thus presuppositions in the plans of the Episcopal Commission to which Lutherans would not agree without much further discussion. In the appointment of a committee the Council left a door open for further negotiations. As we have seen, this was more than was conceded by President Norelius. But though in 1917 the Augustana Synod declined to enter the United Lutheran Church, its members would undoubtedly have approved of the words of Dean Henry E. Jacobs at the first convention of that body, when he asserted that, "sooner or later the Lutheran Church in America must define more adequately its relation to other churches. A new symbolics must be taught in a land where European distinctions are greatly modified by the attrition between diverging Christian forces. May we not expect that the Lutheran Church of America, combining fidelity to its confession with kindly consideration of other churches, may attain results on American soil, not hitherto reached in Europe? And may we not hope, and should we not pray that American Evangelical Protestantism may learn to appreciate more fully what we have found so precious in the Gospel, until the great Head of the Church, to whom nothing is impossible, shall, in His own time and way, bring about a union far wider than that we have today formed?"[8]

Before American Lutherans could speak unitedly to and with other churches, either in America or Europe, on the subject of ecumenicity, it was necessary that they learn to understand each other. Probably some of the reluctance of Lutherans to participate in unity movements was due to an unquiet mind concerning relationships within the household of the Lutheran faith. The inclusion of this paragraph in the General Council's Committee statement of 1913, wherein the Council gave its reply to the Faith and Order invitation,

---

[8]*Minutes of the First Convention of the United Lutheran Church in America*, New York City, 1918, p. 17.

seems significant: "The General Council believes that it is its first duty, and the first duty of every particular Church, to seek to gain a unity in the true faith among those of its own household, that is, among all Lutherans throughout the world, and promises solemnly to set itself to the great work of bringing the many ecclesiastical divisions of Lutheranism throughout the world into fuller consciousness of the unity of the one and same faith in which they stand, and, on the basis of that same pure faith, into the unity of fellowship with each other."[9]

Two hundred and seventy-five years of Lutheran history in America lay back of that statement. In all those years there had never been a united Lutheranism, and the prospect in 1913 was not clear. The Swedish Lutherans on the Delaware had maintained themselves from 1638 to the days of Muhlenberg a century later. There had been some negotiations for a close cooperation between the Swedish and the German churches in Pennsylvania, Delaware, and New Jersey,[10] but to no avail, and the Swedish congregations were gradually absorbed by the Anglican Church. The German colonists organized the Ministerium of Pennsylvania (1748) and embarked on a program of expansion and inward development which affected all the subsequent synods in the East. Meanwhile great migrations of European Lutherans were colonizing the Mississippi Valley, but these colonies had little in common. Coming from diverse Lutheran countries in Europe, they knew little or nothing of other Lutherans than those in their homeland. There the Lutheran Church had practically no intercourse with Lutherans in other countries. Bearing an isolationist tradition, these colonists proceeded to restrict still further the dimensions of their faith by cutting the ties which bound them to the

[9]*Minutes,* Toledo, 1913, p. 227.
[10]Acrelius, I. *A History of New Sweden,* trans. by W.M. Reynolds, Hist. Society of Penn., 1847, pp. 245f.

larger Lutheranism of their homeland. Partly, this was due
to sharp doctrinal differences with the parent church as in
the case of the Missouri Synod (1847) and the Iowa Synod
(1854). The Norwegian settlements perpetuated and intensified their different traditions in Eielsen's (1846) and the
Norwegian Synod (1853); the Swedish congregations found
most of their needs fulfilled in the Augustana Synod (1860),
which during its first decade included a Norwegian group.
The Danes, the Finns, even the Icelandic group, considered
size no element in the concept of the church and followed
the example of the more numerous European Lutheran
bodies in creating their own autonomous synods. W. H.
Greever[11] has tellingly contrasted the apparent purpose of
Midwest Lutherans of the nineteenth century with the motto
of Muhlenberg a century earlier. While the latter proclaimed as his motto, *Ecclesia plantanda est*, the unexpressed
motto of the former groups seemed to be, "The church must
be transplanted." The result was a garden with all the
varieties of Europe plus indigenous types which developed
under the conditions of the New World environment.

Yet something of the attractive force of Christian unity
brought scattered parts of the church together in more or
less enduring union. The first comprehensive organization of
Lutherans in America took the name of "The General Synod"
(1820). It was essentially a federation of autonomous synods
and from the start was subject to withdrawals. But for the
first time a vision appeared of a united Lutheranism in
the New World. Theological dissension and suspicion of
encroachments on congregational independence limited the
effectiveness of the synod, but in the field of theological
education, home missions and charities, permanent results
were achieved. The revival of Lutheran self-consciousness
reached American Lutheranism both directly from European

---

[11]*Lutheran World Almanac*, 1934-1937, pp. 92-93.

movements and, indirectly, through the spirit and the purpose of the newer emigrants into the West. The ferment of a conservative, orthodox theology, combined with a spirit of independent Lutheranism over against unionistic movements in American Protestantism, finally split the General Synod. In 1867 the General Council became the spokesman of that large part of the Lutheran Church in America which was intent on conserving the verities of the sixteenth-century Reformation in the new American environment. It could not gain, however, the adherence of those Lutherans who saw in the Missouri Synod a bulwark against unionism, on the one hand, and the rise of a centrally organized church, on the other. These included some Norwegians, but were mainly German in origin, and in 1872 they founded the third general group of Lutherans with the designation of "Synodical Conference." This body has maintained itself up to the present. The General Synod and the General Council merged in 1917 with the Synod of the South which consisted of district synods in the South who withdrew during the Civil War from the General Synod to form the United Lutheran Church. Two-thirds of American Lutheranism had thus found congenial relationships in these two organizations.

The greater part of the remaining third is at present seeking more effective unity in the American Lutheran Conference. The composition of this rather loose federation is interesting. The Norwegians in the Norwegian Synod had joined the Synodical Conference in 1872, but most of them withdrew in 1883, only to have their own ranks split in 1887 by the separation of the Anti-Missourian party. This party in 1890 joined with the Norwegian Augustana Synod and the Danish-Norwegian Conference (both organized 1870) to form the United Norwegian Lutheran Church of America. But the union did not include the Norwegian Synod nor the Hauge Synod, which had absorbed most of the Eielsen

Synod; these remained independent until their merger in 1917 with the United Church, which now was renamed the Norwegian Lutheran Church of America.[12] But even this union was incomplete, for the Norwegian Free Church, which had withdrawn in 1896 from the United Church of 1890, declined to join the united church of 1917. But the Free Church was willing to accept membership along with the Norwegian Lutheran Church of America in the American Lutheran Conference in 1930.

A third element in this Conference is the Augustana Synod, which had belonged to the General Council between 1870 and 1917. The American Lutheran Church, a fourth member, was a consolidation of the former Ohio and Iowa Synods who had been unable to find congenial relationship either with the General Council or the Synodical Conference and merged with the Buffalo Synod in 1930 into one body. The fifth member is the United Danish Church, which has its name from a union in 1886 of former members of the Danish-Norwegian Conference and a party protesting against the doctrinal stand and practices of the Danish Lutheran Church (organized in 1872).

All of these bodies had developed within the century before the organization of the American Lutheran Conference in 1930. They represented the newer Lutheran immigration of the nineteenth century—Norwegian, Swedish, German, Danish—which had not been willing to join either with the older American Lutherans of the East nor the newer orthodoxy as developed and interpreted by the Missouri Synod. They were affected by, and they themselves affected the other great groups. In the Conference they found much in common though it is not at all clear that this position is more than a temporary and transitional one.

This hasty review of the changing relationships of the

---

[12]Since 1945 the Evangelical Lutheran Church in America.

many Lutheran groups in America suggests that, though history and geography may have isolated them in various ways, they have not been happy in isolation. Each in its own manner has tried to express the underlying conviction that a unity of faith calls for an embodiment of such unity. Illustrative of the general attitude are statements which are part of the records of the major organizations. The Ministerium of Pennsylvania in 1818 resolved that "in its judgment, it would be well if the different Evangelical Lutheran synods in the United States were to stand, in some way or other, in true union with one another."[13] Almost half a century later, in 1866, the representatives of the synods who gathered to organize the General Council agreed to this preamble:

"We are fully persuaded that with our communion scattered over a vast and ever-widening territory, with the ceaseless tide of immigration to our shores, with the diversity of surrounding usages and of religious life, with our various nationalities and tongues, our crying need of faithful ministers, our imperfect provision for any and all of the urgent wants of the Church, there is danger that the genuinely Lutheran elements may become gradually alienated, that misunderstandings may arise, that the narrow and local may overcome the broad and general, that the unity of the Spirit in the bond of peace may be lost, and that our Church, which alone in the history of Protestantism has maintained a genuine catholicity and unity, should drift into the sectarianism and separatism which characterize and curse our land."[14]

Those who did not unite with the Council but after half a dozen years formed another general body, the Synodical Conference, felt they must justify their action. Dr. W. Sihler, at the organization meeting of the new body, admitted "frankly that we are perfectly satisfied with the doctrinal basis officially adopted by that body (the General Council) and could enter into affiliation with the Council on that

---

[13]Jacobs, H. E., A *History of the Evangelical Lutheran Church in the United States*, 2nd ed., p. 357.
[14]*Proceedings of the Convention Held by Representatives from Various Evangelical Lutheran Synods*, Reading, Pa.: 1866, p. 9.

basis." But he and the other founders of the Synodical
Conference claimed that the Council was unwilling to
discipline synods in its membership whose actions were not
in conformity with the professions of the Council. Furthermore, the Missouri Synod wanted no "open" questions but
definite answers to questions on the Church, the Ministry,
Church Government, the Antichrist.[15]

It was from the General Council and General Synod that
forces came which made these organizations means to greater ends. The General Council had resulted from the defects
of the General Synod. Yet the latter had made significant
contributions to the character of American Lutheranism.
"The General Synod," in the judgment of H. E. Jacobs, "was
a protest against the socinianizing tendency in New York
and the schemes of a union with the Reformed in Pennsylvania and with the Episcopalians in North Carolina. It stood
for the independent existence of the Lutheran Church in
America, and the clear and unequivocal confession of a positive faith. It failed, as its founders in the several synods had
failed, in specifically determining the contents of this faith."[16]

A decade after the formation of the Council steps were
taken to bring closer together the Council, the Synod, and
the Synod of the South. The three bodies worked together
on a common liturgy, a common hymnbook, in deaconess
and mission work. "In 1911 the doctrinal differences between
the three General Bodies were removed by constitutional
amendment in the General Synod, and the greatest confessional barrier in the way of Lutheran unity between them
was eliminated."[17] The approaching quadricentennial observance of the Reformation proved a powerful stimulus as

---

[15]"The Organization of the Synodical Conference," A. W. Meyer,
in *Ebenezer,* ed. by W. H. T. Dau, St. Louis: 1922, pp. 321-332.
[16]Jacobs, *op. cit.,* p. 362.
[17]*Minutes of the First Convention of the United Lutheran Church
in America,* 1918, pp. 38-39.

well as an excellent opportunity for the merger, which, in fact, was achieved in 1917. The president of the General Council in the last presidential report of the Council estimated that "the steady influence of the General Council during a half century toward a true and sound Lutheran Confession and Praxis, as thus now finally expressed in the common faith of all the bodies intending to unity, is perhaps the greatest achievement of the General Council as a body."[18]

The resulting United Lutheran Church was in a position to affect greatly the Council, which in 1918 grew out of the National Lutheran Commission for Soldiers' and Sailors' Welfare. The first officers of the National Lutheran Council were from the United Lutheran Church and the Norwegian Lutheran Church of America, which had consummated its union half a year before the United Lutheran Church. The new Council was a common agency of the cooperating synods in dealing with social and secular problems, especially such as arose out of the war. It won the adherence of most of the Lutheran synods in America, the largest group not cooperating being the Synodical Conference. The National Lutheran Council, even though its activities are restricted, represents the most comprehensive union of Lutherans in America, bridging the gap that separates the synods of the United Lutheran Church from those in the American Lutheran Conference.

The Council naturally became the means whereby communication might be carried on between the Lutherans in America and those in Europe. Some contacts had been maintained in earlier generations. The Norwegians, especially those of the Norwegian Synod, had kept in touch with the Church of Norway. The Augustana Synod had enjoyed visits by Swedish bishops; even Archbishop Nathan Soderblom had come on the Synod's invitation in 1923. So also

---

[18]*Minutes of the General Council*, 1917, p. 23.

the Danes and the Finns had been unwilling to disinherit
themselves from their European heritage. The newer German groups had been in close contact with Lœhe in
Germany even as the older groups had felt bound to Halle.
The Missouri Synod gave support to the "Evangelical Lutheran Synod of Saxony and other States," which it had
itself been instrumental in establishing.[19]

But the most significant manifestation of interest in
European Lutheranism was the membership of the General
Council in the *Allgemeine Konferenz.*[20] The *Konferenz* had
been created in the same year as the General Council held
its first convention, 1867. Its purpose was to bring together
German Lutherans who opposed the efforts of the Prussian
Unionists to impose their form of church organization on the
churches of the German Empire. The larger organization
contained as its core an *Engere Konferenz* of eighty members, who elected nine men as an executive committee. In
1901 the *Konferenz* met at Lund in Sweden, where it
widened its basis of membership and became international.
The General Council was frequently represented at the
meetings. But after 1907 the relations became strained. The
Engere Konferenz in that year was opened to members of
the Prussian Union Church though neither Lutherans in the
Union nor in free churches could be members of the executive committee. This seemed to be a concession to the Union
which the General Council could not approve, and it continued to make representations to officers of the *Konferenz* until
the war suspended the activities of this European federation.
President Schmauk in 1915 advocated that the *Konferenz*
should include all Lutherans, organized as American, Scandinavian, and Oriental branches beside the parent German

---

[19]Brunn, Arthur, "Our Transoceanic Connections," in *Ebenezer,*
pp. 467ff.
[20]"Historical Summary," in *Minutes of the General Council,* 1913,
pp. 276-285.

branch. "The time would seem to be auspicious," he said, "after peace is once again declared, for proposing this matter to that body (the *Allgemeine Konferenz*), with a view to such an inter-linking of Lutheranism, in the circle of a World Conference, as will be universal, and in which all Lutherans in the world on a sound doctrinal basis can unite on equal terms, and can secure a basis of equitable representation, such a basis as alone befits the Church of Christ, and as alone will render such a movement permanently successful."[21]

The National Lutheran Council did take up the matter after the war and together with the *Allgemeine Konferenz* made arrangements for a world conference of Lutherans, meeting at Eisenach, Germany, in August, 1923. "One hundred and sixty delegates and representatives of the Lutherans of the world, from twenty-two or more nations, with the exception of a small minority, the Synodical Conference of North America with about a million members, they represented the Lutherans of the world, or about 80,000,000 members."[22] A second world convention followed in 1929, at Copenhagen, where both the organization and the purpose of the world gathering of Lutheranism were more clearly defined. The principles were thus enunciated by the executive committee.

"1). That the continuation work of the Lutheran World Convention be spiritual and churchly in character, being governed and determined by the truth as it is in Jesus Christ, revealed in the Holy Scriptures and witnessed to positively by Luther's Small Catechism and the Augsburg Confession. The discovery and furtherance of inner unity in the truth in loyalty to the confessional principle therefore is a primary object. 2). The Lutheran World Convention shall be of the nature of a free conference or a free association of Lutheran Churches and organizations. 3). The complete autonomy of all existing organized Evangelical Churches shall be fully recognized and shall under no circumstances be interfered with. 4). The Lutheran World Convention shall exclude politics, national or international, from its pro-

[21]*Minutes of the General Council*, 1915, pp. 18-19.
[22]*Lutheran World Almanac.* 1924-1926. p. 26.

grams of discussion and work, confining its activities to the spiritual
interests of the Church and the Kingdom of God. 5). In all of its work
of serving love, the Lutheran World Convention and its Committees
shall, so far as the means are available, assist the needy and deserving
Churches of the faith without respect to race, language, or political
alignment. 6). Looking unto God for wisdom and strength, it shall be
the declared purpose of the Lutheran World Convention and its
authorized committee or committees to become the servant of all in
the Gospel and in the faith that worketh by love. 7). Since the power
is of God and His word, the utmost simplicity in organization is right
in principle and wise in the present situation."[23]

The Copenhagen convention attracted, besides 147 official
representatives from 21 countries, a very large number of
visitors.

The executive committee acted as a continuation committee, meeting from year to year in various countries until
a third world convention was assembled in Paris in 1935.
The attendance was entirely official, about 100, and the
sessions concentrated on specific topics. Among the decisions
was one that a general secretary should be elected by the
executive committee (six members). Dr. Hans Lilje of Berlin
was chosen for this position at the committee's meeting in
New York in the fall of 1936. The same group set forth a series
of resolutions on the relationship of Lutherans to ecumenical
movements. They defined the principles which Lutherans
should maintain in such relationships, called for common
Lutheran action, and declared "that recognizing that there
are true Christians in every Church of whatever name, the
Lutheran Churches of the world should approach the question of their relationship with general movements in the
spirit of catholicity and without hostility or prejudice. While
they should make no effort to gloss genuine difference they
should nevertheless proceed in the sincere and humble desire
to render service and cooperate in works of Christian love."[24]

---

[23]*Lutheran World Almanac,* 1929-30, p. 23.
[24]*Lutheran World Almanac,* 1934-37, p. 37.

Plans to hold a fourth world convention of Lutherans in Philadelphia in 1940 were under way when the second world war caused an indefinite postponement of most international activities. The National Lutheran Council has gradually become the accepted spokesman of American Lutherans in the world convention and has acted in that capacity though the exact status of the Council in the world organization is still under debate.[25]

While during the period between the world wars the Lutherans of the world were thus achieving a sense of solidarity and some measure of effective united action, Lutherans of various countries were also taking part in the ecumenical movements which had gathered force with the coming of peace after the first war. It was a Lutheran who had been leader in an effort to unite the churches of the world on a common program of social and economic action in the face of the problems of the modern world. Gradually Nathan Soderblom, Archbishop of Sweden, had won support for his *Life and Work* program. He was not uninterested in the *Faith and Order* movement, but the Church of Christ, he held, could not wait to act together on certain issues until it was fully agreed on doctrine and organization. Encouraged especially by help from the World Alliance of Friendship Through the Churches, and the American Federal Council, Soderblom arranged the great Stockholm Conference in 1925, the first large-scale meeting of the churches of Christendom since the medieval councils. The Lutheran Churches of Europe were generally represented. Only two American bodies had sent delegates: The United Lutheran Church and the Augustana Synod.

These same bodies were also the only American Lutheran participants in the world conference of the Faith and

[25] cf. *Minutes of Annual Meetings of the National Lutheran Council,* 1940-43 (mimeographed).

Order movement at Lausanne in 1927. This meeting was a goal toward which the Episcopal Church of America had striven under Bishop Brent's leadership ever since 1910. The war had prevented the full development of plans, but preparations went ahead in peacetime, and what Stockholm meant to *Life and Work*, Lausanne meant to *Faith and Order*. Both branches of the ecumenical movement continued their respective programs and a decade later met again in world conferences, Stockholm being continued by Oxford, Lausanne by Edinburgh. The list of official delegates at Edinburgh indicates how general Lutheranism outside of the United States took part in these ecumenical gatherings: Church of Norway, Church of Denmark, Lutheran Church of Finland, the Evangelical Lutheran Churches of Estonia, Latvia, France, Hungary, the Netherlands, the Church of Sweden, the German Evangelical Church in Bohemia, Moravia, and Silesia, the Evangelical Church in Slovakia, the Evangelical Augsburg Church in Poland, the Church of the Confession of Augsburg in Alsace and Lorraine, the Tamil Evangelical Lutheran Church.[26] Through membership on the continuation committee of *Life and Work* and *Faith and Order* the United Lutheran Church and the Augustana Synod have been parties to the formation of the World Council of Churches (Utrecht, 1938), and members of these bodies have served on various committees and commissions such as the Joint Committee, the American Theological Commission, the Commission on Intercommunion. Their respective bodies are as yet the only American Lutheran groups who are members of the World Council of Churches.

From the foregoing the emerging picture discloses a restless endeavor on the part of Lutherans in America to obtain fuller organic relationship. There is evidence for the

---

[26]*The Second World Conference on Faith and Order,* ed. by L. Hodgson, p. 282.

oft-repeated statement that Lutheranism is not sectarian but fundamentally ecumenical. Very few Lutheran groups have been satisfied with an independent, isolated status. The majority has always been seeking means of union. The General Synod did not succeed. The General Council succeeded only partially. The United Lutheran Church was only partly a "united" church. The Norwegians have employed the word "United," so also the Danes. The Iowa and Ohio merger resulted in an "American" Lutheran Church though none could claim the term as all-inclusive. The American Lutheran Conference has had some thought of embracing all Lutherans in America, but the development of the Conference since 1930 gives little ground for supposing that such will be its destiny. Rather, the National Lutheran Council has proved to be the most national and the most effective of all common endeavors, and current proposals to enlarge its scope and its authority are but an outgrowth of successful enterprises already a part of its history.

In any closer fellowship of American Lutherans there will assuredly be voices raised in behalf of an ecumenicity which extends beyond synodical mergers. It is already clear that Lutherans in America wish to renew the bonds of faith which existed in earlier generations with the homelands of Lutheranism. Lutheran world conventions have only begun. The center of the world church may already be in America, which has had to furnish funds and leadership for times of reconstruction. Closer ties with the Scandinavian, the German, the minority and the younger churches of the mission fields are necessary if the church of the Reformation is to give united testimony in a broken and despairing world. The real ecumenicity of the Lutheran Church will reveal itself in the breadth of sympathy and largeness of outlook which the postwar years will demand of any communion that claims universality.

But does ecumenicity stop for Lutherans even in a world convention of those who subscribe to the doctrinal declaration of the Eisenach convention? "The Lutheran World Convention acknowledges the Holy Scriptures of the Old and New Testaments as the only source and infallible norm of all church doctrines and practice, and sees in the Confessions of the Lutheran Church, especially in the Unaltered Augsburg Confession and Luther's Small Catechism, a pure exposition of the Word of God."[27] Or is there an interpretation of the ecumenical spirit which finds some relationship short of organic union possible with those who "accept our Lord Jesus Christ as God and Savior"?[28]

Surely, the Lutherans in America will not agree to enter into any organic union with other Christians on terms such as those S. S. Schmucker proposed almost a century ago. But if the discussions and the meetings of the past generation have taught anything at all, it is that sincere Christians in various communions desire to find some *modus vivendi* which at least will not deny to the world the unity that actually does exist between Christians of different churches. Though we do not believe that a unity of "Order, or the union of the Church Visible, *i.e.*, of ecclesiastical denominations, is the unity to which our Savior referred in His prayer to the Father,"[29] yet one might ask: "Why all the constant search of Lutherans for formulæ of agreements among themselves? Do the Lutheran bodies not, by their very uneasiness in isolation, proclaim that the Lord wills that such unity as exists shall be made evident?"

Those who established the American Lutheran Conference put into their constitution the declaration that "in the providence of God, the time appears to have come when

---

[27]*Lutheran World Almanac,* 1929-1930, p. 24.
[28]The doctrinal basis of the World Council of Churches.
[29]Schmauk, in President's Report, *Minutes of the General Council,* 1911, p. 13.

Lutheran Church bodies in America that are one in faith and that have declared pulpit and altar fellowship with one another should manifest their oneness by seeking to foster fraternal relations and by cooperating in the extension of the kingdom of Christ."[30] By what reasoning can it be said that it is not the will of God that Christians in America and in the world should "manifest their oneness"? That oneness may not be the same as the oneness of those who have adopted the Eisenach formula. But it is ecumenical to participate in the efforts of the various communions to discover what "oneness" they do share. The Church of Sweden replied to one of the questions raised at Lausanne in words that seem altogether in harmony with ecumenical Lutheranism.

"We are convinced that it is possible to reach the goal of our aspirations only by the road of federation. We are quite aware that there are those who are of opinion that such a federative unity—a league of churches with an executive council—would fall short of the goal. We should not be satisfied with anything less than full organic union, and should carefully avoid every substitute for this. We find, however, in a league of churches not a substitute for an organic union but a temporary stage of evolution, a fellowship in service, necessary for solving the practical problems of the church, which, through more intimate conviction and mutual knowledge, is calculated to prepare and advance the highest form of organic unity which is the ultimate goal. It would be a step for reaching the goal, and according to our conviction a necessary step. Through manifold divisions we have been disunited and have developed differently, each in a special way. It is not possible for us to be organically reunited save by growing together little by little. This process of growing together has begun most hopefully. We must carefully avoid being too rash in quickening this process in a way incompatible with the nature of life, which is to develop step by step until perfection is reached."[31]

The same spirit which urges Lutherans on to unity with those who are in Christ is the spirit which would seek a unity beyond the barriers of geography and history with the

---

[30]*Journal of the American Lutheran Conference,* Vol. II, No. 3, (March, 1937) p. 9.
[31]*Convictions,* ed. by L. Hodgson, pp. 160-161.

saints of all times and places. This communion of saints is a reality even in this life, and somehow those who are of the household of Christ, who knows His own, should discover and learn to live with His other children. Never will those who participated at Edinburgh in 1927 forget nor regret that moment when 414 delegates from 22 Christian communions in 43 different countries gave their adherence in the following affirmation. It is a document which bears witness to the truth that a principle of unity dwells within Protestantism despite its divisions,[32] and that Christianity is the ultimate principle of unity even as Christ is one, and salvation is one in Him.

"We are one in faith in our Lord Jesus Christ, the incarnate Word of God. We are one in allegiance to Him as Head of the Church, and as King of kings and Lord of lords. We are one in acknowledging that this allegiance takes precedence of any other allegiance that may make claims upon us.

"This unity does not consist in the agreement of our minds or the consent of our wills. It is founded in Jesus Christ Himself, who lived, died and rose again to bring us to the Father, and who through the Holy Spirit dwells in His Church. We are one because we are all the objects of the love and grace of God, and called by Him to witness in all the world to His glorious gospel.

"Our unity is of heart and spirit. We are divided in the outward forms of our life in Christ, because we understand differently His will for His Church. We believe, however, that a deeper understanding will lead us towards a united apprehension of the truth as it is in Jesus.

"We humbly acknowledge that our divisions are contrary to the will of Christ, and we pray God in His Mercy to shorten the days of our separation and to guide us by His Spirit into fulness of unity.

"We are thankful that during recent years we have been drawn together; prejudices have been overcome, misunderstandings removed, and real, if limited, progress has been made towards our goal of a common mind.

"In this Conference we may gratefully claim that the Spirit of God has made us willing to learn from one another, and has given us a fuller vision of the truth and enriched our spiritual experience.

"We have lifted up our hearts together in prayer; we have sung the same hymns; together we have read the same Holy scriptures. We

---

[32]Cf. McNeill, J. T., *Unitive Protestantism*, 1930.

recognize in one another, across the barriers of our separation, a common Christian outlook and a common standard of values. We are therefore assured of a unity deeper than our divisions.

"We are convinced that our unity of spirit and aim must be embodied in a way that will make it manifest to the world, though we do not yet clearly see what outward form it should take.

"We believe that every sincere attempt to cooperate in the concerns of the kingdom of God draws the severed communions together in increased mutual understanding and goodwill. We call upon our fellow-Christians of all communions to practise such cooperation; to consider patiently occasions of disunion that they may be overcome; to be ready to learn from those who differ from them; to seek to remove those obstacles to the furtherance of the gospel in the non-Christian world which arise from our divisions; and constantly to pray for that unity which we believe to be our Lord's will for His Church.

"We desire also to declare to all men everywhere our assurance that Christ is the one hope of unity for the world in face of the distractions and dissensions of this present time. We know that our witness is weakened by our divisions. Yet we are one in Christ and in the fellowship of His Spirit. We pray that everywhere, in a world divided and perplexed, men may turn to Jesus Christ our Lord, who makes us one in spite of our divisions; that He may bind in one those who by many worldly claims are set at variance; and that the world may at last find peace and unity in Him; to whom be glory for ever."[33]

---

[33]*The Second World Conference on Faith and Order,* ed. by L. Hodgson, 275-276.

BIBLIOGRAPHICAL NOTE

The material used in this article is based on official reports contained in the proceedings of the bodies concerned. The references to the *Minutes* of the Augustana Synod are to the published records of the annual conventions, which in earlier years were in Swedish, *Referat af förhandlingarna vid Augustana Synodens—årsmöte,* published by the Augustana Book Concern, Rock Island, Illinois.

The proceedings of the General Council of the Evangelical Lutheran Church in North America (organized 1867) are printed in the *Minutes* of the Council's biennial conventions up to the merger of the Council with the General Synod of the Evangelical Lutheran Church in the United States of America (organized 1821) and the United Synod of the Evangelical Lutheran Church in the South (organized 1886) in 1918. The merged bodies became the United Lutheran Church in America, and the proceedings then appear as the *Minutes of the Convention of the United Lutheran Church in America* (First Convention, New York City, 1918).

The Lutheran World Almanac was first published in 1921 by the National Lutheran Council, which has issued subsequent volumes at irregular intervals. References are made to these volumes by year or years (thus 1934-37 is one volume). The Minutes of the annual meetings of the National Lutheran Council are available only in mimeographed form.

The Journal of the American Lutheran Conference is a publication of the American Lutheran Conference, formed in 1930 by bodies not in the United Lutheran Church or the Synodical Conference. *Ebenezer* is a memorial volume of the Missouri Synod, published on the occasion of the synod's seventy-fifth anniversary, in St. Louis, in 1922, edited by W. H. T. Dau.

The Second World Conference on Faith and Order is the title of a volume edited by L. Hodgson, covering the proceedings of the conference in Edinburgh, 1937, under the auspices of the Faith and Order Movement. This same movement published *Convictions,* a volume of responses from the Churches to points raised at the first conference at Lausanne in 1927.

Other volumes cited in this paper are: Acrelius, I., *A History of New Sweden,* trans. by W. M. Reynolds, Historical Society of Penna., 1847. Jacobs, H. E., *A History of the Evangelical Lutheran Church in the United States,* 2nd ed., 1899. McNeill, J. T., *Unitive Protestantism,* 1930.

WORSHIP

LUTHER D. REED

The place and the scope of liturgics in theological education should be proportioned to the importance of worship itself in the history and the life of the church.

Public Worship Essential, Universal, Unique

The current "Liturgical Movement" is a new interest for some. Leaders in many communions are seeking to recover lost or impaired qualities of reverence and beauty and to lift public worship above the uncertainty and the mediocrity of individualism. There is an increasing appreciation of literary values and of art and music, with resulting impatience with crudity and ugliness.

For the historic liturgical churches, however, the maintenance of ordered and beautiful services has ever been a matter of study and endeavor. For them corporate worship is an essential and unique institution of the whole church. From the beginning believers have maintained fellowship with God and with each other by common assemblies of worship. At no time or place has the church developed without such assemblies. Organized Christianity could not long exist anywhere without them.

This public worship of Almighty God has no counterpart in secular experience. The Lord's House, the Lord's Day, the Lord's Service are not duplicated anywhere. In public worship the church, as the Body of Christ in the world, exercises and develops its spiritual powers and best impresses its claims upon the non-Christian world.

Reality in worship is attained by faith. Without this worship would be fantasy or pageantry. Back of common

(391)

prayer and the common faith are the revelation of God in Jesus Christ and the divine energy of the Holy Spirit, who "calls, gathers, enlightens, and sanctifies the whole Christian Church on earth." Faith thus rooted and grounded brings Christians together for praise and prayer, fills the House of God with melody and beauty, and carries the inspiration of the sanctuary into the home, the community, and everyday life. Thus worship has its monuments—its churches and cathedrals, its liturgies and hymnals, its music and art—in every clime and time.

The separate aspects of worship—adoration, confession, commemoration, thanksgiving, sacrifice, supplication, and intercession—are merged and heightened in our conception of it as communion, an idea which is particularly stressed in the Lutheran system. The thought of communion is evident in the church's doctrines of the Person of Christ, the Church, Baptism, and the Lord's Supper. Luther with great simplicity said, "These are the two priestly offices, *viz.*, to hear God speak and to speak to God who hears us." And again at the dedication of the Castle Church at Torgau in 1544, in speaking of the nature and the aim of worship, he said these were "that we assemble together at a common time and place; that we hear God's word and lay before God our own needs and those of other people . . . and that we celebrate God's blessings with thanksgiving." The fundamental principle of all worship, as we understand it, is this "balanced pattern of initiation and response" which comprehends the objective or sacramental gifts of God on the one hand and our subjective or sacrificial response in canticles, hymns, prayers, and offerings on the other hand.

The gospel and the sacraments are individualized in a special way in the services of worship which culminate in the Holy Communion. St. Augustine recognized this as "the sacrament of unity" in that it realizes a double fellowship, the communion of believers as the Body of Christ and their corporate communion with Christ, their Exalted Head. In this atmosphere of religious collectivity and group experience the convictions and the aspirations of individuals are nourished, elevated, and intensified. Distinctions so important in the outside world fall away. Here the rich and the poor, the strong and the weak are of equal stature before God. Together they gain strength as they unite in a common service of devotion which has greater significance and scale than the private devotions of any individual in the group could possibly attain.

Corporate worship is thus one of the great, constructive factors in Christian experience. Because of its importance, its universality, and its uniqueness the church makes every effort to preserve the purity of its worship with respect to content and form and to raise it above the levels of the secular and the commonplace. Thus, apart from spiritual and social considerations, more time, thought, and wealth are regularly expended in the building of churches and the maintenance of services of worship, the installation of altars, organs, and other liturgical appointments, the remuneration of organists, choirmasters, singers, sextons, etc., than in the work of missions, religious education, and all other practical activities of the church combined.

Significance of the Liturgy

With relatively few exceptions Christian worship has been and is liturgical, that is, ordered, with forms and usages prescribed by authority and accepted and used over wide areas by member groups in some general church body. The historic churches—Eastern, Roman, Lutheran, and Anglican—all have their historic liturgies. The "Free Churches," a minority in Christendom, have developed more or less stereotyped forms and orders of worship for local and limited use.

The liturgies of the historic churches are works of large dimension and universal significance. They differ materially from the orders of worship of the Free churches, which individual pastors prepare according to "psychological patterns" for the use of particular congregations. These "worship programs" usually consist of lessons, responsive readings, hymns, and prayers selected from various sources and interspersed with organ and choral numbers. Such "devotional exercises" preliminary to the sermon, however balanced, beautiful, and edifying in themselves, have no connection with the services of other congregations and little connection with other services in the same congregation.

The liturgy is something different. It is not a sheaf of pretty autumn leaves but a noble, living tree. It is the work and the possession of the whole church. It is used by thousands of congregations over continental areas. Its plan is not limited to a single service but encompasses the cycle of a year. It provides a fixed framework for every service throughout the year but inserts in this fixed form rich selections of variable material appropriate for particular festivals and days. Its invariable Order for Confession, its Kyrie, its Gloria and other canticles of praise, its Creed, Common Preface, Sanctus, Lord's Prayer, and Words of Institution express the universal beliefs and needs of all men at all times. Its ever-changing "propers"—Lessons, Introits, Graduals, Collects and Prayers, Sermons, Hymns, and choral music— unfold the themes of particular days or seasons. Each individual service is thus a spoke in a wheel, a polished and balanced order complete in itself but related to the other services in its season and to the whole cycle of the Christian Year.

Formal perfection and polish, however, are not the chief qualities in the liturgy. Its essential significance lies in its content rather than in its form. It is rich in Scriptural thought and phrase. It contains gems from the Psalms, the

Prophets, the Gospels, and other books of the New Testament set in the golden fabric of its own confessions and thanksgivings, its collects and prayers, its canticles of praise. But apart from this Scriptural content and tone its carefully prepared outline presents a complete summary of the Christian faith and life as a basis for common edification and instruction. As the Liturgical Year unfolds it reveals God's eternal plan of salvation in the life, teaching, death, and resurrection of Jesus Christ, our Lord. The liturgy is the guardian of the faith. It omits no essential part of the gospel and includes nothing unimportant or unworthy. Its supreme function is to present and to administer, with all possible beauty and holy joy, the divine gifts of grace in Word and sacrament and to afford an opportunity for response in united prayer, praise, and thanksgiving. Because of its confessional character it provides a wealth of illustration and information for the student of dogmatic theology.

As the product and possession of the universal church the liturgy enshrines the faith of every age and continent. It preserves features of Jewish as well as of early Christian worship. Its Gloria in Excelsis, the General Prayer, the Preface, and the Sanctus are contributions from the Eastern Church; its Order of Confession and its series of Introits, Graduals, Collects, Proper Prefaces, and Liturgical Lessons are developments of the Western Church. In the simplification and the purification of its text, the use of the vernacular, the development of the sermon, and its wealth of congregational song and artistic choral music we have products of the Reformation.

Enhanced by all the arts, the liturgy comes to us a gift of the Christian centuries to our own time. It is to be treasured, enriched, and transmitted to those who come after us. But it is more than a high heritage. It is a living, flexible, powerful instrument for today, which expresses the individual's spirit of devotion in forms richer and more satisfying than he himself could fashion and which unites all worshippers in a great spiritual transaction. It promotes church consciousness and church unity by lifting the individual congregation above parochial and local levels. It brings the church of today into conscious fellowship with the church of the past and enables it to commune in faith and in hope with the church triumphant. It acquaints the youth with the most important parts of God's Word and impresses upon them the duty and the privilege of corporate devotion. Its power of suggestion enforces the truths which education labors to implant more directly. Its forms satisfy the needs and the aspirations of mature Christians of every station.

Liturgical Art

The liturgy is more than a literary product. Its use invites the aid of art in many forms.

As soon as the early church was freed from persecution it built its basilicas and decorated them with ever-increasing richness. It rejected the pagan temple along with paganism itself and developed a new type of building. Eventually the influences of the classic era declined, and the church, as the one stable and permanent factor in the civilization of the time, brought all art into its service, fostered it in its monasteries, and gave it a definitely Christian spirit and aim. Even lay craftsmen and artists in their powerful guilds strove to exalt the honor of the church and the glory of its worship. The churches and cathedrals of that era amaze us by their perfection of plan, variety and beauty of detail, and strength of construction. Their exterior proportions dominated their surroundings, and their interiors were sumptuously decorated and furnished with carvings of wood and stone, paintings on walls and canvas, altars and reredoses, roodscreens and choir stalls, fonts and ciboriums, crosses and chalices, service books, vestments and embroideries, and innumerable creations in silver and gold, in glass and mosaics, in enamel and bronze.

The church furnished the themes for this mighty effort, and her liturgical life determined its forms. Through the use of a universally understood symbolism art became the teacher of her children and the preacher of the gospel to all men. Poetry fashioned the liturgy, hymns, and sequences. Music, developing the early Greek modes and recitative, clothed the liturgy in the melodies of the Plain Song system and finally blossomed forth in harmony and counterpoint in the loveliness of the Netherlands School of the fifteenth century and the spirituality of the Palestrina School of the sixteenth century.

The Renaissance profoundly influenced art and the church alike. Its revival of classic culture and its promotion of intellectual and artistic endeavor outside the church developed individual technical proficiency and led to a freer appreciation of nature. In exploring these new fields, however, art lost much of its spiritual motivation and ministry.

In the era of the Reformation the spirit of Zwinglianism and Calvinism was hostile to liturgical art. Luther and his followers on the contrary appreciated it. They preserved and purified the liturgy, kept alive the liturgical principle, and fostered the development of liturgical art. Luther as the leader in this type of conservative reform preserved the ancient Plain Song, laid the foundations of the German Chorale, encouraged the composition of artistic polyphonic music for choirs, and prepared the way for the eventual development of a great musical literature for the organ. Influences which sprang from his leadership enabled the Lutheran Church in its subsequent history to make contributions of

the greatest importance to the literature of church music in
a movement which culminated in the choral preludes, canta-
tas, and mighty organ fugues of Johann Sebastian Bach.

Formal worship and church art languished in all communions in the days of Pietism and Rationalism. It remained
for the liturgical revival of the nineteenth century, with the
aid of contemporary Romanticism, to awaken interest in the
liturgy and to rouse the church to the recovery of its forgotten treasures in architecture, music, painting, and the minor
arts. This churchly revival, manifest in the Roman as well as
the Lutheran and the Anglican communions for the past
century, is still gaining momentum. The radical objections of
the Zwinglians and the Puritans have lost their force, and
practically all Christian groups today welcome the aid of art
in worship. Inspiration and leadership in this field will,
however, of necessity remain in the liturgical communions.

There are philosophical considerations which explain the
long and intimate association of art with worship. Art
belongs to the completeness, the wholeness of life. Worship,
like life itself, is incomplete and imperfect if it lacks beauty.
Art has supreme powers of expression. In worship it is art
which enables the truth and the goodness of the Christian
faith to express themselves significantly and beautifully.

Art preserves and interprets quality; it impresses, suggests, evokes. The Nicene Creed is a theological formula
which confesses the divinity of our Lord. The Te Deum is a
great hymn which expresses precisely the same truth in
a worshipful and a vital way. The beauty of its text and the
power of its music give it wings. The Augsburg Confession
and the Decrees of Trent give theological definitions regarding the Lord's Supper. The Holy Communion, as celebrated
by Christian congregations, gives the picture of our Lord's
breaking, blessing, and distributing the bread and the wine
to His disciples and at the same time vividly suggests signifi-

cant meanings of the Sacrament for all believers. It is this
power to impress and to suggest as well as to exalt that
makes liturgical art so valuable a servant ... the temple.[1]

Liturgics in Theological Education

Thus corporate worship is not only an experience of the
individual and of the group but an institution of the church.
The liturgy is the mother of all liturgical art. The liturgy and
liturgical art must be studied and practiced. Their history
must be traced, their principles clarified, their material organized, and their techniques perfected and exemplified. This is
the function of the science of liturgics. This science should
have its rightful place in the curriculum and the life of the
seminary beside the other recognized theological disciplines.

Unfortunately, this subject receives little or no scientific
treatment in most Protestant seminaries. Worship generally
seems to be thought of as something subjective, individual,
emotional, occasional. Even in Lutheran seminaries its
objective character and scope, its importance as a historical
institution, and the essential unity of liturgics and liturgical
art are not generally appreciated.

In preparation for the study of the English Bible we lay
foundations and build backgrounds; we study the original
languages of Scripture and develop principles of exegesis.
In theology proper we are not concerned primarily with
current discussions and theories but with the mastery of
distinct doctrines and systems of historical and universal
significance. Similarly in the matter of worship, while
appreciating its personal and practical aspects, we should
develop our study along scientific lines. We should acquaint
our students with its history and its monuments in the great

---

[1]The thoughts briefly presented so far in this chapter are fully
developed in *The Lutheran Liturgy*, a book by the author, which may
be expected from the press shortly.

liturgies, prayer collections, and hymnals of the church, the vast literature of church music and the significant church buildings of all periods with their wealth of symbolism and architectural detail. These are some of the greatest creations of the Christian spirit. The Missal and the Breviary, the great cathedrals and churches, and the vast literature of Plain Song and polyphonic music are, in strength of conception and elaboration of detail, as massive and as mighty as are the contemporary theological systems of Thomas Aquinas or Peter Lombard, and quite as worthy of study. Liturgical practice, liturgical development, liturgical reform are all expressions of the church's life, which life flows out through worship as truly as through doctrine or through missions, education, and Christian social service.

In spite of its historical and practical importance, however, worship as a subject is the stepchild of the theological curriculum. In most seminaries the part time of a professor whose real strength is devoted to homiletics, church history, religious education, or something else is given to worship. A professional musician may also give an hour or two in church music, and some other professor may have a course in hymnology. Church architecture is usually neglected entirely in spite of the fact that ministers have the responsibility of spending their people's money wisely and of instructing architects precisely concerning the liturgical appointments of the church building.

Study of the curriculum offerings in the latest catalogs of the ten largest Lutheran seminaries, representing all the major bodies in the country, shows that there is no uniform treatment of subjects in this field. The offerings range from two required semester hours in one seminary to ten required and six elective in another. With the exception of one or at most two seminaries liturgics and liturgical art everywhere receive far less consideration than is accorded other important subjects.

Four seminaries require as little as two semester hours of liturgics with no electives. Five seminaries give no more than an additional hour to either church music, church architecture, hymnology, or church art proper; three seminaries give two hours to these subjects as a group; two give six hours. One seminary, which has given departmental status to liturgics and church art for the past thirty-three years, offers six required hours and four elective hours in liturgics proper, two required hours in church architecture, one required hour in church music, one required hour in hymnology, and two elective hours in church art.

Departmental status for the subject of worship is urged, not simply because of the importance of worship in general, but because of the importance of the Lutheran liturgy and the distinctive contributions of the Lutheran Church to liturgical art. The Lutheran liturgy is a type, one of the three great, distinctive liturgies of the Western Church. Its character has developed from principles inherent in Lutheranism itself. The Reformers, who restated the doctrines of the church in the sixteenth century, were equally concerned with its worship. The typical Lutheran liturgy, which developed under their active leadership in Germany and in Scandinavia between the years 1523 and 1539, became at once a classic expression of the Lutheran faith comparable to the Confessions themselves. Moreover, it was the first successful attempt to purify and to simplify the historic services of the church and to give them expression in the vernacular, antedating by several decades the corresponding achievement of the Church of England in its Book of Common Prayer.

Unfortunately, in their preparation of the church orders the Reformers generally gave only an outline of the services, counting upon familiarity with the historic liturgical books and the weight of liturgical tradition to enable the evangelical pastors to conduct the services properly without complete textual and rubrical detail. The Thirty Years' War destroyed the old office books and disorganized church life. Pietism and Rationalism ignored or rejected the historic liturgy; the liturgical tradition was broken, and liturgical art languished. The nineteenth-century revival of confessionalism and church life was real and powerful, but recovery of historic values in the field of worship was slow and partial. In the Common Service the Lutheran Church in America has recovered the historic services of our fathers. In scholarly and popular understanding of these services, in conforming our worship in all consistency to our doctrine, in the use of proper evangelical ceremonial, and in the enrichment of our services and our sanctuaries by significant and beautiful forms of art we are still beneath the levels of achievement attained by our church in the cities and large towns of Germany and Scandinavia in the sixteenth century.

We have much ground to recover, and eventually we shall have a great field to cultivate and to develop. Recovery and development should center in the seminaries, where the entire subject can be integrated with other departments of theological education and held in balance with other aspects of Christian thought and life. We should encourage serious study of the liturgy and related subjects by pastors and laymen in local societies and groups, for we cannot hope for growth and proper development in this field except at the hands of those who know and love the subject. But we must recognize the fact that organized, aggressive leadership by individuals and groups outside the seminaries frequently focuses upon externals and promotes confusion and controversy.

The history and the genius of our church, as well as the requirements of our future ministry, call for adequate instruction and training in these subjects. Our smaller institutions should offer more required courses in this field and integrate them thoroughly. The larger seminaries should give the subject departmental status, supplementing adequate required courses by elective and seminar offerings. The professor in charge should be responsible, not only for instruction in the classroom, but for the supervision of the daily and special services of the institution.

Liturgical Life in the Seminary

The daily services of the seminary are or should be a very important factor in seminary life, for spiritual values should crown the intellectual and the practical activities of every church school.

The seminary community contains able men of the church as teachers, and the flower of the church's youth as students. This group of spiritually minded men in close association day by day should strive to realize the church's ideals in every department of life. Its devotional ideals and its traditional forms of worship should be made real, attractive, and powerful, particularly in the larger institutions which are able to employ the resources of art.

Every member of the faculty should feel that the chapel services are as important as work in the classroom and should manifest his interest by regular attendance. The authorized liturgical appointments in the church's Service Book should be mastered by the students who themselves should conduct most of the chapel services under the direction of the chaplain. No matter what modifications may have to be made later under abnormal parish conditions, every student while in the seminary should become thoroughly familiar with the structure and the details of The Service, Matins, Vespers, the Suffrages, the Litany, the Bidding Prayer, and the Occasional Services, and should be taught how to conduct them to the edification of congregations.

Four important results may be expected from chapel services of this sort. The faculty and the student body will be knit together in new bonds of understanding and spiritual unity; the spiritual life of everyone will be deepened by daily use of approved and perfected forms; the students, particularly as they employ these historical forms to express their own devotion, will be brought into conscious fellowship with the Holy Catholic Church, the Communion of Saints; and they will receive the training in leadership in public worship which will enable them in their future ministry to be as proficient in their practice as is the lawyer, the surgeon, the architect, or the engineer in his special field.

The chapel services will also provide the setting for inspiring messages by able speakers. The climax of their spiritual influence and power will be realized in frequent administrations of the Holy Communion. The seminaries which regularly bring teachers and students together before the altar of God in the devout reception of the Holy Communion know, indeed, that the Sacrament is a means of grace in their own community life.

The seminaries may also well provide opportunities for the holding of retreats and quiet days to which upon occasion the alumni and the local clergy may be invited. The chapel or some other appropriately furnished room should also be available at other times for private meditation and prayer.

The Lutheran Church is an historic, liturgical church with a truly worshipful spirit. Our liturgy in its complete provisions challenges us to renewed efforts. We must be worthy of our heritage, and we must use and develop it. If the seminaries provide leadership and inspiration, the church will respond with understanding and gladness of heart in rich offerings of talent, wealth, and consecrated endeavor.

THE LITERATURE OF LITURGICS

This is extensive, and only a few important and valuable works in Liturgics proper can be mentioned. Most of them have appeared since 1925, and to save space, dates of publication are omitted except in the case of some important earlier works.

AUTHORITATIVE ARTICLES in Herzog-Hauck, *Realencyklopadie* (24 vol.); *The Catholic Encyclopedia* (17 vol); Smith, William & Cheetham, Samuel, ed. *A Dictionary of Christian Antiquities* (2 vol., 1880).

GENERAL INTRODUCTION, with full historical treatment: Duchesne, L., *Christian Worship, Its Origin and Evolution* (invaluable to the eighth century); Underhill, Evelyn, *Worship;* Hislop, D. H., *Our Heritage in Public Worship;* Maxwell, W. D., *An Outline of Christian Worship;* Hardman, Oscar, *A History of Christian Worship* (the last two brief but good), and Rietschel, Georg, *Lehrbuch der Liturgik* (2 vol. 1900-09).

Noteworthy works with philosophical, theological, and historical approach: Will, Robert, *Le culte* (3 vol.); Kirk, K. E., *The Vision of God;* Sperry, W. L., *Reality in Worship.* Daniel, H. A., *Codex Liturgicus* (2 vol. 1847-53) inaugurated comparative study of the great liturgies; recent stimulating studies in this field by Heiler, Friedrich, *The Spirit of Worship,* and Brilioth, Yngve, *Eucharistic Faith and Practice, Evangelical and Catholic.*

THE EARLY CHURCH: Oesterley, W. O. E., *The Jewish Background of the Christian Liturgy;* Schaff, Philip, *The Teaching of the Twelve Apostles* (3rd ed., 1899); Easton, B. S., tr., *The Apostolic Tradition of Hippolytus;* Leitzmann, Hans, *Messe und Herrenmahl;* Warren, F. E., *The Liturgy and Ritual of the Ante-Nicene Church* (2nd ed.); Srawley, J. H., *The Early History of the Liturgy;* Maclean, A. J., *The Ancient Church Orders;* Cabrol, Fernand, *The Prayer of the Early Christians.*

PRE-REFORMATION AND ROMAN sources: Feltoe, C. L. *Sacramentarium Leonianum* (1896); Wilson, H. A., ed., *The Gelasian Sacramentary* (1894) and *The Gregorian Sacramentary; Missale Romanum; Breviarium Romanum* (4 vol.); *Rituale Romanum* (1914). History and discussion: Thalhofer, Valentin, *Handbuch der katholischen Liturgik,* hrsg. von Lugwig Eisenhofer; an exhaustive work in 2 vol. (1912); Gihr, *Holy Sacrifice of the Mass;* Frere, W. H., *Studies in the Early Roman Liturgy;* Fortescue, Adrian, *The Mass,* a scholarly work in very readable form; Cabrol, Fernand, *The Mass of the Western Rites;* Baümer, Suitbert, *Geschichte des Breviers* (1905); Batiffol, Pierre, *History of the Roman Breviary* (1912); Bishop, Edmund,

Liturgica Historica (1918), an extensive collection of learned essays. The Ceremonial: Fortescue, Adrian, *The Ceremonies of the Roman Rite Described* (1920); O'Connell, J., *The Celebration of the Mass* (3 vol.).

LUTHERAN sources: *Dr. Martin Luther's Werke,* Weimar edition (1883-1939); Luther, Martin, *Works* (6 vol.), Philadelphia (1915-32); Richter, Ludwig, *Die evangelischen Kirchenordnungen des sechszehnten Jahrhunderts* (1846), the earliest collection with many texts incomplete; Sehling, Emil, ed., *Die evangelischen Kirchenordnungen des XVI. Yahrhunderts* (1902-13), a monumental work complete so far as its six published volumes go.

HISTORY AND DISCUSSION on the Church Orders: Fendt, Leonhard, *Der lutherische Gottesdienst des 16. Yahrhunderts* (1923); Höfling, J. W. F., *Liturgisches Urkunden Buch* (1854). General Discussion: Kliefoth, Theodor, *Liturgische Abhandlungen* (1854-61), an exhaustive work in 8 vol.; Alt, Heinrich, *Der Christliche Cultus* (3 vol., 1851-60); Schoeberlein, Ludwig, *Schatz des liturgischen Chor— und Gemeindegesangs* (1865-72), historical music of the liturgy; Rietschel, *Lehrbuch der Liturgik,* presents the best in these earlier works and organizes the material in the entire field, including not only the Liturgy, Matins and Vespers and the Occasional Services, but Church Architecture and Church Music. This is still the best all-round work though limited in usefulness for Lutherans in America by its preoccupation with details of the provincial state churches in Europe. Loehe, Wilhelm, ed., *Agende für Christliche Gemeinden des Lutherischen Bekenntnisses* (1844) with its reconstruction of the historical Lutheran liturgy was very influential.

ON THE SWEDISH CHURCH: Bergendoff, Conrad, *Olavus Petri and the Ecclesiastical Transformation in Sweden,* 1521-1552; Wordsworth, John, *The National Church of Sweden* (1911); Yelverton, E. E., *The Swedish Rite* (1921); also *The Mass in Sweden* (1919); Quensel, Oscar, *Bidrag till Svenska Liturgiens Historia.*

ON THE COMMON SERVICE AND THE LUTHERAN CHURCH IN AMERICA IN GENERAL: Reed, L. D., ed., *Memoirs of the Lutheran Liturgical Association* (7 vol., 1906); Strodach, Paul Z., *Manual on Worship; The Church Year;* Kretzmann, *Christian Art;* Lochner, Friedrich, *Der Hauptgottesdienst der Evangelisch-Lutherischen Kirche* (1895); Reed, L. D., *The Lutheran Liturgy,* to be published shortly.

ANGLICAN: The best historical introduction to the Book of Common Prayer is Proctor, W. H. and Frere, Francis, ed., *A New History of the Book of Common Prayer.* An equally valuable work with admirable introduction and tables of sources is Brightman, F. E., *The English Rite* (2 vol., 1915). *The Prayer Book Dictionary,* ed. by Harford, G., Stevenson, M., and Tryer, J. W.; and *Liturgy and Worship* by Clarke, W. K. L. and Harris, Charles, contain valuable articles by specialists. Dearmer, Percy, *The Parson's Handbook,* now in its 14th ed., supplies a practical directory with historical background. Bishop Dowden's *Workmanship of the Prayer Book, Further Studies in the Prayer Book,* and *The Church Year* are works of sound scholarship. Jacobs, H. E., *The Lutheran Movement in England* (1894), first disclosed important Lutheran influence on the Prayer Book. Scuddamore, W. E., *Notitia Eucharistica* (1876), is an erudite work which explores the ancient sources. Parsons, E. L. and Jones, B. H., *The American Prayer Book,* is a work of independent value.

SPECIAL STUDIES: Heiler, Friedrich, *Prayer;* Brown, W. A., *The Life of Prayer in a World of Science;* Goulburn, E. M., *The Collects of the Day* (2 vol., 1883); Althaus, Paul, *Zur Einführung in die Quellengeschichte der Kirchlichen Kollekten in den Lutherischen Agenden des 16. Jahrhunderts* (1919); Strodach, *The Collect;* Drews, Paul, *Beiträge zu Luthers Liturgischen Reformen* (1910); Gummey, H. R., Jr., *The Consecration of the Eucharist* (1908); Frere, W. H., *The Anaphora;* Linton, Arthur, *Twenty-five Consecration Prayers;* Webber, F. R., *Studies in the Liturgy;* Lowrie, Walter, *The Lord's Supper and the Liturgy.*

CHURCH MUSIC

Its Place in Lutheran Worship

W. G. POLACK

Martin Luther placed music next to theology as a great gift of God to man. "It is the gift and grace of God," he said, "not an invention of man." Another poet called music the "heavenly maid." Carlyle stated that "music is the speech of angels." The Book of Job reminds us that music accompanied the creation when "the morning stars sang together, and all the sons of God shouted for joy," and the Apocalypse tells us that the Heavenly City, the New Jerusalem, resounds with the strains of the "new song" sung by the redeemed to the praise and glory of the Lamb that sitteth on the throne, described by Milton thus:

> "That undisturbed song of pure concent,
> Ay sung before the sapphire-colored throne,
> To Him that sits thereon,
> With saintly shout and solemn Jubily,
> Where the bright Seraphim in burning row
> Their loud uplifted Angel trumpets blow,
> And the Cherubick host in thousand quires
> Touch their immortal Harps of golden wires,
> With those just Spirits that wear victorious Palms
> Hymns devout, and holy Psalms
> Singing everlastingly."

Music has an important place in the world. It has rightly been said: "We live in a singing world. Nature is full of music. The soughing of winds, the ripple of streams, the roar of waterfalls, the call of birds—these are about us in the wild places. And in the places of men's habitation the very noises which, near at hand, disturb us sometimes, blend at a distance into weird and subtle harmonies. . . . Moreover to sing is as instinctive with mankind as to

(408)

breathe. . . . Children often sing before they talk." Horace Bushnell said, "Everything the sun shines upon sings, or can be made to sing, and can be heard to sing."

> "Music is in all growing things;
> And, underneath the silky wings
> Of smallest insect, there is stirred
> A pulse of air that must be heard;
> Earth's silence lives, and throbs, and sings."

As the music of the earth and heaven rises in praise of God, the children of God on earth have ever brought their sacrifices of thanksgiving and praise to Him on the wings of music.

> "Saints below, with heart and voice,
> Still in songs of praise rejoice;
> Learning here, by faith and love,
> Songs of praise to sing above."

Music and song played an important part in the worship of God's children in the Old Covenant, and from the days of our Lord and His apostles on the members of the New Testament Church have been "singing and making melody in their hearts to the Lord." A church without music is as unthinkable as a bird without wings.

The Lutheran Church, from its beginning, has also given music and song a prominent place in its worship, and for this reason it has been called the "singing church."

The place of music in the Lutheran Church is intimately related to its conception of worship and liturgy. Worship is properly held to be a corporate act of the congregation, pastor and people. It is not merely a priestly function for the people. God's people, led by their minister, hold communion with Him. Thus the principle of direct access on the part of the believer to the Father without the mediation of a priestly office is carried out in practice. The believer is himself a king and priest before the Lord.[1] This is typical of the spirit of Lutheran worship.

---

[1] I Pet. 2:9.

In Luther's view the external act of worship in prayer,
praise, Scripture lesson, etc., is designed as a testimony of
the Christian's faith, a natural outgrowth of his justification,
an evidence of his gratitude to God for His infinite grace in
Christ, and as a means of edification and of kindling the
devotional spirit through the reactive influence of its audible
expression.[2] The substance of worship, he said, is "that our
dear Lord speaks with us through His Holy Word, and we in
return speak with Him through prayer and song of praise."

In keeping with this conception of worship Luther in
publishing his first liturgical work, his *Formula Missæ*
(Order of the Mass), 1523, while retaining the Latin language and the main parts of the Roman Mass, removed
everything from it that tended to characterize the Mass as a
priestly, sacrificial act and whatever was erroneous or superstitious in its doctrine. Then in his *Deutsche Messe* (German
Mass) of 1526 he further simplified the service, put it into
the vernacular, and gave a prominent place to congregational song. Thus, as Merle D'Aubigne said: "The Church was
no longer composed of priests and monks; it was now the
congregation of believers. All were to take part in worship,
and the chanting of the clergy was to be succeeded by the
psalmody of the people. Luther, accordingly, in translating
the Psalms, thought of adapting them to be sung by the
Church. Thus a taste for music was diffused throughout
the nation. From Luther's time the people sang; the Bible
inspired their songs. . . . Hymns were multiplied; they
spread rapidly among the people, and powerfully contributed to rouse it from sleep."[3]

Luther's work as a hymn writer and a compiler of hymnbooks, which had its beginning between the publication of
the *Formula Missæ* and the *Deutsche Messe,* went hand in

---

[2]Dickinson, *Music in the History of the Western Church,* p. 245.
[3]Merle D'Aubigne, *History of the Reformation,* Vol. III, p. 211.

hand with his liturgical work for the churches. Thus "in poetry, music, and the several details of church worship, Luther recast the old models, and gave them to his followers with contents purified and adapted to those needs which he himself made them realize,"[4] and the Lutheran Church, in the main, has to this day been true to the ideals of congregational worship set up by the great Reformer.

The Lutheran Hymn

We do not acclaim Luther as the founder of German or Protestant hymnody. Many German hymns were written and sung before Luther. Moreover, the work of the Bohemian Brethren in the field of hymnody was considerable even before Luther set his own hand to the task of writing hymns for his congregational worship. Yet we may call him the father of congregational song. "The new conceptions of the relationship of man to God, which so altered the fundamental principle and the external forms of worship under the Lutheran movement, manifested themselves most strikingly in the mighty impetus given to congregational song. Luther set the national impulse free, and taught the people that in singing praise they were performing a service that was well-pleasing to God and a necessary part of public communion with Him. It was not simply that Luther charged the popular hymnody with the energy of his world-transforming doctrine—he also gave it a dignity which it had never possessed before, certainly not since the apostolic age, as a part of the official liturgic song of the Church."

"The church hymn in the strict sense of the term, as a popular religious lyric in praise of God to be sung by the congregation in public worship, was born with the German Reformation, and most extensively cultivated ever since by the Evangelical Church in Germany. The Latin hymns of Hilary, Ambrose, and others, were indeed used in public worship before, but only by the priests and choristers,

'Dickinson, *op. cit.*, pp. 242-243.

not by the people, who could not understand them any more than the Latin Psalms and the Latin Mass. . . .

"The treasury of German hymnody has enriched churches of other tongues and passed into Swedish, Norwegian, Danish, and modern English and American hymnbooks. John Wesley was one of the first English divines who appreciated its value. . . . The Reformation of the 16th century taught or revived the primitive idea of the general priesthood of believers, and introduced the language of the people into public worship. It substituted a vernacular sermon instead of the Latin Mass, and congregational singing for the chanting of priests and choirs. The results were far-reaching and of the utmost benefit to the Church of Christ. The leader of the Reformation was also the first Evangelical hymnist. To Luther belongs the extraordinary merit of having given to the German people in their own tongue the Bible, the Catechism, and the hymnbook, so that God could speak directly to them in His Word, and they might directly answer Him in their songs. Luther was also a musician and composed tunes to his best hymns. Some of them are immortal. . . . He is the Ambrose of German hymnody. His hymns are characterized by simplicity and strength and a popular churchly tone. They breathe the bold, confident, joyful spirit of justifying faith, which was the beating heart of his theology and piety. He had an extraordinary faculty of expressing profound thought in the clearest language. In this gift he is not surpassed by any uninspired writer, and herein lies the secret of his power. . . ."[5]

The hymns of Luther and his co-workers in the field are genuine church hymns, "in which the common faith is expressed in its universality, without the subjective feeling of personality." Koch, in his great work on the hymns of the evangelical church, characterizes these hymns thus:

"It is always we, not I, which is the prevailing word in these songs. The poets of this period did not, like those of later times, paint their own individual emotions with all kinds of figurative expressions, but, powerfully moved by the truth, they sang the work of redemption and extolled the faith in the free, undeserved grace of God in Jesus Christ, or gave thanks for the newly given pure Word of God in strains of joyful victory, and defied their foes in firm, godly trust in the divinity of the doctrine which was so new and yet so old. Therefore they speak the truths of salvation, not in dry doctrinal tone and sober reflection, but in the form of testimony or confession, and although in some of these songs are contained plain statements of belief, the reason therefore is simply in the hunger and thirst after the pure doctrine. Hence

---

[5]John Julian, in *Dictionary of Hymnology*, p. 412 (Edition 1915).

the speech of these poets is the Bible speech, and the expression forcible and simple. It is not art, but faith, which gives these songs their imperishable value."

We see that the emphasis in Lutheran worship, both liturgically and hymnodically, is on congregational participation. It is church worship in the best sense of the term. It is singing or chanting which the members share in common by experience: their common faith, their common love, their common hope, their common trust, their common praise. It means de-emphasizing that which is individualistic and stressing that which is corporate.

The Lutheran ideal has been well stated by Dr. Jowett in his book, *The Preacher, His Life and Work:*

"Many hymns are characterized by an extreme individualism which may make them unsuitable for common use in public worship. I know how singularly sweet and intimate may be the communion of the soul with our Lord. I know that no language can express the delicacy of the ties between the Lamb and His bride. And it is well that the soul, laden with the glorious burden of redeeming grace, should be able to sing its secret confidence and pour out the strains of its personal troth to the Lord. . . . But still I think that these hymns of intense individualism should be chosen with prayerful and scrupulous care. Public worship is not a means of grace wherein each may assert his own individuality and help himself from the common feast: it is a communion where each may help his brother to 'the things which the Lord hath prepared for them that love Him.' A congregation is not supposed to be a crowd of isolated units, each one intent upon a personal and private quest. The ideal is not that each individual should hustle and bustle for himself, stretching out his hand to touch the hem of Christ's garment, but that each should be tenderly solicitous of every other, and particularly mindful of those with 'lame hands' who are timid and despondent even in the very presence of the Great Physician. And so the ideal hymn in public worship is one in which we move together as a fellowship, bearing one another's sins, sharing one another's conquests, 'weeping with them that weep, and rejoicing with them that do rejoice.' "

The Chorale

Accordingly, the music that has a rightful and a proper place in Lutheran worship must be church music. And it was this ideal of worship that produced the Lutheran chorale. "The chorale originated by Luther cannot be surpassed for dignity and simple devotional earnestness. The chorale melodies of the Lutheran Church have exerted a powerful influence on classical music."[6] "He practically created the chorale. Like a second Ambrose, he possessed in a preeminent degree a gift of writing hymns of the liturgical type. Even his paraphrase of parts of Holy Scripture were so free, so poetically powerful in the idiom of the people, that they are really new creations. . . . When there is added to this a positive genius for trenchant and forceful melody, supported by adequate musical training, and an almost unparalleled personal force, we are no longer surprised at the tremendous hold that Luther's hymns soon obtained in Germany, or at their influence on the Christian world, which is still increasing."[7]

What is a chorale?

"The chorale is a fusion of various types. . . . It has a dignified strength, such as no other church song for congregational purposes possesses. It has an inherent dignity that defies cheap familiarity, much as a magnificent cathedral defies flippant familiarity. This is a heritage from plain song. . . . From folksong the chorale inherited rhythm and melody, which plain song did not possess, and which is also an echo of Ambrosian song. Natural folk rhythm adds interest and feeling and makes the melody more congregational than it would be otherwise. . . . The fourth mark of the chorale is its objective spiritual fervor. To be warm and fervent spiritually, yet be objective about it and avoid sentimentality is a mark of musical greatness. The chorales, words and music both, have achieved this."[8]

We need to mention only a few of these great chorales by way of example. Luther's "A Mighty Fortress" and his "Our Father, Thou in Heaven Above"; Decius' "All Glory be to God on High"; Graumann's "My Soul, Now Bless Thy

---

[6]Grove's *Dictionary of Music.*
[7]Winfred Douglas, *Church Music in History and Practise,* p. 210.
[8]Howard R. Kunkle, in *Sursum Corda.*

Maker"; Speratus' "Salvation Unto Us Has Come"; Behm's "Lord Jesus Christ, My Life, My Light"; Nicolai's "How Lovely Shines the Morning Star" and his "Wake, Awake, for Night Is Flying." These are representative of the best in Lutheran hymnody.

These high ideals of Lutheran worship and song have been maintained by the Lutheran Church in America. The Common Service, which represents the consensus of the Lutheran liturgies of the sixteenth century, and which is in use in most of the American Lutheran synods today, is a service that is truly congregational. Textually and musically it is in keeping with that dignified, objective, and reverential spirit that makes for fitting corporate worship. There is nothing cheap and tawdry, nothing frothy or sentimental about it. It is elevating in style and in sentiment, and it produces in the house of God that which is fitting and proper for the worship of the Most High. The official hymnals of the various Lutheran synods likewise present a body of hymns, to be used with the liturgy of the worshiping congregation, suited to the high standards of the liturgy. In them the Lutheran chorale has a prominent place. Some official hymnals have more, some less; but in them all the chorale is well represented. We believe that this is not only an indication of a deep appreciation of the Lutheran Church's great history in this respect but also proof of a desire to perpetuate that heritage for posterity.

What Are the Chief Characteristics of Lutheran Hymnody?

It is not a simple matter to describe the characteristics of Lutheran hymnody, for it naturally has certain things in common with all true Christian hymnody in all ages and sections of the church. Nor will the characteristics to which we shall point be found in every hymn that has a Lutheran origin. Furthermore, it will not be difficult to find hymns of non-Lutheran origin that have the characteristics of the Lutheran hymn. That is why, as mentioned above, our Lutheran hymnals also contain hymns written by men and women of other than Lutheran connections. Nevertheless, as there are certain characteristics that will label a hymn Roman Catholic or Episcopalian or Methodist or Pentecostal, so the Lutheran hymn may be recognized by certain earmarks.

In endeavoring to point out that which distinguishes Lutheran hymns as a class from the hymns of other denominations we should say that the Lutheran hymn is primarily a vehicle of the Lutheran faith. The Lutheran poets express themselves in the form of testimony or confession. The faith that animates their hearts is clearly defined in their hymns. Their statements are not a vague groping after something undefined, not pious mouthings of a religious sentimentality, not pietistic expressions of extremely individualistic spiritual experiences. That is the reason the Lutheran hymn is sometimes criticized for being too dogmatical, a criticism which is sometimes justified. For example, Luther's hymn on the Ten Commandments, "That Man a Godly Life Might Live," which was, however, probably never intended for use as a congregational hymn but rather for use by children in the church school.

Two hymns of the Reformation period may be cited as excellent hymns of a strongly confessional character. One is by Luther himself, "Dear Christians, One and All Rejoice," the other is by Paul Speratus, "Salvation unto Us Has Come." In them we have a vigorous outpouring of the heart in which the truth of salvation in Christ alone, by God's free grace, is presented. Here we find a faith-consciousness, common to all true believers, that is nevertheless objectively expressed. The subjective element of individualistic experience is absent. The common experience of all believers is emphasized.

Then there are hymns that emphasize the faith of the church, but from another angle, namely, to the praise of God for the salvation which is in Christ Jesus. Among these are many of the hymns written for Christmas, Epiphany, Easter, Ascension, and Pentecost, to say nothing of hymns like C. L. Scheidt's "By Grace I'm Saved, Grace Free and Boundless" or Lazarus Spengler's "All Mankind Fell in Adam's Fall" or L. F. Lehr's "My Savior Sinners Doth Receive."

Other hymns, in the full assurance of faith, voice the confident trust of the believer that God will not forsake His own, and that He will stand by His children. Luther's "A Mighty Fortress" is, of course, the outstanding example of this type; but there are many others, for example, Altenburg's "O Little Flock, Fear Not the Foe" or J. J. Schuetz's "All Praise to God Who Reigns Above" or Paul Gerhardt's "I Will Sing My Maker's Praises."

Finally, these hymns, in the form of petitions or prayers that seek, even implore, God's help against opposition, in times of trouble, temptation, distress, persecution, and sorrow, basing their requests on the promises and the assurances of God's Word, are also examples of the outpourings from the heart of those who rest their hope on "nothing less than Jesus' blood and righteousness." To quote just a few examples: Martin Schalling's "Lord, Thee I Love with All My Heart" or Paul Gerhardt's "If God Himself Be for Me" or Luther's "O Lord, Look Down from Heaven, Behold" or George Neumark's "If Thou but Suffer God to Guide Thee." All of them again submerge the subjective element and move in the sphere of the Christian's common experience and avoid all moroseness, sentimentality and are at the same time full of feeling so that they strike a responsive chord in the hearts of the believers who likewise are bowed down under the cross.

Thus the Lutheran hymns breathe a spirit of testimony to the truth of God's Word. In them moves a faith that is firmly grounded in that Word and the certainty of ultimate victory over every evil in the power of God. The language of these hymns is Biblical; their style is simple and popular; their presentation is lively; and their tone is truly churchly and devotional. They are centered, not in man, but in God and in His Word, and they are conducive to worship and edification.

The Inclusiveness of Lutheran Hymnody

As a cursory examination of any official American Lutheran hymnal will show, the Lutheran Church in our country does not confine itself exclusively to the use of the chorale, for the hymnals include hymns of the ancient and medieval church and hymns of English and American origin as well as Plain Song melodies, Psalm tunes, and modern English hymn tunes. This does not necessarily mean a departure from the traditional standards of Lutheranism, nor does it imply a lack of appreciation of the Lutheran chorale. Here, too, our modern Lutheran hymnals follow the example set by the great Reformer. For Luther had a deep love for the Latin medieval hymns, and he would have his followers love them, too. So for those who knew Latin or who were learning Latin, like the youth in school, he prescribed the singing of these hymns in the original. For those not familiar with Latin he himself translated some of these hymns in order to keep them in use in the church.

Our modern Lutheran hymnals would lack completeness, therefore, if they did not contain such hymns of medieval origin as "O Sacred Head, Now Wounded," "Jerusalem the Golden," "All Glory, Laud, and Honor," "Come Holy Ghost, in Love," "A Hymn of Glory Let Us Sing," etc. The same is true of the more modern English and American hymns, which have been included in our American Lutheran hymnals. Our hymnody has not been degraded but rather enriched thereby. Who of us would want to be deprived of the privilege of singing in our churches such pearls of English and American hymns as "When I Survey the Wondrous Cross," "Holy, Holy, Holy, Lord God Almighty," "Rock of Ages," "Come, Thou Almighty King," "At Even, When the Sun Did Set," "My Faith Looks Up to Thee," "How Firm a Foundation, Ye Saints of the Lord," and a host of others that might be named! The same is true in another respect.

The Lutheran Church has not confined herself to the use of hymns of Lutheran origin although self-evidently the bulk of its hymnody is made up of those hymns which were composed in her own household of faith, whether of German or Slovak or Scandinavian or American origin. It makes no difference that "Thee Will I Love, My Strength, My Tower," was written by Johann Scheffler after he had left the Lutheran Church to join the Roman Catholic communion, or that "Praise To the Lord, the Almighty," flowed from the pen of Neander of the German Reformed Church, or that "O Come, All Ye Faithful," came to us from Roman Catholic sources, or that "In the Cross of Christ I Glory" originated in the heart of a professed Unitarian. It is rather a reason for rejoicing on our part that children of God in other church groups expressed their faith and love and hope and trust in so beautiful a style and sentiment that we can use their hymns to give utterance to our own thoughts and emotions. "For even as the Church of Jesus Christ knows no race, no color, no nationality, no language, no male or female, no social status, no class, no age, but draws its adherents from all the children of men, from all walks of life, so the Christian hymn is also truly universal, truly catholic, truly cosmopolitan, truly Pentecostal in the original sense of the term."[9]

---

[9]L. Blankenbuhler, in *The Christian Hymn*, p. 44.

It is well that we be reminded again of the treasury of our hymnals. Peter C. Lutkin has rightly said:

"The average churchgoer places but scant value on the hymnbook he casually uses. He ordinarily fails to appreciate that he holds in his hands a remarkable collection of religious experiences. In no inconsiderable measure a good hymnbook is a history of religious emotions—a history of the reaction of the human mind to the truths of religion. From the earliest days of the Christian Church to our own day, devout and faithful souls have voiced their penitence, their prayers, their hopes, and their praise in appealing and at times impassioned verse. Throughout all these ages the church musician has rejoiced in reinforcing the message of the poet with the power and expression of his own art, and this joint product has been a real and living force in both establishing and maintaining the faith."[10]

What is true of our hymns is also true of the tunes to which we sing our hymns and of the melodies to which we chant our liturgy. All periods of church history and composers of many Christian nations have contributed to the musical treasure of our Lutheran Church. Here again the music, acceptable to the church, exhibits an ecumenicity that is inspiring and together with the texts of the hymns giving us a glorious treasure

"Born of the power of Christian faith, arising spontaneously out of the living experience of God's bountiful mercies our hymnody unites in one corporate body the whole invisible Church universal, the spiritual priesthood of all believers, singing the new song which only the ransomed of the Lord can sing, experiencing a foretaste of that new song which St. John in the heavenly Jerusalem heard sung before the throne by them which were redeemed, praise and honor and glory and thanksgiving to the Lamb and to the Father and to the Holy Spirit."[11]

The Choir

What is true of hymns and chants sung by the worshipping congregation is true also of the music presented in the service by the choir. It must fit into the picture. It

---

[10]Peter Christian Lutkin, in *Hymns and Hymn-singing*, p. 5.
[11]L. Blankenbuhler, in *The Christian Hymn*, p. 61.

must be in harmony with the ideals and the standards of a true worship service.

In the Lutheran Church the choir is not a clerical choir but a congregational or church choir. The choir does not perform for the congregation but worships with the congregation and as a part of the congregation. The worshipping choir, therefore, does not face the congregation but the altar. Its great purpose is not to entertain or to make a display of skill. It sings to the glory of God and leads the congregation in offering its sacrifice of praise. The anthem or solo which intrudes the personality of the singer, either because of a peculiarly personal sentiment, mannerisms of pose or vocal style, sudden and violent changes of rhythm or tempo—such defeats the very purpose of church song which is to arouse and sustain religious emotion.

Centuries ago the church father Jerome, commenting on Eph. 5:19, set up standards for choir singing which are still true today when he said:

"Let our youths hear this; let those hear it whose office it is to sing in the church. Not with the voice, but with the heart must we make melody to the Lord. We are not like comedians, to smooth the throat with sweet drinks, in order that we may hear theatrical songs and melodies in the church; but the fear of God, piety, and the knowledge of the Savior should inspire our songs; so that not the voice of the singer, but the divine matter expressed, may be the point of attraction; so that the evil spirit which entered into the heart of a Saul may be expelled from those who are in like manner possessed by him, rather than invited by those who would turn the house of God into a heathen theatre."

The Lutheran worship centers in Word and sacrament. The work of the choir may serve this objective in several ways. It may help to prepare the minds and the hearts of the hearers for a reverent reception of the means of grace. It may enhance the beauty of the service. It may intensify the devotion of the people as they bring their sacrifice of praise, prayer, and thanksgiving. The order of worship provides a number of opportunities for the cooperation of the choir by giving to the choir those portions of the liturgy which usually lie beyond the ability of the average congregation to do. In the Order of the Holy Communion the choir may properly chant the Introit and the Gradual for the Day, the Seasonal Sentence or the Sequence. In the Orders of Matins and Vespers the canticles may well be chanted by the choir as they are usually done rather haltingly and clumsily by the average congregation. In these items of the service the choir has a legitimate function.

The Organ

Finally we come to the part of the organ in a Lutheran service. What has been said above applies equally to the music of the organ. The organist of the church is by virtue of his position a "person of more than passing importance, for upon him is largely dependent the proper expression of public worship, and in him is vested an educational power which is wielded, not only over a few individuals, but over the entire congregation. . . . From the organ loft he rules, for weal or woe, over the most subtle influence, temporally speaking, that is brought to bear upon the people."[12]

We realize this more fully when we pause to consider just what we expect of the organist in the service: he opens the service with a prelude and closes it with a postlude. In between the opening and the closing of the service he is constantly at work except when the minister is reading the lessons and preaching the sermon. He must tie together the liturgy of the service, accompany the singing of the people and the choir, and modulate properly from one part to the next so as to leave no awkward pauses and no spots of dead silence. The good organist will, like the choir director (which he usually is also), acquaint himself with the ideals

---

[12]Gomer C. Rees, *Memoirs, Lutheran Liturgical Association,* Vol. III, pp. 47f.

and the standards of Lutheran worship and then strive to make everything he does in the service measure up to them. His preludes will at once strike the dominant tone of the particular service, whether it be praise, penitence, trust, comfort, etc., and in his postludes he will put a fitting musical period to the service which is now over. His interludes between the liturgy and the hymnody will be musically neutral so as not to break the spell that is being woven with the various parts of the service. In his voluntary after the sermon he will use a selection that will help to emphasize or intensify the impression of the sermonic message that has just been delivered. In short, the true organist is not a performer in the service who will try to impress the people with his skill or versatility but is a servant, a minister in the service, a minister in the field of sacred music, whose one high aim is always to help the people of God in their worship and to edify them with the medium of that art which, next to theology, is God's greatest gift to man.

BIBLIOGRAPHY

Douglas, *Church Music in History and Practice*, Scribner's.

Richardson, *Church Music*, Longmans.

Dearmer, *Songs of Praise Discussed*, Oxford.

Breed, *History and Use of Hymns and Hymn-Tunes*, Revell.

Dickinson, *Music in the History of the Western Church*, Scribner's.

Davison, *Protestant Church Music in America*, E. C. Schirmer.

Lutkin, *Music in the Church*, Young Churchman Co.

Memoirs of the Lutheran Liturgical Association.

LUTHERAN PIETY

N. C. CARLSEN

Lutheran piety is well grounded in the Word of God. Accepting Holy Scripture as the inspired and inerrant Word of God and as the only sufficient and infallible rule and standard of faith and practice, Lutheran piety is well rooted in Scripture. While Lutheran piety is orthodox, it is not of a one-sided, intellectual type which stresses only indoctrination and neglects the practice of Christian virtues. The Lutheran Church places great emphasis on indoctrination. We cannot stress knowledge of the Word of God and pure doctrine too much. Without purity of doctrine we cannot conceive of a healthy Christian life. It is the truth only that can set a sinner free.

But doctrine is not life. Christ only is life. There is an emphasis on doctrine which leads to building on pure doctrine rather than on Christ, the only Savior of man. There may be those within the Lutheran Church who base their faith on their knowledge of pure doctrine, who have never come to know Christ as their personal Savior. That is not Lutheran piety.

The fact must not be overlooked that faith is not merely a matter of the intellect. It is also a matter of the emotions and will. Faith is not mere knowledge; it is also assent and confidence. The man who possesses true Lutheran piety will not consider his duty fully discharged merely by having taught and preached the pure Word of God. But what more can he do? To convert a sinner is the work of the Holy Spirit. The pastor cannot convert anybody, but he can permit himself to be used as an agent of the Holy Spirit to bring a conversion about. This he will do, not only by his preaching, but also by his work as a *"Seelsorger."* Imbued with genuine piety, he will, like a good physician, endeavor to diagnose the spiritual state of the soul that he may know what in the Word of God to apply in each particular case to effect a soul cure.

A man, pastor or layman, is not a pietist simply because he is zealous to reach the individual soul so that it may be saved. Such zeal, combined with zeal for pure doctrine, is good Lutheran piety. Where that kind of zeal is absent, doctrinal preaching becomes cold and perfunctory. Of this Dr. G. H. Gerberding writes in his book *Lutheran Fundamentals:* "Oh, how cold, how formal, how external, how heavy, how purely intellectual is much of the preaching on faith and justification. And this is unhappily true of the preaching in many orthodox Lutheran pulpits. It is head, head, head! The preacher doesn't even seem to know that 'with the heart man believeth.' Luther's living, loving, burning words on the faith that justifies made John Wesley write into his *Journal,* where he tells of hearing Luther's 'Preface to the Epistle to the Romans,' 'I felt my heart strangely warmed. I felt that I was justified.'" Cold, intellectual preaching is not the type that generally reaches the hearts of men.

On the other hand, Lutheran piety is not of the highly emotional type. This assertion must not be interpreted to mean that it is unemotional. Sorrow for sin and the joy of salvation involve our feelings to a greater or a less degree. But Lutherans are averse to that type of preaching which aims at man's emotions rather than his conscience. We have observed how a person may be moved to hasty action by a highly emotional type of preaching from which permanent results are generally meager. Feelings are like shifting sand. Under a stirring sermon, playing on man's feelings, he may feel as though he were lifted into the seventh heaven today, but by tomorrow his happy feelings may have vanished as dew before the morning sun. The preaching, which has been aimed primarily at his emotions, did not reach his conscience and his will. When his feelings have vanished, he is quite at sea as to his relation to God. He has no solid ground on which to stand.

Dr. Karl Ermisch has said of the emotionalists: "Through their revivalistic methods they are able to kindle a fire, but it often is a straw fire of short duration. The firm foundation which can be laid only through indoctrination is lacking. And because they are lacking in indoctrination, they have to build on emotions—on feelings rather than on the objective Word of God. And the house which is built on sand is not able to weather the storms of daily life with all its trials and temptations. Oh yes, there are exceptions. Begbie, in his book *Twice Born Men,* gives us fine examples, but we cannot speak here of exceptions, only of the rule."

Lutheran piety embraces man's whole personality—his will, his thinking, and his emotions. Dr. O. H. Pannkoke writes: "In an organic view of faith as the moving force of personality in life, faith is more than knowledge of God, more than assent to Christian truth, more than trust in God's grace. It is an act of commitment to God, as a soldier gives allegiance to his commander. It is a new attitude, a new alignment, a new purpose in life. Man hears God's will. He breaks with the past. He follows God. That is the dynamic element in faith."

Its Source Is the Grace of God only

Lutheran piety has its source in the saving grace of God in Jesus Christ alone. This is particularly manifest in our conception of regeneration in baptism. This is especially true in the case of infant baptism, in which God alone is active. We believe that we are born again in holy baptism. Jesus said, "Except one be born of water and the Spirit, he can not enter into the kingdom of God."[1] The apostle calls baptism the "washing of regeneration and renewing of the Holy Spirit."[2] We believe that God wills that even infants should be born again in baptism because Jesus said, "Go ye therefore and make disciples of all nations, baptizing them into the name of the Father and of the Son and of the Holy Spirit," and most certainly the children constitute a part of the nations. In baptism the child is born again and adopted as a child of God. The infant is born again. This is one of the mysteries of God. He works in His mysterious ways. It is enough for us to take Him at His Word and believe that He receives us into a state of grace in the holy sacrament of baptism.

When we again go back to the great commission we find that we are to make disciples, not merely by baptizing, but also by "teaching them to observe all things whatsoever I have commanded you."[3] The spiritual life which was born in baptism is at that time in its infancy. Hence it must be nurtured with the bread of life, the Word of God, that it may grow into beautiful Christian youth; strong, stalwart Christian manhood; and ultimately into the full stature of Christ. It is characteristic of Lutheran piety that we do not look at baptized children as heathen whom we hope to win for Christ. We believe they belong to Him. They are God's children. It, therefore, simply devolves on parents and the church to nurture their spiritual life that they may grow in grace, to nurture their Christian life that they may abide in Christ always even as they in baptism were grafted into Him.

Growing into Conscious Faith

If a right Christian atmosphere is created, and if the church as well as the parents faithfully nurture the spiritual

---

[1]John 3:5.   [2]Titus 3:5.   [3]Matt. 28:20.

life of the children, it is to be expected that they will gradually grow and develop in a beautiful Christian life. On the one hand they will grow in consciousness of and sorrow for sin, and on the other hand in confident trust in the saving and sustaining grace of God. Penitence for sin and faith in Christ grow with the years.

Luther, in his small Catechism, asks, "What does such baptism with water signify?" He answers: "It signifies that the old Adam in us, together with all sins and evil lusts, should be drowned by daily sorrow and repentance, and be put to death; and that the new man should daily come forth and rise to live before God in righteousness and holiness forever."

Whoever is thus nurtured by the Word of God grows in daily repentance by daily drowning of the old Adam, grows in faith and rises with Christ to newness of life, remains in covenant relationship with God. He learns to hate sin and increases in his trust in Christ. He loves his Savior. Dr. G. H. Gerberding writes of such a one, "He is in a state of conversion and needs no other conversion." The Holy Spirit works penitence for sin and faith in Christ in the soul of the baptized child so that it may remain in communion with God. He works penitence and faith in the soul of the prodigal so that he may return to God.

The mysteries of the conception and the growth of spiritual life are illustrated in a striking way in a parable found in Mark: "And He said, So is the kingdom of God, as if a man should cast seed upon the earth, and should sleep and rise night and day, and the seed should spring up and grow, he knoweth not how. The earth beareth fruit of herself, first the blade, then the ear, then the full grain in the ear. But when the fruit is ripe, straightway he putteth forth the sickle, because the harvest is come."[4]

---

[4]Mark 4:26-29.

Thus God works in His mysterious way in the soul of believers by the means of grace. The germ of spiritual life is planted in baptism. Nurtured by the Word of God, it sprouts, and the blade appears. The sprouting and the appearance of the blade may illustrate a certain crisis that often occurs in more or less pronounced form, usually in the early youth of the baptized believer.

In the period of adolescence there are many new experiences and changes that enter into both the physical and the mental sphere of life. If God may have His way, similar changes will occur in the spiritual life. There are two things which characterize the young in the age of adolescence. The one is self-examination. In his childhood the young person busied himself mostly with his outward experiences. He did not give much thought to an analysis of his feelings and emotions. In the adolescent age he begins to think about himself in a way he never did before. He is conscious of feelings previously unknown to him. He is aware of new powers, and he feels that he should throw his energy into the real things of life. He begins to examine himself. This makes him self-conscious, introspective, and often bewildered.

Then there is also a developing of self-determination. He wants to think for himself and to make his own decisions. We have now the awakening of the natural capacities. He is becoming an adult. When the physical and the mental faculties are thus awakened, there should be a corresponding awakening of the spiritual life as well. This is not only possible, but it is to be expected where the spiritual environment is favorable, and where the Christian life has been properly nurtured with the means of grace.

There will come a similar awakening of the religious consciousness if the nurture of spiritual life has been effective. There will be introspection or self-examination with the awakening of the spiritual life to a more conscious state.

Though the child under spiritual nurture becomes conscious of sin very early in life, it is more its outward manifestation such as cursing, swearing, and lying—sins of the tongue and the hands—but not so much a consciousness of the sinful state of the heart. But when the Holy Spirit, through the Word of God, guides the young in their self-examination, they discover that their sins are but the outward growth of the evil of their hearts. God would have man realize that the law requires not merely an outward obedience but a heart that is pure and holy. Finding that they lack such purity of heart, the law becomes a tutor to Christ. They have been awakened to a consciousness of what sin really is, and more than ever they experience their need of the saving grace of God.

This is a critical period in the life of the young. They are now conscious of the fact that they should not only abstain from sin but hate it. But they find that they often love what they ought to hate and hate what they ought to love. They feel that they are not conscious of as much sorrow for sin as they ought to feel. Their greatest sorrow is that they are not penitent enough. Here is the crisis. Their faith will grow into conscious assurance, or they will go the way of the prodigal. The forces of darkness put forth every effort to cast doubt into their hearts and to lead them away from God while the Holy Spirit is active to finish the work which He has begun in their souls.

The second factor in the period of adolescence is self-determination. That also applies to the spiritual sphere of life. The youth will now become definitely fixed in his spiritual course; and if he does not reject the guidance of the Holy Spirit he can pursue but one course, namely, to rest his case in his Savior's hand, trusting that the grace of God in Christ Jesus is sufficient unto salvation. Tears or no tears, feelings or no feelings, the grace of God is sufficient.

When we rest our case in the hand of Christ, the Holy Spirit will finish the work He has begun. The weak and trembling faith will grow into the blessed assurance of being a child of God, purchased with the blood of Jesus and baptized to be His own. That I have written at length about the development of the life which was born in holy baptism into a conscious Christian life is due to the fact that we here have the source and the growth of a piety which is distinctively Lutheran in as much as it is based on the conviction that baptism is a means of grace, the sacrament of the new birth.

Conversion

It is a deplorable fact that many, very many of those who were baptized, have gone the way of the prodigal because of a lack of nurture of their spiritual life. The atmosphere in their home was unfavorable. Instruction in the Word of God was neglected. An unchristian example was constantly before them. They neglected the means of grace and grew indifferent, cold, and worldly. They have come to live as if they had never been touched by divine grace. All such need conversion as well as those who were never baptized or instructed in the Word of life.

How is conversion brought about? Can a man convert himself? Most emphatically, no. "No man can say that Jesus is Lord but by the Holy Spirit." Luther writes in his explanation to the Third Article of the Apostles' Creed: "I believe that I can not by my own reason or strength believe in Jesus Christ my Lord, or come to Him." Conversion is a divine work. The Holy Spirit must bring it about. He works through the means of grace. Through the Word he calls and enlightens the sinner and reveals unto him his sin and his consequent need of a Savior. He induces man to believe. He enables man to believe. Faith is a gift of God. To this truth the apostle Paul bears witness, "By grace have ye been saved through faith and that not of yourselves, it is the gift of God."⁵

Are we to interpret this to mean that man is not responsible, and that his will plays no part at all in conversion? By no means. While it is true that, if a man is converted, it is wholly due to the work of the Holy Spirit, and all honor and glory are due to God, it is also true that, if he is not converted he himself must shoulder the responsibility. The Holy Spirit works in the soul of the unconverted through the Word of God. He sounds a ringing call to repentance. "Seek the Lord while He may be found, call upon Him while He is near." "Repent and believe the gospel." While it is true that nothing in man enables him to repent and to believe, the Word of God bestows grace to do the very thing it demands. With the call to repentance and faith there follows grace to repent and to believe. By nature man has the power to resist and to harden his heart. By the grace of God he can cease resisting. Not by his own power but by the power given through the Word he can repent, believe, and become converted.

It is not our task in this treatise to enter into a full discussion of conversion. Suffice it to say that it is fundamentally repentance and faith—a change of heart which implies a change of direction. That statement will be generally accepted by all evangelical Christians. However, there are certain conceptions pertaining to conversion which are distinctively Lutheran. The fact that we believe that we were born again in baptism means much to the Lutheran who has been awakened from his sleep in sin and unbelief. It is reassuring to him that he was not only purchased with the redeeming blood of Jesus Christ, but that he was also born a child of God in baptism. He is, therefore, not to return to a stranger but to his Father. He is still a son

---

⁵Eph. 2:8.

though an estranged son who finds his return open to his Father, who will not disown him but receive him. Conversion returns him to his baptismal grace. In the case of an unbaptized adult the Word of God works as the regenerating means.[6] When a soul is thus led to conversion, his regeneration is consummated in baptism. "He that believeth and is baptized shall be saved."[7]

Lutheran Christians are not all cast in the same mold. Although penitence and faith always characterize conversion, we recognize that there are varied phenomena incident to that experience. "There are diversities of operation, but it is the same God, which worketh all in all."[8] Temperaments differ. Therefore the experience of conversion differs. In some cases the emotions are stirred with a heart-rending sorrow for sin while others never shed a penitential tear though their penitence may go deeper than it does in the case of the former. Some are awakened largely by the thunder of Sinai while others are converted primarily by the love of God as revealed in Jesus Christ. Both find peace only in the grace of God. Some are converted in a day while in the case of others it requires a longer period of time before peace comes to their souls. Some know the day and the hour of their conversion, others do not. But the question is not whether or not our experiences are identical. The question simply is, "Do we have the assurance that we are the children of God, justified freely by His grace through the redemption that is in Christ Jesus, whom God set forth to be a propitiation through faith in His blood"?[9] Justification by faith. This is the fountain from which our piety springs.

Conception of Sin

Lutheran piety is unique in its conception of sin. While some Christians hold that we are born into this world as

[6] I Pet. 1:23.   [7] Mark 16:16.   [8] I Cor. 12:6.   [9] Rom. 3:24, 25.

innocent creatures, the Lutheran Christian is convinced that he is born with original sin or sin of inheritance. The Word of God is clear enough also on that point. "Behold, I was brought forth in iniquity, and in sin did my mother conceive me."[10] "We . . . were by nature children of wrath, even as the rest."[11] Luther says, "This hereditary sin is so deep a corruption of nature that no reason can understand it, but it must be believed from the revelation of Scriptures."

Sin is more than a moral breach. It is more than so many evil incidents in the life of man. Sin is the outgrowth of the evil of man's heart. "The heart is deceitful above all things, and it is exceedingly corrupt: who can know it!"[12] The apostle does not exclude himself. He writes, "Wretched man that I am: Who shall deliver me out of the body of this death?"[13] Who is this Paul who has such a keen consciousness of sin? One should think that he was an immoral character, a thief or a robber, an outcast among men. But such was not the case. In the eyes of man he was good, righteous, blameless. Nevertheless, he includes himself when he writes, "All have sinned and come short of the glory of God."

The same applies to Martin Luther. He quotes from Isaiah: "We are all become as one that is unclean, and all our righteousnesses are as a polluted garment."[14] On that text he comments out of the conviction of his heart: "Observe that the prophet excepts nobody, but says, 'we are all of us unclean,' and yet he was a holy prophet. Again, if our righteousness is unclean and a stench in God's nostrils, what will unrighteousness be? Moreover, he says, 'All righteousness,' none excepted. So then, if there is such a thing as a good work without sin, this prophet lies, which God forbid. Is not this passage of Isaiah clear enough?"

---

[10]Ps. 51:5.
[11]Eph. 2:3.
[12]Jer. 17:9.

[13]Rom. 7:24.
[14]Isa. 64:6.

Sin does not consist of a number of evil works. These spring from a common source in which every individual sin originates. That source is the perverted will of man. In its final analysis sin is selfishness. All sinful acts are the outgrowth of man's desire to please his sinful self.

We rejoice that we are justified freely by grace through faith in Jesus Christ. We believe that the righteousness of Jesus Christ is imputed to all those who believe on Him, and that we stand acquitted before God as though sin had never entered our hearts. We have the assurance that God, for Christ's sake, has accepted us into a state of grace. However, we realize that the forgiveness of sin does not imply that we have been relieved of our sinful nature. Though we have been given newness of life and really desire to live a life worthy of our high calling we, nevertheless, find that we fall far short of the ideal. Time and again we find that the words of Paul apply to us, "For the good which I would I do not, but the evil which I would not, that I practice."[15] Therefore we are not satisfied that all is well. We want to rise to higher planes in our Christian life. Hence the Lutheran Christian finds himself in harmony with the words of Paul when he writes: "Not that I have already obtained, or am already made perfect, but I press on, if so be that I may lay hold on that for which also I was laid hold on by Christ Jesus."[16]

Unsatisfied with self, grieving that sin plays such a big part in his Christian life, the Lutheran Christian nevertheless rejoices in the Lord. He is happy in the assurance that the grace of God in Christ Jesus is sufficient to save and to sustain him in faith until the crown is won. He rejoices in the assurance: "We were buried with Christ through baptism unto death, that like as Christ was raised from the dead, by the glory of the Father, so we might also walk in

---

[15]Rom. 7:20.   [16]Phil. 3:12.

the newness of life."[17] While the Old Adam is still active, we experience more and more that there is in our risen Savior a victorious power by which the Old Adam is put to death and the new man lives and grows. "Being confident of this very thing, that He who began a good work in you will perfect it until the day of Jesus Christ."[18]

While, with the deeper sense of sin, Lutheran piety is characterized by a certain soberness, it is at the same time normally marked by the joy of salvation. It may not always appear that way because Lutheran piety is not of the highly emotional type. It is a joy which is based on positive Christian conviction rather than on a display of emotions. It is a more abiding joy because its foundation is not anything self-induced but the work of Christ in those He has made His own.

Lutheran piety rejoices in Christian liberty. That must not be interpreted to mean that we are antinomistic. The law of God still has its place. It is a tutor to lead us to Christ, and it serves as a guide for Christian living. But when we endeavor to live according to the law of God, it is not in order to be saved by the law, but rather because we are saved by grace. The believer concerns himself about the will of God. When we say that Lutheran piety is not legalistic we mean that it does not consist of "no's" and "don'ts." It is not a catalogue of negatives. It is a living, growing faith in Christian liberty. Jesus said, "He whom the Son maketh free is free indeed."[19] Of this Köberle writes: "The liberty of faith does not give a license to sin, but it gives a license to do all kinds of good works and to suffer all things as they come to hand, so that no one is bound exclusively to one sort or to several kinds of works." The more faith grows, the more accompanying good works will increase. In the same degree as the selfish desires, which so completely

---

[17]Rom. 6:4.   [19]John 8:36.
[18]Phil. 1:6.

dominate us in our natural state, are broken, the will becomes free to carry out the will of God.

Lutheran piety is not austere and puritanical. It is not characterized by the severity of asceticism. It does not consist in the enforced, perfunctory service of the slave but the free, willing obedience of the son. Lutheran piety rejoices not only in spiritual gifts but in God's gifts in nature as well. Of this Martin Luther himself is an example. Koestlin writes of him: "With childlike joy he recognized God's gifts in nature, in garden and field, plants and cattle. He was enraptured with the beauties of spring, the bloom of the flowers, and the song of the birds." He said on a fine spring day to Justus Jones, in that tone of mingled melancholy and joy which sometimes overpower man in the joys of spring: "If there were neither sin nor death, we might be satisfied with this paradise. But all shall be more beautiful still when the old world shall have been removed, and a new spring shall open and remain forever." He loved home, wife, and children. He would play with children as though he were a child himself. He loved friends and cherished their company. In the evening, after hard studies, he would gather in the social circle with his friends and his family. He would play the lute; other members of the family and friends would join with other instruments, or they would lift their voices in song. Once, when he had the singers at the table sing beautiful motets with him, he said with emotion: "As our Lord pours out such noble gifts upon us in this life, how glorious will be eternal life! This is only the beginning." This joyous nature of Luther's Christian life normally characterizes Lutheran piety.

Manifestations of Lutheran Piety

It is natural to look for manifestations of Lutheran piety. The Lutheran Church is a singing church. More than that of any other church her piety finds expression not only in hymns and chorals but in instrumental music as well. "The Lutheran Church," says Dr. Schaff, "draws the fine arts into the service of religion and has produced a body of hymns and chorals which in riches, power, and unction surpasses the hymnology of all other churches in the world. She has sung the most fervent hymns to the Savior and holds sweet, childlike intercourse with the heavenly Father." This is the testimony of a non-Lutheran theologian.

Lutheran piety finds its outward expression in particular in its missionary activities. The Lutheran Church has always assumed a leading role in modern evangelical missions. Consult the chapter on missions for a detailed presentation of Lutheran missionary endeavors.

Lutheran piety has borne fruit in works of mercy. This is manifested in the founding of children's homes, homes for the aged, hospitals, and deaconess institutes. It is well known that the first and greatest children's home was founded in Halle, Germany, by the Lutheran Francke. At the time of his death it provided for 2,000 orphans. It was the forerunner of hundreds of such homes scattered all over the world. The first institution for Protestant deaconesses was founded by the Lutheran Pastor Fliedner at Kaiserswerth, Germany.

Dr. Schaff writes: "Lutheran piety has its peculiar charm, the charm of Mary, who sat at Jesus' feet and heard His Word. It has a rich inward life." The deep, rich spiritual life of Lutheran Christians is due to the fact that they are like Mary, devoting themselves to the one thing needful, conscious of their constant need of the ministry of Christ that they might grow strong in the Lord and in the power of His might.

BIBLIOGRAPHY

Elert, W., *Morphologie des Luthertums*.

Fischer, E. E., *Social Problems: The Christian Solution*.

Frank, F. H. R., *System der Christlichen Sittlichkeit*.

Haas, J. A. W., *Freedom and Christian Conduct*.

Haering, Th., *Das Christliche Leben*, 1926.

Hallesby, O., *Conscience*.

Koeberle, A., *The Quest for Holiness*.

Löber, Richard, *Das innere Leben*.

Löhe, Wilhelm, *Drei Bücher von der Kirche*.

Luthardt, Chr., *Geschichte der Christlichen Ethik*.

Mattson, A. D., *Christian Ethics*.

Wuttke, Adolf, *Handbuch der Christlichen Sittenlehre*.

Minutes Lutheran World Convention: Eisenach, 1923; Copenhagen, 1929; Paris, 1935.

THE LUTHERAN VIEW OF CHRISTIAN ETHICS

C. C. RASMUSSEN

Not all Lutherans have exactly the same viewpoint on Christian Ethics. Such diversity is, for instance, illustrated in the brief discussion of Christian Ethics which *Credo Ecclesiam,* in February, 1942, presented as the late Dr. J. O. Evjen's "last written work." There the writer called attention to variant views: Hans Michael Müller's *Die Verleugnung Luthers im heutigen Protestantismus,* Paul Althaus' *Der Geist der lutherischen Ethik im ausburgischen Bekenntnis,* Emanuel Hirsch's *Leitfaden zur christlichen Lehre,* Nygren's *Philosophical and Christian Ethics,* and Bohlin's *The Fundamental Problem of Ethics.*

Yet that which is common to Lutheran minds is more significant than that in which they differ. It is this common element which we hope to set forth. The following pages will present an interpretation which seems to the writer to belong to the genius of Lutheran thought.

There are two great categories of ethical viewpoints, the naturalistic and the theistic.

Here it may only be pointed out that naturalistic or philosophical ethics finds both the content and the sanctions of ethics in man: his apprehension of *a priori* truths as in rationalism; his natural, psychological constitution as in hedonism and its child, utilitarianism; his status in natural evolution: his conditioning at the hands of society. Whether or not advocates of one or another of these views be personally theistic is irrelevant. The sanctions and the contents of their systems of ethics are located only in the horizontal frame of reference; the vertical dimension of man's relation

to God is not determinative. If such spokesmen introduce
God, it is because they are troubled by the inadequacy of
the naturalistic position.

Theistic ethics lays two charges against naturalistic systems. On the one hand, they are not true to fact; for
whether or not the fact be denied, man does inevitably live
under God. And on the other hand, no nontheistic ethics can
adequately answer the deepest ethical questions: what
makes right right and wrong wrong; why the individual
"ought" to do the right and not the wrong; and whence man
gets the ability to do the right and to avoid the wrong.

The meaning of the right and the dynamic for the accomplishment thereof both lie in the nature of God and of man's
relationship to Him.

The theistic ethics is independent of the philosophical
or naturalistic ethics. It does not necessarily contradict a
judgment of secular ethics on a given issue, but it is not
dependent on such.

Theistic ethics must, in turn, be divided into two types.

There is, on the one hand, the nomos ethics. It is the
ethics of law, rooting in the sovereign will of God. God
has prescribed the moral code, it is held, and man's standing before God is contingent on his conformity with such
ethical precepts.

Such is the ethics of the Old Testament and of the
religion whose sacred Scriptures the Old Testament was.
It is central to the mutuality of obligation obtaining in the
covenant relation into which God entered with Israel. It was
the outlook of the Torah, of the Mishna, of the Targums, and
of the Talmud—authoritative rabbinic commentaries on the
Torah and the Mishna. "The righteousness of the Pharisee
was secured through the fulfilment of the Torah in all its mi-
nutiæ—written and oral—the doing of the works of the Law."[1]

---

[1]Bowman, *The Intention of Jesus*, p. 23.

Reference to nomos ethics is relevant to our discussion because much that has been offered as Christian ethics is of this type.

Dibelius[2] recognizes that this was true of Thomas Aquinas. The way to eternal happiness was by obedience to *præcepta*, moral rules; and besides *præcepta* there were *concilia*, which were more and higher rules for those who would achieve a higher perfection—poverty, chastity, and obedience, best kept by withdrawal from this world.

In the Roman Catholic Church, which gives to Aquinas his recognized theological authority, one is not surprised to find a thoroughgoing legalism. A perusal of Father Connell's *The New Baltimore Catechism, No. 3,* is illuminating. "Besides believing what God has revealed, what else must we do to be saved?" The answer is, "We must keep His law."[3] Chapters are devoted to the exposition of such laws. Laws of God and laws of his Church are alike mandatory. "We are bound under pain of sin to obey the laws of the Church, since it is by the authority of God that the Church commands us to observe these laws."[4] That the Roman Church is thoroughly committed to the nomos type of ethics is unmistakably shown by its pervasive belief in the saving merit of man's good works.

But it is not in Romanism alone that legalistic ethics is encountered. Calvin's overshadowing emphasis on the sovereignty of divine will and the correlative social theory of his hagiocracy at Geneva illustrate this point. It is not accidental that "blue laws" have played so eminent a role among Calvin's followers.

A liberal Protestant like Knudson shows that his ethics rests on the same foundation when he says of Jesus, "He

---

[2]Dibelius, *The Sermon on the Mount,* p. 110.
[3]Father Connell, *The New Baltimore Catechism, No. 3,* p. 121.
[4]*Ibid.,* p. 179.

laid down moral principles and set up ethical standards."[5] Nor is the outlook of the book the less legalistic because of the sad confession that, conditions being what they are, "We simply have to acknowledge the indeterminateness of the moral law and decide for ourselves, as best we can, what we ought to do."[6]

To differentiate the Lutheran concept of Christian ethics (and it is not meant to imply that what we here call "spiritual ethics" is found only among Lutherans) from nomos ethics is not to deny a proper place to law but rather to affirm that a Christian's highest ethics takes him beyond the mandate of law, code, or principle. But the difference is not quantitative, a more or a less of the same thing. There is a sharp distinction between law and gospel, and the place of each is defined. It is hardly too strong to say that the one is regarded as necessary as the other. Both are necessary because their effects are not interchangeable, and the effects of both are necessary if man is to be saved. The law can never save. That is true not only because man is unable not to violate it but because it is always a mandate from without, not a creative power within. But, on the other hand, the gospel cannot save if the law has not done its work. Sinful man cannot be saved without faith—the grateful apprehension of the presence of God and man's responding commitment of himself to Him of whom he is apprehended. And sinful man is not brought to faith without repentance. It is not merely that God requires penitence. It is rather that, lacking repentance, man continues to keep self at the center of his life; hence the heart is not open to God. It is the accusing voice of the law that brings man to repentance. Without the law's "pedagogic" ministry there is no salvation.

The respective ministries of law and gospel find expression in Luther's view of the two kingdoms to which the

---

[5]Knudson, *Principles of Christian Ethics*, p. 35.   [6]*Ibid.*, p. 134.

Christian belongs—the kingdom of law and the kingdom of grace. In the latter man is ruled only by the Word of God; in the former he is constrained by the enforcement of law.

It is by the will of God that the two kingdoms coexist in this fallen world. The worldly kingdom is not redemptive; but if it were not beside the spiritual kingdom, the unrestrained wickedness of unregenerate man would destroy all order and make the ministry of the Word impossible. Worldly government thus exists by the will of God. The legal order in which God has set man is both penalty for man's sin and opportunity for man in the midst of sin.

The proclamation that the gospel sets man free from the law is misunderstood when it is construed in an antinomian sense. Luther's discussion of the Ten Commandments shows this clearly enough. And Melanchthon's affirmation that "the law ought to be begun in us, and be kept by us more and more,"[7] finds many iterations in the Lutheran Confessions.

God is Himself the author of the natural law on which the political order rests. He has made this law of nature as inclusive as the cosmos. His universe is not morally neutral. It imposes its consistent moral imperatives. The state must ever be summoned to make its positive legislation true to this God-made law. The body politic is not within its rights if, in violation of this law, it enacts statutes for the reason that they seem desirable to the sovereign, be that an individual, a class, a party, or a majority. The sovereign stands under the judgment of the law of nature which God has built into existence.

This is properly called a natural law, for it is true of the behavior of the created order—and that whether man apprehends it or not. Indeed, man's sin dims his eyes so that this law, of divine origin, is often seen but darkly.

It would be false to say that, because this law is natural, it is not revealed. It is both natural and revealed. God

---

[7]The Apology, Chapter III, Article VI.

ceaselessly affirms it and calls upon man to live by it lest in defying it he be crushed by it. And "holy men" have heard the divine call and proclaimed what His will is. The Decalogue, for instance, is an example of natural law that is revealed. Luther said that the Ten Commandments really ought not to be called the Law of Moses because "even if there had been no Moses, they were inevitably regnant in all men from the beginning."[8]

There is manifestly no inclination on the part of Lutheran ethics to ignore the mandate of this all-pervasive law. Christian ethics speaks for both kingdoms.

But the point which it is particularly important to stress, in view of the persistence with which ethics is legalistically conceived, is that no ethics which stops on the level of law, or code, or principle is sufficiently Christian. There is a higher ethics. The kingdom of God never rests on a basis of law but of grace. This was as true before the incarnation as it is after Bethlehem. That is the message of the eleventh chapter of Hebrews. To the same effect Melanchthon says that the Old Testament "fathers were also justified, not by the law, but by the promise and faith."[9]

The result of this realization brings what Nygren calls "a revolutionary change" in ethical concept. "The question of the good is no longer envisioned from the point of view of the isolated individual, but is widened to cover the relations of man with God and with his fellow men."[10]

When Christian ethics speaks to us about the Christian's highest ethics, it is, of course, the ethics of the kingdom of God. It presents the quality of the conduct of the man who is "in Christ," and, because he is in Christ, in the relation of love with all who are Christian. It is not that he does not

---

[8]W. A., 50, 330.
[9]The Apology, Chapter II, Article IV.
[10]Nygren, *Agape and Eros*, Part I, p. 30.

love those who are not Christians. He does. Love is not exclusive. But the mutuality of relationship which is true of all who are in the kingdom of God is refused by him who is without even while he is himself the object of the fellowship's love.

The Christian's action is action in the spirit and the fact of the *agape*-relation. He who lives in this relation is in the kingdom of God, and he who is in the kingdom of God does live in this relation. The quality of the action is regulated, not by law or rule, but by the fact that the regenerated person has become a participant in a new relationship. "That mind which was also in Christ Jesus" is the spirit of the fellowship, and Christ is, in the most literal and present sense, the central person in that κοινωνία (*koinonia*). All who are within it are of one mind, and that not because it is required of them, but because the fellowship and that mind are one indivisible fact.

The recognition of this fellowship is absolutely central in Lutheran thought. It is of one and the same thing that we speak, whether we say the *koinonia*, the communion of believers, the kingdom of God, or the church. In Chapter IV of the Apology, for instance, Melanchthon says, "The church is the kingdom of Christ"; and "the church which is truly the kingdom of Christ is properly the congregation of saints." It is the fact by whose coming to us we are made Christians. In his treatment of Article III of the Apostles' Creed, Luther said, "Outside of this Christian Church, where the gospel is not, there is no forgiveness, as also there can be no sanctification." The truth is not that the individual reaches a Christian conclusion and therefore decides to unite with the church. The truth is that the church, with Christ ever in the midst, comes to the unregenerate and by its coming proffers to him a fellowship which he may share but which he could never enter except for this "prevenient grace."

This is salvation. This is translation from the kingdom of darkness into the kingdom of Christ. This is justification. This is reconciliation. As Melanchthon says, "Justification is reconciliation."[11] And the cardinal meaning of this for ethics is that the redeemed person's action is no longer an obeying of rules or laws—even of laws or rules given by Christ! It is, as Luther affirmed, that the Christian, through the Holy Spirit and faith, is of such nature that "he does the right better than one could instruct him with all the commandments, and stands in personal need of neither law nor court."[12] By virtue of the fact that he shares the life of the communion the Christian's life is motivated from within. It is the expression of the new person that he is.

"If any man is in Christ, he is a new creature." What is the fact that is there affirmed? A person is not made new by a divine alchemy, a mysterious soul-chemistry, or an *ex nihilo* creative act of God. It is precisely by the fact of the acceptance of the proffer of new relationship and self-commitment thereto—forever impossible for the sinner but for the condescending grace in which Christ brings the proffer—that personality is made new. And the quality of the "new" person is the fruit of the character of the relationship.

In all this there is no disposition to overlook the fact that man's sharing in the mind of Christ is imperfect and in variable degree. There is no occasion for complacency. To stand in reconciliation with God is the Christian's most moving joy. But in his joy he knows himself as still a sinner. To be sure, between the sins of the defiant and of the repentant who lament and hate their sins in the very doing to which weakness leads them there is the difference between hell and heaven. The one is estranged from God, and the other reconciled. "Although the grace of God is secured through Christ, and sanctification is wrought by the Holy

---

[11]The Apology, Chapter III, Article VI.　　[12]W. A., 11, 250.

Ghost through the Word of God in the unity of the Christian Church, yet on account of our flesh which we bear about with us we are never without sin."[13]

Professor Soe rightly makes the twofold affirmation that the good is possible only as the fruit of justification, and the good is the inevitable fruit of justification.[14] The unregenerate—all they who have not been brought into grateful commitment of self to Him of whom they are apprehended—are indeed bound by the law which God has built into the fiber of existence. It is their highest ethics—unless and until they be "reconciled to God." Theirs is the morality which is the content of all secular systems of ethical thought. Christian ethics, as we have seen, recognizes the reality of that law and the fact that when the Christian wavers from the kingdom's fellowship he is himself again under the yoke of that law. But he knows that it is not the Christian's ethics. It is but the highest morality of those who are still estranged from God. Out of Christ there is no freedom therefrom.

Further light can probably be shed on the spirit of Christian ethics by reply to such criticisms as Schopenhauer has made.[15] When he argued that submission to the will of another, as to God, is not truly ethical, the answer is that the Christian is in harmony with God rather than in submission. He acts as a Christian, not because it is demanded of him by God, but because he stands in unity of spirit with God. He is in society with God, and the attitude of that society is his own attitude. He has entered into it, and its spirit lives in him. It does not coerce him.

Christian ethics rejects the further charge that it is low ethics because it acts under rewards and punishments. That consequences, happy or tragic, follow upon one's conduct

---

[13]Luther, *The Larger Catechism,* Article III of the Creed.
[14]*Erkendelsen og Virkeliggorelsen af det Gode,* p. 131.
[15]Knudson, *Principles of Christian Ethics,* Chapter I.

the Christian of course recognizes. He rejoices in "the fruit of the Spirit." And he knows that "the wages of sin is death." But he does not act to gain reward or to avoid punishment. His joy is to stand in fellowship with God and the redeemed society. But the mainspring of his action is the spirit which he shares, not the joy that inevitably comes to him because he does so. The reward does not fail him, to be sure, but it is the more sure because his spirit is above the seeking of it. He has a purpose deeper than personal reward, and the by-product that comes to his self-denial illustrates the divine observation that "he that loseth his life for My sake and the gospel's shall find it."

Nor is Schopenhauer closer to the truth when he says that Christianity, being other-worldly, cripples effectiveness. Christian ethics does not indeed forget that this life stands in relation to the next. But it is not thereby less concerned about the present. On the contrary, since its very essence is a quality of relationship between persons, it shows itself wherever the Christian stands in relation with others. Not to be interested in the next life is to be less than Christian, but to be indifferent to the ethical in this life is to be unchristian.

But how can the Christian answer the question as to the right in any given situation if it be true that "reconciliation" ethics does not offer code or precept? The answer gives none of the neat definiteness which another view of ethics demands. As Melanchthon said of the Romanists, "The adversaries select the law, because human reason naturally understands it."[16] But an ethics which supplies the Christian with no code leaves him with the necessity to decide what is the right in any situation. The basis for such decision must, for one who is God's, be the spirit of God's dealing with persons. God is love. All that God does with man He does for the

---

[16]The Apology, Article IV.

sake of man even as "the Sabbath was made for man, and
not man for the Sabbath." For man, God is ever the
unwearying Seeker. For man, God became incarnate, no
less absolute method sufficing for His redemptive purpose.
For man, the Son of God died, His absolute quest not even
stopping short of that.

This is the "mind" of the fellowship of those that are
God's, its quality "caught" from the heart of God who is
Himself in the midst.

And here is the criterion by which the Christian reaches
the ethical decisions inseparable from his relation with others.
The quality of his conduct is not conformed to an external
demand; it obeys an inward quality which is his because he
is at home in the spiritual fellowship which is "His body."
Here is "the liberty wherewith Christ has made us free."

One way of stating the criterion of the Christian's ethics
is to say that he determines the rightness of an action by its
consequences, its total consequences, to all persons involved
in the action. Each of the consequences, and all of them, are
judged by the question of their conformity with that which
agape, love, would do to all who are touched by the action,
remotely as well as immediately. Love is indeed the fulfilling of the only "law" that regulates Christian action.

It may not be amiss to state that this is something quite
different from the call of exponents of philosophical ethics
for conduct in conformity with a "principle" of love. The
Christian, as Christian, does not act under the mandate of a
principle, for that, too, is a rule of conduct lying outside
himself. The Christian's spring of action is the inner spirit
which became his when he was taken into Christ's fellowship.

Even the New Testament does not supply the Christian
with rules for Christian living. The New Testament is not a
new and better law. Christ is not there a lawgiver, nor is He
a "blueprint," specifying that the Christian must do as He

did—in marriage, parenthood, property, citizenship, occupation, diet, and such. He is the Head of the fellowship and
the matchless illustrator of its spirit. The Sermon on the
Mount, for example, is "not a program for the reform of this
world."[17] It is a presentation of the pure will of God as to the
spirit in which the Christian lives in all his relationships. Its
very spirit is lost if it be construed as a set of rules. One
could turn the other cheek, or go two miles when one was
asked, and yet have nothing of the mind of Christ.

The specific content of the Christian's ethics rests on
love's verdict as to the effect of an action on persons. For
example, the Christian judges hate, or adultery, or any other
forbidden act or attitude wrong for a deeper reason than
that it is forbidden. It is in love's judgment that Christ
"forbids." The Christian's motivation is other-regarding and
self-forgetting. His action is not even dictated by desire for
good standing in the kingdom of God. To act even from
that measure of self-seeking is, by so much, less than the
mind of Christ and the Christian's highest ethics.

It would be facile shallowness to brush aside this view
as unrealistic idealism. Any profound study of personality
shows that it is true to life where life is seen at its highest.
The place to look for that is not in realms that are ruled by
law or contract. "The letter killeth." It is a commonplace of
human conduct that many a man who is warm and generous
in certain of his associations can, when his work takes him
back to "business," be as cold and ruthless as an avalanche.

The place to see human fellowship at its best is where
the fellowship is not built on law but on spontaneous
mutuality of spirit. The relationships in a good family, for
instance, are not regulated by law or rule. Love "prevents"
law—in both senses of that verb—and far exceeds what any
rule could rightly ask. It is only when willingness of spirit

---

[17]Dibelius, *The Sermon on the Mount,* p. 136.

fails that laws are necessary, and that necessity is evidence that the relationship has been broken.

This view is misunderstood if it be regarded as leaving man "on his own" and without divine help in his ethical judgments. On the contrary, it puts its reliance in the Spirit, not in the letter. The Christian does not look at Christ afar off and make choices which will make him like his great Exemplar. "He is not far from us, but in Him we live, and move, and have our being." Psychology recognizes that all thought is social and not merely individual. No one thinks in isolation. It is not only that one's language, concepts, and attitudes are borrowed from his milieu. All thinking goes on in a meeting of minds, harmonious or clashing. Even so the Christian's thinking is a thinking in which the fellowship of believers is in the deepest sense participant; and the pre-eminent participant is the Christ who in deepest truth is "in the midst." There is no fact more central to the Christian life than the mutual communion of Christ and those that are His. This fact is declared in many Scriptural assurances. "I am with you alway." "I have yet many things to say unto you." "Abide in Me and I in you." "The Spirit . . . will guide you into all truth."

Such assurances are taken seriously in the Lutheran view of ethics. The Christian makes his moral decisions, not only in the spirit of Jesus, but with the Spirit of Jesus. Far from being unguided, he is guided of God. And it is guidance, not rules, that he receives. He is, indeed, of all men most free, for he acts out of an inner fact, his fellowship with Christ.

The ethical emphasis here given is in keeping with the recognized *Innerlichkeit* of the Lutheran understanding of Christianity. Inwardness does not mean, as some have mistakenly concluded, neglect of life's outward relationships. No one, for instance, was more insistent than Luther on the Christian's temporal responsibilities. *Innerlichkeit* means that the quality of the Christian's action in all relationships, human and divine, comes from the inward fact of reconciliation, from citizenship in the kingdom of God.

Because the issue has been raised whether the ethics of Jesus was an "interim" ethics, in force only till He shall come again to fulfill his kingdom, it should be pointed out that the Christian ethics is rather an eternal ethics. It is the spirit of all person-to-person relationships in the kingdom of God. It is "that mind which was also in Christ Jesus," and that shall never pass away or cease to be the spirit of the redeemed society.

What is the possibility of a systematic ethics? The question has been answered variously, depending on what is meant by the term. It must be said that there can be no systematic ethics on the interpretation herein presented if by the term is meant that ethics can offer a formulated system of precepts to prescribe conduct in the various areas of social contacts—family, state, economics, etc. But an affirmative answer is not impossible if one means a systematic study of the Christian's problems in such areas with a view to supplying light for ethical decisions by pointing out the loci of ethical issues and presenting descriptive suggestion of the way such issues are met by Christians. Professor Soe, of the University of Copenhagen, deplores[18] the position of Bultmann and Gogarten, "at least in his earlier views," that a Christian ethics is not possible. He is fearful that the result will be that the determination of ethical issues will be left to unregulated subjectivity. But his own presentation seems to espouse nothing more than a systematic study of ethical problems in the light of the practice and the counsels of leading Christian minds, met in Scripture and in subsequent religious thought. But this is assuredly not to espouse something small, for in the field of ethics there could be

---

[18]*Erkendelsen og Virkleggorelsen af det Gode,* pp. 106ff.

nothing greater. It is not moral legislation. It is the sharing of insights as to life's deepest ethical issues and the contagion of life that flows forth from that inner compulsion which spiritual status supplies.

BIBLIOGRAPHY

A. ON RELIGION AS PERSONAL RELATIONSHIP

Baillie, John, *Our Knowledge of God*, New York: Scribner, 1939.

Brunner, Emil, *The Divine-Human Encounter*, Philadelphia: Westminster, 1943.

Oman, John, *Grace and Personality*, Cambridge University, 1925.

B. NATURALISTIC ETHICS

Titus, Harold Hopper, *Ethics for Today*, American Book Co., 1936.

Seth, James, *Ethical Principles*, New York: Scribner's, 1908.

Dewey and Tufts, *Ethics*, New York: Henry Holt, 1908.

Bentham, Jeremy, *Principles of Moral Legislation*, Oxford: 1907.

Mill, John Stuart, *Utilitarianism*, New York: Dutton & Co., 1920.

Spencer, Herbert, *Data of Ethics*, New York: A. L. Burt.

C. NOMOS ETHICS

Knudson, Albert C., *Principles of Christian Ethics*, New York: Abingdon-Cokesbury, 1943.

Smyth, Newman, *Christian Ethics*, New York: Scribner's, 1901.

Schmid, Chr. Fr., *Christian Ethics*, Philadelphia: 1872.

D. SPIRITUAL ETHICS

Althaus, Paul, *Grundriss der Ethik*, 1931.

Bring, Ragnar, *Forhallandet Mellen Tro Och Garning Inom Luthersk Theologie*, Stockholm: 1933.

Brunner, Emil, *The Divine Imperative*, 1937.

Dibelius, Martin, *The Sermon on the Mount*.

Ehlert, Werner, *Morphologie des Luthertums*, Munich: Beck, 1932.

Köberle, Adolf, *The Quest for Holiness*, New York: Harper, 1936.

Müller, Hans Michael, *Die Verleugnung Luthers im Heutigen Protestantismus*.

Niebuhr, H. Reinhold, *Interpretation of Christian Ethics*, New York: Harper, 1935.

Nygren, Anders, *Agape and Eros*, New York: Macmillan, 1941.

Soe, N. H., *Erkendelsen og Virkeliggorelsen af det Gode*, Copenhagen: G. E. C. Gads, 1937.

THE CHURCH AND SOCIETY

A. D. MATTSON

In this chapter we deal with the relation and the responsibility of the church to society. The term "society" includes the state, by which is meant the political community, but one of the following chapters will deal with the relation of the church to the state, and we shall therefore not directly consider the relation of the church to the political community. There are certain social relationships in life which are not amenable to the immediate will of the individual such as war, the conflict between capital and labor, the liquor traffic, problems created by extreme wealth, problems created by poverty, divorce, child labor, race prejudice, the immigrant, lawlessness, amusements, and the problem of population. The state will be concerned with most, if not all, of these problems, but also the church has an interest in all of them. No clear line of distinction can therefore be drawn between the relation of the church to society and the relation of the church to the state. It is nevertheless possible, on the one hand, to consider in a general way the relation of the church to society, which includes the political organization, and, on the other hand, to consider specifically the relation of the church to the political community.

Every individual has his private realm of experience. Whether he recognizes it or not, every man also stands in a certain relationship to God. Every man lives also in the sphere of certain corporate relationships with his fellow men. All who are interested in religion will agree that the church is concerned with the first two relationships, but it is in the third realm that various attitudes are discernible among religious people. We shall consider our subject by a

(455)

discussion of two attitudes which have prevailed with respect to the relationship of the church to society. These two attitudes were clearly discernible at the Stockholm Conference on Life and Work in 1925. Two types of Protestantism have developed with respect to attitudes to the relation of the church to society. One of these types is individual and eschatological, emphasizing the transcendent aspects of the kingdom of God, and assumes a rather pessimistic attitude to the world. At Stockholm this attitude was revealed among the German, French, and Scandinavian delegates to a large degree. The other type of piety is more social in its emphases, stressing the immanent aspects of the kingdom of God and assuming a more optimistic attitude toward the world. This attitude was evident particularly among the Anglo-Saxons.

In the first place, there have been those who have held that the church is not directly concerned with the problems of society. Arguments have been advanced against any social application of the gospel. The command to engage in missionary activity is very clear in the last verses of the Gospel of Matthew, and yet many arguments were advanced against foreign missionary activity by leaders in the church from the sixteenth century to relatively modern times. The chief objection to missionary activity was that man must not interfere with God's providence. It is interesting to note that the same arguments which were used against missionary activity are now often used against the social application of the gospel.

The Lutheran Church has often been accused of being quietistic.[1] Dean Inge wrote in 1930:

Luther's "doctrine, sometimes explicitly stated, sometimes merely assumed, is that Christianity is, on the moral side, a system of individual ethics, a principle of personal conduct, but that it is not concerned with national and international politics, in which the interests of the State are the supreme law. . . . 'When the authority of the pope in international politics was repudiated, there was nothing

---

[1] See Garvie, *The Christian Ideal for Human Society*, p. 22.

to take its place.' Grotius and others did their best to formulate principles of international law; but there was no clear doctrine of the
supremacy of the Gospel over the relations of peoples. Luther and
the Lutheran Church have been, I think, especially unfortunate in
handling this problem, and their ready acceptance of war as a permanent necessity for human societies has been a weapon in the hands of
militarist parties. Even before the war I have read strangely unethical
utterances by responsible and representative Germans on this subject."[2]

Barry says that "Protestantism in both its leading forms,
and perhaps most markedly in its Lutheran version, has been
prone to combine orthodoxy in belief and intense devotion
in personal religion with inertia, and at times with a shame-
less cynicism, in the sphere of economics and politics and
the great issues of public morality."[3]

Reinhold Niebuhr in his book, *Does Civilization Need
Religion?* says that "Lutheranism is the Protestant way of
despairing of the world and of claiming victory for the
religious ideal without engaging the world in combat."[4]
Again he says that "unfortunately, Lutheran piety, at its
best, is too pure to affect the world."[5]

Schaff says that "Luther and his followers carefully ab-
stained from politics."[6] Karl Barth in a letter to the French
Protestants in 1939 spoke of "Martin Luther's error on the
relation between the temporal and the spiritual order and
power."

Quotations similar to those given might be multiplied at
great length, but the gist of them all is that the Lutheran
Church has been quietistic, and that it has theoretically and
practically failed to influence society as it ought to have
done. It may be that the least satisfactory aspect of Luther's
thought and writings is to be found in his dealing with the
relation of the church to society and the state. It may be

---

[2] *Christian Ethics and Modern Problems,* pp. 237, 238.
[3] *Christianity and New World,* pp. 25, 26.
[4] p. 110. [5] *Christendom,* I, 3, p. 474.
[6] *Creeds of Christendom,* Vol. I, p. 218.

that the reason it is so difficult to understand Luther at this point is that he lacks consistency in dealing with the matter. It has been pointed out that, in connection with the peasants' revolt, Luther could, on the one hand, tell the peasants to govern themselves according to the Sermon on the Mount and, on the other hand, when writing to the princes he completely ignored these injunctions.

However, a distinction must be made between Luther and Lutheranism in dealing with the matters involved. The context of a statement or an attitude must determine its significance. The Roman Church had during the Middle Ages tried to influence public morality and had, to a certain extent, influenced group life, socially, economically, and nationally. The ideal had been a state controlled by the church. It enforced what moral justice could be enforced; it mitigated the evils of war; it developed science, furthered medicine and surgery; it founded and nurtured universities; it build up systems of philosophy; it produced poets such as Dante; it moralized Arabic chivalry; it fostered the feudal system; it helped build up the guilds; and it forbade the lending of money on interest. Charles Clayton Morrison has stated:

"For a thousand years Christianity had accepted this responsibility [for the character of civilization]. No sphere of life was untouched by its influence. No sphere claimed autonomy for itself; it was a part of a larger unity. Education was a function of religion. Art not only drew its chief materials from the Christian legend, but its outlook and inspiration were religious. Science stood within the Christian tradition and accepted a theological framework as marking the boundaries of its domain. Business derived its ethical standards from the Church. Theology was the queen of the sciences. Religion had the last word, as it had the first, in all human affairs. One may not like the kind of religion which existed during the thousand years of the middle ages, nor the kind of organization through which it exercised its dominance, but it did give a spiritual solidarity, a unity, a soul, to western society."[7]

This was the environment in which Luther lived, spoke,

---

[7]*Christendom*, I, 3, p. 498.

and wrote, and all of his statements must be viewed in the light of that background and context.

Luther did individualize religion and ethics, but he never conceived of a situation where religion would become a kind of epiphenomenon to life. For Luther it was an axiom that religion would exert its influence upon society. No one can read Luther without sensing that fact. Luther certainly never contemplated a society in which the church was not to exert its influence. That religion has nothing to do with society was an idea absolutely foreign either to Luther or to any of his contemporaries. That religion and the church have no obligation to society is an absolutely modern idea. It is true that Luther did not place his emphasis in this sphere, but it is likewise true that he accepted it as an axiom.[8]

Luther went even farther in stressing the social implications of Christianity than many of his contemporaries. Roman Catholic catechims had explained the Fourth Petition of the Lord's Prayer as referring to the Lord Jesus Christ as bread for the soul. In his catechism of 1520 Luther follows the Roman tradition and says that "the bread is our Lord Jesus Christ, who feedeth and comforteth the soul." In 1529 he interpreted "daily bread" to mean "everything that is required to satisfy our bodily needs; such as food and raiment; house and home; fields and flocks; money and goods; pious parents; children and servants; godly and faithful rulers; good government; seasonable weather; peace and health; order and honor; true friends; good neighbors; and the like." In this explanation is to be found a summary of all the social problems of the time, and here Luther certainly connects the religious interest with the problems and the needs of the social order.

Luther was a monk, and the greatest of all problems for Luther, as a monk, was the salvation of his soul. When he

[8]Cf. "Letter to the Christian Nobility."

was finally assured of the salvation, it became for him the "pearl of great price," and it was only natural that the chief emphasis in his preaching and his writing should revolve about this fact. This does not mean that Luther did not recognize that the church had obligations and responsibilities to society. That fact Luther took for granted because it was not questioned in his day. Luther was also conservative politically, and the feudal pattern of society supplied the background for his thinking, but that Luther advocated an exclusively other-worldly type of religion cannot be maintained.

However, when we commence a historical survey of Lutheranism we often find attitudes to society which Luther never contemplated. It is possible to use Luther as a kind of legal guide in a situation and an environment which Luther did not face, and to quote Luther in such a new environment will bring results never contemplated by him. It is also possible to use Luther's emphasis, without producing what he contemplated, when the environment in which he found himself does not exist. Luther never knew, in a practical way, such a separation of church and state as has developed among us. In our situation we need Luther's emphasis upon salvation through grace by faith plus an emphasis upon the responsibility of the church to society which was an axiom for Luther and his contemporaries.

A legalistic use of Luther has led to some very strange attitudes on the part of Lutherans. Some years ago a questionnaire was circulated among Lutheran pastors on the problem of the relation of the church to society. One man answered that his "church makes it a point to adhere to the spirit of the U. S. Constitution and the teachings of the Word of God by refraining from mingling with the affairs of the State. . . . My business is to preach the Word of God only and to concern myself with the spiritual welfare of my parishioners." It might be asked what this man might mean by "preaching the Word of God." Another pastor answered, "Tell me, what has this to do with me or my position as a pastor, or what has this to do with the preaching of the cross?" A great number of such replies might be quoted, but these are sufficient to emphasize that there are those who would say that the church has no responsibility to society.

It has often been said that the church's only business is to bring about the salvation of the individual, and then the social problem will automatically take care of itself. Certainly, the church is and ought to be interested in the salvation of the individual. However, the individual Christian does not live his life in a vacuum. It is lived in a society. The patterns of society differ, and in some of these patterns it is possible to live the Christian life, and in others it is not possible to do so. Some patterns of society are more adaptable for an expression of the Christian life than others. A cannibal cannot continue to live in the social patterns of his tribe if he is to be a Christian. He must change the customs of his tribe if he is to stay with it and live a Christian life. Farm tenancy is creating a problem for the rural church, but the fact that individuals are converted will not automatically solve the tenancy problem. Techniques must be developed if the problem is to be solved. Furthermore, Christians must consider the problems of society in order that they may reach a common mind on what the Spirit of Christ demands of us in our social situation.

Christians cannot wait until all men have become Christians to assume responsibility for the character of society. The Christians' obligation is as great at present in this realm as it will ever be for any future generation. It is not necessary to be an impractical Utopian dreamer in order to sense the obligation of the church to society. The leaven of Biblical religion has been at work in the world, and the things which we cherish most in our civilization are due to the influence of that religion. In many respects the attitudes and the ideals of people who profess no religion have been molded by Biblical religion. No one knows how much of society will ever be influenced by the principles of the kingdom of God, but the obligation of Christians to strive toward that end is nevertheless clear.

The Lutheran Church has been engaged in a great deal of inner mission work. It has done a great deal by way of rescuing the victims of sin. It has, however, done less by way of preventing people from falling into sin. The former should be done while not leaving the latter undone. It is the duty of the church to rescue the man who fell among robbers on the road between Jerusalem and Jericho, but it is also the duty of the church to try to see to it that the road is made safe so that men will not fall among robbers. It is the duty of the church to rescue the man who has become a drunkard, and it is likewise the obligation of the church to do something about the liquor traffic which manufactures drunkards. The latter may not be as spectacular as the former, but it may be a great deal more effective in the long run. It is true that many individuals have risen above great combinations of adverse circumstances, through the Christian gospel, but it is not the rule. All of us realize to what a great extent we are creatures of our environment. The influence of Christianity in the home, through the church, through companions, and in society has had a great deal to do with the shaping of our characters. Society can tear down more than the church can build of character unless the church exerts its influence upon society. The church cannot, if it be true to its nature, function as a political unit, but through the preaching of the Word the light of God's will must be cast upon the problems of society.

In some strange manner the idea has also developed that what is spiritual is somehow to be contrasted with the problems of society. The spiritual is looked upon as something exclusively other-worldly or that which belongs to the so-called realm of the inner life. This attitude follows the example of asceticism. It never comes to grips with the social problem but withdraws from it. Whatever else the spiritual may be, it must be considered as a quality of life, and as such it must influence the social order. Luther rejected the ethical dualism of Roman Catholic ethics and insisted that a man could serve God in his vocation. Luther's emphasis upon the vocation was a return to Biblical Christianity, for Paul had said, "Let each man abide in that calling wherein he was called."[9] Luther did not consider it necessary to withdraw into a monastery or a convent in order to serve God wholeheartedly. He put it thus: "To serve God is for everyone to remain in his vocation and calling, be it ever so mean and simple."[10] Again he said, "When a poor servant maid sweeps the house and does it because God has commanded her, she does a better work and renders God a greater service than did Anthony in the desert." Luther certainly did not consider the spiritual to be something divorced from society.

If Luther's attitude to the spiritual implications of man's vocation were consistently followed, the common distinctions between sacred and secular would cease to exist. The secular is life or any area of life which is lived without reference to God. For the Christian no area of life should be lived without reference to God. The Christian must, therefore, be interested in establishing a social order in which he can manifest the spirit of Christ in his vocation. The dynamic and the insights for such a life must come from the church.

The Lutheran Church accepts the Bible as the Word of God and as its rule of faith and practice. The Bible does have something to say about society and social problems. No

---

[9] I Cor. 7:20.　　　　[10] *Table Talk*, tr. by Hazlitt, p. 447.

one can read the great prophets of the Old Testament without realizing that they were concerned about practically all of the social problems of their day. The land question, the liquor problem, child labor, poverty, wealth, slavery, and injustice in all its social forms, were dealt with by the prophets. In the New Testament Jesus taught His disciples to pray that the will of God might be done "on earth." The social interest of the writers of the Bible is apparent on almost every page, and it would be a strange preaching of that Word if the problems of society were to be ignored. If the Bible is the rule of faith and practice, those who ignore social problems in their preaching of the Word are not preaching the Word of God in its fulness. Religion must give meaning and direction to life if it is to function vitally and according to its nature. Such meaning cannot be given to life if the problems of society are ignored because the Christian lives his life in a social order. Without Christian individuals there would be no application of Christian principles in society, but the Christian individual repents in a social order; he exercises his faith in a social order; and he lives the sanctified life in a social order. The church has an obligation and a responsibility to society to supply the dynamic and the insights, through the preaching of the Word, for the creation of an environment in which the Christian ethical life can be lived, and the Spirit of Christ can be manifested.

The quietistic attitude is not satisfactory from the Christian point of view with respect to the relationship of the church and society. An exclusively transcendental emphasis is not true to the genius of Christianity. The historical process must somehow be brought within the orbit of the religious interest. God is the Creator of the world and the Lord of history. The doctrine of the incarnation of God in Jesus is a historical fact, and that incarnation took place in history. God is somehow related to the historical process, and the historical process is somehow related to God's goals and purposes for the human race and his kingdom.

The social problem is an ethical problem. Christian Sociology is simply Christian Social Ethics. There are those who have held that all that is of value in religion is the moral. There are also those who have placed such an emphasis upon social ethics that religion has almost been lost, and practically nothing but an ethical system has remained. This was a danger which was very close at hand for many adherents of the so-called "social-gospel" movement. Here we have an attitude at the opposite extreme from the attitude which we have been considering. This attitude involves such an emphasis upon the social problem that religion becomes little more than a system of social ethics. American humanism is a typical example.

Humanism could not long hold the field because it failed to answer the question as to the cosmic place of the moral. The moral must be grounded in the very nature of things if it is to have a claim upon us. Ethics without religion is in the same position as physics without astronomy. The obligations inculcated by ethics must be related to the Power that rules the world, or it is difficult to see why men should be obligated to obey them. Religion has found the clue to the meaning of life, apart from which it is difficult to see how morality could either arise or function.

Moral values are, in the last analysis, dependent upon the wider outlook of religion. Religion has something to say about the nature of reality and the disposition of the universe and thus gives meaning to life and direction to ethics. Any ethical system which has divorced itself from religion can rest only on a hedonistic or utilitarian basis. Hedonism and utilitarianism reduce the sense of obligation, which is fundamental for ethics, to something other than what is given in the sense of obligation. The moral is something *sui generis* and stands in its own right. It is a category which cannot be reduced to anything else. The sense of obligation involves that it is assigned to us by the nature of reality itself, and thus it leads us into the realm of religion.

Morality cannot exhaust the meaning of religion from other points of view as well. For morality the good is a task to be achieved. Morality functions with a certain tension and effort. From the moral point of view our goal can be achieved only at the end of the process. For religion the good is something given and is a present possession. Religion gives to the soul a peace and a joy which the moral struggle itself can never give. Ethics cannot take the place of religion in the great crises of life. It has little comfort to offer in suffering, in bereavement, or in the face of death.

Ethics cannot solve the question as to what shall be done with sin which has already been committed. How shall the sense of guilt be lifted from the soul? Christianity offers forgiveness of sins and is the gospel of a new start. Reconciliation with God is a religious experience which ethics by itself could not give. Religion lifts the burden from man's soul. Religion is something greater than ethics even though it includes the latter, and the latter can never take the place of the former. Religion involves a response to fundamental needs of the human soul which ethics cannot satisfy.

The church must not become a glorified social service club. It is with religion that the church must reach out and touch the various relationships of society. Religion is the dynamic in the church's relationship to society. Social service may not be Christianity even though Christianity, if it be true to its genius, will render service to society. To strive to live according to Christian principles is not the whole of Christianity, and it may not even be a part of it.

For Luther God was the "Living God." Following Luther, one of the characteristics of Lutheranism has been its emphasis upon the divine initiative and the divine activity. For Luther revelation was divine activity manifesting itself to and comprehended by men. In considering the meaning of baptism Luther placed the emphasis upon the divine initiative rather than upon the psychological aspects of it. It was Luther's experience of the Lord's presence in the Sacrament of the Altar that led to his irreconcilable attitude to Zwingli. He confessed that it was not through his own reason or strength that he had come to faith in the Lord Jesus Christ, but the Holy Spirit had called him through the gospel. This awareness of God in an existential manner is that which makes religion. Luther and Lutheranism have been correct in placing their emphasis at this point. God's activity in Christ brought Christianity into being, and it created the church, and still creates the church.

There is a serious danger in the tendency to separate activity in the church from its roots in the divine grace. There is also a danger in emphasizing the divine initiative and activity in such a manner that it leads to quietism. Both tendencies are apparent in the history of the church, and we need to be on our guard against them both. The point is well illustrated by a parody of Dr. Merrill's well-known hymn:

> Rise up, O men of God,
> His Kingdom tarries long,
> *Bring in* the day of brotherhood,
> And end the night of wrong.

A Scotch student felt that the Continental theologians would have to sing it this way:

> Sit down, O men of God,
> His Kingdom He will bring
> Whenever it may please His will;
> You cannot do a thing.[11]

---

[11]Quoted from Horton, *Contemporary Continental Theology*, p. XVI.

If the attitudes expressed in this chapter seem like paradoxes, they can be resolved by the recognition of the fact that the good which Christians do is the work of God in them.

The heirs of Luther have a contribution to render to the church universal through their insistence upon the fact that Christian activity must always be founded in the divine grace. On the other hand, Lutherans need to learn from some of the more activistic Protestant groups that the church cannot remain satisfied with a mere private type of piety but must insist that the will of God be done not only in the private but also in the public affairs of men.

In considering the relation of the church to society we are led to the position that neither a passive quietism nor an activism, which fails sufficiently to emphasize man's relationship to God, is a satisfactory solution of the problem. The chief concern of the church is religion, and "let the church be the church." The church cannot identify itself with any parties or pressure groups but must pass judgment upon them all from the point of view of the Word of God. The determining factor for the message of the church is the Word of God, and no party loyalties should be allowed to color that message.

The Word of God is, however, no legal code which the church can apply to society. Christianity is not a new law but a spirit. Jesus never gave us a code of laws as regulative for conduct, and He never outlined any program for His followers. He did give us a spirit, and that spirit we are to apply to our various social problems. That spirit is applicable to all times, all problems, all conditions. Had Jesus given us a code of laws, His religion might have easily become a brake to progress and the exponent of a static culture, but His spirit is adaptable to an ever-changing environment and has a message for all times and conditions. We are not even called upon slavishly to follow Christ in

His manner of life but rather to lay hold of His spirit and to apply that to our problems and conditions. That spirit is a spirit of love and involves everything that Christianity means by the word love. Christians are not called to an outward imitation of Christ but to obedience to Jesus' inner spirit. Jesus is our model in disposition in relation to God and man. The chief characteristic of the Christian spirit is the experience of God pressing in upon human conduct and exerting His influence upon it.

Because of the very nature of Christianity the message of the church must become, for the Christian, an integrating center for all life. With its gospel the church must reach out and touch all of the relationships of society. The church cannot function, if it is to remain true to its nature, as a political unit, but it can and should quicken and enlighten the consciences of its members in order that the spirit of Christ may increasingly be incorporated in the various social relationships which these members touch. This the church can do through its preaching and its teaching ministry. The church will thus function as a conscience for society. The church has the remedy for our social maladjustments, and it has the only remedy which will keep society from disintegrating.

BIBLIOGRAPHY

Rauschenbusch, Walter, *Christianity and the Social Crisis; Christianizing the Social Order; The Social Principles of Jesus.*

Sharpe, Dores Robinson, *Walter Rauschenbusch.*

Bodein, Vernon Parker, *The Social Gospel of Walter Rauschenbusch.*

Hopkins, Charles Howard, *The Rise of the Social Gospel in American Protestantism.*

Temple, William, *Christianity and the Social Order.*

Oldham, J. H., *The Oxford Conference.*

Johnson, F. Ernest, *The Social Gospel Re-examined.*

Husslein, Joseph, *The Christian Social Manifesto* (Roman Catholic).

Jones, E. Stanley, *Christ's Alternative to Communism.*

Macintosh, D. C., *Social Religion.*

Brown, William Adams, *Church and State in Contemporary America.*

Means, Paul B., *Things That Are Caesar's.*

McNeill, John T., *Christian Hope for World Society.*

Visser 'T Hooft, W. A., and Oldham, J. H., *The Church and Its Function in Society.*

Plowright, B. C., *Rebel Religion.*

Vollmer, Philip, *New Testament Sociology.*

Bennett, John C., *Social Salvation.*

Demant, V. A., *God, Man, and Society.*

Lingle, Walter T., *The Bible and Social Problems.*

Trueblood, D. Elton, *The Predicament of Modern Man.*

Wood, H. G., *Christianity and Communism.*

CHURCH AND FAMILY

BERNHARD M. CHRISTENSEN

I. The Family, a Cornerstone of Society

For the Christian the fundamental character of the family as an institution in human society is clearly indicated by the fact that the Scriptures repeatedly make use of figures drawn from family life to suggest the basic relationships that should prevail within the spiritual order. In the Old Testament, Jehovah is again and again called the "husband" of Israel. In the New, Jesus reveals Him as "the Father." The church is the "bride" of Christ. Christians are exhorted to be "loving as brethren" toward one another, for they are all called to be members of "the household of God." In one of His most revolutionary and revealing statements our Lord declares that "whosoever shall do the will of God, the same is My brother, and sister, and mother." He could find no more perfect earthly picture of the harmonious fellowship among persons which His coming and kingdom were to mediate than those suggested by true family relations.

This conception of the family as occupying a fundamental place in all human society, so clearly implied in the Scriptures, is confirmed by scholars in the field of sociology and anthropology. There is no society known, either in the past or the present, where the institutions of marriage and the family have not been recognized as playing an important part in the social order. The forms of marriage and of family life have, of course, differed widely in the various cultures. Monogamy, polygymy, polyandry have prevailed at various times and places, and all are still to be found today. And in inclusiveness the family organization may vary from the simplest form of one parent and one child living together to much more complex structures involving a large group of married sons (or daughters) and their respective "families," all sharing one patriarchal home.

But whatever the specific form or pattern of organization, the family unit is everywhere—even in the most primitive or savage cultures—known and recognized, and definite laws and customs are enforced for its protection and its preservation. On the basis of the past history of the race every attempt to discredit or destroy the family would seem, therefore, to be definitely foredoomed to failure. The very nature of human life, involving, as it does, a long period of helpless infancy and comparatively helpless childhood, necessitates the preservation of some type of family organization if mankind is to continue to exist.

The universality and the necessity of family organization do not, of course, indicate that all family relationships exemplify the high ideals of personal fellowship enjoined in the Scriptures, including the teachings of Christ Himself. It is, however, highly significant that Christ and the Bible should repeatedly stress the necessity of cultivating the type of relations characteristic of a social unit which humanity has so clearly demonstrated that it cannot live without. It would seem to point to the profound truth that the human race will ultimately have to learn that its very existence can be preserved only by cultivating family-like relations among all groups and individuals. At any rate, sacred and secular scholarship agree that marriage and the family constitute one of the chief foundation stones in the structure of human society, and no one who desires to contribute effectively to humanity's social good can afford not to give major attention to this basic human relationship.

II. LUTHER'S EMANCIPATION OF THE FAMILY

Both the possibility and the necessity of family life are rooted in the fact of sex. In every age and in every clime and culture the regulation and the control of sex life have constituted one of mankind's chief problems, both for the individual and for the social group. Even the "advanced" groups who have attempted to deny the existence of any special problems connected with sex have not been able long to maintain this attitude of seeming unconcern. For sex and sex life are so intimately bound up with the innermost secret of personal human existence on earth that only in a sinless world could there be no special problems connected with them. And the fact that sex problems have perpetually troubled and tormented men therefore only confirms the teaching of Scripture that the race is enmeshed in sin and is living under the judgment of God. Man's struggle with sex is in reality but one peculiarly important aspect of his struggle with life itself. The area of sex experience is one of the major arenas for the testing and the disciplining of human personality in its earthly existence. Practically every adult person who has honestly faced the ethical and the spiritual issues in his own life can bear witness to the truth of this statement. And it is clearly and repeatedly suggested in the Scriptures, beginning with the very earliest stories in Genesis. The difficulties which men meet in the realm of sex are not in themselves evil; they are intended to serve the creative and the disciplinary purposes of God.

In an endeavor to escape from the problems connected with sex men have tended to adopt one or the other of two extreme views and then to carry out the consequences of these views in countless variations, ever seeking the freedom and the happiness which are man's perennial quest. On the one hand men have sought to deny the validity of any abiding moral principles with reference to sex and have

plunged themselves into abysses of self-indulgence, frequently overleaping or temporarily disregarding the more
regularized family organization referred to above. The number of those who have sought liberty through varying
degrees of libertinism is legion in every generation.

On the other hand, a host of men have sought refuge
from the sex problem along exactly the opposite road, namely through ascetic self-denial. By these sex and sex life are
regarded as something evil or at least representative of a
lower type of life than that which is purely "spiritual," and
celibacy is exalted as being on a higher ethical and spiritual
plane than marriage. And, as is well known, from the early
beginnings of the church and throughout its history this
view has had considerable prevalence within Christendom
and was thought to be rooted in the teachings of Christ and
the New Testament. How widely accepted is this mistaken
conception of the teachings of Christianity even in our own
day is indicated by the fact that a reputable sociologist—and
his view is not unique but rather representative—can publish
a statement like the following in a widely used college textbook: "Thus, one influence of Christianity was to establish
the idea of sex as a purely physical experience, devoid of
spiritual significance. It is impossible to estimate the amount
of serious damage which this view has done to human lives."[1]

The first sentence in this quotation is completely mis-
leading with reference to the actual teachings of Scripture
and certainly of Christ—and, we may well add, of St. Paul,
whose discussions of the problems of sex and marriage have
been subject to such widespread misinterpretation. It is
true, however, that many of the Church Fathers, including
even as great a teacher as St. Augustine, held views concerning sex which did not do justice to the positive and realistic
teachings of the Bible, and, as a result, relatively early in

---

[1]Nimkoff, *The Family*, p. 149.

the Christian era a warped and false view of sex and
marriage gained widespread acceptance and held sway for
centuries, doing untold harm to human life and society, not
to speak of the hindrance it caused to a deeper understanding of the essential nature of the Christian gospel.

One of the most significant achievements of the Reformation, and particularly of its great leader, Martin Luther, was
the rediscovery and restoration of a wholesome and Scriptural view of sex and marriage and of the place and importance of family life. Luther has, it is true, like St. Paul, been
criticized for his realistic approach to the sex problem. And
he certainly made mistakes. Few there are today, even among
his most ardent followers, who would defend his counsel to
Henry VIII or to Philip of Hesse.[2] And his language in dealing with sex matters, particularly where passages are quoted
out of their context, may well be a stumbling block to
modern readers.

Nevertheless, it remains true that in relation to marriage,
as in so many other areas of ethical teaching, Luther effectively led the revolt against the false and superficial moralism that characterized much of medieval Scholastic teaching
and demonstrated in cogent arguments that came to mark a
milestone in the development of ethical theory that the
truest service of God is not to flee from the world and its
obligations but gladly to assume the burdens of human life
and to live out the implications of Christian love in all
normal human relationships. In order to give his teaching
with regard to the ethics of sex and family life practical
embodiment Luther himself married and lived a happy
home life, which has since been a pattern and an inspiration
not only to unnumbered other Christian pastors but to
Christians in every calling, who through the teachings of

---

[2] For an excellent brief presentation of what is to be said in
Luther's defense in the Philip of Hesse case, however, see Lenski:
Marriage in the Lutheran Church, especially Chap. VIII.

the Reformers have found liberation from the false standards of asceticism and a new entrance into the experience
of evangelical freedom.

Not that Luther or the teachings of the Reformation gave
a final "solution" to the problems of sex and marriage. There
is no final and universally applicable solution for these in a
world where sin prevails. But Luther at least placed sex and
marriage in a new positive light, as an area of human experience to be entered into with faith and courage and not to be
fled from by those who desire to live on the highest ethical
and spiritual planes. He rediscovered the foundation stones
of Christian home and family life and boldly invited all Christians to build upon them even though he at the same time fully
recognized that the intricacy and the complexity of the sex
problem would always preclude its solution through any single simple and neat formula. Luther reannounced the emancipation of sex and marriage as one of the great ethical and
spiritual blessings and high prerogatives of the Christian life.

III. PRESENT PERILS THREATENING FAMILY AND HOME LIFE

Because of the basic character of sex and marriage the
welfare of both the secular state and the Christian Church
are inseparably linked with the stability and the strength of
the marriage and family ties that prevail among a given
people or nation. The ancient commandments, "Honor thy
father and thy mother, that it may be well with thee and
thou mayest live long in the land," and, "Thou shalt not
commit adultery," are concerned with the very foundations
of social living. Well does the Fourth Commandment connect both personal prosperity and national well-being with
the observance of law and order learned first in the family
fold through obedience to parents. Life is not atomized in
its spiritual structure but deeply interrelated. What is sown
in the seedbeds of home is easily transplanted to bear its

fruitage, good or evil, in the harvest fields of the world. Nor
is it strange at all that this should be so if marriage and the
family are as integral among the institutions of human society
as both secular and sacred scholarship agree that they are.

We may well be disturbed, therefore, as we regard
developments in our country in recent years in this area of
social life. It has become almost trite to make the statement
that the American home is disintegrating. Yet this undeniable
fact needs to be sharply driven home to the conscience of
our people and particularly to the conscience of leaders in
every area of social and spiritual life. As a single glaring
example of the present trend we may mention that just as
this paper was being prepared for publication the figures
concerning marriages and divorces for 1944 in the writer's
home city (Minneapolis) were announced: only a little
more than three marriages for each divorce took place in
this city of many Christian churches, this stronghold of
Lutheranism, in 1944! And although this is an even higher
divorce rate than that of the country as a whole—partly due
to the fact that much of our country is still rural—the
disintegration of American family life is certainly one of
the major problems facing both church and nation.

It is scarcely necessary to attempt to catalog the various
influences which have helped to promote this lamentable
condition. Among them the results of the world war loom
large with its myriad attendant tensions and disruptions in
the world's homes. The tragedy of broken homes due to the
strains of prolonged absences has become almost a commonplace as our chaplains know all too well. Hasty marriages,
built on emotional quicksands, give little assurance of
stability in long years of testing, and a surge of postwar
divorces is generally, and rather tepidly, accepted as inevitable. Add to these conditions the problems of the homes
which find themselves deprived of a father's guidance or

a son's strength in facing the years of readjustments before us, and we may well dread the seeds of evil sown by the war in the modern home.

Closely associated with the war, though preceding it, is the serious problem of juvenile delinquency in America, a present and potent threat to creative Christian home life in our country as well as one of the bitter fruits of the lack of such homes. The amazing statistics concerning our very young "criminals" have been variously explained. Economic insecurity, slum dwellings, a prevailing atmosphere of moral laxity, a philosophy of education minimizing the factor of discipline, have undoubtedly contributed their large share to the prevailing delinquencies of youth. But the problem addresses itself primarily to the parents and to the homes and can best find its solution there. A new emphasis is needed in our day upon the duty of obedience of children toward their parents. There is no easy or abbreviated route leading to social and national stability. It can be secured only through the patient and often arduous inculcation of ideals of obedience in the life of the younger generation.

This does not mean, of course, that parents and homes and home life cannot be immeasurably helped by improvements in many economic and educational and social areas of human life. Economic conditions, for instance, can drastically affect a family's life. It is everywhere acknowledged that too long hours of work, financial insecurity, crowded living conditions tend to vitiate and destroy true home life.

One of the most revolutionary economic problems in many homes today is that connected with the so-called "emancipation of womanhood." In itself it is, of course, gratifying that woman is achieving a new freedom, that many new areas of experience and service have been opened to her, and that complete masculine domination of the home is becoming outmoded. But simultaneously has come a widespread and dangerous tendency to disparage the importance of the contribution of the faithful wife and mother as compared with that of the business or professional woman. Far too often a selfish desire for the comforts which the additional earnings of the wife can purchase is present, and far too often the sad cost of such selfishness is a neglected home. And under wartime conditions these particular sources of difficulty are aggravated a hundred fold in practically every community.

But perhaps the most insidious and destructive of all the influences which have tended to undermine the home in this age has been a resurgence, throughout the modern western world, of pagan ethics of sex, both in theory and in practice. This development has been closely associated with the general secularization of life, which has characterized modern times, and has been promoted by a great deal of quasi-scientific research. The more popular forms in which it has expressed itself are widely varied and very familiar: literature, from the most-heralded best-sellers to the cheap drugstore magazine; the stage and screen; teaching in the classrooms of both high school and university; unnumbered forms of coarsened commercialized amusements; the blatant appeal of advertising; the alarming divorce rate—these are but a very few of the most evident manifestations. As in the early Christian era, so also today, the light of Christ's teaching concerning sex and its control and expression shines into a very murky and turgid atmosphere of sin.

IV. The Christian Conception of Marriage and the Family

Over against this whole trend of modern paganism the Christian Church proclaims the pure and enduring teachings of Christ and the New Testament with regard to sex and marriage. Basic to all these teachings is the view of man as essentially a spiritual being. In the Christian doctrine of man central place is given to personality. Men are not merely animals nor discarnate spirits but persons, essentially spiritual even while clothed in flesh and blood. Therefore, also, sexual sin is primarily a spiritual matter. Adultery is first and foremost a matter of personality relationships. "Whosoever looketh on a woman to lust after her hath committed adultery with her already in his heart." Christ places sex in its rightful perspective, as but one rich aspect of total personality. To give expression to sex life except as the outflow of true personality life is the betrayal of one of life's sacred citadels.

Yet it must be given equally strong emphasis that the Christian view of marriage does not neglect or despise the flesh. "Marriage is holy." The physical body, as Luther constantly reiterated, must be given its legitimate place as a divinely ordained part of the created order. Through His incarnation Christ entered into human flesh and lifted it up to His own spirit heights. Not man's sex life but his self-centered ego, in rebellion against God and His laws, is the essential seat of sin in the human heart. The human body, too, has been redeemed from sin to be the instrument of the Spirit, the temple of God.

As mentioned above, in the New Testament marriage is frequently presented as a symbol of the church's union with Christ. While marriage embraces and includes every aspect of the personalities concerned, spirit and mind and body, its deepest essence is a spiritual union in holy love rooted in God Himself. Every attempt to solve the problems and the difficulties which beset marriage in modern life will inevitably fail unless first of all this basic fact is taken into consideration. Marriage from the Christian point of view involves the right relation of two souls to God.

From premises such as these we are inevitably led to the

position, so unequivocally enunciated in the teaching of
Christ, that marriage, by its very nature, is the indissoluble,
lifelong union of one man and one woman. Though other
forms of marriage have widely prevailed, though even in the
Old Testament polygamy was accepted as divinely sanc-
tioned by outstanding leaders and men of God, and divorce
was stamped with Mosaic authority, yet Christ's teaching is
very clear that "from the beginning it was not so": such less
perfect forms of marriage were permitted only "because of
the hardness of your hearts," because of the ravages of sin
in the life of humanity.

Numberless arguments have, of course, at various times
been advanced seeking to justify not only divorce as such
but easy divorce and remarriage. Neither history nor experience, however, indicates that easy divorce contributes
toward either human happiness or social stability. Decidedly
the contrary. It is true that the state, where many of its
members are unchristian, cannot be expected to enforce
Christian standards of marriage morality. The state must
still, as in the days of Christ, recognize and deal with the
reality of broken marriages. But the church must maintain
the ideal of Christ: in marriage "the two shall be one" until
death separates them.[3] Whenever divorce occurs, the church
can only regard it as a fruit of sin and deal with the parties

---

[3]Piper's pointed summarizing statements on this point are illuminating even when it is admitted that the exegetical problems concerning Christ's teaching as to divorce are extremely difficult of solution:
"Jesus did not content Himself with making divorce difficult; He
forbade it outright. . . . Even if the recognition of immorality in Matthew 5:32; 19:9, as a reason for divorce, is to be traced back to Jesus
(the parallels in Luke 16:18 and Mark 10:12 do not admit it, as is
well known), the case would remain in principle the same. For if the
married woman plays the prostitute (adultery alone is not in question
as many exegetes think), she is no longer really living in marriage with
her husband; and the purpose of forbidding divorce, that the woman
might not be seduced into temptation to have sex intercourse with
other men, is in such a case abrogated by the very fact of the wife's
conduct." Piper: *The Christian Interpretation of Sex,* p. 160 and note.

concerned in that light. The recent official pronouncement on this subject by the convention of the American Lutheran Conference gives adequate and realistic recognition to the actual fact that divorce occurs and is widely prevalent and still reasserts the Christian position of the essential indissolubility of the marriage tie:

"We recognize . . . that because of sin, situations arise in the married state which so disrupt the marital relationship that separation or divorce seem to afford the only relief, and that, for the sake of the spiritual and physical well-being of either or both spouses, a dissolution of the marriage bond will be sought. But where cases of marital tension, estrangement or threatened estrangement come within the purview of the church, the Christian teachings of family life, marriage and divorce must be emphasized and every means at the disposal of the pastor exhausted in efforts to bring about reconciliation, so that separation and divorce may, if possible, be avoided. It should in this connection be brought out that Christ and the New Testament lay down the principle, valid for all time, that marriage, according to its ideal and God's plan, is a lifelong union between one man and one woman, and that divorce therefore, no matter for what reason, is a violation of this principle."[4]

In this connection it needs to be said too, however, that although the severing of a marriage tie is an unspeakably tragic occurrence and contrary to the will and the purpose of God, yet the Bible also teaches clearly that marriage is an earthly, not an ultimate spiritual, good. Therefore, if a marriage bond is broken, though it bring sorrow and untold suffering, it need not lead to despair even though the circumstances are such that remarriage is ethically impossible.[5]

---

[4]Official minutes, Seventh Biennial Convention of the American Lutheran Conference (1944).

[5]Lutheran theologians have commonly admitted the right to remarry to the innocent party in a divorce granted upon the "Biblical" grounds of adultery or malicious desertion. The present writer regards the Biblical basis of this position as questionable. With those who have become entangled in the meshes of sin in this area the church must deal upon the basis of divine grace and forgiveness as she does in other areas of life. Indeed, it is well for us to remember, as Christ suggested in his word about "casting the first stone," that the sex life of each one of us stands in need of the cleansing forgiveness of God.

The church cannot admit modern paganism's surrender to the conception of man as primarily physical. On the contrary, difficult as it may be, it is not impossible that a tragic experience of marriage may even lead to a new vision of the love of God as, for example, in the case of the Prophet Hosea.

Every husband and every wife should regard it as their calling from God, unless prevented by illness or physical disability, to rear a family. A primary end of marriage is the bearing of children and thus the continuing of the race. The rapidly declining birth rate in many of the Western countries today should be a cause for concern not only to statesmen and students of society but even more to the Christian Church which knows that man's obligations for the continuation of the race are God-given, and that man is also here responsible to God as a steward. While the rearing of children entails additional economic burdens, faithful obedience to this aspect of God's will for man brings its own compensating rewards and joys. It becomes, too, an avenue of entering more deeply into the life of God Himself who has taught us that His nature and His love are best expressed in the word "Father."

Many a home has been brought to ruin because the husband and the wife were not willing to assume the physical and economic and social burdens connected with the bearing and the rearing of children. In relation to this whole modern trend and to all the related problems of "planned parenthood" the Christian Church must strongly reassert the high, Scriptural view of marriage as a spiritual reality given for the propagation of the race, for the completion and the unfolding of human personality, and for the spiritual and the moral discipline of humanity. In the degree in which any agency related to marriage detracts from these ends it detracts from the sanctity of marriage as ordained by God. And for the Christian the primary problem in this area of life must ever remain the unselfish fulfilment of his part in the life of the race, rendered in loving obedience to God and in a form which contributes to his own spiritual upbuilding.

The whole teaching of Christ concerning sex and its control and expression is indeed a "hard saying." But we need to be reminded that that is merely one side of the picture. The other is that the gospel of Christ has redeemed the sex life of man from the slavery of sin and given it a new birth of sacred freedom in the Christian family. Within the sacred precincts of home and family provision is made for the deepest needs, physical, social, and spiritual, of both parents and children. There both children and adults are to be nurtured in the most intimate earthly school—a school which in truth ministers to the whole personality. There, above all, the Word of God is to be transmitted to the oncoming generations: "One generation shall declare Thy works to another."

The very center of the Christian home is the family altar. It is the duty and the high privilege of Christian parents to implant in the hearts of their children the everlasting Word and to nurture them in the fear of the Lord. We need look for no widespread spiritual awakening in the world except in connection with a re-establishment of true religion in the home. Parents should assume as their very first and highest obligation and privilege the instruction of their children in the things of Christ. From the Christian point of view the Word of God is as necessary as daily bread. And as the church seeks to plant the seeds of the kingdom in the world it can surely have no stronger ally than the consecrated Christian home. And in the degree in which the two divinely ordained institutions of "church" and "family" are wedded together in their efforts and their programs the social future for mankind will grow brighter.

No finer flower grows from the seed of the gospel than

the Christian home. It is the practical earthly consummation of the teaching of Christ on the subject of sex. Theoretical considerations weigh heavily in its favor, whether viewed by the social or theological sciences, but the full weight of its importance for human happiness can be obtained only empirically. In the struggle of conflicting moralities it is in the arena of life itself, not in theoretical discussion, that the final battle will be waged. The relative strength of purity and impurity, of Christian marriage and pagan licentiousness, will be tested in the fires of actual human experience. Time, as well as eternity, will tell.

V. The Church's Obligation to the Homes of Tomorrow

If these be the convictions of the Christian Church with regard to sex and marriage and their place in human life, what steps ought the church to take in order to make this point of view more dynamically effective in the life of mankind today? We may summarize our suggestions toward an effective program under the three general heads of evangelization, education, and legislation. In the present age the church cannot escape responsibility in any of these three though her contribution may bulk larger in one than in the others.

1. *Evangelization.* It is almost a Christian truism to say that the primary need of mankind is not social improvement or amelioration but spiritual redemption. Christ was not primarily concerned with attempting a reorganization of human society but with bringing individual men and women into a living fellowship with God. He sought to purify the sources of human life, knowing that if that were done, the stream itself would be pure also. Even secular philosophers have often seen that the real problem of building a better social order is basically the problem of getting better men. In the gospel of Jesus Christ, which reaches deep into the heart

of man, revitalizing the very springs of his existence, the church has in its hands the force for spiritual renewal which alone can minister effectively to this fundamental need of society. The preaching of the gospel, therefore, and the building of the living church are the best possible basis also for a renewal of a high morality in the realm of sex and marriage.

Many qualified writers on the problems of sex and marriage maintain that the most effective sex education is by no means simply the impartation of informational content concerning this aspect of life but rather the general building of individual character. For sexual behavior is not determined by the amount of information a person possesses but rather by the quality of his character as a whole. It has been pointedly remarked that, if information were the primary requisite, medical students should be pre-eminently moral whereas investigations prove that they are not more so than other groups of students.

Neither better information nor improved social conditions are sufficient bulwarks against temptation. In themselves they can never spiritualize the habits and the ideals of men in society. The gospel of Christ, which demands the surrender of the innermost citadel of the soul to God, is the only basically effective means for the purification of human morality in the realm of sex. The first and highest duty of the church in this connection is, therefore, to carry on its spiritual mission to mankind and especially to its own membership with consecrated zeal for winning the souls of men to complete devotion to Christ. The Word and the sacraments are the abiding means of grace also in this area of human life.

2. *Education.* What has just been said is intimately related to the whole matter of the church's attitude toward sex education. In general the main point to be emphasized is this, that the most valuable education in the realm of sex is

not direct and informational but an indirect building of the will and the character. Much of what today passes for sex education does far more harm than good because it consistently isolates certain facts from their larger relationships and draws glaring attention to processes which belong appropriately in the shadows of the subconscious. Many of the best medical authorities hold this view to be fundamental. Not the opinions of medical science, however, are decisive for us in dealing with questions of an ethical nature but rather the teachings and the attitude reflected in the Scriptures. The same high realism, the openness with restraint, with which sex matters are there treated, constitute a standard of approach which we will do well to follow in trying to formulate tenable principles of education for marriage and home life—as well as in the whole practice of pastoral counselling in the realm of marriage relationships.

In a spirit of chaste thoughtfulness and wonder education for Christian marriage should begin with the child in the home. There character is to be built by the discipline of true Christian devotion. There the values of life are to be gradually unfolded in their proper sequence and relationship. There life is to be seen, at first fragmentarily, then ever more as a whole. In that process education concerning sex life will also have its natural place. It should be surrounded by no special mysteriousness, tantalizing the curiosities of childhood and youth. Yet it is well that it be permitted to preserve its own deep and unsearchable mystery as one of the sanctuaries of life. In the confidential comradeship of parents with children questions concerning sex may be freely answered as they arise. Admittedly, not least in modern urban life, there are countless dangers to the unfolding life of the child. But in the Christian home, with wholesome family life, with wide and cordial friendship circles, with a vital family altar, with wholesome literature and music, with the high example of parents who have learned to combine true devoutness with a natural and open fellowship with their children—here is a garden of God where the unfolding personalities may grow up in the disciplined liberty which is the essence of the Christian life.

It is true that this is a highly idealized picture of the Christian home, a picture which comparatively seldom can be fully realized in actual practice. And precisely here lies the great need for the ministry of the church if the citadel of the family is to be built strong and effective for its service to human needs. Both in the public preaching of the Word and in the instruction of youth in catechetical classes, both in the social contacts of his everyday life and in the private confessional hours where he ministers to individual souls, the Christian pastor has a large responsibility to fulfil in counselling his people, young and old, married and unmarried, concerning the Christian conception of marriage and family life.

It is probably not too much to say that most church groups have barely made a beginning in this challenging phase of the church's ministry. Whatever methods are utilized, it behooves the pastor to be both well-informed and wise in his approach and his counsel. He should be a light bearer in the dark places of human life. The theological seminaries have a special obligation in seeking to train candidates for the ministry who shall be able to be such light bearers. Yet, let it be repeated, a reverent restraint needs to be exercised at all times by spiritual counsellors. The pastor is not called to take the place of the physician.

The importance of the right type of literature concerning marriage and the home can scarcely be overemphasized. The floods of impurity that sweep the world of literature today are the cause of thousands of shipwrecked lives and homes. The power of the printed word as a guide of life cannot be overestimated. The church, not least the Protestant Church, in our day has been too negligent in the production and the distribution of suitable literature of this type—literature which is authentic, modern, helpful, and still preserves the high Christian idealism of sex, marriage, and family life.

3. *Legislation.* Inspired by Christ's passionate zeal for justice and love, the church cannot remain placid in the midst of social conditions which place overwhelming obstructions and temptations in the path of men. Christ's claim to universal dominion imposes upon her the task of influencing the whole life of society. Through awakening her membership as active voting members of society; through the adoption of programs of action when expedient and in harmony with the nature and principles of the church; through declarations of position on specific questions; through timely protest—through these and other means the church can do much to affect legislative measures which will have a far-reaching influence toward creating favorable environmental conditions for the building of the Christian home. Among the more important of these areas of influence the following may be mentioned: laws concerning marriage, divorce, and birth control; slum clearance; public recreation facilities; public care of health; motion pictures and the press; moral conditions in prisons and in other public institutions; labor conditions; and general social security.

Such legislative efforts must, of course, remain subsidiary to the main purpose and emphasis of the church's message. The kingdom of God does not come by political force or legislative enactment. The standards of the Sermon on the Mount cannot be forced upon unregenerate men. Though Christian action is desperately and consistently needed in the battle between the "new" paganism and the Christian ethic of sex, such action cannot be carried out primarily by means of legislation; and its goal will neither be perfectly comprehended nor perfectly realized in the realm of time.

In conclusion: Reverent and thoughtful consideration of both the rich possibilities and the high prerogatives as well as the subtle temptations and dangers inherent in marriage and family life lead us to the conviction that the only adequate answer to the problems in these areas of human experience is a God-centered faith and God-centered life, mediated by the ministry of a consecrated and socially concerned church. The root problems of sex and marriage lie in the inherent selfishness of the human heart. Man must be saved from himself if he is to be saved from the specific aspects of his sinful nature. We cannot by thinking, even Christian thinking, completely solve the problems of living. It is in the fellowship of the Living Christ in whom the Word became flesh that the problems of our human flesh find their abiding solution. And it is through the ministry of the Living Church that our earthly families and homes, so fundamental in the unfolding history of mankind on earth, may find their highest meaning as creative "cells" in the eternal family of God.

SELECTED REFERENCES

Bosanquet, Helen, *The Family*, London and New York: Macmillan, 1906, 344 pp.

Bruce, G. M., *Marriage and Divorce*, Minneapolis: Augsburg, 1930, 196 pp.

Cabot, Richard C., *Christianity and Sex*, New York: Macmillan, 1937, 78 pp.

Cope, H. F., *Religious Education in the Family*, Chicago: Univ. of Chicago Press, 1915, 289 pp.

Doms, Herbert, *The Meaning of Marriage* (Engl. trans.), New York and London: Sheed & Ward, 1939, 229 pp.

Fiske, George W., *The Changing Family*, New York and London: Harpers, 1928, 320 pp.

Foerster, F. W., *Marriage and the Sex Problem*, New York: Stokes, 1936, Tr. by Meyrick Booth, 228 pp.

Goodsell, Willystine, *A History of Marriage and the Family*, New York: 1934, 563 pp.

Groves, E. R., *Christianity and the Family*, New York: Macmillan, 1942, 224 pp.

Groves, Ernest R., *The Family and Its Social Functions*, Philadelphia: Lippincott, 1940, 611 pp.

Groves, Ernest R., *The American Family*, Chicago and Philadelphia: Lippincott, 1934, 461 pp.

Groves, Gladys Hoagland, *Marriage and Family Life*, New York: Houghton Mifflin, 1942, 564 pp.

Holl Karl, *Gesammelte Aufsätze zur Kirchengeschichte I*, Luther, Tübingen: J. C. B. Mohr, 1927, 582 pp.

Lenski, G. E., *Marriage in the Lutheran Church*, Columbus: Lutheran Book Concern, 1936, 377 pp.

Nimkoff, *The Family*, New York: Houghton Mifflin, 1934, 513 pp.

Overton, Grace Sloan, *The Home in a Changing Culture*, New York: Revell, 1935, 156 pp.

Piper, Otto A., *The Christian Interpretation of Sex*, New York: Scribner's, 1941, 219 pp.

Westermarck, Edward, *Marriage*, New York: Jonathan Cape and Harrison Smith, 1929, 115 pp.

CHURCH AND STATE

GEORGE F. HALL

The modern state is an artificial sovereignty confined to boundaries which are the products of the fortuities of history and the circumstances of geography. Every person is a member of some state. A Christian is by his physical nature confined to earth and is hence subject, as all men are, to the state. But at the same time the Christian is a member of the all-transcending spiritual kingdom of Christ, which commands his highest allegiance. The church proclaims that its kingdom is a kingdom of the spirit of Christ—a kingdom which recognizes no territorial bounds or confines.

Church and state are segments of the much larger group concept of a society which embraces all men in all conditions of life. The state is composed of people within a certain territory or those professing citizenship in a certain territory although temporarily they may not be abiding in it. The church transcends territorial limitations but is limited by 1) the extent to which the gospel has been proclaimed throughout society and 2) the response which individuals have given to that gospel if they have come under its influence, and only those who have responded affirmatively and have complied with the conditions for membership are included in its fold.

Church and state are both social concepts. A Louis XIV may venture to say, "I am the state," but no one is convinced, neither can anyone properly say, "I am the church."[1] Two or three gathered anywhere in Christ's name constitute the

---

[1] McGovern, W. M., *From Luther to Hitler*, Houghton, 1941. Winfield, O. A., *The Control of Lutheran Theological Education in America*, Augustana Book Concern, Rock Island, Ill., 1933.

(492)

church. It is, therefore, in the world but not of it. It disagrees with the world but yet must live in it. Its sovereign is the Christ, and allegiance is due primarily to Him. Each Christian has a dual citizenship, one in the kingdom and one in the state. As such his obedience is required by both.

The existence of the state rests on the solid ground of necessity. Aristotle noted that man is by nature a political creature. As a result man has formed many types of associations with his fellows. Rules and regulations governing conduct are instituted and enforced. The power to make and to enforce such regulations constitutes the very essence of the state. Although the state by its very necessity is an instrument for the common good of its subjects, it is obvious that all political sovereignties have not at all times been guided in their activities either by the common good or the spirit of Christ. A serious problem then arises for the Christian when he is called upon to serve two masters who give conflicting instructions. The solution does not lie in the abolition of the state. Consequently, the dilemma arising from the conflicting aims and purposes of the church and the state remains.

The Teaching of Jesus

That Jesus was not exempt from these tensions of allegiance and conduct is apparent in the records about His life. One of the temptations confronting Him immediately after His baptism was to worship Satan.[2] His temptation was a choice between alternatives, both professing to have a good end in which the wrong choice is baited by glittering inducements. The inducement was world dominion. The end, universal salvation through universal dominion, could sanctify the means. Here was the temptation to be the kind of Messiah the Jews sought after in conformity with many Old

---

[2]Luke 4:7.

Testament patterns. He was tempted to be a Messiah with a kingdom on earth such as David had, to lead a revolution, like the Maccabees, that would restore the kingdom and the worship to the Jews. But He refused the inevitable compromise involved in political and legal dominion of the world by a religious leader. Instead, using somewhat the same terminology, He proclaimed a kingdom, eschatological in nature, that would permeate the structure of all society like the yeast in the dough which, when the lump was fully leavened, would have an abrupt, cataclysmic ending with universal judgment. When that time came, all temporal arrangements would vanish, and the state would be no more.

Because His kingdom was not of this world, He did not use the method of the state, *i.e.*, force. He taught instead the futility of resisting force with force. Perhaps He had a vivid recollection of those days in His youth when hopes ran so high in Galilee for another successful Maccabean revolution centered in Sepphoris just an hour's walk from Nazareth. These hopes were cruelly dashed with the complete destruction of that city and the exile into slavery of its remaining population. Jesus' teaching of nonresistance has never been fully tried by any state of consequence.

The night before His crucifixion He was sorely tried in spirit. He won eventual victory through submissive prayer in the Garden of Gethsemane. Prior to this season of prayer He spoke about needed preparations with His disciples, commanding them to secure swords as though He contemplated resisting force with force. But when the disciples thought the implications of His command warranted the use of the sword in defense to prevent His arrest, they were rebuked by the saying that those taking to the sword would perish by it, and the one wound that resulted was healed.[3]

---

[3] Luke 22:36-38; Matt. 26:52.

That Jesus did not accept force as an instrument for the accomplishment of His kingdom's intent is without an opposing argument. Just as clear is His teaching that He did not intend to establish a world state, not even a theocracy according to the Old Testament pattern in the same sense that David, Alexander the Great, Cæsar, Napoleon, Hitler, or the British Empire might be considered representative. If He had a world state at all in mind, it was to come through the slower but more effective application of Christian love in contrast with the crude and bitter employment of the sword. Christian love should supplant the dissipating force of brute strength. If truly Christian states should ever arise, it would come as the inevitable product of the Christianization of society, not as the fulfillment of the primary intention of Jesus.

The dilemma of the Jewish patriot and religionist was placed squarely before Jesus the last week of His ministry.[4] The three accounts vary as to who the questioners were and their motive, but they do not vary as to the issue at point: the payment of taxes. The solution to "render unto Cæsar the things that are Cæsar's and unto God the things that are God's" related strictly to taxes. By this Jesus taught that there was no ethical inconsistency in supporting financially these diverse and contradictory powers, pagan Rome and the Jewish Temple.

It was a principle of Jewish jurisprudence that whoever minted the coinage also had the right of taxation, hence the Temple was also engaged in minting its own coinage the use of which was compulsory in the Temple area. Money-changers were a practical necessity on the Temple grounds for that reason. By the same standards the Roman tax was also legal. The coin with Cæsar's superscription was symbolic

---

[4]Matt. 22:15-22; Mark 12:13-17; Luke 20:20-26.

of the services rendered the Jewish people by the Roman occupation.

Theories of taxation have been based upon the premise that all earthly possessions are by permission of the state; consequently citizens pay interest or usury to the state for the right of ownership. In America, where the right of private property is highly respected by the state, taxes cannot be considered as tribute or interest. The state is an agency for collective action to provide certain goods and services which otherwise would not be provided at all, or, if left to the individual initiative, such services could be provided only with a greater expenditure of effort. The state performs many valuable functions which add to the general well-being. Taxes are payments to support these socially desirable activities of the state.

That tax funds may be used by a Louis XIV or a Cæsar in a trivial, wasteful, and harmful manner cannot be gainsaid. The way to combat such abuses, however, is not by the refusal to pay taxes, which would strike at the very heart of social organization, but patiently to await the reformation of the state through preaching and living the principles of the Sermon on the Mount. Although Roman taxes collected in Palestine may well have served to tighten the Roman yoke upon the Jews as a subservient people, Jesus did not advocate even this form of resistance.

There is hardly a saying of Jesus that has been misinterpreted with as serious consequences to Christianity as the unqualified, "Render unto Cæsar the things that are Cæsar's." This text, like all texts, needs a control. That control is provided by the text itself—that Jesus referred only to taxation. There is no exegetical warrant for making a universal from this teaching to apply to all possible requirements of the state or Jewish Temple. For instance, although a party of

Jewish Christians sought to bind all Christians with all the provisions of the Jewish religious law, the Christian Church under pressure from Paul and others soon released itself from that accumulation of sacerdotal laws.

While there is a great deal in Jesus' teaching that applies to the gradual transformation of society by the power of the gospel, it is hardly possible by honest historical exegesis to develop any specific doctrine of state from His teachings.[5] The general principles of His gospel which can be applied to all human institutions can also be applied to the state.

The Apostles

It will be recalled that the important statement, "We ought to obey God rather than men"[6] was spoken in a clash with religious authorities. To identify the commands of the sacerdotalists with that of man instead of God, whose spokesmen they claimed to be, was itself a sweeping assertion of no little consequences. Relationships with civil governments are pictured as fair and understanding in Acts, this in spite of the fact that many principals of primitive Christianity had been put to death by civil authorities prior to its writing. There is no trace of a spirit of vindictiveness directed toward the government for the death of Jesus, Peter, and Paul. The statements by Paul in Romans[7] are

---

[5]Speculation as to why Jesus did not teach more about the state perhaps has no place in this study, but because it is so provocative, we may venture some explanations scholars have advanced. 1) He was in the ranks of the artisan, the subject of the state who yields to all ordinary demands, does not question the origin or authority of the state, and pays the taxes and the services required. 2) He was an eschatologist who believed in the imminent passing of all nations and kingdoms. It was futile, therefore, to consider reform of political institutions with the end of the world so near at hand. His teaching was then primarily for this interim period. 3) If He had taught a theory of the state He would have become a political messiah quite similar to the common run of revolutionary messiahs, 150 B.C.-135 A.D.

[6]Acts 5:29.

[7]Rom. 13:1-10.

in harmony with this position. His teaching there about the state has these essential principles:

1. Obedience is required of all persons including Christians, for whoever resists the authorities is resisting God.

2. Authority exists with God's permission and was established by Him.

3. The intent of government is to do good to those who deserve it.

4. Government has the right to use force for punitive purposes, to collect taxes, and to demand respect.

5. The Christian spirit of love will fulfill all possible demands of the state.

The Petrine passage[8] has these commands:

1. Submit to all human authority and ordinances for the Master's sake.

2. God works through the state to punish evildoers and to encourage those doing good.

3. Christian freedom is not an excuse for breaking the laws of the empire.

4. The emperor is entitled to respect as a duty of the Christian parallel to love of the brotherhood and reverence of God.

The Book of Revelation pictures the ultimate destruction of the kingdom of the world and of Rome in particular. Apocalyptic by nature, it contributes little to a Christian view of the state except as a description of God's judgment upon worldly powers.

The scantiness of the New Testament in direct references to the state should not blind us to the important implications of the statements that are included. Stanley's statement in *Essays Chiefly on Questions of Church and State* may well be repeated: "There is no existing institution which can claim from the Bible so distinctly sacred a character" as the state.

---

[8] I Pet. 2:1-3.

Augustine

Most political scientists and Augustine would not agree with this.[9] Augustine's *City of God* distinguishes between *civitas terrena* and *civitas Dei* and does not consider both to have a divine origin. The earthly city was founded in the fratricidal act of Cain. This archetype of crime was repeated in the founding of Rome. The Roman Empire is identified as the earthly city.[10] With the imminence of the fall of Rome before the barbarians Augustine proclaimed that the earthly city had been committed to the extreme penalty for its sins. The City of God, however, was eternal. Christians as members of both the city of God and the earthly city participate in the strife and hatred of the earthly city but are cleansed through repentance.

In later centuries the Roman church identified Augustine's ideal city with the visible ecclesiastical empire of Rome. Submission of the kings to the pope and the exemption from state duties and immunity from the state's laws of the clergy came through this avenue.

The two swords which the company of Jesus had the night of His arrest[11] were given an interpretation enhancing the power of the papacy during the middle ages. It was held that these two swords were given to Peter, one to be wielded by the church for the church and the other to be given by the church to a world emperor and by him to be wielded over the secular realm for the church. Pope Gregory VII, following Augustine's idea, maintained that the state originated in man's pride, worldliness, and ignorance, and was the work of sin and the devil. Civil government was evil

---

[9]Jean Bodin's theory of the origin of the state in force is similar to Augustine's view. See *From Luther to Hitler*, McGovern. Political scientists for the most part ignore the divine origin of the state because it is open for serious misconstruction when identified with a certain person or family in leadership such as divine right of kings.

[10]*City of God*, XV, 4-6.   [11]Luke 22:38.

and could be sanctified only by the authorization and the blessing of the church. Defenders of civil government in answer maintained that the two swords were two distinct and independent powers, both instituted by God Himself, *i.e.*, church and state. The idea of the doctrine of the orders comes through Augustine, but his dualism is unlike Luther's, for Augustine clearly placed the church in the position of temporal supremacy while Luther in civil relationships placed the secular authority above the clergy. Luther did not consider the state's origin to be evil.

Luther

Luther's doctrine of orders is simply this:[12] There are two kingdoms, the kingdom of God and the kingdom of the world. Those belonging to the kingdom of God are true believers in Christ and are subject to Christ. These have the Holy Spirit in their hearts, who instructs them and causes them to wrong no one, to love everyone, willingly and cheerfully to suffer injustice and even death from everyone. Therefore it is not possible for the secular sword and the law to find any work to do among Christians since of themselves they do much more than its laws and its doctrines can demand.

All who are not Christians belong to the kingdom of the world and are under the law. Since few believe and still fewer live a Christian life, do not resist the evil, and themselves do no good, God has provided for non-Christians a different kingdom outside the Christian's estate and God's kingdom and has subjected them to the sword so that, even

---

[12]Works of Martin Luther, 6 vols. Philadelphia: A. J. Holman Co., 1915-1932. "Secular Authority: To What Extent It Should Be Obeyed," iii, pp. 223ff. (1523). On Luther's view of the state see Carlson, Edgar M., *The Interpretation of Luther in Modern Swedish Theology*, unpublished dissertation, University of Chicago, 1944, pp. 106ff; McGovern, *From Luther to Hitler;* Waring, Luther Hess, *The Political Theories of Martin Luther*, New York: Putnam, 1910.

though they would do so, they cannot practice their wickedness, and that, if they do, they may not do it without fear nor in peace and prosperity. For this reason God has ordained the two governments: the spiritual and the secular.

This secular government is indispensable. The masses are and always will be unchristian. The venture to rule a country or the world with the gospel would be like a shepherd who should place in one fold wolves, lions, eagles, and sheep and freely let them mingle with one another and say: "Help yourselves and be good and peaceful among yourselves. The fold is open; there is plenty of food. Have no fear of dogs and clubs." The sheep would keep the peace and would allow themselves to be governed in peace, but they would not live long; nor would any beast keep from molesting another.

That is why the two kingdoms must be sharply distinguished and both be permitted to exist: the one to produce piety, the other to bring about external peace and prevent evil deeds. Neither is sufficient in the world without the other.

Christians are not to use secular law to settle differences among themselves, but they are subject to secular authority in love. They need no sword for their personal interests, but they bear it for the common good. Wielding the sword is a divine service when it is done for the state to punish wickedness, but it is forbidden to wield the sword for personal revenge or gain. Individual ethics are not applicable to the state. Secular authority does not extend over the soul but is limited to property, service, and life.

Did Luther have in mind that the church and the kingdom of God are the same in this dualism? The church, he taught, is the assembly of all believers in Christ upon earth, the communion of saints.[13] This community consists of all

---

[13]"The Papacy at Rome," Holman i, pp. 349ff. It has not been in the province of this paper to discuss the state-church which arose in the visitations of 1526-29. Our approach is confined to the American problem.

who live in true faith, hope, and love so that the essence, life, and nature of Christendom are not a bodily assembly but an assembly of hearts united in one baptism, one faith, one Lord. Though a thousand miles apart in body, they are called an assembly in spirit because each one preaches, believes, hopes, loves, and lives like the other. This unity is of itself sufficient to make a church. External or outward unity does not make a church. Just as being in the Roman unity does not make one a Christian, so being outside of that unity does not make one heretic or unchristian.

The external communion is only a figure of the Christian, spiritual community. If the church were a bodily assembly, one could tell by looking at the body whether anyone were Christian, Turk, or Jew just as one can tell whether that person is male or female, adult or child, white or black.

The head of the church is Christ. The church cannot have an earthly head. The head must give life to the body, and neither pope nor bishop can produce faith in a man's heart nor anything else a Christian member should have. If a man were its head here, Christendom would die as often as a pope dies. The external marks of the spiritual community are the Word, baptism, and the Sacrament of the Altar. Where baptism and the gospel are, no one may doubt that there are saints even if it were only the babes in their cradles. The only Lutheran requirement for unity in the church is agreement on the doctrine of the gospel and the right administration of the sacraments.[14]

The external church in the doctrine of orders is the external symbol of the kingdom of God having the means of grace whereby God's will and command are given to mankind. The "true" church, if such could be determined, would correspond with the kingdom of God in its present state. The church and the state are both instituted by God

---

[14]Augsburg Confession, VII.

to serve His purposes, ideally along parallel lines. This was Luther's ideal of the separation of church and state.

Luther's thinking is dualistic and full of tensions. Church and state compose one of these tensions in his thought. He had lived under the tyranny of the sacerdotal system over which there seemed to be no check or control. His only hope to curb a corrupt church satiated with power was the temporal authorities. At other periods in history the only hope to curb temporal powers in their tyranny has been the church. This tension is commonly expressed in the current phrase that the church is the conscience of the state.

The Sovereignty of the State

The power of the papacy was supposed to be checked by three methods: 1) the temporal power; 2) the Scriptures; and 3) the councils of the church.[15] We have already indicated the interpretation of Gregory VII, which placed the spiritual over the temporal power. Luther restored temporal power to its place by means of the doctrine of the orders, in part, to serve as a control over the external church when adulterated. To assure temporal authorities that they had this right to challenge the church he wrote a document which politically was as significant as the *Ninety-five Theses* was religiously, namely the *Open Letter to the Christian Nobility* of 1520.

By teaching the priesthood of all believers he shows that temporal authorities by virtue of baptism are priests and bishops charged, not with the administration of the Word of God and the sacraments, but to bear the sword and the rod. Temporal power was ordained of God to punish evildoers and to protect them that do well and should therefore be

---

[15]"Open Letter to the Christian Nobility," Holman ii, pp. 65ff. For a recent discussion of sovereignty see Freeman, H. A. (ed.), *Peace Is the Victory*, New York: Harpers, 1944. Also address by Harold Stassen, March 7, 1945.

left free to perform its office without hindrance throughout
the whole body of Christendom with no respect of persons
even if it affected pope, bishops, priests, monks, nuns, or
anyone else. Whoever was guilty of breaking the law of the
state should suffer. "Let every soul," he said quoting Paul
and adding in parenthesis, "(I take that to mean the pope's
soul also) be subject to the higher powers."

In this appeal Luther proclaimed the sovereignty of the
state over all persons, clergy, and laity alike. In the church
he proclaimed that there was no "authority save for edification." The sovereignty of the law of the land was placed
above the power of ecclesiastical courts. Luther himself
expressed his willingness to appear before an unfriendly
emperor.[16] He insisted that an emperor must be respected
and obeyed until he is formally and legally deposed. Yet, for
all of this emphasis on the authority of the sovereign, Luther
cannot be said to have taught *absolute* submission to the
state, nor can he be quoted in support of absolute tyranny.

Objectives of the State

The state is a necessity born out of the common good.
Government is to be in the interests of the governed. Whatever its form may be, it is a sacred trust to be executed
as a government for the people.

Civil authority has jurisdiction over all matters involving
money, property, person, and honor. But the ruler is not to
rely on force. All works not done in love are cursed. Government is established and administered in love when it is
carried on, not for selfish pleasure, use, honor, and con-
venience, but for the benefit, honor, and safety of others.
The prince must hold justice firmly in his grip and mete it
out sternly on the one hand and tempered with mercy on the

---

[16]Letters of November 28, 1529, and March 6, 1530.

other hand as good reason may dictate so that justice may
rule in all things, and that reason may remain the highest
law and master of laws. He is not to think, "Land and
people are mine, I will do with them as I please"; but, "I am
of this land and of the people, and I must act in such a way
as to be of benefit and service to them." He is to imitate the
spirit and the example of Christ. His duty is fourfold:
1) toward God with confident trust and devout prayer;
2) toward his subjects with love and Christian service;
3) toward his counsellors and mighty men with clear
mind and unprejudiced judgment; and 4) toward evildoers
with discriminating earnestness and firmness.

Luther did not hesitate to be critical of princes and rulers
and to urge them to be more considerate of their subjects.[17]
He enunciated the principle of social reconstruction that we
are not competitors but brothers, and it is our highest
privilege to serve God by serving one another. He did not
aim to present a theory of state but in all things was a
theologian, a preacher, and a pastor. All objectives of the
state were to come from Christian principles derived from
the Scriptures. He did not attempt to set up a bibliocracy as
Calvin did who sought to find the answers to all external
questions in the Bible. The Bible was not such a book to
Luther. The law of Moses, for instance, had nothing whatever to do with a Christian as a Christian. The Biblical
materials do not constitute an absolute and eternal standard
for community living but are instructive examples of how
such questions of Christian common life can be treated. The
duty of the community, council, or government is to prevent
and to abolish anything that is contrary to God's will and
harmful to men in body and in soul. The righteous state is
the external servant of God.

[17]"Admonition to Peace: A Reply to the Twelve Articles of The
Peasants in Swabia," Holman, iv, 220ff.

Specific Areas of State Direction or Supervision

In the appeal to the Christian nobility in sermons and pamphlets relative to education and in the writings centering in the Peasant's War, 1525, Luther indicated certain areas in which the state was responsible. Some of these areas as the special obligation of the state to control are still under discussion.

Education

Luther recommended compulsory education for all persons under the direct supervision of the local governments or councils. However, as the educational process went on it should become more and more selective, and only the best should be permitted to be students in the universities.

He made suggestions about books and the approach that was used, the place of Aristotle,[18] etc. The purpose of education was to prepare intelligent and moral citizens for their places in society. Luther did not have confidence in placing governmental matters in the hands of everyone until the general level of education had been raised sufficiently to remove the hazards of it. Luther was the father of the modern public school and compulsory universal education.

Business

Wealth itself, honestly acquired and honorably employed, is a great good.[19] The state, however, should prohibit its improper use such as in extortion, gambling, and usury. The state may fix and regulate prices. Monopolies must be restrained; domestic industries should be encouraged and

---

[18]Dean E. C. Colwell's witty analysis of Luther and education: "I particularly enjoyed Adam Smith and Martin Luther on the universities and what they should be. Although Luther did not like Aristotle ('God sent him on us as a plague'), he nevertheless borrowed a lot of ideas from Robert M. Hutchins." *The Divinity School News,* Chicago: February 1, 1945.

[19]"On Trading and Usury and A Treatise on Usury," Holman, iv, p. 12.

cultivated. He preached the golden rule as the highest standard of business conduct. He felt that buying on credit cultivated the spirit of avarice. He denounced agreements between merchants to regulate or control high prices. He said it was the duty of the princes to expose, punish, and prohibit unfair and unjust methods of trade. He spoke for the small merchant and businessman who were driven out of business by the large combinations which controlled the market. He urged pastors to preach against usury. But he also made an important distinction between usury and interest. Interest, which represents the damage or loss the lender may have sustained in making the loan, was an honorable service and good work. The amount of such interest should be determined by the jurists.

Apparently Luther is not to be quoted in behalf of extreme economic individualism,[20] but he favored control of trade for the benefit of the greatest number and the protection of the public from fraud.

Public Morality

The state must forcibly control and abate social immoralities. Luther recommended that the civil government should encourage marriage and forbid prostitution. Luther repudiated the church laws relative to marriage that gave the church the sole right to perform legal marriages. Marriage as the basis of family rights was within the province of the state and must be regulated by it. Marriage and the married state were civil matters in the management of which priests and ministers were not to intermeddle. But when required, either before the church or in the church, to bless the pair, to pray over them, or even to marry them, it was the bounden duty of the clergy to do so.

---

[20]"If Luther were living today," remarked an economics professor after reading some of his views, "he perhaps would be a radical new dealer like Henry A. Wallace!"

Pauperism

Pauperism was the problem of mendicant monks, wandering students, aimless beggars, vagrants, and shiftless criminals. Luther urged in his *Appeal* that all begging be abolished. Every town should feed its own poor. An overseer or guardian (social worker) should know the poor, inform the council or priest of the requirements that provision might be made for their aid. To warn the naive about the knavery of beggars he republished with his own preface a book *Liber Vagatorum,* ancient in vintage, which exposed the tricks of the begging trade. He demanded that as the state had the right to conscript men for military purposes it should also conscript the idle for productive work. He blamed pilgrimages to Rome for much vagabondage and stated the principle that no one should travel except he could afford to do so.

Sumptuary Laws

Luther believed that the state should enact laws against profusion and extravagance in dress, the use of spices, and excesses in eating and drinking. He wanted the abolition of all holy days except Sunday. He said they promoted idleness and gluttony.

The Limits of the State's Jurisdiction

Luther's doctrine of the orders has been misinterpreted to such an extent in recent years that a restatement of the limitations of authority he placed on the state is a necessity.

The one broad area in which the state has no jurisdiction, said Luther, was that of the soul. He went to considerable pains to show that the words of Peter and Paul used to formulate the doctrine of orders did not include the affairs of faith. Heresy never flourishes so much, he said, as when opposed by force. Temporal rulers who interfere with matters of faith will find themselves utterly destroyed eventually in punishment for their meddling. "If a temporal prince requires you to hold to the pope, to believe this or that, or to give up certain books, one should say, 'Dear Lord, I owe you obedience in life and goods; command me within the limits of your power on earth, and I will obey. But if you command me to believe and to put away books, I will not obey; for in this case you are a tyrant and overreach yourself and command where you have neither right nor power.' If he should take away your property for this, blessed are you! Thank God that you are worthy to suffer for the sake of the divine Word, and let him rave, fool that he is. He will meet his judge. For I tell you, if you do not resist him and let him take your faith or your books, you have really denied God."

He also classified cases in which it would be justifiable for the individual to resist judges and courts in their acts and decisions. Even in temporal matters the Christian had the right of self-defense, and especially so in case of tyranny. He insisted that there was no difference between an emperor's committing murder or theft when acting beyond the jurisdiction of his office and the individual's doing the same.

The state cannot force a person to do that as the state's agent which is contrary to the individual conscience. An illustration is that of compulsory military duty.[21] Luther justified war in some cases, in other instances he definitely took the position that it was unjust, and a Christian should not participate. Revolution is definitely forbidden except when a tyrant has lost his reason (insanity). Tyranny is not a just cause for rebellion, for the tyrant has his conscience and knowledge and knows that he does wrong. There is hope that he will do better. Besides, tyranny cannot be exactly defined and limited, and to allow rebellion for tyranny's sake would permit rebellion whenever the mob wishes to have one. Even the pretext of an unchristian ruler's

---

[21] "Whether Soldiers, Too, Can Be Saved," Holman, v, p. 68.

persecuting the gospel is not sufficient warrant for rebellion. Wars not to be justified are those against superiors by inferiors (rebellion) even when the inferiors are princes. Just wars between equals cannot be wars of aggression, nor should a war of defense be carried on in the spirit of pride. Putting down rebellion and defense are just causes of war and must be done in humility and fear of God, that is, penitently.

A soldier who is convinced that his superior is in the wrong must not fight but must object conscientiously, taking whatever punishment is meted to him for this cause with the true martyr spirit. If the soldier is in doubt about the justness of a particular war he should trust his superior's cause implicitly and thus fight with a clear conscience. A soldier is to fight God's fight and not to have the motives of glory, reward, and riches.

Reformation of the State

Armed rebellion as a way of changing the state was forbidden by Luther. He was not seeking to maintain by that token that improvement was not necessary or desirable. There are only two ways of reforming a government, the way of peace or the way of war. The latter is revolution, hence only the first was recognized by Luther.

Three crises in the Reformation during Luther's lifetime called for the consideration of reform of existing authorities by means of force. In 1520, in his *Answer to Prieras,* he suggested that the temporal authorities should rise up against the Roman papacy and decide the matter, not by words, but by the sword. "If we punish thieves with the axe, heretics with fire, why do we not rather attack these masters of perdition, these cardinals, these popes, and the whole rabble of the Roman Sodom, and wash our hands in their blood, and thus free ourselves from the common and most dangerous conflagration of all?" This prospect did not materialize. This suggested course of action was not rebellion to Luther because the papal authority was not duly constituted in his opinion.

Ulrich von Hutten and Franz von Sickingen offered their support to him in 1520; and Silvester von Schaumburg offered him safe retreat in this eventuality and expressed the hope of rallying a hundred of his nobility to Luther's defense. In January, 1521, when Luther wrote to Spalatin, it was clear that his opinion expressed in the *Answer to Prieras* was changed. He wrote: "You see what Hutten wants. I would not have the gospel defended by violence and murder. By the Word the world was conquered; by the Word the church was preserved; by the Word she will be restored. Antichrist, as he began without violence, will be crushed without violence, by the Word."

In 1525 the second crisis occurred in the peasants' rebellion. Prior to the actual rebellion Luther sought by peaceful methods to show the wrong and the right on both sides, writing just as harshly to both princes and peasants. When warfare broke out, he unhesitatingly took the side of duly constituted authority on the basis that no rebellion was ever permissible. He believed that the Word would accomplish all reform, and until that time came, one should suffer in patience.

The third crisis following the year 1530 (Augsburg) was found in the possibility of the emperor's waging a war against the Protestant princes, the Schmalkald defensive league. In the years prior to this he had taught clearly that inferiors had no right to fight against their legal superiors. He now declared the right of the civil government to protect itself if an attempt was made to force it to accept idolatry and forbidden worship. He wrote a warning to his beloved Germans in January, 1531, telling them why they should not obey the emperor if he should wage war against them. Three reasons were advanced: first, that the people and the emperor had vowed never to persecute the gospel but instead to defend it; second, even if the Protestant teaching were not true, by such participation on the side of the emperor they would become guilty of all of the sins of the papacy; and third, that they would root up and destroy the good that had been produced and done through the holy gospel.

This position has been criticized as an inconsistency on Luther's part with the position he had taken on rebellion. Two considerations, however, show this to be untenable. His recommendation was only in the case of defensive war in which the emperor had struck first; second, it was the duty of the temporal authorities to preserve freedom of conscience and soul, using the sword if necessary to do so. The state, in his thinking, was the guardian of the right of the individual to follow his conscience and to have religious liberty.

The state has no right to do wrong. It is wrong for a citizen to refuse obedience to that which is right; it is right to refuse obedience to that which is wrong. This is not resisting the ordinance of God. A people has the right to reform its government, constitution, and laws.

The Cardinal Doctrines of the Reformation and the Doctrine of Church and State

Luther's doctrine of church and state is an application of the principles enunciated throughout his reform. His thinking, conditioned throughout by the central thesis of justification by faith, is Christ-centered, and the Christ spirit of love is the answer to all problems where that spirit will be allowed to speak. Elsewhere the law of force and retribution must have its way.

Justification by faith alone is basic in his appeal for reform.

The authority of the Scripture is noted in his sincere

attempt to derive principles for a political government from the teachings of the Bible. At the same time, however, he did not use the Bible in a legalistic sense as a guide and a rule in every particular for his times. He sought to follow the gospel and law tension but did not consider Moses binding for the contemporary scene, for Christ had superseded Moses.

The priesthood of all believers' principles broke the power of the clergy in secular matters and gave the secular authorities the right to check the church in its abuses. His appeal to the nobility was based upon this.

The ethics of the citizen who is also a Christian are developed in the tension of Christian liberty. The Christian man, although the free lord of all, subject to none, was yet in his social and his civil relations the perfectly dutiful servant of all, subject to all.

It is clear that Luther's doctrine of church and state was not isolated from his other theological thinking. His approach to the problem was theological. He was not a political economist but a pastor trying to point out a Christian solution for the turbulent affairs of church and state that he was witnessing, and about which his counsel was sought.

The Contemporary Scene and Luther

Lutherans of today do not presume that Luther has done all of their theological and political thinking for them, or that his teachings are a necessary rule and guide for them. Where Luther is wrong or archaic in terms of today, he is relegated to a historical curiosity because Lutheranism, for the most part, has tried to be objective and critical about Luther.

Luther did not envisage a world temporal state. His situation was not identical with ours. Only recently has the world become small enough through communication to render isolation a near impossibility. Duly constituted and

with the consent of the governed and respect for the rights
of the individual conscience, there are few reasons, possibly
none of them theological, why Lutherans should not encourage such a world temporal state.

The church has an obligation to the state. It is the
conscience of the state that at no time should it participate
as a church in party politics. The church should instruct
Christians rightly to evaluate the state, to give it the position of honor as an instrument of God to do good. The
church should teach *reverence* for the state as a necessary
human institution. It may be necessary for the church to be
critical of a particular government or form of government
but it can never speak disparagingly of the state as such.

The young people of the church should be encouraged
by the church to consider the possibility of adopting politics
as a profession that is pleasing in God's sight and an avenue
of service to God.[22] Every man's duty to the state must be
emphasized as a Christian's duty as well.

Definite encouragement should be given to sincere plans
and attempts to restore the Bible to its rightful place in the
curriculum of public schools, high schools, and universities.
In most instances this is an affair of the local community and
prospers and fails to the extent that the Christian spirit is applied in the human relationships of the various personalities,
church organizations, and school administration involved.

Social legislation should be encouraged that will combat
pauperism and yet perform the necessary services to the
needy. The church should continue to train in its colleges
social workers for this work of the state. The social work of
the church must also be continued and expanded as the
needful expression of Christian love and kindness.

Christians should constantly engage in redemptive activ-

---

[22]Luther thought the best students should become servants of the
state. "An Exposition of the Eighty-Second Psalm," Holman, iv, pp.
285ff.

ity, cleansing the state of that which is unworthy of its high calling. This should not be done with the false notion of winning the world for Christ by civil legislation or of ushering in Utopia.

In this world conflict Lutherans have apparently followed Luther. Perhaps common sense and Christianity have dictated no other possible course. In Germany, Norway, and Denmark temporal authority has been resisted by leaders of the church when it has infringed upon the matters of the soul and the individual conscience. They have paid the price in martyrdom for this important truth that the state has its limitations of power. Lutheran bodies, such as the Augustana Evangelical Lutheran Church of North America,[23] have supported with their prayers and their means the young men and women who have been inducted into the armed forces and have also supported officially in much the same manner the young people of the church who have not been able to participate in war because of conscientious objection. Both courses of action have been honored as Scriptural, Lutheran, and American. The attitudes of Christian fairness and concern shown by the government of the United States, its Selective Service Boards, and judges in the great majority of these cases should elicit from all Christians an appreciation and a thankfulness for such a state. Nor should it be forgotten that the freedom for which the Allied armies fought is in large part the freedom Luther described as the right of everyone.[24]

---

[23]P. O. Bersell, Annual Messages to Augustana Lutheran Synod. Lindsborg, Kansas, 1939; Rock Island, Illinois, 1940; Minneapolis, Minnesota, 1941.

[24]Federal Council of Churches, Theologians' report on "The Christian Faith and the War," 297 Fourth Ave., New York 10. Excerpts in Christian Century, December 20, 1944, and editorial comment in issue of December 6, 1944. The Cleveland Report, "The Churches and the World Order," January 16-19, 1945. The Lutheran Outlook, February, 1945. Hutchinson, Paul, From Victory to Peace, Chicago: Willett, Clark, 1943.

War and force as a means of settling international dis-
putes should not be a necessary evil. The church must
always proclaim the teachings of Christ that negotiation in
love is the best policy. The church must hold out for the
possibility of peace until open conflict has rendered it impossible. It must, therefore, seem always to proclaim the
lost cause of amity between nations. It must be the conscience of the state, preaching the folly of war, destruction,
and hate. It must approach this problem of church and
state religiously first but also as scientifically as the labo-
ratory worker seeking to isolate the causes of war like the
germs and causes of disease, aiming to control the spread of
infection and seeking in love its prevention. Emotional
exhortations against the curse of war can make people
aware of the problem but have as little to do with its actual
elimination as similar protests against cancer. The church
must not isolate itself from the state, no matter how wicked
the government may be, but must pray for it, put the best
construction upon its deeds (at least before the full truth is
shown), and teach all men to respect it. If the church
sincerely desires to play a vital part in the world of today it
should endeavor to stimulate, as never before, the social
consciousness of all Christians. This, in itself, is not enough,
however, since the shouldering of social responsibilities requires a broad horizon and a considerable knowledge of the
mechanism of human organization. We cannot content ourselves only with doing good in an immediate small community, thus failing to comprehend the broader scope of
the national and the world community in which we live.
Christianity calls for a loyalty beyond that of friends in
the home community.

The world is so interrelated today that a ripple initiated
in a small part of the globe carries on in accelerated power
throughout the rest of the world. People who are peace-

loving at heart my form policies which make war all but inevitable. For example, many Christians believe in protective tariffs, yet an unimpassioned study of tariffs can lead only to the conclusion that such measures result in international friction. Should the Christian favor tariff legislation because it will protect him or his friends from foreign competition and permit him to exploit the consumer? Economists have pointed out the naive, obvious fallacies of protectionism since the days of Adam Smith. If the Christian is informed about such national policies, it seems that he should act in the interest of general welfare.

Our silver policy after 1934 did irreparable damage to the Chinese. In the silver states it is quite probable that Christians favored the silver policy. Christians did not know the ultimate effect of this program.

What should be the Christian attitude toward high-pressure salesmanship and advertising? What about slum clearance, social security, and labor problems? The church may stand aloof as an organization, but its individual members have convictions on these questions. They are favorably or unfavorably disposed toward governmental action of one kind or another.

The obligation of the church to the state is part of its total obligation to society. As the church stimulates thinking in the area of Christian ethics as applied to practical, everyday life as the way of applying the leaven to society, the problems of state will also be affected. The gospel enunciated from the pulpit and the Bible has a place in the market place and the halls of government. The legislator sweating under the tug and pull of pressure groups in a democracy needs the clear light of Christian ethics and the best scientific knowledge available in the areas of politics, economics, and sociology to determine how to cast his vote so that the state might serve the best interests of its people.

BIBLIOGRAPHY

Augustine, *The City of God.*

Hutchinson, Paul, *The New Leviathan,* Chicago: Willett, Clark, 1946.

Luther, Martin, *Works,* Philadelphia: A. J. Holman, 1915-1932, 6 vols.: "The Papacy at Rome," Vol. 1, pp. 327ff.; "Open Letter to the Christian Nobility," Vol. 2, pp. 57ff.; "The Babylonian Captivity of the Church," Vol. 2, pp. 167ff.; "Secular Authority: To What Extent It Should be Obeyed," Vol. 3, pp. 201ff.; "An Earnest Exhortation for All Christians, warning them against insurrection and rebellion," Vol. 3, pp. 201ff.; "The Right and Power of a Christian Congregation or Community to judge all teaching and to call, appoint, and dismiss teachers, established and proved from Scripture," Vol. 4, pp. 73ff.; "A Sermon on Keeping Children in School," Vol. 4, pp. 133ff.; "Admonition to Peace: A Reply to the Twelve Articles of the Peasants in Swabia," pp. 205ff.; "Against the Robbing and Murdering Hordes of Peasants," Vol. 4, pp. 247ff.; "An Open Letter concerning the Hard Book Against the Peasants," Vol. 4, pp. 257ff.; "Whether Soldiers, too, can be saved," Vol. 5, pp. 29ff.; "On War Against the Turk," Vol. 5, pp. 75ff.; "On the Councils and the Churches," Vol. 5, pp. 125ff.

McGovern, W. M., *From Luther to Hitler,* Houghton Mifflin, 1941.

Niebuhr, Reinhold, *The Nature and Destiny of Man,* II Human Destiny, pp. 244ff., New York: Scribners, 1943.

Troeltsch, Ernst, *Social Teachings of the Christian Churches,* Vol. 2, New York: Macmillan, 1912.

Waring, Luther Hess, *The Political Theories of Martin Luther,* New York: Putnam, 1910.

LUTHERAN PARISH EDUCATION

O. FREDERICK NOLDE

What do Lutherans have to say about parish education? This is not an easy question to answer. In matters of doctrine, notwithstanding large agreement on the confessional writings, there are varying approaches to the study of the Bible and to the interpretation of its teachings. In matters of educational practice, with no formal agreement to fix the limits of procedure, even wider differences are to be encountered. A measure of uniformity has been gained within separate Lutheran bodies. Cooperative ventures which are now under way may extend that uniformity beyond hitherto fixed lines of separation. At the present stage of development, however, no one description of parish education would be generally applicable. Accordingly, this article cannot speak for all Lutherans. It is intended to emphasize what the writer believes to be significant characteristics of the program of education in a parish. It takes its point of departure and finds its justification in confessional Lutheranism. In the spirit of ecumenical Christianity it seeks to encourage such views and practices as will make Christian education a vital force in our day.

THE CHRISTIAN COMMUNITY

What Lutherans have to say about parish education is premised on what they have to say about the church. For the historical and contemporaneous reality of the church establishes the base from which parish education emerges. In this connection "they teach that one holy church is to continue forever."[1] In union with all Christians they refer

---

[1] Augsburg Confession, Article VII.

to this one holy church as catholic or Christian: they acknowledge "the Communion of Saints." The community or communion to which the label catholic-Christian may be correctly ascribed derives its genius, its objectives, its incentives, its life, and its hope from a historical and ever-contemporaneous person—Jesus, the Christ. Here is the primary distinguishing mark of the Christian Church.

Within the limiting arc described from this primary distinguishing mark there is to be found a wide variety of views concerning the exact nature of the church and the specific ways in which its life is to be developed. This variety stems in part from differing interpretations of the will and the activity of God as expressed in Christ and in part from historical circumstances which brought fragments of the total Christian community into separate organizations. Lutherans hold that the church is "the congregation of saints, where the gospel is rightly taught and the sacraments rightly administered."[2] Even within this more limiting construction wide differences are recognized with respect to the interpretation of the gospel and the use of the sacraments. These differences have resulted in varying institutional forms. Through almost endless variety the one holy church nevertheless manifests its distinguishing mark. It is built upon the cornerstone of Jesus Christ.

EDUCATION IN RELATION TO THE CHRISTIAN COMMUNITY

The educational work of a parish normally reflects the point of view of the denomination or the segment of the total Christian community with which the parish is affiliated. This does not mean that the parish may carry on its work merely to propagate itself or its own church group. Only when the denomination's educational program is viewed as

---

[2] loc. cit.

a contributing testimony to the truth of the gospel which the entire Christian community is proclaiming is its own peculiar emphasis justifiable. Such emphasis may be permitted when the denominational educational program seeks to relate men to God through Jesus Christ with the view to advancing the total Christian community. Thus the Lutheran view of parish education must be cast on the background of Lutheran heritage. Be it remembered, however, that there is one holy church throughout the world. This conviction is a part of Lutheran heritage. It must never be lost sight of in the Lutheran view or the Lutheran practice of parish education.

When Christian education is thus rooted in the life of the Christian community it includes more than has usually been associated with modern religious education. It is not merely the work done by Sunday schools, weekday schools, or auxiliary organizations. These agencies ought to exist only because of and for the sake of the church. From earliest times the church interpreted the mind of its Lord as commanding: "Go you therefore, and teach all nations, baptizing them in the name of the Father, and of the Son, and of the Holy Ghost; teaching them to observe all things whatsoever I have commanded you: and, lo, I am with you alway, even unto the end of the world." The teaching function is primary in the effort of the Christian community to win new believers and to direct those already in faith to "observe all things." Christian education is therefore concerned with the full truth of God as revealed in Christ; with the individual in his relations to God, fellow men, and the material world; with the corporate life of the church; with the expansion of the church through efforts to reach those who have not yet had the benefit of the gospel; and with the church's testimony to the world by word and by life.

This inclusive view is not dictated by a presumption to have religious education pre-empt all other fields of Christian thought and practice. On the contrary, it arises from the conviction that the Christian community must be the determining factor in all that touches the lives of its members. It seeks to subordinate Christian education to the church. It seeks to integrate education with all other efforts of the parish. And what is more important, it seeks to utilize the best leadership and scholarship in the church—Biblical, theological, practical—for the development of the church's educational program. Only in this way can the vagaries which sway many "specialists" in religious education be counteracted. Only in this way can the historical accidents which continue to live in our varied "schools, organizations, and agencies" become intrinsic and component parts of the parish.

Parish Education as a Process

The general purpose of Christian education, understood as a responsibility of the entire parish, is to see to it that the growth of all its members to Christian maturity is made as certain as possible. Education in the parish must therefore be looked upon, first of all, as a process. It is the process of directing growing persons to an understanding of the truth about God, man, and the world; to Christian attitudes, convictions, and appreciations; and to certain forms and manners of expression in life. As a result of this direction the conduct of the believer is to be shaped and controlled. An enriched interpretation of his experiences with God, man, and the universe is to be enabled. Direction is the evangelical process; control and enrichment are the anticipated general results.

Parenthetically, it may be noted that, whereas religious education is fundamentally a process, it may also be viewed as a science. When methods and procedures have been used often enough to demonstrate their adequacy they may be set forth as general principles. Such general principles will never stand as purely scientific. For there are too many uncertainties in human nature and in environment with which education must contend. They will, however, serve to acquaint leaders of parish education with procedures that are most likely to accomplish desired results. They tend to shape the process of parish education.

In the process of parish education a number of factors play a part. These will now be briefly considered, as follows: the Bible, objectives, curriculum, leadership, pupil constituency, and organization.

1. *The Bible*

The church, by practice and by formal decision, recognizes the Bible as the basic source of information to direct growing pupils to Christian maturity. In the Bible, Christians find the Word of God. The revelation of God, which began at the beginning of human history, continued throughout the ages, and reached its fullness in Jesus Christ—*revelation in history*—is the Word of God; for it is the experience medium through which man first came to know the God in whom he trusted. The writings of the Bible, which faithfully record that revelation—*the Scriptures*—are the Word of God; for they constitute the ever-present medium through which man comes to know the God in whom he may trust. The gospel, which is the message concerning Jesus Christ, His life, His work, His teachings, His suffering and death, His resurrection and ascension for our sakes—*the gospel*—is the Word of God in the most real sense; for, while its historical and geographical roots are preserved, *as a message*, it is freed from the distracting limitations of time and place.

The Bible came from the community—first the Hebrew, then the Christian. The books which it now contains were written at different periods of history, under the influence of distinctive environmental conditions, and by the use of varying literary forms. In the main they were written with the purpose of accomplishing definite ends, which the community or leaders of the community were seeking. For example, the writings of the New Testament were the verbal witness to Jesus Christ as Lord and Savior. They took form in the effort to win men to faith and to strengthen them in Christian life. They were a means to an end, not an end in themselves.

The Bible is now the possession of the community, of the Christian community of our day. It is to be used in our time, not as an end in itself, but first of all as a means to an end, as a means of apprehending the gospel. It is also to be used as the standard for judging all teachers and all doctrines. To see to it that the Bible is intelligently used in these two ways—as a means to the gospel and as a standard of judgment—is the responsibility of every generation of Christians. In the effort to meet this responsibility Christians may not rest content with the methods whereby the Bible was used in earlier generations. With that use they must be thoroughly familiar. However, they must also take into account such developments and findings as will shed new light upon Biblical literature.

Christians of our generation have the task of making the gospel a living and an effective force in our own time. To do this they must appraise different kinds of values contained in the Bible. On the one hand, they must see that certain religious and moral teachings had worth only for a bygone generation. These teachings continue in importance primarily because they illuminate the progressive revelation which derived from an intermingling of divine initiative and human response. On the other hand, they must discern such teachings as incorporate abiding worth. These teachings they must interpret and apply with a consideration of present circumstances. Briefly, they must distinguish between temporary and permanent values, between values that are accidental and those that are essential. They also have the task of passing to a next generation the full heritage which they received together with their interpretations of it and their contributions to it.

As Christian leaders of our generation use the Bible to direct growing pupils to Christian maturity they ought to employ the historical, literary, and scientific findings which aid in differentiating between accidental and essential values. They ought not only to permit but to encourage an approach to Biblical literature similar to that which is used in connection with all documents of antiquity. In doing this they will demonstrate a confidence that the Bible can stand on its own merit. The following principles of interpretation, drawn with a view to the study of Biblical writings, are given to illustrate the manner in which historical, literary, and scientific findings may be applied.

(1) Interpretation ought to be historical—
  a. with a consideration of the age of writing.
  b. with a consideration of the author who wrote or edited a work.
  c. with a consideration of the people addressed.
  d. with an understanding of the purpose of the writer.
  e. in the light of progressive revelation and apprehension.
(2) Interpretation ought to be made with a consideration of literary form.
(3) It ought to be made with an appreciation of the Oriental character of the writings.
(4) It ought to be in relation to the context.
(5) It ought to be made by comparative study, that is, a study of parallel passages, both similar and analogous.
(6) It ought to be made with the Christo-centric and Theo-ultimate conceptions clearly in mind.

(7) It ought to be made reverently and with an open
mind.

Used in this fashion, the Bible, first of all, reveals the ends
to be sought in parish education. More will be said later concerning the use of the Bible as a direct medium of instruction.

2. *Objectives*

As the Bible came from individuals in the corporate life
of the Christian community, so it is to return its benefits to
the individual in the corporate life of the community. Christian leaders, whose faith and life have been molded by contact with God's Word, identify the ends which they believe
ought to be sought in pupils through the program of parish
education. They do this in the light of their own experience,
of their understanding God's will and activity as manifest in
the continuing stream of experience in the Christian community, and of the particular needs which current environmental conditions reveal. In general they desire (1) that
pupils shall face life, both present and future, realistically;
(2) that pupils shall understand their Christian heritage as
it pertains to life needs; (3) that they shall take over and,
with God's help, develop their heritage; (4) that they shall
be imbued with such dynamic as will make Christian faith a
force for righteousness in the world and an avenue to eternal
fellowship with God through Christ. When they have made
specific such ends as are implied in their statements, they
must test their formulation by the use of the Bible, soundly
interpreted, as a norm.

This view of objectives emphasizes results which are to
be sought in the experience of the learner. It stands in sharp
contrast with the view that the objective is to study the
Bible or to learn its stories and its facts. There is no denial
that a reasonable mastery of content is imperative. Christian
attitudes and habits must be grounded on sound knowledge.

But content mastery is not the real objective. The final result sought is in the reaction of the pupil to essential truths and in his use of these truths to govern his relations with God and man.

By way of illustration two groups of objectives are given here. The first has been selected because it represents a cooperative undertaking of the United Lutheran Church, the American Lutheran Church, and the Augustana Synod. It sets forth the ends which are sought in the experience of growing Christians through the study of a series of courses designed for use in Sunday church schools, *The Christian Growth Series.*

(1) *Fellowship with God.* A sense of fellowship with God—the Father, Jesus, the Holy Spirit. (2) *Christian Faith.* An understanding and personal acceptance of the Christian faith. (3) *Christian Living.* The expression of Christian faith in Christian living, both personal and social. (4) *Christian Adjustment.* Christian poise or adjustment in a continuously changing world. (5) *Church Membership.* An intelligent and wholehearted participation in the life and the work of the church. Effective church membership. (6) *Use of the Bible.* Regular, intelligent, and fruitful use of the Bible. (7) *Use of Christian Resources.* Regular, intelligent, and fruitful use of such Christian resources as prayer, the Catechism, church history, hymns, devotional literature, and religious art.

The second has been selected because it attaches to a rather distinctive emphasis in Lutheran educational practice. It presents outcomes which may be sought through catechetical instruction, the instruction which is immediately preparatory to confirmation. These outcomes are in the form of an analysis of Christian experience, conceived as a complex personal response to the gospel. Christian experience varies with different personalities, different races, and different ages. It nevertheless contains common elements which, with necessary adaptations, appear in all its forms and manifestations.

(1) *A sense of relationship with God as Father.* Basic to the experience of the Christian is the ever-present conviction of the Father-child relationship as it is realized through Jesus Christ. (2) *Fellowship or prayer life.* Out of the basic relationship grows a prayer life or fellowship with God through Christ. (3) *Convictions and their profession.* From a continuing fellowship there develops an increasingly intelligent faith and a desire to express that faith. (4) *Standards of conduct to serve as a guide and a measure.* Mere verbal expression of faith is inadequate. A life expression is essential. In the life expression of faith it is necessary to have standards or guides harmonizing with God's will. The Christian strives to live in accordance with these standards. When he recognizes his inability fully to have met them he becomes conscious of an infringement of his initial relationship with God. He needs to be assured of God's forgiveness and continued love. He needs God's strength for renewed endeavors. (5) *Forgiveness and strength.* He may find the assurance of God's forgiveness and love in his faith generally but also in the provision of particular opportunities in the church. Having received this assurance, he then enters more richly into the relationship with God which is basic to his life.

In both these illustrations the emphasis is not laid on the presentation and the interpretation of subject matter. It rests rather on the results which are to be achieved in the experience of the learner. Subject matter is one of the media through which these results may be attained. It is not an end in itself, nor is the mastery of it by pupils the major goal to be sought. The subject matter, including the Bible and all other sources of content information, is a means to an end. This is in harmony with the Lutheran conception of the gospel.

3. *Curriculum*

Inseparably related to objectives is the curriculum by which they are to be achieved. The mere phrasing of objectives in terms of experience offers no guarantee that the provisions for learning will move the pupil in the proper direction with the greatest effectiveness and economy. The curriculum is the course which pupils will run in order to arrive at successful points of achievement. In the judgment of mature Christians these points of achievement mark the hoped-for Christian growth. Too often a wide gap has remained between the purposes as framed and the procedures as actually provided and used in practice. In order to clarify the desired relationship between objectives and curriculum three theses are here advanced. They do not take the form of steps in curriculum building. They are given to identify significant characteristics of the curriculum as an operating medium.

(1) *The life of the Christian community is the primary curricular agent by which progress toward Christian goals is made possible.* By Christian community is here meant, first of all, the local parish. As already indicated, the Christian community in its more inclusive aspects must be taken into account. Further reference to this will be made in the conclusion.

Christianity has propagated itself essentially through the impact of the Christian community upon the individual and through its success in incorporating the individual in its life. In other words, growing persons learn more from people and happenings than they do from formal courses of study. The attitudes and the habits of parents, pastor, teachers, adults, and associates are more influential in shaping the life of the pupil than the procedures of the classroom. Imitation, whether viewed as a process consciously indulged or as the unwitting response to an environment of persons, is the major factor contributing to the formation of character.

The course which pupils follow in the achievement of desired outcomes is, first of all, blocked out and colored by the life of the Christian community. An adequate curriculum of parish education therefore demands an awareness on the part of the community of the pre-eminent part which its life plays. Strong effort is under way to stimulate this awareness in the people who comprise the parishes and to place all more specific procedures in proper relationship to the potentiality of Christian group life.

(2) *The major objectives of parish education are normally in harmony with or similar to the common ends of the one holy church throughout the world; the differentiating interpretations of denominational groups are introduced through the content of the curriculum.* A brief scrutiny of the outcomes sought through the *Christian Growth Series* will reveal their acceptability in practically all Christian circles. The same agreement would, in all probability, not be found with respect to the detailed materials and the interpretations contained in the separate courses.

The unity and the diversity here noted can be more clearly seen in the illustration dealing with catechetical instruction. The results to be sought in experience may be described in many different ways. Nevertheless, they will remain essentially the same: a sense of relationship with God as Father, built up and maintained through faith in Jesus Christ; an expression of this relationship through a continuing fellowship in spoken prayer or in companionship without words; a growing clarity of conviction and a desire to testify thereto; a recognition that, in facing the problems of life, there is a will of God made known in Christ, which serves both as a guide for conduct and as a measure of worth; a realization of personal inadequacy, of the need for forgiveness and strength, of the joy of an ever-renewed relationship. This can be taken to represent substantial unity.

A degree of unity continues in the "subject matter" which is a partial instrument for the attainment of these results. The Lutheran Church uses Martin Luther's *Small Catechism* as a basis for catechetical instruction. The five parts of the Catechism—The Ten Commandments, The Apostles' Creed, The Lord's Prayer, Baptism, and the Lord's Supper—are a common Christian heritage. With the explanation of these five parts other denominations may not agree. Here diversity becomes apparent. The Lutheran Church offers its testimony to the gospel by interpretations which derive from its heritage. In this fashion it contributes to the testimony made by the one holy church. It seeks to relate men to God through Jesus Christ with a view to advancing the total Christian community.

Thus, while the Lutheran Church teaches its own view of baptism, the primary objective it seeks approaches an experience common to all Christians: a sense of the covenant relationship with God through Christ. The same connection between distinctive material and primary objective obtains in the other parts of the Catechism. The Lord's Prayer, as a model prayer, is the means for awakening or strengthening the pupils' prayer life. The Apostles' Creed becomes a vehicle for common expression of faith and also a guide for personal, informal expression. The Ten Commandments, with Jesus' interpretation, serve as a guide for the life the pupil is to live and also as a means for measuring his life. The Lord's Supper offers a particular opportunity to enter into joyful fellowship with God through Christ and to be assured of God's forgiveness and continued love.

It is important to recognize this diversity in unity, or, better, this unity in diversity. In shaping the curriculum of parish education effort may validly be made to set forth the distinctive contribution which a denomination has to make to the interpretation and the expression of Christianity. Significant differences need not and ought not to be over-looked. They will lend varying shades of color to experience. But the extent to which the experiences are essentially the same must be increasingly made known, and the sense of oneness in Christianity increasingly stressed. This is a demand which our belief in the one holy church makes of us.

(3) *In more formal instruction, such as is provided in the organizations and schools of the parish, the sequence of curricular materials and the selection of learning methods are governed by the outcomes sought.* In the schools, as well as in the life of the total community, the personality of the leader is a significant factor in the learning process. Only because consecrated, mature Christians have taught in Sunday church schools has any success been possible in the face of unsatisfactory equipment, inadequate courses, and meager teaching skill. The leader's personality will always be counted on as an indispensable aid to successful work in the church school.

The Christian community can reasonably be expected to provide its schools with more than consecrated leaders. Through cooperative effort it must prepare the kind of curriculum that will lend pupils every assistance in achieving desired goals. These goals, it must be remembered, are to be found in the experience of the learner. Courses of study must draw upon the basic sources of Christian truth to stimulate and direct the pupils' progress. But courses of study cannot slavishly follow the sequence and the methods of presentation in the basic sources and pretend to psycho-logical adequacy for our day.

The literary form in which our Christian heritage has been transmitted to us is not adequate as a text for study.

The books of the Bible as they now stand were not prepared as courses for twentieth-century schools. It is even more apparent that the sequence of books in the Bible does not of necessity lend itself to the steps which pupils must follow in order to cultivate Christian experience. To contend that the pupil's progress from Genesis to Revelation with sufficient frequency will guarantee Christian character ignores both the known facts about the growth of the Bible and the fairly substantiated information about ways in which experience is formed.

To be sure, at some time pupils ought to attain thorough familiarity with the Bible in its present form. This is desirable in the interest of literary and historical appreciation. It is necessary in order that pupils may be equipped to use the Bible for themselves. It is essential so that Christian attitudes and habits may be grounded on a thorough understanding of facts. However, when the objective sought has to do with Christian character, the desired experiences of pupils take precedence over form and sequence of content. The anticipated use of what is to be learned must be taken into account in the procedures of learning.

The curriculum, inclusively understood, is the pathway which pupils follow to achieve the goals of a parish. Brief attention must now be given to the leaders who use the curriculum, to the pupils for whose growth they are responsible, and to the organization through which they work.

4. *Leaders*

In a sense every more mature Christian is a leader of the more immature. Practically all members of a parish therefore have leadership responsibilities. An understanding of this fact will do much to realize the potentiality of the entire Christian community as the primary educational agent.

More specialized leadership training demands attention

in order that all agencies in the parish may utilize their opportunities. The Lutheran Church has long contended that a full college and theological education is an indispensable requisite for the pastor. It recognizes, too, that education of leaders for work in the schools of the congregation is needed. Moreover, much is now being done to prepare church councilmen, leaders of organizations for young people and adults, choir directors, administrators, and the like for an intelligent and efficient approach to their tasks.

Religious education, more narrowly understood, has a general contribution to make as the whole Christian community approaches its leadership problems. It ought to encourage the use of such procedure and techniques as educators and psychologists have found to be helpful. Religious education has a distinctive task in developing consecrated and efficient leaders for the schools of the parish.

5. *Pupils*

Leaders deal with pupils in order that, through the curriculum or course of study, the essential objectives of Christian growth may be attained. All members of the parish are pupils—from the cradle to the grave. In attempting to direct the growth of pupils differences in age, mentality, emotionality, and environment must be taken into account. These differences will affect not only the learning process but also the product of learning.

Pure individualism, however, does not represent a satisfactory Christian emphasis. The individual is a member of the community. He derives his benefits from the community. He owes a responsibility to the community. Accordingly, both in the pupil's learning and in his expression of what he has acquired, the ends which are sought in the life of the Christian community must always remain prominent.

6. Organization.

Little will here be said about organization except by way of caution. No one form of organizing a parish to conduct its educational program is of necessity satisfactory. Reduced to minimum essentials, the sympathetic leader and the interested pupil make the organization.

There is need for continuing scrutiny of existing organizations. Many of them came into being to meet a previously unmet need. In too frequent cases they have pursued their independent course without fitting themselves into the life of the parish. In some instances, while still acceptable, they could conceivably be supplanted by more effective agencies. The criterion governing organization must always be found in the readiness with which the ends of the parish or of the Christian community can be accomplished.

THE CHURCH AND THE WORLD

With such help as the broader Christian community may provide a parish develops and administers its own program of education. It recognizes the Bible as the basic source of information to direct growing pupils to Christian maturity. It determines the objectives which are essential to Christian faith and life. It plans or takes over the curriculum and courses of study to accomplish these objectives. It educates leaders to work with pupils individually and through its schools and its organizations. The parish is in itself a manifestation of the Christian community. It fashions and pursues its own program of education. This is its privilege and its responsibility.

If the parish does nothing more than this it is woefully lacking in Christian perspective. When a Christian becomes a member of a parish he becomes a member of his distinctive communion. He also becomes a member of the one holy church throughout the world. Of his relation to the broader

Christian community he should be clearly conscious. The sense of world Christian fellowship must be instilled through education, not only to offset provincialism but also to realize what the church is actually meant to be.

The local parish touches the world through its direct and indirect participation in evangelistic effort, that is, in the effort to reach those who are not yet committed to the Christian way of life. Its direct part relates to people within the community where the parish is located. Its indirect part has to do with the responsibility assumed in behalf of missionary enterprise. The primary task of the Christian Church is to make better people. Whether this is being done through activity at home or abroad, it is a part of the educational responsibility of the church.

The church also has a provisional witness to make in the form of an impact upon the world. While its major task is to bring people to Christian faith and life, it recognizes that this task is importantly conditioned by the environment in which Christians move. Accordingly, the church becomes a witness to Christian truth as related to social, political, and economic life. It seeks to educate its own constituency for living in the world of our day. It seeks to testify to the world of our day concerning the conditions which are favorable to Christian living.

Whether Christian ends are attainable in human relations when God works merely through feeble man, no one can say. One conclusion is certain. Man must make every effort to utilize what God has placed at his disposal for the achievement of a Christian society. No guarantee can be offered that man's effort will win success at any period of history. There is a sure conviction, however, that God's cause will ultimately be victorious. The Christian is sustained by the hope that "The kingdoms of this world (shall) become the kingdoms of our Lord, and of his Christ." For the realization of this hope the Christian must strive with God's help, in season and out of season.

REFERENCES

Luther, Martin, "A Sermon on Keeping Children in School," *Works*, with Introduction and Notes, Vol. IV, Philadelphia: Holman Press, 1915-32.

Sherrill, L. Y., *The Rise of Christian Education*, New York: Macmillan Company, 1944.

Offermann, H. F., "The Place of Biblical Criticism in a Lutheran Seminary," *Lutheran Church Quarterly*, 1937, Vol. 12, pp. 396-410.

Offermann, H. F., "An Interpretation of the Baltimore Declaration," *Lutheran Church Quarterly*, 1939, Vol. 12, pp. 279-287.

Fischer, E. E., "Implications of the Baltimore Declaration for Dogmatics," *Lutheran Church Quarterly*, 1939, Vol. 12, pp. 287-296.

Nolde, O. F., "Implications of the Baltimore Declaration for Christian Education," *Lutheran Church Quarterly*, 1939, Vol. 12, pp. 296-302.

Bell, G. K. A., *The Stockholm Conference on Life and Work*, London: Oxford University Press, 1925, pp. 561-627.

Oldham, J. H., *The Oxford Conference*, Chicago: Willet, Clarke and Company, 1937, pp. 55-64; 113-150; 172-223.

Religious Education. Jerusalem Meeting of International Missionary Council. Vol. II. New York: International Missionary Council, 1928.

The World Mission of the Church, Findings and Recommendations of the International Missionary Council (Madras), New York: International Missionary Council, 1938, pp. 73-78.

The Life of the Church, Madras Series, Vol. IV, New York: International Missionary Council, 1938, pp. 51-161.

Nolde, O. F., *Guidebook in Catechetical Instruction*, Philadelphia: U.L.P.H. Board of Publication, 1939.

Nolde, O. F. and Hoh, P. J., *My Preparation*, Philadelphia: U.L.P.H. Board of Publication, 1935.

LUTHERANS AND GENERAL EDUCATION

A. R. WENTZ

What Lutherans have to say about education in general
varies from place to place and from time to time. Their attitudes and their utterances are determined for the most part
by the special situation which they face locally at the time. To
recount all the varied theories that have come to expression
in Lutheran circles during the past four centuries, or to set
forth even in outline all the different policies and practices
that Lutherans have ever developed with reference to the general education of man would require a series of large volumes.

It will be possible in this brief essay to do no more than
to sketch some of the fundamental pedagogical principles
that seem to be the corollaries of Lutheran teaching and
attitudes. We can undertake no effort to record the history
of elementary or higher education among Lutherans. Even
a bare enumeration of parochial schools or higher educational institutions under Lutheran auspices would require
more space than is here available. But the distinctive tenets
of the Lutheran faith do involve certain attitudes toward the
school, certain definite ideals and methods and content of
general education, and these we can easily detect in any
Lutheran household of faith, past or present.

By general education in this chapter we mean education
through the schools and other cultural agencies that lie
beyond the congregation or parish, beyond the theological
seminary or religious training institute, outside the church
college or the church-related college. This is only by way of
definition and does not involve any judgment of those Lutherans who are convinced that general education on the

(538)

elementary level must not be permitted to get away from the church and its parish and who are willing not only to pay their taxes for the support of the public schools but also to devote great energy and substance to the maintenance of parochial schools. The results of the parochial schools for the Lutheran churches that maintain them have always abundantly justified the great sacrifice of funds and the devotion of man power. But these schools do not come within the purview of this essay. Their history, their theory, and their problems would warrant a separate chapter in any complete narrative of Lutheran thinking and acting.

We propose only to inquire into the attitude of typical followers of Martin Luther with reference to the general education of the common man, the training and the culture he receives outside the parish and beyond the church. Just as we cannot speak of Lutheran agriculture or Lutheran chemistry or Lutheran trees, so it would not be entirely accurate to speak of Lutheran general education, because general education by its very definition cannot be labelled with the name of a church or a theological or doctrinal system. But we may speak of the Lutheran attitude toward general education. We may study the pedagogical implications of the distinctively Lutheran understanding of the Christian gospel.

These general pedagogical implications of Lutheranism can best be discerned in the life and the work of the founder of Lutheranism. The circumstances under which Luther began his work, the manner in which he carried it through to success, the various forms of his own thought and action along pedagogical lines—all these constitute our sources of information concerning the implications of the Lutheran faith for the education of the average man. In varying degrees and with many modifications because of changing times and circumstances Lutherans through more than four centuries have reflected these ideas of Martin Luther in their philosophies of education, in their utterances on pedagogical subjects, and in their plans for schools of every grade. We turn, therefore, to a consideration of the philosophy of general education as it was developed back at the very beginnings of historical Lutheranism.

The Lutheran Church was born in a university. How often Lutherans have made this boast, both to themselves and to others! If it means that the principles of the Lutheran Reformation were born in the heart of a man who was teaching in a university, it is very true, and it certainly has its implications and admonitions.

Luther was a university professor first and a reformer afterward. The character of his Reformation was determined by the fact that he was a teacher of the Bible at the time his revolutionary convictions settled upon him. Luther's Reformation moved on the wings of the teaching-learning process. It was carried to success by the vehicles of enlightened thought, of clear reasoning, and the products of the printing press. That kind of Reformation left a distinctive heritage in the sphere of education. It is seen in the educational theory and practice of Luther's followers in our day.

In their theories of general education Lutherans today draw the implications of Luther's reforms. And Luther was as great an educational reformer as he was a religious reformer. In fact, his activities as a pioneer in educational standards and methods are part and parcel of his activities as a pioneer in religious thought and practice. Luther's interest in education was very practical; it centered in the crying needs of religion in his day. So, too, were his plans and his methods. But his intense nature and his profound insight led him to fundamental principles that are reflected in general education among Lutherans to this day. His influence on the progress of education in general was clear and strong and abiding, and the philosophy of education that prevails among Lutherans in our time can best be understood if we first examine Luther's motivation, his principles, and his practice in educational reforms.

As Luther denied the authority of tradition and recognized the sole authority of the Word of God in matters of religion he naturally wanted the people to read the Bible for themselves. He knew that the pope's stranglehold on the people was tightened by the superstition of the masses. He saw that the strongholds of the hierarchy were fortified by the dense ignorance of the people as a whole. He realized, therefore, that his most powerful ally in overcoming the abuses in the church and in securing the triumph of the precious gospel would be the spread of enlightenment through popular education. Christian liberty will not dwell together with a darkened mind. If the universal priesthood of believers is to be realized in practice, one of the first steps must be the emancipation of the intellects of men.

The material principle of the Reformation, namely, that man is saved only by faith in Christ without the mediation of priest or ceremony or church, carries with it a pedagogical corollary. It lays upon every individual the responsibility for his own salvation and the necessity for watching over his own religious faith and practice. This calls for a certain degree of intelligence, a higher degree certainly than is required when all responsibility concerning the soul can be delegated to the priest.

Moreover, there is a certain intellectual element in the Protestant conception of faith. The intelligent assent of the believer is required. This, too, carries an impetus to know and a stimulus to learn. The gospel is no longer merely external; it is a glorious, transforming truth that permeates the entire thought and feeling of the Christian. It begets a Christian consciousness with a sense of individuality and personal responsibility.

Moved by such considerations, Luther early began to labor for the establishment and the improvement of schools. As early as 1520, in his "Address to the Christian Nobility of the German Nation," he made an appeal for the establishment of good schools everywhere. The great need that he saw during his visitation of the churches of Saxony led him to prepare in 1529 his two catechisms for the instruction of the clergy and the laity. In 1534 he completed and published his translation of the entire Bible, and its educational influence was very great. Everywhere in his writings and his addresses occur extended references to educational organization and pedagogical principles. Repeatedly he makes appeals on behalf of better schools and more of them. But the clearest statement of his ideas on the question of schools is found in two of his writings devoted entirely to the subject: first, his "Letter to the Mayors and Aldermen of all the Cities of Germany on Behalf of Christian Schools" (1524); and second, his "Sermon on the Duty of Sending Children to School" (1530). These two documents are the chief sources of our information as to Luther's plans and methods for education.

The great Reformer urged many considerations for the establishment of Christian schools. They were always practical considerations. He never urged education merely as a matter of abstract and formal discipline. He would never have agreed with the advocates of the pedagogical doctrine of "mental discipline" who hold that it makes no difference what you study provided you study it well. The actual content of the educational process was of supreme importance in Luther's estimation, and in this respect he stood diametrically opposed to the educational theory of the Middle Ages. Among the scholastics it was the theory of mental calisthenics that dominated the schools and determined their practice. The chief study was logic and the chief pastime theoretical controversy. Now Luther, after his emancipation, violently rejected Aristotle and the entire mediæval system of aprioristic thinking and theoretical education. He was bitterly opposed to scholastic Latin, scholastic disputing, scholastic theology, in short, the entire scholastic curriculum and method.

In his underlying motive for education Luther went back beyond the Middle Ages and took his stand with those ancients who held that education is the process of bringing the mind of the learner into contact with the body of usable knowledge and letting him learn it for himself. In this respect Luther was in thorough accord also with the very best educational theory of his day as held in the revival of ancient learning known as the Renaissance. In the Revival of Learning the ideals of education were self-culture and preparation for usefulness and success in the world that now is. These ideals were a clear break with mediæval authority and traditions in which the monastic ideal of life and the mental attitude of the self-abasing monk dominated all thinking and all learning. When Luther discarded the ascetic ideal and the grindstone theory of education, when he gave very practical reasons for the establishment of schools, when he urged thorough preparation for intelligent service in the church, in the state, and in society in general he threw into discard a thousand years of educational practice, popularized the ideals of the Renaissance, and took a long step forward in the direction of the modern school.

Luther advocated popular education for two main reasons, for the sake of the church and for the sake of society in general. His reasoning along both lines has its bearing upon the educational theory and practice of Lutherans during the past four centuries.

For the sake of the church as an institution Luther argued that effective Christian schools must be maintained.

Such schools will help the church, he said, by enabling parents to teach their children, by preparing useful teachers, and by equipping faithful pastors and preachers. The church will not prosper unless Christian parents have the intellectual equipment to take their places as the heads of their families. "If the kingdom of God is to come in power, we must begin with children and teach them from the cradle." Moreover, good Christian schools must be maintained in order that a continuous line of teachers may be trained up.

But above all, Christian schools are needed by the church in order to furnish men for the ministerial office. Luther set a very high value on the divine institution of the ministry. Nothing can exceed the vigor with which he urges parents to give their sons to that high calling. Here are some of his words on the subject: "God needs pastors, preachers, schoolteachers in His spiritual kingdom, and you can provide them. If you do not, behold, you rob, not a poor man of his coat, but the kingdom of God of many souls." "You have children," he says, "and can give them, but you will not do it; thus, so far as you are concerned, the ministry falls to the ground."

"We must have persons qualified to dispense the Word of God and the sacraments and to be pastors of the people. But where will we obtain them if schools are not established on a more Christian basis since those hitherto maintained, even if they do not go down, can produce nothing but depraved and dangerous corrupters of youth? There is consequently an urgent necessity, not only for the sake of the young, but also for the maintenance of Christianity and of civil government, that this matter be immediately and earnestly taken hold of, lest afterward, although we would gladly attend to it, we shall find it impossible to do so, and be obliged to feel in vain the pangs of remorse forever."

But Luther greatly broadened the range and the responsibility of education when he emphasized the need of popu-

lar education for the sake of society in general. He laid
upon the municipal authorities the responsibility for the
maintenance of schools for all classes and all vocations. For
he writes: "The highest welfare, safety, and power of a city
consists in able, learned, wise, upright, and cultivated
citizens, who can secure, preserve, and utilize every treasure
and advantage." He saw very clearly that the welfare of a
state depends on the intelligence and the virtue of its
citizens; and so he says: "Even if we had no souls, and
schools and languages were not needed for God's sake and
the Bible's, there would still be ground enough for establishing the best possible schools both for boys and girls, for
the world needs fine and capable men and women to
conduct its affairs and to regulate its households. Such
men are made of boys and such women of girls, and hence
it is necessary to educate the boys and girls properly." This
thought occurs repeatedly.

Schools are necessary in order to make good men and
women, capable of self-restraint, upright conduct, and noble
service to their fellow men. The peace and the permanence
of the social order and the happiness of its citizens depend
upon the degree of intelligence that is abroad in the land. In
his Sermon on the subject the Reformer says: "Though there
were no soul, nor heaven, nor hell, but only the civil government, would not this require good schools and learned
men more than do our spiritual interests? Hitherto the
Papists have taken no interest in civil government, and have
conducted the schools so entirely in the interests of the
priesthood, that it has become a matter of reproach for a
learned man to marry, and he has been forced to hear
remarks like this: 'Behold, he has become a man of the
world and cares nothing for the clerical state,' just as if the
priestly order were alone acceptable to God, and the secular
classes, as they are called, belonged to Satan and were

unchristian. But in the sight of God the former rather belong to Satan while the despised masses (as happened to the people of Israel in the Babylonian captivity) remain in the land and in right relations with God." And again, "If you look about you you will find innumerable offices that will need learned men in less than ten years, and yet but few young people are being educated for them."

In his concern for the education of all men in the interest of the state, Luther gave expression to an idea that was little heard in his generation. But it is an idea that is taken for granted in all modern education, namely, that the welfare of a state depends upon the intelligence and the virtue of its citizens. In Luther's judgment no calling, whether in church or state, was higher than the calling to be a man and a Christian. And the ideal purpose of education that he always had before him was the training of boys and girls, of men and women, for this high calling. He sought to foster the general culture of all human faculties and all human capacities. He looked upon schools as laboratories in which boys and girls might be made into skillful men, steady citizens, pious women, and good mothers. In his study of classic antiquity he had learned to know the fine training which the Greeks and the Romans gave their children, a training particularly calculated to prepare them thoroughly for all the duties of life. This ideal of school training lay behind all of Luther's practical utterances on the subject.

Not only for the sake of providing intelligent citizens and guaranteeing the security of peaceful occupations, but also for the purpose of training wise rulers, Luther urged the maintenance of efficient schools. "We know, or ought to know, how necessary and useful a thing it is, and how acceptable to God, when a prince, lord, counsellor, or other ruler is well trained and skilful in discharging in a Christian way the functions of his office." Just as parents who withhold their promising sons from the preparation for the ministry are responsible for any general decline in religion, so parents who keep back their sons from preparation for civil office are, in theory at least, guilty of anarchy. "Think of your son," Luther writes, "as a messenger in the empire, an apostle of the emperor, a cornerstone and foundation of temporal peace on earth! God looks upon the service in this light. For though we cannot be justified and secure salvation by such works, it is still a joyful comfort that these works are well-pleasing to God, especially when such a man is a believer and a member of Christ's kingdom."

Because of the great value of education to the state and its citizens in maintaining a peaceful and an orderly society Luther taught that the state itself is responsible for the Christian nurture and the general culture of the young. This does not mean that he advocated the secularization of the schools; such an idea was far from his mind. It means that he regarded the civil government as a divine institution, a necessary arrangement for social order and happiness. He says: "Secular authority is an image, shadow, or figure of the authority of Christ; for the ministerial office brings and imparts eternal righteousness, eternal peace, and eternal life, but secular government maintains temporal and transitory peace, life, and law. . . . Therefore, as it is the function of the ministerial office to make saints out of sinners . . . so it is the function and honor of the civil government to make men out of wild animals. But who will maintain it except us men to whom God has committed it? . . . It must be done by means of knowledge and books; men must learn and understand the law and wisdom of our empire."

So Luther urges the Christian education of all citizens and urgently lays it upon the hearts of all rulers, in whatever degree of authority, to exercise the greatest care over the young. The honor and the happiness of the city, the nation, the empire, depend upon the Christian schools of general culture. The richest treasures of a city are not its firm walls, its beautiful houses, or its abundant munitions of war, but its able, learned, wise, upright, cultivated citizens. God will hold all rulers to account for the training of such citizens through Christian schools.

Thus the Reformation made education a public duty. That was a very long step forward. It helped to dignify labor and to sanctify every human relation. It helped to bridge the chasm that yawned between the clerical estate and the mere layman's estate. It developed that healthy interest in the conquest of secular culture that has always been normative among the followers of Luther and indeed has distinctly marked the direction of western civilization during the past four centuries.

In consonance with his emphasis upon Christian schools as agents of good citizenship and general culture Luther insisted upon universal education, *i.e.*, the education of all classes and both sexes. He was the first to plead for an education of the whole people without regard to class or special lifework. No educator, ancient or modern, has set forth a more important pedagogical principle. It grew out of the Reformer's teaching that all men are equal before God. The principles of the Reformation concern man as an individual soul, irrespective of the accidents of outward condition. The Protestant ideal of life is the faithful discharge of every duty, both private and public, in the fear of God. Thus instruction becomes a practical necessity to every individual. The educational plan of the Middle Ages was directed almost exclusively to the preparation for the priesthood. The rank and file of common people were woefully neglected. But Luther insists that every man, rich or poor, high or low, regardless of race or color, rank or station or calling, has a right to be instructed so that he may become an intelligent child of God and a useful citizen in society.

But Luther went farther. In order that no class might be left in ignorance but that every person might have at least an elementary education he taught that it is the duty of the state to establish schools and compel attendance. "If the government can compel such citizens as are fit for military service to bear spear and rifle, to mount ramparts, and perform other martial duties in time of war; how much more has it a right to compel the people to send their children to school, because in this case we are warring with the Devil, whose object it is secretly to exhaust our cities and principalities of their strong men, to destroy the kernel and leave a shell of ignorant and helpless people, whom he can sport and juggle with at pleasure."

Compulsory education, Luther argued, should be maintained by general taxation. Those who enjoy the privileges of a country such as roads and bridges, public tranquility and general intelligence, ought to be obliged to contribute to the cost of these privileges. For more than a thousand years before this there had been no such suggestion of a system of education supported and controlled by the state. But shortly after Luther this idea was destined to become general throughout Germany and then among Protestants throughout the world. As late as 1864 the Roman pope stigmatized as an "error" the idea that "the entire direction of public schools belongs to the civil power." But Lutherans have always opposed the papal effort at church control of general education, and today it is a maxim both in politics and in education that the state must in self-interest educate all its citizens, even by compulsory means if necessary. The modern elementary vernacular school is recognized by students of educational history to be essentially a product of the Protestant Reformation.

But it must be emphasized that when Luther advocated tax-supported schools he had no thought of removing religion from the education of youth. The secularized school of our day never entered his mind. He thought of his schools of general culture as distinctly Christian in character. The religious motive was always primary in his own life, and he regarded it as the basis of all worthy living. It was only natural, therefore, that religious instruction should take precedence over all other instruction in his educational plans. The Bible is to be the chief branch of study in schools of every grade. That would be his unequivocal answer to a problem that is pressing for solution in our school system today.

At the same time it should be kept clear that Luther and Lutherans do not depend upon the public school as the primary agency for the Christian training of the young. The church must have its own schools, and Luther would heartily approve of the modern efforts among Lutherans to provide for more adequate parish education. And the family, as the most fundamental element in society, must carry a primary burden of responsibility in the religious training and the personality development of the young. Lutherans of today are good followers of Luther in their concern for the general enlightenment of the whole family.

The home must cooperate with the school in the training of the child, so Luther taught. As inefficient schools and godless homes will cause the downfall of both church and state, so effective schools and pious homes will guarantee the security of both church and state. The Reformer labored incessantly to secure harmony of action on the part of family, church, and state, which he called "the three hierarchies established by God." He was most emphatic, therefore, in his insistence upon careful home training. In a multitude of ways he tried to impress upon parents their obligation to bring up their children in the nurture and admonition of the

Lord. Family government, he pointed out, is the basis of all other government, and, therefore, parents can perform no greater service for the commonweal than to enforce obedience in the home and govern the household in wisdom, tenderness, and love. Parents have a very serious responsibility before God to bring up their children in wisdom and the knowledge of God and, if they have talents, to have them instructed and trained in a liberal education.

Another essential element in the religious tone and content of popular education is the Christian character of the teacher. Luther frequently emphasized the fundamental importance of the teaching vocation. The general character of the schoolteachers of the Middle Ages had brought the profession into disrepute. They were poorly compensated, and their work was regarded as menial. From this low estate Luther sought to redeem the office of schoolteacher. Because of its tremendous possibilities for popular education in the common schools he regarded the work of the schoolmaster as important to a city as the work of a pastor. "If I had to give up preaching and my other duties, there is no office I would rather have than that of schoolteacher. For I know that next to the ministry it is the most useful, greatest, and best; and I am not sure which of the two is to be preferred." This high estimate of the position of the teacher of schools in general education is of great importance for succeeding generations, especially in the modern democracies where the chief hedge against the complete paganization of the schools is the Christian character of the average schoolteacher.

The methods of general education that Luther advocated anticipated in many respects the requirements of present-day pedagogical psychology. He urged, for example, that the natural activity and acquisitiveness of the child be used in educating him. He recommended that all methods of instruction be adapted to the nature of the child, and that all learning be made pleasant for the child. The individuality of the child must be utilized and developed, and he must be educated through self-activity. He condemned harsh discipline and urged the utmost kindness. Luther realized that play is the serious work of the child's life and forms the foundation of his future character, and he urged, therefore, that the child's play should not be repressed but should be skillfully utilized and properly directed in the schools. He first applied the dialogue method of instruction to the common man and in the vernacular. He called for the utmost simplicity of method. In advocating these natural methods of education Luther set a pattern for the Lutherans of today and deserves to rank among the greatest educational reformers of modern times.

It should be emphasized that in all his writing and planning about schools, whether elementary or secondary or of university grade, Luther regarded Christian education as the foundation of all education. When he argued for schools for everyone as training centers for enlightened citizenship he was thinking of distinctively Christian citizenship. His schools were organized under secular control, but they were not what we call today "secularized"; they had Christian foundations, Christian teachers, Christian textbooks, Christian goals. Church and state were to work together as partners in different spheres, and the jurisdiction of general education was not taken out of the hands of the civil authorities because the princes and other secular authorities were simply outstanding members of the church and therefore accountable to God for the Christian use of their powers and privileges. It was their Christian duty to maintain schools and to fill them with Christian quality.

This constant emphasis upon the religious quality of the common school distinguishes Luther from John Calvin. It distinguishes the general tone of educational theory among Lutherans today from that among other Protestants. It grows out of a difference in their general attitude toward the world. Calvin's interest in civil and economic problems, in national and international politics, was almost as great as his interest in religion and education. He would have religion taught rather than caught in the schools. The civil government, he said, must serve the Christian religion in its own right, and he would provide ecclesiastical oversight to see that what was taught was also practiced. His conception of the relation between church and school was much like the Hebrew idea of the socio-religious community. The emphasis is upon ethics and moral conduct rather than the attitude of the heart, upon the reorganizing and molding of the whole life of a people rather than the deepening of convictions or the enrichment of spiritual fellowship.

This difference in the general tone of their educational theory has persisted between Lutherans and Calvinists through the past four centuries and may be discerned today even in America. It grows out of a difference in their conceptions of God and of His relation to the world. Lutheranism emphasizes God's immanence in the world, His omnipotent love, while Calvinism emphasizes God's transcendence and majesty. Luther's God is the Father who begets and sustains, who is always near and full of love. Calvin's God is the majestic Creator who demands implicit obedience and unceasing service and calls upon His devotees to make all worldly power and glory subject to His ineffable personality. The Calvinist therefore feels that the world must be God's, and to that end he must teach each new generation how to conquer the world and subdue it. But for the Lutheran the world is already God's, and the creation sanctified through Christ is the delight of the soul. The joys of the world

Lutherans accept as good gifts bestowed by God's hand. For them "natural law" has a very different meaning from that which Calvinists ascribe to it.

These fundamental differences are reflected not only in the Lutheran and Reformed systems of theology, in their varied conceptions of the church and discipline, in their services of worship, in their works of charity and benevolence, in their attitudes toward industrial and social life, but also in their ideas concerning pedagogy and the schools. The Lutheran would emphasize the elements of religion rather than the elements of ethics. He will never be satisfied with a system of general education that aims only to make one good; he will insist upon a system that is calculated to reach the heart and save the soul. He will seek to center the personality of the pupil not primarily in the present currents of environmental life but in the historical revelation of God's love in Christ. The true follower of Luther may be impolitic, unsophisticated, unskilled in organization, but he always stands ready to draw the pedagogical implications of the Lutheran Reformation. He will labor constantly for universal education to match the universal priesthood of believers, for general enlightenment to make possible the propagation of God's Word, and for a culture that applies first and last to the very heart of the personality where faith resides, that personal commitment to Christ which alone binds a soul in saving relation with his God.

BIBLIOGRAPHY

Bruce, G. M., *Luther as an Educator*, Minneapolis: 1928.

Cubberley, E. P., *History of Education*, Boston: 1920.

Eby, F., *Early Protestant Educators*, New York: 1931.

Mertz, G. K., *Das Schulwesen der deutschen Reformation im 16ten Jahrhundert*, Heidelberg: 1902.

Monroe, Paul, *A Textbook in the History of Education*, New York: 1906.

Monroe, P. (editor), *Cyclopedia of Education*, 5 vols., New York: 1911-13.

Painter, F. V. N., *Luther on Education*, Philadelphia: 1889.

Reisner, Edward H., *Historical Foundation of Modern Education*, New York: 1927.

Schmid, K. A., *Geschichte der Erziehung*, Vol. II, Pt. 2, Stuttgart: 1889.

Watson, F. (editor), *Encyclopedia of Education*, 4 vols., London and New York: 1921-22.

LUTHERAN MISSIONS

R. A. SYRDAHL

The Reformation and Missions

The Lutheran churches in America have their heritage from Europe, and their roots and spirit go back to the Reformation in which the church was brought back to its apostolic foundation. Belonging to the basic concept of the apostolic church was an urgency in proclaiming the word of salvation that ushered in the most spectacular growth of the Christian Church on record. This concept was inherent in the Church of the Reformation but was slow in making itself manifest because of external circumstances.

At the time of the Reformation missions were in a period of extreme sterility. The apostolic urge to bring Christ to the people and to establish His kingdom in the world had given way to an ecclesiastical program. For five hundred years, roughly from 1000 to 1500, missionary efforts were at first weak and sporadic, later being discontinued as an activity of the church. But for the occasional independent action of a few individuals and monastic orders missionary activity had ceased.

The change that was brought about with the Reformation, coming, as it did, at the time of great geographical discoveries, not only changed the basis of mission theory but also gave a new urge that startled the church into new missionary zeal. The Roman Church, losing territory to the Protestant churches in Europe, looked about for new fields. These she found in the lands claimed by Spanish and Portuguese explorers, who were also considered missionaries of the Church. They took possession of the lands for the Church of Rome as they planted the flags of their respective nations in the newly discovered territories. In 1541, twenty-four years after the beginning of the Reformation, the Jesuit order initiated a missionary drive. In 1622, about a hundred years after the Reformation, the first Jesuit pope was elected, and the mission work became an arm of the church under the Society for the Propagation of the Faith.

Meanwhile mission interest sprang up in the newborn Protestant Church. The most immediate contribution to missionary endeavor was the restoration of the apostolic principles of the gospel and the church and the distribution of the Bible. Direct mission activity was delayed by the necessity of the organization of a church and the formulation of doctrines and principles, by the lack of access to the newly discovered countries, and by the lack of such organizations as the monastic orders that had previously carried on mission work in the Roman Church. However, Luther was awake to the missionary responsibility of the new church, writing a tract urging the conversion of the Jew and several times calling attention to the duty of Christians to evangelize the Moslems by the Word of God rather than by the sword. In several sermons he spoke of the missionary responsibility of the Christians, refuting the theory of the scholastic period, then in vogue, that the missionary commission was fulfilled at the time of the apostles. Mentioning the many lands and islands that had not yet received the gospel, he declared: "Shall they believe, then they must first hear His Word and by it receive the Holy Ghost, who cleanses and enlightens their hearts through faith. Are they to hear His Word, then preachers must be sent who shall declare to them the Word of God."[1] Several attempts to reach tribes and groups of people outside the pale of the church were made by Lutherans during the lifetime of Luther and for a short time after his death.

---

[1] W. A. xxxi 1, pp. 228, 33-229, 20.

This initial interest in missions by the Church of the Reformation was short-lived. The period of orthodoxy and rationalism followed too soon after the church had been formed to permit its missionary impetus to live through times of difficulty. Missions were frowned upon, and exponents of missionary endeavor were treated as fanatics. The experiences of Von Weltz, who was ridiculed because of his writings to stir up the missionary zeal and died a lonely death on the shores of Patagonia lacking all support, typifies the spirit of this brief period.

Revived during the period of pietism, the church gradually reverted to its original evangelical zeal. The first serious missionary effort in India was begun by Ziegenbalg, Pluetschau, and Schwartz, Lutheran missionaries from Germany, supported by the Danish king and a Danish missionary society. One of the first missionaries to China was the legendary hero, Karl Gützlaff, who travelled up and down the continent of Europe stirring up mission zeal among all denominations. Preceding Livingstone we have Krapf and Rebmann, the first explorers of note of interior Africa and the first to begin mission work in Eastern Africa. They were from Basel but were supported by the newly formed Church Missionary Society of England. In all about eighty missionaries were sent out at the beginning of the nineteenth century from Father Jænicke's mission school in Berlin, organized in 1800. Many of these became the first Protestant missionaries sent to West Africa, supported by the Church Missionary Society. Wars, economic difficulties on the Continent, and lack of colonial possessions on the part of Lutheran countries hampered the work. But there was a growing activity, and much zeal on the part of the early Lutheran missions stirred up sympathetic chords in other groups, and many Protestant missionary societies were begun as a result of their activity.

Mission interest was inherent in the early immigrants who came to America from Lutheran lands. Again there was a pause, however. The Lutheran groups found themselves a minority in many sections of America, often facing a militant exclusiveness that was built up about the dominant faith of a colony. For that reason they had to struggle to build their own church, sometimes against the spirit of compromise on the part of some of their own numbers and sometimes against laws of intolerance against them. They first had to consolidate their own ranks and organize their church groups before any extensive aggressive work could be accomplished.

Some notable work was carried on among the American Indians by the Lutherans at an early date. This work was generally of short duration at the various places it was attempted, however, and this was true of much of the Indian work at the time of immigration movements westward into the lands of the Indians. The main emphasis was originally on reaching out to other numbers of their own racial and spiritual fellows. This was accomplished with little support from the homelands of the immigrants and was hampered by lack of trained men for the task of missionary and pastoral work. Divisions by racial differences and doctrinal variations also tended to weaken the various groups so that the impact they might have made both in America and abroad was lessened. The first main step of each group was home missions. Foreign mission interest did not die out, but as soon as the various congregations were organized well enough for a consideration of mission needs, they supported the mission programs of the mother churches in Europe. They were acquainted with these fields, and with racial and religious ties still strongly binding them to the "old country," they satisfied their missionary urge by sending funds to assist in the work on established fields under established European boards.

With the foreign missionary interest thus satisfied, it was only gradually that the desire for independent mission fields was awakened. Missionary expansion in this country was a natural development that followed along with the increasing numbers of immigrants that came in succeeding waves. As these new groups of immigrants arrived they were directed into new sections of the country. These formed the natural spots for the expansion of the church and automatically determined the direction of the expansion.

Home Missions

The history of the expansion of the church in America is really the story of home missions seen in retrospect. It has been estimated that from four-fifths to nine-tenths of the Protestant churches in the United States are of home mission origin.[2] It is a distinctly American activity, reaching the unchurched masses in a country where the free-church system is the only one in vogue. Its purpose is to win the unchurched of all conditions to Christ and to the church. To the Lutheran Church in America this has always been an evangelical task, seeking regeneration and not merely reform, seeking regenerate members of the church and not only new members of an organization. It has a special significance in the Lutheran Church. Most of the Lutherans that came to this country were from state churches. Few of them were of dissenter groups that had their organizations perfected before they came, and the motive for immigration was more economic than religious. For that reason, though the majority may have been deeply religious, they did not transplant the church with them, nor were they immediately organized into churches. Their faith was on the basis of individual conviction or of smaller group solidarity in the faith of their homeland. There were many defections to

---

[2]Clark, *Leavening the Nation,* p. 330.

other church bodies, but those that remained true to their religious convictions began to effect organizations, secure pastors, and gradually establish their own churches with centers in this country. This was a slow development through the long pioneer period when many other problems faced the newcomers.

When there was enough of a solidarity of religious impact established, the first move was one of reaching out to their own nationals of their faith to gather them in. This took place in two directions—in ministering to immigrants that had already settled in various communities and in winning the ever-increasing flow of new immigrants to these settlements. When the communities that were well-established had been reached, centralization and organization of the church proceeded to create an American base for future expansion.

The next step was an expansion of the church into frontier areas to reach more of the nationals of the home church in areas that lay outside the already established nucleus of the church. This period continued beyond the time of the frontier expansion as the church had not been able to keep abreast of the waves of immigration to reach all groups that came in such rapid succession. It kept the church on the national basis of the Old World church. The Lutherans were decentralized on the point of nationality and in most cases kept the mother tongue in its earlier ministrations. Lutheran services were conducted in nineteen tongues. This was a logical tendency as the finest ministration could be given in the tongues of the people that settled in the new land. It was a natural bond among the people and a natural social unit. It barred the church from an extended ministry among the American-speaking groups, however, and created natural limits for its expansion. Added to the language barrier were the different backgrounds from the various European lands according to varying emphases on doctrine and practice and in forms of church worship. These differences were also transplanted to the new soil.

The third period was a period of nationalization. This period began at the close of the first generation of immigrants; but as the waves of immigration were drawn out for a long period of years, nationalization was deferred in many sections until the beginning of the twentieth century. The first step was the change of language. This did not immediately change the outlook of the churches as practices built up in the country after the pattern of the initial pioneer groups continued to give each Lutheran group its special characteristics even though all now used the one language of their adopted country. This feeling has not yet been entirely removed and may not be for some time.

The fourth stage of home missions was entered before the third was completed. This was a reaching out to the unchurched everywhere, irrespective of race or heritage. This last aim has been greatly accelerated by the war conditions which created a flux of population that broke up old ties of churches in fixed areas. In meeting this situation the National Lutheran Council arranged for intersynodical services for Lutheran groups for the great defense areas. At the same time the challenge of a wider service to all unchurched in the areas touched by these programs was recognized. Having already been recognized by all synods, the impetus to serve whole communities irrespective of former racial or synodical relationships has been intensified. Elements of the last two stages are now present in the American Lutheran churches with a growing emphasis on areas rather than on groups.

In the development referred to above there has been a companion movement under the auspices of the American Lutheran Conference and the National Lutheran Council to intersynodical coordination of Lutheran home mission activity. As the old backgrounds began to diminish in importance, it was considered a duplication and a waste of man power and effort to have all Lutheran churches proceed with home mission programs in a given area that became competitive in character. The results were often many weak Lutheran churches of several synodical affiliations in some areas with other sections neglected by all synods instead of strategically placed churches covering all the areas of need without duplication. Attempts at general understanding between synods to avoid duplication were made, and this led to the formation of intersynodical home mission committees. There are now twenty-five Regional Home Mission Committees covering the areas of the United States and Western Canada under the National Lutheran Council. Two representatives of each cooperating body serve on each regional committee. No mission work is begun by any of the synods affiliated in the National Lutheran Council without the approval of the regional committee. This assures an objective study of the field to decide the need and the most effective body to minister to the field before work is begun. In this way duplication of home mission efforts is avoided in all new ventures of these synods. Not all Lutheran bodies are members to this agreement, however, and there are instances where other considerations step in to interfere with the practical working of this plan. It is working increasingly well, however, under a developing intersynodical consciousness.

Each Lutheran synod has its own home mission board and its own home mission budget; so individual initiative is not stifled. Each church can put forth as much effort as it deems wise in each field under the cooperative planning of the regional committees.

Lutheran World Action, the movement that has sponsored the service to migrant workers, has also sponsored an intersynodical approach to the servicemen through Lutheran service centers. The Lutheran World Action publicity and appeal, as well as its actual contacts throughout the many branches of its service, have intensified the united approach of Lutherans to the problem of missions both at home and abroad.

The last available statistics will indicate that home mission work is carried on by some branch of the Lutheran Church in every state of the Union, in Washington, D.C., in Canada, and in Alaska. Not every synod carries on this work in every state, the greatest number being touched by the Missouri Synod which does work in forty-two states. The Augustana Synod and the United Lutheran Church carry on work in thirty-five states, and the American Lutheran Church and the Norwegian Lutheran Church of America in twenty-five states each. Analysis will show that the northcentral, northwest, and the three Pacific board tiers of states receive the greatest attention, plus Texas in the deep South and New York, Pennsylvania, and New Jersey on the Atlantic board. The deep South is generally but lightly touched. This picture holds true fairly well as to the proportion of home mission expenditures for all the synods except for the United Lutheran Church which has paid more attention to the Atlantic Coast than have the other synods. Thus there will seem to be no general geographic division of synods of the Lutheran Church in the home mission effort. As the various synods threw off their nationalistic backgrounds they also began to discount all barriers, so the spread became general.

Annual expenditures for the home mission programs of the Lutheran churches in the United States amount to over two and a half million dollars a year. Approximately one half of this sum represents the expenditure of the Missouri Synod. The expenditures of the other major Lutheran synods vary from $150,000 to $400,000 annually.

Lutheran Welfare

(Inner Missions)

A new approach to social welfare was made in the spirit of the Reformation under the direction of Luther. His insistence on the availability of the Word of God for every person of every class gave new nobility to the individual soul in its direct contact with God. It also prepared for the equality of men in a common brotherhood that has remained the key of Lutheran preaching and social work. Social work has remained primarily a matter of correcting the individual in the light of his relationship to God. It has been recognized that this "correction" lies deeper than social and economic factors, and that power to make a permanent adjustment of man to God and to his environment lies in the regeneration of the individual soul and a redirection of his entire being in the ways of righteousness in the power of God.

Luther was also interested in the more purely economic and social conditions of the people within his range of contact, however, and felt the responsibility of facing needs that called for alleviation or adjustment. His program, though not organized, was found basically to consist in a cooperation of the church and the state in specific cases with the state, as a divinely instituted organ, bearing the chief load of responsibility before God for the economic conditions of the people. In his treatise, "An Open Letter to the Christian Nobility," we find this pronouncement:

"One of our greatest necessities is the abolition of all begging throughout Christendom. Among Christians no one ought to go begging! It would also be easy to make a law, if only we had the courage and the serious intention, to the effect that every city should provide for its own poor, and admit no foreign beggars by whatever name they might be called, whether pilgrims or mendicant monks. Every city could support its own poor, and if it were too small, the people in the surrounding villages also should be exhorted to contribute, since in any case they have to feed so many vagabonds and knaves in the guise of mendicants. In this way, too, it could be known who were really poor and who not.

"There would have to be an overseer or warden who knew all the poor and informed the city council or the priests what they needed; or some other better arrangement might be made."[3]

He speaks further of the evil of living in idleness at the discomfort of others and scores the social ills of the day, among them unnecessary luxuries in eating, excessive drinking, and the social abuses of the day.[4]

Bereft of the large institutions of the day that were the usual instrument of ministration in the social and economic sphere, the Church of the Reformation was thrown back on the more immediate and personal way of dealing with cases that need adjustment in these spheres, more in accord with the spirit and the practice of the church in the apostolic age. Under the state church system, however, an increasing amount of this responsibility was left with the state. Though much relief work and other welfare activity were carried on informally by the church and church people, it was not till the beginning of the nineteenth century that the church awoke to the fact that the state was not meeting the needs and that deplorable conditions in many spheres had sprung up that needed the attention of the church for the spiritual, moral, and physical betterment of its people. At this time giants of faith rose to meet the challenge, men like Spener, Francke, Wichern, Fliedner, Lœhe, Bodelschwing, Stœker, Uhlhorn, and others. They led the church in its return to the care of the neglected fields of ministration so that work was rapidly begun in many areas: family welfare, child welfare, child caring, youth guidance, religious education, care of the sick and inebriate, city missions, care of prisoners and discharged prisoners, rescue homes, etc. It was natural

---

[3]Works of Martin Luther, Vol. 2, pp. 134-135. A. J. Holman Co., 1915.
[4]Ibid., pp. 158, 161, 162.

that the pattern of larger institutions would in part be followed, but the education of individuals in specialized work and a greater amount of attention to needs and individuals in a curative and preventative way brought an improvement that continued to develop.

Luther's emphasis on a gospel-centered ministration was retained. Soul cure was uppermost in all contacts and was the ultimate goal as individuals and groups were readjusted economically, physically, or morally that they might be useful citizens of the kingdom of God as well as of society. It served among those who nominally did or should belong to the state church but who had been lost to its immediate ministering influence. It differed from home missions both in method and in aim. It did not normally seek to establish new congregations but sought to draw in those that were not being reached by the normal contacts of the church to the already existing congregations.

The "Inner Mission" philosophy and practice were transplanted to America, where they found fertile soil in the Lutheran churches that had been organized here. Many works of charity had been carried on spontaneously by the Lutherans of America since the time of the early immigrants, but the organized work of this branch of church activity was introduced by Passavant who, with the help and the guidance of Fliedner, brought over the first deaconesses to America in 1849. Hospital work, deaconess homes, orphanages, educational institutions, and other mission institutions to fill a void in the Lutheran churches of several racial backgrounds were begun in rapid succession. At its inception this work was especially centered around institutions and the deaconess organizations. Later local and regional Lutheran groups, some under the direct support of the church, others forming independent associations, developed in all main spheres of the welfare activity of that age.

Child-caring agencies and institutions were the first to receive the general attention of the Lutherans. One agency that is still in existence was organized in 1808, and more than half of the eighty such institutions and agencies listed today were organized before 1900. Few institutions of welfare were organized before 1850, but in the twenty-five year periods following that date we see an increasing number in each period till the peak is reached in the period from 1900 to 1924. During that period over half of the 105 homes for the aged that are now in existence were founded, one-fourth of the institutions and agencies for child care, about one-third of the seamen's missions, and one-half of the present eighty hospitals, sanataria, and invalid homes. There are today a total of 426 agencies, societies, institutions, and special activities in the field of social welfare within the Lutheran churches of America, staffed by 12,520 paid workers and 1,955 volunteers. More than one million persons annually receive service in some manner through their facilities. The annual expenditure for the services given amounts to $18,395,622.

To begin with most of the services offered were rendered through independent organizations and institutions within the various synods or were extrasynodical. Individual synods later stepped in and took over the responsibility for some of the institutions and the services and developed these under synodical sponsorship and management. Meanwhile the other type of organizations has continued and has increased, full freedom for such institutions being maintained within the church.

Several developments have been noted throughout the history of Lutheran welfare. We generally see a change in the type of institutions. The larger institutions that offer many services under one roof and management are yielding to the smaller, specialized institutions under specialized management. Numerous larger institutions are continuing very commendable service in many spheres but in many cases with a more careful breakdown of services offered. Instead of the larger orphanages the cottage type of institution is favored where possible, some of the older institutions being reorganized on a system bearing some of the features of the cottage plan by divisions of facilities and supervision. This is true to a less degree of the homes for the aged.

The orphanages are in many cases changing their character as new methods are developed. They are taking more and more care of such children as cannot or should not for some reason be placed for adoption—whether either physical, social, or moral habits make adoption impractical; where there are several members of one family who should not be separated from each other; or where the dependency of the children might be of a temporary nature. Thus children's receiving homes have come into vogue where smaller groups of children are cared for with the purpose of study and corrective treatment so that they can either be placed for adoption or placed in boarding homes or permanent, specialized institutions. Receiving homes also care for cases of temporary dependency. In this way a specialization of area of service has developed in each case.

Another development has been a great increase in services rendered through a development of agencies that serve in the field of social service, not necessarily connected with any institution but using existing institutions and adding some as needs developed. Trained social workers have been used largely for these services and have worked in the areas of family welfare, child welfare, and juvenile groups. The services branched out into big-sister services, court service, summer camps for children, city missions, radio evangelism, and other allied branches, including the more generally accepted services already mentioned as well as hostels for young men and women, homes for unmarried mothers, adoption services, boarding homes, public clinics.

Simultaneously with this change the character of the service organizations was broadened into intersynodical or extrasynodical ventures. It was found that most of these services could best be given in a cooperative manner between various synodical groups of Lutherans. In 1922 the National Lutheran Inner Mission Conference was organized in Pittsburgh, Pa., to coordinate services and to share experiences of the various local, regional, or state groups that were in the field of service. The name of this organization was changed to Lutheran Welfare Conference in America in 1940 under the National Lutheran Council.

> "It serves in a consultative capacity and shall seek to further the development of Christian welfare service through the churches, and to bring into cooperative relationships the inner mission, charitable, and social welfare work of the cooperative bodies."[5]

A similar organization of national scope has been created for the Synodical Conference though in some cases the Missouri Synod also affiliates with the Lutheran Welfare organization of an area or a state. The result has been a unification of services and an extension of state and area Lutheran welfare organizations that had already begun to come into existence at the beginning of the century.

Many of the institutions remain under the ownership and the control of individual synods or special groups within the synods as before, but wider use is made of them, and extended services are offered by this broader service group. The national Lutheran welfare organization has conducted surveys of existing organizations and services and has tried to unify standards and aims as well as to coordinate all services offered.

---

[5]Report by Dr. C. E. Krumbholz in the twenty-third annual meeting of the National Lutheran Council, January 22-23, 1941, Columbus, Ohio.

With the latter development we find a more popular appeal and representation that have made it possible for the church groups to utilize services offered by the state, county, or local service groups, to cooperate with these groups for the administration of their services more effectively among Lutheran constituencies and to receive support from the community chests and treasuries of these groups. Added recognition of the services given by the Lutheran groups has led to a hearty understanding and support by the agencies referred to. This has increased the effectiveness and the scope of services offered by the Lutheran service groups. In this way Luther's principle of sharing of responsibility between state and church has been placed on a workable plane where mutual benefits and blessings are assured without the danger of neglect that grew up in a post-Reformation era.

Similar changes have taken place within the diaconate of the Lutheran Church. It is still felt that the institutional system is best suited for the organization, but at the last survey it was found that deaconesses are now serving in twenty-seven different areas of inner mission and social service. There has been a marked decrease in the appeal of the deaconess movement among the young women of today. This has perhaps been augmented by the multitude of opportunities in the social service field for young women wishing to serve their church and society, but the deaconess movement is still an important arm of the church that can well fit into the present developments and render increased service. This is recognized both by the organization itself and by the church at large.

Foreign Missions

Though the bonds to the mother churches in Europe held the immigrant churches closely for a long period and served as outlets for their foreign mission interest, it was not long till the independence of the churches in the new country manifested itself. While the immigrants were still pressing westward, and new log and sod huts were springing up in widely scattered communities, creating vast problems for the home mission interests of newly organized church bodies, the Lutheran churches of America began to reach across the seas into mission lands.

The first definite action in forming a Lutheran mission society in America was taken in 1835 when an appeal went out among the General Synod congregations to set aside the first Monday of each month for intercession that the "missionary spirit" might grow among them. That year, with John C. F. Heyer presiding, "The Central Missionary Society" was formed, which was to work for both home and foreign missions. At this time appeals came from Rhenius in India and Gützlaff in China for the support of the Lutherans in America. These appeals stirred the interested groups in America to form the "German Foreign Missionary Society," supported by members of the General Synod, the Ministerium of Pennsylvania, the Ohio Synod, and the German Reformed group. When the Reformed group dropped out, it was reorganized as "The Foreign Missionary Society of the Evangelical Lutheran Church in the United States." It decided to support Rhenius who had been educated in the Jænicke Institute of Germany but had been sent out and supported by the Church of England Missionary Society. Differences in doctrine and in practice had caused his dismissal from the British society, and he had formed an independent Lutheran mission in the Tinnevelly district. When Rhenius died in 1838, his colaborers and the church they had formed returned to the Church of England Missionary Society.

Meanwhile, in 1836, a mission society had been formed

within the Ministerium of Pennsylvania. Interest aroused for the cause of missions in India by the support of the work there precipitated direct action for the establishment of a mission field of its own. In 1841 "Father" Heyer was called by the General Synod mission society but deferred when he found that he was to go out under the management of the American Board. Offering his services to the Pennsylvania Synod, he was sent out by this body, arriving in India in March, 1842. Journeying northward from Ticiturn through Madras, he headed for the Telugu people and found vast areas that were unreached by the missionary enterprise. He settled in Guntur and there founded the work in which the General Synod cooperated and which became the basis of the future mission field of the Guntur area. Work was begun July 31, 1842.[6]

In Rajahmundry a field was begun under missionary L. M. Valett in 1844. The Bremen Society was also working in this field but turned over its two missionaries and two stations in 1850 when economic difficulties in Germany made it difficult to continue the work. Thus two large districts about 100 miles apart became the field of the Lutheran groups in India. At the time of the division of the Lutherans into the General Council and General Synod, the latter retained the Guntur field, and the General Council became responsible for the Rajahmundry field. These were reunited as one field under the United Lutheran Church.[7] The Augustana Lutheran Church cooperates with the United Lutheran Church in this work, sending several missionaries and assisting generally in the support of the work and specifically in maintaining individual institutions.

The Missouri Synod was the next Lutheran church to enter India from America. Doctrinal differences within the

---

[6]*They Called Him Father,* pp. 115ff; Laury, pp. 123ff.
[7]Cf. Laury, pp. 126, 129.

Leipzig Mission in India caused the dismissal of two of the conservative missionaries. The Missouri Synod was at that time ripe for the beginning of mission work, having for some time considered the desirability of entering Japan with the gospel. Upon hearing of these men they conferred with them and commissioned them in 1894 to begin work in an unevangelized section of India. The central point of the new venture was Krishnagiri, opened as a mission station in 1895. Gradual expansion led into the Kolar gold fields of Mysore, into Travancore and Colombo, Ceylon.

The Joint Synod of Ohio, one of the constituent synods within the present American Lutheran Church, had for a long period of time supported the mission work of the Hermannsburg Society in India. In 1908 the desire to have its own mission field was officially expressed in conference, and negotiations were finally concluded with the Hermannsburg Society for the purchase of Puttur and Kodur stations in 1913. These became the nucleus of its mission field, which was increased by the rest of the Hermannsburg field when it took over the latter during World War I when the German missionaries were withdrawn, and it was found impossible for that society to continue its work.

These three missions lie mostly in the Madras Presidency. The work of the United Lutheran Church and the American Lutheran Church is largely among the Telugu people. The work of the Missouri Synod is among the Tamil-speaking people in its northern field and among the Malayalam-speaking people, with some work among the tribes people. These efforts are a part of the impact on South India and are shared with Lutheran missions of Europe. Most of the Lutheran missions of India, the majority of which are in south India, are united in the Federation of Lutheran Churches in India. The baptized membership of the Lutheran churches in India within this federation is 400,000.[8]

_____

[8] *In Seven Nations*, p. 18.

Besides these missions in south India there is a mission that was begun in 1867 in North India among the Santal people by a Norwegian mission. This mission is organized in India, receiving support from Scandinavian countries and from American Lutherans, mostly among the Scandinavian descendants in America. Its fields lie in Santal Parganas, Sultanabad, Assam, Dinajpur, and Malda. Support of this mission from America was begun in 1884 by Danish Lutheran organizations, spread among the Norwegian groups, and became very general after 1894 upon the visit of its pioneer missionary, Skrefsrud. An American board of this mission is now functioning, and during the war much of the support for the entire field has been received and managed through this board.

These missions have a combined force of 257 missionaries, 194 native pastors, and 2,617 other native workers. The native Christians number 256,164. There are 14,343 congregations and 1,394 primary and elementary schools. One college, three seminaries, and fourteen hospitals are conducted by the missions. The annual budget from American sources amounts to $582,036.

Africa

Lutheran missionaries were among the first of the Protestants to make an impact on Africa. Eighty of the early missionaries sent out by the Church Missionary Society of England were Lutherans, working in Siera Leona and Cambia, East Africa. The first two, who were from Jænicke's mission school in Berlin, arrived in Africa in 1804. Contemporary with Livingstone who arrived in Africa in 1840, there are several Lutheran missionaries of note in West Africa. Krapf, arriving in 1844, and Rebmann in 1846 were the first explorers of note in the interior of Africa, discovering the snow-clad mountains of the Lake Victoria region. These two men, educated at Basel, were also supported by the Church Missionary Society of England. Hans Schreuder arrived in Natal, South Africa, in 1844 to found the Schreuder Mission, for a while conducted by the Norwegian Lutheran Church of America. He began his work among the Zulu people north of Natal where two previous attempts had been unsuccessful in establishing missions. This move was of importance beyond the immediate mission as Bishop Schreuder was instrumental in interesting several continental and American Lutheran missions in beginning work among the Zulus and other peoples of Africa.

The Norwegian Lutheran Church of America supported the work of the Schreuder Mission, conducted from Norway, in increasing proportion from about 1850. Some of the personnel was later sent out from America, and increased support by the American group led to negotiations that were concluded in 1927, giving the field of the Schreuder Mission to the Norwegian Lutheran Church in America. The work among the Zulu people is shared with several other Lutheran and some Reformed groups. Increasing cooperation among the Lutherans has led to joint ventures in higher education and literature and present plans for the formation of Bantu Lutheran Church, which will be an indigenous Lutheran church composed of all Lutheran mission fields in South Africa. The constitution of this new organization has been proposed to the constituent groups, but the ratification has been held up as a result of the war. This mission has twenty-seven missionaries today, and there are fifty-one congregations with a total of 13,926 Christians. The native church has thirteen ordained and 160 unordained native workers.

The next oldest mission conducted by the Lutheran Church groups of America, and the oldest organized by an

American Lutheran church body, is the one conducted in Liberia by the United Lutheran Church of America. Work was begun in 1860 in this country, the only republic of Africa, composed of descendants of released American Negro slaves and native aborigines. The beginnings of the work were among Congoes that had just been released from a slave ship captured enroute to America. David A. Day, who spent 23 years on the field, was the pioneer who laid the foundation of the mission. Because of unhealthful climate and many fevers there has been a rapid turnover of missionaries, and in the early years there were few workers and some gaps with no foreign workers. The field was expanded inland among the primitive tribes in 1908, and there are over seventy organized churches in the field today with 2,889 Christians, two ordained native ministers, and fifty-eight other native workers. There are thirty missionaries.

In the French Cameroon there are two Lutheran missions from America, conducted by the Lutheran Brethren Church and the Sudan Mission. The Church of the Lutheran Brethren decided to affiliate with the Sudan United Mission in beginning work in the French Cameroon in 1917. The first missionary couple was called that same year, and the mission is at present staffed with ten missionaries.

The Sudan Mission is also located in French Cameroon. It was organized as an intersynodical mission in 1918 and began its work in 1923 under the guidance of its pioneer missionary, A. E. Gunderson, who had previously worked independently in Nigeria since 1913. It has twenty-one missionaries at present, most of them from America. The headquarters of the mission is in Minneapolis, Minnesota. This mission has one organized congregation, 200 Christians, and twenty-one unordained native workers.

In Tanganyika, East Africa, there is a cluster of Lutheran missions from Europe. The Augustana Synod of America had been seeking a field in the Sudan, and Mr. Hult, its pioneer missionary, was sent out in 1919. A field was temporarily selected when the plight of German missions in Tanganyika during World War I called the Augustana Synod temporarily to take over the Leipzig Mission in northern Tanganyika, begun in 1893. Postwar readjustments, completed in 1926, allotted the Iramba field in Tanganyika to this body as a permanent field. There are twenty-eight missionaries on the field, 249 ordained native workers, seven congregations, and 7,500 Christians.

The last country in Africa to be entered by the Lutheran Church of America was Nigeria. The Synodical Conference took over a field in the interior, consisting of sixteen congregations and 5,000 souls, that had been formed into a native church but had fallen into a decadent condition because of the lack of workers and supervision. At their request the Synodical Conference stepped in in 1936, and Rev. H. Nau reorganized the field and began the mission that at the present time has seven missionaries, fifty-nine congregations, two ordained native pastors, and one unordained worker. There are 10,106 Christians.

China

China was entered by a Lutheran missionary from Germany, Karl Frederick Guetzlaff, in 1831, who conducted a private mission for some time before the country as such was open to foreign residence and missionary work. His greatest accomplishment was his ability to arouse continental Lutheran groups to active interest in China as a needy mission field. Two Lutheran missions from Germany entered in 1847, a few others followed before the turn of the century, most of them working in South China.

When the American Lutherans began work in China, the interior was opening up to foreign missionaries, and the jumping-off-place that drew them was Hankow, about 700 miles up the Yangtze River. The first American groups that entered were of the church groups that now form the Norwegian Lutheran Church of America. Two fields were selected by them, one in Northwestern Hupeh Province, and one in South Central and South Eastern Honan. They founded the first permanent mission field in Honan Province and drew three other missions near to their centers of work so that the Lutheran impact was concentrated in these central provinces. These groups opened the province of Honan for the gospel and remain an influential group in the missionary personnel of the two provinces mentioned.

The mission of the Hauge Synod with its pioneer, Rev. H. N. Running, and Rev. D. Nelson of the United Norwegian Lutheran Church began working the field in Northwest Hupeh together, the latter finally going into South Central Honan along the route of the proposed Peking-Hankow Railway. This field extended from the southern border of the province northward through several inland cities and eastward to the boundary region of Anhui Province, the eastern portion being later in charge of the Norwegian Synod. The field in Hupeh was extended into Southwest Honan, and these three sections now form the field of the Norwegian Lutheran Church of America.

The Church of the Lutheran Brethren, upon consultation with the two Norwegian Lutheran groups from America already on the field, chose a section of the country bridging the gap between their two fields. They arrived in 1903 and have continued working in that section, partly in Hupeh and partly in Honan Provinces.

The Augustana Synod was the next to join the other Lutheran missions in Central China and with the assistance of the existing missions selected a field in the north central section of Honan Province in 1905, along the Peking-Hankow railway, extending their work westward till it bordered on the fields of Lutheran mission fields of two Norwegian groups. They also gradually extended their field northward, occupying some of the more important Honan towns along the Lung-Hai Railway.

The Missouri Synod entered Hupeh Province in 1913 with headquarters in Hankow. From this Yangtze port city it moved up the river, establishing mission stations at strategic cities along the river. It also has some scattered stations in Anhui and Hopei, where it has made contact with native Christian groups desiring supervision of a mission, and where a nucleus of the converts gained for the church in Hupeh have their permanent residences.

The Lutheran Free Church arrived in China in 1916, settling down in Northern Honan, just a little east of the Augustana field, south of the Lung-Hai Railway. Its field, though limited in size, is in a vital section of Honan, in a pocket but slightly touched by the gospel before its coming.

The last of the American Lutheran churches to enter China was the United Lutheran Church, which took over the field of the Berlin Mission in Shantung in 1925. This work had been begun in 1898, but postwar depression made it necessary to confine the work to South China; so the Berlin Mission gladly yielded this portion of its work to the United Lutheran Church. With the center in Tsingtao, the field stretches inland, covering more heavily populated areas.

The United Danish mission has actively supported the work of the Danish Lutheran Mission in Manchuria and Korea, assisting mostly with funds but also sending some missionary personnel to this field.

The impact of the American Lutheran missions on China has been felt in considerable strength. There are 160 missionaries in their field where 252 congregations with fifty-six ordained and 722 unordained native workers are serving

28,521 baptized Christians and reaching out to the non-Christian areas allotted to them.

These Lutheran groups have developed strong indigenous churches. All have conducted strong educational programs and some medical work together with evangelistic work. The Missouri Synod has been conducting its work separately from the other synods, including seminary and literary work. The others, exclusive of the Lutheran Brethren mission, have united in the Lutheran Church of China, organized in 1912, including all the major Lutheran missions from Europe. These conduct a joint Lutheran theological seminary and have at various times projected joint participation in other institutions of higher education. They have a central board for producing Lutheran literature and have a common liturgy and Lutheran church hymnal. The Lutheran Church of China is nation-wide in its scope, and the eleven mission churches have a unified organization with a president and all necessary functionary committees and boards. This indigenous national church embraces mission fields from southern China to northern Manchuria, and though each mission field forms its own synod, all the fields are amalgamated into this central national organization.

Japan

Protestant missions followed on the heels of Commodore Perry when he reopened Japan to the western world after 230 years of self-imposed quarantine. The United Synod of the South, now a part of the United Lutheran Church, was the first Lutheran group to enter Japan, two missionaries arriving in 1892, beginning work in Saga and Kumumoto on the island of Kyushu. In 1898 the United Danish Church sent its first missionaries who settled in the city of Kurume on the same island. These missions have joined hands in the work, conducting a seminary and other institutions together

and coordinating the evangelistic work in the various centers. Tokyo, where the seminary is located, has also been
included as one center of the work. Institutions of mercy
are specially stressed in Japan since they appeal to the
people and open wide avenues of Christian work. The
Evangelical Lutheran Church in Japan was organized in
1934 under its own constitution and native leadership. This
organization was strong enough to receive special attention
and insist on its prerogatives before the national government
of Japan for a considerable period of time before all
churches were forced to become a part of the general
Christian Church in Japan during the war years. There are
eighty-six missionaries, forty-five congregations, 5,240 Christians, twenty-seven ordained, and 201 unordained national
workers in this joint mission venture.

Madagascar

The island of Madagascar has a long history of Lutheran
missions, the Norwegian Mission Society entering the capital city, Tananarive, in 1866. The southern half of the island
was allotted to it as its field. It, in turn, gave the southern
tip of the island to the Norwegian Lutheran churches of
America. This was entered by the first Lutheran from
America in 1887. When the Lutheran Free Church was
organized in 1894 it desired a section of this field as some of
the early missionaries there became members of this church.
Division was made in 1904 whereby the Norwegian Lutheran Church in America now has the eastern portion of the
field and the Lutheran Free Church the western. Though a
national Lutheran Church of Madagascar has not yet been
fully organized, much union work is conducted by the three
Lutheran groups on the island. The Lutheran seminary originally conducted by the Norwegian Mission Society since
1871 became a Lutheran venture in 1923. Other union activi-

ties include literature, a union hymnbook and common form of liturgy, and an inter-Lutheran conference to which both missionaries and national workers are elected as delegates.

The American Lutheran missions have fifty-seven missionaries, 185 organized churches, 15,338 Christians, thirty-five ordained, and 245 unordained national workers on the island.

New Guinea

The only island in the Pacific that has active Lutheran missionary work of American Lutherans is New Guinea. Groups from Germany and the Lutherans of Australia share in the work on this island. Work begun there by German Lutherans in 1887 was in dire stress during the first world war and was sustained financially by the Australian Lutheran and the Iowa Synod of America. The control of the combined missions of the Rhenish, Hermannsburg, and Neuendettelsau fields was under the joint administration of the Australian Lutherans and the Iowa Synod since 1921. The formal transfer of the mission to their control came in 1926. The first American Lutheran missionaries arrived in 1921. After the postwar readjustments made the return of German missionaries possible, an adjustment of the field was made granting the American Lutheran Church (originally the Iowa Synod) the Madang mission area as its field. This final action was taken in 1932. This field has been extended along the Rai coast, inland, and on islands along the coast. There are fifty-three missionaries, sixteen organized congregations, 16,000 Christians, three ordained, and 220 unordained native workers here. Cooperation between all the Lutheran missions in New Guinea is very close and cordial.

South America

The Lutheran Church has a long history in South America. In 1665 Baron Justinianus von Weltz made an abortive effort at conducting mission work in Suranim in the Guianas. In 1741 the first Lutheran congregation was established at Paramaribo, and in 1743 one was established in New Amsterdam. The latter city is the center of mission work now conducted in British Guiana by the United Lutheran Church of America. The pastor of this congregation became a member of the East Pennsylvania Synod in 1890, and in 1915 the congregation and its mission field were transferred to the Board of Foreign Missions of the General Synod. There are now seven missionaries with nineteen organized congregations, 1,750 members, two ordained, and twenty unordained national workers. A national church has been organized there, and it is now indigenous in its control and expanding program.

Argentina has two Lutheran missions, the United Lutheran Church and the Missouri Synod, both with headquarters at Buenos Aires. Both of these missions began with the purpose of ministering to the German and other European Lutheran immigrant groups, branching into mission work among the Spanish-speaking nationals as the need for this work became evident. The actual mission work of the United Lutheran Church among the nationals began in 1919, and that of the Missouri Synod in 1927. The earlier work among the immigrants was begun shortly after the turn of the century (Missouri Synod, 1905; United Lutheran Church of America, 1908). There are in these missions thirty-seven missionaries, eighty-four congregations, 8,417 Christians, and forty-three national workers in Argentina.

The Missouri Synod began work among the German Lutherans in Brazil in 1900; this work was soon developed into mission work among the nationals also. Seminary training on the field was begun in 1903, but the first full-time missionary among the natives was not appointed till 1918.

There are fifty-four missionaries, 212 organized churches, ten national workers, and a membership of 45,000.

Bolivia was not entered by any Lutheran missionary group till 1938 when an independent intersynodical Lutheran mission, the World Mission Prayer League, began work in districts east of La Paz. Its work is among the Spanish people and the Indian tribes and is conducted in five main stations. It has fourteen missionaries, 100 members of the church, and one ordained national worker.

Colombia was entered by a similar group, the Colombia Evangelical Lutheran Mission of South America. Its field lies in the Boyaca and the Arauca Districts where work was begun in 1938. It has nine missionaries working in five centers. The Norwegian Lutheran Church of America and the United Danish Church decided to begin work in South America jointly in 1943. At present the seven missionaries of these missions are cooperating in the work on the field of the above mission in Colombia.

Lutheran World Action

The latest venture in foreign missions of the Lutheran churches in America has been under the direction of the Lutheran World Convention. Under the activity called Lutheran World Action the various synods have cooperated in supporting and conducting mission fields of Lutheran missions of European countries that were shorn of support from their home churches because of the war. This great venture has been carried in addition to all regular synodical commitments in such a manner as to receive the commendation of international mission bodies as well as the groups receiving aid. This act has tended to cement the kinship of Lutherans over the entire world and has opened the vision of American Lutherans to increased possibilities of service through missions to other lands.

BIBLIOGRAPHY

I. INTRODUCTORY AND GENERAL

Luthers Werke, Weimar Edition.

Works of Martin Luther, Vol. 2, Philadelphia: A. J. Holman Co., 1916.

Holl, Karl, *Gesammelte Aufsätze zur Kirchengeschichte.* Tübingen: J. C. B. Mohr, 1928.

Ussing, Henry, *Evangeliets Seiersgang,* Kobenhavn: G. E. C. Gad, 1924.

Ussing, Henry, *Den Evangeliske Mission i vor Egen Tid,* Kobenhavn: G. E. C. Gads Forlag, 1924.

Interpretive Statistical Survey of the World Mission of the Christian Church, New York: International Missionary Council, 1938.

Latourette, Kenneth Scott, *A History of the Expansion of Christianity,* seven volumes, New York: Harper Bros.

Glover, Robert Hall, *The Progress of World Wide Missions,* New York: Harper Bros., 1939.

Pfeiffer, Edward, *Mission Studies,* Columbus, Ohio: Lutheran Book Concern, 1931.

Aberly, John, *An Outline of Missions,* Philadelphia: Muhlenberg Press, 1945.

Warneck, Gustav, *Outline of a History of Protestant Missions,* New York: Fleming and Co.

Long, Ralph H., *A Statistical Bulletin,* New York: National Lutheran Council, 1945.

Burgess, Andrew, *In the Lands of Pagodas, Temples, and Mosques,* Minneapolis, Minn.: Augsburg Publishing House, 1945.

II. GENERAL LUTHERAN AND SYNODICAL MISSIONS

Laury, Preston A., *A History of Lutheran Missions,* Reading, Pa.: Pilger Publishing House, 1905.

Drach, George, *Our Church Abroad,* Minneapolis, Minn.: Augsburg Publishing House, 1926.

Drach, George, ed., *In Seven Nations,* Baltimore, Md.: Board of Foreign Missions of the U.L.C.A., 1941.

Hauge, Osborne, *Lutherans Working Together,* New York: National Lutheran Counncil, 1945.

Fiedler, Fred. J., *Then the Light Came,* Philadelphia, Pa.: Muhlenberg Press, 1941.

Bachmann, E. Theodore, *They Called Him Father,* Philadelphia, Pa.: Muhlenberg Press, 1942.

Gotwald, L. A., *What Hath God Wrought!* Guntur, India: U.L.C. Mission Press, 1941.

Syrdahl, Rolf A., *American Lutheran Mission Work in China.* Unpublished thesis, 1942.

White Unto Harvest in China, Minneapolis, Minn.: Board of Foreign Missions of the N.L.C.A., 1934.

Burgess, Andrew, *Zanahary in South Madagascar,* Minneapolis, Minn.: Augsburg Publishing House, 1932.

Burgess, Andrew, *Unkulunkulu in Zululand,* Minneapolis, Minn.: Augsburg Publishing House, 1934.

Gronli, J. E., *Kumbulani,* Minneapolis, Minn.: Board of Foreign Missions of the N.L.C.A., 1945.

Sheatsley, C. V., *Our Mission Field in India,* Columbus, Ohio: Lutheran Book Concern, 1921.

Braun, F., and Sheatsley, C. V., *On Both Sides of the Equator,* Columbus, Ohio: Lutheran Book Concern, 1937.

Lund, G. Albert, ed., *After Seventy-Five Years,* Rock Island, Ill.: Augustana Book Concern.

Sandgren, Carl H., ed., *My Church,* Rock Island, Ill.: Augustana Book Concern.

Eckman, F. M., *Our First Decade in China,* Rock Island, Ill.: China Mission Board of the Augustana Synod, 1915.

Carlberg, Gustav, *Our Second Decade in China,* Rock Island, Ill.: China Mission Board of the Augustana Synod, 1925.

Carlberg, Gustav, *Thirty Years in China,* Rock Island, Ill.: China Mission Board of the Augustana Synod, 1937.

Ditmanson, Frederick, *In Foreign Fields,* Minneapolis, Minn.: Lutheran Board of Missions, 1927.

On Wings of Faith, St. Louis, Mo.: Concordia Publishing House, 1943.

Christiansen, G. B., *Recollections of Our Church Work,* Blair, Nebr.: Danish Lutheran Publication House, 1930.

Association of Lutheran Brotherhoods, *Our Church at Work,* Blair, Nebr.: Danish Lutheran Publication House, 1940.

Vig, P. S. and Hanson, I. M., *Danske i Amerika,* Vol. 1, Minneapolis, Minn.: C. Rasmussen Pub. Co., 1907.

Nau, Henry, *We Move into Africa,* St. Louis, Mo.: Concordia Publishing House, 1945.

Gausdal, Johannes, *Santalmisjonens Historie,* Oslo, Norway: Santalmisjonens Forlag, 1937.

Malme, Anders, *The Pioneer Era of the Santal Mission of the Northern Churches,* Unpublished thesis, 1945.

Oversikt over Brodersamfundets Kinamission, Minneapolis, Minn.: Missionstyrelsen, 1914.

Annual Reports of the Lutheran Foreign Missions Conference of North America.

Annual reports, yearbooks, statistical reports of the various synodical activities of the Lutheran churches in America.

Synodical periodical literature.

III. HOME MISSIONS

Hunt, J. R. E., *Lutheran Home Missions*, Rock Island, Ill.: Augustana Book Conncern, 1913.

Hunt, J. R. E., *Thy Kingdom Come*, Rock Island, Ill.: Augustana Publishing House, 1920.

The Challenge of Lutheran Home Missions, Lutheran Home Missions Council.

Horine, John W., *A Home Enterprise*, Philadelphia, Pa.: United Lutheran Publication House, 1925.

Norlie, O. M., *The United Church Home Missions*, Minneapolis, Minn.: Augsburg Publishing House, 1909.

Preus, J. C. K., *Widening the Frontier*, Minneapolis, Minn.: Augsburg Publishing House, 1929.

Goodykoontz, Colin B., *Home Missions on the American Frontier*, Caldwell, Idaho: The Caxton Printers, 1939.

Bachman, E. Theodore, *They Called Him Father*, Philadelphia, Pa.: Muhlenberg Press, 1942.

Wentz, Abdel R., *The Lutheran Church in American History*, Philadelphia: United Lutheran Publishing House, 1923.

IV. INNER MISSIONS (WELFARE)

Ohl, J. F., *The Inner Mission*, Philadelphia, Pa.: The United Lutheran Publication House, 1911.

Gerberding, George, *The Priesthood of Believers*, Philadelphia, Pa.: Inner Mission Board of the U.L.C.A., 1920.

Lutheran Welfare Conference in America, annual regional and national reports.

Gerberding, G. H., *The Life and Letters of W. A. Passavant*, Greenville, Pa.: The Young Lutheran Co., 1906.

Wurster, Paul, *Die Lehre von der Inneren Mission*, Berlin: Verlag von Reuther & Reichard, 1895.

Pfatteicher, E. P., *Christian Social Science*, New York: Falcon Press, 1933.

Faris, Ellsworth, *Intelligent Philanthropy*, Chicago: University of Chicago Press, 1930.

Wacker, Emil, *Diakonissegjerningen*, Minneapolis, Minn.: Oscar W. Lund's Publishing House, 1898.

Reports of individual institutions and annual reports of the various synods as well as of independent institutions.

BIOGRAPHICAL NOTES

W. ARNDT is professor of New Testament exegesis at Concordia
Seminary, St. Louis, Mo. He is also the managing editor of *The
Concordia Theological Monthly*. Dr. Arndt is one of the members
of the Missouri Synod's Committee on Doctrinal Unity in the Lutheran
Church in America.

E. THEODORE BACHMANN is professor of church history at Chicago
Lutheran Theological Seminary. He has done postgraduate work at the
Universities of Erlangen, Tuebingen, and Chicago. He is the author
of *They Called Him Father*, a centennial biography of C. F. Heyer.

CONRAD BERGENDOFF is president of Augustana College and Theo-
logical Seminary, Rock Island, Ill. He has done graduate work in the
Universities of Uppsala and Lund, Sweden, Berlin, Germany, and
Chicago. He is the author of a book on Olavus Petri and was a dele-
gate to the ecumenical conferences of Oxford and Edinburgh in 1937.
He is president of the American Association of Theological Schools.

JULIUS BODENSIECK is president of Wartburg Theological Seminary,
Dubuque, Iowa, where he teaches in the fields of Old and New Testament interpretation. He was editor of the *Kirchenblatt* from 1930 to
1940, before becoming president of Wartburg Seminary. He is also
director of the Luther Academy, a summer theological seminar for
pastors, patterned after the famed Luther Akademie of Sondershausen,
Germany.

C. G. CARLFELT is professor of systematic theology at Augustana
Theological Seminary in Rock Island, Ill. His graduate work was
done at Uppsala, Lund, and Chicago. He is a frequent contributor
of articles to the *Augustana Quarterly*.

N. C. CARLSEN is the president of the United Evangelical Lutheran Church with offices in Blair, Neb. He is one of the theologians
whose historical antecedents are rooted in the Danish Lutheran Church.

BERNHARD M. CHRISTENSEN is president of Augsburg College and
Seminary in Minneapolis, Minn. His graduate studies took him to
Princeton, Berlin, Goettingen, and Hartford. He is the author of *Fire
Upon the Earth*. He has taken an active part in Lutheran educational
conferences.

W. H. T. DAU was for many years a professor of theology at
Concordia Seminary, St. Louis, Mo., before becoming president of
Valparaiso University. He retired from active service in 1929 but

continued writing many articles in his special field of research, Luther. Dr. Dau died in 1945.

J. A. DELL is professor of practical theology at the Capital University Theological Seminary, Columbus, Ohio. He was editor of the *Journal of the American Lutheran Conference* for four years and is the author of *I Still Believe in God*. He also edited Luther's Small Catechism for juniors and seniors.

EDWARD C. FENDT is dean and professor of systematic theology at Capital University Theological Seminary, Columbus, Ohio. Before joining the seminary faculty in 1936 he taught in the department of Bible at Capital University.

E. E. FLACK is dean and professor of exegetical theology in Hamma Divinity School, Springfield, Ohio. He is a member of the Board of Social Missions and the Commission on World Conference on Faith and Order of the United Lutheran Church in America. He is co-editor with H. C. Alleman of the *Old Testament Commentary* now being published.

THEODORE GRAEBNER is professor of philosophy and New Testament interpretation at Concordia Seminary, St. Louis, Mo. For many years he has been one of the editors of the *Lutheran Witness*. He is the author of *God and the Cosmos*. He has been active in the field of Lutheran apologetics, having written hundreds of articles in defense of Biblical Christianity.

T. F. GULLIXSON is president of Luther Theological Seminary, St. Paul, Minn., where he also teaches in the field of pastoral theology. He is the author of *Christus Emptor*. He has been active in the formation and the growth of the American Lutheran Conference.

GEORGE F. HALL is professor of Christianity at Gustavus Adolphus College, St. Peter, Minn. He pursued graduate studies at Chicago and Union. He is a frequent contributor to religious journals.

ALBERT A. JAGNOW is professor of church history at Wartburg Seminary, Dubuque, Iowa. His special field of investigation has been the theology of Herrmann and Barth. At Yale he wrote his doctor's dissertation on the concept of revelation as found in the writings of these two theologians.

T. A. KANTONEN is professor of systematic theology at Hamma Divinity School, Springfield, Ohio. His graduate work took him to Harvard, Boston, and the University of Minnesota. He is the author of *The Message of the Church for the World Today* and a contributor to the *Encyclopedia of Religion*.

THEODORE S. LIEFELD is professor of New Testament at Capital University Theological Seminary, Columbus, Ohio. Prior to his seminary professorship he was instructor in psychology and Bible at Capital University.

A. D. MATTSON is professor of ethics and sociology in Augustana Theological Seminary, Rock Island, Ill. He is the author of the textbook *Christian Ethics*. He is a frequent contributor to religious journals, usually writing on the problems of the church and the labor movement and the rural church.

J. T. MUELLER is professor of doctrinal and exegetical theology at Concordia Seminary, St. Louis, Mo. His *Christian Dogmatics* is a translation of Pieper's *Christliche Dogmatik*. He is the author of *The Concordia New Testament with Notes* and *The Concordia Bible with Notes*. He is a frequent contributor to the religious journals of the Missouri Synod.

O. FREDERICK NOLDE is professor of Christian education at the Lutheran Theological Seminary, Philadelphia, Pa. He is a member of the Commission to Study the Bases of a Just and Durable Peace and was a consultant at the San Francisco Conference of the United Nations in 1945. He is the author of *Christian World Action* and *Christian Messages to the Peoples of the World*.

W. G. POLACK is professor of church history at Concordia Seminary, St. Louis, Mo. He was editor-in-chief of the *Lutheran Hymnal* of the Missouri Synod and author of the *Handbook* to the Lutheran Hymnal. He is an associate editor of the *Lutheran Witness* and the *Cresset*.

C. C. RASMUSSEN is professor of systematic theology at the Lutheran Theological Seminary, Gettysburg, Pa. Before becoming professor at Gettysburg in 1940 he was pastor of Luther Place Memorial Lutheran Church, Washington, D. C. He was active in the National Preaching Mission and the National Christian Mission.

LUTHER D. REED is professor of liturgics and church art at the Lutheran Theological Seminary, Philadelphia, Pa., where he also served as president until 1945. He is chairman of the Common Service Book Committee of the United Lutheran Church and a member of the Commission on Intercommunion, World Conference on Faith and Order. He has written many articles on church music, liturgics, and church art. His latest book is *The Lutheran Liturgy*.

ROLF A. SYRDAHL is professor of missions and New Testament at Luther Theological Seminary, St. Paul, Minn. He worked for seven years as a missionary in China, then taught Bible at St. Olaf College for four years before assuming his professorship in 1941.

T. G. TAPPERT is professor of Christian history at Lutheran Theological Seminary, Philadelphia, Pa. He is the managing editor of the *Lutheran Church Quarterly*. He translated Sasse's *Here We Stand* and translated and edited the *Journals of Henry Melchior Muhlenberg*. He wrote the *Church Through the Ages* in 1941.

E. H. WAHLSTROM is professor of New Testament language and literature in Augustana Theological Seminary, Rock Island, Ill. He did graduate work at Yale, Chicago, and Union. He is a member of the American section of the World Conference on Faith and Order, where his special field of research has been the church.

A. R. WENTZ is president of Lutheran Theological Seminary, Gettysburg, Pa., and has been professor of church history there for more than 30 years. He is the author of the *Lutheran Church in American History*. He is a member of the committee which edited the Revised Standard Version of the New Testament. He has also been active in the American Association of Theological Schools.

C. UMHAU WOLF is professor of Old Testament interpretation at Chicago Lutheran Seminary. His graduate work was done at Johns Hopkins, Ohio State, and Hartford. He is a frequent contributor to religious journals.